# DIPLOMA IN CORPORAT

## PAPER 1 – CORPORATE FIN
## TECHNIQUES AND THEORY



## STUDY TEXT

APPROVED WORKBOOK

ICAEW
PARTNER IN LEARNING

BPP
LEARNING MEDIA

Published March 2017

ISBN 9781 5097 0977 9
eISBN 9781 5097 0916 8

British Library Cataloguing-in-Publication Data
A catalogue record for this book
is available from the British Library

Published by

BPP Learning Media Ltd
BPP House, Aldine Place
London W12 8AA

www.bpp.com/learningmedia

Printed in the United Kingdom by RICOH UK Limited

Unit 2
Wells Place
Merstham
RH1 3LG
United Kingdom

Your learning materials, published by BPP Learning Media Ltd, are printed on paper obtained from traceable sustainable sources.





BPP
LEARNING MEDIA

# CONTENTS

**Introduction**

**Module 1 – Financial Statement Analysis** **Page 1**

Chapter 1 – Accounting for Revenue 3
Chapter 2 – Accounting for Cash Flow 13
Chapter 3 – Off-Balance Sheet Financing 21
Chapter 4 – Group Accounting 43
Chapter 5 – Accounting for Taxation 75
Chapter 6 – Ratio Analysis 87
Chapter 7 – Analysis of Financial Statements Case Study 141

**Module 2 – Valuation** **Page 155**

Chapter 8 – Traditional Methods of Equity Analysis 159
Chapter 9 – Understanding Risk and Return 181
Chapter 10 – The Capital Asset Pricing Model 213
Chapter 11 – Calculating the Cost of Capital 241
Chapter 12 – Free Cash Flow 259
Chapter 13 – Other Valuation Techniques 277

**Module 3 – Debt and Equity** **Page 291**

Chapter 14 – Financial Instruments 295
Chapter 15 – Unquoted Sources of Finance 339
Chapter 16 – Public Equity 367
Chapter 17 – Pension Schemes 391
Chapter 18 – Derivatives 401

**Module 4 – Mergers, Aquisitions and Disposals** **Page 421**

Chapter 19 – Making Aquisitions 425
Chapter 20 – Deal Structuring 441
Chapter 21 – Disposals and Demergers 453
Chapter 22 – Public Deals 465

**Module 5 – Regulation, Governance and Ethics** **Page 475**

Chapter 23 – The Takeover Code 479
Chapter 24 – The Listing Rules 513
Chapter 25 – Other Corporate Finance Regulation 539
Chapter 26 – Ethics and Market Abuse 553

**Index** **Page 573**

## Updates

From time to time we may need to publish updates to one of our titles. This can be for a variety of reasons, from a small change in regulation to the identification of errata.

You should check our updates/errata page regularly for anything that may affect your learning materials. All updates are available free of charge on our updates page on our website at:

http://www.bpp.com/about-bpp/aboutBPP/StudentInfo#q4

# 1 Introduction

Welcome to the study text for the Corporate Finance Diploma Paper 1 – Techniques and Theory.

# 2 Outline of the Corporate Finance Diploma Programme

Candidates embarking on the programme will have passed CISI Certificate in Corporate Finance or be qualified accountants.

The programme comprises two stages as follows:

- **Paper 1** - focused on developing the understanding and application of techniques, theories and issues in a range of practical corporate finance situations.
- **Paper 2** - focused on advanced issues and practice for the experienced practitioner seeking to move into the top tier of the corporate finance field.

Successful completion of the programme, paired with appropriate practical experience, leads to the awarding of the CF designation.

The programme aims:

- to provide a practically grounded, transactions-orientated, international qualification in corporate finance recognised as the standard bearer for professionals across the industry and across the world
- to underpin, via a staged qualification, the increasing knowledge and skill requirements of corporate finance executives from industry entrants to those on the verge of appointment to director or vice president level
- to enhance the scope and depth of knowledge and skills of corporate finance professionals benchmarked against current industry practice
- to reinforce and enhance the key skills required for senior corporate advisory work
- to provide a common knowledge base and internationally recognised qualification that establishes and maintains high standards of professional skill and care in all corporate finance transactions.

Paper 1 requires candidates to pass a three-hour examination paper. Paper 2 requires candidates to pass a Case Study which comprises information and an examination paper. The examination lasts four hours.

## Syllabus

### Aim

To provide students with a thorough understanding of techniques, theories and issues found in practical corporate finance situations.

# 3 DIPLOMA IN CORPORATE FINANCE

### Paper One: Corporate Finance Techniques and Theory

1 Financial Statement Analysis

2 Valuation

3 Debt and Equity

4 Mergers, Acquisitions and Disposals

5 Regulation, Governance and Ethics

### Paper Two: Corporate Finance Strategy and Advice

**Content**

1 Corporate Strategy

2 Mergers and Acquisitions

3 Corporate Performance and Reconstructions

4 Supporting material for sections 2 and 3

**Integrated skills**

Case study

## Aim

The Diploma in Corporate Finance aims to ensure that students possess the knowledge and skills to respond effectively to complex situations found in corporate finance activity.

## Structure

The syllabus has been designed to develop core technical, commercial, and ethical skills and knowledge for those working in the field of corporate finance. Knowledge of fundamental techniques, theories and issues gained at the Techniques and Theory level supports the handling of complex corporate finance scenarios at the Strategy and Advice level.

## Syllabus

This document presents the learning outcomes for the Corporate Finance Techniques and Theory and Strategy and Advice modules.

# 4 CORPORATE FINANCE TECHNIQUES AND THEORY

## Aim

To provide students with a thorough understanding of techniques, theories and issues found in practical corporate finance situations.

On completion of this module, students will be able to:

- undertake a high level of financial statement analysis
- value a range of undertakings across industry sectors
- conduct an advanced analysis of debt and equity requirements in given situations
- establish how, and whether, value is created in mergers, disposals and acquisitions
- detect the relevance of UK and EU regulatory requirements to current situations and proposed actions.

## Entry to Corporate Finance Techniques and Theory

Students embarking on this module of the Diploma in Corporate Finance will have passed CISI Certificate in Corporate Finance or the ACA.

## Assessment

The module will draw from across the syllabus and be assessed through short scenario style questions in a three hour open book examination. Candidates will be expected to demonstrate that they can apply their understanding to a range of practical scenarios.

The examination will comprise:

Section A – worth 50 marks.

Candidates answer five questions from a choice of seven, each question worth ten marks

Section B – worth 50 marks.

Candidates answer two scenario style questions in this section from a choice of three, worth 25 marks each. The questions in this section will combine and test knowledge from different parts of the syllabus.

## Specification grid

This grid shows the relative weightings of topics within this module and should guide the relative study time spent on each. Over time the marks available in the assessment will equate to the weightings below, while slight variations may occur in individual assessments to enable suitable questions to be set.

| Syllabus area | Weighting (%) |
|---|---|
| Financial Statement Analysis | 25 |
| Valuation | 25 |
| Debt and Equity | 15–20 |
| Mergers, Acquisitions and Disposals | 15–20 |
| Regulation, Governance and Ethics | 15–20 |

## Knowledge Levels

The level of knowledge required in this module is that required for the solution of complex problems except where indicated with a **(G)**, where knowledge is required only at a level for the solution of straightforward problems.

## Content

### Financial Statement Analysis

Candidates will be able to undertake an advanced level of financial statement analysis and will be able to recognise the particular analytical problems of different types of domestic and international industry sector and business entity.

In the assessment, candidates may be required to:

(a) Use ratio analysis and other techniques on the financial statements of single companies and groups, including the use of cash to measure return

(b) Interpret financial statements of single companies and groups, and explain the implications of accounting standards on the financial statements

(c) Take account of the following aspects and issues in the analysis of financial statements:

- Revenue recognition
- Revenue recognition principles in different sectors
- Reporting deferred and accrued income
- Revenue recognition versus cash flow
- Off-balance-sheet financing
- Operating versus finance leases
- Informative notes to the financial statements
- Group accounting, including intra-group activity and taxation
- Accounting for acquisitions, disposals and mergers.
- impact of FRS102 on financial statements

### Valuation

Candidates will be able to undertake an advanced level of valuation and will be able to recognise the particular valuation problems of different domestic and international industry sectors and types of business entity.

In the assessment, candidates may be required to

(a) Use and appraise methods of equity analysis for different types of business entity and industry sectors, indicating each methods' problems and limitations:

(b)

- Traditional methods:
  - Earnings per share (EPS)
  - Return on capital employed (ROCE)
  - Price/book, price/sales and the price/earnings ratios
- Adjusted traditional methods:
  - EV and EBITDA
  - EV and EBIT
  - Turnover

- Other 'rule of thumb' methods
- Advantages and disadvantages of an enterprise based approach to evaluation
- The treatment of synergies

- The cost of equity:
  - The capital asset pricing model (CAPM)
  - Systematic and business risk
  - Application of beta
  - The dividend valuation model (DVM)
  - Alternative measures of the cost of equity **(G)**
  - Arbitrage pricing theory and its limitations **(G)**
- The cost of debt
  - Calculating the required yield on debt
  - Considerations of currency and inflation matching
- Weighted average cost of capital (WACC)
  - Calculation and limitations
  - Gearing and its impact on WACCs and values
- Free cash flow (FCF)
  - Applying discounted cash flow (DCF) techniques to FCF
  - FCF for equity holders
  - FCF for the enterprise
  - Key economic assumptions used to structure a forecast
  - The treatment of synergies
  - Terminal values and their derivation from both multiples and DCF
  - Sensitivity analysis and its interpretation
- Economic value added (EVA) **(G)**
- Real options and options-based valuation models **(G)**
- Methodologies in the valuation of mineral rights **(G).**

## Debt and Equity

Candidates will be able to explain and evaluate advanced aspects of domestic and international debt instruments and equity issues, to judge when and where to use debt and/or equity, the appropriate mix of debt and equity, and when to use certain types of debt instrument.

In the assessment, candidates may be required to

(a) Summarise the terms, rights, conditions of use and the factors concerning value of the following instruments:

- Ordinary shares
- Preference shares
- Debt
- Convertible loans
- Warrants
- Options
- Bonds including debt capital markets

(b) Critically evaluate the following unquoted sources of finance

- Private equity, including VCTs
- Private placings
- Enterprise investment schemes

- Banks
- Financial leases
- Project finance
- Senior, mezzanine and other debt
- Sovereign wealth funds
- Family offices

(c) Evaluate the appropriateness of unquoted finance for the following:

- Start-ups/early stage
- Development capital
- Management buy-outs/buy-ins
- Public companies

(d) Determine financing options, including rights issues, placings and vendor placings, for a company by evaluating a company's financing needs.

(e) Determine financing options for a company by examining the financial implications of pension schemes, with particular reference to: **(G)**

- Defined contribution schemes
- Defined benefit schemes
- Valuation of assets and liabilities
- Deficit funding
- Rights of pension holders
- Asset based finance
- Bonds

(f) Explain the use of the following derivatives in debt and equity and incorporate these instruments in financing options in straightforward situations: **(G)**

- Forwards and futures
- Options
- Swaps

## Mergers, Acquisitions and Disposals

Candidates will be able to assess how, and whether, value is created by domestic and international mergers, acquisitions and disposals, including the effect on a group's financial statements (including IBO's, management buy-outs and other variants),

In the assessment, candidates may be required to:

(a) Evaluate or construct commercial and financial rationale for acquisitions and disposals in a given scenario.

(b) Explain in detail how the following disposal processes are carried out and apply this knowledge to a given scenario

- The sale process (initiation only)
  - Traditional and alternative disposal methods
  - Identifying and short-listing purchasers
  - Approaching potential purchasers
- The auction process
  - No-names teasers
  - Confidentiality undertakings
  - The information memorandum
  - Inviting and evaluating offers

(c) Explain in detail how the following stages in an acquisition are carried out and apply this knowledge to a given scenario:

- Identifying potential acquisition targets
- Initial evaluation of targets
- Approaching the target: considerations and best practice

(d) Explain in detail the following aspects of mergers, acquisitions and disposals and apply this knowledge to a given scenario

- Public deals
  - Transaction process overview
  - Outline of regulatory issues
  - Defence and bid strategies
- Due diligence
  - Scope of due diligence
  - Vendor due diligence and data rooms
  - Purchaser due diligence
- Legal documentation
  - Heads of agreement
  - Break clauses and exclusivity agreements
  - Sale and purchase agreement
  - Warranties, indemnities, representations and disclosures
  - Conditions precedent and subsequent
  - Exchange and completion
  - The completion meeting and problem areas
  - 'Locked box' mechanisms versus completion accounts
  - Other post completion mechanisms
- Deal structuring
  - Buying and selling assets versus shares
  - Cash, loan stock, shares and alternatives as consideration
  - Earn-outs, options and deferred consideration
  - Tax considerations for the vendor and purchaser
  - Hedging foreign exchange rate risk
  - Hedging interest rate risk.

## Regulation, Governance and Ethics

Candidates will be able to describe UK regulation and the regulatory regimes in different jurisdictions, recognise the applicability of regulation in given scenarios and apply that knowledge to given scenarios.

In the assessment, candidates may be required to

(a) Specific rules and practice statements will be tested. Also candidates should be able to describe the following aspects of the Takeover Code and assess their relevance to a given scenario

- The structure of the Code
- The spirit of the Code
- The structure of the Panel and its powers
- Statutory status
- Companies to which the code applies
- Independent advice
- Irrevocable undertakings
- Financing arrangements
- Offers for different classes of shares
- Concert parties

- Special deals and management incentives
- Accuracy and content of documents
- The creation of false markets
- Restrictions and frustrating actions
- Consideration
- Mandatory offers
- The timetable of an offer
- EU implications
- Consulting the Panel
- Schemes of arrangement

(b) Listing:

(i) Describe the following aspects of the FCA Listing Rules and assess their relevance to a given scenario

- The structure of the UK Listing Authority Rules
- Overview of the Disclosure Guidance and Transparency Rules
- Prospectus rules
- Standard and premium listing options
- The minimum requirements for listing
- Prospectuses
- Timetable for listing
- Sponsor's obligations
- Announcements and circulars to shareholders
- Continuing obligations
- Class tests
- Share buybacks
- Secondary offerings

(ii) AIM and ISDX Rules and other junior UK markets **(G)**

(c) Describe the following areas relevant to corporate finance activity and assess their relevance to a given straightforward scenario **(G)**

- Corporate governance
  - The UK Corporate Governance Code (including the implications for smaller companies)
  - The overlap with the FCA Disclosure Guidance and Transparency Rules
  - EU implications
- Competition regulation
  - The general purpose of competition regulation
  - EU implications
- Ethics
  - Fiduciary duties to the client
  - Bribery Act
  - Ethics – with knowledge of your professional body's code of ethics, eg CISI Code of conduct or ICAEW code of ethics
- Market abuse
  - Insider trading
  - Price sensitive information
  - Misleading statements
  - Financial promotions
  - EU implications
- Companies Act

Candidates should be able to demonstrate an awareness of US and other extraterritorial regulations which might impact upon a UK transaction.

MODULE 1

# FINANCIAL STATEMENT ANALYSIS

## INTRODUCTION

The material in this section assumes that you possess a good level of knowledge of financial statements, in particular the mechanics of the income statement, balance sheet and cash flow statement, including how the statements inter-relate. You should also be comfortable with the main accounting ratios and their calculation and interpretation. If in doubt, a review of the accounting sections in the Certificate of Corporate Finance (Unit 2) would be helpful.

The syllabus concentrates on more advanced accounting issues, as relevant to corporate financiers, and their impact on financial analysis. The study material incorporates worked examples and tasks for you to undertake. Even if you are very familiar with accounts, it is still recommended you complete all tasks to ensure revision of the skills required for the exam. A full analysis case study is included in Chapter 7 and should be attempted by all.

Where reference is made in the study material to accounting standards, these are based on international accounting standards, namely IAS (International Accounting Standards) and IFRS (International Financial Reporting Standards).

The syllabus requirements relating to Financial Statements Analysis are shown below. The relevant chapters of the study material are highlighted next to each section for your information.

## SYLLABUS – FINANCIAL STATEMENT ANALYSIS

### Aim

Candidates will be able to undertake an advanced level of financial statement analysis and will be able to recognise the particular analytical problems of different types of domestic and international industry sector and business entity.

Financial statement analysis questions will make up approximately 20% of the total marks in the examination.

### Syllabus and BPP Study Text Coverage

In the assessment, candidates may be required to:

| SYLLABUS | BPP STUDY TEXT |
|---|---|
| **a. Use ratio analysis and other techniques on the financial statements of single companies and groups, including the use of cash to measure return** | Chapters 6 & 7 |
| **b. Interpret financial statements of single companies and groups, and the explain the implications of accounting standards on the financial statements** | Chapters 1–7 |
| **c. Take account of the following aspects and issues in the analysis of financial statements:** | |
| • **Revenue recognition** | Chapter 1 |
| • **Revenue recognition principles in different sectors** | Chapter 1 |
| • **Reporting deferred and accrued income** | Chapter 1 |
| • **Revenue recognition versus cash flow** | Chapter 2 |
| • **Off-balance-sheet financing** | Chapter 3 |
| • **Operating versus finance leases** | Chapter 3 |
| • **Informative notes to the financial statements** | Chapters 1–7 |
| • **Group accounting, including intra-group activity and taxation** | Chapters 4 & 5 |
| • **Accounting for acquisitions, disposals and mergers** | Chapter 4 |

# ACCOUNTING FOR REVENUE

chapter 1

Contents


| | | |
|---|---|---|
| 1 | Revenue Recognition | 4 |
| 2 | Revenue Recognition Principles in Different Sectors | 4 |
| 3 | Reporting Deferred and Accrued Income | 9 |

# 1 Revenue Recognition

IAS 18 governs the recognition of revenue in specific (common) types of transaction. Generally, revenue should be recognised when it is probable that **future economic benefits** will flow to the enterprise and when these benefits can be **measured reliably**.

Income, as defined by the IASB's *Framework* document, includes both revenues and gains. Revenue is income arising in the ordinary course of an enterprise's activities and it may be called different names, such as sales, fees, interest, dividends or royalties.

## Definitions

The following definitions are given in IAS 18.

**Revenue** is the gross inflow of economic benefits during the period arising in the course of the ordinary activities of an enterprise when those inflows result in increases in equity, other than increases relating to contributions from equity participants.

**Fair value** is the amount for which an asset could be exchanged, or a liability settled, between knowledgeable, willing parties in an arm's length transaction. *(IAS 18)*

Revenue **does not include** sales taxes, value added taxes or goods and service taxes which are only collected for third parties, because these do not represent an economic benefit flowing to the entity.

## Measurement of revenue

When a transaction takes place, the amount of revenue is usually decided by the **agreement of the buyer and seller**. The revenue is actually measured, however, as the **fair value of the consideration received**, which will take account of any trade discounts and volume rebates.

# 2 Revenue Recognition Principles in Different Sectors

The revenue recognition rules in different sectors, depend upon the nature of the business activities taking place. The key distinction made in the accounting standards is between the sale of goods and the rendering of services. In addition, revenue can arise from use of a company's assets, giving rise to interest, royalties or dividends. Each of these scenarios is considered below.

## Sale of goods

Revenue from the sale of goods should only be recognised when *all* these conditions are satisfied.

- The enterprise has transferred the **significant risks and rewards** of ownership of the goods to the buyer.
- The enterprise has **no continuing managerial involvement** to the degree usually associated with ownership, and no longer has effective control over the goods sold.
- The amount of revenue can be **measured reliably**.
- It is probable that the **economic benefits** associated with the transaction will flow to the enterprise.
- The **costs incurred** in respect of the transaction can be measured reliably.

The transfer of risks and rewards can only be decided by examining each transaction. Mainly, the transfer occurs at the same time as either the **transfer of legal title**, or the **passing of possession** to the buyer – this is what happens when you buy something in a shop.

If **significant risks and rewards remain with the seller**, then the transaction is *not* a sale and revenue cannot be recognised, for example if the receipt of the revenue from a particular sale depends on the buyer receiving revenue from his own sale of the goods.

It is possible for the seller to retain only an **'insignificant' risk of ownership** and for the sale and revenue to be recognised. The main example here is where the seller retains title only to ensure collection of what is owed on the goods. This is a common commercial situation, and when it arises the revenue should be recognised on the date of sale.

## Rendering of services

When the outcome of a transaction involving the rendering of services can be estimated reliably, the associated revenue should be recognised by reference to the **stage of completion of the transaction** at the balance sheet date. The outcome of a transaction can be estimated reliably when *all* these conditions are satisfied.

- The amount of revenue can be **measured reliably**.
- It is probable that the **economic benefits** associated with the transaction will flow to the enterprise.
- The **stage of completion** of the transaction at the balance sheet date can be measured reliably.
- The **costs incurred** for the transaction and the costs to complete the transaction can be measured reliably.

The parties to the transaction will normally have to agree the following before an enterprise can make reliable estimates.

- Each party's **enforceable rights** regarding the service to be provided and received by the parties.
- The **consideration** to be exchanged.
- The **manner and terms of settlement**.

There are various methods of determining the stage of completion of a transaction, but for practical purposes, when services are performed by an indeterminate number of acts over a period of time, revenue should be recognised on a **straight-line basis** over the period, unless there is evidence for the use of a more appropriate method. If one act is of more significance than the others, then the significant act should be carried out *before* revenue is recognised.

In uncertain situations, when the outcome of the transaction involving the rendering of services cannot be estimated reliably, the Standard recommends a **no loss/no gain approach**. Revenue is recognised only to the extent of the expenses recognised that are recoverable.

This is particularly likely during the **early stages of a transaction**, but it is still probable that the enterprise will recover the costs incurred. So the revenue recognised in such a period will be equal to the expenses incurred, with no profit.

Obviously, if the costs are not likely to be reimbursed, then they must be recognised as an expense immediately. **When the uncertainties cease to exist**, revenue should be recognised in accordance with the stage of completion.

## Interest, royalties and dividends

When others use the enterprise's assets yielding interest, royalties and dividends, the revenue should be recognised on the bases set out below when:

- It is probable that the **economic benefits** associated with the transaction will flow to the enterprise; and
- The amount of the revenue can be **measured reliably**.

The revenue is recognised on the following bases.

- **Interest** is recognised on a time proportion basis that takes into account the effective yield on the asset.
- **Royalties** are recognised on an accruals basis in accordance with the substance of the relevant agreement.
- **Dividends** are recognised when the shareholder's right to receive payment is established.

## Revenue recognition: practical example

The extract below is from the 2014/15 Annual Report of Kingfisher plc and gives the group's revenue recognition policy. The extract highlights different methodologies used for separate income streams.

**Kingfisher Revenue Recognition Policy**

Sales represent the supply of home improvement products and services. Sales exclude transactions made between companies within the Group, Value Added Tax, other sales-related taxes and are net of returns, trade and staff discounts.

Sales of in-store products are generally recognised at the point of cash receipt. Where award credits such as vouchers or loyalty points are provided as part of the sales transaction, the amount allocated to the credits is deferred and recognised when the credits are redeemed and the Group fulfils its obligations to supply the awards.

For delivered products sales are recognised either when the product has been delivered or, for installation income, when the service has been performed. Sales from delivered products and services represent only a small component of the Group's sales as the majority relates to in-store purchases of products.

### TASK

Choose a quoted company that interests you and use the internet to find its latest annual report and accounts. Find its revenue recognition policy in its accounting policies and map how the policy fits with the requirements of IAS 18.

## Revenue recognition – long term contracts

A specific application of revenue recognition policies occurs for companies with long term contracts, namely those straddling more than one accounting period. IAS 11 Construction Contract deals with how companies should recognize the revenue, expenses and resulting profits from long term contracts in the construction industry.

Imagine that you work in the finance department of a construction company. Your company is building a large tower block that will house offices, under a contract with an investment company. It will take three years to build the block and over that time you will obviously have to pay for building materials, wages of workers on the building, architects' fees and so on. You will receive periodic payments from the investment company at various predetermined stages of the construction. How do you decide, in each of the three years, what to include as income and expenditure for the contract in the income statement?

This is the problem tackled by IAS 11 Construction Contracts.

## EXAMPLE

Suppose that a contract is started on 1 January 2015, with an estimated completion date of 31 December 2016. The final contract price is £1,500,000.

In the first year, to 31 December 2015:

- Costs incurred amounted to £600,000.
- Half the work on the contract was completed.
- Certificates of work completed have been issued, to the value of £750,000. (Note. It is usual, in a construction contract, for a qualified person such as an architect or engineer to inspect the work completed, and if it is satisfactory, to issue certificates. This will then be the notification to the customer that progress payments are now due to the contractor. Progress payments are commonly the amount of valuation on the work certificates issued, minus a precautionary retention of 10%.)
- It is estimated with reasonable certainty that further costs to completion in 2016 will be £600,000.

### Required

What is the contract profit in 2015, and what entries would be made for the contract at 31 December 2015 if

(a) Profits are deferred until the completion of the contract?

(b) A proportion of the estimated revenue and profit is credited to the income statement in 2015?

## SOLUTION

(a) If profits were deferred until the completion of the contract in 2016, the revenue and profit recognised on the contract in 2015 would be nil, and the value of work in progress on 31 December 2015 would be £600,000. IAS 11 takes the view that this policy is unreasonable, because in 2016, the total profit of £300,000 would be recorded. Since the contract revenues are earned throughout 2015 and 2016, a profit of nil in 2015 and £300,000 in 2016 would be contrary to the accruals concept of accounting.

(b) It is fairer to recognise revenue and profit throughout the duration of the contract.

As at 31 December 2015 revenue of £750,000 should be matched with cost of sales of £600,000 in the income statement, leaving an attributable profit for 2015 of £150,000.

The only balance sheet entry as at 31 December 2015 is a receivable of £750,000 recognising that the company is owed this amount for work done to date. No balance remains for work in progress, the whole £600,000 having been recognised in cost of sales.

## What is a construction contract?

A contract which needs IAS 11 treatment does not have to last for a period of more than one year. The main point is that the contract activity starts in one financial period and ends in another, thus creating the problem: to which of two or more periods should contract income and costs be allocated? In fact the definition given in the IAS of a construction contract is very straightforward.

> A contract specifically negotiated for the construction of an asset or a combination of assets that are closely interrelated or interdependent in terms of their design, technology and function or their ultimate purpose or use. (*IAS 11*)

Construction contracts may involve the building of one asset, eg a bridge, or a series of interrelated assets, eg an oil refinery. They may also include rendering of services (eg architects) or restoring or demolishing an asset.

## Contract revenue

Contract revenue will be the amount specified in the contract, subject to variations in the contract work, incentive payments and claims if these will probably give rise to revenue and if they can be reliably measured. The result is that contract revenue is measured at the fair value of received or receivable revenue.

## Contract costs

Contract costs consist of:

- Costs relating directly to the contract.
- Costs attributable to general contract activity which can be allocated to the contract, such as insurance, cost of design and technical assistance not directly related to a specific contract and construction overheads.
- Any other costs which can be charged to the customer under the contract, which may include general administration costs and development costs.

## Recognition of contract revenue and expenses

Revenue and costs associated with a contract should be recognised according to the stage of completion of the contract at the balance sheet date, but only when the outcome of the activity can be estimated reliably. This is often known as the percentage of completion method. If a loss is predicted on a contract, then it should be recognised immediately.

The percentage of completion method is an application of the accruals assumption. Contract revenue is matched to the contract costs incurred in reaching the stage of completion, so revenue, costs and profit are attributed to the proportion of work completed.

We can summarise the treatment as follows.

- Recognise contract revenue as revenue in the accounting periods in which the work is performed.
- Recognise contract costs as an expense in the accounting period in which the work to which they relate is performed.
- Any expected excess of total contract costs over total contract revenue should be recognised as an expense immediately.

- The figure to appear in the balance sheet either:
  - Gross amount owed by customer; or
  - Gross amount due to customer.
- These are calculated as costs incurred plus recognised profits less recognised losses less progress billings.

### Determining the stage of completion

How should you decide on the stage of completion of any contract? The Standard lists two methods.

- Surveys of work carried out (work certified).
- The proportion that contract costs incurred for work carried out to date bear to the estimated total contract costs.

## 3 Reporting Deferred and Accrued Income

We can make a distinction between 'accrued' and 'deferred' income. Both types of income are an application of the 'accruals' concept of accounting and relate to scenarios where cash is received by an entity in a different period to where it is actually earned.

**Accrued income** arises when revenue or other income has been earned by an entity but not yet received as cash. The company concerned will include this income as part of its income statement for the year and show a corresponding receivable for the period in its balance sheet. To show accrued income, the company must be confident that the cash will actually be received; if this subsequently is in doubt, then a bad debt must be reflected, giving an expense in the income statement and removing the receivable in the balance sheet.

A distinction can be drawn with **deferred income** which is income where the cash has been received but the revenue or other income has not yet been earned by the company. For instance, an upfront payment has been made by a customer to a company for a service to be performed by the company in a future accounting period. Following the accruals concept, no entry should be made in the company's income statement for the period as the income has not yet been 'earned'. Instead, cash is increased in the balance sheet and a corresponding payable entry is given within liabilities. This payable is usually show within current liability payables under the heading 'accruals and deferred income'. In subsequent accounting periods, when the revenue is earned, there will be a reduction in the deferred income liability and a corresponding increase in income in the income statement.

The main issue for the analyst with accrued and deferred revenue is that what is reported in the income statement may not give a fair reflection of the cash position for the year. Accrued income can also give a distorted picture when you are undertaking ratio analysis.

**TASK**

### Question

What is the impact on the return on capital employed ratio and gearing ratio (debt-to-equity) of a company if it includes the following in its financial statements for the period:

(i) Accrued income
(ii) Deferred income

### Solution

Accrued income gives rise to higher profits and larger net assets in the period of recognition. This will have an uncertain impact on return on capital employed (both profits and capital employed rise), but will reduce gearing (borrowings remain unchanged but equity rises). Accrued income can thus have the effect of making a company appear to have lower financial risk. Deferred income has no impact on capital employed or gearing (profits and net assets unchanged).

## Deferred revenue: practical example

The following are extracts from the 2014 Annual Report of TUI Travel plc relating to revenue recognition and deferred income.

**Extracts from TUI Travel plc Annual Report & Accounts 2014**

**(i) Revenue recognition**

Revenue is recognised in the consolidated income statement when the significant risks and rewards of ownership have been transferred to the buyer. Travel agency commissions and other revenues received from the sale of third party product are recognised when they are earned, typically on receipt of final payment. Revenue in respect of our own holidays and services is recognised on the date of departure. Revenue from individual travel modules directly booked by the customer with airlines, hotels and incoming agencies is recognised when the customer departs or uses the respective service. Revenue from the sale of travel insurance is recognised at the point of sale.

No revenue is recognised if there are significant uncertainties regarding recovery of the consideration due or associated costs.

**(ii) Client monies received in advance (deferred income)**

Client monies received at the balance sheet date, relating to holidays commencing and flights departing after the year end, are deferred and included within trade and other payables.

## Chapter Roundup

### Module 1, Chapter 1: Accounting for Revenue

#### Revenue Recognition Principles

You need to be clear on the accounting rules in this area and, in particular, the impact that different sectors have on the different revenue recognition rules.

- International accounting rules on revenue regulation are governed by the need to **reflect economic substance** rather than pure legal form.
- Revenue should only be included in the income statement when it is probable that future economic benefits will flow to the enterprise.
- The amount quantified as revenue should reflect the fair value of the consideration received, net of any discounts or rebates.
- Revenue recognition principles differ, dependent on the nature of the business operations.
- Where the revenue results from the sale of business services, the revenue recognised must relate to the stage of completion of the transaction.
- Revenue, and costs, (thus profits) resulting from long term contracts should be recognised according to the stage of completion of the transaction using the 'percentage of completion' method. Losses should be recognised immediately.

#### Deferred and Accrued Income

You need to be confident in the difference between accrued and deferred income and how they impact on financial analysis.

| | Accrued income | Deferred income |
|---|---|---|
| Definition | Revenue has been earned but is not yet received as cash | Cash has been received but the revenue has not yet been earned (there has been an upfront payment) |
| Accounting treatment: **income statement** | Recognise revenue | No recognition of revenue |
| Accounting treatment: **balance sheet** | Show a receivable | Cash increases current assets<br>Deferred income increases current liabilities |
| Other points | Recognise a bad debt immediately if recoverability of cash is in doubt | As revenue is earned, deferred income reduces and revenue shown in the income statement |
| Impact on financial analysis in the year of recognition | Increases profits and net assets | Profits and net assets unchanged |

# ACCOUNTING FOR CASH FLOW

chapter 2

Contents

1 Revenue Recognition v Cash Flow 14

# 1 Revenue Recognition v Cash Flow

Revenue is recorded on an accruals basis which can often differ from the cash position. This is why both the income statement and cash flow statement are important documents for the analyst which provide information about different aspects of the company's performance and position at the balance sheet date. It is perfectly possible for a company to be both highly profitable and have a very poor liquidity (cash flow) position.

Trade certainly causes cash to flow, for example when customers pay or suppliers are paid, therefore trade does impact on cash flows. However, not all income statement items result in an immediate cash flow or even any cash flow at all, for example:

- **Depreciation** – The cash flow arises when the original non-current asset is purchased from the supplier, the income statement depreciation charge is *not* a cash flow.
- **Sales on credit/purchases on credit** – Cash flows in relation to these items arise when the amounts are actually received/paid, which is after they have been credited/charged within the income statement.
- **Accrued expenses/prepaid expenses** – Cash flows arise when these expenses are settled which, again, differs from when they are recognised in the income statement.

Cash also moves for other reasons, for example buying subsidiaries, raising share capital/loans, etc.

The following are all important advantages that come from the availability of cash flow information and justify the requirement for a statement of cash flows.

- Cash is highly relevant to a company's survival. Lenders foreclose due to inadequacies of cash to service debt.
- Many users, especially lenders, make their business decisions based on cash flow analysis.
- It may be possible to identify creative accounting through a comparison of cash flow with profits.
- The format of the statement of cash flows under IAS 7 assists analysis, enabling the analyst to identify the level of reinvestment, non-discretionary demands on the company, and so on.

## The cash flow statement

The aim of IAS 7 is to provide information to users of financial statements about the entity's **ability to generate cash and cash equivalents**, as well as indicating the cash needs of the entity. The statement of cash flows provides *historical* information about cash and cash equivalents, classifying cash flows between operating, investing and financing activities.

A statement of cash flows should be presented as an **integral part** of an entity's financial statements. All types of entity can provide useful information about cash flows as the need for cash is universal, whatever the nature of their revenue-producing activities. Therefore **all entities are required by the Standard to produce a statement of cash flows**.

The use of statement of cash flows is very much **in conjunction** with the rest of the financial statements. Users can gain further appreciation of the change in net assets, of the entity's financial position (liquidity and solvency) and the entity's ability to adapt to changing circumstances by affecting the amount and timing of cash flows. statement of cash flows **enhance comparability** as they are not affected by differing accounting policies used for the same type of transactions or events.

Cash flow information of a historical nature can be used as an indicator of the amount, timing and certainty of future cash flows. Past forecast cash flow information can be **checked for accuracy** as actual figures emerge. The relationship between profit and cash flows can be analysed as can changes in prices over time.

## Definitions

The Standard gives the following definitions, the most important of which are **cash** and **cash equivalents**.

**Cash** comprises cash on hand and demand deposits.

**Cash equivalents** are short-term, highly liquid investments that are readily convertible to known amounts of cash and which are subject to an insignificant risk of changes in value.

**Cash flows** are inflows and outflows of cash and cash equivalents.

**Operating activities** are the principal revenue-producing activities of the entity and other activities that are not investing or financing activities.

**Investing activities** are the acquisition and disposal of non-current assets and other investments not included in cash equivalents.

**Financing activities** are activities that result in changes in the size and composition of the equity capital and borrowings of the entity. *(IAS 7)*

The Standard expands on the definition of cash equivalents: they are not held for investment or other long-term purposes, but rather to meet short-term cash commitments. To fulfil the above definition, an investment's **maturity date should normally be within three months from its acquisition date**. It would usually be the case then that equity investments (ie shares in other companies) are *not* cash equivalents. An exception would be where preferred shares were acquired with a very close maturity date.

**Loans and other borrowings** from banks are classified as financing activities. However, **bank overdrafts** are repayable on demand and are treated as part of an entity's total cash management system. In these circumstances an overdrawn balance will be included in cash and cash equivalents.

**Movements** between different types of cash and cash equivalent are not included in cash flows. The investment of surplus cash in cash equivalents is part of cash management, not part of operating, investing or financing activities.

**TASK**

**Preparing a cash flow statement**

You should be familiar with the relationship between the income statement and cash flow statement from your studies in the Certificate of Corporate Finance (or similar). Use the following example to test your knowledge of this important area.

Using the information below, prepare a cash flow statement for the year ended 31 December 2015.

**Income Statement for the Year Ended 31 December 2015**

| | £'000 |
|---|---|
| Revenue | 1,450 |
| Cost of sales | (900) |
| Gross profit | 500 |
| Distribution costs | (100) |
| Administrative expenses | (50) |
| Operating profit | 400 |
| Finance costs | (150) |
| Profit before taxation | 250 |
| Taxation | (100) |
| Profit for the period | 150 |

**Note.** During the year a dividend of £50,000 was paid in cash. This represents the dividend proposed out of the profits of the year ended 31 December 2014. The directors propose to pay a dividend of £60,000 out of the current period's profits. This will be considered for approval by shareholders at the AGM to be held in May 2016.

**Balance Sheets as at 31 December**

| | 2015<br>£'000 | 2014<br>£'000 |
|---|---|---|
| Non-current assets | | |
| Cost | 1,100 | 950 |
| Depreciation | 390 | 330 |
| | 710 | 620 |
| Current assets | | |
| Inventories | 80 | 60 |
| Receivables | 110 | 95 |
| Cash at bank and in hand | 30 | 20 |
| | 220 | 175 |
| **Total assets** | **930** | **795** |
| Current liabilities | | |
| Trade payables | (25) | (13) |
| Bank overdraft | (39) | (35) |
| Tax payable | (100) | (80) |
| | (164) | (128) |
| Non-current liabilities | | |
| Loans | (300) | (351) |
| **Total liabilities** | **(464)** | **(479)** |
| **Net assets** | 466 | 316 |
| Share capital | 200 | 150 |
| Retained earnings | 266 | 166 |
| **Equity** | **466** | **316** |

## SOLUTION

**Cash Flow Statement for the Year Ended 31 December 2015**

| | £'000 | £'000 |
|---|---|---|
| *Net cash from operating activities* | | |
| Operating profit | | 400 |
| Depreciation (390–330) | | 60 |
| Increase in inventories (80–60) | | (20) |
| Increase in receivables (110–95) | | (15) |
| Increase in payables (25–13) | | 12 |
| | | 437 |
| Income taxes paid | | (80) |
| *Net cash provided by operating activities* | | 357 |
| *Investing activities* | | |
| Non-current assets purchased (1,100–950) | | (150) |
| *Financing activities* | | |
| Dividends paid | (50) | |
| Interest paid | (150) | |
| Proceeds of issue of shares | 50 | |
| Repayment of loans (351–300) | (51) | |
| | | (201) |
| *Increase in cash and cash equivalents* | | *6* |
| Represented by | | |
| Increase in cash at bank (30–20) | | 10 |
| Increase in overdraft (39–35) | | (4) |
| | | 6 |

**Note.** This solution has classified interest paid as a financing cash outflow. IAS 7 allows interest paid to be treated as an operating cash outflow. Similarly this answer treats dividends paid as a financing item. IAS 7 also offers the possibility of reporting dividends paid as operating cash outflows.

## TASK

**Reading a cash flow statement**

The following is an extract from the Kingfisher plc Annual Report and Accounts 2014/15.

Read the cash flow statement and pick out the important cash flow themes for the business. What conclusions can you draw about the liquidity position of the group?

### Consolidated cash flow statement

Year ended 31 January 2015

| £ millions | Notes | 2014/15 | 2013/14 |
|---|---|---|---|
| **Operating activities** | | | |
| Cash generated by operations | 31 | **806** | 976 |
| Income tax paid | | **(146)** | (142) |
| **Net cash flows from operating activities** | | **660** | 834 |
| **Investing activities** | | | |
| Purchase of businesses, net of cash acquired | 33 | **–** | (28) |
| Disposal of Hornbach | | **198** | – |
| Disposal of China (deposit received) | | **12** | – |
| Purchase of property, plant and equipment, investment property and intangible assets | 4 | **(275)** | (304) |
| Disposal of property, plant and equipment, investment property, property held for sale and intangible assets | | **50** | 12 |
| Increase in short-term deposits | | **(48)** | – |
| Interest received | | **5** | 8 |
| Dividends received from joint ventures and associates | | **7** | 11 |
| **Net cash flows from investing activities** | | **(51)** | (301) |
| **Financing activities** | | | |
| Interest paid | | **(10)** | (12) |
| Interest element of finance lease rental payments | | **(3)** | (4) |
| Repayment of bank loans | | **(2)** | (89) |
| Repayment of Medium Term Notes and other fixed term debt | | **(73)** | (33) |
| (Payment) / receipt on financing derivatives | | **(9)** | 6 |
| Capital element of finance lease rental payments | | **(14)** | (13) |
| New shares issued under share schemes | | **6** | 5 |
| Own shares issued under share schemes | | **2** | 8 |
| Purchase of own shares for ESOP trust | | **(17)** | (24) |
| Purchase of own shares for cancellation | | **(100)** | – |
| Special dividend paid to equity shareholders of the Company | | **(100)** | – |
| Ordinary dividends paid to equity shareholders of the Company | | **(234)** | (224) |
| **Net cash flows from financing activities** | | **(554)** | (380) |
| **Net increase in cash and cash equivalents and bank overdrafts** | | **55** | 153 |
| **Cash and cash equivalents and bank overdrafts at beginning of year** | | **534** | 398 |
| Exchange differences | | **(62)** | (17) |
| **Cash and cash equivalents and bank overdrafts, including amounts classified as held for sale, at end of year** | | **527** | 534 |
| Cash and cash equivalents classified as held for sale (China) | | **(57)** | – |
| **Cash and cash equivalents and bank overdrafts at end of year** | 32 | **470** | 534 |

Analysing the cash flow statement for Kingfisher plc gives us the following information:

- The group generated £806m cash on its operations in the period 2014/15, which was a 17.4% decrease on the prior year.
- The tax cash outflow as a proportion of cash generated by operations has increased, from 14.5% in 2013/14 to 18.1% in 2014/15.
- The net cash flow from operating activities of £660m, has been predominantly utilised for financing purposes. A net cash outflow of £554m was spent on financing in the period.

- Financing cash flows comprised £234m paid out as an ordinary dividend to shareholders and a further £200m paid out as a special dividend and a share repurchase. Kingfisher has significant net cash on its balance sheet and it is returning a proportion of the cash generated this period to its shareholders.
- The net cash outflow from investing activities was £51m. This was comprised £275m spent on capital expenditure, offset by a £210m cash disposal proceeds.
- Net cash on the balance sheet at the end of the period was £470m, compared to £534m the prior year. The decrease has been due to exchange differences on translation of the balance sheet at the end of the reporting period.
- In conclusion, Kingfisher has significant balance sheet liquidity, and has returned a significant proportion of the cash generated in the period to shareholders. Excess liquidity can have a negative impact on the business' return on capital employed.

## TASK

**Reviewing a cash flow statement**

Choose a quoted company that interests you and use the internet to find its latest report and accounts. Read the cash flow statement and use it to identify the main themes for the company in the period. What is your overall conclusion on its liquidity position for the current year?

## CHAPTER ROUNDUP

**Module 1, Chapter 2: Accounting for Cash Flow**

- The income statement and balance sheet is prepared on an accruals basis, which can differ from the cash position.
- A statutory cash flow statement is divided into three headings:
  - **cash flow from operating activities** – the cash generated from operations or trading;
  - **cash flow from investing activities** – includes net capital expenditure on purchases and sales of non-current assets and investments; and
  - **cash flow from financing activities** – cash inflows and outflows from debt refinancing, repayment and draw-downs of borrowings, new equity issues and share redemptions. Movements in the overdraft are excluded.
- The statutory cash flow statement shows the net change of cash and cash equivalents in the period, including overdrafts and short-term (less than three months) highly liquid investments.
- You should be confident in both preparing and interpreting a statutory cash flow statement (ie using the appropriate headings in the prescribed format).

# Off-Balance Sheet Financing

chapter 3

Contents


| | | |
|---|---|---|
| 1 | Introduction | 22 |
| 2 | Basic Principles | 23 |
| 3 | Recognition | 24 |
| 4 | Common Forms of Off-Balance Sheet Finance | 24 |
| 5 | Operating versus Finance Leases | 31 |

# 1 Introduction

In the past, companies have attempted to acquire or use assets in such a way that the financing for those assets was not recognised on the balance sheet. The resultant asset and liability figures did not realistically represent the value of assets or debt being used within the business.

This type of activity is known as **off-balance sheet financing** – the financing of the activities of the company while keeping some or all of the finance off the balance sheet.

Why might company managers wish to enter into such transactions?

- In some countries, companies traditionally have a lower level of gearing than companies in other countries. Off-balance sheet finance is used to **keep gearing low**, probably because of the views of analysts and brokers.
- A company may need to keep its gearing down in order to stay within the terms of **loan covenants** imposed by lenders.
- A quoted company with high borrowings is often expected (by analysts and others) to declare a **rights issue** in order to reduce gearing. This has an adverse effect on a company's share price and so off-balance sheet financing is used to reduce gearing *and* the expectation of a rights issue.
- Analysts' short-term views are a problem for companies **developing assets** which are not producing income during the development stage. Such companies will match the borrowings associated with such developing assets, along with the assets themselves, off-balance sheet position.

  They are brought back on balance sheet once income is being generated by the assets. This process keeps return on capital employed higher than it would have been during the development stage.
- In the past, groups of companies have excluded **subsidiaries** from consolidation in an off-balance sheet position transaction because they carry out completely different types of business and have different characteristics. The usual example is a leasing company (in say a retail group) which has a high level of gearing.

You can see from this brief list of reasons that the overriding motivation is to avoid **misinterpretation**. In other words, the company does not trust the analysts or other users to understand the reasons for a transaction and so avoids any effect such transactions might have by taking them off-balance sheet. Unfortunately, the position of the company is then misstated and the user of the accounts is misled.

Not all forms of 'off-balance sheet finance' are undertaken for cosmetic or accounting reasons. Some transactions are carried out to **limit or isolate risk**, to reduce interest costs and so on. In other words, these transactions are in the best interests of the company, not merely a cosmetic repackaging of figures which would normally appear in the balance sheet.

The result of the use of increasingly sophisticated off-balance sheet finance transactions is a situation where the users of financial statements do not have a proper or clear view of the state of the company's affairs. The disclosures required by national company law and accounting standards did not in the past provide sufficient rules for disclosure of off-balance sheet finance transactions and so very little of the true nature of the transaction was exposed.

Whatever the purpose of such transactions, insufficient disclosure creates a problem. This problem has been debated over the years by the accountancy profession and other interested parties and some progress has been made. However, company collapses during recessions have often revealed much higher borrowings than originally thought, because part of the borrowing was off-balance sheet.

The *Framework*, issued by the IASB, states that information contained in the financial statements should be **relevant and reliable**. One of the key features of reliable information is that it accords with the **commercial reality or substance** of the circumstances. Thus the *Framework* effectively elevates this concept to the status of a fundamental principle that is required to be followed in the financial statements.

This concept, of **commercial substance over legal form**, forms the basis for the treatment of leases and other problematic transactions.

The IASB *Framework* states that accounting for items according to substance and economic reality and not merely legal form is a key determinant of reliable information.

- For the majority of transactions there is **no difference** between the two and therefore no conflict arises.
- For other transactions **substance and form diverge** and the choice of treatment can give different results due to non-recognition of an asset or liability even though benefits or obligations result.

Full disclosure is not enough: all transactions must be **accounted for** correctly, with full disclosure of related details as necessary to give the user of accounts a full understanding of the transactions.

## 2 Basic Principles

How does the *Framework* enforce the substance over form rule? Its main method is to define the elements of financial statements and therefore to give rules for their recognition. The key considerations are whether a transaction has **given rise to new assets and liabilities**, and whether it has **changed any existing assets and liabilities**.

The characteristics of transactions whose substance is not readily apparent are as follows.

- The **legal title** to an item is separated from the ability to enjoy the principal benefits, and the exposure to the main risks associated with it.
- The transaction is **linked to one or more others** so that the commercial effect of the transaction cannot be understood without reference to the complete series.
- The transaction includes **one or more options**, under such terms that it makes it highly likely that the option(s) will be exercised.

### Definitions

These are perhaps the most important definitions.

An **asset** is a resource controlled by the entity as a result of past events and from which future economic benefits are expected to flow to the entity.

A **liability** is a present obligation of the entity arising from past events, the settlement of which is expected to result in an outflow from the entity of resources embodying economic benefit.

*(Framework)*

Identification of **who has the risks** relating to an asset will generally indicate **who has the benefits** and hence **who has the asset**. If an entity is in certain circumstances unable to avoid an **outflow of benefits**, this will provide evidence that it has a liability.

The definitions given in the IASB *Framework* of income and expenses are not as important as those of assets and liabilities. This is because income and expenses are **described in terms of changes in assets and liabilities**, ie they are secondary definitions.

**Income** is increases in economic benefits during the accounting period in the form of inflows or enhancements of assets or decreases of liabilities that result in increases in equity, other than those relating to contributions from equity participants.

**Expenses** are decreases in economic benefits during the accounting period in the form of outflows or depletions of assets or incurrences of liabilities that result in decreases in equity, other than those relating to distributions to equity participants. *(Framework)*

The real importance, then, is the way the *Framework* defines assets and liabilities. This forces entities to acknowledge their assets and liabilities regardless of the legal status.

It is not sufficient, however, that the asset or liability fulfils the above definitions; it must also satisfy **recognition criteria** in order to be shown in an entity's accounts.

# 3 Recognition

**Recognition** is the process of incorporating in the balance sheet or income statement an item that meets the definition of an element and satisfies the criteria for recognition set out below. It involves the depiction of the item in words and by a monetary amount and the inclusion of that amount in the balance sheet or income statement totals.

The next key question is deciding **when** something which satisfies the definition of an asset or liability has to be recognised in the balance sheet. Where a transaction results in an item that meets the definition of an asset or liability, that item should be recognised in the balance sheet if:

- It is **probable that a future inflow or outflow** of benefit to or from the entity will occur; and
- The item can be **measured at a monetary amount with sufficient reliability**.

This effectively prevents entities abusing the definitions of the elements by recognising items that are vague in terms of likelihood of occurrence and measurability. If this were not in force, entities could **manipulate the financial statements** in various ways, eg recognising assets when the likely future economic benefits cannot yet be determined.

**Probability** is assessed based on the situation at the balance sheet date. For example, it is usually expected that some customers of an entity will not pay what they owe. The expected level of non-payment is based on past experience and the receivables asset is reduced by a percentage (the general bad debt provision).

**Measurement** must be reliable, but it does not preclude the use of **reasonable estimates**, which is an essential part of the financial statement preparation.

Even if something does not qualify for recognition now, it may meet the criteria **at a later date**.

# 4 Common Forms of Off-Balance Sheet Finance

How does the theory of the *Framework* **apply in practice**, to real transactions? The rest of this section looks at some complex transactions that occur frequently in practice.

## Consignment inventory

Consignment inventory is an arrangement where inventory is held by one party (say a distributor) but is owned by another party (for example, a manufacturer or a finance company). Consignment inventory is common in the motor industry and is similar to goods sold on a 'sale or return' basis.

To identify the correct treatment, it is necessary to identify the point at which the distributor or dealer acquired the benefits of the asset (the inventory) rather than the point at which legal title was acquired. If the manufacturer has the right to require the return of the inventory, and if that right is likely to be exercised, then the inventory is *not* an asset of the dealer. If the dealer is rarely required to return the inventory, then this part of the transaction will have little commercial effect in practice and should be ignored for accounting purposes. The potential liability would need to be disclosed in the accounts.

## Summary of indications of asset status

The following analysis summarises the range of possibilities in such a transaction.

| Indications that the inventory is *not an asset* of the dealer at delivery | Indications that the inventory *is an asset* of the dealer at delivery |
|---|---|
| Manufacturer can require dealer to **return inventory** (or transfer inventory to another dealer) without compensation. | Manufacturer cannot require dealer to **return or transfer inventory**. |
| **Penalty paid** by the dealer to prevent returns/transfers of inventory at the manufacturer's request. | **Financial incentives** given to persuade dealer to transfer inventory at manufacturer's request. |
| Dealer has unfettered **right to return inventory** to the manufacturer without penalty and actually exercises the right in practice. | Dealer has **no right to return inventory** or is commercially compelled not to exercise its right of return. |
| Manufacturer bears **obsolescence risk**, eg<br>Obsolete inventory is returned to the manufacturer without penalty; or<br>Financial incentives given by manufacturer to prevent inventory being returned to it (eg on a model change or if it becomes obsolete). | Dealer bears **obsolescence risk**, eg<br>Penalty charged if dealer returns inventory to manufacturer; or<br>Obsolete inventory cannot be returned to the manufacturer and no compensation is paid by manufacturer for losses due to obsolescence. |
| Inventory **transfer price** charged by manufacturer is based on manufacturer's list price at date of transfer of legal title. | Inventory **transfer price** charged by manufacturer is based on manufacturer's list price at date of delivery. |
| Manufacturer bears **slow movement risk**, eg transfer price set independently of time for which dealer holds inventory, and there is no deposit. | Dealer bears **slow movement risk**, eg<br>Dealer is effectively charged interest as transfer price or other payments to manufacturer vary with time for which dealer holds inventory; or<br>Dealer makes a substantial interest-free deposit that varies with the levels of inventory held. |

## Required accounting

The following apply where it is concluded that the inventory **is in substance an asset** of the dealer.

- The inventory should be recognised as such on the dealer's balance sheet, together with a corresponding liability to the manufacturer.
- Any deposit should be deducted from the liability and the excess classified as a trade payable.

Where it is concluded that the inventory is **not in substance an asset** of the dealer, the following apply.

- The inventory should not be included on the dealer's balance sheet until the transfer of risks and rewards has crystallised.
- Any deposit should be included under 'other receivables'.

## TASK

Review the following example and decide in each case if the asset and liability should be recognised by Daley Co at the date of delivery.

Daley Motors Co owns a number of car dealerships throughout a geographical area. The terms of the arrangement between the dealerships and the manufacturer are as follows.

(a) Legal title passes when the cars are either used by Daley Co for demonstration purposes or sold to a third party.

(b) The dealer has the right to return vehicles to the manufacturer without penalty. (Daley Co has rarely exercised this right in the past.)

(c) The transfer price is based on the manufacturer's list price at the date of delivery.

(d) Daley Co makes a substantial interest-free deposit based on the number of cars held.

## SOLUTION

(a) Legal form is irrelevant.
(b) Yes: only because rarely exercised (otherwise 'no').
(c) Yes.
(d) Yes: the dealership is effectively forgoing the interest which could be earned on the cash sum.

Overall it can be seen that the asset and liability should be recognised at the date of delivery.

### Consignment stock: practical example

The extract below is from the accounting policies given in the 2010 Annual Report of Inchcape plc.

**Inchcape consignment stock**

Vehicles held on consignment which are deemed in substance to be assets of the Group are included within 'inventories' with the corresponding liability included within 'trade and other payables'.

## Sale and repurchase agreements

These are arrangements under which the company sells an asset to another person on terms that allow the company to **repurchase the asset** in certain circumstances. A common example is the sale and repurchase of maturing whisky inventories. The key question is whether the transaction is a **straightforward sale**, or whether it is, in effect, a **secured loan**. It is necessary to look at the arrangement to determine who has the rights to the economic benefits that the asset generates, and the terms on which the asset is to be repurchased.

If the seller has the right to the benefits of the **use of the asset**, and the repurchase terms are such that the **repurchase is likely** to take place, the transaction should be accounted for as a **loan**.

## Summary of indications of the sale of the asset

The following summary is helpful.

| Indications of *sale* of original asset to buyer (nevertheless, the seller may retain a different asset) | Indications of *no sale* of original asset to buyer (secured loan) |
|---|---|
| | Sale price does not equal **market value** at date of sale. |
| No commitment for **seller to repurchase** asset, eg call option where there is a real possibility the option will fail to be exercised. | Commitment for **seller to repurchase** asset, eg<br>Put and call option with the same exercise price.<br>Either a put or a call option with no genuine commercial possibility that the option will fail to be exercised; or<br>Seller requires asset back to use in its business, or asset is in effect the only source of seller's future sales. |
| Risk of **changes in asset value** borne by buyer such that buyer does not receive solely a lender's return, eg both sale and repurchase price equal market value at date of sale/repurchase. | Risk of **changes in asset value** borne by seller such that buyer receives solely a lender's return, eg<br>Repurchase price equals sale price plus costs plus interest.<br>Original purchase price adjusted retrospectively to pass variations in the value of the asset to the seller.<br>Seller provides residual value guarantee to buyer or subordinated debt to protect buyer from falls in the value of the asset. |
| Nature of the asset is such that it will be used over the life of the agreement, and seller has no rights to **determine its use**. Seller has no rights to determine asset's development or future sale. | Seller retains right to **determine asset's use**, development or sale, or rights to profits therefrom. |

### Required accounting

Where the substance of the transaction is that of a **secured loan**:

- The seller should continue to recognise the original asset and record the proceeds received from the buyer as a liability
- Interest, however designated, should be accrued
- The carrying amount of the asset should be reviewed for impairment and written down if necessary.

Where the transaction is a **sale and leaseback** under a finance lease, then no profit should be recognised on entering in to the arrangement and no adjustment made to the carrying value of the asset. As stated in IAS 17, this represents the substance of the transactions, namely the raising of finance secured on an asset that continues to be held and that is not disposed of.

Where the **seller has a new asset or liability** (eg merely a call option to repurchase the original asset), it should recognise or disclose that new asset or liability on a prudent basis in accordance with accounting standards relating to financial instruments. In particular, the seller should recognise (and not merely disclose) a liability for any kind of unconditional obligation it has entered into. Where doubts exist regarding the amount of any gain or loss arising, full provision should be made for any expected loss; but recognition of any gain, to the extent that it is in doubt, should be deferred until it is realised.

## Task

A construction company, Mecanto Co, agrees to sell to Hamlows Bank some of the land within its landbank. The terms of the sale are as follows.

(a) The sales price is to be at open market value.

(b) Mecanto Co has the right to develop the land on the basis that it will pay all the outgoings on the land plus an annual fee of 5% of the purchase price.

(c) Mecanto has the option to buy back the land at any time within the next five years. The repurchase price is based on:

- Original purchase price
- Expenses relating to the purchase
- An interest charge of base rate + 2%
- Less amounts received from Mecanto by Hamlows

(d) At the end of five years Hamlows Bank may offer the land for sale generally. Any shortfall on the proceeds relative to the agreed purchase price agreed with Mecanto has to be settled by Mecanto in cash.

Should the asset continue to be recognised by Mecanto Co and the sales proceeds treated as a loan?

## Solution

(a) No: the sales price is as for an arm's length transaction.

(b) Yes: Mecanto has control over the asset.

Yes: Mecanto has to pay a fee based on cash received.

(c) Yes: interest is charged on the proceeds paid by Mecanto.

Yes: the repurchase price is based on the lender's return

(d) Yes: options ensure that Mecanto bears all the risk (both favourable and unfavourable) of changes in the market value of the land.

The asset should continue to be recognised and the sales proceeds treated as a loan.

## Factoring of receivables/debts

Where debts or receivables are factored, the original creditor **sells the debts to the factor**. The sales price may be fixed at the outset or may be adjusted later. It is also common for the factor to offer a credit facility that allows the seller to draw upon a proportion of the amounts owed.

In order to determine the correct accounting treatment it is necessary to consider whether the benefit of the debts has been passed on to the factor, or whether the factor is, in effect, providing a loan on the security of the receivables balances. If the seller has to **pay interest** on the difference between the amounts advanced to him and the amounts that the factor has received, and if the seller bears the **risks of non-payment** by the receivable, then the indications would be that the transaction is, in effect, a loan. Depending on the circumstances, either a linked presentation or separate presentation may be appropriate.

### Summary of indications of appropriate treatment

The following is a summary of indicators of the appropriate treatment.

| Indications the debts are *not an asset* of the seller | Indications that the debts are an *asset* of the seller |
|---|---|
| Transfer is for a single non-returnable fixed sum. | Finance cost varies with speed of collection of debts, eg<br>By adjustment to consideration for original transfer; or<br>Subsequent transfers priced to recover costs of earlier transfers. |
| There is no recourse to the seller for losses. | There is full recourse to the seller for losses. |
| Factor is paid all amounts received from the factored debts (and no more). Seller has no rights to further sums from the factor. | Seller is required to repay amounts received from the factor on or before a set date, regardless of timing or amounts of collections from debtors. |

### Required accounting

Where the seller has retained no significant benefits and risks relating to the receivables and has no obligation to repay amounts received from the factors, the receivables should be removed from its balance sheet and no liability shown in respect of the proceeds received from the factor. A profit or loss should be recognised, calculated as the difference between the carrying amount of the receivables and the proceeds received.

**EXAMPLE**

If trade receivables of £100m are sold for £98m without recourse the following accounting entries would happen.

| | |
|---|---|
| Reduce trade receivables | £100m |
| Increase cash flow | £98m |
| Increase expenses in income statement | £2m |

Where the seller does retain significant benefits and risks, a gross asset (equivalent in amount to the gross amount of the receivables) should be shown on the balance sheet of the seller within assets, and a corresponding liability in respect of the proceeds received from the factor should be shown within liabilities. The interest element of the factor's charges should be recognised as it accrues and included in the income statement with other interest charges. Other factoring costs should be similarly accrued and included in the income statement within the appropriate caption.

**EXAMPLE**

If the trade receivables are sold for £100m with full recourse, the following accounting entries would happen.

| | |
|---|---|
| Increase cash | £100m |
| Increase liabilities | £100m |

## Securitised assets

Securitisation is very common in the financial services industry, and the assets that are most commonly securitised are mortgages and credit card accounts, although hire purchase loans, trade receivables and even property and inventories are sometimes securitised. **Blocks of assets** are thus financed, rather than the company's general business.

The normal procedure is for the assets to be transferred by the person who held them (the originator) to a special purpose company (the issuer) in exchange for cash. The issuer will use the proceeds of an issue of debentures or loan notes to pay for the assets. The shares in the issuer are usually held by a third party so that it does not need to be consolidated. The issuer will usually have a very small share capital, and so most of the risk will be borne by the people who lent it the money through the debentures to pay for the assets. For this reason there is usually some form of insurance taken out on the assets to give some security for the lenders.

### Summary of indications as to accounting treatment

The following is a summary of indications of the appropriate treatment.

| **Indications that the securitised assets are *not assets* of the originator** | **Indications that the securitised assets are *assets* of the originator** |
|---|---|
| Originator's individual financial statements | |
| Transaction price is arm's length price for an outright sale. | Transaction price is not arm's length price for an outright sale. |
| Transfer is for a single, non-returnable fixed sum. | Proceeds received are returnable, or there is a provision whereby the originator may keep the securitised assets on repayment of the loan notes or re-acquire them. |
| There is no recourse to the originator for losses. | There is or may be full recourse to the originator for losses, eg<br>Originator's directors are unable or unwilling to state that it is not obliged to fund any losses.<br>Noteholders have not agreed in writing that they will seek repayment only from funds generated by the securitised assets. |
| Originator's consolidated financial statements | |
| Issuer is owned by an independent third party that made a substantial capital investment, has control of the issuer, and has the benefits and risks of its net assets. | Issuer is a subsidiary or quasi-subsidiary of the originator. |

### Required accounting: originator's financial statements

Where the originator has retained no significant benefits and risks relating to the securitised assets and has no obligation to repay the proceeds of the note issue, the asset should be removed from its balance sheet, and no liability shown in respect of the proceeds of the note issue. A profit or loss should be recognised, calculated as the difference between the carrying amount of the assets and the proceeds received.

Where the originator has retained significant benefits and risks, a gross asset (equal in amount to the gross amount of the securitised assets) should be shown on the balance sheet of the originator within assets, and a corresponding liability in respect of the proceeds of the note issue shown within liabilities. No gain or loss should be recognised at the time the securitisation is entered into (unless adjustment to the carrying value of the asset independent of the securitisation is required).

### Required accounting: issuer's financial statements

The requirements set out in the paragraphs above for the originator's individual financial statements also apply to the issuer's financial statements. In most cases the issuer will be required to show the gross amounts, as explained above.

### Loan transfers

These are arrangements where a loan is transferred to a transferee from an original lender. This will usually be done by the **assignment of rights and obligations** by the lender, or the **creation of a new agreement** between the borrower and the transferee. The same principles apply to loan transfers as to debt factoring and securitised assets.

### Summary of indications of appropriate treatment

The indications may be summarised as follows.

| Indications that the loan is *off* the lender's balance sheet | Indications that the loan is *on* the lender's balance sheet |
|---|---|
| Transfer is for a single, non-returnable fixed sum. | The proceeds received are returnable in the event of losses occurring on the loans. |
| There is no recourse to the lender for losses from any cause. | There is full recourse to the lender for losses. |
| Transferee is paid all amounts received from the loans (and no more), as and when received. Lender has no rights to further sums from the loans or the transferee. | Lender is required to repay amounts received from the transferee on or before a set date, regardless of the timing or amount of payments by the borrowers. |

### Required accounting

Where the lender has retained no significant benefits and risks relating to the loans and has no obligation to repay the transferee, the loans should be removed from its balance sheet and no liability shown in respect of the amounts received from the transferee. A profit or loss may arise for the lender. Where the profit or loss is realised in cash it should be recognised, calculated as the difference between the carrying amount of the loans and the cash proceeds received. Where, however, the lender's profit or loss is not realised in cash and there are doubts as to its amount, full provision should be made for any expected loss but recognition of any gain, to the extent it is in doubt, should be deferred until cash has been received.

Where the lender has retained significant rights and benefits, a gross asset (equivalent in amount to the gross amount of the loans) should be shown on the balance sheet of the lender within assets, and a corresponding liability in respect of the amounts received from the transferee should be shown within liabilities. No gain or loss should be recognised at the time of the transfer (unless adjustment to the carrying value of the loan independent of the transfer is required).

## 5 Operating versus Finance Leases

In a leasing transaction there is a **contract** between the lessor and the lessee for the hire of an asset. The lessor retains legal ownership but conveys to the lessee the right to use the asset for an agreed period of time in return for specified rentals. IAS 17 *Leases* standardises the accounting treatment and disclosure of assets held under lease. IAS 17 defines a lease and recognises two types.

## Definitions

**Lease**. An agreement whereby the lessor conveys to the lessee in return for a payment or series of payments the right to use an asset for an agreed period of time.

**Finance lease**. A lease that transfers substantially all the risks and rewards incidental to ownership of an asset. Title may or may not eventually be transferred.

**Operating lease**. A lease other than a finance lease. *(IAS 17)*

A **finance lease** may be a **hire purchase agreement**. The difference is that under a hire purchase agreement the customer eventually, after paying an agreed number of instalments, becomes entitled to exercise an option to purchase the asset. Under other leasing agreements, ownership remains forever with the lessor.

To expand on the definition above, a finance lease should be presumed if at the inception of a lease the **present value of the minimum lease payments** is approximately equal to the **fair value of the leased asset**.

The present value should be calculated by using the **interest rate implicit in the lease**.

- **Minimum lease payments**. The payments over the lease term that the lessee is or can be required to make, excluding contingent rent, costs for services and taxes to be paid by and be reimbursed to the lessor, together with
  - For a lessee, any amounts guaranteed by the lessee or by a party related to the lessee.
  - For a lessor, any residual value guaranteed to the lessor by one of the following.
    - The lessee
    - A party related to the lessee
    - An independent third party financially capable of meeting this guarantee

  However, if the lessee has the option to purchase the asset at a price which is expected to be sufficiently lower than fair value at the date the option becomes exercisable for it to be reasonably certain, at the inception of the lease, that the option will be exercised, the minimum lease payments comprise the minimum payments payable over the lease term to the expected date of exercise of this purchase option and the payment required to exercise it.

- **Interest rate implicit in the lease**

  The discount rate that, at the inception of the lease, causes the aggregate present value of:
  - The minimum lease payments; and
  - The unguaranteed residual value

  to be equal to the sum of
  - The fair value of the leased asset; and
  - Any initial direct costs of the lessor.

## Accounting for leases: lessees and lessors

**Operating leases** do not really pose an accounting problem. The lessee pays amounts periodically to the lessor and these are **charged to the income statement** on a straight-line basis over the term of the lease.

The accounting impact is as follows.

- Income statement – operating costs
- Balance sheet – cash down

For assets held under **finance leases** (including hire purchase) this accounting treatment would not reflect the commercial reality of the situation.

A **lessee** may use a finance lease to fund the 'acquisition' of a major asset which he will then use in his business, perhaps for many years. **The substance of the transaction is that he has acquired a non-current asset**, and this is reflected in the accounting treatment prescribed by IAS 17, even though in law the lessee may never become the owner of the asset.

The revised IAS 17 states that when classifying a lease of **land and buildings** the **land** element is normally classified as an **operating lease unless title passes to the lessee** at the end of the contract.

## Accounting treatment – balance sheet

**IAS 17** requires that, when an asset is the subject of a **finance lease**, **lessor and lessee should account for the transaction as though it were a credit sale**. In the lessee's books therefore

- Increase assets
- Increase liabilities

The amount to be recorded in this way is the **lower of** the **fair value** of the leased asset and the **present value** of the **minimum lease payments**.

IAS 17 states that it is not appropriate to show liabilities for leased assets as deductions from the leased assets. A distinction should be made between **current and non-current** lease liabilities, if the entity makes this distinction for other liabilities.

The asset should be **depreciated** (on the bases set out in IAS 16 and IAS 38) over the shorter of:

- The lease term
- The asset's useful life

## Apportionment of rental payments

When the lessee makes a rental payment under a finance lease it will comprise two elements.

- An **interest charge** on the finance provided by the lessor. This proportion of each payment is interest payable in the income statement of the lessee.
- A repayment of part of the **capital cost** of the asset. In the lessee's books this proportion of each rental payment must be debited to reduce the outstanding liability.

The accounting problem is to decide what proportion of each instalment paid by the lessee represents interest, and what proportion represents a repayment of the capital advanced by the lessor. There are two apportionment methods used.

- **Actuarial method**
- **Sum-of-the-digits method**

## EXAMPLE

On 1 January, a company acquires an asset with a cash price of £255,000 under a lease. The terms of the lease are that five six-monthly instalments of £60,000 are to be paid in arrears, ie a total of £300,000 must be paid. In addition, we can extend the lease to a full four years and will probably do so, as we believe the asset will continue to be useful to us for that time.

The rent for this secondary period is negligible.

How will this be reflected in the accounts of the company for the next four years?

**NB:** The rate of interest implicit in the lease is 5.7% per instalment.

## SOLUTION

**Classification – Finance/Operating lease**

The present value of the minimum lease payments is approximately equal to the fair value of the asset so we will assume this is a finance lease.

**Value Capitalised**

We will base the value capitalised on the cash price of £255,000. The impact on the accounting equation on 1 January will be

- Non-current assets up £255,000. (**Debit**: Non current assets)
- Liabilities up £255,000 (representing the finance lease liability now payable). (**Credit**: liabilities)

**Lease Term**

**Primary term – for finance charge allocation**

In this Example, we have a primary lease term of 2½ years and should therefore allocate the total finance charge over this period. The total finance charge is the difference between the total amount being paid and the capitalised value of the asset (which equals the initial value of the loan). In this example, the total finance charge is £45,000 (£300,000 – £255,000).

**Full lease term – for depreciation**

The full lease term in this Example is four years, the period over which we can, and are expected to want to use the asset. This, therefore, represents the time over which we should depreciate the asset, ie our annual depreciation charge should be £63,750 (£255,000 ÷ 4 years) assuming straight-line depreciation.

Over the next four years, this asset will appear on the balance sheet as follows.

| Non-Current Assets | Year 1 (£'000) | Year 2 (£'000) | Year 3 (£'000) | Year 4 (£'000) |
|---|---|---|---|---|
| Cost | 255.00 | 255.00 | 255.00 | 255.00 |
| Depreciation | (63.75) | (127.50) | (191.25) | (255.00) |
| Net Book Value | 191.25 | 127.50 | 63.75 | – |

## Analysis of payments

Remember that the idea is that we calculate how much of the finance charge is allocated to each payment by one of two methods.

- The actuarial method
- The sum-of-digits method

We will illustrate both to show that they show substantially similar results.

### Actuarial method

Using the rate of interest implicit in the lease of 5.7% per instalment we can calculate the following repayment schedule.

| Period | Lease Liability b/f (£'000) | Finance Charge at 5.7% (£'000) | Paid (£'000) | Difference (Capital Repaid) (£'000) | Lease Liability c/f (£'000) |
|---|---|---|---|---|---|
| **Year 1** | | | | | |
| 1 Jan–30 June | 255.0 | 14.5 | (60.0) | 45.5 | 209.5 |
| 1 July–31 Dec | 209.5 | 11.9 | (60.0) | 48.1 | 161.4 |
| **Year 2** | | | | | |
| 1 Jan–30 June | 161.4 | 9.2 | (60.0) | 50.8 | 110.6 |
| 1 July–31 Dec | 110.6 | 6.3 | (60.0) | 53.7 | 56.9 |
| **Year 3** | | | | | |
| 1 Jan–30 June | 56.9 | 3.1 | (60.0) | 56.9 | – |
| | | 45.0 | 300.0 | 255.0 | |

We can see from this that over the primary term of 2½ years, £300,000 is paid in total, which we can split into £45,000 total finance charge and £255,000 capital repaid, as we wanted.

Looking down this table we can see that the loan balance outstanding at the end of Year 1 is £161,400. Looking further down the table, we can see that £56,900 is still outstanding at the end of Year 2 and that the liability is cleared during Year 3. These, therefore, represent our full year-end liabilities at those dates.

What we need to do is split these balances between amounts current and non-current liabilities.

| Liabilities | Year 1 (£'000) | Year 2 (£'000) | Year 3 (£'000) | Year 4 (£'000) |
|---|---|---|---|---|
| Current | 104.50 | 56.90 | – | – |
| Non-current | 56.90 | – | – | – |
| Total liability | 161.40 | 56.90 | – | – |

### Sum-of-digits method

To utilise this alternative method we firstly need to add up the digits corresponding to the number of payments we are making, ie 5 + 4 + 3 + 2 + 1 = 15. We will then use this to allocate the total finance charge of £45,000 as follows.

Alternatively the sum of digits can be calculated using the following formula.

$$\frac{n(n+1)}{2}$$

where 'n' is the number of instalments. Therefore, in our example

$$\frac{5(5+1)}{2} = 15$$

| Payment | Finance Charge | (£'000) |
|---|---|---|
| 1 | 5/15 × 45,000 | 15 |
| 2 | 4/15 × 45,000 | 12 |
| 3 | 3/15 × 45,000 | 9 |
| 4 | 2/15 × 45,000 | 6 |
| 5 | 1/15 × 45,000 | 3 |

Hence, our repayment schedule on this basis looks as follows.

| Period | Lease Creditor b/f (£'000) | Finance Charge (£'000) | Paid (£'000) | Difference (Capital Repaid) (£'000) | Lease Creditor c/f (£'000) |
|---|---|---|---|---|---|
| **Year 1** | | | | | |
| 1 Jan–30 June | 255 | 15 | (60) | 45 | 210 |
| 1 July–31 Dec | 210 | 12 | (60) | 48 | 162 |
| **Year 2** | | | | | |
| 1 Jan–30 June | 162 | 9 | (60) | 51 | 111 |
| 1 July–31 Dec | 111 | 6 | (60) | 54 | 57 |
| **Year 3** | | | | | |
| 1 Jan–30 June | 57 | 3 | (60) | 57 | – |
| | | 45 | 300 | 255 | |

As we can see, the figures are substantially similar to those calculated under the actuarial method, with a liability at the end of Year 1 of £162,000, compared to £161,400 under the actuarial method.

We can also see that the finance charge for this year is very similar under both methods, being £27,000 (£15,000 + £12,000) under the sum-of-digits method and £26,400 (£14,500 + £11,900) under the actuarial method.

## SOLUTION

Using the actuarial method, we can produce the following extract from the balance sheet and income statement.

**Balance sheets**

| **Non-Current Assets** | Year 1 (£'000) | Year 2 (£'000) | Year 3 (£'000) | Year 4 (£'000) |
|---|---|---|---|---|
| Cost | 255.00 | 255.00 | 255.00 | 255.00 |
| Depreciation | (63.75) | (127.50) | (191.25) | (255.00) |
| Net Book Value | 191.25 | 127.50 | 63.75 | 0.00 |
| **Liabilities:** | | | | |
| Current | 104.50 | 56.90 | – | – |
| Non-Current | 56.90 | – | – | – |
| **Total Liability** | 161.40 | 56.90 | – | – |

**Income statements**

| | Year 1 (£'000) | Year 2 (£'000) | Year 3 (£'000) | Year 4 (£'000) |
|---|---|---|---|---|
| Depreciation | 63.75 | 63.75 | 63.75 | 63.75 |
| Finance lease charges | 26.40 | 15.50 | 3.10 | – |
| | 90.15 | 79.25 | 66.85 | 63.75 |

## Finance leases – analysis points

A number of accounting ratios are impacted upon as a result of treating a lease as a finance lease rather than an operating lease.

**TASK**

Describe the impact of including a finance lease in a company's accounts on the following ratios:

(a) Return on capital employed
(b) Gearing
(c) Interest cover
(d) Current and quick ratio

**SOLUTION**

(a) **Return on capital employed**

Treating the lease as a finance lease results in a non-current asset being added to the trading assets and a finance lease liability being added to the loans. As a result, the capital employed will be larger and hence the return on capital employed may be lower than would be the case were we accounting for the lease as an operating lease.

(b) **Gearing**

There will be no change in shareholders' funds as a result of acquiring this asset, however, there will be an increase in the level of borrowings as the finance lease liability is added to the debt. As a result, gearing will apparently be higher.

(c) **Interest cover**

Since the finance lease charges will be added to the interest payable in the income statement, the interest cover is liable to be reduced.

(d) **Current/Quick ratios**

Part of the finance lease liability will be recorded within current liabilities. There will be no corresponding increase in the current assets, thus the current and quick ratios will both be reduced, deteriorating the apparent liquidity position of the company.

## Accounting for operating leases

The substance of an operating lease is that the risks and rewards of ownership remain with the lessor and therefore the lessee is simply hiring the equipment as opposed to effectively 'acquiring' it.

The accounting treatment for operating leases is simply to treat the full rent as an expense as incurred, with any rent paid in advance or in arrears appearing as a balance sheet prepayment (current asset) or accrual (current liability) respectively.

## Disclosure requirements for finance leases

IAS 17 (revised) requires the following disclosures by lessees in respect of finance leases.

- The **net carrying amount** at the balance sheet date for each class of asset.
- A **reconciliation** between the total of minimum lease payments at the balance sheet date, and their present value. In addition, an entity should disclose the total of minimum lease payments at the balance sheet date, and their present value, for each of the following periods.
  - Not later than one year
  - Later than one year and not later than five years
  - Later than five years
- **Contingent rents** recognised in income for the period.
- Total of **future minimum sublease payments** expected to be received under non-cancellable subleases at the balance sheet date.
- A **general description** of the lessee's significant leasing arrangements including, but not limited to, the following.
  - The basis on which contingent rent payments are determined.
  - The existence and terms of renewal or purchase options and escalation clauses.
  - Restrictions imposed by lease arrangements, such as those concerning dividends, additional debt, and further leasing.

IAS 17 encourages (but does not require) further disclosures, as appropriate.

## Disclosure requirements for operating leases

For **operating leases** the disclosures are as follows.

- The total of future minimum lease payments under non-cancellable operating leases for each of the following periods.
  - Not later than one year
  - Later than one year and not later than five years
  - Later than five years
- The total of future minimum sublease payments expected to be received under non-cancellable subleases at the balance sheet date.
- Lease and sublease payments recognised in income for the period, with separate amounts for minimum lease payments, contingent rents, and sublease payments.
- A general description of the lessee's significant leasing arrangements including, but not limited to, the following.
  - The basis on which contingent rent payments are determined.
  - The existence and terms of renewal or purchase options and escalation clauses.
  - Restrictions imposed by lease arrangements, such as those concerning dividends, additional debt, and further leasing.

## Impact on analysis of operating leases

The scale of a company's commitment under operating leases can be gauged from reading the notes to the financial statements. As covered above, a company must disclose its total minimum future commitments under operating leases. These payments represent contractual commitments and it is possible to argue that they are the economic equivalent of interest-bearing liabilities. To consider the impact that this has on financial risk of the group, a revised gearing ratio can be calculated, which includes the total operating lease commitment within the group's borrowings.

### TASK

J Sainsbury plc discloses the following note in its 2015 Annual Report relating to commitments under operating leases:

**33 Operating lease commitments**

The Group leases various retail stores, offices, depots and equipment under non-cancellable operating leases. The leases have varying terms, escalation clauses and renewal rights.

| | 2015 £m | 2014 £m |
|---|---|---|
| Aggregate future minimum lease payments: | | |
| Within one year | **585** | 554 |
| In the second to fifth years inclusive | **2,171** | 2,071 |
| After five years | **7,040** | 6,402 |
| | **9,796** | 9,027 |

Given that the net balance sheet borrowings of the group amounted to £2,343m and net assets were £5,539m at the year end, calculate the gearing ratio for J Sainsbury:

(a) Excluding operating leases
(b) Including operating leases

What is your view of the financial risk of this group? What further information do you require? Are there any limitations of your calculation?

### SOLUTION

(a) Gearing, excluding operating leases:

| | |
|---|---|
| Borrowings | 2,343 |
| Equity | 5,539 |
| **Gearing** | **42.3%** |

(b) Gearing, including operating leases:

| | |
|---|---|
| Borrowings | 2,343 |
| Capitalised operating leases | 9,796 |
| Total borrowings, including operating leases | 12,139 |
| Equity | 5,539 |
| **Gearing** | **219.2%** |

The calculations illustrate that the balance sheet gearing calculation does not adequately reflect the financial risk of the group. J Sainsbury has significant commitments under operating leases which serve to augment the overall financial risk of the business and the potential volatility of profits. It is possible to argue that operating lease payments are the economic equivalent of fixed rate debt, but under prevailing accounting standards this obligation is off-balance sheet.

To assess whether this level of financial risk is manageable, we require further information. In particular, we need sight of the income statement and cash flow statement to assess the level of operating profits and cash flows being generated by the business and how these relate to the finance charges on the debt and the rental payments on the operating leases. If there is adequate payment coverage, then we can conclude that the level of financial risk is manageable.

The revised calculation of gearing has the main limitation that the capitalised value of the operating lease payments is stated at their future value, not the present value equivalent. Borrowings capitalised in the balance sheet are stated at the present value, taking into account the implicit interest rate of the debt. Our revised calculation is likely therefore to have overstated the total financial risk outstanding.

## Chapter Roundup

### Module 1, Chapter 3: Off-Balance Sheet Financing

#### Off-Balance Sheet Financing

You need to be able to define off-balance sheet financing and provide appropriate examples. You need to be able to identify appropriate risk areas from a company's accounts.

- Off-balance sheet financing occurs when the balance sheet does not reflect the true financial risk of the business. A source of financing of the business activities has been excluded from the group liabilities.
- International accounting standards require companies to account for the **commercial substance** of the transaction as opposed to the **legal form**. If the company has the **risks and rewards** of ownership of the asset, then **the asset and its corresponding financing should be included in the financial statements.**
- Examples of off-balance sheet financing could include:
  - **Consignment inventory** – for example, a motor dealership holds a stock of motor cars, but legal title to the vehicles resides with the manufacturer. Who bears the risks and rewards of ownership of the vehicles?
  - **Sale and repurchase agreements** – a company sells an asset (eg property) to a finance provider in return for cash. Is the transaction a genuine commercial sale? Who bears the on-going risks and rewards of property ownership?
  - **Debt factoring –** a company sells debtor assets to a finance provider in return for cash. The commercial substance of the transaction should be assessed by examining with whom the bad debt risk resides.
  - **Securitised asset** – a company transfers an income-generating asset to a special purpose vehicle (SPV) and utilises this SPV to raise cash. The commercial substance of the transaction must be assessed to determine who still bears the risks and rewards of asset ownership (usually the transferring company).

#### Leases

This chapter gives you the key definitions of finance and operating leases and, importantly, their impact on the analysis of consolidated financial statements.

- A **lease** is an agreement whereby the lessor conveys to the lessee in return for a payment or series of payments the right to use an asset for an agreed period of time.
- A **finance lease** transfers substantially all the risks and rewards incidental to ownership of an asset. Title may or may not eventually be transferred.
- An **operating lease** is a lease other than a finance lease.
- A finance lease should be presumed if at the inception of a lease the **present value of the minimum lease payments** is approximately equal to the **fair value of the leased asset**.
  - The present value should be calculated by using the **interest rate implicit in the lease**.
  - **Minimum lease payments**. The payments over the lease term that the lessee is or can be required to make.
  - **Interest rate implicit in the lease.** The discount rate that, at the inception of the lease, causes the aggregate present value of the minimum lease payments and the residual value to be equal to the fair value of the leased asset.

- Analysis points:
  - **Finance leases** increase capital employed and the borrowings of a company. Capitalising finance leases in the balance sheet will thus reduce the return on capital employed ratio and increase gearing. Trading performance will appear worse and financial risk augmented.
  - **Operating leases** are a source of off-balance sheet financing. For analysis purposes, the present value of minimum operating lease commitments is, in substance, financial borrowings and the gearing ratio can be adjusted to reflect the additional debt burden.

# Group Accounting

chapter 4

Contents


| | | |
|---|---|---|
| 1 | Introduction | 44 |
| 2 | Accounting for Investments | 44 |
| 3 | Consolidated Accounts/Group Accounts | 46 |
| 4 | Group Accounts and Parent Company Accounts | 48 |
| 5 | Goodwill Arising on Consolidation | 50 |
| 6 | IFRS 3 Business Combinations | 53 |
| 7 | IFRS 3 and Fair Values in Acquisition Accounting | 57 |
| 8 | Accounting for Associates | 64 |
| 9 | Joint Ventures and Jointly Controlled Entities | 69 |
| 10 | Analysis Points | 69 |
| 11 | Accounting for Disposals and Discontinued Operations | 70 |

# 1 Introduction

The ability to consolidate accounts is a fundamental skill for a corporate financier. You will need to be able to prepare proforma accounts to decide upon an appropriate structure for a proposed transaction and to assess the financial effects of a deal. Please ensure you fully immerse yourself in the detail of this chapter – you need a good grasp of the mechanics and be comfortable with producing consolidated financial statements independently.

This chapter covers accounting for acquisitions, including subsidiaries, associates and joint ventures. We look in detail at the process of consolidation, including calculating minority interest, goodwill, fair value adjustment and dealing with intra-group transactions and mid-year acquisitions. We also cover disposals and specific accounting requirements relating to discontinued operations.

# 2 Accounting for Investments

When a company buys shares in another company it is making an investment. The basic accounting treatment is outlined diagrammatically below.

**Investments**

When we invest, the impact on the accounting equation is

- Cash down (net assets down)
- Investment up (net assets up)

The investment is an asset, but what type?

**Current Asset**

**Definition**

Not a non-current asset investment, ie

- Speculative
- For the purpose of resale

**Accounting treatment**

- Balance sheet at lower of cost and net realiable value (ie net selling cost)
- IS: Dividends received = Income

**Non-Current Asset**

**Definition**

- Long term
- For continuing use, not intended for resale

**Accounting treatment**

- Balance sheet at cost less provision for any impairment
- IS: Dividends received = Income

The above treatment of current asset investments is appropriate as it is very similar to that of holding a unit of inventory for resale. The question is whether this treatment of non-current asset investments is appropriate for different percentage levels of investment?

## Accounting treatment

It certainly seems appropriate for very low levels of investment of, say, one or two per cent of share capital of the company in which the investment is held. However, is it appropriate for higher levels of investment? Will this treatment give a fair presentation of the performance of a company and its position at the year-end for significant levels of investment? We will answer this with an example.

## EXAMPLE

A company (H) was formed ten years ago with the investment of £1,200 cash by the shareholders. Its balance sheet today is

| H's Balance sheet | (£) |
|---|---|
| **Net Assets** | |
| Investment in S | 1,000 |
| Other Non-Current Assets | 800 |
| Current Assets | 1,000 |
| | 2,800 |
| Liabilities | (200) |
| | 2,600 |
| **Shareholders' Funds** | |
| Share Capital | 1,200 |
| Retained Earnings | 1,400 |
| | 2,600 |

The £1,000 investment on the balance sheet of H represents the cost of acquiring 100% of the shares in S, formed on the same day as H itself was set up. Neither H nor S has ever paid any dividends, hence, based on these accounts, the only return that the investors are aware of being generated from their initial £1,200 investment is the £1,400 profit in the books of H, not a very exciting return over ten years!

However, if we are now told that the balance sheet of S is as follows, we see a different picture of how well the original £1,200 investment has been utilised.

| S's Balance sheet | (£) |
|---|---|
| **Net Assets** | |
| Non-Current Assets | 50,000 |
| Current Assets | 120,000 |
| | 170,000 |
| Liabilities | (20,000) |
| | 150,000 |
| **Shareholders' Funds** | |
| Share Capital | 1,000 |
| Retained Earnings | 149,000 |
| | 150,000 |

As we can see, of the original £1,200 invested in H, £1,000 was immediately invested in S and that £1,000 has managed to generate £149,000 profit over the intervening years. The £1,400 profit we see in H's books is the profit that has been generated on the remaining £200 of the initial capital invested.

Since S has never paid any dividends to H (its shareholder), the shareholders of H have had no indication as to how their cash has been used. Since the directors of H control S through their 100% ownership of its shares and the shareholders of H have effectively financed S, does simply showing S being worth £1,000 in the books of H give a fair presentation of the state of affairs of H Limited at that date?

Clearly H's shareholders need more information. One possibility might be to provide them with the financial statements of all companies controlled by H and a commentary explaining the implications. If H had many subsidiaries, this would lead to information overload and shareholders would find it impossible to interpret.

# 3 Consolidated Accounts/Group Accounts

The chosen option has been to aggregate the financial statements of the parent company (also known as the holding company) with those of its subsidiaries into a single set of accounts referred to as either 'group' or 'consolidated' accounts. Group accounts do not reflect the legal position, as the group is not a legal entity, but they present the commercial reality (the substance). Since the parent company's directors control the operating and financial policy decisions taken by subsidiaries there is, in commercial reality, a single business managed by the parent company's board. It follows that there should also be a single set of financial statements for this entity. This is an important example of the accounting convention that prefers to reflect the (commercial) substance of a transaction where this conflicts with its (legal) form – 'substance over form'. Accountants believe that this approach is necessary if a fair presentation is to be given.

## What are group accounts?

The individual financial statements of the parent and its subsidiaries are the starting point for the group accounts. However, these must be adjusted to remove the effects of transactions between them. These intra-group transactions typically include:

- Loans between members of the group
- Share capital of subsidiaries held by the parent
- Purchase and sale of goods and/or services (including management charges)
- Interest and dividends paid and received within the group

These transactions take place within the group and cannot be shown as assets, liabilities, income or expenditure in the group accounts that show that entity's relationship with the outside world.

### Preparation of group accounts

Users of the accounts do not see what adjustments have been made to eliminate intra-group transactions – they are only shown the results of the process. There are three steps in preparing group accounts where the parent owns 100% of the share capital of a subsidiary.

1 Eliminate intra-group transactions.

2 Aggregate remaining assets, liabilities, income and expenses.

3 Calculate group/consolidated retained earnings.

Where a subsidiary is partly owned, ie the parent has a controlling interest but does not own all the subsidiary's share capital, there is a fourth step.

4 Calculate minority interests.

In this case, H owns 100% of the share capital of S and so there are no minority interests.

## EXAMPLE Accounting for a wholly-owned subsidiary

| Balance sheet | H (£) | S (£) |
|---|---|---|
| **Net Assets** | | |
| Investment in S (100%) | 1,000 | |
| Other Non-Current Assets | 800 | 50,000 |
| Net Current Assets | 1,000 | 120,000 |
| | 2,800 | 170,000 |
| **Liabilities** | (200) | (20,000) |
| | 2,600 | 150,000 |
| Shareholders' Funds | | |
| Share Capital | 1,200 | 1,000 |
| Retained Earnings | 1,400 | 149,000 |
| | 2,600 | 150,000 |

**STEP 1** Eliminate intra-group transactions

The investment asset in the balance sheet of H represents the cost (£1,000) of acquiring 100% of S's share capital on its formation ten years ago. At that date, S had no retained earnings as it had not yet started to trade.

H's asset is matched by 100% of S's share capital. Share capital is in the nature of a liability owed by the company to its shareholders although it is not usually expected to be repaid. From the point of view of H and S combined (the group), H cannot own shares in itself and S cannot owe obligations to itself. The adjustment to eliminate these items is

| | |
|---|---|
| Reduce investment in S | £1,000 |
| Reduce share capital of S | £1,000 |

A similar adjustment would be made if H had lent money to S: neither H's loan asset (receivable) nor S's loan liability (payable) would be reported in the group balance sheet.

**STEP 2** Aggregate remaining assets and liabilities

**STEP 3** Calculate group/consolidated retained earnings

Group retained earnings are made up of the parent company's retained earnings plus the group's share of any increase generated in the retained earnings of each subsidiary since it joined the group. In this case, the group's share is 100% and all the retained earnings (£149,000) of the subsidiary have been generated since H acquired its interest ten years ago, before S started to trade.

Thus, the group retained earnings are made up of:

| | | |
|---|---|---|
| H | | £1,400 |
| S | 100% × £149,000 | £149,000 |
| | | £150,400 |

| Group balance sheet | | (£) |
|---|---|---|
| **Net Assets** | | |
| Other Non-Current Assets | (800 + 50,000) | 50,800 |
| Current Assets | (1,000 + 120,000) | 121,000 |
| Liabilities | (200 + 20,000) | (20,200) |
| | | 151,600 |
| **Shareholders' Funds** | | |
| Share Capital | | 1,200 |
| Retained Earnings | (1,400 + 149,000) | 150,400 |
| | | 151,600 |

In a group balance sheet, there is no asset 'investment in subsidiary'. It has been replaced by all of the subsidiary's assets and liabilities as if they were held by the parent itself. It therefore shows all of the assets and liabilities that are effectively under the control of the parent company's directors. The share capital that appears in a group balance sheet is always the share capital of the parent company and the reserves show what the parent's retained earnings would have been if it had earned the profits on its own account, rather than operating through a subsidiary company.

## 4 Group Accounts and Parent Company Accounts

Where a company has subsidiaries, under the Companies Act it is required to prepare two sets of accounts for its shareholders as follows:

- Individual company accounts of the parent company
- Group accounts

The parent company's accounts are relevant mainly for determining the maximum amount of dividend that the company can legally distribute (its distributable profits). The group accounts are used by investors and lenders for valuation, performance measurement and assessing risk.

### Example — Accounting for a partly-owned subsidiary

The previous example (*wholly-owned subsidiary*) shows how the group balance sheet is generated where the parent company acquired 100% of the subsidiary's share capital for £1,000 on the formation of the subsidiary.

This example uses similar figures except for the fact that it is assumed that H acquired 70% of S's share capital at a cost of £700. Other investors contributed £300 for 30% of S's share capital. H's balance sheet therefore records the investment in subsidiary at £700 and its net current assets will be £1,100, not £800, if it only spent £700 on buying shares in S.

| **Balance sheet** | **H (£)** | **S (£)** |
|---|---|---|
| **Net Assets** | | |
| Investment in S (70%) | 700 | |
| Other Non-current Assets | 800 | 50,000 |
| Net Current Assets | 1,100 | 100,000 |
| | 2,600 | 150,000 |
| **Shareholders' Funds** | | |
| Share Capital | 1,200 | 1,000 |
| Retained Earnings | 1,400 | 149,000 |
| | 2,600 | 150,000 |

**STEP 1** Eliminate intra-group transactions

| | |
|---|---|
| Reduce investment in S | £700 |
| Reduce share capital of S | £700 |

This leaves £300 (30%) of the share capital of S, which is not owned by H but by other shareholders in S. These outside shareholders are known as minority shareholders and their proportion of the subsidiary's capital and retained earnings will be shown in the group balance sheet as a separate caption after shareholders' funds.

**STEP 2** Aggregate remaining assets and liabilities

An important principle of consolidation is that 100% of a subsidiary's assets and liabilities (£50,000 and £100,000) are reported in the group balance sheet, even when, as is the case here, the parent does not own all the share capital of the subsidiary. The reason for this is that the group balance sheet must show all the assets and liabilities over which the parent company's directors exercise **control**: whether H owns 100%, 70% or 51% of S's share capital, it is still able to direct the financial and operating policy decisions of S because it only needs a simple majority (more than 50%) of voting power to appoint and remove directors to/from the board of S. The group balance sheet will report all the assets and liabilities of S with H's own and then show how much of S's net assets/shareholders' funds are financed by the minority shareholders in S.

## Minority interests

If a parent company does not own all of the shares of the subsidiary but still controls it, the total assets and liabilities of the subsidiary are included in the consolidated balance sheet. A proportion of the net assets of such subsidiaries in fact belongs to investors from outside the group (**minority interests**).

The net assets of a company are financed by share capital and retained earnings. The consolidation procedure for dealing with partly owned subsidiaries is to **calculate the proportion of ordinary shares, preference shares and retained earnings attributable to minority interests.**

We will now look at a separate example with a minority interest.

### EXAMPLE Minority interests

P Co has owned 75% of the share capital of S Co since the date of S Co's incorporation. Their latest balance sheets are given below.

| **P Co** | **(£)** | **(£)** |
|---|---|---|
| **Net Assets** | | |
| Non-Current Assets | | |
| PPE | 50,000 | |
| 30,000 £1 ordinary shares in S Co at cost | 30,000 | |
| | | 80,000 |
| Current Assets | | 45,000 |
| Current Liabilities | | (20,000) |
| | | 105,000 |
| **Shareholders' Funds** | | |
| Equity | | |
| 80,000 £1 ordinary shares | 80,000 | |
| Retained Earnings | 25,000 | |
| | | 105,000 |

| **S Co Balance sheet** | **(£)** | **(£)** |
|---|---|---|
| **Net assets** | | |
| PPE | | 35,000 |
| Current Assets | | 35,000 |
| Current Liabilities | | (20,000) |
| | | 50,000 |
| **Shareholders' Funds** | | |
| 40,000 £1 ordinary shares | 40,000 | |
| Retained Earnings | 10,000 | |
| | | 50,000 |

#### Requirement

Prepare the consolidated balance sheet.

## SOLUTION

All of S Co's net assets are consolidated despite the fact that the company is only 75% owned. The amount of net assets attributable to minority interests is calculated as follows.

| | (£) |
|---|---|
| Minority share of share capital (25% × £40,000) | 10,000 |
| Minority share of retained earnings (25% × £10,000) | 2,500 |
| | 12,500 |

Of S Co's share capital of £40,000, £10,000 is included in the figure for minority interest, while £30,000 is cancelled with P Co's asset 'investment in S Co'.

The consolidated balance sheet can now be prepared.

| **P Group Consolidated Balance sheet** | **(£)** | **(£)** |
|---|---|---|
| **Net Assets** | | |
| Non-Current Assets (50,000 + 35,000) | | 85,000 |
| Current Assets (45,000 + 35,000) | | 80,000 |
| Current Liabilities (20,000 + 20,000) | | (40,000) |
| | | 125,000 |
| **Shareholders funds** | | |
| Share Capital (P only) | 80,000 | |
| Retained Earnings (25,000 + (75% × £10,000) | 32,500 | |
| | | 112,500 |
| Minority Interest | | 12,500 |
| | | 125,000 |

# 5 GOODWILL ARISING ON CONSOLIDATION

In the examples we have looked at so far, the cost of shares acquired by the parent company has always been equal to the par value of those shares. This is seldom the case in practice and we must now consider some more complicated examples.

## Accounting

To begin with, we will examine the entries made by the parent company in its own balance sheet when it acquires shares.

When a company P Co wishes to purchase shares in a company S Co it must pay the previous owners of those shares. The most obvious form of payment would be in cash. Suppose P Co purchases all 40,000 £1 shares in S Co and pays £60,000 cash to the previous shareholders in consideration. The entries in P Co's books would be

| **Accounting equation** | **(£)** |
|---|---|
| Investment in S Co at cost of | 60,000 |
| Cash down | 60,000 |

However, the previous shareholders might be prepared to accept some other form of consideration. For example, they might accept an agreed number of **shares** in P Co. P Co would then issue new shares in the agreed number and allot them to the former shareholders of S Co. This kind of deal might be attractive to P Co since it avoids the need for a heavy cash outlay. The former shareholders of S Co would retain an indirect interest in that company's profitability via their new holding in its parent company.

Continuing the Example, suppose the shareholders of S Co agreed to accept one £1 ordinary share in P Co for every two £1 ordinary shares in S Co. P Co would then need to issue and allot 20,000 new £1 shares. How would this transaction be recorded in the books of P Co?

The simplest method would be as follows.

| **Accounting equation** | **(£)** |
|---|---|
| Investment in S Co up | 20,000 |
| Share capital up | 20,000 |

However, if the 40,000 £1 shares acquired in S Co are thought to have a value of £60,000 this would be misleading. The former shareholders of S Co have presumably agreed to accept 20,000 shares in P Co because they consider each of those shares to have a value of £3. This view of the matter suggests the following method of recording the transaction in P Co's books.

| **Accounting equation** | **(£)** |
|---|---|
| Investment in S Co up | 60,000 |
| Share capital up | 20,000 |
| Share premium account up | 40,000 |

The second method is the one which should normally be used in preparing consolidated accounts.

## Goodwill on consolidation

The amount which P Co records in its books as the cost of its investment in S Co may be more or less than the book value of the assets it acquires. Suppose that S Co in the previous Example has no retained earnings and no liabilities, so that its share capital of £40,000 is balanced by tangible assets with a book value of £40,000. For simplicity, assume that the book value of S Co's assets is the same as their market or fair value.

Now when the directors of P Co agree to pay £60,000 for a 100% investment in S Co they must believe that, in addition to its tangible assets of £40,000, S Co must also have intangible assets worth £20,000. This amount of £20,000 paid over and above the value of the tangible assets acquired is called **goodwill arising on consolidation** (also sometimes called **premium on acquisition**).

Following the normal cancellation procedure the £40,000 share capital in S Co's balance sheet could be cancelled against £40,000 of the 'investment in S Co' in the balance sheet of P Co. This would leave a £20,000 debit uncancelled in the parent company's accounts and this £20,000 would appear in the consolidated balance sheet under the caption 'Intangible non-current assets: goodwill arising on consolidation'.

## Goodwill and pre-acquisition profits

Up to now we have assumed that S Co did not have any retained earnings when its shares were purchased by P Co. Assuming instead that S Co had earned profits of £8,000 in the period before acquisition, its balance sheet just before the purchase would look as follows.

| **Accounting equation impact** | **(£)** |
|---|---|
| PPE | 48,000 |
| Share Capital | 40,000 |
| Retained Earnings | 8,000 |
| | 48,000 |

If P Co now purchases all the shares in S Co it will acquire total tangible assets worth £48,000 at a cost of £60,000. Clearly in this case S Co's intangible assets (goodwill) are being valued at £12,000. It should be apparent that any **retained earnings** earned by the subsidiary **prior to its acquisition** by the parent company must be **incorporated in the cancellation** process so as to arrive at a figure for goodwill arising on consolidation. In other words, not only S Co's share capital, but also its **pre-acquisition retained earnings**, must be cancelled against the asset 'investment in S Co' in the accounts of the parent company. The uncancelled balance of £12,000 appears in the consolidated balance sheet.

The consequence of this is that **any pre-acquisition retained earnings of a subsidiary company are not aggregated with the parent company's retained earnings** in the consolidated balance sheet. The figure of consolidated retained earnings comprises the retained earnings of the parent company plus the **post-acquisition retained earnings only of subsidiary companies**. The post-acquisition retained earnings are simply retained earnings now *less* retained earnings at acquisition.

## EXAMPLE

Sing Co acquired the ordinary shares of Wing Co on 31 March when the draft balance sheet of each company were as follows.

| **Sing Co balance sheet as at 31 March** | **(£)** |
|---|---|
| **Net Assets** | |
| Non-current Assets | |
| Investment in 50,000 shares in Wing Co at cost | 80,000 |
| Current Assets | 40,000 |
| | 120,000 |
| **Shareholders' Funds** | |
| Ordinary Shares | 75,000 |
| Retained Earnings | 45,000 |
| | 120,000 |

| **Wing Co balance sheet as at 31 March** | **(£)** |
|---|---|
| Net Assets | 60,000 |
| 50,000 ordinary shares of £1 each | 50,000 |
| Retained Earnings | 10,000 |
| | 60,000 |

### Requirement

Prepare the consolidated balance sheet as at 31 March.

**SOLUTION**

The technique to adopt here is to produce a new working: 'Goodwill'. A proforma working is set out below.

| **Goodwill** | **(£)** | **(£)** |
|---|---|---|
| Cost of investment | | X |
| Share of net assets acquired as represented by: | | |
| Ordinary share capital | X | |
| Share premium | X | |
| Retained earnings on acquisition | X | |
| Group share a% | | (X) |
| | | X |
| b% preferred shares | | (X) |
| Goodwill | | X |

Applying this to our Example the working will look like this.

| | **(£)** | **(£)** |
|---|---|---|
| Cost of investment | | 80,000 |
| Share of net assets acquired as represented by: | | |
| Ordinary share capital | 50,000 | |
| Retained earnings on acquisition | 10,000 | |
| | 60,000 | |
| Group share 100% | | 60,000 |
| Goodwill | | 20,000 |

| **Sing Co consolidated balance sheet as at 31 March** | **(£)** |
|---|---|
| **Net Assets** | |
| Non-Current assets: Goodwill arising on consolidation | 20,000 |
| Current Assets (40,000 + 60,000) | 100,000 |
| | 120,000 |
| **Shareholders' Funds** | |
| Ordinary Shares (Sing Co only) | 75,000 |
| Retained Earnings (Sing Co only – no post-acquisition retained earnings in Wing Co) | 45,000 |
| | 120,000 |

# 6 IFRS 3 Business Combinations

Goodwill arising on consolidation is one form of **purchased goodwill**, and is governed by IFRS 3. IFRS 3 requires that goodwill arising on consolidation should **be capitalised in the consolidated balance sheet** and **reviewed for impairment every year**.

## Negative goodwill

Goodwill arising on consolidation is the difference between the cost of an acquisition and the value of the subsidiary's net assets acquired. This difference can be **negative**: the aggregate of the fair values of the separable net assets acquired may exceed what the parent company paid for them.

The treatment of this 'negative goodwill' is:

- An entity should first **re-assess** the amounts at which it has measured both the cost of the combination and the acquiree's identifiable net assets. This exercise should **identify any errors**.
- Any negative goodwill remaining should be recognised immediately in the income statement.

## Practical example

The following is extracted from the accounting policies note in the 2014/15 financial statements of Kingfisher plc. It shows the group's accounting policy relating to goodwill.

**(i) Goodwill**

Goodwill represents the future economic benefits arising from assets acquired in a business combination that are not individually identified and separately recognised. Such benefits include future synergies expected from the combination and intangible assets not meeting the criteria for separate recognition.

Goodwill is carried at cost less accumulated impairment losses. Goodwill is not amortised and is tested annually for impairment by assessing the recoverable amount of each cash generating unit or groups of cash generating units to which the goodwill relates. The recoverable amount is assessed by reference to the net present value of expected future pre-tax cash flows ('value-in-use') or fair value less costs to sell if higher. The discount rate applied is based upon the Group's weighted average cost of capital with appropriate adjustments for the risks associated with the relevant cash generating unit or groups of cash generating units. When the recoverable amount of the goodwill is less than its carrying amount, an impairment loss is recognised immediately in the income statement which cannot subsequently be reversed. Gains and losses on the disposal of an entity include the carrying amount of goodwill relating to the entity sold.

## Consolidation – Intra-group trading

### Unrealised profit

Any receivable/payable balances outstanding between the companies are cancelled on consolidation. No further problem arises if all such intra-group transactions are undertaken at cost, without any mark-up for profit.

However, each company in a group is a separate trading entity and may wish to treat other group companies in the same way as any other customer. In this case, a company (say, A Co) may buy goods at one price and sell them at a higher price to another group company (B Co). The accounts of A Co will quite properly include the profit earned on sales to B Co; and similarly B Co's balance sheet will include inventories at their cost to B Co, ie at the amount at which they were purchased from A Co.

This gives rise to two problems.

- Although A Co makes a profit as soon as it sells goods to B Co, the group does not make a sale or achieve a profit until an outside customer buys the goods from B Co.
- Any purchases from A Co which remain unsold by B Co at the year end will be included in B Co's inventory. Their balance sheet value will be their cost to B Co, which is not the same as their cost to the group.

The objective of consolidated accounts is to present the financial position of several connected companies as that of a single entity, the group. This means that **in a consolidated balance sheet the only profits recognised should be those earned by the group** in providing goods or services to outsiders; and similarly, inventory in the consolidated balance sheet should be valued at cost to the group.

## Example

Suppose that a holding company P Co buys goods for £1,600 and sells them to a wholly-owned subsidiary S Co for £2,000. The goods are in S Co's inventory at the year end and appear in S Co's balance sheet at £2,000. In this case, P Co will record a profit of £400 in its individual accounts, but from the group's point of view the figures are:

| | |
|---|---|
| Cost | £1,600 |
| External sales | nil |
| Closing inventory at cost | £1,600 |
| Profit/loss | nil |

If we add together the figures for retained earnings and inventory in the individual balance sheets of P Co and S Co the resulting figures for consolidated retained earnings and consolidated inventory will each be overstated by £400.

## Solution

A **consolidation adjustment** is therefore necessary as follows

| Accounting equation impact |
|---|
| Group reserves down |
| Group inventory (balance sheet) down |

with the amount of **profit unrealised** by the group.

## Example

P Co acquired all the shares in S Co one year ago when the reserves of S Co stood at £10,000. Draft balance sheets for each company are as follows.

| | P Co | | S Co | |
|---|---|---|---|---|
| | (£) | (£) | (£) | (£) |
| **Net Assets** | | | | |
| Non-Current Assets | | | | |
| PPE | 80,000 | | | 40,000 |
| Investment in S Co at cost | 46,000 | | | |
| | | 126,000 | | |
| Current Assets | | 40,000 | | 30,000 |
| Current Liabilities | | (21,000) | | (18,000) |
| | | 145,000 | | 52,000 |
| **Shareholders' Funds** | | | | |
| Ordinary shares of £1 each | | 100,000 | | 30,000 |
| Reserves | | 45,000 | | 22,000 |
| | | 145,000 | | 52,000 |

During the year P Co sold goods to S Co for £50,000, the profit to S Co being 20% of selling price. At the balance sheet date, £15,000 of these goods remained unsold in the inventories of S Co. At the same date, P Co owed S Co £12,000 for goods bought and this debt is included in the trade payables of P Co and the receivables of S Co. The goodwill arising on consolidation has been impaired. The amount of the impairment is £1,500.

## Requirement

Prepare a draft consolidated balance sheet for P Co.

## SOLUTION

1 **Goodwill**

| | (£) | (£) |
|---|---|---|
| Cost of investment | | 46,000 |
| Share of net assets acquired as represented by | | |
| Share capital | 30,000 | |
| Retained earnings | 10,000 | |
| | 40,000 | |
| Group share (100%) | | 40,000 |
| Goodwill | | 6,000 |
| Less: impairment loss | | (1,500) |
| | | 4,500 |

2 **Retained Earnings**

| | **P Co (£)** | **S Co (£)** |
|---|---|---|
| Retained earnings per question | 45,000 | 22,000 |
| Unrealised profit: 20% × £15,000 | (3,000) | |
| | 42,000 | |
| Pre-acquisition retained earnings | | (10,000) |
| | | 12,000 |
| Share of S Co (post-acquisition) | 12,000 | |
| Goodwill impairment loss | (1,500) | |
| | 52,500 | |

| **P Co consolidated balance sheet** | **(£)** | **(£)** |
|---|---|---|
| **Net Assets** | | |
| Non-Current Assets | | |
| PPE | 120,000 | |
| Goodwill (6,000–1,500) | 4,500 | |
| | | 124,500 |
| Current Assets (W1) | | 55,000 |
| Current Liabilities (W2) | | (27,000) |
| | | 152,500 |
| **Shareholders' Funds** | | |
| Ordinary Shares of £1 each | 100,000 | |
| Retained Earnings | 52,500 | |
| | | 152,500 |

**Workings**

1 **Current Assets**

| | (£) | (£) |
|---|---|---|
| In P Co's balance sheet | | 40,000 |
| In S Co's balance sheet | 30,000 | |
| Less S Co's current account with P Co cancelled | 12,000 | |
| | | 18,000 |
| | | 58,000 |
| Less unrealised profit excluded from inventory valuation | | 3,000 |
| | | 55,000 |

2 **Current Liabilities**

| | (£) |
|---|---|
| In P Co's balance sheet | 21,000 |
| Less P Co's current account with S Co cancelled | 12,000 |
| | 9,000 |
| In S Co's balance sheet | 18,000 |
| | 27,000 |

# 7 IFRS 3 AND FAIR VALUES IN ACQUISITION ACCOUNTING

Fair values are very important in calculating goodwill.

## Goodwill

To understand the importance of fair values in the acquisition of a subsidiary consider the definition of **goodwill**.

Any excess of the cost of the acquisition over the acquirer's interest in the fair value of the identifiable assets and liabilities acquired as at the date of the exchange transaction.

The **balance sheet of a subsidiary company** at the date it is acquired may not be a guide to the fair value of its net assets. For example, the market value of a freehold building may have risen greatly since it was acquired, but it may appear in the balance sheet at historical cost less accumulated depreciation.

## What is fair value?

**Fair value** is defined as follows by IFRS 3 and various other Standards – it is an important definition.

The amount for which an asset could be exchanged, or a liability settled, between knowledgeable, willing parties in an arm's length transaction.

## Fair value adjustment calculations

Until now we have calculated goodwill as the difference between the cost of the investment and the **book value** of net assets acquired by the group. If this calculation is to comply with the definition above we must ensure that the book value of the subsidiary's net assets is the same as their **fair value**.

### EXAMPLE

P Co acquired 75% of the ordinary shares of S Co last year. At that date the fair value of S Co's non-current assets was £23,000 greater than their net book value, and the balance of retained earnings was £21,000. The balance sheets of both companies at the current year end are given below.

S Co has not incorporated any revaluation in its books of account.

| **P Co balance sheet** | **(£)** |
|---|---|
| **Net Assets** | |
| Non-Current Assets | |
| PPE | 63,000 |
| Investment in S Co at cost | 51,000 |
| | 114,000 |
| Current Assets | 82,000 |
| Current Liabilities | (20,000) |
| | 176,000 |
| **Shareholders' Funds** | |
| Ordinary shares of £1 each | 80,000 |
| Retained Earnings | 96,000 |
| | 176,000 |

| **S Co consolidated balance sheet** | **(£)** |
|---|---|
| **Net Assets** | |
| Non-Current Assets – PPE | 28,000 |
| Current Assets | 43,000 |
| Current Liabilities | (10,000) |
| | 61,000 |
| **Shareholders' Funds** | |
| Ordinary shares of £1 each | 20,000 |
| Retained Earnings | 41,000 |
| | 61,000 |

If S Co had revalued its non-current assets at the start of the year, an addition of £3,000 would have been made to the depreciation charged in the income statement for the year.

### Requirement

Prepare P Co's consolidated balance sheet at the year end.

## SOLUTION

S Co has not incorporated the revaluation in its draft balance sheet. Before beginning the consolidation workings we must therefore adjust the company's balance of profits at the date of acquisition and at the balance sheet date.

| S Co Adjusted Balance of Accumulated Profits | (£) | (£) |
|---|---|---|
| Retained earnings brought forward | | 21,000 |
| Consolidation adjustment: revaluation surplus | | 23,000 |
| ∴ Pre-acquisition retained earnings for consolidation purposes | | 44,000 |
| Profit for year | | |
| Per draft accounts £(41,000 – 21,000) | 20,000 | |
| Consolidation adjustment: increase in depreciation charge | (3,000) | |
| | | 17,000 |
| Adjusted balance of retained earnings at the year end | | 61,000 |

In the consolidated balance sheet, S Co's non-current assets will appear at their revalued amount: £(28,000 + 23,000 – 3,000) = £48,000. The consolidation workings can now be drawn up.

**Workings**

1 **Minority interest**

| | (£) |
|---|---|
| Share capital (25% × £20,000) | 5,000 |
| Retained earnings (25% × £61,000) | 15,250 |
| | 20,250 |

2 **Goodwill**

| | (£) | (£) |
|---|---|---|
| Cost of investment | | 51,000 |
| Share of net assets acquired as represented by | | |
| Ordinary share capital | 20,000 | |
| Retained earnings | 21,000 | |
| Fair value adjustment | 23,000 | |
| | 64,000 | |
| Group share (75%) | | 48,000 |
| Goodwill | | 3,000 |

3 **Retained earnings**

| | P Co (£) | S Co (£) |
|---|---|---|
| Per question | 96,000 | 41,000 |
| Pre-acquisition retained earnings | | (21,000) |
| Depreciation adjustment | | (3,000) |
| Post acquisition S Co | | 17,000 |
| Group share in S Co (£17,000 × 75%) | 12,750 | |
| Group retained earnings | 108,750 | |

| P Co consolidated balance sheet at the year end | (£) | (£) |
|---|---|---|
| **Net Assets** | | |
| Non-Current Assets: PPE (63,000 + 48,000) | 111,000 | |
| Goodwill (W2) | 3,000 | |
| | | 114,000 |
| Current Assets (82,000 + 43,000) | | 125,000 |
| Current Liabilities (20,000 + 10,000) | | (30,000) |
| | | 209,000 |

| | | |
|---|---|---|
| **Shareholders' Funds** | | |
| Ordinary shares of £1 each | 80,000 | |
| Retained Earnings (W3) | 108,750 | |
| | | 188,750 |
| Minority Interest (W1) | | 20,250 |
| | | 209,000 |

## The consolidated income statement

The individual income statements are set out side by side and totalled to form the basis of the consolidated income statement.

### EXAMPLE

P Co acquired 75% of the ordinary shares of S Co on that company's incorporation several years ago. The summarised income statements of the two companies for the current year are set out below.

| | P Co (£) | S Co (£) |
|---|---|---|
| Sales revenue | 75,000 | 38,000 |
| Cost of sales | 30,000 | 20,000 |
| Gross profit | 45,000 | 18,000 |
| Administrative expenses | 14,000 | 8,000 |
| Profit before tax | 31,000 | 10,000 |
| Tax | 10,000 | 2,000 |
| Profit for the year | 21,000 | 8,000 |
| Retained earnings brought forward | 87,000 | 17,000 |
| Retained earnings carried forward | 108,000 | 25,000 |

#### Requirement

Prepare the consolidated income statement and movement in retained earnings.

### SOLUTION

| **P Co Consolidated Income Statement for the Year** | **(£)** |
|---|---|
| Sales revenue (75 + 38) | 113,000 |
| Cost of sales (30 + 20) | 50,000 |
| Gross profit | 63,000 |
| Administrative expenses (14 + 8) | 22,000 |
| Profit before tax | 41,000 |
| Tax (10 + 2) | 12,000 |
| Profit after tax | 29,000 |
| Minority interest (25% × £8,000) | 2,000 |
| Group profit for the year | 27,000 |
| Retained earnings brought forward (group share only: 87 + (17 × 75%)) | 99,750 |
| Retained earnings carried forward | 126,750 |

Note how the minority interest is dealt with.

- Down to the line '**profit after taxation**' the **whole** of S Co's results is included without reference to group share or minority share. A **one-line adjustment** is then inserted to deduct the minority's share of S Co's profit after taxation.
- The minority's share (£4,250) of S Co's retained earnings brought forward is **excluded**. This means that the carried forward figure of £126,750 is the figure which would appear in the balance sheet for group retained earnings.

This last point may be clearer if we revert to our **balance sheet technique** and construct the working for group retained earnings.

| | **(£)** |
|---|---|
| **Group reserves** | |
| P Co | 108,000 |
| Share of S Co's post-acquisition retained reserves (75% × £25,000) | 18,750 |
| | 126,750 |

The minority share of S Co's retained earnings comprises the minority interest in the £17,000 profits brought forward plus the minority interest (£2,000) in £8,000 retained earnings for the year.

Notice that a consolidated income statement **links up** with a consolidated balance sheet exactly as in the case of an individual company's accounts: the figure of retained earnings carried forward at the bottom of the income statement appears as the figure for retained earnings in the balance sheet. (*Note.* Under IAS 1 this would be shown as a movement in retained earnings; for convenience the retained earnings movements are shown here with the income statement.)

We will now look at the complications introduced by **inter-company trading** and **mid year acquisition** of the subsidiary.

## Intra-group trading

Like the consolidated balance sheet, the consolidated income statement should deal with the results of the group as those of a single entity. When one company in a group sells goods to another an identical amount is added to the sales revenue of the first company and to the cost of sales of the second. Yet as far as the entity's dealings with outsiders are concerned no sale has taken place.

The consolidated figures for sales revenue and cost of sales should represent **sales to**, and **purchases from, outsiders**. An adjustment is therefore necessary to reduce the sales revenue and cost of sales figures by the value of intra-group sales during the year.

We have also seen in an earlier chapter that any unrealised profits on intra-group trading should be excluded from the figure for group profits. This will occur whenever goods sold at a profit within the group remain in the inventory of the purchasing company at the year end. The best way to deal with this is to **calculate the unrealised profit on unsold inventories at the year end and reduce consolidated gross profit by this amount**. Cost of sales will be the balancing figure.

### EXAMPLE

Suppose in our earlier example that S Co had recorded sales of £5,000 to P Co during the year. S Co had purchased these goods from outside suppliers at a cost of £3,000. One half of the goods remained in P Co's inventory at the year end. Prepare the revised consolidated income statement.

## SOLUTION

The consolidated income statement for the year ended 31 December would now be as follows.

| | (£) |
|---|---|
| Sales revenue (75 + 38 – 5) | 108,000 |
| Cost of sales (balancing figure) or (30 + 20 – 5 + 1) | (46,000) |
| Gross profit (45 + 18 – 1*) | 62,000 |
| Administrative expenses | (22,000) |
| Profit before tax | 40,000 |
| Tax | (12,000) |
| Profit after tax | 28,000 |
| Minority interest (25% × (£8,000 – £1,000*)) | (1,750) |
| Group profit for the year | 26,250 |
| Retained earnings brought forward | 99,750 |
| Retained earnings carried forward | 126,000 |

*Unrealised profit: ½ × (£5,000 – £3,000)

An adjustment will be made for the unrealised profit against the inventory figure in the consolidated balance sheet, as explained earlier in the chapter.

## Accounting for a mid-year acquisition

As explained earlier, the figure for retained earnings at the bottom of the consolidated income statement must be the same as the figure for retained earnings in the consolidated balance sheet. We have seen earlier in this chapter that retained earnings in the consolidated balance sheet comprise

- The whole of the parent company's retained earnings.
- A **proportion of the subsidiary company's** retained earnings. The proportion is the **group's share of post-acquisition retained earnings** in the subsidiary. From the total retained earnings of the subsidiary we must therefore **exclude** both the **minority's share** of total retained earnings and the **group's share of pre-acquisition** retained earnings.

A similar procedure is necessary in the consolidated income statement if it is to link up with the consolidated balance sheet. Previous examples have shown how the minority share of profits is excluded in the income statement. Their share of profits for the year is deducted from profit after tax, while the figure for profits brought forward in the consolidation schedule includes only the group's proportion of the subsidiary's profits.

In the same way, if the subsidiary is **acquired during the accounting year**, it is therefore necessary to apportion its profit for the year between pre-acquisition and post-acquisition elements.

## EXAMPLE

P Co acquired 60% of the equity of S Co on 1 April. The income statements of the two companies for the year ended 31 December are set out below.

| | P Co (£) | S Co (£) | S Co 9/12 (£) |
|---|---|---|---|
| Sales Revenue | 170,000 | 80,000 | 60,000 |
| Cost of Sales | 65,000 | 36,000 | 27,000 |
| Gross Profit | 105,000 | 44,000 | 33,000 |
| Administrative Expenses | 43,000 | 12,000 | 9,000 |
| Profit before tax | 62,000 | 32,000 | 24,000 |
| Tax | 23,000 | 8,000 | 6,000 |
| Profit after tax | 39,000 | 24,000 | 18,000 |
| Dividends (paid 31 December) | 12,000 | 6,000 | |
| Retained Earnings brought forward | 81,000 | 40,000 | |
| Retained Earnings carried forward | 108,000 | 58,000 | |

P Co has not yet accounted for the dividends received from S Co.

### Requirement

Prepare the consolidated income statement and movements in retained earnings.

## SOLUTION

The shares in S Co were acquired three months into the year. Only the post-acquisition proportion (9/12ths) of S Co's income statement is included in the consolidated income statement. This is shown above for convenience.

| **P Co Consolidated Income Statement for the Year Ended 31 December** | **(£)** |
|---|---|
| Sales Revenue (170 + 60) | 230,000 |
| Cost of Sales (65 + 27) | 92,000 |
| Gross Profit | 138,000 |
| Administrative Expenses (43 + 9) | 52,000 |
| Profit before tax | 86,000 |
| Tax (23 + 6) | 29,000 |
| Profit after tax | 57,000 |
| Minority Interest (40% × £18,000) | 7,200 |
| Group Profit for the year | 49,800 |
| Retained Earnings brought forward* | 81,000 |
| Profit for the year | 49,800 |
| Dividends | (12,000) |
| Retained earnings carried forward | 118,800 |

* All of S Co's profits brought forward are pre-acquisition.

# 8 Accounting for Associates

## Definitions

**Associate**. An entity, including an unincorporated entity such as a partnership, over which an investor has significant influence and which is neither a subsidiary nor a joint venture of the investor.

**Significant influence** is the power to participate in the financial and operating policy decisions of an economic entity but is not control or joint control over those policies.

**Joint control** is the contractually agreed sharing of control over an economic activity.

**Equity method**. A method of accounting whereby the investment is initially recorded at cost and adjusted thereafter for the post acquisition change in the investor's share of net assets of the investee. The profit or loss of the investor includes the investor's share of the profit or loss of the investee.

The key to associate status is significant influence.

## IAS 28 Investments in Associates

IAS 28 requires all investments in associates to be accounted for in the consolidated accounts using the equity method, *unless* the investment is classified as 'held for sale' in accordance with IFRS 5 in which case it should be accounted for under IFRS 5.

The use of the equity method should be **discontinued** from the date that the investor **ceases to have significant influence**.

From that date, the investor shall account for the investment in accordance with either IFRS 9 *Financial Instruments* or IAS 39 *Financial Instruments: Recognition and Measurement*. The carrying amount of the investment at the date that it ceases to be an associate shall be regarded as its cost on initial measurement as a financial asset under IFRS 9/IAS 39.

## Separate financial statements of the investor

In the investor's individual accounts the interest is the associate should be treated as follows.

- Accounted for at **cost**; or
- In accordance with **IFRS 9/IAS 39**.

## Application of the equity method: consolidated accounts

Many of the procedures required to apply the equity method are the same as are required for full consolidation. In particular, **intra-group unrealised profits** must be excluded.

**Goodwill** is calculated as the difference (positive or negative) between the cost of acquisition and the investor's share of the fair values of the net identifiable assets of the associate. This should be treated as required by IFRS 3. Appropriate adjustments should be made to the investor's share of the profits or losses after acquisition, to account for depreciation.

## Consolidated income statement

The basic principle is that the investing company (X Co) should take account of its **share of the earnings** of the associate, Y Co, whether or not Y Co distributes the earnings as dividends. X Co achieves this by adding to consolidated profit the group's share of Y Co's profit after tax.

Under equity accounting, the associated company's sales revenue, cost of sales and so on are ***not* amalgamated** with those of the group. Instead the group share only of the associate's profit before tax and tax charge for the year is added to the corresponding lines of the parent company and its subsidiaries.

## Consolidated balance sheet

A figure for **investment in associates** is shown which at the time of the acquisition must be stated at cost. This amount will increase (decrease) each year by the amount of the group's share of the associated company's profit (loss) for the year.

### EXAMPLE

P Co, a company with subsidiaries, acquires 25,000 of the 100,000 £1 ordinary shares in A Co for £60,000 on 1 January. In the year to 31 December, A Co earns profits after tax of £24,000, from which it pays a dividend of £6,000.

How will A Co's results be accounted for in the individual and consolidated accounts of P Co for the year ended 31 December?

### SOLUTION

In the **individual accounts** of P Co, the investment will be recorded on 1 January at cost. Unless there is an impairment in the value of the investment, this amount will remain in the individual balance sheet of P Co permanently. The only entry in P Co's individual income statement will be to record dividends received. For the year ended 31 December, P Co will be

| Accounting Entry | (£) |
|---|---|
| Cash up | 1,500 |
| Retained Earnings – income up | 1,500 |

In the **consolidated accounts** of P Co equity accounting principles will be used to account for the investment in A Co. Consolidated profit after tax will include the group's share of A Co's profit after tax (25% × £24,000 = £6,000). To the extent that this has been distributed as dividend, it is already included in P Co's individual accounts and will automatically be brought into the consolidated results. That part of the group's profit share which has not been distributed as dividend (£4,500) will be brought into consolidation by the following adjustment.

| Accounting Entry | (£) |
|---|---|
| Investment in associates up | 4,500 |
| Retained Profits – income from shares in associates up | 4,500 |

The asset 'Investment in associates' is then stated at £64,500, being cost plus the group share of post-acquisition retained profits.

## Pro-forma consolidated income statement

The following is a **suggested layout** for the consolidated income statement for a company having subsidiaries as well as associated companies.

| | ($'000) |
|---|---|
| Revenue | 1,400 |
| Cost of Sales | 770 |
| Gross Profit | 630 |
| Distribution Costs and Administrative Expenses | 290 |
| | 340 |
| Share of Profit of Associates | 17 |
| | 357 |
| Finance Income | (30) |
| | 387 |
| Finance Costs | 20 |
| Profit before Taxation | 367 |
| Tax | 145 |
| Profit for the year | 222 |
| Attributable to: | |
| Equity holders of the parent | 200 |
| Minority Interest | 22 |
| | 222 |

## Consolidated balance sheet

As explained earlier, the consolidated balance sheet will contain an **asset 'Investment in associate'**.

The amount at which this asset is stated will be its original cost plus the group's share of any **profits earned since acquisition** which have not been distributed as dividends.

### EXAMPLE

On 1 January the net tangible assets of A Co amount to £220,000, financed by 100,000 £1 ordinary shares and revenue reserves of £120,000. P Co, a company with subsidiaries, acquires 30,000 of the shares in A Co for £75,000. During the year ended 31 December A Co's profit after tax is £30,000, from which dividends of £12,000 are paid.

Show how P Co's investment in A Co would appear in the consolidated balance sheet at 31 December.

### SOLUTION

| **Consolidated balance sheet as at 31 December (extract)** | (£) |
|---|---|
| Non-current assets | |
| Investment in associate | |
| Cost | 75,000 |
| Group share of post-acquisition retained profits (30% × £18,000) | 5,400 |
| | 80,400 |

An important point to note is that this figure of £80,400 can be arrived at in a completely different way. It is the sum of

(a) The group's share of A Co's net assets at 31 December, and

(b) The premium paid over fair value for the shares acquired.

This can be shown as follows.

| | | (£) | (£) |
|---|---|---|---|
| (a) | A Co's net assets at 31 December | | |
| | Net assets at 1 January | 220,000 | |
| | Retained profit for year | 18,000 | |
| | Net assets at 31 December | 238,000 | |
| | Group share (30%) | | 71,400 |
| (b) | Premium on acquisition | | |
| | Net assets acquired by group on 1 Jan (30% × £220,000) | 66,000 | |
| | Price paid for shares | 75,000 | |
| | Premium on acquisition | | 9,000 |
| | Investment in associated company per balance sheet | | 80,400 |

## EXAMPLE

Set out below are the draft accounts of Parent Co and its subsidiaries and of Associate Co. Parent Co acquired 40% of the equity capital of Associate Co three years ago when the latter's reserves stood at £40,000.

| **Summarised balance sheets** | **Parent Co & Subsidiaries (£'000)** | **Associate Co (£'000)** |
|---|---|---|
| Tangible non-current assets | 220 | 170 |
| Investment in associate, at cost | 60 | – |
| Loan to associate | 20 | – |
| Current assets | 100 | 50 |
| Loan from parent | – | (20) |
| | 400 | 200 |
| Share capital (£1 shares) | 250 | 100 |
| Reserves | 150 | 100 |
| | 400 | 200 |

| **Summarised income statements** | **Parent Co & Subsidiaries (£'000)** | **Associate Co (£'000)** |
|---|---|---|
| Operating profit | 95 | 80 |
| Tax | 35 | 30 |
| | 60 | 50 |

You are required to prepare the summarised consolidated accounts of Parent Co.

**Notes**

1 Assume that the associate's assets/liabilities are stated at fair value.

2 Assume that there are no minority interests in the subsidiary companies.

## SOLUTION

| Parent Co consolidated income statement | (£'000) |
|---|---|
| Net profit | 95 |
| Share of profit of associated company (50 × 40%) | 20 |
| Profit before tax | 105 |
| Tax | 35 |
| Profit attributable to the members of Parent Co | 80 |

| Parent Co Consolidated balance sheet | (£'000) |
|---|---|
| **Assets** | |
| Tangible non-current assets | 220 |
| Investment in associate (see note) | 104 |
| Current assets | 100 |
| Total assets | 424 |
| **Equity and liabilities** | |
| Share capital | 250 |
| Reserves (W1) | 174 |
| Total equity and liabilities | 424 |

| Note | (£'000) |
|---|---|
| Investment in associate | |
| Group's share of net assets (40% × 200) | 80 |
| Premium on acquisition (W2) | 4 |
| | 84 |
| Loan to associate | 20 |
| | 104 |

**Workings**

1 **Reserves**

| | Parent & subsidiaries (£'000) | Associate (£'000) |
|---|---|---|
| Per question | 150 | 100 |
| Pre-acquisition | | 40 |
| Post-acquisition | | 60 |
| Group share in associate (£60 x 40%) | 24 | |
| Group reserves | 174 | |

2 **Premium on acquisition**

| | (£'000) |
|---|---|
| Share capital | 100 |
| Reserves at date of acquisition | 40 |
| | 140 |
| Net assets acquired (40% × 140) | 56 |
| Cost | 60 |
| Premium on acquisition (goodwill) | 4 |

# 9 Joint Ventures and Jointly Controlled Entities

IFRS 11 *Joint Arrangements* covers all types of joint ventures. It is not concerned with the accounts of the joint venture itself (if separate accounts are maintained), but rather **how the interest in a joint venture is accounted for by each joint venturer** (ie each 'partner' in the joint venture).

The assets and liabilities, income and expenses of the joint venture must be reported in the financial statements of the venturers and investors, whatever the form of the joint venture.

IFRS 11 looks at the contractual rights and obligations agreed between the parties. If the parties only have a right to a share of the outcome of the activities of a jointly controlled entity, their net interest in the arrangement would be accounted for under the equity method.

## Example

Shown below is an extract from the accounting policies note from the 2014/15 Kingfisher Annual Report on associates and joint ventures.

**(ii) Joint ventures and associates**

Joint ventures are entities over which the Group has joint control. Joint control is the contractually agreed sharing of control of an arrangement, which exists only when decisions about therelevant activities require the unanimous consent of the parties sharing control. The equity method is used to account for the Group's investments in joint ventures.

Associates are entities over which the Group has the ability to exercise significant influence but not control, generally accompanied by a shareholding of between 20% and 50% of the voting rights. The equity method is used to account for the Group's investments in associates.

Under the equity method investments are initially recognised at cost. The Group's share of post-acquisition profits or losses is recognised in the income statement within operating profit, and its share of post-acquisition movements in reserves is recognised in reserves. The cumulative post-acquisition movements are adjusted against the carrying amount of the investment. When the Group's share of losses equals or exceeds its interest, including any long-term receivables, the Group does not recognise any further losses, unless it has incurred obligations or made payments on behalf of the joint venture or associate.

Unrealised gains on transactions between the Group and its joint ventures and associates are eliminated to the extent of the Group's interest. Unrealised losses are also eliminated unless the transaction provides evidence of an impairment of the asset transferred. Accounting policies of joint ventures and associates have been changed where necessary to ensure consistency with the policies adopted by the Group.

The equity method of accounting is discontinued from the date an investment ceases to be a joint venture or associate, that is the date on which the Group ceases to have joint control or significant influence over the investee or on the date it is classified as held for sale.

# 10 Analysis Points

## Equity accounting

Equity accounting for associates and JVs advocates a one-line consolidation that provides very little information about the assets or profits of the associate/JV.

In the balance sheet the one-line approach gives no indication of the breakdown of the assets and liabilities. It is quite conceivable that the associate/ JV could be in a desperate liquidity or gearing position but this would not be revealed in the group financial statements.

The treatment in the income statement is very similar in that the group share of the associate's/JV's profit is shown separately from group amounts. The group share of the associate's/JV's tax is added to the other elements of the group tax charge. This provides very little breakdown of how the profit has been generated by the associate or JV.

# 11 Accounting for Disposals and Discontinued Operations

IFRS 5 requires that assets 'held for sale' are presented separately on the face of the balance sheet and the results of discontinued operations to be presented separately in the income statement. The idea here is that users of financial statements will be better able to make projections about the financial position, profits and cash flows.

## Classification of assets held for sale

A non-current asset (or disposal group) should be classified as **held for sale** if its carrying amount will be recovered **principally through a sale transaction** rather than **through continuing use**. A number of detailed criteria must be met.

- The asset must be **available for immediate sale** in its present condition.
- Its sale must be **highly probable** (ie significantly more likely than not).

For the sale to be highly probable, the following must apply.

- Management must be **committed** to a plan to sell the asset.
- There must be an active programme to **locate a buyer**.
- The asset must be marketed for sale at a **price that is reasonable** in relation to its current fair value.
- The sale should be expected to take place **within one year** from the date of classification.
- It is unlikely that significant changes to the plan will be made or that the plan will be withdrawn.

## Definitions

The following are key IFRS 5 definitions.

**Fair value**: the amount for which an asset could be exchanged, or a liability settled, between knowledgeable, willing parties in an arm's length transaction.

**Costs to sell**: the incremental costs directly attributable to the disposal of an asset (or disposal group), excluding finance costs and income tax expense.

**Recoverable amount**: the higher of an asset's fair value less costs to sell and its value in use.

**Value in use**: the present value of estimated future cash flows expected to arise from the continuing use of an asset and from its disposal at the end of its useful life. (IFRS 5)

## Measurement of assets held for sale

A non-current asset (or disposal group) that is held for sale should be measured at the **lower of** its **carrying amount** and **fair value less costs to sell**. Fair value less costs to sell is equivalent to net realisable value. If fair value less costs to sell is lower than the carrying value an impairment loss is recognised in the income statement.

## Discontinued operations – definitions

**Discontinued operation**: a component of an entity that has either been disposed of, or is classified as held for sale, and

- Represents a separate major line of business or geographical area of operations
- Is part of a single co-ordinated plan to dispose of a separate major line of business or geographical area of operations; or
- Is a subsidiary acquired exclusively with a view to resale.

**Component of an entity**: operations and cash flows that can be clearly distinguished, operationally and for financial reporting purposes, from the rest of the entity.

## Presenting discontinued operations

An entity should **present and disclose information** that enables users of the financial statements to evaluate the financial effects of **discontinued operations** and disposals of non-current assets or disposal groups.

An entity should disclose a **single amount** on the **face of the income statement** comprising the total of:

- The post-tax profit or loss of discontinued operations; and
- The post-tax gain or loss recognised on the measurement to fair value less costs to sell or on the disposal of the assets or disposal group(s) constituting the discontinued operation.

## Analysis of discontinued operations figure

An entity should also disclose an **analysis** of this single amount into:

- The revenue, expenses and pre-tax profit or loss of discontinued operations
- The related income tax expense
- The gain or loss recognised on the measurement to fair value less costs to sell or on the disposal of the assets of the discontinued operation
- The related income tax expense

This may be presented either on the face of the income statement or in the notes. If it is presented on the face of the income statement it should be presented in a section identified as relating to discontinued operations, ie separately from continuing operations. This analysis is not required where the discontinued operation is a newly acquired subsidiary that has been classified as held for sale.

**EXAMPLE**

The following example is taken from the implementation guidance to IFRS 5. Profit for the period from discontinued operations would be analysed in the notes.

**XYZ Group**

**Income Statement for the Year Ended 31 December 2015**

| | **2015 (£'000)** | **2014 (£'000)** |
|---|---|---|
| Continuing operations | | |
| Revenue | X | X |
| Cost of sales | (X) | (X) |
| Gross profit | X | X |
| Other income | X | X |
| Distribution costs | (X) | (X) |
| Administrative expenses | (X) | (X) |
| Other expenses | (X) | (X) |
| Finance costs | (X) | (X) |
| Share of profit of associates | X | X |
| Profit before tax | X | X |
| Income tax expense | (X) | (X) |
| Profit for the period from continuing operations | X | X |
| Discontinued operations | | |
| Profit for the period from discontinued operations | X | X |
| Profit for the period | X | X |
| Attributable to: | | |
| Equity holders of the parent | X | X |
| Minority interest | X | X |
| | X | X |

An alternative to this presentation would be to analyse the profit from discontinued operations in a separate column on the face of the income statement.

## Presentation of a non-current asset or disposal group classified as held for sale

Non-current assets and disposal groups classified as held for sale should be **presented separately** from other assets in the balance sheet. The liabilities of a disposal group should be presented separately from other liabilities in the balance sheet.

- Assets and liabilities held for sale should not be offset.
- The major classes of assets and liabilities held for sale should be separately disclosed either on the face of the balance sheet or in the notes.

## Chapter Roundup

**Module 1, Chapter 4: Group Accounting**

- Consolidated accounts provide a true and fair view of the risks and rewards of a group of companies, by showing the user of the accounts the combined assets, liabilities and trading performance of all subsidiaries.
- You need to be able to produce a consolidated balance sheet or a pro-forma statement of net assets for a group, including dealing with:
  - Minority interest. **Minority interest** arises with subsidiaries that are not 100% owned by the group. It represents the non-group shareholders' interest in the subsidiary's profit or loss and net assets.
  - Goodwill and fair values. **Goodwill** is the excess of the cost of the acquisition over the acquirer's interest in the fair value of the identifiable assets and liabilities acquired as at the date of the exchange transaction. **Fair value** is the amount for which an asset could be exchanged, or a liability settled, between knowledgeable, willing parties in an arm's length transaction.
  - **Intra-group trading**. All intra-group sales, asset transfers, dividends and loans must be excluded prior to consolidation. The consolidated financial statements show the group performance and position versus the outside world ie excluding any movements of resources within the group.
  - The impact of **mid-year acquisitions and disposals** on the balance sheet and income statement. The income statement results must be pro-rated to reflect the period of ownership. The balance sheet must show the position at the balance sheet date, in other words will incorporate 100% of the assets and liabilities of a subsidiary acquired in the year. This can give a mismatch with the income statement when calculating ratios.

# ACCOUNTING FOR TAXATION

chapter 5

Contents


| | | |
|---|---|---|
| 1 | Corporation Tax | 76 |
| 2 | Accounting for Tax Charge | 76 |
| 3 | Accounting for Tax Payment | 76 |
| 4 | Corporation Tax on Dividends and Interest | 78 |
| 5 | Overseas Tax | 78 |

# 1 Corporation Tax

Since 1 April 1964, all UK resident companies have been subject to a single tax, corporation tax, on all their profits (income and chargeable gains) wherever generated (either in the UK or overseas). Any income generated abroad may also be subject to overseas tax.

In calculating the corporation tax payable, Her Majesty's Revenue and Customs (HMRC) work on a strict legal basis, ie individual companies (separate legal entities) are assessed separately for tax purposes. In a group situation, tax is *not* levied on group profits (though some concessions may ultimately be available from group membership). Tax is levied on the individual group members based on their individual profits, the group tax charge being an accumulation of these separate amounts. Hence, with reference to group tax situations:

- UK subsidiaries are subject to UK corporation tax based on their own profits.
- Overseas subsidiaries are subject to their own relevant country's corporate taxes based on their individual profits, these profits will not automatically be subject to UK corporation tax as we discuss later.
- The overall group tax charge is an accumulation of UK and overseas taxes, as all other figures, eg turnover, are an accumulation of UK and overseas figures.

# 2 Accounting for Tax Charge

Tax accrues through the accounting period as the company generates taxable profits. However, for accounting purposes the tax is only formally calculated at the end of the accounting period. The estimated charge is accounted for as follows.

- Tax charge is increased in the income statement (profit and shareholders' funds reduced).
- Tax liability is increased on the year-end balance sheet (liabilities increased).

# 3 Accounting for Tax Payment

Corporation tax is paid over four instalments, two within the current accounting period and two after the end of the accounting period.

When tax is paid, the following accounting entry will be made.

- Cash balance decreased
- Tax liability decreased

In practice, the company will be paying some of its tax charge before providing for the full year tax charge at year end. However, the year-end balance sheet will show the net tax liability, being the total estimated charge for the year minus the two instalments paid to date.

The accounting regulations are governed by IAS 12 *Income Taxes*.

The tax charge in the income statement for a particular year will probably just be one figure, though this will be analysed in the notes. The headings that may be included in this note are

| | (£) |
|---|---|
| UK corporation tax at X% | X |
| Less: Relief for overseas tax | (X) |
| | X |
| Overseas tax | X |
| Deferred tax | X |
| Adjustments related to prior years | X |
| Total income statement tax charge | X |

The corporation tax charge is a percentage applied to the **taxable profits**. These taxable profits are not necessarily the same as accounting profits.

Accounting profits can, to a very large extent, be dependent on the accounting policies adopted by the company (eg depreciation rates, etc). HMRC does not want companies to be able to manipulate their tax charge by use of creative accounting policies, hence profits are recalculated based on HMRC's own standards to arrive at the taxable profits figure. This recalculation is done by taking the original profit as reported by the company and adjusting it to apply tax rules.

There are two types of difference between taxable and accounting profits.

## Taxation: permanent differences

Permanent differences are one of the following.

- Income which is never subject to corporation tax, eg dividends from UK companies. As a result, a company may have reported profits but no tax charge.
- Expenses which are never allowed, eg entertaining, fines, etc. Expenses are deducted from revenue to calculate profit, however, HMRC does not allow the deduction of these particular expenses and hence, the taxable profits are higher.

As a result of these items, the corporation tax charge will seldom simply be the financial accounting profits multiplied by the prevailing tax rate.

## Taxation: timing differences

Items where the:

- Profit effect is in one period when the revenue or cost is recognised on the basis of the fundamental accounting concepts
- Tax effect is in another period based on tax legislation

The result being that the items are taxed, but the tax charged does not match against the profits for the year to which they relate. Examples of such items include:

- Royalties payable and receivable (short-term timing differences)
- Capital allowance and depreciation
- Revaluations of non-current assets
- Losses

### EXAMPLE

This is an example of an adjustment to profits calculation.

| | P/T | £'000 |
|---|---|---|
| Profit before tax per the financial statements | | 2,400 |
| Less: Income not subject to corporation tax | | |
| – Dividends received from UK companies | P | (500) |
| Add: Expenditure not allowed for tax | | |
| – Entertaining | P | 60 |
| – Fines | P | 40 |
| – Depreciation | T | 500 |
| | | 2,500 |
| Less: Capital allowances | T | (1,000) |
| Profits chargeable to corporation tax | | £1,500 |
| Corporation tax at 30% (1,500 × 30%) | | £450 |

The P/T column indicates Permanent/Timing difference.

As we can see from this example, the effective tax rate has turned out to be 18.8%, (450 ÷ 2,400), significantly less than the nominal or statutory tax rate for that financial year of 30%.

# 4 Corporation Tax on Dividends and Interest

## Dividends paid and payable

Dividends are a means by which the company distributes profits to the shareholders. As such, they do not represent a tax-allowable expense and are therefore paid out of profits after the tax charge for the accounting period has been deducted.

## Dividends received

If dividends have been received from another UK company, the profits out of which they are being paid will already have been taxed. Therefore, the recipient company is not required to pay any further tax to HMRC.

It is required that companies show dividends received as being the net cash amount received above the tax line, with no tax implications for the income statement tax charge.

## Interest receivable

Interest receivable is treated as investment income in the income statement and is chargeable to tax. It is shown as a gross figure in the income statement, with the tax charge thus being higher as a result of the additional taxable income.

## Interest received net of withholding tax

It is, however, often the case that interest income is paid net of a withholding tax, with the recipient therefore in a similar position to having received a dividend net of the 'tax credit'. Although these situations appear similar, interest income is required to be grossed up in the income statement to include the tax withheld. This treatment is disallowed for dividend income, which should be included in the income statement as a net amount received, as detailed above.

The tax charge must include the tax withheld on the interest income, although, as this tax has already been deducted by the paying company, it will never actually be paid by the recipient company.

# 5 Overseas Tax

## How overseas tax arises

A UK company may become subject to overseas tax when it conducts part of its operations abroad, eg through the operations of an overseas branch.

In a group situation, the profits of any overseas subsidiaries will be subject to overseas tax, ie the corporate tax regime of the country in which it is incorporated and operates, not UK corporation tax.

Remember that tax is calculated on a strict legal basis, ie individual companies profits are taxed separately, we do not tax group profit.

For these reasons, the tax charge in both the individual company's accounts ,or group accounts may include an element of overseas tax.

## Double tax relief

You will recall that UK companies are subject to corporation tax on *all* their profits wherever generated in the world. As a result, if we have set up a branch in, say, France, the UK tax authorities will wish to subject the profits of that branch to UK corporation tax. We may also find, however, that the French authorities wish to tax the profits that have been generated on their soil. Hence, these profits are taxable twice.

In a group situation, the profits of the overseas subsidiaries will have been subject to overseas taxes when earned. If a dividend is paid from these subsidiaries out of their after-tax profits to the UK holding company, then this income received by the UK holding company will be subject to UK corporation tax. Hence, effectively the income from which the dividend that has been paid has been taxed twice: once overseas and once when remitted as a dividend to the UK parent.

This problem is not just confined to the UK, but is quite common internationally. Clearly, such double taxation, were it to stand, would be a distinct disincentive to overseas investment. As a concession in these situations, HMRC authorities of most countries have developed tax treaties alleviating this problem and ensuring that the income is only taxed once.

In the UK, the effect is that the income will be subject to UK corporation tax, but then double tax relief will be given. The tax charge and corresponding liability will be reduced by the lower of

- The overseas tax paid.
- UK corporation tax on the same profits.

If the figures are material then the tax note will then disclose three items.

- Corporation tax charge.
- Overseas tax charge.
- Overseas or double tax relief as a reduction against the corporation tax charge.

## Deferred tax

**Deferred tax** is an accounting adjustment used to match the tax effects of transactions with their accounting impact.

When a company recognises an asset or liability, it expects to **recover or settle the carrying amount** of that asset or liability. In other words, it expects to sell or use up assets, and to pay off liabilities. What happens if that recovery or settlement is likely to make future tax payments larger (or smaller) than they would otherwise have been if the recovery or settlement had no tax consequences? In these circumstances, IAS 12 requires companies to recognise a **deferred tax liability** (or **deferred tax asset**).

**Deferred tax liabilities** are the amounts of income taxes payable in future periods in respect of taxable temporary differences.

**Deferred tax assets** are the amounts of income taxes recoverable in future periods in respect of:

- Deductible temporary differences
- The carry-forward of unused tax losses
- The carry-forward of unused tax credits

**Temporary differences** are differences between the carrying amount of an asset or liability in the balance sheet and its tax base. Temporary differences may be either:

- **Taxable temporary differences**, which are temporary differences that will result in taxable amounts in determining taxable profit (tax loss) of future periods when the carrying amount of the asset or liability is recovered or settled

- **Deductible temporary differences**, which are temporary differences that will result in amounts that are deductible in determining taxable profit (tax loss) of future periods when the carrying amount of the asset or liability is recovered or settled

The **tax base** of an asset or liability is the amount attributed to that asset or liability for tax purposes.

*(IAS 12)*

## Taxation: temporary differences

Accounting profits form the basis for computing **taxable profits**, on which the tax liability for the year is calculated; however, accounting profits and taxable profits are different. There are two reasons for the differences.

- **Permanent differences**. These occur when certain items of revenue or expense are excluded from the computation of taxable profits (for example, entertainment expenses may not be allowable for tax purposes).
- **Temporary differences**. These occur when items of revenue or expense are included in both accounting profits and taxable profits, but not for the same accounting period. For example, an expense which is allowable as a deduction in arriving at taxable profits for 20X7 might not be included in the financial accounts until 20X8 or later. In the long run, the total taxable profits and total accounting profits will be the same (except for permanent differences) so that temporary differences originate in one period and are capable of reversal in one or more subsequent periods. Deferred tax is the tax attributable to **temporary differences**.

Temporary differences are known as timing differences in the UK.

### EXAMPLE

A company buys a machine for £160,000, which it expects to last for three years and then have a residual value of £70,000.

What will be the reported profits and balance sheet position at the end of each of the three years both without and with deferred tax? Assume that profits before tax are £100,000 in each year. Assume the applicable corporate tax rate is 30%.

## SOLUTION

### Without deferred tax

The corporation tax charge will be based on taxable profits (an adjustment to accounting profits) and will result in the following.

| | Year 1 (£) | Year 2 (£) | Year 3 (£) | Total (£) |
|---|---|---|---|---|
| **Income statement** | | | | |
| Profit before tax | 100,000 | 100,000 | 100,000 | 300,000 |
| Corporation tax | (27,000) | (30,000) | (33,000) | (90,000) |
| Profit after tax | 73,000 | 70,000 | 67,000 | 210,000 |
| **Balance sheet extract** | | | | |
| Corporation tax liability | 27,000 | 30,000 | 33,000 | |

The corporation tax charge has been based on the following adjustment to profits.

**Adjust to Profit & Tax**

| | Year 1 (£) | Year 2 (£) | Year 3 (£) | Total (£) |
|---|---|---|---|---|
| Profit before tax | 100,000 | 100,000 | 100,000 | 300,000 |
| Add: Depreciation | 30,000 | 30,000 | 30,000 | 90,000 |
| Less: Capital allowances | (40,000) | (30,000) | (20,000) | (90,000) |
| Profit chargeable to tax | 90,000 | 100,000 | 110,000 | 300,000 |
| Tax at 30% | 27,000 | 30,000 | 33,000 | 90,000 |

We can see that in total the tax charge of £90,000 represents 30% of the total profits of £300,000. Ideally, therefore, to apply the matching concept the tax charge for each year would be £100,000 × 30% = £30,000. Capital allowances are assumed at 25% on a reducing balance basis.

**Tax Charge**

| | Year 1 (£) | Year 2 (£) | Year 3 (£) |
|---|---|---|---|
| Ideal wanted | 30,000 | 30,000 | 30,000 |
| Corporation tax charge | (27,000) | (30,000) | (33,000) |
| Difference | 3,000 | 0 | (3,000) |

Hence, the tax charge is £3,000 too low in Year 1 but correspondingly £3,000 too high in Year 2.

### With deferred tax

We can use deferred tax to recognise an extra £3,000 in Year 1.

- Deferred tax charge up £3,000
- Deferred tax liability up £3,000

Resulting in a lower profit after tax and a deferred tax liability on the balance sheet.

In Year 2, no change is made to the deferred tax provision as this year the actual tax charge is the same as the ideal charge wanted.

In Year 3, we take a deferred tax credit, the effect on the accounting equation being:

- Deferred tax charge down £3,000 (profits, hence shareholders' funds up)
- Deferred tax liability down £3,000 (liabilities down)

Thus cancelling the deferred tax liability established in Year 1 down to zero and giving the following income statement and balance sheet figures.

| | Year 1 (£) | Year 2 (£) | Year 3 (£) | Total (£) |
|---|---|---|---|---|
| Income statement | | | | |
| Profit before tax | 100,000 | 100,000 | 100,000 | 300,000 |
| Corporation tax | (27,000) | (30,000) | (33,000) | (90,000) |
| Deferred tax | (3,000) | – | 3,000 | – |
| Total tax charge | (30,000) | (30,000) | (30,000) | (90,000) |
| Profit after tax | 70,000 | 70,000 | 70,000 | 210,000 |
| Balance sheet extract | | | | |
| Corporation tax liability | 27,000 | 30,000 | 33,000 | |
| Deferred tax liability | 3,000 | 3,000 | – | |

We can see that now the total tax charge each year is the same at £30,000. Likewise, the corresponding profits after tax are identical each year at £70,000 as could reasonably be expected when the business has performed the same each year.

Once more, this Example shows that the deferred tax charge or credit is based on any timing differences that arise. In Year 1 of this Example, we have accounting profits of £100,000 and taxable profits of £90,000 – a £10,000 timing difference has arisen and hence a £3,000 (£10,000 × 30%) deferred tax charge results.

## TASK

The following extracts are the income taxes note and deferred tax note from Kingfisher 2014/15 annual report.

Use this financial information to answer the following questions:

(a) What is the charge for taxation that has been included in Kingfisher's income statement for the 2014/15 period?

(b) What is the effective tax rate for Kingfisher in 2014/15?

(c) Explain why this differs from the actual corporation tax prevailing in the year.

(d) What is the deferred tax asset or liability included in the balance sheet for Kingfisher at the 2014/15 period end?

(e) What are the main reasons for this asset or liability?

(f) What impact will the asset/liability have on the following ratios for the group?

- (i) Return on capital employed
- (ii) Gearing
- (iii) Current ratio

## 9 Income tax expense

| £ millions | 2014/15 | 2013/14 |
|---|---|---|
| **UK corporation tax** | | |
| Current tax on profits for the year | **46** | 47 |
| Adjustments in respect of prior years | **(96)** | (7) |
| | **(50)** | 40 |
| **Overseas tax** | | |
| Current tax on profits for the year | **138** | 131 |
| Kesa demerger French tax case | – | (118) |
| Other adjustments in respect of prior years | **(6)** | (11) |
| | **132** | 2 |
| **Deferred tax** | | |
| Current year | **(12)** | 16 |
| Adjustments in respect of changes in tax rates | **1** | (9) |
| | **(11)** | 7 |
| **Income tax expense** | **71** | 49 |

### Factors affecting tax charge for the year

The tax charge for the year differs from the standard rate of corporation tax in the UK of 21% (2013/14: 23%). The differences are explained below:

| £ millions | 2014/15 | 2013/14 |
|---|---|---|
| Profit before taxation | **644** | 759 |
| Profit multiplied by the standard rate of corporation tax in the UK of 21% (2013/14: 23%) | **135** | 175 |
| Share of post-tax results of joint ventures and associates | **(1)** | (2) |
| Net income not chargeable for tax purposes | **(5)** | (16) |
| Temporary differences: | | |
| – Net gains on property | **(4)** | (3) |
| – Losses not recognised | **11** | 9 |
| Foreign tax rate differences | **36** | 31 |
| Adjustments in respect of prior years | **(102)** | (136) |
| Adjustments in respect of changes in tax rates | **1** | (9) |
| Income tax expense | **71** | 49 |

## 25 Deferred tax

| £ millions | 2014/15 | 2013/14 |
|---|---|---|
| Deferred tax assets | **10** | 12 |
| Deferred tax liabilities | **(329)** | (251) |
| | **(319)** | (239) |

Deferred tax assets and liabilities are offset against each other when they relate to income taxes levied by the same tax jurisdiction and when the Group intends to settle its current tax assets and liabilities on a net basis.

| £ millions | Accelerated tax depreciation | Gains on property | Provisions | Tax losses | Post-employment benefits | Other | Total |
|---|---|---|---|---|---|---|---|
| At 2 February 2014 | **(151)** | **(114)** | **19** | **7** | **(5)** | **5** | **(239)** |
| (Charge)/credit to income statement | **(6)** | **8** | **8** | **(2)** | **(1)** | **4** | **11** |
| Charge to equity | – | – | **(1)** | – | **(92)** | **(19)** | **(112)** |
| Transfers to liabilities held for sale (China) | – | **9** | – | – | – | – | **9** |
| Exchange differences | **13** | **6** | **(3)** | **(1)** | **(3)** | – | **12** |
| At 31 January 2015 | **(144)** | **(91)** | **23** | **4** | **(101)** | **(10)** | **(319)** |
| | | | | | | | |
| At 3 February 2013 | (136) | (132) | 20 | 8 | (57) | 11 | (286) |
| (Charge)/credit to income statement | (24) | 17 | 2 | – | 2 | (4) | (7) |
| (Charge)/credit to equity | – | – | (1) | – | 51 | (2) | 48 |
| Acquisition of subsidiaries | – | (3) | – | – | – | – | (3) |
| Exchange differences | 9 | 4 | (2) | (1) | (1) | – | 9 |
| At 1 February 2014 | (151) | (114) | 19 | 7 | (5) | 5 | (239) |

## SOLUTION

(a) The charge for taxation in the income statement for 2014/15 is £71m (ie the current year UK and overseas tax charge, including deferred tax expense and prior year adjustments).

(b) The effective tax rate is a calculated as follows:

| | |
|---|---|
| Income tax charge | 71 |
| Profit before taxation | 644 |
| **Effective tax rate** | **11.0%** |

(c) The actual corporation tax prevailing in the year is 21%, which is considerably higher than the group's effective rate. The main reason that the group has a lower effective tax rate is because of adjustments in respect of prior years.

(d) The group has a net deferred tax liability in its balance sheet of £319m in 2014/15.

(e) The main reasons for the net deferred tax liability are timing differences relating to accelerated tax depreciation (capital allowances are available at a faster rate than accounting depreciation), timing differences relating to retirement benefits and a liability relating to gains on property.

(f) The liability will have the following impact on these ratios:

(i) There will be no impact on return on capital employed (operating profit unchanged; capital employed unchanged, as long term liabilities increase and equity reduces)

(ii) Gearing will increase (borrowings unchanged; equity reduced)

(iii) There will be no impact on the current ratio (current assets and current liabilities unchanged)

## TASK

Choose a company which interests you and find its latest financial statements on the internet. Use the annual report to answer questions (a) to (f) above. Contrast the tax position with that of Kingfisher above.

## Examples of deferred tax liabilities

The following are examples of circumstances that give rise to deferred tax liabilities.

## Transactions that affect the income statement

- **Interest revenue** received in arrears and included in accounting profit on the basis of time apportionment. It is included in taxable profit, however, on a cash basis.
- **Depreciation** of an asset is accelerated for tax purposes. When new assets are purchased, allowances may be available against taxable profits which exceed the amount of depreciation chargeable on the assets in the financial accounts for the year of purchase.
- **Development costs** which have been capitalised will be amortised in the income statement, but they were deducted in full from taxable profit in the period in which they were incurred.
- **Prepaid expenses** have already been deducted on a cash basis in determining the taxable profit of the current or previous periods.

## Transactions that affect the balance sheet

- **Depreciation of an asset** is not deductible for tax purposes. No deduction will be available for tax purposes when the asset is sold/scrapped.
- A borrower records a **loan** at proceeds received (amount due at maturity) less transaction costs.

The carrying amount of the loan is subsequently increased by amortisation of the transaction costs against accounting profit. The transaction costs were, however, deducted for tax purposes in the period when the loan was first recognised.

## Fair value adjustments and revaluations

- **Financial assets or investment property** are carried at fair value. This exceeds cost, but no equivalent adjustment is made for tax purposes.
- Property, plant and equipment is **revalued** by an entity (under IAS 16), but no equivalent adjustment is made for tax purposes.

## Examples of deferred tax assets

The deferred tax asset must also satisfy the **recognition criteria** given in IAS 12. These state that a deferred tax asset should be recognised for all deductible temporary differences to the extent that it is **probable that taxable profit will be available** against which it can be utilised. This is an application of prudence.

## Transactions that affect the income statement

- **Retirement benefit costs** (pension costs) are deducted from accounting profit as service is provided by the employee. They are not deducted in determining taxable profit until the entity pays either retirement benefits or contributions to a fund. (This may also apply to similar expenses.)
- **Accumulated depreciation** of an asset in the financial statements is greater than the accumulated depreciation allowed for tax purposes up to the balance sheet date.
- The **cost of inventories** sold before the balance sheet date is deducted from accounting profit when goods/services are delivered, but is deducted from taxable profit when the cash is received.
  (**Note.** There is also a taxable temporary difference associated with the related trade receivable.)
- The **net realisable value (NRV)** of inventory, or the **recoverable amount** of an item of property, plant and equipment falls and the carrying value is therefore **reduced**, but that reduction is ignored for tax purposes until the asset is sold.
- **Research costs** (or organisation/other start-up costs) are recognised as an expense for accounting purposes but are not deductible against taxable profits until a later period.
- Income is **deferred** in the balance sheet, but has already been included in taxable profit in current/prior periods.
- A **government grant** is included in the balance sheet as deferred income, but it will not be taxable in future periods.
  (**Note.** A deferred tax asset may *not* be recognised here according to the Standard.)

## CHAPTER ROUNDUP

**Module 1, Chapter 5: Accounting for Taxation**

- A company's tax charge is calculated based on its reported profits for the period, using taxation rules (not accounting rules).
- The tax charge shown in the income statement comprises the tax due to the taxation authorities, together with other adjustments, including deferred taxation.
- Deferred tax is an accounting adjustment which aligns the cash tax payment with the accounting profits, using the accruals concept.
- Deferred tax arises because of timing differences between when an item is recognised for accounting or taxation purposes. These are termed 'temporary differences'.
  - **Deferred tax liabilities** are the amounts of income taxes payable in future periods in respect of taxable temporary differences.
  - **Deferred tax assets** are the amounts of income taxes recoverable in future periods in respect of
    - Deductible temporary differences.
    - The carryforward of unused tax losses.
    - The carryforward of unused tax credits.
  - **Temporary differences** are differences between the carrying amount of an asset or liability in the balance sheet and its tax base (its value for tax purposes).
- Particularly important in this chapter, is the ability to understand and interpret taxation disclosures in consolidated financial statements.

# Ratio Analysis

chapter 6

## Contents


| | | |
|---|---|---|
| 1 | Financial Statements | 88 |
| 2 | Ratios | 88 |
| 3 | Profitability Ratios | 89 |
| 4 | Liquidity Ratios | 95 |
| 5 | Capital Structure | 104 |
| 6 | Earnings per Share | 111 |
| 7 | Other Investment Ratios | 121 |
| 8 | Analysis Considerations | 127 |
| 9 | Other Tools of Interpretation | 130 |

# 1 Financial Statements

The financial statements, namely the income statement, the balance sheet, the cash flow statement and all the associated notes, contain a vast amount of information. It is the role of the financial analyst to use this information to develop a substantiated view on the company's past performance and whether this can be used as a prediction of future performance.

The financial statements are primarily prepared for the shareholders. However, they may have several other users such as lenders, creditors, the government, tax authorities, and so on. Each of these will be looking to use the accounts to get some indication of the:

- Returns they are receiving
- Risks they are facing

A number of fairly standard ratios have been developed to assist with this process.

# 2 Ratios

A ratio is a calculation which compares different elements of the financial statements. Ratios are very convenient for summarising and presenting information. In general they are easy to understand and they help to focus attention on the important aspects of business performance and risk (trading or financial).

A ratio is, however, **meaningless in isolation**. In order to be useful, a ratio must have some reasonable comparative, for example:

- Prior year figures
- Competitors' figures
- Target figures

We can then review how the company is doing compared with, say, the previous year. The ratio itself is not an answer, simply a means to an end. If all of our ratios this year are the same as they were last year, then our returns and risks for all interested parties are unaltered.

Ratios can be used to highlight trends over a number of years, which may not be so apparent from the figures themselves. These trends can then be used by the analyst's client to assess how the company is performing.

When using ratios to focus our attention for analysis purposes, we will essentially be looking for:

- **Discontinuities**, ie large changes in the ratios from one year to the next, or large variances of the ratio against competitors or budgets. These, in all probability, will be highlighting some anomaly.
- **Trends** illustrated by the ratios over a period of time. These may be upward/downward trends in terms of returns being achieved, or the risks people face.

## Definition of ratios

Other than earnings per share, there is **no strict definition of any ratio**. What we describe below are standard methods of calculating ratios, but how certain elements should be treated can be open to debate. It is your job as the analyst to determine the best way to deal with these items in any particular scenario, although the most important factor is that you are **consistent in how you treat them** from one year to another or from one company to another.

## Ratio groupings

Ratios are commonly grouped under four headings. This classification is important; if the examiner uses these terms, you will be expected to know which ratios to calculate.

| | |
|---|---|
| **Profitability** | Measures to assess the trading or operating performance of the company, ie levels of trading profits generated and the effectiveness of the use of trading assets. Sometimes described as 'performance' ratios. |
| **Liquidity** | Measures to assess the trading risk of the company. This is the risk that, as a result of trading activities, the company may be unable to pay its suppliers as the debts fall due and cease to exist. |
| **Investors' ratios** | Measures to assess the returns to providers of finance, who may be either shareholders or lenders. |
| **Capital structure** | Measures to assess the risks to the providers of finance due to the company's level of borrowing (ie gearing). These ratios can also be termed 'financial risk' ratios or 'solvency' ratios. |

There are effectively two sides to a business – a trading side and the financing side.
A company raises finance then uses this to enable it to trade. Our analysis will be used to measure the risks and returns on each side.

# 3 Profitability Ratios

The aim of profitability ratios is to measure the underlying trading performance of the business itself regardless of how it is financed. A common starting point is a calculation of return on capital employed (ROCE). ROCE is a very useful ratio to summarise the overall performance of the business in the period.

## Return on capital employed

### Basic calculation

The return on capital employed is calculated as

$$\text{ROCE} = \frac{\begin{array}{c}\text{Profit from operations + Interest receivable}\\ \text{and other income receivable}\end{array}}{\text{Capital employed}} \times 100\%$$

### Considerations

This profit figure can be viewed as operating profit plus interest receivable and income from other investments, ie the profits that management has generated from the resources it has available. It is calculated before interest payable since that will clearly be dependent on the financing of the business – the larger the loans, the larger the interest payable.

The capital employed figure is the total trading assets (or total financing since they are equal) that can be identified by rearranging the balance sheet. Rather than showing net assets and shareholders' funds as two sides of the balance sheet, we can rearrange the assets, liabilities and equity to show the trading assets on one side and all the financing on the other. Effectively, this involves shifting all the non-current liabilities from the top of the balance sheet to the bottom of the balance sheet.

## EXAMPLE Calculating capital employed

We have the following initial balance sheet showing net assets and shareholders' funds.

| **Balance sheet** | **£'000** |
|---|---|
| **Net Assets** | |
| Non-Current Assets | 50 |
| Current Assets | 60 |
| Non-Current Liabilities (provisions and borrowings) | (30) |
| Current Liabilities (trade and other payables) | (45) |
| | 35 |
| **Shareholders' Funds** | |
| Share Capital | 12 |
| Reserves | 23 |
| | 35 |

Rearranging to find capital employed:

| **Rearranged balance sheet** | **£'000** | **£'000** |
|---|---|---|
| **Total Trading Assets** | | |
| Non-Current Assets | | 50 |
| Current Assets | 60 | |
| Current Liabilities | (45) | |
| Net Current Assets | | 15 |
| | | 65 |
| **Total Financing** | | |
| Share Capital | | 12 |
| Reserves | | 23 |
| Non-Current Liabilities | | 30 |
| | | 65 |

Based on this, capital employed can be calculated from the financing side as

Capital employed = Shareholders' funds + Non-current liabilities + Borrowings in current liabilities

or from the trading side as

Capital employed = Total assets – Current liabilities
(excluding borrowings in current liabilities, such as overdrafts, finance lease obligations)

## EXAMPLE Calculating capital employed

This example uses information from the illustrative financial statements included in the Appendix to this chapter.

***ROCE – after exceptional items***

$$\text{ROCE} = \frac{6,484 + 62 + 303}{33,041 + 4,445 + 137 + 16,942} \times 100\%$$

$$\text{ROCE} = \frac{6,849}{54,565} \times 100\%$$

ROCE = 12.6%

***ROCE – before exceptional items (included in administration costs)***

$$\text{ROCE} = \frac{6,849 + 3,192}{54,565} \times 100\%$$

ROCE = 18.4%

For this example, we have calculated the capital employed as shareholders' funds, including minority interest, non-current liabilities and the bank overdraft and finance lease liabilities. These liabilities are being treated as part of the financing of the company, not the trading assets.

The ratio can be calculated either before or after 'exceptional items'. These are items which are one-off in nature, such as restructuring costs or gains/ losses on disposal of an asset. Ratios calculated on a pre-exceptional basis can be more useful for analysing trends. However, the analyst needs to consider if the exceptional item is actually a one-off item or a regular feature of the income statement.

### Potential problems

Ideally, it would be best to use the average capital employed for the calculation, as our aim is to match the profits generated throughout the year to the capital or assets that have been used to generate them, or the total financing of the business.

It is unlikely that this information will be available, and normally the calculation would be based on year-end figures. This can lead to some **major distortions in our ratios**, especially if there have been large changes in capital employed during the year, ie from the acquisition of a subsidiary or the raising of funds near the year end.

### Analysis points

Having established the return on capital employed, we now need to consider what has caused the ratio to change from one year to the next.

The return on capital employed ratio can be disaggregated into its component parts.

- Profit margin (showing business profitability)
- Asset turnover (showing business efficiency)

The following diagram illustrates this disaggregation.

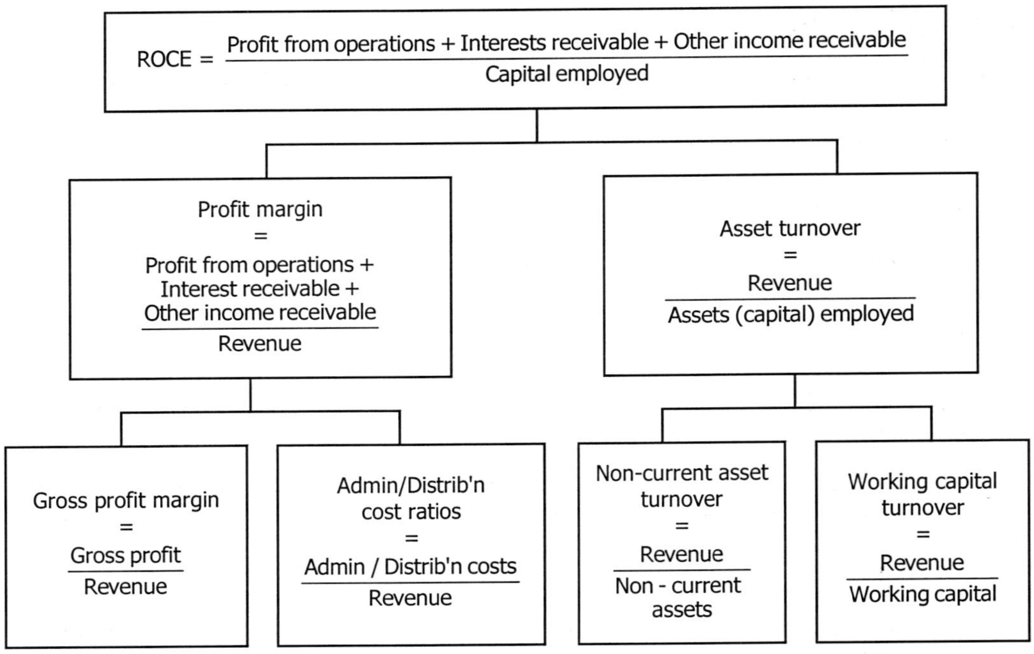


If we multiply the profit margin by the asset turnover, we get back to the return on capital employed since the revenue figures will cancel. We will now consider each of these ratios in more detail. Understanding changes in each of these ratios will help us to see what is driving the overall change in return on capital employed.

## Profit margins

A profit margin is a measure of the profit achieved per £1 sale generated.

$$\text{Profit margin} = \frac{\text{Profits}}{\text{Revenue}} \times 100\%$$

### Considerations

From our diagram above we have taken profit as profit from operations and other income. This ensures that the ratios exactly 'interlock'. However, this brings with it the problem that not all elements of this profit as defined here have any relationship to the levels of revenue. For example, this profit is stated after:

- Interest receivable
- Income from non-current asset investments
- Share of profits of associated undertakings

None of the above three are related to revenue. In some cases it might be better, therefore, particularly if examining the profit margin in isolation, to use the operating profit figure only. However, we will continue using our 'full' PBIT figure for now.

**EXAMPLE**

Again, using information contained in our illustration financial statements at the end of this chapter.

$$\text{Profit margin} = \frac{\text{£6,849 (see ROCE above)}}{\text{£135,761}} \times 100\%$$

Profit margin = 5.0%

### Analysis points

Once we have calculated this ratio, we need to make something meaningful out of it. When doing this, it is important to consider the causes and possible consequences, not just the numbers.

Rising profit margins are good news – higher levels of profits. However, these higher profits may mean that the company loses customer loyalty if they perceive that they are being exploited. Alternatively, high prices may attract competitors into the field, in which case the company may lose a substantial amount of market share.

Conversely, margins going down may normally be perceived as bad news. However, it may be as a consequence of a policy of penetration pricing; or it may be that the company is incurring high development costs and future years' profitability will be that much higher as a result.

## Asset turnover

The asset turnover ratio assesses the effectiveness of the use of the trading assets available.

$$\text{Asset turnover} = \frac{\text{Revenue}}{\text{Assets (capital) employed}}$$

### Considerations

To make these ratios exactly interlock, as in the diagram above, we would need to take all the capital employed as being the denominator in this calculation. However, again, some assets bear no relationship to turnover whatsoever, eg:

- Investment in associated undertakings
- Short-term investments

It may therefore be more appropriate to take just those trading assets that have contributed to turnover.

**EXAMPLE**

Using information from our illustration financial statements (Section 9)

$$\text{Asset turnover} = \frac{\text{£135,761}}{\text{£54,565 (see ROCE above)}}$$

Asset turnover = 2.49×

51.2

52.3 41.71. 36.37.

### Potential problems

Again a problem with this ratio, in common with the problem of return on capital employed, is that we are comparing a full year's transactions (revenue) to a year-end balance sheet figure (assets employed). Unless this year-end figure is representative of the assets employed throughout the year, we will not exactly be comparing like-with-like and there may be some distortions.

For example, if the company buys a subsidiary or raises new finance close to the year end, then the year-end assets employed would be substantially higher than the general level throughout the year.

Another problem is the impact of accounting policies. If, for example, non-current assets are revalued this year then this will have two effects.

- Profits will be down due to increased depreciation charges.
- Capital assets employed will be up due to the increase in non-current asset net book values.

The result will be that the return on capital employed and asset turnover figures will be reduced, although the effectiveness of the business, in truth, may be unaltered. It is very difficult to remove these distorting effects. It is probably more convenient to calculate the ratios but to note any distortions.

### Analysis points

Again, when considering this ratio, it may be tempting just to state the obvious – but take care. We should **consider the causes**, not just the numbers.

Considering just the numbers, it would be tempting to believe that increased asset turnover is a positive thing. However, it may arise from

- Overtrading, which would result in liquidity problems.
- A deterioration of the capital base, ie sales are not rising, rather the asset base is falling.

As the diagram above illustrates, this ratio may be further sub-analysed into, for example, working capital turnover and non-current asset turnover; each of which may be an appropriate ratio for a particular sort of industry. Non-current asset turnover may be an appropriate ratio in a capital-intensive industry where a large amount of the capital of the business is tied up in non-current assets. The analyst needs to decide which ratios to use and how to use them.

## Operational gearing

The operational gearing ratio gives the percentage change in profits per 1% change in revenue, which may be calculated as

$$\text{Operational gearing ratio} = \frac{\text{Revenue} - \text{Variable costs}}{\text{Profit}}$$

### Considerations

This ratio is a measure of operational risk, ie risk to the operating profit figure, and is assessing the levels of variable and fixed operating costs in the business. Variable costs are costs whose level varies directly with the level of output, hence if sales increase/(decrease) then variable costs increase/(decrease), eg raw material costs. Fixed costs are costs whose level remains constant regardless of output levels, eg rent, rates, depreciation.

The greater the level of fixed costs in the business, the **greater the variation in the profit figure** as a result of revenue changes. Businesses with high fixed cost bases have high operational gearing.

**EXAMPLE**

A company sells its product for £10 per unit, has variable costs of £6 per unit and fixed costs of £15,000 per annum. The normal level of output is 10,000 units p.a., but if output levels vary, we will see the following.

| Output (Units) | 8,000<br>£'000 | 10,000<br>£'000 | 13,000<br>£'000 |
|---|---|---|---|
| Revenue | 80 | 100 | 130 |
| Variable costs | (48) | (60) | (78) |
| | 32 | 40 | 52 |
| Fixed costs | (15) | (15) | (15) |
| Profit before tax | 17 | 25 | 37 |

The operational gearing calculated at the normal output level of 10,000 units is

$$\text{Operational gearing ratio} = \frac{100-60}{25} = 1.6\times$$

What we can see is that a 20% fall in revenue (down to 8,000 units from 10,000) results in a 32% (20% × 1.6) fall in profits, a fall of £8,000 (25,000 × 32%) from £25,000 to £17,000.

Similarly, a 30% increase in revenue (up to 13,000 units from 10,000) results in a 48% (30% × 1.6) increase in profits, a rise of £12,000 (25,000 × 48%) from £25,000 to £37,000.

What this ratio is considering is the levels of profit generated by the company before (the top line) and after (the bottom line) suffering the fixed costs.

### Potential problems and analysis points

The difficulty that we have in applying this idea in the analysis of the accounts of a company is that the accounts do not reveal the extent of the fixed and variable costs. An income statement by function of expense breaks down the operating costs into cost of sales, distribution costs and administrative expenses. Within each of these headings there may be an element of variable costs and an element of fixed costs. An income statement analyses the expenses in a manner that may enable this ratio to be calculated, however, this is still doubtful.

Operational gearing is more a factor to consider given the nature of the business, rather than a statistic that can be calculated. For example, capital intensive businesses will suffer from high fixed costs due to the depreciation of their non-current assets. We can conclude therefore that capital intensive businesses are more likely to have high operational gearing and thus more profit volatility due to the high proportion of fixed costs in their cost base.

# 4 LIQUIDITY RATIOS

## Introduction

There are two main sources of information relating to the liquidity position of a company.

- The balance sheet
- The cash flow statement

The ratios we look at below aim to establish one of two things.

- Do we have the resources to meet our liabilities in hard cash terms?
- Are we realising those resources quickly enough to pay off the liabilities as they fall due?

As we will see, some of these ratios are rather blunt tools but they are useful for showing trends and are frequently used in loan agreements.

## Current ratio

The purpose of this ratio is to see whether the current assets recoverable within one year are sufficient to cover the liabilities that fall due within one year.

$$\text{Current ratio} = \frac{\text{Current assets}}{\text{Current liabilities}}$$

**EXAMPLE**

Using information from our illustration at the end of this chapter

$$\text{Current ratio} = \frac{£57,653}{£43,666}$$

Current ratio = 1.32×

### Potential problems and analysis points

Other practical problems when calculating or using this ratio are as follows.

- **Overdrafts** will be included within current liabilities but are frequently payable after more than one year in practice. Banks frequently allow companies to extend overdrafts for several years.
- **Realisation of inventory** – inventory is contained within current assets and is therefore almost automatically assumed to be realisable within one year, but this may not necessarily be the case. Unlike receivables there will be no note anywhere indicating the recoverability or likely time scale for the realisation of inventories.
- This ratio completely ignores the **timing of cash flows** within the period. In theory it could be possible that all the liabilities are payable now and all the assets are recoverable in 12 months' time. Although in total terms they match, in actual cash flow terms they do not.

Interpretation of this ratio is tricky. A high current ratio implies high liquidity, as current assets provide good coverage to current liabilities. However, high liquidity can be also inefficient as we will see when we discuss working capital in this section below. What we are looking for as a balance between adequate liquidity and ensuring there is an efficient usage of assets in the business.

The current ratio is very sector dependent. Current ratio 'norms' vary significantly depending on the underlying business model. A current ratio less than one arises if a company has greater current liabilities than current assets. This, in itself, does not necessarily mean liquidity problems. There are many sectors for which a current ratio less than one is the norm (eg retail – this sector is typically characterised by low receivables and inventory, but high levels of payables).

## Quick ratio

The quick ratio is an adaptation of the current ratio designed to remove the problem of inventory.

$$\text{Quick ratio} = \frac{\text{Current assets} - \text{Inventory}}{\text{Current liabilities}}$$

### Considerations

The quick ratio considers just the readily realisable assets (cash, investments and receivables) and whether they are sufficient to cover the short-term liabilities of the business. Being a modification of the current ratio, it suffers from the same problems, excluding realisability of inventory.

**EXAMPLE**

Using information from our illustration at the end of this chapter.

$$\text{Quick ratio} = \frac{£57,653 \text{ (see above)} - £19,420}{£43,666}$$

$$\text{Quick ratio} = \frac{£38,233}{£43,666}$$

Quick ratio = 0.88×

Our company has a quick ratio of less than one. This does not mean that it is insolvent and unable to pay off its liabilities. However, depending on the type of business, it may be a sign of liquidity problems.

As discussed above, the current and quick ratios will be influenced by the sector in which the company operates. For example, a supermarket group may have a current and quick ratio of less than one. Supermarkets usually have very low receivables because most customers pay for their goods immediately. Inventory is normally kept at low levels by using a just-in-time system, which delivers the inventory shortly before the sale. This results in low levels of current assets compared to current liabilities, which in turn gives rise to low current and quick ratios.

## Inventory turnover

This measure gives an indication of how quickly a business is selling its inventory.

$$\text{Inventory turnover} = \frac{\text{Cost of sales}}{\text{Inventory}}$$

The cost of sales figure shows the total cost value of the goods sold in the year. The inventory figure shows the total cost value of the goods still held at the year end. This ratio therefore shows how many times during a year we can expect to sell our normal holding of inventory. For example, if this ratio was 6, then it takes us two months to sell our inventory on average; if the ratio was 12 it takes us one month, and so on.

### Considerations

Within any business the ideal is to hold no inventory whatsoever, ie any item arrives from our supplier exactly at the time the customer walks in through the door to buy it, so they can specifically be matched one to another and the company need not hold any inventory at all. However, this is unlikely to be the case in practice.

In practice, companies will need to hold inventory on the shelves for customers to select, but they have got to make sure they do not hold too much inventory. Holding too much inventory will tie up much of the company's resources in goods for resale, and may lead to high insurance costs and high inventory obsolescence. Similarly, too little inventory will mean that customers cannot be served and may choose to go elsewhere. There needs to be a good balance somewhere in between.

**EXAMPLE**

Using information from our illustration financial statements at the end of this chapter

$$\text{Inventory turnover} = \frac{£83{,}604}{£19{,}420}$$

$$\text{Inventory turnover} = 4.31\times$$

### Potential problems

This ratio, in common with others, is comparing a full year's transactions (cost of sales) to a year-end balance that may not be representative of the levels of inventory throughout the year. This would especially be the case in a business with seasonal demand and hence seasonal inventory levels.

### Analysis points

Inventory turnover indicates the amount of inventory we are holding in terms of the time it may take to realise it, and any movement in this ratio from one year to the next may indicate whether we are tending to hold too much or too little inventory.

As we have already pointed out, the ideal amount of inventory and the inventory turnover rate are dependent on the business circumstances. For example

- A supermarket would expect a very high inventory turnover for its milk – perhaps as high as 365×.
- A whisky distiller whose inventory takes several years to mature would expect an inventory turnover rate of say 0.1×.

Hence, we should always consider the nature of the business.

However, care needs to be taken in stating what the ratio is showing. For example, an increased inventory turnover may naively be considered fairly good, and viewed as confirming increased levels of revenue. However, it may be a result of holding very low levels of inventory, which, as we have just noted, may be commercially bad.

## Receivables' collection period

This measure gives an indication of how quickly a business is realising its trade receivables, ie turning them into cash.

$$\text{Receivables' collection period} = \frac{\text{Trade receivables}}{\text{Revenue}} \times 365 \text{ days}$$

### Considerations

Assuming all sales are made on credit, the revenue figure will represent the total invoiced sales in the year, the trade receivables' figure will represent the unpaid invoices at the year end. Hence, receivables over revenue shows the proportion of the year's sales that have not been paid for, ie the credit period we are offering.

**EXAMPLE**

Using information from our illustration financial statements at the end of the chapter

$$\text{Receivables' collection period} = \frac{£21,753}{£135,761} \times 365 \text{ days}$$

Receivables' collection period = 58.5 days

### Potential problems and analysis points

Again, the problem with this ratio is that we are comparing the year-end balance (receivables) to a year's transactions (revenue), which could lead to some distortions if, for some reason, these figures are not representative.

For example, if sales are very seasonal, they may peak at one time in the year and reach a low point at another time in the year. We would expect our receivables to be correspondingly high at one point in the year and low at another point in the year. The revenue figure would be the sum total of all the sales in the year, regardless of the seasonal nature. Clearly, however, we would show substantially different receivables' collection periods if our year end was when we had a high receivables' figure or when we had a low receivables' figure.

## Payables' payment period

This measure shows how quickly a business is settling its liabilities.

$$\text{Payables' payment period} = \frac{\text{Trade payables}}{\text{Cost of sales}} \times 365 \text{ days}$$

### Considerations

This ratio, in a very similar way to the receivables' collection period, measures the amount of credit we are taking from our suppliers. To be a worthwhile and valid comparison, we really need to try to compare invoiced payables to invoiced costs. Remember, however, that in a manufacturing business the cost of sales may include such things as wages and salaries of the production staff, which will distort the ratio unless care is taken.

**EXAMPLE**

Using information from our illustration financial statements at the end of this chapter

$$\text{Payables' payment period} = \frac{£18,702}{£83,604} \times 365 \text{ days}$$

Payables' payment period = 81.6 days

### Potential problems and analysis points

The problems with the use of this ratio are identical to those identified for the receivables' collection period above.

## Working capital cycle

The previous three ratios are really looking at the speed of cash flow around the working capital cycle.

- The **inventory turnover ratio** shows how quickly inventory is being turned into a sale (receivables).
- The **receivables' collection period** shows how quickly those receivables are being turned into cash (in days).
- The **payables' payment period** shows the time scale over which we have to pay off our suppliers.

An organisation should always look to **maintain a balance** in these areas. In particular, between the collection period for receivables and the payment period for payables, assuming they are of a similar scale.

If we are forced by our customers to increase the credit period we offer, we must endeavour to increase the credit period we can get from our suppliers in turn. Otherwise, we will find ourselves with a cash flow problem, since we will have to settle our liabilities without having the cash available to do so.

This is quite a frequent problem for businesses that fall into the liquidity trap. Such businesses, in an effort to boost sales, may extend credit terms to their customers. This has the effect of increasing the sales as anticipated. However, it causes the mismatch of the cash flows in from receivables and out to payables, and subsequent liquidity problems may arise.

## Analysing the statement of cash flows

No analysis of liquidity would be complete without a review of the company's cash flow statement. One of the objectives of statement of cash flows is to ensure that it is relatively easy to read. IAS 7 achieves this objective by requiring companies to adopt a standardised format which contains a wealth of useful information.

## Cash flow from operations

When analysing cash flow from operations, it is important to understand how the cash flows have been generated and why they differ from the previous year. This can be done by looking at the reconciliation of operating profits to cash flow from operations. Reasons for changes in cash flow include the following.

- Changes in operating profits.
- Changes in working capital levels.

## Changes in operating profits

The underlying profits of the business may have changed. The reasons for this will be apparent from the analysis of the income statement. For example, margins or volumes may have changed. Changes in volumes can be linked into other areas of the statement of cash flows, such as purchases of non-current assets and changes in levels of working capital in the business.

## Changes in working capital levels

Even if profits have risen, cash flow may not benefit if there has been a significant increase in receivables over the year, or the company has built up its inventory to meet anticipated future demand.

It is often the case that, as businesses expand, they suffer a severe strain on their cash resources since they have to pay cash out up front, buying non-current assets and inventory, but only receive cash later after they make the sales and receive payments from their customers. This may only be a short-term problem as the cash flows from receivables are received. However, if a business does not have sufficient finance from shareholders and banks to cover the initial cash outflows, it may become insolvent. This is known as 'overtrading' and is a common cause of insolvency for start-up and small expanding companies.

Conversely, a business may suffer poor profits but still generate operating cash in the short term by squeezing working capital levels. For example, a company could take longer to pay its suppliers, reduce inventory levels and pressurise its customers to pay more quickly. In the short term, this will give improved cash flow. However, it will only give a one-off benefit to the company, since working capital cannot be squeezed indefinitely, and may result in higher cash outflows in future years, if working capital is restored to its previous levels. As a result, high cash flow due solely to falling working capital levels should not always be viewed as being good news for a company.

## Non-cash items in profit

Apart from working capital, there are various non-cash items in profit, such as depreciation and provisions. If a company has high depreciation charges, then its operating cash flow will be higher than its profits in the statement of cash flows. Note, however, that such a company must have high non-current assets and therefore some of this operating cash flow will need to be used to pay for replacement of non-current assets, covered in the investing activities section of the statement of cash flows.

## Interest paid

The level of interest paid should be compared to the previous year and reasons for differences identified. This may be due to changes in interest rates or levels of borrowings over the year. If borrowings have increased, then the use of the borrowed funds should be identified. If borrowings have fallen, then the source of cash to repay the borrowings should be identified.

The amount of interest paid should be compared to the interest charge in the income statement and explanations found for any significant differences. These may be due to the accruals concept. For example, where interest is paid annually on a bond, if it is issued one month into the year, then the income statement will show 11 months of interest charge accrued while no interest has yet been paid. Alternatively, the company may be capitalising interest as a non-current asset, rather than charging it as an expense in the income statement (this will be apparent from the interest note to the income statement). Another possibility is that the company has issued a zero-coupon bond, where interest is being charged to the income statement over the bond's life, but no interest is paid until redemption.

A comparison of interest paid and interest charged to the absolute level of borrowings in the statement of financial position is also useful. For example, if the interest paid/charged seems very low compared to the closing borrowings level, it may be that the borrowings were made very late in the year. This will be reinforced by looking at the opening borrowings, if they are significantly lower than the closing borrowings.

The company's level of gearing can be assessed by looking at the level of interest paid relative to the level of operating cash flow available to cover the interest.

The level of interest cover in cash terms can be assessed by calculating the following ratio, the result of which shows the number of times the interest payments could have been made out of operating cash flows. The higher this figure is, the less of a concern there would be about the ability of the company to service its debt.

$$\text{Interest cover in cash flow} = \frac{\text{Operating cash flow}}{\text{Interest paid}}$$

## Preference dividends paid

Preference dividends paid are non-discretionary. The cash outflow should therefore be fairly constant year on year. An increase may indicate additional preference shares issued in the year, whereas a decrease could be from a redemption of existing shares or, more worryingly, be indicative of an inability to declare a dividend as a result of poor cash flow or insufficient profits.

## Investment income

A company with high levels of investment income will presumably have high levels of surplus cash on its statement of financial position. While this means that the company is in a very strong financial position, whether or not it is effectively using the cash being generated should be considered. It may be that the business needs cash balances for the future or it may be that the company has insufficient investment opportunities that yield acceptable returns. In this case, there will be a case for returning surplus cash to shareholders to reinvest elsewhere.

## Taxation

The level of tax paid should be considered in relation to the tax charge and the profits of the company. In doing this, the analyst will need to consider the source of the tax payments.

- Corporation tax in the UK, which will be based on the quarterly instalments per the tax regime.
- Overseas tax, which will depend on the overseas regimes in which the company is operating.

## Capital expenditure and financial investment

The level of capital expenditure should be evaluated, to establish if the company is replacing its non-current assets and maintaining its level of underlying capital employed. A simple test here is to compare the depreciation charge with the level of capital expenditure. The idea is that the depreciation charge indicates the level of capital expenditure required to replace non-current assets and maintain the asset base, called maintenance capital expenditure.

For example, a company has non-current assets with a two-year life, which cost £1,000 each. The company has two assets and it replaces these in alternate years, ie it buys one new asset a year. The cost of buying the asset each year will be £1,000. This is the same as the annual depreciation charge for two assets of £1,000.

This simple idea has several limitations.

- Inflation is ignored.
- It is assumed that the depreciation charge and the capital expenditure relate to the same assets, whereas the company may be contracting one area of its business and expanding in another, or replacing existing expensive non-current assets with newer assets that are more efficient to operate (meaning we need less) but cheaper to buy.

The level of capital expenditure can also indicate whether a company has expanded its operations significantly over the year or is in a process of contraction. In either case, the reasons for this, the business areas in which it is occurring and the implications for the company need to be considered.

Cash flows from financial investment will indicate the extent to which the company is lending funds to other entities and whether those loans are being repaid. Large loans to other entities may be indicative of a long-term cash surplus, which could be better utilised by acquisitions or return of funds to shareholders.

## Acquisitions and disposals

Purchase and sale of businesses will highlight several important issues.

- Acquisitions may indicate that the company is attempting to utilise a cash surplus in order to provide greater returns to shareholders. Alternatively, the company may be attempting to gear up its position where its current debt levels are considered too low.
- Disposals may be indicative of a strategy to release funds from non-core businesses in order to invest in growth within the main business areas. Alternatively, the company may be in urgent need of cash to bolster funds available for operations.
- The cash flows in this area need to be reviewed in conjunction with the financing section (to determine how acquisitions have been funded or disposals from sale used to reduce borrowing) and the purchase of non-current if funds from disposals have been used for financing organic growth.

## Equity dividends paid

Dividends paid will link in closely to the profit performance of the company. If a company has increasing profits, it is likely that dividends per share will be increased. Notwithstanding this, it is often the case that companies may suffer falls in profits but maintain the dividend to avoid incurring the wrath of their shareholders, at least for the short term. The statement of cash flows can be used to assess whether the business has the underlying ability to generate cash to justify paying a dividend.

## Financing activities

Having generated its operating cash flows and paid interest, dividends, tax and capital expenditure, a company will either have surplus cash or a deficit. Surplus cash will need to be utilised in some respect and a deficit will need to be financed. The financing activities section and the change in cash and cash equivalents will tell us how this has happened.

Surpluses may have been used to repay debt or complete a share repurchase operation, in which case, this will be apparent from the financing activities. Alternatively, they may have been used to increase cash balances or decrease overdrafts and short-term borrowings, which will be evident from the change in cash and cash equivalents. This can be determined from the statement of financial position.

Deficits may have been funded by an increase in borrowings, a share issue or a change in cash and cash equivalents. Each of these can be identified from the statement, as with the use of surpluses.

Even if the company has no significant surplus or deficit from its operations for the year, the financing and change in cash and cash equivalents may indicate a change in the source of finance, for example, short-term borrowings may have been repaid through a share issue or a long-term borrowing.

# 5 Capital Structure

## Introduction

Capital structure ratios consider the composition of the financing side of the capital employed equation and address the relationships between:

- Interest-bearing borrowed capital, on which the return must be paid
- Shareholders' capital, on which the return is optional

Capital structure ratios can also be described as financial risk ratios; solvency ratios and gearing ratios.

## Borrowings and financial risk

It is generally accepted that high levels of borrowings imply high financial risk for the company. What do we mean by financial risk and why is it a problem? Let us consider this with two examples.

### Example 1

Consider an individual who buys a £32,000 house with a £30,000 mortgage and £2,000 of his own cash, then subsequently sells it in five years' time for

(a) **£64,000 (ie the price has doubled – a 100% increase)**

Here the individual is walking away with a £32,000 profit on effectively a £2,000 investment – a 1,600% return.

(b) **£16,000 (ie the price has halved – a 50% decrease)**

Here, the individual has lost £16,000 on his £2,000 investment – an 800% loss.

The scale of the profits and losses is significantly greater than the change in the house price. If risk is viewed as the variability of returns, we can see that the risk to the investor is much greater than the basic risk in house prices.

### Example 2

A company has interest payable of £30,000 per annum. In three different years, it generates three different levels of operating profits as shown below.

| | **Year 1 (£'000)** | **Year 2 (£'000)** | **Year 3 (£'000)** |
|---|---|---|---|
| Operating profits | 50 | 100 | 150 |
| Interest | (30) | (30) | (30) |
| Profit before tax | 20 | 70 | 120 |

We can see from the above that when operating profits fluctuate 50% up or down from their normal level of £100,000, the profit before tax fluctuates by 71.43% from its normal level, ie profits before tax are **significantly more volatile** than operating profits themselves, and this volatility increases as the interest charge (or gearing) rises.

**NB**: Financial gearing is not necessarily introducing risk in itself. Financial gearing is augmenting or amplifying the risk inherent in the basic operations. If our operating profit did not vary from £100,000, the profit figure before tax would always be £70,000. If there is no risk in operating profit, there is no risk in the profit before tax introduced by the gearing.

The level of gearing does, however, amplify the effect of changes in operating profit on changes in profit before tax. Work out for yourself what the variability would be if the interest paid each year was £40,000 (answer +/– 83.33%).

## Gearing ratio

The gearing ratio examines the proportion of borrowings (debt) in the company's capital structure versus equity shareholders' funds.

$$\text{Debt to equity} = \frac{\text{Interest bearing loans} + \text{Preference share capital}}{\text{Equity shareholders' funds}} \times 100\%$$

### Considerations

We consider only interest-bearing debt (ie exclude all non-interest bearing liabilities) since this is what is causing the risk to profit before tax, hence ultimately the profits after tax and amounts available for payment as dividends to our shareholders.

Interest-bearing debt includes: loans, overdrafts (usually), bonds, debentures, leases.

Equity (the denominator) comprises share capital and all other reserves.

**EXAMPLE**

Using information from our illustration financial statements at the end of this chapter,

$$\text{Debt to equity} = \frac{16,942 + 137 + 1,356 + 1,016 + 837}{32,138 - 837} \times 100\%$$

$$\text{Debt to equity} = \frac{20,288}{31,301} \times 100\%$$

$$\text{Debt to equity} = 64.8\%$$

### Potential problems

#### Accounting policies

The gearing ratio can be greatly influenced by the **accounting policies**. For example, if non-current assets are revalued upwards then shareholders' funds will rise (since the revaluation surplus has increased) but there will be no change in the debt figure, hence the gearing ratio will fall. If we consider the impact of this on our interest cover (see below), however, a larger value of non-current assets will result in a larger depreciation figure in subsequent years. Hence, a lower operating profit and therefore a lower interest cover in subsequent years. Therefore, if a policy of revaluation is adopted in a year, it will distort both the balance sheet and income statement ratios compared to the previous years.

### Analysis points

'Is there an optimal gearing ratio?' is a question frequently asked. The answer is no, not a general one, but certainly the level of gearing a business can stand can be determined in some way. As our example above shows, if there is no variability in operating profit, then financial gearing is of no consequence whatsoever.

Financial gearing is only a factor to consider if operating profits do vary, in which case **financial gearing amplifies that variation**. Therefore, in more stable businesses, such as utilities, with steady levels of earnings, they can stand a higher level of gearing than in a volatile industry, such as high technology businesses.

As with all ratios, again, the most important thing is not the absolute value but the trend that we are seeing. Are we seeing a trend of increasing financial risk or a trend of reducing financial risk?

## Net debt to equity ratio

This is an alternative to the above which takes account of the cash that a business may also hold which could be used to repay debt.

$$\text{Net debt to equity} = \frac{\text{Debt as above} - \text{Cash and current asset investments}}{\text{Equity shareholders' funds}} \times 100\%$$

### Considerations

We should consider the ability of the company to use the cash it has available to repay debt. For example, it may be that some of the cash we hold is cash received on account from customers that we cannot use for the repayment of debts in general.

**EXAMPLE**

$$\text{Net debt to equity} = \frac{20{,}288 \text{ (as above)} - 6{,}425 - 3{,}926}{31{,}301} \times 100\%$$

$$\text{Net debt to equity} = \frac{9{,}937}{31{,}301} \times 100\%$$

Net debt to equity = 31.7%

## Lenders' debt to equity ratio

This is a relationship that our unsecured lenders would consider as a measure of the risk to their returns.

$$\text{Lenders' debt to equity} = \frac{\begin{array}{c}\text{Total borrowings}\\ \text{(including non-interest bearing debt)}\end{array}}{\begin{array}{c}\text{Total shareholders' funds}\\ \text{(including preference shares)}\end{array}} \times 100\%$$

### Considerations

Here, total debt equals debt as defined above plus non-interest-bearing debt, ie we consider all obligations to pay all liabilities. This is therefore useful to lenders, who are just one of the many creditors of a company, all of whom need to be paid off.

**EXAMPLE**

$$\text{Lenders' debt to equity} = \frac{43,666 + 4,445}{32,138} \times 100\%$$

$$\text{Lenders' debt to equity} = \frac{48,111}{32,138} \times 100\%$$

Lenders' debt to equity = 149.7%

### Potential problems and analysis points

The same problems arise in the context of this ratio as with the debt to equity ratio above.

## Interest cover

This ratio considers gearing from the viewpoint of the income statement.

$$\text{Interest cover} = \frac{\text{Profit from operations + Interest receivable + Other income receivables}}{\text{Interest payable}}$$

### Considerations

The interest cover gives a measure of the ability of the company to pay the fixed interest on borrowings out of its profits for the year. Clearly, the higher the level of interest cover, the less risk there is to either shareholders or lenders. However, again there is no optimal level.

**EXAMPLE**

$$\text{Interestcover} = \frac{\text{£6,849 (see ROCE above)}}{\text{£3,176}}$$

Interest cover = 2.16×

### Potential problems and analysis points

As above for debt to equity ratios.

## Asset cover (or capital cover)

In the same way that lenders are concerned about the interest cover, they may also be concerned over the safety of the loan itself as demonstrated by the assets available to repay it. The asset cover is calculated as

$$\text{Asset cover} = \frac{\text{Total assets} - \text{Current liabilities}}{\text{Loans payable}}$$

### Considerations

If there are a number of loans with different priorities of repayment in a winding up, the asset cover is calculated for each of them in priority order on a cumulative basis.

**EXAMPLE**

In order of priority, our debt can be analysed as

| Debt | Value (£'000) | Cumulative (£'000) |
|---|---|---|
| Finance lease (secured on asset) | 1,153 | 1,153 |
| Unsecured loans and bank overdraft | 18,298 | 19,451 |

Our total assets less current liabilities excluding current instalments due on loans and finance leases is £81,152 – 43,666 + £16,942 + £137 = £54,565.

Hence, asset covers are

Finance lease = 54,565 ÷ 1,153 = 47.3×

Loans = 54,565 ÷ 19,451 = 2.81×

## Task

The following five-year summary relates to Wandafood Products plc, and is based on financial statements.

| | | | 20X5 | 20X4 | 20X3 | 20X2 | 20X1 |
|---|---|---|---|---|---|---|---|
| **Financial ratios** | | | | | | | |
| Profitability | | | | | | | |
| Margin | Operating profit / Revenue | % | 7.8 | 7.5 | 7.0 | 7.2 | 7.3 |
| Return on capital employed | PBIT / Capital employed | % | 16.3 | 17.6 | 16.2 | 18.2 | 18.3 |
| Interest and dividend cover | | | | | | | |
| Interest cover | PBIT / Net finance charges | times | 2.9 | 4.8 | 5.1 | 6.5 | 3.6 |
| Dividend cover | Earnings per ordinary share / Dividend per ordinary share | times | 2.7 | 2.6 | 2.1 | 2.5 | 3.1 |
| **Debt to equity ratios** | | | | | | | |
| | Net borrowings / Shareholders' funds | % | 65.9 | 61.3 | 48.3 | 10.8 | 36.5 |
| | Net borrowings / Shareholders' funds + Minority interests | % | 59.3 | 55.5 | 44.0 | 10.1 | 33.9 |
| **Liquidity ratios** | | | | | | | |
| Quick ratio | Current assets - Inventories / Current liabilities | % | 74.3 | 73.3 | 78.8 | 113.8 | 93.4 |
| Current ratio | Current assets / Current liabilities | % | 133.6 | 130.3 | 142.2 | 178.9 | 174.7 |
| **Asset ratios** | | | | | | | |
| Operating asset turnover | Revenue / Capital employed | times | 2.1 | 2.4 | 2.3 | 2.5 | 2.5 |
| Working capital turnover | Revenue / Working capital | times | 8.6 | 8.0 | 7.0 | 7.4 | 6.2 |
| **Per share** | | | | | | | |
| Earnings per share | | | | | | | |
| Pre-tax basis | p | | 23.62 | 21.25 | 17.96 | 17.72 | 15.06 |
| Net basis | p | | 15.65 | 13.60 | 10.98 | 11.32 | 12.18 |
| Dividend per share | p | | 5.90 | 5.40 | 4.90 | 4.60 | 4.10 |
| Net assets per share | p | | 102.10 | 89.22 | 85.95 | 85.79 | 78.11 |

### Requirements

Prepare a report on the company, clearly interpreting and evaluating the information given.

## SOLUTION

**Wandafood Products – Five-Year Summary: 20X1 to 20X5**

**Prepared by**: An Accountant

**Date**: 28 February 20X6

**Introduction**

This report discusses the trends shown in the five-year summary prepared from the published accounts for the five years ended 31 December 20X5. It also considers how price changes over that period may have limited the usefulness of the historical cost data provided.

**Profitability**

The net profit margin has remained fairly constant, although it dropped in 20X3. Asset turnover has decreased over the five years, pulling back a little in 20X4. Return on capital employed, the primary ratio produced by combining these two secondary ratios, has therefore decreased over the period but was at its lowest in 20X3.

These findings seem to indicate that assets are not being used more efficiently and that this has caused the decrease in return on capital employed. Inflation may be responsible for increases in revenue, which would mask even worse decreases in efficiency.

**Interest and Dividend Cover**

Interest cover improved markedly between 20X1 and 20X2, falling back a little in 20X3 and 20X4, but now below the 20X1 level, indicating increases in debt and/or interest rates. Dividend cover, however, after dropping below 20X1 levels for three years, has now recovered some lost ground. In both cases, cover was adequate, even at the lowest points; however, since there has been a substantial increase in gearing, interest cover ought to be watched carefully. Profits may be available to cover interest and dividends, but this must be matched by good cash flow.

**Debt to Equity**

Debt:equity fell in 20X2 but has steadily increased until, in 20X5, it was almost double its 20X1 level. Minority interests appear to have remained a relatively insignificant element in the group's funding. It is more likely that debt has increased than that equity has decreased (for example, because of a purchase or redemption of own shares). Interest cover has fallen in line with this increase in borrowing as a proportion of long-term capital.

**Liquidity**

Both the current and the quick ratios have declined over the period, although in 20X2, they both improved. However, they have been fairly constant between 20X3 and 20X5 and are quite high, although comments on the adequacy of these ratios are of very limited utility in the absence of information about the company's activities and industry averages.

The reduction may have been planned to reduce the costs involved in maintaining high levels of inventory and allowing generous credit to customers. From the differential between the quick and current ratios, it would seem that inventory is a significant asset here. However, current liabilities must not be allowed to increase to the extent that current assets (and especially liquid assets) are insufficient to cover them, as this can lead to a liquidity crisis. Worsening liquidity ratios can be an indicator of overtrading, but this most often arises when expansion is funded from short-term borrowings whereas, here, new long-term capital in the form of debt appears to have been found.

Because working capital has fallen in size, it is now being used more efficiently, generating more sales from a reduced base. It would seem likely, given the slight fall in asset turnover, that non-current asset turnover has worsened considerably and that the improvement in working capital turnover has compensated for this in calculating total asset turnover. It may be that long-term borrowings have financed capital expenditure which has not yet affected operations (an increase in the amount of non-current assets would decrease non-current asset turnover if turnover did not increase correspondingly).

**Investors' ratios**

Earnings, dividends and net assets per share have all increased over the period. There has therefore been no need to increase dividends regardless of fluctuations in earnings.

The increase in net assets per share seems to indicate either that retained profits and borrowings have been used to increase capital expenditure or (less likely) that assets have been revalued each year.

**Conclusion**

The group would appear, from this superficial analysis, to be a steady performer but not expanding fast. This may be an advantage in times of recession: debt is probably not so high as to cause liquidity problems nor have shareholders come to expect a high payout ratio. The possible recent expansion of non-current assets may help it to grow in future, as will its improved working capital management.

# 6 Earnings per Share

## Investors' ratios

Investors want a good return, either as income now or capital growth, or some combination of both, plus security of their investment. Investors' ratios are designed to consider these factors. One of the key investor ratios is earnings per share.

## Earnings per share

The calculation of earnings per share is specified in IAS 33 – *Earnings per Share.*

Earnings per share (EPS) is the one ratio for which there are some rules regarding its calculation. These are laid out in IAS 33, which basically defines the EPS as

$$\text{EPS} = \frac{\text{Net profit / loss attributable to ordinary shareholders}}{\text{Weighted average number of ordinary shares outstanding during the period}}$$

### Considerations

What the Standard does is define each of these terms and what adjustments should be made to them under certain circumstances, such as the issue of shares during the year. It also details disclosure requirements.

## Earnings

Earnings represent the profit available to pay out to the ordinary shareholders, ie after all deductions excluding ordinary dividends.

**EXAMPLE**

$$EPS = \frac{£2,301 - £84}{17,925 \text{ shares}}$$

$$EPS = \frac{£2,217}{17,925}$$

$$EPS = 12.37p$$

## Number of shares

### Introduction

The number of shares is the number of equity shares in issue. So long as there have been no changes in the number of shares during the year, no problems will arise. However, if there have been any issues of shares, some adjustment will be required.

The purpose of the adjustments will be:

- To ensure the ratio for the current year is valid by comparing the full year's earnings to the representative number of shares in issue during the year, not simply the number of shares in issue at the year end, which may be distorted by an issue near to year end
- To ensure that previous years' earnings per share figures have been calculated on a similar basis, and thus ensure that they are comparable to this year's earnings per share figure, ie we may need to restate previous years' EPS figures

Each possible circumstance is outlined below.

## Earnings per share: full price issue

When shares are issued at full value part way through the year, then the new finance raised at that point is available to generate new profits from that point in the year. Hence, the level of earnings and number of shares will rise from the date the shares are issued.

To ensure we make a like-for-like comparison in the earnings per share calculation, we will need to compare the earnings for the year to a representative number of shares throughout the year, rather than simply the year-end number. This representative number is the **weighted average number of shares** in issue during the year.

For a full price issue **no adjustment to prior years' figures** is required since the shares were not in issue and will have had no impact on previous years.

**EXAMPLE**

***Earnings***

Profit attributable to the group = £2,217 as used above.

***Number of shares***

If the company issued three million shares on 31 August (year end 31 December), then the weighted average number of shares is

| Dates | Total Number | Time Apportion | Weighted Average |
|---|---|---|---|
| 1 Jan–31 Aug | 14,925 | $\times \frac{8}{12}$ | 9,950 |
| 31 Aug issue | 3,000 | | |
| 1 Sept–31 Dec | 17,925 | $\times \frac{4}{12}$ | 5,975 |
| | | | 15,925 |

***EPS***

$$\text{EPS} = \frac{£2,217}{15,925}$$

EPS = 13.92p

The comparative EPS would remain unaltered.

## Issue to acquire a subsidiary

When we issue shares as part of the purchase consideration to acquire a subsidiary, the treatment is exactly the same as a full price issue.

From the date we acquire the subsidiary, we will start to consolidate into the group accounts the profit of the subsidiary, ie from the date of acquisition group earnings will rise by the earnings generated by the subsidiary. We therefore want to take the number of shares as having risen from that date also; ie we need to take the **weighted average number of shares**.

## Earnings per share: bonus issues and share splits

When we make a bonus issue, we are not actually altering the operating assets of the business at all; all we are doing is restructuring shareholders' funds.

A bonus issue does not raise any new cash and therefore will not generate any new earnings. The bonus issue has the effect of increasing share capital and reducing reserves, ie restructuring shareholders' funds, but causes no change in the total shareholders' funds or total net assets. From an operational viewpoint, these bonus shares may as well have been issued at the same time as the underlying shares on which they are now being 'paid'.

This last point really gives an indication of the treatment where there is a bonus issue. Specifically we backdate the bonus and pretend that those **shares had always been in issue**. As a result an adjustment will be required to the number of shares previously in issue by use of the bonus fraction, which is

$$\text{Bonus fraction} = \frac{\text{Number of shares after the issue}}{\text{Number of shares before the issue}}$$

**EXAMPLE**

***Earnings***

Profit attributable to the group = £2,217 as used above.

***Number of shares***

On 1 January, the company had 14,340 shares in issue. It made a 1 for 4 bonus issue on 31 August (year end 31 December), the bonus fraction being

$$\text{Bonus fraction} = \frac{5}{4}$$

since one new share is issued for every four currently in issue. The calculation of the weighted average is as follows.

| Dates | Total Number | Bonus Fraction | Time Apportion | Weighted Average |
|---|---|---|---|---|
| 1 Jan–31 Aug | 14,340 | $\times \frac{5}{4}$ | $\times \frac{8}{12}$ | 11,950 |
| 31 Aug issue | 3,585 | | | |
| 1 Sept–31 Dec | 17,925 | | $\times \frac{4}{12}$ | 5,975 |
| | | | | 17,925 |

You will notice that the number of shares that we arrive at is, in fact, the year-end number and this calculation proves to be unnecessary. It has been included here to illustrate an idea we will come back to when we consider a rights issue.

A quicker method of doing the calculations in the circumstance of a bonus issue is to simply take the year-end number of shares.

***EPS***

$$\text{EPS} = \frac{£2,217}{17,925}$$

$$\text{EPS} = 12.37\text{p}$$

In addition, we would need to **update last year's original EPS** of 12.43p in the Example to make it appear to have been based on 17,925 shares rather than the 14,340 actually in issue (ie we need to scale the EPS down – spread the same earnings over more shares).

We can do this by multiplying last year's EPS by the inverse of the bonus fraction $\left(\text{ie } \frac{1}{\text{Bonus fraction}}\right)$, sometimes referred to as the adjustment factor, giving a comparative EPS of

$$\text{EPS (comparative)} = 12.43 \times \frac{4}{5} = 9.94\text{p}$$

## Earnings per share: rights issue

Rights issues are typically made at a discount to the full market price. The purpose of a rights issue is to raise some new finance in order to undertake a project, hence, from the date of the issue we can imagine that earnings will rise. This is similar to the full price issue situation.

However, the increase in earnings will be less than it would have been had we made a full price issue since less cash is raised per share. We can consider a rights issue at a discount, as getting somebody to pay the full price for a proportion of the shares and then giving away the rest, ie we can consider the rights issue as being the equivalent of:

- Part of the issue being at the full price
- Part of the issue being a bonus

As such, we would need to apply both the above ideas to the issue, specifically:

- We need to calculate the weighted average number of shares this year for the full price issue element
- We need to backdate the bonus element and revise the prior year figures

We therefore need a method to split the full issue into those two components. Fortunately, we can calculate the bonus element by use of a simple formula.

$$\text{Bonus fraction} = \frac{\text{Actual price before the issue (cum – rights price)}}{\text{Theoretical price after issue (ex – rights price)}}$$

We will firstly show how to calculate these figures, then why this formula actually works.

## EXAMPLE

***Earnings***

Profit attributable to the group = £2,217 as used above.

***Number of shares***

On 1 January, the company had 14,340 shares in issue. It made a 1 for 4 rights issue at a price of £1.20 on 31 August (the full share price on that date is £2.20). The bonus fraction for this can be calculated as follows.

| | Number of Shares | Price (£) | Value (£) |
|---|---|---|---|
| Before | 4 | 2.20 | 8.80 |
| Issue | 1 | 1.20 | 1.20 |
| After | 5 | | 10.00 |

Hence, the theoretical ex-rights price (price after the issue) is £2.00 (£10.00 ÷ 5 shares), giving a bonus fraction of

$$\text{Bonus fraction} = \frac{2.20}{2.00} = 1.1$$

From this, we can calculate the appropriate number of shares (backdating the bonus element) as

| Dates | Total Number | Bonus Fraction | Time Apportion | Weighted Average |
|---|---|---|---|---|
| 1 Jan–31 Aug | 14,340 | $\times \frac{2.20}{2.00}$ | $\times \frac{8}{12}$ | 10,516 |
| 31 Aug issue | 3,585 | | | |
| 1 Sept–31 Dec | 17,925 | | $\times \frac{4}{12}$ | 5,975 |
| | | | | 16,491 |

***EPS***

$$\text{EPS} = \frac{£2{,}217}{16{,}491}$$

EPS = 13.44p

Again here, we would need to update last year's EPS to make it appear to have been based on a larger number of shares due to the bonus element of the issue. We do this by multiplying last year's EPS by the inverse of the bonus fraction $\left(\text{ie } \dfrac{1}{\text{Bonus fraction}}\right)$; again this is sometimes referred to as the adjustment factor, giving a comparative EPS of

$$\text{EPS (comparative)} = 12.43 \times \frac{2.00}{2.20} = 11.30\text{p}$$

***Proof of bonus fraction***

By taking the bonus fraction as 1.1, we are stating that the rights issue is the equivalent of a 1 for 10 bonus issue plus a full price issue for the remainder of the shares.

Considering an individual who held 40 shares before the rights issue, this would mean taking a bonus of four shares and paying the full price for six (taking his year end holding up to 50 shares as would be the case following the 1 for 4 rights issue). We will show that the share price under this alternative is the same as we calculated above and hence the two are equivalent.

| | Number of Shares | Price (£) | Value (£) |
|---|---|---|---|
| Held | 40 | 2.20 | 88.00 |
| Bonus | 4 | – | – |
| | 44 | | 88.00* |
| Full price | 6 | 2.00* | 12.00 |
| New holding | 50 | | 100.00 |

* Following the bonus element of the issue, our share price falls to £2.00 (£88 ÷ 44 shares), which must be the price for the full price element of the issue.

We can see from this that our shareholder is in exactly the same position following either the rights issue or the bonus issue plus the issue at full price. Specifically, he holds 50 shares worth £2.00 each. The two are therefore equivalent and our bonus fraction applies.

## Earnings per share: post-balance sheet events

The basic EPS is required to be altered to incorporate the effect of certain share issues on the number of ordinary shares where the issue occurs between the balance sheet date and the date on which the accounts are approved.

Where the company undertakes a bonus issue, share split or consolidation, or where there is a bonus element to another issue (eg rights issue) the number of shares must include the extra shares now in issue after the event.

In the case of an issue that impacts on earnings, such as a rights issue, only those shares that have no earnings impact should be included in the EPS calculation. For a rights issue, this would be just the 'bonus' element.

## Alternative measures of earnings

### Maintainable earnings

Earnings per share is widely used as a performance measure from the point of view of equity shareholders. It is also the denominator in the Price/Earnings ratio (see below).
An Accounting Standard (IAS 33) regulates how earnings per share must be calculated and disclosed in financial statements. It aims to ensure that calculations and disclosures are consistent across companies.

Basic EPS takes account of *all* transactions that have affected the profit or loss for the period. Financial analysts and other users of the financial statements may not find the IAS 33 published figures ideal for their purposes. For example, the current period's results may reflect some unusual one-off transactions. If EPS is being measured to monitor the trend in shareholders' profits, the trend will be distorted by including the non-recurring item in one period. Similarly inter-company comparisons may be distorted. If EPS is to be used for calculating and comparing Price/Earnings multiples it makes sense to adjust for one-offs. The point is that users would like to know the extent to which profits are derived from a business's core operating activities and are maintainable or likely to recur. In principle, this is about establishing those earnings that are of the highest quality and therefore most valuable to investors. Published EPS per IAS 33 cannot do this job, nor does it claim to.

IAS 33 recognises that companies may want to disclose additional measures of EPS and allows them to do so providing that these are

- Presented in the notes to the accounts, not on the face of the income statement.
- Reconciled to the basic and diluted figures per IAS 33.

This leaves preparers with scope to come up with different (and usually higher) EPS non-GAAP measures, frequently described as 'underlying EPS' or something similar. However, by definition these need not be calculated consistently between companies. This leaves individual users to develop their own measures of EPS; arguably that is what analysts are paid to do. The point is that no single measure of EPS can be the correct figure for all purposes and for all users.

## Diluted earnings per share

The purpose of publishing the diluted earnings per share figure is to warn shareholders of potential future changes in the earnings per share figure as a result of events that have already happened. There are two possible factors that could cause a diluted earnings per share to arise.

- Convertible loan stock or convertible preference shares in issue.
- Options or warrants in issue.

Each of these circumstances may potentially result in more shares being issued and ranking for a dividend in future years, hence leading to a dilution of the current earnings per share.

The diluted EPS figure, although a theoretical calculation based on assumptions about the future, is considered of such importance to the reader of the accounts that its **calculation and disclosure is required** by IAS 33 – *Earnings Per Share*.

### Calculation

To calculate diluted earnings per share, we take the basic earnings and the basic number of shares and make suitable adjustments to account for the changes that will occur if and when the new shares are issued.

## Diluted earnings per share: convertible preference shares and convertible loan stock

When there are convertibles in issue (either loan stock or preference shares) the holder of this stock has, at their option, the opportunity to convert into ordinary shares, hence the number of ordinary shares will be increased if the conversion option is taken up.

Often the number of shares into which convertibles may convert will change with time. Generally speaking, the number of shares that a bond holder can convert into will fall the longer the bond is held, as it is anticipated that the share price will rise over that time.

To warn current shareholders of the maximum possible diluting effect of any conversion of any loan stock or convertible preference shares in existence at the year end, the number of ordinary shares to be issued will be calculated based on the maximum possible number they could convert into in the future.

Conversion will also affect the earnings figure. With any convertible loan stock we will currently be paying interest, with any convertible preference shares we will currently be paying a preference dividend. If we bear in mind that the earnings figure is profit after tax, after minority interest, and after preference dividends, then we can see that the adjustments required will be as follows.

## Earnings

For loan stock, add to earnings the after corporation tax interest charge that will no longer be suffered once conversion takes place. Currently, the profit before tax is reduced by the interest payment and the tax charge is also reduced as the interest charge attracts tax relief. This net reduction in profit will no longer occur, hence we need to add the net figure back.

For preference shares, when the preference shares convert we will no longer pay the preference dividend, hence we need to add the preference dividend currently payable to the basic earnings.

## Number of shares

Add to the basic number of shares the greatest number of equity shares that may be issued in the future upon conversion of the loan stock or convertible preference shares in issue at the year end.

### EXAMPLE

The debt financing of the company at the year end includes £500,000 10% convertible loan stock, which was issued on 30 June this year. The terms of conversion for every £100 nominal value of loan stock are

| | |
|---|---|
| 31 December this year | 120 |
| 31 December next year | 115 |
| 31 December in two years | 110 |

Assume corporation tax at the rate of 30%.

***Earnings***

| | (£'000) | (£'000) |
|---|---|---|
| Basic earnings | | 2,217 |
| Dilution | | |
| Interest saved $\left(£500{,}000 \times 10\% \times \frac{6}{12}\right)$ | 25 | |
| Tax (£25,000 × 30%) | (8) | |
| | | 17 |
| Diluted earnings | | 2,234 |

***Number of shares***

Since the £500,000 of convertible loan stock is in issue at this year end, we know that these stockholders have not taken the option of converting to 120 shares. The best option that remains for them is to convert to 115 shares, resulting in a further 575,000 shares being issued, hence

| | Number |
|---|---|
| Basic number | 17,925 |
| Dilution $\left(575 \times \frac{6}{12}\right)$ | 288 |
| Diluted number | 18,213 |

***EPS***

$$\text{Basic EPS} = \frac{£2{,}217}{17{,}925} = 12.37\text{p}$$

$$\text{Diluted EPS} = \frac{£2{,}234}{18{,}213} = 12.27\text{p}$$

The dilution is only assumed to occur for half a year, since the convertibles were only issued six months into the year. In subsequent years, the dilution calculation would assume dilution for the whole year.

## Diluted earnings per share: options and warrants

When a company has options or warrants in issue, it specifies a number of shares that a person can take up and the price at which they can exercise the option. The calculation of diluted earnings per share will assume exercise of the warrants or options. The assumed proceeds on exercise should be treated as having been received from the issue of shares at fair value. The difference between the number of shares issued and the number of shares that would have been issued at fair value is treated as an issue of shares for no consideration.

Fair value of the shares should be based on the **average price of the shares** over the year.

Since any shares issued at fair value would also cause an increase in earnings, they are excluded from the diluted calculation on the basis that any increase in earnings would counterbalance the increase in shares, causing no change to earnings per share.

The shares issued for free will be added to the weighted average of shares from the basic calculation.

## Earnings

There will be no change to earnings in the diluted calculation.

## Number of shares

Add to the basic number of shares the number of shares that would be issued on exercise of the warrants or options less the number of shares that would be issued at fair value, given the proceeds on exercise.

**EXAMPLE**

Assume that the company has options in issue to subscribe for one million new shares at £1.20 per share. The average share price over the year has been £2.00.

***Earnings***

Earnings are left unchanged at £2,217,000.

***Number of shares***

On the assumed exercise of the options, the company would receive £1.2m. Using the average share price over the year, this would imply the issue of 600,000 shares at fair value. This indicates that, when the shares are being issued, 600,000 are being issued at a fair price and 400,000 are being issued for free.

| | **Number** |
|---|---|
| Basic number | 17,925 |
| New shares issued | 1,000 |
| Shares that would have been issued at fair value | (600) |
| Diluted number | 18,325 |

***EPS***

$$\text{Basic EPS} = \frac{£2,217}{17,925} = 12.37\text{p}$$

$$\text{Diluted EPS} = \frac{£2,217}{18,325} = 12.10\text{p}$$

## Disclosure

IAS 33 requires the disclosure of basic and diluted earnings per share on the face of the income statement, both for net profit or loss for the period and profit or loss for continuing operations.

Any additional information, such as alternative methods of calculating the EPS, can only be disclosed by way of a note to the accounts.

A note needs to be included in the accounts detailing the basis upon which the calculations are done, specifically the earnings figure used and the number of shares figure used within the calculation, both for this year and the comparative year.

### TASK

What will be the impact on **return on capital employed** and **earnings per share** of the following changes in a set of accounts?

(a) Revaluation of property plant and equipment.
(b) Increasing the useful life of a non-current asset.
(c) Capitalisation of development costs.
(d) Treating a lease as a finance lease rather than an operating lease.

**SOLUTION**

| | Impact on earnings per share | Impact on profit before interest | Impact on capital employed | Impact on return on capital employed |
|---|---|---|---|---|
| **Revaluation of PPE** | Higher depreciation therefore lower earnings<br>EPS falls | Higher depreciation therefore lower profit before tax | Higher asset values increases capital employed | Lower ROCE |
| **Increasing asset's useful life** | Lower depreciation gives higher earnings<br>EPS rises | Higher profit before interest | Higher capital employed since lower depreciation gives higher net book value | Uncertain |
| **Capitalisation of development costs** | Higher earnings due to lower expenses<br>EPS rises | Higher profit before interest | Higher capital employed due to higher assets | Uncertain |
| **Finance lease** | Uncertain effect<br>Earnings increase due to the elimination of rental expenses but decrease due to the inclusion of depreciation and interest | Higher profit before interest probably, since finance lease expense will partly be finance charges | Higher capital employed due to the inclusion of a non-current asset financed by long-term obligations probably | Uncertain |

# 7 Other Investment Ratios

## Return on equity

The return on equity ratio is calculated as follows.

$$\text{Return on equity} = \frac{\text{Earnings attributable to ordinary shareholders}}{\text{Equity shareholders' funds}} \times 100\%$$

### Considerations

The return on equity ratio measures the percentage return that the company is generating on the book (or balance sheet) value of equity shareholders' funds invested in the business.

It is, therefore, a measure assessing profitability from the viewpoint of the owners of the business (the shareholders) and thus the return measure used in the ratio is the same as the earnings figure used in calculating EPS. The equity shareholders' funds figure used will consist of ordinary share capital plus the reserves of the business.

**EXAMPLE**

If we take the earnings figure used in the EPS calculation together with the shareholders' funds figure excluding preference share capital and minority interest, the calculation will be as follows.

$$\text{Return on equity} = \frac{2,217}{31,301} \times 100 = 7.1\%$$

### Potential problems

This ratio suffers, in the same way as EPS, from one-off gains and losses introducing volatility into the earnings figure. For trend analysis, therefore, it may be better to strip out the post-tax impact of gains and losses recognised in the income statement that are considered to be non-recurring.

The measurement of earnings and shareholders' funds is distorted by accounting policy choices (such as revaluations and recognition of development costs as an intangible asset) and therefore reduces comparability between different companies.

### Analysis Points

Shareholders are looking for a rising trend of returns on equity in order to provide them with increasing levels of dividend income and/or growth in the share price.

Returns across different companies in the same sector can be compared but it should be noted that this ratio does *not* produce a yield or return on investment measure. To obtain such a number, it would be necessary to use the market value of equity as opposed to the book value (as used to calculate earnings yield).

## Price/Earnings ratio (P/E)

The Price/Earnings ratio is calculated as follows.

$$\text{Price / Earnings} = \frac{\text{Current market price per share}}{\text{Earnings per share}}$$

### Considerations

The P/E ratio gives a market 'rating' for the company – how much is the stock market prepared to pay for the earnings stream? A high P/E ratio indicates that the company's earnings are more 'expensive'.

**EXAMPLE**

If we take our current share price as £2.20 and our EPS figure as 12.37p, then the P/E ratio is

$$\text{Price/Earnings} = \frac{220}{12.37}$$

$$\text{Price/Earnings} = 17.78\times$$

### Potential problems

The P/E ratio is **difficult to use in isolation** as a result of accounting choices distorting the profit measurement basis for different companies, even those operating in the same sectors. In addition, the globalisation of many industries now requires comparisons on a cross-border basis between companies reporting under different GAAP regimes. The resultant variability in reported profits can be huge and the resultant P/E comparisons would be virtually meaningless.

In order to overcome these problems, various other measures of earnings are used by both analysts and increasingly companies, to measure and analyse profit performance. These are discussed in more detail below.

### Analysis points

The significance of a P/E ratio can only be judged in relation to the ratios of other companies in the same type of business. If the median P/E ratio for an industry sector was 8, then a ratio of 12 for a particular company would suggest that the shares of that company were in great demand possibly because a rapid growth of earnings was expected. A low ratio, say 4 for example, would indicate a company not greatly favoured by investors, which probably has poor growth prospects.

## Enterprise value multiples

The following earnings multiples measuring corporate performance are used frequently by analysts as an **alternative to the P/E ratio**.

$$\text{Enterprise value to EBIT} = \frac{\text{Enterprise value}}{\text{Earnings before interest and tax}}$$

$$\text{Enterprise value to EBITDA} = \frac{\text{Enterprise value}}{\text{Earnings before interest, tax, depreciation and amortisation}}$$

$$\text{Enterprise value to sales} = \frac{\text{Enterprise value}}{\text{Revenue}}$$

### Considerations

These earnings multiples work in the same way as the P/E ratio, in that they compare an historic earnings or revenue figure to the market value of the business. Thus, the higher the multiple the more growth expectation is factored into market values and the more positively the company is viewed in relation to its peers.

However, the market value used in these ratios is not the market value of equity, which is used for the P/E ratio. Instead, the **enterprise value** (EV) is used, which is the market value of equity plus the market value of net debt (in other words, the value of the business to all providers of finance).

The rationale for using the EV is that this is a figure that is not distorted by the gearing of the business, and therefore can be used to more directly compare companies with different financing strategies. Therefore, while the P/E ratio focuses only on earnings available to equity shareholders, EV multiples look at earnings available to all finance providers, being earnings before all dividends and before interest payments.

It is possible to use different earnings figures in the multiple, depending on which potential distorting factors need to be removed. Tax, for example, is distorted by the tax rules and rates in the countries in which profits are generated. Earnings performance is therefore distorted by the countries in which a company operates, making global comparisons more difficult. Thus, earnings figures used in EV multiples tend to be pre-tax.

It is also possible for companies to apply different rules on depreciation and amortisation of tangible and intangible non-current assets respectively, depending on the GAAP regime under which they report.

Therefore, many analysts and companies are turning to measures of **earnings before interest and tax (EBIT)** or **before interest, tax, depreciation and amortisation (EBITDA)**. These measures are therefore used for the following reasons.

- To eliminate distortions caused by different financing structures, tax regimes, depreciation mechanisms and amortisation periods.
- To facilitate cross-border comparisons.
- To obtain an earnings figure that is closer to a cash measure (after adjustment for two major non-cash expenses, depreciation and amortisation).
- To calculate meaningful multiples for companies in high growth sectors, such as telecommunications and technology, where traditional P/E measures are not able to be calculated due to the businesses currently being loss-making.

There is a further measure, **EV to sales**, that is used mainly for companies in the early stages of growth and thus any form of profit figure tends to be relatively meaningless. By using sales, or revenue, as the historic measure of performance, all distortions to profit are stripped out. In addition, the calculation of sales will be very similar across almost all major reporting regimes.

## EXAMPLE

Assume that there is a charge of £14,500,000 for depreciation and £8,250,000 for amortisation included within the operating costs and that the book value of debt as stated on the balance sheet is equivalent to its market value. The current share price is £2.20, making the market value of equity £39,435,000 (£2.20 × 17.925m shares).

Enterprise value is therefore calculated as follows.

| | **(£'000)** |
|---|---|
| Market value of equity | 39,435 |
| Market value of debt (= book value) | 19,451 |
| Less: Cash and liquid investments | (10,351) |
| Enterprise value | 48,535 |

$$\text{Enterprise value to EBIT} = \frac{48,535}{3,673 + 3,176 - 303} = 7.4\times$$

$$\text{Enterprise value to EBITDA} = \frac{48,535}{3,673 + 3,176 - 303 + 14,500 + 8,250} = 1.7\times$$

$$\text{Enterprise value to sales} = \frac{48,535}{135,761} = 0.4\times$$

### Potential problems

The following problems may arise when using EV multiples.

- It may appear that a company with a high EV multiple is successful and profitable, when in fact at the post-tax level it may be loss-making.

- EBITDA as a measure ignores important real costs associated with running a business. Both depreciation and amortisation represent assets being used up in the business and ignoring them both can lead to misleading results. Tax is also a real cost and a cash outflow for companies.
- EV to sales is a measure that can be influenced by companies entering into barter transactions with the intention of increasing the sales figure, reducing the size of the multiple and thus appearing to be better value (or alternatively prompting an upward rerating of the share price).

### Analysis points

EV multiples should be analysed in the same way as P/E multiples, to compare different companies within the same sector. Therefore, the same comments can be made, and conclusions drawn, as were discussed for the P/E ratio.

## Earnings yield

The earnings yield expresses the most recent earnings per share as a percentage of the current market price as follows.

$$\text{Earnings yield} = \frac{\text{Earnings per share}}{\text{Current market price per share}} \times 100\%$$

**EXAMPLE**

$$\text{Earnings yield} = \frac{12.37}{220} \times 100\%$$

$$\text{Earnings yield} = 5.62\%$$

### Analysis points

The earnings yield is **almost the inverse of the P/E ratio**, hence similar comments apply. If the median earnings yield for an industry sector was 10%, then a yield of only 6% for a particular company would suggest that the shares of that company were in great demand possibly because a rapid growth of earnings was expected. A higher yield, say 18% for example, would indicate a company not greatly favoured by investors which probably has poor growth prospects.

In practice, the earnings yield is used less frequently than the P/E ratio.

## Dividend yield

The dividend yield of an ordinary share is calculated as follows.

$$\text{Dividend yield} = \frac{\text{Dividend per share}}{\text{Current market price per share}} \times 100\%$$

**EXAMPLE**

$$\text{Dividend yield} = \frac{6.25}{220} \times 100\%$$

$$\text{Dividend yield} = 2.84\%$$

### Analysis points

A high dividend yield implies that the company is paying reasonable levels of income but not particularly highly regarded for its growth prospects and *vice versa*. If the figures show a high yield then the share price is relatively low, implying that the main factor attracting shareholders to the company is the reasonably high current level of income. Investors who believe that the company has good growth prospects would buy the share, driving the price up and reducing the yield.

It is therefore also true that companies with high P/E ratios tend to have low dividend yields and *vice versa*.

## Dividend cover

Dividend cover is used as an attempt to assess the likelihood of the existing dividend being maintained. The dividend cover is calculated as follows.

$$\text{Dividend cover} = \frac{\text{Earnings per share}}{\text{Net dividend per share}}$$

**EXAMPLE**

$$\text{Dividend cover} = \frac{12.37}{6.25}$$

$$\text{Dividend cover} = 1.98\times$$

### Analysis points

An unusually high dividend cover implies that the company is retaining the majority of its earnings, presumably with the intention of reinvesting to generate growth.

A company may alternatively pay a larger dividend than the year's earnings, in which case it is drawing on past reserves and is said to be paying an uncovered dividend.

## Net asset value/Net assets per share

The net asset value or net assets per share is calculated as

$$\text{Net asset value} = \frac{\text{Net assets attributable to ordinary shareholders}}{\text{Number of ordinary shares in issue}}$$

### Considerations

The net asset value represents the 'intrinsic' worth of the shares in terms of the net assets that support that value. This could show an unrealistically low figure in terms of current worth if a strict policy of historical cost accounting has been applied. The shareholder may be more interested in the asset values if the company adopts a policy of revaluation.

**EXAMPLE**

$$\text{Net asset value} = \frac{£32{,}138 - £837}{17{,}925}$$

$$\text{Net asset value} = \frac{£31{,}301}{17{,}925}$$

$$\text{Net asset value} = £1.75$$

Note that the net assets figure is after deducting those due to the preference shareholders.

### Analysis points

While the company continues to trade, the net assets per share might be considerably higher or lower than the market value of those shares. This is because investors do not think that all of the assets will be sold and they are basing the value of the company on its ability to generate returns using those assets. The 'asset backing' tends to become more significant in the event of a potential takeover. It is also of regular concern to property companies and investment trusts.

# 8 Analysis Considerations

## Introduction

With the exclusion of the earnings per share figures, none of the ratios we have described above have hard and fast definitions, hence there is no right answer to a question such as 'what is the return on capital employed?' It could depend on how you treat bank overdrafts, and so on as discussed earlier in the chapter.

Despite this, ratios do provide a useful tool. We can calculate the ratios and, with the aid of useful comparatives that are essential for this process, we can look for trends or discontinuities from one year to the next.

Always remember, however, that the **ratio is not the answer in itself**, simply a tool to help us identify important factors. For example, has the return on capital employed gone up because the return has gone up or because the capital employed has gone down? They clearly imply different things about the company.

When carrying out an analysis exercise there are a number of factors we need to consider.

## Who is the information for?

We need to satisfy the requirements of our clients and hence concentrate on those areas that are of concern to them. If, for example, our client is a shareholder, then we would probably concentrate initially on the investors' ratios.

However, we should never adopt a blinkered approach to analysis. When looking at an investors' ratio we may consider, for example, the earnings per share figure. The earnings per share figure clearly depends on the profits and the number of shares. If the earnings per share figure is changed because profits have changed, we may well wish to go and consider further the profitability of the business. Hence our client tells us the starting point for our analysis, but we should be prepared to be taken off in different directions depending on what we find being highlighted by the ratios we initially consider.

## Practical circumstances

In order to appreciate and understand the trends and ratios we are seeing, we need to consider the **practical circumstances of the business**.

## Profitability

How did the business make its profits? Is it a 'stack 'em high, sell 'em fast', high volume, low margin retailer or is it a high margin, low turnover business, such as a jeweller?

What is the nature of the earnings and the dependency of those earnings on economic factors such as exchange rates, general state of the economy, recession, etc. For example, supermarkets largely provide necessities, hence in a recession we would expect their profits to remain fairly level. However, for luxury car manufacturers, we would expect their profits to decline substantially in a recession as demand for their goods drops.

## Liquidity

In considering the liquidity of the business under consideration we should try to imagine its working capital cycle. We should try to picture in our minds what we expect to see or what we can see as the norm by considering the working capital cycle of the peer group. In this way we will be in a decent position to comment on what we are actually finding in the company under consideration.

## Accounting policies

The **accounting policies adopted** by any company can significantly impact on its ratios.

If we revalue non-current assets, then our depreciation charge will be higher. Hence, profits will be lower, but on the balance sheet, more non-current assets means a higher capital employed figure. Hence, our return on capital employed will be reduced (lower profits divided by higher capital employed).

If we are comparing two companies, one that does revalue non-current assets and one that does not, or if we are comparing one company to a previous year when we have revalued non-current assets in between, then we would expect to see a distortion between the ratios as a result of this accounting policy.

## Window dressing

Window dressing techniques incorporate some dubious financing methods, hence they are worthy of consideration here.

Window dressing transactions are **transactions intended to mislead the user** of the accounts. We outline below two basic window dressing transaction types.

## Circular transactions

In a circular transaction, Company A sells goods to Company B who in turn sells them back to Company A. The purpose of undertaking these transactions is simply to boost reported revenue, which in turn would boost such measures as asset turnover, distorting the view of the user as to the effectiveness of the management of the company.

Clearly, such a transaction is totally fictitious. It is likely that the transactions would have to be disclosed as a result of the rules in IAS 24 *Related Party Disclosures*, assuming that the two companies are in some way connected.

## Bed and breakfast transactions

A bed and breakfast transaction is very much like a circular transaction that is undertaken over a year end, ie Company A sells to Company B before the year end, then repurchases after the year end. This will not only boost Company A's revenue for the year but also their reported profits if the goods have been sold at a profit.

Again, the transaction is totally fictitious and only designed to mislead the user of the account. As above, the transactions are likely to be disclosed as being with a related party.

## Possible distorting effects

When calculating any ratios we should always try to look for **possible distorting effects** that impact on our analysis. Factors to consider would be as follows.

## Comparing a full year's transactions to year end balances

One of the biggest possible distortions that is only tackled in the earnings per share calculation as a matter of course, is that we compare a full year's worth of transactions to a year-end balance sheet figure with a number of the ratios. What we really should be doing is comparing a full year's transaction to a representative balance throughout the year. For example, ideally we should compare the full year's profits to a representative amount of capital employed to get return on capital employed.

When analysing a set of financial statements, it is highly unlikely that you will be able to calculate the representative amount of capital employed throughout the year, hence you may only be able to work out the return on capital employed based on start of the year or end of the year capital employed figures.

The problem is not only confined to return on capital employed, it is true for any ratio that compares a full year's transaction to a year-end figure, for example receivables' collection period, payables' payment period or inventory turnover rate. Hence, these ratios can be distorted by such things as

- **Subsidiary acquired near year end** – profits up only from the date of acquisition, capital up at the year end by the full amount.
- **Funds raised near year end** – capital employed higher, return increased by only a small amount based upon what the funds have managed to generate in the short period of time to year end.
- **Seasonal sale** – the receivables' collection period compares the year-end receivables to the year's sales. If sales are seasonal in nature then, depending on when the year end is, the receivables may be very significant or very small compared to the year's revenue.

## Comparing like-with-like

All of our ratios should endeavour to **compare like-with-like**. For example, when considering the payables' payment period, we should try to compare the invoiced payables to the invoiced cost of sales. When calculating profit margins, we should compare the profit to the revenue that has generated that profit.

We should, therefore, always be looking for factors that cause any distortions in these ratios. For example, income from associated undertakings boosts the profits before tax, however, it has no revenue implications and therefore a simple calculation of profit margins based on profits before tax and revenue will incorporate a distorting effect.

The method of equity accounting for associates on the balance sheet will similarly distort any asset turnover calculation, since this particular element of capital employed does not contribute to revenue. When considering any ratio the aim should always be to compare like-with-like.

### Ability to realise assets

When considering any ratios, in particular liquidity, it may be very difficult for us to get any indication as to the **potential ability to realise assets**.

#### Cash

We would normally assume that we can get hold of any cash immediately. However, it is quite possible that a company may have significant amounts of cash held overseas that it cannot remit to the UK for certain reasons particular to the country concerned. Alternatively, a proportion of the cash a company is in possession of may not be freely available for its own use to repay debts. For example, a manufacturer may have received cash in advance that can only be used to fund a specific project and is not available to settle other debts.

#### Inventory

Inventory is shown on the balance sheet under the heading current assets, which leads to the reasonable assumption that it is likely to be converted into cash within 12 months. However, this may not always be the case. In such industries as high technology or fashion, inventory may become unsaleable very rapidly. The financial statements give no indication as to what the inventory is, to enable you to assess any potential problems regarding realisation.

## 9 Other Tools of Interpretation

### Introduction

In addition to ratios, there are a number of other tools of interpretation, specifically:

- Trend statements
- Common size statements
- Multivariate analysis

### Trend statements

Trend statements are more commonly prepared for income statement information, by choosing one year as the base year and expressing similar items of other years as a percentage of that base year.

## EXAMPLE

We are given the following five-year summary information for a company.

| | 2014 (£'000) | 2015 (£'000) | 2016 (£'000) | 2017 (£'000) | 2018 (£'000) |
|---|---|---|---|---|---|
| Revenue | 800 | 880 | 1,040 | 1,280 | 1,600 |
| Gross profit | 90 | 100 | 110 | 150 | 190 |
| Profit before tax | 40 | 46 | 52 | 90 | 130 |
| Dividends | 4 | 5 | 6 | 9 | 15 |

We may prepare a trend statement for these five years with the 2014 figures taken as 100% as follows.

| | 2014 (%) | 2015 (%) | 2016 (%) | 2017 (%) | 2018 (%) |
|---|---|---|---|---|---|
| Revenue | 100 | 110 | 130 | 160 | 200 |
| Gross profit | 100 | 111 | 128 | 167 | 211 |
| Profit before tax | 100 | 115 | 130 | 225 | 325 |
| Dividends | 100 | 125 | 150 | 225 | 375 |

This is a useful approach when analysing performance from the five-year summary as it provides a convenient way of presenting data for a large number of years, and can be helpful in highlighting trends. In the above example, we can see that as revenue doubles, profit before tax more than trebles, indicating a reasonable degree of fixed costs since they have not increased in line with the increase in revenue.

Alternatively, when presented with data in this form it is sometimes useful if we recompute each individual year's movement as compared with the previous year.

## EXAMPLE

We are presented with the following trend data for the sales of two companies, A and B, over a five-year period.

| | 2014 (%) | 2015 (%) | 2016 (%) | 2017 (%) | 2018 (%) |
|---|---|---|---|---|---|
| A | 100 | 110 | 130 | 160 | 200 |
| B | 100 | 150 | 210 | 240 | 250 |

If we restate this data in terms of the **increase** in sales achieved by each company we would show

| | 2015 | 2016 | 2017 | 2018 |
|---|---|---|---|---|
| A | +10% | +18% | +23% | +25% |
| B | +50% | +40% | +15% | +4% |

The trend statement indicated that, to each year, it would be correct to state that Company B had expanded sales more rapidly than Company A since 2014. On the other hand, the data on the increase in sales each year indicate that the rate of increase in sales is on the rise for Company A and on the decline for Company B, with the former company now increasing sales at a much faster rate.

Thus, both types of analysis can give us a useful insight when we are analysing performance over a number of years.

## Common size statements

A common size statement expresses the amounts of successive years as a proportion of one figure in the accounts. Such statements are normally prepared in relation to the balance sheet, relating each amount to the balance sheet totals.

### EXAMPLE

We are provided with the following data in relation to a company.

| | 2011 (£'000) | 2012 (£'000) | 2013 (£'000) | 2014 (£'000) | 2015 (£'000) |
|---|---|---|---|---|---|
| **Total assets** | | | | | |
| Non-current assets | 180 | 240 | 250 | 280 | 310 |
| Current assets | 175 | 185 | 220 | 300 | 370 |
| | 225 | 295 | 330 | 421 | 501 |
| **Financing** | | | | | |
| Share capital | 100 | 100 | 100 | 150 | 150 |
| Reserves | 50 | 79 | 110 | 166 | 241 |
| Shareholders' funds | 150 | 179 | 210 | 316 | 391 |
| Loans | 60 | 100 | 100 | 80 | 80 |
| Current liabilities | 145 | 146 | 160 | 184 | 209 |
| | 355 | 425 | 470 | 580 | 680 |

From which, we can prepare the following common size statement taking each figure as a percentage of total assets.

| | 2011 (%) | 2012 (%) | 2013 (%) | 2014 (%) | 2015 (%) |
|---|---|---|---|---|---|
| Trading assets | | | | | |
| Non-current assets | 51 | 56 | 53 | 48 | 46 |
| Current assets | 49 | 44 | 47 | 52 | 54 |
| | 100 | 100 | 100 | 100 | 100 |
| Financing | | | | | |
| Share capital | 28 | 24 | 21 | 26 | 22 |
| Reserves | 14 | 18 | 23 | 28 | 35 |
| Shareholders' funds | 42 | 42 | 44 | 54 | 57 |
| Loans | 17 | 24 | 21 | 14 | 12 |
| Current liabilities | 41 | 34 | 35 | 32 | 31 |
| | 100 | 100 | 100 | 100 | 100 |

This is a valuable tool for identifying changes in the way in which assets employed are financed and the breakdown of the assets employed.

In this Example, we can now more readily identify the relative decline in the level of non-current assets and the impact on gearing of the raising of a loan in 2012 and the issue of shares, which is partly used to repay the loans in 2014.

## Cash flow statement

The cash flow statement is in itself a potentially valuable aid in the interpretation of accounts. This statement is a reanalysis of the data given in the income statement and balance sheet, designed to give a view of the flow of cash through the business.

IAS 7 requires most limited companies to present a cash flow statement in a standard format. This format can provide some very useful input to any analysis we do as it closely ties in with the four main analysis areas we have been highlighting, as follows.

| Analysis Area | Cash Flow Heading |
|---|---|
| Trading performance | Operating activities |
| Financial performance | Investing activities |
| Financial position | Financing activities |

For example, the financing activities cash flows can help us identify causes for any changes in the gearing position of the company as it details all the finance raised and repaid in one place.

It will also be possible to make a year-on-year or cross-company cash flow comparison by using a common size balance sheet.

## Z-scores

One way of using ratios is to identify several ratios that reflect on a particular aspect of a business and produce a single, combined, 'multivariate' ratio that represents some kind of weighted average.

Most research in this field has focused on identifying liquidity problems, using ratios to identify companies that will have problems in meeting their obligations.

One example of multivariate ratio analysis is the 'Z score' system. This is a composite ratio calculation derived by Altman (1983) which is designed to assess the solvency of a particular company. Depending on the number calculated by the formula, its 'Z score', a conclusion could be reached on the likelihood of bankruptcy. Altman's Z score is worked out as follows:

**Z = 0.717A + 0.847B + 3.11C + 0.420D + 0.998E**

Each of the letters in the formula represents a different financial ratio:

**A = net working capital/total assets**

**B = retained earnings/total assets**

**C = earnings before interest and tax (EBIT)/total assets**

**D = shareholders' equity/total liabilities**

**E = sales/total assets**

The results can be interpreted as follows:

Z score < 1.20; bankruptcy is predicted

Z score > 1.20 but < 2.90; the position is unclear (ie a grey area)

Z score > 2.90; the company is safe with no risk of bankruptcy

The ratios A to E are deemed to provide an insight into a company's solvency.

**Net working capital/ total assets:** working capital is calculated by deducting current liabilities from current assets. The higher this ratio is, the greater the working capital, and thus the greater the balance sheet liquidity. The current ratio or quick ratio gives a similar measure of liquidity. High balance sheet liquidity lowers the bankruptcy risk.

**Retained earnings/total assets**: the higher the level of retained earnings, the greater the 'creditors' buffer' and thus the lower the bankruptcy risk.

**EBIT/total assets**: an indicator of profitability and efficiency. Making a reasonable return should make a business more able to meet the demand of creditors. Altman accords this ratio the highest weighting in his formula. A profitable business is more likely to survive going forward.

**Shareholders' equity/total liabilities**: how does the shareholders' investment in the company compare to the amount owed by the business? The greater the proportion of shareholders' equity, the lower the bankruptcy risk.

**Sales/total assets**: this is the asset turnover ratio, which is a measure of efficiency. Are the assets of the business productive in generating revenue? Higher capital efficiency lowers bankruptcy risk.

## EXAMPLE

The following is extracted from the accounts of Whiskey plc:

| | **2015 (£m)** | **2016 (£m)** |
|---|---|---|
| Revenue | 123 | 220 |
| Profit before interest and tax | 24 | 43 |
| Working capital | 48 | 72 |
| Total assets | 135 | 155 |
| Total liabilities | 97 | 123 |
| Retained earnings | 25 | 27 |
| Shareholders equity | 60 | 52 |

Calculate and interpret the Z score for Whiskey plc in 2015 and 2016.

## SOLUTION

| | **Weights** | **2015** | **2016** |
|---|---|---|---|
| Net working capital/total assets | 0.72 | 0.36 | 0.46 |
| Retained earnings/total assets | 0.85 | 0.19 | 0.17 |
| Earnings before interest and tax/total assets | 3.11 | 0.18 | 0.28 |
| Shareholders' equity/total liabilities | 0.42 | 0.62 | 0.42 |
| Sales/total assets | 1.0 | 0.91 | 1.42 |
| **Z score** | | **2.15** | **2.94** |

The Z score indicates that the company's financial position has changed from showing a possible bankruptcy risk in 2015 to no forecast risk of bankruptcy based on 2016's results. This improvement has been driven by a significant improvement in the efficiency of the business, with higher levels of revenue and profit being generated from the asset base. This is demonstrated by the increases in the asset turnover ratio (sales/ total assets) and in EBIT/total assets ratio.

## Summary

Any analysis should consist of the following points.

- What we have seen, stating the obvious, the limitations of our analysis and any further information needed.
- The possible causes of what we have seen, again stating the obvious possible causes but also thinking more broadly and trying to imagine alternative possible causes that are not highlighted by the accounts.
- Any impact of accounting policies or other distorting effects.
- The implications for the future.

Therefore, we need to build up from the factual details of the past, through possible causes of the past, to speculation of the implications for the future.

# Appendix

## Illustrative Financial Statements

**EXAMPLE**

| **Balance sheet as at 31 December** | **(£'000)** | **(£'000)** |
|---|---|---|
| **Non-Current Assets** | | |
| Intangible | | 3,926 |
| Property, Plant and Equipment (PPE) | | 18,731 |
| Investments | | 842 |
| | | 23,499 |
| **Current Assets** | | |
| Inventory | 19,420 | |
| Trade Receivables | 21,753 | |
| Other Receivables | 6,129 | |
| Investments | 3,926 | |
| Cash | 6,425 | |
| | | 57,653 |
| **Total Assets** | | 81,152 |
| **Non-Current Liabilities** | | |
| Loans | (1,356) | |
| Finance Leases | (1,016) | |
| Deferred Tax | (1,484) | |
| Provision for reorganisation costs | (589) | |
| | | 4,445 |
| **Current liabilities** | | |
| Bank Overdraft | (16,942) | |
| Finance Lease Obligation | (137) | |
| Trade Payables | (18,702) | |
| Tax | (1,625) | |
| Others | (6,260) | |
| | | (43,666) |
| **Net Assets** | | 33,041 |
| £1 Ordinary shares | | 17,925 |
| Preference shares | | 837 |
| Share Premium | | 2,455 |
| Revaluation Reserve | | 2,681 |
| Retained Earnings | | 8,240 |
| | | 32,138 |
| **Minority Interest** | | 903 |
| **Shareholders' Funds** | | 33,041 |

| Income Statement for the Period Ended 31 December | (£'000) |
|---|---|
| Revenue | 135,761 |
| Cost of sales | (83,604) |
| Gross profit | 52,157 |
| Distribution costs | (22,961) |
| Administration costs | (22,712) |
| Profit from operations | 6,484 |
| Income from associate | 62 |
| Interest receivable | 303 |
| Interest payable | (3,176) |
| Profit before taxation | 3,673 |
| Tax | (1,164) |
| Profit after taxation | 2,509 |
| Minority interest | (208) |
| Preference share dividends | (84) |
| Profit attributable to the group | 2,217 |
| Dividends – Ordinary | 1,120 |
| Earnings per share | 12.37p |
| Dividend per share | 6.25p |

Last year, the earnings per share was quoted as 12.43p. Included in administration costs is an exceptional expense of £3,192,000.

## Ratios summary

- **Profitability ratios**

ROCE $= \dfrac{\text{Profit from operations + Interest receivable and other income receivable}}{\text{Capital employed}} \times 100\%$

Profit margins $= \dfrac{\text{Profit}}{\text{Revenue}} \times 100\%$

Asset turnover $= \dfrac{\text{Revenue}}{\text{Assets (capital) employed}}$

Operational gearing ratio $= \dfrac{\text{Revenue} - \text{Variable costs}}{\text{Profit}}$

- **Liquidity ratios**

Current ratio $= \dfrac{\text{Current assets}}{\text{Current liabilities}}$

Quick ratio $= \dfrac{\text{Current assets} - \text{Inventory}}{\text{Current liabilities}}$

Inventory turnover $= \dfrac{\text{Cost of sales}}{\text{Inventory}}$

Receivables' collection period $= \dfrac{\text{Trade receivables}}{\text{Revenue}} \times 365 \text{ days}$

Payables' payment period $= \dfrac{\text{Trade payables}}{\text{Cost of sales}} \times 365 \text{ days}$

- **Capital structure**

Debt to equity $= \dfrac{\text{Interest bearing loans + Preference share capital}}{\text{Equity shareholders' funds}} \times 100\%$

Net debt to equity $= \dfrac{\text{Debt as above} - \text{Cash and current asset investments}}{\text{Equity shareholders' funds}} \times 100\%$

Lenders' debt to equity $= \dfrac{\text{Total borrowings (including non-interest bearing debt)}}{\text{Total shareholders' funds (including preference shares)}} \times 100\%$

Interest cover $= \dfrac{\text{Profit from operations + Interest Receivables + Other income receivables}}{\text{Interest payable}}$

Asset cover $= \dfrac{\text{Total assets} - \text{Current liabilities}}{\text{Loans payable}}$

- **Investors' ratios and EPS**

EPS $= \dfrac{\text{Net profit / loss attributable to ordinary shareholders}}{\text{Weighted average number of ordinary shares outstanding during the period}}$

Return on equity $= \dfrac{\text{Earnings attributable to ordinary shareholders}}{\text{Equity shareholders' funds}} \times 100\%$

Price/Earnings $= \dfrac{\text{Current market price per share}}{\text{Earnings per share}}$

Enterprise value to EBIT $= \dfrac{\text{Enterprise value}}{\text{Earnings before interest and tax}}$

Enterprise value to EBITDA $= \dfrac{\text{Enterprise value}}{\text{Earnings before interest, tax, depreciation and amortisation}}$

Enterprise value to sales $= \dfrac{\text{Enterprise value}}{\text{Revenue}}$

Earnings yield $= \dfrac{\text{Earnings per share}}{\text{Current market price per share}} \times 100\%$

Dividend yield $= \dfrac{\text{Dividend per share}}{\text{Current market price per share}} \times 100\%$

Dividend cover $= \dfrac{\text{Earnings per share}}{\text{Net dividend per share}}$

Net asset value $= \dfrac{\text{Net assets attributable to ordinary shareholders}}{\text{Number of ordiary shares in issue}}$

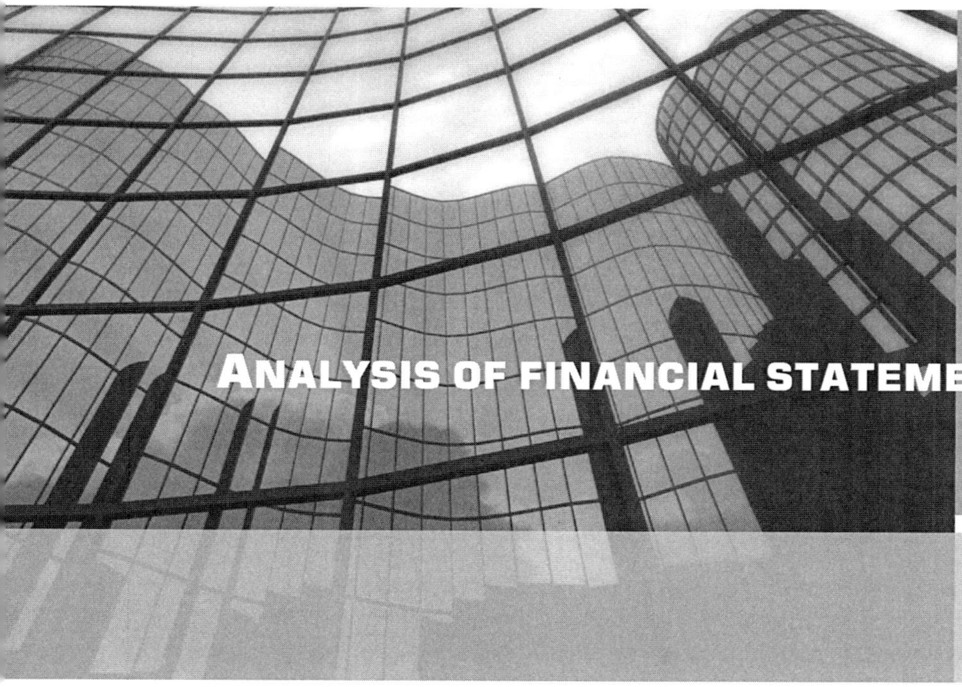

# ANALYSIS OF FINANCIAL STATEMENTS CASE STUDY

chapter 7

Contents


| | | |
|---|---|---|
| 1 | Introduction | 142 |
| 2 | Case Study Company Information | 142 |
| 3 | Sample Solution - Analysis Report | 147 |

# 1 Introduction

This chapter will help you put into practice the ratio analysis techniques taught in the previous chapter. Being able to provide detailed and meaningful financial analysis is a key skill for the exam. You should attempt the case study below before you read through the suggested solution provided.

# 2 Case Study Company Information

Set out below are extracts from the 2010/11 Annual Report of Kingfisher plc. Kingfisher is a large international home improvement retail group, with almost 860 stores in eight countries in Europe and Asia. Key brand names are: B&Q and Screwfix in the UK/Ireland and Castorama and Brico Depot in France and Poland.

## Requirements

Use the Annual Report extracts to undertake a ratio analysis of Kingfisher, giving your opinion of the group's trading performance; liquidity and capital structure for 2010/11. Ensure all ratio calculations are explained and that you discuss relevant trends and conclude as to what you see as the most important themes for this business. You should include comments on the performance of the different geographic segments of Kingfisher, as well as discussing the group performance as a whole. What further information do you require?

***Tutor note:***

*Before you start writing, think about the layout of your report. A clear structure, including a conclusion will have most impact for the reader of the report. Ensure your narrative is split into the different areas of analysis as detailed in the requirement and accompanied by suitable ratio calculations. Try and support all calculations by an insightful comment ie not just specifying that the trend is up or down but is it positive/ negative and why is it happening? Workings must be shown for all ratios, but it is probably most helpful to the reader if you include these as a separate section at the end of the report. Don't forget a conclusion to tie the main points of your report together and to finish on a decisive note.*

## Case Study - Kingfisher Financial Statements

Kingfisher plc
Annual Report
and Accounts
2010/11

# Consolidated income statement



Year ended 29 January 2011

| £ millions | Notes | 2010/11 Before exceptional items | Exceptional items (note 5) | Total | 2009/10 Before exceptional items | Exceptional items (note 5) | Total |
|---|---|---|---|---|---|---|---|
| Continuing operations: | | | | | | | |
| **Sales** | 4 | 10,450 | - | 10,450 | 10,503 | - | 10,503 |
| Cost of sales | | (6,545) | - | (6,545) | (6,706) | - | (6,706) |
| Gross profit | | 3,905 | - | 3,905 | 3,797 | - | 3,797 |
| Selling and distribution expenses | | (2,739) | (9) | (2,748) | (2,712) | - | (2,712) |
| Administrative expenses | | (527) | - | (527) | (536) | - | (536) |
| Other income | | 34 | (3) | 37 | 31 | 17 | 48 |
| Share of post-tax results of joint ventures and associates | 17 | 31 | - | 31 | 26 | - | 26 |
| **Operating profit** | | 704 | (6) | 698 | 606 | 17 | 623 |
| Analysed as: | | | | | | | |
| **Retail profit** | 4 | 762 | (6) | 756 | 664 | 17 | 681 |
| Central costs | | (41) | - | (41) | (41) | - | (41) |
| Share of interest and tax of joint ventures and associates | | (17) | - | (17) | (17) | - | (17) |
| Finance costs | | (46) | - | (46) | (76) | - | (76) |
| Finance income | | 19 | - | 19 | 19 | - | 19 |
| Net finance costs | 6 | (27) | - | (27) | (57) | - | (57) |
| **Profit before taxation** | 7 | 677 | (6) | 671 | 549 | 17 | 566 |
| Income tax expense | 9 | (183) | 3 | (180) | (174) | (7) | (181) |
| **Profit for the year** | | 494 | (3) | 491 | 375 | 10 | 385 |
| Attributable to: | | | | | | | |
| Equity shareholders of the Company | | | | 494 | | | 388 |
| Non-controlling interests | | | | (3) | | | (3) |
| | | | | 491 | | | 385 |
| **Earnings per share** | 10 | | | | | | |
| Basic | | | | 21.0p | | | 16.5p |
| Diluted | | | | 20.7p | | | 16.4p |
| Adjusted basic | | | | 20.5p | | | 16.4p |
| Adjusted diluted | | | | 20.2p | | | 16.3p |

The proposed final dividend for the year ended 29 January 2011, subject to approval by shareholder at the Annual General Meeting, is 5.145p per share.

# 58 Consolidated balance sheet

Year ended 29 January 2011

Kingfisher plc
Annual Report
and Accounts
2010/11

| £ millions | Notes | 2010/11 | 2009/10 |
|---|---|---|---|
| **Non-current assets** | | | |
| Goodwill | 12 | 2,395 | 2,395 |
| Other intangible assets | 13 | 86 | 70 |
| Property, plant and equipment | 14 | 3,632 | 3,612 |
| Investment property | 15 | 32 | 24 |
| Investments in joint ventures and associates | 17 | 259 | 234 |
| Deferred tax assets | 25 | 27 | 27 |
| Derivatives | 23 | 62 | 81 |
| Other receivables | 19 | 15 | 22 |
| | | 6,508 | 6,465 |
| **Current assets** | | | |
| Inventories | 18 | 1,791 | 1,545 |
| Trade and other receivables | 19 | 513 | 494 |
| Derivatives | 23 | 15 | 24 |
| Current tax assets | | 45 | 58 |
| Cash and cash equivalents | 20 | 731 | 1,260 |
| | | 3,095 | 3,381 |
| **Total assets** | | 9,603 | 9,846 |
| **Current liabilities** | | | |
| Trade and other payables | 21 | (2,519) | (2,374) |
| Borrowings | 22 | (196) | (647) |
| Derivatives | 23 | (11) | (25) |
| Current tax liabilities | | (372) | (348) |
| Provisions | 26 | (27) | (36) |
| | | (3,125) | (3,430) |
| **Non-current liabilities** | | | |
| Other payables | 21 | (76) | (74) |
| Borrowings | 22 | (577) | (883) |
| Derivatives | 23 | (17) | (47) |
| Deferred tax liabilities | 25 | (238) | (197) |
| Provisions | 26 | (52) | (62) |
| Post employment benefits | 27 | (58) | (198) |
| | | (1,018) | (1,461) |
| **Total liabilitities** | | (4,143) | (4,891) |
| **Net assets** | 4 | 5,460 | 4,955 |
| **Equity** | | | |
| Share capital | 28 | 371 | 371 |
| Share premium | | 2,194 | 2,191 |
| Own shares held | | (42) | (54) |
| Retained earnings | | 2,390 | 1,921 |
| Other reserves | 29 | 539 | 516 |
| **Total attributable to equity shareholders of the Company** | | 5,452 | 4,945 |
| Non-controlling interests | | 8 | 10 |
| **Total equity** | | 5,460 | 4,955 |

Kingfisher plc
Annual Report
and Accounts
2010/11

# Consolidated cash flow statement

Year ended 29 January 2011

59

| £ millions | Notes | 2010/11 | 2009/10 |
|---|---|---|---|
| **Operating activities** | | | |
| Cash generated by operations | 31 | 763 | 1,130 |
| Income tax paid | | (133) | (151) |
| French tax receipt | 9 | - | 148 |
| **Net cash flows from operating activities** | | 630 | 1,127 |
| **Investing activities** | | | |
| Purchase of property, plant and equipment investment property and intangible assets | 4 | (310) | (256) |
| Disposal of property, plant and equipment investment property and intangible assets | | 87 | 59 |
| Interest received | | 19 | 14 |
| Dividends received from joint ventures and associates | | 6 | 5 |
| **Net cash flows from investing activities** | | (198) | (178) |
| **Financing activities** | | | |
| Interest paid | | (33) | (72) |
| Interest element of finance lease rental payments | | (5) | (5) |
| Repayment of bank loans | | (57) | (150) |
| Repayment of Medium Term Notes and other fixed term debt | | (696) | (500) |
| Receipt on financing derivatives | | 6 | 78 |
| Capital element of finance lease rental payments | | (12) | (14) |
| Issue of share capital under share schemes | | 3 | - |
| Purchase of own shares | | - | (7) |
| Disposal of own shares | | 1 | - |
| Dividends paid to equity shareholders of the Company | | (129) | (125) |
| **Net cash flows from financing activities** | | (922) | (775) |
| **Net (decrease)/increase in cash and cash equivalents and bank overdrafts** | | (490) | 174 |
| **Cash and cash equivalents and bank overdrafts at beginning of year** | | 1,135 | 994 |
| Exchange differences | | (9) | (33) |
| **Cash and cash equivalents and bank overdrafts at end of year** | | 636 | 1,135 |

## Extracts from Kingfisher Notes to the Accounts

4 Segmental analysis

**Income statements**

| | | | | | 2010/11 |
|---|---|---|---|---|---|
| | UK & | | Other International | | |
| £ millions | Ireland | France | Poland | Other | Total |
| **Sales** | 4,333 | 4,204 | 1,062 | 851 | 10,450 |
| **Retail profit** | 243 | 348 | 134 | 37 | 762 |
| Exceptional items | | | | | (6) |
| Central costs | | | | | (41) |
| Share of interest and tax of joint ventures and associates | | | | | (17) |
| **Operating profit** | | | | | 698 |
| Net finance costs | | | | | (27) |
| **Profit before taxation** | | | | | 671 |

| | | | | | 2009/10 |
|---|---|---|---|---|---|
| | UK & | | Other International | | |
| £ millions | Ireland | France | Poland | Other | Total |
| **Sales** | 4,442 | 4,242 | 1,012 | 807 | 10,503 |
| **Retail profit** | 217 | 322 | 125 | - | 664 |
| Exceptional items | | | | | 17 |
| Central costs | | | | | (41) |
| Share of interest and tax of joint ventures and associates | | | | | (17) |
| **Operating profit** | | | | | 623 |
| Net finance costs | | | | | (57) |
| **Profit before taxation** | | | | | 566 |

**Balance sheet**

| £ millions | UK & Ireland | France | Other International Poland | Other International Other | 2010/11 Total |
|---|---|---|---|---|---|
| **Segments assets** | 1,172 | 1,233 | 512 | 560 | 3,477 |
| Central liabilities | | | | | (426) |
| Goodwill | | | | | 2,395 |
| Net cash | | | | | 14 |
| **Net assets** | | | | | 54,60 |

| £ millions | UK & Ireland | France | Other International Poland | Other International Other | 2009/10 Total |
|---|---|---|---|---|---|
| **Segments assets** | 997 | 1,187 | 463 | 562 | 3,209 |
| Central liabilities | | | | | (399) |
| Goodwill | | | | | 2,395 |
| Net cash | | | | | (250) |
| **Net assets** | | | | | 4,955 |

6 Net finance costs

| £ millions | 2010/11 | 2009/10 |
|---|---|---|
| Bank overdrafts and bank loans | (18) | (25) |
| Medium Term Notes and other fixed term debts | (27) | (43) |
| Financing fair value remeasurements | 7 | 2 |
| Finance leases | (5) | (5) |
| Unwinding of discounts on provisions | (3) | (4) |
| Expected net interest charge on defined benefit pension schemes | (7) | (4) |
| Capitalised interest | 1 | 3 |
| **Finance costs** | (46) | (76) |
| Cash and cash equivalents and current other investments | 19 | 19 |
| **Finance income** | 19 | 19 |
| **Net finance costs** | (27) | (57) |

11 Dividends

| £ millions | 2010/11 | 2009/10 |
|---|---|---|
| **Dividends to equity shareholders of the Company** | | |
| Final dividend for the year ended 30 January 2010 of 3.575p per share (31 January 2009: 3.4p per share) | 84 | 80 |
| Interim dividend for the year ended 29 January 2011 of 1.925p per share (30 January 2010: 1.925p per share) | 45 | 45 |
| | 129 | 125 |

The proposed final dividend for the year ended 29 January 2011 of 5.145p per share is subject to approval by shareholder at the Annual General Meeting and has not been included as a liability in these financial statements.

Aggregate amounts relating to joint ventures and associates:

| £ millions | 2010/2009/10 Joint ventures | Associates | Total | Joint ventures | Associates | Total |
|---|---|---|---|---|---|---|
| Non-current assets | 29 | 277 | 306 | 26 | 240 | 266 |
| Current assets | 54 | 297 | 351 | 52 | 283 | 335 |
| Current liabilities | (49) | (212) | (261) | (42) | (176) | (218) |
| Non-current liabilities | (2) | (135) | (317) | (9) | (140) | (149) |
| **Share of net assets** | 32 | 227 | 259 | 27 | 207 | 234 |
| Sales | 165 | 569 | 734 | 132 | 562 | 694 |
| Operating expenses | (151) | (535) | (686) | (122) | (529) | (651) |
| Operating profits | 14 | 34 | 48 | 10 | 33 | 43 |
| Net finance costs | (1) | (5) | (5) | (2) | (8) | (10) |
| Profit before taxation | 13 | 29 | 42 | 8 | 25 | 33 |
| Income tax expense | (3) | (8) | (11) | (1) | (6) | (7) |
| **Share of post-tax results** | 10 | 21 | 31 | 7 | 19 | 26 |

19 Trade and other receivables

| £ millions | 2010/11 | 2009/10 |
|---|---|---|
| **Non-currents** | | |
| Prepayments | 13 | 18 |
| Property receivables | 2 | 2 |
| Other receivables | - | 2 |
| | 15 | 22 |
| **Current** | | |
| Trade receivables | 72 | 69 |
| Provision for bad and doubtful debts | (16) | (15) |
| Net trade receivables | 56 | 54 |
| Property receivables | 2 | 2 |
| Prepayments | 137 | 124 |
| Other receivables | 318 | 314 |
| | 513 | 494 |
| **Trade and other receivables** | 528 | 516 |

21 Trade and other payables

| £ millions | 2010/11 | 2009/10 |
|---|---|---|
| **Currents** | | |
| Trade payables | 1,366 | 1,323 |
| Other taxation and social security | 218 | 207 |
| Deferred income | 187 | 178 |
| Accruals and other payables | 748 | 666 |
| | 2,519 | 2,374 |
| **Non-current** | | |
| Accruals and other payables | 76 | 74 |
| **Trade and other payables** | 2,595 | 2,448 |

Accruals include allowance for customer returns, representing the estimate of future sales returns at the year end.

The fair values of trade and other payables approximate to their carrying amounts

22 Borrowings

| £ millions | 2010/11 | 2009/10 |
|---|---|---|
| **Currents** | | |
| Bank overdrafts | 95 | 125 |
| Bank loans | 89 | 136 |
| Medium Term Notes and other fixed term debt | - | 374 |
| Finance leases | 12 | 12 |
| | 196 | 647 |
| **Non-current** | | |
| Bank loans | 15 | 18 |
| Medium Term Notes and other fixed term debt | 504 | 812 |
| Finance leases | 58 | 53 |
| | 577 | 883 |
| **Borrowings** | 773 | 1,530 |

31 Cash generated by operations

| £ millions | 2010/11 | 2009/10 |
|---|---|---|
| **Operating profit** | 698 | 623 |
| Share of post-tax results of joint ventures and associates | (31) | (26) |
| Depreciation and amortisation | 238 | 260 |
| Impairment losses | 14 | 4 |
| Loss/(profit) on disposal of property, plant and equipments, investment property and intangible assets | 4 | (1) |
| Share-based compensation charge | 21 | 20 |
| (Increase)/decrease in inventories | (238) | 234 |
| Increase in trade and other receivables | (10) | (18) |
| Increase in trade and other payables | 107 | 102 |
| Movement in provisions | (21) | (24) |
| Movement in post employment benefits | (19) | (44) |
| **Cash generated by operations** | 763 | 1,130 |

# 3 Sample Solution - Analysis Report

Ratio calculations are provided in the appendix to this report.

## Profitability

Group revenue performance in the period was flat. 2010/11 revenue recorded was £10,450m, down 0.5% from 2009/10 recorded revenue of £10,503m. This limited growth could be put in the context of difficult economic conditions which have impacted the retail sector generally.

Total operating profit increased from £623m in 2009/10 to £698m in 2010/11, a rise of 12.0%. Excluding the impact of the exceptional gain in 2009/10 and the exceptional loss in 2010/11, the rise in total operating profit was greater at 16.2%. As revenue was flat, operating margins on a pre-exceptional basis have been boosted from 5.8% to 6.7%. Despite the improvements, operating margins remain at low levels in absolute terms.

Asset turnover for the group improved from 1.5× (2009/10) to 1.6× (2010/11) indicating better sales generation on capital invested. This trend, combined with the rise in pre-exceptional operating margins, led to an increase in pre-exceptional return on capital employed from 9.1% (2009/10) to 11.1% (2010/11). This indicates the group is making more efficient use of its invested funds.

Profits before taxation, on a pre-exceptional basis, rose from £549m in 2009/10 to £677m in 2010/11. This is an increase of 23.3%, which outstrips the increase in pre-exceptional operating profit of 16.2%. The profits before taxation increase has been fuelled by the reduction in debt levels (and consequently interest payable) as well as the improved profitability of the business. Pre-exceptional return on equity rose from 7.6% (2009/10) to 9.0% (2010/11) reflecting these trends.

### Exceptional items

Kingfisher splits its results in the income statement between 'before exceptional items' and 'total'. The group chooses to highlight 'before exceptional items' figures, as it believes these give a fairer depiction of performance in the period and provide a more meaningful basis to compare the figures year-on-year. Pre-exceptional results also assist analysts in forecasting future performance. 'Exceptional' items are more likely to be 'one-offs' and less likely to reoccur. Pre-tax exceptional items totalled an expense of £6m in 2010/11 and a gain of £17m in 2009/10.

## Segmental analysis

Segmental results provide an analysis of certain key figures in the financial statements, allowing the user of the accounts to assess performance of the business on a divisional basis. The group discloses three different segments, namely UK/ Ireland; France and Other international, which includes Poland.

### Profitability

'Result' = retail profit, namely operating profit excluding exceptional items, central costs and group share of interest/tax of joint ventures and associates.

| (£m) | % of 2010/11 revenue | 2010/11 Revenue | % of 2010/11 result | 2010/11 Result | 2010/11 Margin (%) | 2009/10 Revenue | 2009/10 Result | 2009/10 Margin (%) |
|---|---|---|---|---|---|---|---|---|
| UK/ Ireland | 41.5 | 4,333 | 31.9 | 243 | 5.6 | 4,442 | 217 | 4.9 |
| France | 40.2 | 4,204 | 45.7 | 348 | 8.3 | 4,242 | 322 | 7.6 |
| Poland | 10.2 | 1,062 | 17.6 | 134 | 12.6 | 1,012 | 125 | 12.4 |
| Other | 8.1 | 851 | 4.9 | 37 | 4.3 | 807 | – | n/a |
| Total | 100 | 10,450 | 100 | 762 | 7.3 | 10,503 | 664 | 6.3 |

### Efficiency

Segmental total assets are calculated as segment net assets excluding central liabilities, goodwill and net cash.

| (£m) | 2010/11 Revenue | 2010/11 Total assets | 2010/11 Asset turnover (x) | 2009/10 Revenue | 2009/10 Total assets | 2009/10 Asset turnover (x) |
|---|---|---|---|---|---|---|
| UK/ Ireland | 4,333 | 1,172 | 3.7 | 4,442 | 997 | 4.5 |
| France | 4,204 | 1,233 | 3.4 | 4,242 | 1,187 | 3.6 |
| Poland | 1,062 | 512 | 2.1 | 1,012 | 463 | 2.2 |
| Other | 851 | 560 | 1.5 | 807 | 562 | 1.4 |
| Total | 10,450 | 3,477 | 3.0 | 10,503 | 3,209 | 3.3 |

**Performance**

ROA is return on assets. Assets equate to segmental net assets excluding central liabilities, goodwill and net cash. Result is retail profit, namely operating profit excluding exceptional items, central costs and group share of interest/tax of joint ventures and associates.

| (£m) | 2010/11 Result | 2010/11 Total assets | 2010/11 ROA (%) | 2009/10 Result | 2009/10 Total assets | 2009/10 ROA (%) |
|---|---|---|---|---|---|---|
| UK/ Ireland | 243 | 1,172 | 20.7 | 217 | 997 | 21.8 |
| France | 348 | 1,233 | 28.2 | 322 | 1,187 | 27.1 |
| Poland | 134 | 512 | 26.2 | 125 | 463 | 27.0 |
| Other | 37 | 560 | 6.6 | – | 562 | n/a |
| Total | 762 | 3,477 | 21.9 | 664 | 3,209 | 20.7 |

## UK/ Ireland

The UK/Ireland division is the largest contributor to revenue, with 41.5% of total 2010/11 revenue. Reported sales fell from £4,442m in 2009/10 to £4,333m in 2010/11, a decline of 2.5%. Whereas the UK/Ireland division contributes the highest proportion of revenue to group results (41.5%), it contributes only 31.9% to retail profit in 2010/11. This is however an improvement from 2009/10, with retail profit rising 12.0% from £217m to £243m in the period.

UK retail profit margin was 5.6% in 2010/11 which remains significantly below the group overall retail margin of 7.3%. UK retail profit margin has risen from 4.9% in 2009/10, which has contributed to the rise in group total retail profit margin for the period, up from 6.3% (2009/10) to 7.3% (2010/11). Divisional profitability remains low in absolute terms.

Divisional asset turnover has fallen slightly, from 4.5× in 2009/10 to 3.7× in 2010/11, reflecting the slight decline in sales. Divisional asset turnover is better than the group position of 3.0× in 2010/11. Return on total assets for the UK/Ireland has declined slightly from 21.8% in 2009/10 to 20.7% in 2010/11. The 12.0% rise in retail profit has been outstripped by the 17.6% rise in segment assets.

## France

The next largest segment in revenue terms is France with 40.2% of total revenue in 2010/11. Sales were down slightly from the previous year at £4,204m (2010/11) compared to £4,242m (2009/10). French retail profit grew by more than revenue, with profit margins rising from 7.6% to 8.3%. This division has profit margins in excess of the group profit margin of 7.3% in 2010/11.

Divisional asset turnover was down slightly from 3.6× (2009/10) to 3.4× (2010/11), reflecting the slight increase in divisional assets. On an overall performance basis, however, return on assets increased from 27.1% (2009/10) to 28.2% (2010/11), with the increase in retail profit outstripping the increase in divisional assets. French return on assets is the highest for the whole group and significantly above the Kingfisher average of 20.7% (2009/10) and 21.9% (2010/11).

## Other international

Other international provides the smallest contribution to group results. Poland is the most material segment and results for this country are disclosed separately. The Other International division accounts for the remaining 18.3% of group revenue and 22.4% of group retail profit. On its own, Poland is 10.2% of revenue and 17.6% of retail profit.

Retail profit margins were up slightly in Poland, with margins at 12.6% (2010/11) compared to 12.4% (2009/10). This is significantly better than the group profit margin of 7.3% and over double the UK profit margin of 5.6%. The rest of the division recorded a net profit in the current period, compared to a loss the previous period. Profit margins for this division, excluding Poland, were 4.3% in 2010/11.

Asset turnover has remained steady at 2.1× in Poland (2.2× in the previous year) and 1.5x in the remainder of the division (1.4× in the previous year). Overall, return on assets was 26.2% in Poland, which is better than the group overall return on assets of 21.9%. Other return on assets was just 6.6% in 2010/11, reflecting the low profit margins.

## Liquidity

### Balance sheet

The current ratio has remained steady at 1.0x but the quick ratio has declined slightly from 0.5× (2009/10) to 0.4× (2010/11). The main component of current assets is inventory and inventory levels have increased in the year. In absolute terms the quick ratio is low, with the level of current liabilities around twice that of current assets minus inventory. This is typical for a retailer, where it would be inefficient to hold high levels of working capital on balance sheet. Overall levels of current assets and liabilities have fallen in the period, reflecting the use of cash and cash equivalents to pay down short term borrowings.

Higher levels of inventory have caused inventory days to rise from 84.1 days to 99.9 days, which seems high in absolute terms. The rise in inventory levels will have had a detrimental impact on operating cash flow.

Trade receivables are extremely low as typical for a retailer (rather than a wholesaler). Trade payable days were up from 72.0 days (2009/10) to 76.2 days (2010/11), which will have positive implications for cash flow.

Given the low margins prevailing in the income statement, management of working capital is a crucial factor for this business.

### Cash flow

Cash flow generated from operations before interest and tax was £763m in 2010/11, down by 32% from 2009/10 when £1,130m operating cash flow was generated. This was despite an improved operating profit performance of £698m in 2010/11 (2009/10: £623m).

The driver of this change is cash generated from working capital. In 2010/11, changes in receivables, payables and inventory led to a net cash outflow of £141m. This is the opposite picture from 2009/10, when changes in receivables, payables and inventory led to a working capital net cash inflow of £318m.

Consequently the cash conversion ratio declined from 1.8× to 1.1×, despite the improved position at operating profit level. Changes in working capital levels have thus had a very material impact on group results. In 2009/10, net operating cash flow was also boosted by a one-off tax receipt from the French tax authorities amounting to £148m.

£198m of operating cash flow has been used to fund net investing activities in 2010/11 (2009/10: £178m net investing cash flow). In the current financial period, gross capital expenditure was £310m.

The net cash outflow from financing activities was £922m in 2010/11 and an outflow of £775m in 2009/10. Financing cash flow has been used to repay debt, specifically medium term notes and other fixed term debt; debt repayment excluding finance leases amounted to £630m in 2009/10 and a further £753m in 2010/11. In addition, a cash outflow relating to dividends of £129m was included in 2010/11 (2009/10: £125m).

This net financing cash outflow has been financed partly by operating cash flow, with the balance coming from retained cash. Cash and cash equivalents (net of overdrafts) fell from £1,135m in 2009/10 to £636m in 2010/11.

Taking into account operating, investing and financing flows, the net cash outflow in 2010/11 was £490m (2009/10: net cash inflow of £174m).

## Capital structure

There has been a substantial repayment of bank loans in the year with debt levels halving from gross borrowings of £1,530m in 2009/10 to £773m in 2010/11. Consequently the gross gearing ratio fell from 30.9% to 14.2% and the net gearing ratio fell from 5.4% to 0.8%. The repayments have been largely funded from surplus cash and cash equivalents on the balance sheet.

Interest cover on a profits basis increased from 8.5× (2009/10) to 15.9× (2010/11), and on a cash flow basis from 14.7× (2009/10) to 20.1× (2010/11).

The coverage ratio shows that financial risk is now low, with both operating profit and operating cash flow being comfortably in excess of interest charges/ payments.

Of the £773m debt outstanding at the 2010/11 year end, 75% of it is classified as non-current.

## Conclusion

The group has increased operating profit by 12% on the back of flat revenues, giving a rise in operating margins. Asset turnover has increased too which has led to a rise in return on capital employed up from 9.1% to 11.1% on a pre-exceptional basis. Performance has thus improved in the current period.

Operating cash flow declined from prior year levels, due to increases in inventories. The group has net cash on the balance sheet but has been utilising this to pay down debt. Over £1billion of borrowings have been repaid in the last two years. Financial risk has thus reduced and gearing is now low with high interest coverage.

## Further information requirements

***Tutor note:***

*This section is important. It is a vital skill for the analyst to detail limitations in scope and be able to come up with a list of further information requirements and explain why the items detailed are relevant to the case study*

The following further information would enable us to carry out a more detailed financial analysis and assist with the explanation of the business trends that we have identified.

- The management narratives accompanying the financial statements. These could be used to help us provide explanations for the trends identified from our ratio analysis.
- List of accounting policies. It would be helpful to review the accounting policies to help identify the impact that these might have on the ratios we have calculated.
- Complete financial notes to the accounts. Further supplementary information would help us better understand the three main financial statements. For instance we would like to review the note on operating lease commitments (to give a fuller picture of the financial risk faced by the group); financial instruments (to understand the make-up of the borrowings and the terms attached to the debt); pensions (to see why the group's pension deficit has reduced in the year).
- Details about the company's selling space (ie square meterage of stores). This would enable us to calculate some sector specific ratio analysis (eg sales/ square metre) which could be used to compare the different operating segments of Kingfisher and also to contrast Kingsfisher with other retail companies in its peer group (eg Dixons; Home Retail Group)
- Like-for-like sales figures. The revenue figures as reported are distorted by new openings and stores that have been closed in the year. Like-for-like sales enable a better understanding of the underlying trend of the business, by only including stores that have been open for both periods under consideration.

- Share price information to enable investor ratios to be calculated (multiples) and market information, so we can assess relative performance.
- Financial information from Kingfisher competitor companies and also the sector (eg market growth rates) to help put results in context.
- Results at constant currency. Income statement figures may be distorted by changes in exchange rate. Kingfisher is an international group and operating performance may have improved because of favourable changes in the exchange rate.

## Appendix – Ratio calculations

| | | 2010/11<br>£m | 2009/10<br>£m |
|---|---|---|---|
| 1 | **Pre-exceptional return on capital employed** | | |
| | Pre-exceptional operating profit | 704 | 606 |
| | Add: share of JV/ associate interest and tax | 17 | 17 |
| | Add: Finance income | 19 | 19 |
| | Operating profit plus finance income and JVs | 740 | 642 |
| | Total assets less current liabilities | 6,478 | 6,416 |
| | Add: borrowings in current liabilities | 196 | 647 |
| | Capital employed | 6,674 | 7,063 |
| | Pre-exceptional ROCE | **11.1%** | **9.1%** |
| 2 | **Return on equity** | | |
| | Pre-exceptional profit after taxation | 494 | 375 |
| | Equity | 5,460 | 4,955 |
| | ROE | **9.0%** | **7.6%** |
| 3 | **Growth rates** | | |
| | Revenue | 10,450 | 10,503 |
| | Decline (%) | **–0.5%** | – |
| | Pre-exceptional operating profit | 704 | 606 |
| | Increase (%) | **+16.2%** | – |
| | Operating profit | 698 | 623 |
| | Increase (%) | **+12.0%** | – |
| | Gross profit | 3,905 | 3,797 |
| | Increase (%) | **+2.8%** | – |
| 4 | **Pre-exceptional operating profit margin** | | |
| | Pre-exceptional operating profit | 704 | 606 |
| | Revenue | 10,450 | 10,503 |
| | Operating profit margin | **6.7%** | **5.8%** |
| 5 | **Gross profit margin** | | |
| | Gross profit | 3,905 | 3,797 |
| | Revenue | 10,450 | 10,503 |
| | Gross profit margin | **37.4%** | **36.2%** |
| 6 | **Asset turnover** | | |
| | Revenue | 10,450 | 10,503 |
| | Capital employed (ratio 1) | 6,674 | 7,063 |
| | Asset turnover | **1.6×** | **1.5×** |
| 7 | **Current ratio** | | |
| | Current assets | 3,095 | 3,381 |
| | Current liabilities | 3,125 | 3,430 |
| | Current ratio | **1.0×** | **1.0×** |

| | | 2010/11 £m | 2009/10 £m |
|---|---|---|---|
| 8 | **Quick ratio** | | |
| | Current assets | 3,095 | 3,381 |
| | Less: Inventory | (1,791) | (1,545) |
| | Quick assets | 1,304 | 1,836 |
| | Current liabilities | 3,125 | 3,430 |
| | Quick ratio | **0.4×** | **0.5×** |
| 9 | **Trade receivables collection period** | | |
| | Net trade receivables | 56 | 54 |
| | Revenue | 10,450 | 10,503 |
| | Collection period | **2.0 days** | **1.9 days** |
| 10 | **Trade payables' payment period** | | |
| | Trade payables | 1,366 | 1,323 |
| | Cost of sales | 6,545 | 6,706 |
| | Payment period | **76.2 days** | **72.0 days** |
| 11 | **Inventory days** | | |
| | Inventories | 1,791 | 1,545 |
| | Cost of sales | 6,545 | 6,706 |
| | Inventory holding period | **99.9 days** | **84.1 days** |
| 12 | **Cash conversion ratio** | | |
| | Cash generated from operations before tax and interest | 763 | 1,130 |
| | Operating profit | 698 | 623 |
| | Cash conversion ratio | **1.1×** | **1.8×** |
| 13 | **Gross gearing** | | |
| | Borrowings | 773 | 1,530 |
| | Equity | 5,460 | 4,955 |
| | Gross gearing (%) | **14.2%** | **30.9%** |
| 14 | **Net gearing** | | |
| | Gross borrowings | 773 | 1,530 |
| | Cash and cash equivalents | (731) | (1,260) |
| | Net debt | 42 | 270 |
| | Equity | 5,460 | 4,955 |
| | Net gearing (%) | **0.8%** | **5.4%** |
| 15 | **Interest cover** | | |
| | Total operating profit | 698 | 623 |
| | Interest expense | 44 | 73 |
| | Interest cover | **15.9×** | **8.5×** |
| 16 | **Interest cover in cash flow statement** | | |
| | Cash generated from operations before tax and interest | 763 | 1,130 |
| | Cash interest paid | 38 | 77 |
| | Interest cover in cash flow statement | **20.1×** | **14.7×** |
| 17 | **Dividend cover** | | |
| | Basic earnings per share (pence) | 21.0 | 16.5 |
| | Dividend per share (pence) | 7.07 | 5.5 |
| | Dividend cover | **3.0×** | **3.0×** |

# MODULE 2

## VALUATION

# INTRODUCTION

The material in this section assumes that you possess a current knowledge of basic valuation techniques. If in doubt, a review of the valuation sections in the Certificate of Corporate Finance (unit 2) would be helpful.

# SYLLABUS – VALUATION

## Aim

Candidates will be able to undertake an advanced level of valuation and will be able to recognise the particular valuation problems of different domestic and international industry sectors and types of business entity.

## Syllabus and BPP Study Text coverage

In the assessment, candidates may be required to

| SYLLABUS | BPP STUDY TEXT |
|---|---|
| **a. Use and appraise methods of equity analysis for different types of business entity and industry sectors, indicating the methods' problems and limitations:** | |
| **Traditional methods:**<br>• **Earnings per share (EPS)**<br>• **Return on capital employed (ROCE)**<br>• **Price/book, price/sales and the price/earnings ratios** | Chapter 8 |
| **Adjusted traditional methods:**<br>• **EV and EBITDA**<br>• **EV and EBIT**<br>• **Turnover**<br>• **Other 'rule of thumb' methods**<br>• **Advantages and disadvantages of an enterprise approach to evaluation**<br>• **The treatment of synergies** | Chapter 8 |
| **The cost of equity:**<br>• **The capital asset pricing model (CAPM)**<br>• **Systematic and business risk**<br>• **Application of beta**<br>• **The dividend valuation model (DVM)**<br>• **Alternative measures of the cost of equity (G)**<br>• **Arbitrage pricing theory and its limitations (G)** | Chapters 9 & 10 |
| **The cost of debt**<br>• **Calculating the required yield on debt**<br>• **Considerations of currency and inflation matching** | Chapter 11 |
| **Weighted average cost of capital (WACC)**<br>• **Calculation and limitations**<br>• **Gearing and its impact on WACCs and values** | Chapter 11 |

| SYLLABUS | BPP STUDY TEXT |
|---|---|
| **Free cash flow (FCF)**<br>• **Applying discounted cash flow (DCF) techniques to FCF**<br>• **FCF for equity holders**<br>• **FCF for the enterprise**<br>• **Key economic assumptions used to structure a forecast**<br>• **The treatment of synergies**<br>• **Terminal values and their derivation from both multiples and DCF**<br>• **Sensitivity analysis and its interpretation** | Chapter 12 |
| **Economic value added (EVA) (G)**<br>**Real options and options-based valuation models (G)**<br>**Methodologies in the valuation of mineral rights (G)** | Chapter 13 |

# TRADITIONAL METHODS OF EQUITY ANALYSIS

chapter 8

Contents


| | | |
|---|---|---|
| 1 | Investment Appraisal | 160 |
| 2 | Appraisal of Traditional Methods of Equity Analysis | 165 |
| 3 | Adjusted Traditional Methods | 172 |
| 4 | Earnings Before Interest and Tax Multiple | 176 |
| 5 | Earnings Before Interest, Tax, Depreciation and Amortisation Multiple | 176 |
| 6 | Industry 'Rule of Thumb' Methods | 177 |

# 1 Investment Appraisal

Two main cash flow techniques are used to appraise investment opportunities: the internal rate of return and the net present value. It is assumed you are familiar with these techniques from your earlier studies.

We consider below the internal rate of return in more detail and introduce the new concept of 'modified internal rate of return'.

## Internal rate of return

The internal rate of return (IRR) of any investment is the discount rate at which the net present value (NPV) of the cash flows is equal to zero. A project will only be selected if its internal rate of return exceeds the cost of capital or target rate of return. The IRR is used to calculate the exact discount rate at which NPV is equal to zero.

If calculating IRR manually, we can use the interpolation method. That is, we evaluate the NPV at two different costs of capital and then, by assuming a straight-line relationship between NPV and cost of capital, estimate where the NPV becomes zero. The formula for this is

$$IRR = R1 + \left[ \frac{N_1}{N_1 - N_2} \times (R_2 - R_1) \right]$$

where

$R_1$ = first selected cost of capital

$R_2$ = second selected cost of capital

$N_1$ = NPV of the project when discounted at $R_1$

$N_2$ = NPV of the project when discounted at $R_2$

Interpolation means finding a result between the two figures that we have chosen, ie selecting $R_1$ and $R_2$ such that the IRR falls in between. The IRR can also be estimated using extrapolation: estimating a figure outside of that range, ie selecting values for $R_1$ and $R_2$ such that the IRR does not fall in between. Interpolation will usually give the more accurate solution, hence we should always try to achieve this if possible.

## IRR of a perpetuity

There is a short cut for calculating the IRR of a perpetuity.

**TASK**

We will invest £100,000 and receive back £10,000 in perpetuity. What is the IRR?

**SOLUTION**

We can establish the following table to calculate the project's NPV.

| Time | Cash Flow £ | Discount Factor | Present Value £ |
|---|---|---|---|
| 0 | (100,000) | 1 | (100,000) |
| 1-∞ | 10,000 | ? | 100,000 |
| Net present value | | | – |

If the flows are discounted at the IRR, we know that they must by definition give a NPV of nil. Since the present value of the flow at Time 0 has to be £100,000, the present value of the annual flows from Time 1 to infinity must also be £100,000. This means that we can work out the IRR exactly, since we know that the discount factor for a perpetuity is of the form $\frac{1}{r}$, hence

$$£10,000 \times \frac{1}{r} = £100,000$$

$\Rightarrow r = 0.1$ or 10% p.a.

Effectively, we have simply taken the annual inflow (£10,000) and divided by the initial outflow (£100,000). This is exactly what you would do if you were trying to work out the percentage return on such an investment and it helps to explain why the IRR is often known as the **yield.**

## The multiple IRR problem

The IRR and the NPV methods of investment appraisal produce the same result only when the project has normal cash flows, ie a negative initial cash flow followed by a series of positive cash flows. If the cash flows change signs, then the IRR may not be unique. This is the multiple IRR problem. The multiple IRR occurs when cash flows change sign and result in more than one value for the IRR.

**EXAMPLE**

Consider the following example, where the cash flow for the second year is negative. Note that in this case the NPV is equated to zero for two values of IRR, when IRR = 5.1% and when IRR = 39.8%.

| Time | Cash Flow £ | Discount Factor | Present Value £ |
|---|---|---|---|
| 0 | –245,000 | 1 | –245,000 |
| 1 | 600,000 | 0.909 | 545,455 |
| 2 | –360,000 | 0.826 | –297,521 |
| | | | 2,934 |

If we plot the NPV for this project at various different discount rates, we find the following:

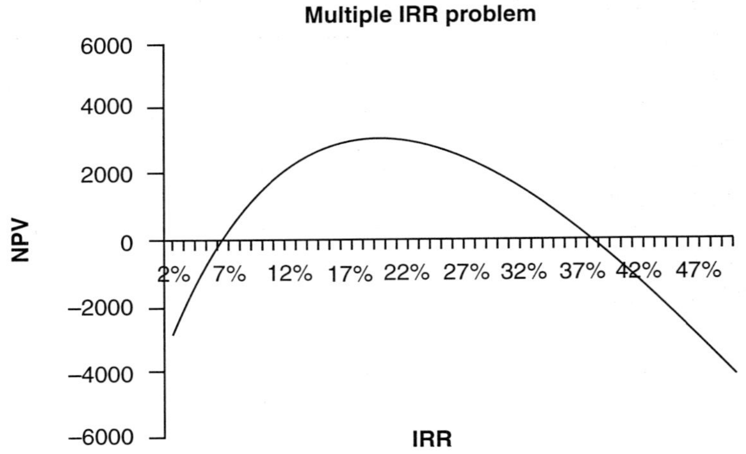


The NPV is initially negative, increases and becomes positive, reaches a maximum value and then declines and becomes negative again. According to the decision rule, we should accept projects for which IRR > discount rate. However, the IRR takes two values.

## Comparison of NPV and IRR

The rule for making investments under the NPV method is that where investments are mutually exclusive, the one with the higher NPV should be preferred. Where investments are independent, all investments should be accepted if they have positive NPVs. The reason for this is that they are generating sufficient cash flows to give an acceptable return to providers of debt and equity finance. This is known as the NPV rule.

The IRR rule states that, where an investment has cash outflows followed by cash inflows, it should be accepted if its IRR exceeds the cost of capital. This is because such investments will have positive NPVs.

## Limitations of the IRR technique

Where we are dealing with independent investments, the IRR should usually come to the same decision as the NPV approach. However, it cannot be used to distinguish between mutually exclusive investments. This is because it merely indicates whether or not a project has a positive NPV. It does not tell us the magnitude of the NPV. Hence, it cannot decide which is the superior project.

## Mutually exclusive projects

We have two projects that both require an initial investment of $10,000. Project A has an IRR of 25% per annum, project B has an IRR of 20% per annum. Which project should we select?

The answer may appear fairly clear cut, ie that we select the project with the higher IRR. However, we are also told that the company's cost of capital is 10% and are provided with the following data.

| Time | Project A | Project B |
|---|---|---|
| 0 | (10,000) | (10,000) |
| 1 | 12,000 | 1,000 |
| 2 | 625 | 13,200 |

It is incorrect to decide between these alternatives based on IRRs. If we were to work out the NPVs of these two projects, we could then summarize the findings as follows:

| | Project A | Project B |
|---|---|---|
| NPV@10% | 1,426 | 1,818 |
| IRR | 25% | 20% |

What we can see is that project A has the higher IRR of 25%, but it has a lower NPV at the company's cost of capital. This means that at a 10% cost of capital, project B is preferable, even though it has the lower IRR. However, when the cost of capital is 20% project A would be preferred since project B would then have a NPV of zero while project A must still have a positive NPV. It can be seen that the decision depends not on the IRR but on the cost of capital being used.

Considering this example more fully, if we calculate the NPVs at various costs of capital we find the following.

| Rate (%) | Project A NPV | Project B NPV |
|---|---|---|
| 5.0 | 1,995 | 2,925 |
| 7.5 | 1,704 | 2,353 |
| 10.0 | 1,426 | 1,818 |
| 12.5 | 1,160 | 1,319 |
| 15.0 | 907 | 851 |
| 17.5 | 665 | 412 |
| 20.0 | 434 | 0 |
| 22.5 | 212 | (387) |
| 25.0 | 0 | (752) |
| 27.5 | (204) | (1,096) |
| 30.0 | (399) | (1,420) |

**TASK**

Plot the data in the above table on a graph. You will need some graph paper.

What information about the projects can be derived from the graphs? What would you identify as the changeover point?

You should find that up to a cost of capital of just over 14%, project B has the highest NPV. Above that cost of capital, project A has the greater NPV and would, therefore, be preferable. For both the above projects, the NPV profile is that the NPV falls as the discount rate increases.

## Reasons why the NPV profiles differ

The NPV profiles cross over at a discount rate of approximately 14%. There are two reasons why this may occur.

- Differences in the timing of the cash flows for each project
- Differences in the project sizes (or project scales)

In our example, there is no difference in project size, with both projects having an initial investment of $10,000. However, there are differences in the timing of the cash flows, with project B having high cash flows in Year 2 and project A having high cash flows in Year 1.

Look again at your graph. You should see that the NPV profile for project B shows a far steeper line. This is because it has higher cash inflows in the more distant year. Therefore, it is much more affected by an increasing discount rate. In contrast, project A has higher value cash flows in the earlier year. This means that it is less affected by the increase in discount rate.

## Conflicting rankings using the NPV and IRR methods

Note that, where the discount rate is greater than 15% (the changeover or crossover rate), selecting an investment based on either the higher NPV or the higher IRR will give the same answer. In this case, for discount rates between 15% and 20%, project A has the higher NPV and it also has the higher IRR.

For discount rates of less than 15%, selecting an investment based on the higher IRR gives an answer which conflicts with the NPV method, since it will select project A, although project B has the higher NPV.

## Re-investment rate

The problem with selecting investments based on the higher IRR is that it makes an assumption that cash flows can be reinvested at the IRR over the life of the project. In contrast, the NPV method assumes that cash flows can be reinvested at the cost of capital over the life of the project.

## Modified internal rate of return

The modified internal rate of return (MIRR) is the IRR that would result if it was not assumed that project proceeds were reinvested at the IRR. The MIRR overcomes the problem of the reinvestment assumption and the fact that changes in the cost of capital over the life of the project cannot be incorporated in the IRR method.

$[PVR/PVi]^{1/n} \times (1+r_e) - 1$

Where $PV_R$ = is the present value of the return phase (the phase of the project with cash inflows)

$PV_I$ = is the present value of the investment phase (the phase of the project with cash outflows)

$r_e$ = the cost of capital

**EXAMPLE** **MIRR calculations**

Consider a project requiring an initial investment of $24,500, with cash inflows of $15,000 in years 1 and 2 and cash inflows of $3,000 in years 3 and 4. The cost of capital is 10%.

**SOLUTION**

Calculate present value of the investment phase and the return phase:

PVR = Total PV for years 1 – 4 = $30,327

PVI = Cost of investment = $24,500

MIRR = $[30{,}327/24{,}500]^{1/4} \times (1+0.1) - 1$

= 16%

The MIRR is calculated on the basis of investing the inflows at the cost of capital.

### Advantages of MIRR

MIRR has the advantage of IRR that it assumes the reinvestment rate is the company's cost of capital. IRR assumes that the reinvestment rate is the IRR itself, which is usually untrue.

In many cases where there is conflict between the NPV and IRR methods, the MIRR will give the same indication as NPV, which is the correct theoretical method. This helps when explaining the appraisal of a project to managers, who often find the concept of rate of return easier to understand than that of net present value.

### Disadvantages of MIRR

However, MIRR, like all rate of return methods, suffers from the problem that it may lead an investor to reject a project which has a lower rate of return but, because of its size, generates a larger increase in wealth. In the same way, a high-return project with a short life may be preferred over a lower-return project with a longer life.

## ANNEX A: INVESTMENT APPRAISAL

## 2 APPRAISAL OF TRADITIONAL METHODS OF EQUITY ANALYSIS

The study of equity analysis is concerned with valuation techniques and methodologies for appraisal of different investment opportunities. The study material begins with a consideration of 'traditional' methods of equity analysis, namely:

- Earnings per share (EPS)
- Return on capital employed (ROCE)
- Price/book ratio
- Price/sales ratio
- Price/earnings (the 'P/E ratio')

We have considered the first two of these, EPS and ROCE, as part of our toolkit to analyse the financial statements of companies and form an opinion on performance for a give historical period. We consider here whether it is valid to extend the use of these measures as valuation and investment appraisal techniques.

### Earnings per share

Earnings per share (EPS) is a measure of the historic performance of a company and as such is an important financial analysis tool. EPS numbers are disclosed prominently in financial statements and EPS data is widely available and often used by analysts as part of headline results summaries.

A consideration of earnings is also important for equity analysis. The earnings of a business are widely recognized as a key driver of value. Trends in EPS are important for assessing the credibility of forecasts and in forming judgments about likely future attainment.

The calculation of earnings per share is specified in the accounting standards (IAS 33). Whilst this provides an objective framework, underlying subjectivity remains as the calculation is based on net income. As such, EPS is subject to distortion from the company's choice of accounting policies and other factors, including the occurrence of exceptional items in the year and changes in the tax rate.

It is common therefore for analysts to consider a 'normalized' or 'adjusted' earnings per share number, as well as the IAS 33 figure. This normalized figure adjusts the earnings per share to give what is perceived to be a more useful figure for financial analysis purposes. The revised figure gives an EPS calculation which is more closely associated with the operating/ trading activities of the period and eliminates any items which might distort the results.

Common adjustments in calculating normalized EPS are as follows:

- The exclusion of exceptional items, such as restructuring costs and profits or losses on the disposal of non-current assets;
- The removal of amortization and impairment charges;
- The exclusion of fair valuing income/expenses in the income statement, such as those relating to financial instruments or currency gains/losses; and
- The exclusion of any income or losses relating to discontinued or soon to be discontinued operations.

This revised EPS figure gives a more sustainable number and thus makes a better starting point for preparing forecasts and other valuation exercises. The number is also likely to be closer to the cash equivalent figure and thus a better basis for valuation. Revised EPS figures also make comparisons between peer group companies easier, as they help smooth out distortions caused by different accounting policy choices.

## Return on capital employed

We calculated return on capital employed in the previous section as a way to appraise the return generated by a company versus the overall funds invested, its 'capital employed'. In a similar vein, we can use the return on capital employed ratio to assess the profitability of an investment (the return) against the size of the investment made (the capital employed). ROCE here is being used as an investment appraisal technique and is also known as 'Return on Investment' (ROI) and 'Accounting Rate of Return' (ARR).

### Basic calculation

For a project with an expected life of several years, ROCE would be calculated based on the estimates of the returns over that time as follows.

$$\text{ROCE} = \frac{\text{Average annual profit before interest payable and tax}}{\text{Capital employed}} \times 100\%$$

**EXAMPLE**

It is estimated that a company will receive income net of direct costs of £100,000 p.a. over the three-year life of a project, Project A. An alternative three-year project, Project B, will generate £324,000 at the end of the third year.

The initial capital required for either project is £240,000, which will be used to acquire a machine that will be fully depreciated and scrapped at the end of this time.

Which project, if either, should be undertaken, on the basis that the alternative use for this cash is to place it on deposit for three years earning compound interest at 10% p.a.?

## SOLUTION

***Project A***

| **Over Three Years** | **£** |
|---|---|
| Total net income | 300,000 |
| Total depreciation | (240,000) |
| Total profit before interest payable | 60,000 |
| Average annual profit | £20,000 |

ROCE $= \frac{£20,000}{£240,000} \times 100\%$

**= 8.33% p.a.**

***Project B***

| **Over Three Years** | **£** |
|---|---|
| Total net income | 324,000 |
| Total depreciation | (240,000) |
| Total profit before interest payable | 84,000 |
| Average annual profit | £28,000 |

ROCE $= \frac{£28,000}{£240,000} \times 100\%$

**= 11.67% p.a.**

Clearly, Project B appears better than Project A under this criterion, but should it be undertaken?

Having calculated the ROCE for our projects, we need a required rate for comparison purposes in order to make our decision. This could be the bank account return of 10% compound interest, which gives the following.

***Bank Account***

| **Year** | **Balance B/F** | **Interest for Year** | **Balance C/F** |
|---|---|---|---|
| | **£** | **£** | **£** |
| 1 | 240,000 | 24,000 | 264,000 |
| 2 | 264,000 | 26,400 | 290,400 |
| 3 | 290,400 | 29,040 | 319,440 |
| | | 79,440 | |
| Average annual profit | | 26,480 | |

ROCE $= \frac{£26,480}{£240,000} \times 100\%$

**= 11.03% p.a.**

As we can see, Project B generates a higher return than this, hence in the absence of any other information, we should accept Project B.

## Advantages and disadvantages of ROCE

### Advantages

ROCE has a number of advantages that make it useful for investment appraisal purposes.

- **Easy to calculate**

  This may seem a somewhat fatuous comment, since a 'correct' decision would be rather more important than saving time. However, given that we are likely to be dealing with rough estimates of anticipated profitability, there could certainly be occasions where a 'rough and ready' measure would be quite sufficient.

- **Easy to understand**

  This again may seem irrelevant, but at the end of the day, it is management who have to make the decision and shareholders who have to be convinced. We cannot expect that all management and shareholders should be skilled in corporate finance techniques.

- **Clearly illustrates profitability**

  If high profits are required, this is certainly a way of selecting the project that will achieve them.

### Disadvantages

- **Timing of profits**

  It is an average, and hence takes no account of the timing of the profits throughout the project period.

- **Lives of projects**

  As an average, it takes no account of the lives of the projects being considered, which may be different.

- **Size of investment**

  As a relative measure (percentage) it takes no account of the size of the initial investment required.

  This is mainly a problem when comparing alternative projects. If Project A required an investment of £100,000 and yielded a ROCE of 10%, whereas Project B required an investment of only £10,000 but yielded 20%, it would not be possible to say that in all circumstances B was the better.

  In order to be able to reach a decision, we would need to know what return the remaining £90,000, not invested in Project B, could be expected to yield.

- **Assumes we invest for profit**

  It is a profit measure and as such is only a worthwhile measure if high profits are the investor's main objective. In most circumstances, cash flow is usually more important than profits. However, if profits are roughly equivalent to cash flows, then ROCE may also maximise cash returns to investors.

## Price to book ratio

The price to book ratio calculates a relationship between the market value of the equity of a company and its accounting value in the balance sheet, the 'book value'. We can calculate the ratio as follows:

Price to book ratio = Equity value/ equity shareholders' funds or net assets

**EXAMPLE**

A manufacturing company has net assets of £75.2m and a share price of £3.95, with 20.75 million ordinary shares in issue. What is its price to book multiple?

**SOLUTION**

Price to book multiple = market value of equity/net asset value

= (3.95 × 20.75)/75.2

= 81.9625/75.2

= 1.1×

The answer calculated is a 'multiple', in other words, it gives a number of 'times' the market value of a company is greater than the book value. It gives a rating – the higher the multiple calculated, the more expensive the share is compared to its net asset value.

In our example, the market value of the company is 1.1× greater than the value of its net assets. The value of the company is in line with its net assets value, which is more likely with a capital intensive business where the assets are a factor determining overall value.

The ratio means little in isolation; a comparative price to book ratio is required. This could be a sector company comparable or an industry or market average. To be meaningful, an analyst must take care to choose comparables so as to minimise differences in net asset value attributable to accounting policy choices or business operations. If we knew that the sector average price to book multiple for competitor companies was 0.8x, we could conclude that our company is more highly rated (ie expensive) than its peers.

It is possible to adjust the balance sheet net asset value to make it more meaningful. Net assets can be adjusted to reflect differences in accounting policy and also to include any assets or liabilities that are off balance sheet. Both sets of adjustments would make the net asset values of a peer group more comparable.

### Advantages

- Net asset value is calculated based on **objective accounting standards** and this provides a means of comparison between companies. Assuming the companies are drawn from a peer group sharing common characteristics, eg sector, then we may be able to draw meaningful conclusions about the relative rating and value of different equity investments.
- In some **sectors**, net assets may be a good guide to value. This is more likely for more capital intensive companies eg manufacturing.
- Analysts do use price to book multiples as an indication of the 'underlying' **security** in a share. High price to book multiples flag up scenarios where market values are not represented by underlying net assets. This may not be problematic but it highlights cases which required further investigation by analysts.
- Price to book multiples can be a means to assess relative **size differentials** of two entities in a proposed merger of companies.

### Disadvantages

- **Empirical evidence** shows that net asset multiples do not work. In general, the accounting value of a business is not a good guide to its stock market value. The composition of the balance sheet does not determine the value a business generates. Value is often driven by intangible assets (such as technical know-how; market position; branding; internally-generated goodwill) which are off balance sheet. Any adjustments to make the net asset value a more reflective figure and include intangibles will be highly subjective and difficult to quantify.

- Net asset value is an **accounting measure** and thus accounting policy choices made by companies will distort comparability in any peer group.

### Different uses of asset-based valuations

- For some **sectors**. Price to book multiples are important in sectors where assets determine business performance, such as property companies, banks and investment trusts.
- To establish **the net realisable value of a business**. The net asset value of the business is of relevance to existing shareholders, since it represents a starting point for the minimum sum for which they should be prepared to sell the company. There is no point in accepting £1m for a business when the assets could have been sold off separately for £3m.
- As a measure of **security** in a share value. The calculation provides an assessment of the asset backing of the company.
- For companies with **low or no profits or cash flows**. Net assets may be positive where profits are negative meaning that price/net asset ratios may be used instead of price/earnings ratios in these circumstances.
- In addition, the net asset value can be useful for businesses in **financial difficulties**. It establishes whether a business has a higher value as a going concern or on liquidation. If a company's cash flows from its operations have a lower present value than the liquidation value, then the company should be wound up and the proceeds reinvested in a more profitable area.

In calculating realisable values, care needs to be taken in assessing the values of non-current assets and inventories. If the break-up of the company is occurring over a rapid timescale or as a result of a forced sale, then values will be lower than if the business were run down in an orderly fashion over a period of time. In addition, any costs of disposal will need to be taken into account. These may include, for example, redundancy costs and taxation on asset disposals.

## Price to sales ratio

The price to sales ratio compares the market value of equity of a business to the revenue earned as follows

Price to sales ratio = Equity value/revenue

The multiple thus demonstrates the relationship between the share price and the company's recorded sales. The price to sales ratio is sometimes abbreviated as 'P/S' or 'PSR'. As with the price to book ratio, this multiple gives an idea of the relative rating of a particular business. A relatively low PSR can imply an under-rated business. The multiple can be analysed by breaking it down into two further ratios:

Price to sales = equity value/earnings × earnings/revenue

ie Price to sales = PE ratio × net profit margin

### Advantages

- The sales figure tends to be less volatile than other headings in the financial statements, eg earnings, and thus is easier to forecast and to compare between companies.

- The price to sales multiple is helpful for businesses which are in the early stage of development, perhaps with operating losses and very little debt. The current operating performance might thus be a very poor predictor of long-term profitability and value.
- If companies in a sector have very different accounting policies or use different accounting regulations, revenue can be the easiest and 'cleanest' figure to compare.
- The sales multiple approach might be particularly useful for owner-managed businesses, where the cost structure may not be reflective of business operating performance. For example, the level of salaries/ drawings may be unusually high or low, making earnings an unreliable figure.

### Disadvantages

- The ratio **ignores the cost structure** of the business. It is very difficult to reach valuation conclusions without taking into account the running costs and profitability of the business.
- Price to sales also **excludes capital structure**. The numerator takes into account the company's capital structure whereas the denominator does not. The price to sales multiple is therefore really only helpful if comparing two companies with the same capital structure – which is unlikely to be the case.

Both of these weakness are addressed by the price earnings ratio.

## Price-to-earnings ratio

The typical method of valuing a company based on its earnings levels is to use the price-to-earnings (P/E) ratio, calculated as

$$\text{P/E ratio} = \frac{\text{Price per share}}{\text{Earnings per share}} = \frac{\text{Equity value}}{\text{Net income}}$$

The P/E ratio for a similar quoted company can be inserted into the formula along with the earnings per share of a company we wish to value. The required valuation will be the missing figure.

### Advantages

- The P/E multiple is commonly used as it is based on earnings, which is recognised as the key driver of value (earnings power). The key assumption underlying the P/E valuation approach is that earnings yields are similar for comparable quoted and unquoted companies. This may be appropriate where earnings are a good indicator of value, ie not distorted by dubious accountancy practices, and of high quality, ie a good indicator of underlying or trend earnings and not distorted by one-off exceptional items.
- It also requires that the comparables being used are similar, not only in terms of their business mix, but also in their capital structure and choice of accounting policies.

## Problems with using P/E ratios

Finding wholly comparable companies in a peer group is difficult due to:

- Differences in accounting policies
- Different growth levels
- Different levels of gearing
- Different levels of liquidity
- Different levels of business risk

One of the reasons that earnings-based approaches work is that a company's earnings can be virtually equivalent to its cash flow. This may be the case for a company that is in a stable market and is not expanding significantly. However, it will be a less reliable indicator of value where a company's cash flows and earnings are significantly different. This may occur due to dubious accounting practices, creation of provisions, high levels of capital expenditure and increases in working capital levels. It may be better for analysts to base the P/E calculation on an 'adjusted' or 'headline' measure of EPS, rather than the IAS 33 reported EPS. An adjusted EPS should be prepared so as to focus on the trading performance of the business in the period and, as such, it eliminates one-offs such as exceptional items and revaluation gains and losses. Care must be taken, though, that all adjustments really are 'one-offs'; for example a company that incurs restructuring costs every year should treat them as part of recurring earnings.

Moreover, the P/E approach cannot be used for loss-making companies (PSR, asset based or cash flow based valuations will be more appropriate). The earnings per share figure is extremely susceptible to differences in accounting policies. It is affected by different inventory valuation, provisioning, depreciation and deferred taxation policies. Empirical studies show that P/E ratios diverge widely both between and within sectors. The P/E ratio is therefore very subjective and difficult to compare between companies, sectors and countries.

Ideally, the P/E ratio could be adjusted to reflect these differences. For example, it is usually the case that unlisted companies are valued at, say, a 30% discount to an equivalent listed company to reflect the lack of liquidity in the shares. However, the assumptions that need to be made and the theoretical nature of such adjustments means that, if additional sophistication is required, it may be better to use a cash-based approach to valuation from the very start.

P/E ratios may also be based on 'pro-forma' earnings that have been adjusted to take account of the transaction under consideration. An example might be a flotation where the finance being raised is, for the most part, being used to reduce the indebtedness of the company. This is a common situation where the floating company was originally a management buy-out. The earnings are restated to allow for a much lower interest charge.

# 3 Adjusted Traditional Methods

The limitations of P/E ratios are to some extent addressed by using other multiples such as those based on operating profit (earnings before interest and tax). Before we consider these multiples we need to review some important definitions of value. Not all multiples give the same measure of value and we need to be able to recognize the differences and adjust between the two.

## Different measures of value

There are two key measures of value: enterprise and equity value. A distinction is also made with the concept of 'transaction value'.

### Enterprise and equity value

**Enterprise value** represents the total value of a business or enterprise to all providers of capital, including equity investors, preference share investors, debt investors and minority interests. It can be calculated by adding the company's market capitalisation and the market value of its gross borrowings, and deducting any cash balances. Short-term liquid financial investments that can readily converted to cash are also deducted. Any additional sources of capital should also be added, ie the market value of preference shares and minority interest. In practice we may not have the information to put all sources of finance at market value, and so we can assume the latest balance sheet is a reasonable proxy where market value information is not available.

Enterprise value = Market capitalisation + Gross debt – Cash + Preference shares – Minority interest

**Equity value** represents the value of the business to the providers of equity finance. It is calculated after deducting the values of debt, preference shares and minority interests from enterprise value.

Equity value = Number of ordinary shares x share price

**In essence therefore:**

| | |
|---|---|
| Enterprise value | x |
| Less: Value of net debt | x |
| Equity value | x |

Although it may seem more appropriate to focus on equity values at first sight, since we are trying to identify the value of the business to its equity investors, enterprise value has an important part to play in the valuation process. The reason for this is that it **ignores the level of gearing** and other related financial factors when calculating the value of any business. As such, it can be an easy and consistent way to value equity – first through calculating the enterprise value and then deducting the value of other sources of finance.

In addition, enterprise value is a useful benchmark for comparisons across companies. Since many companies in different countries will have different gearing levels, even though they are in the same industry, it will not be easy to compare their businesses based on equity values. A more appropriate comparison would be to look at multiples based on enterprise values. For example, multiples based on revenue, research and development costs, number of locations, etc, can be calculated and compared across the international sector.

When calculating a multiple on the basis of equity value, an earnings figure relevant to equity should be used (ie after tax and minority interests such as P/E ratio). Where the comparison is being made on the basis of enterprise value, an earnings figure should be based upon profits available to all providers of finance (ie before interest and tax such as EBIT).

Finding a company on either a high or low multiple relative to its sector does not, of course, tell you whether or not the company is a good buy. An expensive company may be justifiably on a high multiple due to expectations of growth arising from its competitive advantages in the market place in question. A cheap company may be on a low multiple because it has no distinguishing characteristics and can offer no competitive threat. Alternatively, it may be that the stock market has failed to value the company in question correctly. One of the objectives of analysis is to identify which is likely to be the correct answer.

## Enterprise-based valuations

### Advantages of using an enterprise-based methodology

- It values the business as a whole, regardless of how it is being financed. It therefore can provide a measure of value which is independent of how the business is financed.
- It allows better comparison between different companies in the same sector, as it excludes the level of gearing in the different businesses.
- It allows a multiple to be calculated based on both EBIT and EBITDA, thus giving a relative valuation based on the trading activities of the business.
- It allows the valuer to focus on multiples where accounting differences between businesses may be minimised, for example EBITDA multiples.
- It allows the valuer to exclude non-core assets from the valuation.
- Enterprise value is useful for valuing businesses where a change of control is envisaged. It allows the potential purchaser to impose their own required capital structure.

### Disadvantages of using an enterprise-based methodology

- It can be difficult to establish the market value of the borrowings, to deduct from enterprise value before arriving at the market value of the equity. Subtracting the book value of debt is not always a good proxy as interest rates may have changed and the accounts may be out-of-date.
- It can also be difficult to establish a reasonable valuation for other sources of finance, such as minority interest and pension liabilities.
- Forecast EBIT and EBITDA measures are less readily available than forecast price earnings ratios.

## TASK

Use the balance sheet of Kingfisher and the market data below to estimate the equity value and enterprise value of Kingfisher.

## Consolidated balance sheet

At 31 January 2015

| £ millions | Notes | 2014/15 | 2013/14 |
|---|---|---|---|
| **Non-current assets** | | | |
| Goodwill | 12 | **2,414** | 2,417 |
| Other intangible assets | 13 | **258** | 222 |
| Property, plant and equipment | 14 | **3,203** | 3,625 |
| Investment property | 15 | **30** | 50 |
| Investments in joint ventures and associates | 16 | **28** | 32 |
| Post-employment benefits | 27 | **194** | – |
| Deferred tax assets | 25 | **10** | 12 |
| Derivative assets | 23 | **52** | 40 |
| Other receivables | 18 | **7** | 15 |
| | | **6,196** | 6,413 |
| **Current assets** | | | |
| Inventories | 17 | **2,021** | 2,054 |
| Trade and other receivables | 18 | **537** | 590 |
| Derivative assets | 23 | **70** | 5 |
| Current tax assets | | **6** | 15 |
| Short-term deposits | 19 | **48** | – |
| Cash and cash equivalents | 20 | **561** | 535 |
| Assets held for sale | 34 | **274** | 208 |
| | | **3,517** | 3,407 |
| **Total assets** | | **9,713** | 9,820 |

| | | | |
|---|---|---|---|
| **Current liabilities** | | | |
| Trade and other payables | 21 | **(2,323)** | (2,486) |
| Borrowings | 22 | **(105)** | (94) |
| Derivative liabilities | 23 | **(10)** | (27) |
| Current tax liabilities | | **(87)** | (175) |
| Provisions | 26 | **(13)** | (8) |
| Liabilities held for sale | 34 | **(195)** | – |
| | | **(2,733)** | (2,790) |
| **Non-current liabilities** | | | |
| Other payables | 21 | **(64)** | (86) |
| Borrowings | 22 | **(232)** | (230) |
| Deferred tax liabilities | 25 | **(329)** | (251) |
| Provisions | 26 | **(34)** | (46) |
| Post-employment benefits | 27 | **(82)** | (100) |
| | | **(741)** | (713) |
| **Total liabilities** | | **(3,474)** | (3,503) |
| **Net assets** | 4 | **6,239** | 6,317 |
| **Equity** | | | |
| Share capital | 28 | **369** | 373 |
| Share premium | | **2,214** | 2,209 |
| Own shares held in ESOP trust | | **(26)** | (35) |
| Retained earnings | | **3,661** | 3,495 |
| Other reserves | 29 | **11** | 266 |
| **Total attributable to equity shareholders of the Company** | | **6,229** | 6,308 |
| Non-controlling interests | | **10** | 9 |
| **Total equity** | | **6,239** | 6,317 |

**Balance sheet**

Other market data:

Number of ordinary shares in issue: 2,350 million

Share price: 353.93pAssume all borrowings in the balance sheet are stated at current market value

## SOLUTION

Equity value = £ £3.5393 x 2,350m = £8,317.36m

Enterprise value:

| | **£m** |
|---|---|
| Equity value | 8317.36 |
| Short term borrowings | 105 |
| Long term borrowings | 232 |
| Minority interests | 10 |
| Cash and cash equivalents | (561) |
| Enterprise value | £8,103.36 |

## Transaction value

Transaction value assumes a **change of control**. It reflects the cost of buying the entire company and as such the enterprise value should be the starting point when calculating it. In addition, transaction value should reflect that the acquirer of the company will need to pay a control premium, to reflect the value of a controlling stake. The acquirer will justify this to acquiring company shareholders by the synergistic benefits expected from the transaction.

When applying a control premium to the value of a company, the premium should be applied to the equity value rather than the enterprise value. The reason for this is that it is equity that controls the business rather than debt. As a result, there is no reason to pay a control premium for the debt element of the business.

Transaction value = (Equity value + control premium) + Gross debt – Cash + Preference shares + Minority interest

**TASK**

Calculate a transaction value for Kingfisher, using the data above and using a control premium of 30%.

**SOLUTION**

Transaction value = (8317.36 × 1.3) + 105 + 232 + 10 – 561 = £10,598.57m

## 4 Earnings Before Interest and Tax Multiple

Instead of using P/E ratios, which rely on a post-tax figure for earnings, it is possible to do a similar calculation based upon earnings before interest and tax (EBIT). Published EBIT multiples are not so widely available as P/E ratios.

$$\text{EBIT multiple} = \frac{\text{Enterprise value}}{\text{EBIT}}$$

The idea of the EBIT multiple is that it removes distortions caused by the company's gearing structure or tax position, which may change if the company is acquired and merged into a larger group.

Since the EBIT multiple is being based on an earnings figure before interest is paid, it is effectively valuing the whole of the firm rather than just the part of the firm that belongs to equity investors. The earnings before interest need to be used to pay off providers of debt as well as equity finance. In order to find the value of the firm's equity, the value of the debt financing will need to be deducted from the enterprise value calculated.

As with the P/E ratio, the EBIT multiple has problems of comparability across companies. Even though it is based on a pre-interest figure, it is nevertheless affected by the level of gearing, since it is possible that high levels of gearing may adversely affect the operating cash flows of the business.

## 5 Earnings Before Interest, Tax, Depreciation and Amortisation Multiple

It is possible to base earnings multiples on various other definitions of earnings. For example, a multiple based on earnings before interest, tax, depreciation and amortisation (EBITDA).

$$\text{EBITDA multiple} = \frac{\text{Enterprise Value}}{\text{EBITDA}}$$

The benefit of EBITDA multiples is that they strip out the accounting items of depreciation and amortisation, which may vary substantially between companies. EBITDA therefore provides a better basis for comparison between companies, as well as offering the same advantages as the EBIT multiples in that the multiples exclude the impact of a company's gearing structure or tax position. In addition, by excluding two of the main non-cash expenses, the EBITDA multiple is moving towards a normalised cash-based figure for the company in question.

# 6 Industry 'Rule of Thumb' Methods

Industry rules of thumb provide an alternative valuation method. Rules of thumb are sector-specific benchmarks against which valuations of companies can be compared. They are based on a key driver of value in a particular industry. Some examples of industry rules of thumb are:

- Airlines – £ per revenue passenger mile (RPM);
- Oil industry – £/barrel.
- Professional firms and retail stores – multiple (×) of revenue.
- Fund managers – multiple (×) of funds under management.
- Internet service providers and mobile phone companies – £/subscriber.
- Hotels – £/room.

The use of such valuations is similar to earnings-based multiples in that they give a quick and easy, rough indication of value. They can be used as a way to explain valuation in terms of industry metrics that will be widely understood. Rules of thumb are however too broad brush to be considered in isolation. They may be useful as a final cross-check on a valuation derived from a different method.

## Task

Use the following information to derive an Equity Value range for Build Limited, based on multiples calculated for:

(a) EBIT
(b) EBITDA
(c) Revenue
(d) Net asset value

The following financial information is available for Build.

**All figures in £m**

| | **2015 Historic** | **2016 Forecast** |
|---|---|---|
| Revenue | 39.6 | 42.1 |
| Operating profit | 8.7 | 9.2 |
| Depreciation | 0.5 | 0.6 |
| Amortisation | 0.3 | 0.3 |
| Net asset value | 24.4 | |
| Net debt | 13.0 | |

The closest comparable company to Build Limited has been identified as its competitor House plc, for which you have been able to ascertain the following financial data.

**All figures in £m**

| | **2015 Historic** | **2016 Forecast** |
|---|---|---|
| Revenue | 57.7 | 61.9 |
| Operating profit | 10.0 | 12.6 |
| Depreciation | 2.2 | 2.2 |
| Amortisation | – | – |
| Net asset value | 48.1 | |
| Net debt | 25.0 | |

Today's share price for House plc is 175p. House has 27,300,000 shares in issue.

## Solution

**Stage One – Calculating multiples for House plc**

Equity value = £1.75 × 27.3m = £47.8m

Enterprise value = £47.8m + £25.0m = £72.8m

| | 2015 | 2016 |
|---|---|---|
| EBIT multiples | 72.8/10= 7.3× | 72.8/12.6= 5.8× |
| EBITDA multiples | 72.8/(10+2.2)= 6.0× | 72.8/(12.6+2.2)= 4.9× |
| Revenue multiples | 72.8/57.7= 1.3× | 72.8/61.9= 1.2× |
| NAV multiples | 47.8/48.1= 1.0× | |

**Stage Two – Apply multiples to value Build**

| Valuation based on: | 2015 | 2016 |
|---|---|---|
| EBIT | 7.3× × £8.7m= £63.5m (EV) | 5.8× × £9.2m= £53.4m (EV) |
| EBITDA | 6.0× × £9.5m= £57.0m (EV) | 4.9× × £10.1m= £49.4m (EV) |
| Revenue | 1.3× × £39.6m= £51.4m (EV) | 1.2× × £42.1m= £50.5m (EV) |
| NAV | 1.0× × £24.4m= £24.4m (MV) | |

EV = Enterprise value

MV = Equity value

Suggested valuation range (EV): £50m – £55m; (MV) £37m – £42m

With a discount of 30% for a private company valuation, reflecting lack of marketability of the shares (MV): £26m – £30m

## Valuation of synergies

Synergies are the financial benefits arising as a result of a transaction. They need to be quantified as part of the valuation process. As discussed above, an acquiring company is likely to have to pay a bid premium as part of the transaction value for a deal. This is to compensate target company shareholders for relinquishing control of their business. Paying a bid premium needs to be justified to acquiring company shareholders by the value that will be generated from the acquisition in the way of synergies. Acquiring company shareholders will place a ceiling on the level of acceptable bid premium equal to the present value of the synergies expected to be received.

Synergies are derived from three sources.

- Cost savings.
- Revenue enhancement.
- One-off cash inflows.

### Cost savings

Synergistic cost savings can arise in the combined operations from operational reasons, such as eliminating duplication in the merged entity, as well as improvements in the financing structure of the business.

Examples of both types of cost savings are as follows.

- Reducing head-count in administrative functions.
- Economies of scale leading to improved production efficiencies.

- Gaining critical mass and market dominance, giving ability to set prices and negotiate bulk ordering discounts.
- Eliminating excess production capacity.
- Reducing the group's effective tax rate. This could for example result from acquiring foreign operations that are taxed at a lower rate than the UK.
- Improving free cash flow. The acquisition may have the effect of reducing business seasonality, leading to an improvement in the entity's credit rating and an overall cheaper cost of debt.

### Revenue enhancement

The merged entity can benefit from the following.

- Cross-selling products to two separate customer bases.
- Common distribution channels.
- Common advertising, sales promotion and warehousing.

### One-off cash inflows

Non-recurring cash savings arise from the following.

- Disposal of surplus assets.
- One-off tax credits.
- Disposal of non-core elements of the business.

## Quantifying synergies

Once the source of the synergies has been highlighted, it is necessary to estimate the financial effect and also the timing of the cash inflows. A discounted cash flow forecast can then be prepared which computes a present value of the synergies.

Synergies can be cash outflows as well as cash inflows. The valuer should also include the negative impact of the transaction, for example, cash outflows arising due to reorganisation and redundancies or delays in anticipated revenue streams being realised.

## Chapter Roundup

**Module 2, Chapter 8: Traditional Methods of Equity Analysis**

You are required to **calculate** and **comment on your conclusions** from using the following methods of equity analysis:

1 Earnings per share
2 Return on capital employed
3 Price/book ratio
4 Price/sales ratio
5 Price/earnings ratio

In each case, you need to be able to discuss **when the use of the measure is appropriate**. You also need to be able to state the **advantages** of the method and provide a list of **reservations** and **assumptions**.

The calculations here tend to be straight-forward. Most credit from the examiner will thus be awarded for relevant discussion around the techniques, involving your views on the suitability of the method and your opinion on the insightfulness of your results.

# UNDERSTANDING RISK AND RETURN

chapter 9

## Contents


| | | |
|---|---|---|
| 1 | Introduction | 182 |
| 2 | Return | 182 |
| 3 | Risk | 184 |
| 4 | Indifference Curves | 188 |
| 5 | Investment Appraisal Problems | 192 |
| 6 | Conclusion | 192 |
| 7 | Combining Investments' Risks and Returns | 193 |
| 8 | Portfolio Selection – The Efficient Frontier | 201 |
| 9 | Risk-Free Investments – The Capital Market Line | 206 |

# 1 Introduction

In a certain world, the return from an investment would always be exactly as expected and there would be no risk. The investor would merely have to compare the returns available on different investments and choose those that offered the highest returns.

Unfortunately, the existence of uncertainty means that the returns on investments are not always as expected, and there is some risk involved.

Almost all investment opportunities involve a risk. All securities quoted on the Stock Exchange are subject to risk. Different types of security will have different kinds of risk attached to them, for example, UK government securities do not suffer a significant risk of default but are vulnerable to changes in interest rates. However, the effect of all these different kinds of risk is the same, in that the actual returns achieved will be different from those expected by the investor. The riskier the investment, the more likely it is that the expected return will not be reached or that the shortfall from the return will be greater.

A key assumption is that investors are rational and risk averse. Note that risk adversity does not mean that an investor is not prepared to take on risk. It merely implies that an investor will seek compensation for risk by means of a higher return. But how do we measure risk and how can we relate risk and return?

If we are to undertake a systematic appraisal of an investment opportunity, we must be able to incorporate all relevant factors. In order to incorporate these factors into our analysis, we must be able to quantify them. Our concern here is what causes risk and how risk and return can be quantified in a standardised way.

# 2 Return

## Holding period return

### Introduction

When deciding on which investments to hold in a portfolio, an investor has to be able to compare them directly. One measure of the return from an investment would be the holding period return.

**TASK**

Suppose investment A cost £100 and at the end of six months returns £10, before being sold for £110. How can it be compared with investment B, bought at £50, held for one year and then sold for £70 with no income paid out? Obviously, the different costs must be taken into account, as well as the different returns and time periods involved.

### Basic calculation

Calculating the percentage holding period return for each investment avoids the problem of comparing different size investments. This return is simply the gain during the period held (money received less cost) divided by the initial cost, ie

$$r_p = \frac{D_1 + P_1 - P_0}{P_0} \times 100\%$$

where

$r_p$ = holding period return

$D_1$ = any returns paid out during the period

$P_0$ = the cost

$P_1$ = the value of the investment at the end of the holding period

**SOLUTION**

Using this equation, the holding period returns of investments A and B can be calculated as follows.

***Investment A***

$$r_a = \frac{D_1 + P_1 - P_0}{P_0} \times 100\%$$

$$r_a = \frac{10 + 110 - 100}{100} \times 100\% = 20\% \text{ in six months}$$

***Investment B***

$$r_b = \frac{D_1 + P_1 - P_0}{P_0} \times 100\%$$

$$r_b = \frac{0 + 70 - 50}{50} \times 100\% = 40\% \text{ in a year}$$

### Using the Results – Annualising

The holding period returns of A and B are not yet directly comparable, since B was invested for twice as long as A. When A was sold, the proceeds could have been reinvested for another six months. To compare the returns they must be for a standard period. This is achieved by using the equivalent period interest rate formula to annualise the returns as follows.

**SOLUTION**

***Investment A***

$r_a$ = 20% in six months

Hence, annualising this return, we get

$1 + r = (1 + R)^n$

$1 + r = 1.2^2 = 1.44$

$r = 0.44$ or 44% p.a.

***Investment B***

$r_b$ = 40% p.a.

We have now got a standardised measure of return, being either the internal rate of return (IRR) or the holding period return. However, the point is that we do not know the return with certainty on the day we invest. We must, therefore, use the values that we expect to arise, but how can these be calculated? We consider this below.

# 3 RISK

## Types of risk

### Introduction

There are several different types of risk that can lead to variability in return on an investment. Some investments, such as gilts, will have few risks attached to them, whereas company shares will be subject to many possible reasons for fluctuations in return.

### Uncertainty of income

The risk of uncertainty of income is a risk to which all Ordinary shareholders are subject. This can be seen by looking at the holding period return on an Ordinary share, which can be written as

$$rp = r_p \frac{D_1 + P_1 - P_0}{P_0} \times 100\%$$

If we are investing now, all we know for certain is P0, the current market price. We have no idea what the price will be when we sell, nor what income payments we will receive. This uncertainty could be caused by such factors as the following.

### Interest rates

Changes in interest rates are liable to impact upon the future returns resulting from an investment opportunity either through:

- Impacting on the returns that are paid; or
- Impacting on the market value at the end of the period.

For example, increased interest rates tend to have an adverse impact on a company's trading performance, as more profits are consumed in servicing any debt financing. Of course, the opposite is true for net lenders.

In addition, increased interest rates will, in all probability, increase investors' required rates of return, reducing the market values of both equity and debt investments.

### Inflation

Inflation may have two effects on any investment opportunity.

- Increase the nominal cash flow returns from the investment.
- Increase the investor's required rate of return.

### Exchange rates

The main way in which the government attempts to control exchange rates is by the use of interest rates. If UK interest rates are high, relative to those in other countries, then sterling will be an attractive currency in which to invest. This demand for sterling should boost or support the exchange rate.

From the point of view of companies and share performance, a high exchange rate will make imports cheaper and exports more expensive abroad. As a result, we could expect importers' profits to rise and exporters' profits to fall.

For international groups, there will be another effect on their reported assets and profits arising from overseas subsidiaries. As sterling strengthens, the value of anything denominated in a foreign currency will fall, ie the reported assets and profits of overseas subsidiaries will fall.

### Tax rates

An increase in tax rates due to, say, the adoption of a tight fiscal policy by a government will have the effect of reducing the returns from any investments (unless they are tax free). This means that share prices will probably fall as corporate tax as well as personal tax reduces investors' returns.

### Economic state

The general economic state (boom to recession) is likely to impact on the demand for company products driving equities up (boom) or down (recession).

It will be the expectations of the future economic environment that will have an effect on prices now.

### Default risk

If a company does badly, it may be unable to pay the interest on a fixed interest security or to repay the principal on maturity. In the UK, only gilts (fixed interest securities issued or guaranteed by the UK government) are not subject to default risk – the government is the only borrower that can always avoid default in the last resort by printing more money.

All types of fixed interest corporate debt are subject to default risk, from debenture stocks secured on the assets of the company to unsecured loan stocks, but each will be subject to a different level of risk.

On default, debenture holders can appoint a receiver whose job it is to realise the security they hold and, if it is worth at least the sum they are owed on realisation, they will suffer no loss. Unsecured loan stock holders have no security and rank equal with the other unsecured creditors of the company.

Ordinary shareholders do not suffer default risk since they are not entitled to any particular level of income or to any specified capital repayment that might run the risk of not being paid.

Preference shareholders lie somewhere between fixed interest debt holders and Ordinary shareholders. They are entitled to fixed dividend payments if any dividends are paid. However, if these are not made, the company is not legally in default, since preference shareholders are part-owners and not creditors of the company.

### Summary of other influences

| | Equity Prices | Bond Prices | Currency |
|---|---|---|---|
| **Real GDP** | | | |
| Up | Up | Down | Up |
| Down | Down | Up | Down |
| **Consumer prices** | | | |
| Up | Up | Down | Down |
| Down | Down | Up | Up |
| **Trade balance** | | | |
| Improves | Up | Up | Up |
| Worsens | Down | Down | Down |
| **Money supply growth** | | | |
| Up | Neutral | Down | Down |
| Down | Down | Up | Up |

| **Retail sales** | | | |
|---|---|---|---|
| Up | Up | Down | Up |
| Down | Down | Up | Down |
| **Industrial production** | | | |
| Up | Up | Down | Up |
| Down | Down | Up | Down |

## Measurement of expected return and risk

Having identified the different types of risk which exist and realising that they are the result of the possibility of different states of the world occurring in the future, how can we quantify the risk and likely return of any investment?

We can use probabilities to describe the likelihood of each possible state of the world occurring and estimate the returns and values arising, given that state of the world. We can then establish:

- An expected return
- A measure of risk

### Task

The shareholders in an ungeared company have a required rate of return of 10% per annum. The company can invest £100 in a one-year project, for which the holding period returns are expected to fall within the following range of possibilities.

| Probability | Return £ |
|---|---|
| 25 | 100 |
| 45 | 110 |
| 30 | 120 |

Should the investment be undertaken?

### Solution

First, we could calculate the expected rate of return as

| Probability % | Return % | Expected % |
|---|---|---|
| 25 | 0 | 0.0 |
| 45 | 10 | 4.5 |
| 30 | 20 | 6.0 |
| Expected return $(\bar{r})$ = | | 10.5 |

On the basis that the expected return is 10.5% and the required rate of return of the shareholders 10%, we may be tempted to believe that we should accept the project. The problem is that while returns considerably in excess of 10% could occur, there is also a possibility that returns could be considerably below 10%, which may not be acceptable.

This variability is the risk that we face and in deciding on any investment we have to cope with the fact that there is a range of possible outcomes.

In determining their required return from the company of 10%, the shareholders will have taken account of the risk that they expect to face from its current operations, ie the variability of the current returns. However, that is unlikely to be identical to the risk from this project, hence the 10% cost of capital may not be appropriate. If the project is more risky, the investors would require a higher return as we noted above.

Thus, we need to quantify the level of risk involved.

## Variance and standard deviation

To measure the degree of variability of an investment (i), we normally use either:

- The variance ($\sigma_i^2$); or
- The standard deviation ($\sigma_i$);

where each possible return $r_i$ occurs with probability p and the expected return is denoted by $\bar{r}_i$.

The variance is the expected value of the squares of the deviations of possible returns about the expected return $\bar{r}_i$. The standard deviation is the square root of the variance.

As a result, each summarises, as a single figure, the variability of the return (either up or down) about the expected value.

The standard deviation has the benefit that it is expressed in the same units as the returns (% in the example above), whereas the variance is in the original units squared. The standard deviation can be thought of as the average deviation from the expected value.

Other single measures could be calculated, for instance, by only looking at variances below the expected value, but none is as widely used as variance and standard deviation.

### Task

For the above example, determine the expected return and the standard deviation.

### Solution

| Probability (p) | Return $r_i$ | Expected Value | $r_i - \bar{r}_i$ | $(r_i - \bar{r}_i)^2$ | $p(r_i - \bar{r}_i)^2$ |
|---|---|---|---|---|---|
| % | % | % | | | |
| 25 | 0 | 0.0 | –10.5 | 110.25 | 27.5625 |
| 45 | 10 | 4.5 | –0.5 | 0.25 | 0.1125 |
| 30 | 20 | 6.0 | +9.5 | 90.25 | 27.0750 |
| Expected return ( $\bar{r}_i$ ) = | | 10.5 | Variance ($\sigma_i^2$) = | | 54.7500 |

Variance of returns ($\sigma_i^2$) about $\bar{r}_i$ = 54.75

Standard deviation of returns $\sigma_i = \sqrt{54.75} = 7.399\%$

### Interpretation of the result

Being able to calculate the expected return and associated risk is one thing, interpreting and using those results is another. How can we compare the project's expected returns and risk with the investors' required rate of return.

From the above example we have

- Expected net return $\bar{r}_i$ = 10.5%
- Associated risk $\sigma i$ = 7.399%
- Company's required rate of return is 10%

It is clear that the expected return does exceed that currently required by the company's shareholders, but how can we take account of the level of risk? What happens if the project increases the shareholders' risk? Is the extra return sufficient compensation?

In order to answer these questions, we need to look at the idea of risk-return **indifference curves** in general.

## 4 INDIFFERENCE CURVES

### Introduction

Consider an investor comparing a number of possible investment opportunities. For each investment the expected return and risk (standard deviation) could be measured, but we would still need a way of finding out the best combination of risk and return for that investor.

An indifference curve shows combinations of return and risk that are perceived as equivalent by an individual. The investor is indifferent between any investment opportunities lying on the same indifference curve. As such, they may be useful in choosing between different investments offering both differing risks and returns. They may not be necessary to make a decision in certain circumstances, but they are in others.

We will illustrate what indifference curves are and the advantages of using them in the following example.

**TASK**

Consider an investor who has the following choices of mutually exclusive investments that offer the following returns from an investment of £100.

| Probability | Return ($\bar{r}$) | | Risk ($\sigma$) | |
|---|---|---|---|---|
| % | £ | % | £ | % |
| A | 110 | 10 | 6 | 6 |
| B | 111 | 11 | 5 | 5 |
| C | 119 | 19 | 11 | 11 |
| D | 120 | 20 | 10 | 10 |

Assuming that our investor is rational and risk averse, which project will he choose?

## SOLUTION

We can represent the options we have on the following graph.

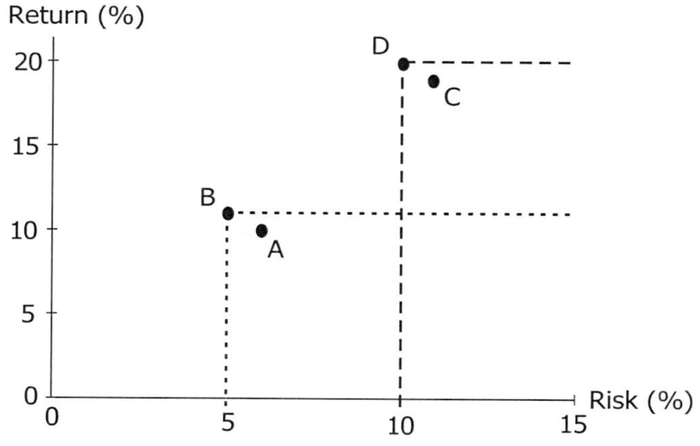


***Comparing Investments in Turn***

*A and B*

Comparing A and B, it is clear that B is preferable because it has a higher return for a lower level of risk. In fact, B dominates all investments in the rectangle shown (with B in the top left-hand corner).

*C and D*

Similarly, D will dominate C and any others in its rectangle.

*B and D*

But which of B and D is preferable? Whilst D offers the higher return, it does so at a higher risk than B. Which combination of return and risk is preferable to the investor?

We cannot answer this question without further information about this particular investor's reaction to risk.

This information, assuming it can be obtained, can be represented by a series of indifference curves.

## Indifference curves

If our rational and risk averse investor was able to obtain a risk-free return of £100 or an investment with a risk ($\sigma_i$) of £5, we would expect him to require a somewhat higher expected return from the risky investment for it to be as attractive as the investment with zero risk. He may, for instance, require an expected return of £107 to be indifferent.

Continuing this idea by considering more investments with higher level of risk, we would expect our investor to require still higher returns to make them as attractive as the initial risk-free £100 investment and we would perhaps end up with the following results.

| Return £ | Risk £ |
|---|---|
| 100 | 0 |
| 107 | 5 |
| 121 | 10 |
| 142 | 15 |
| 170 | 20 |
| 205 | 25 |

Our particular investor is indifferent between each of these investments and would, in each case, regard the extra return as exactly compensating for the additional risk.

Having ascertained our investor's attitude to risk, we could plot this on a graph as follows.

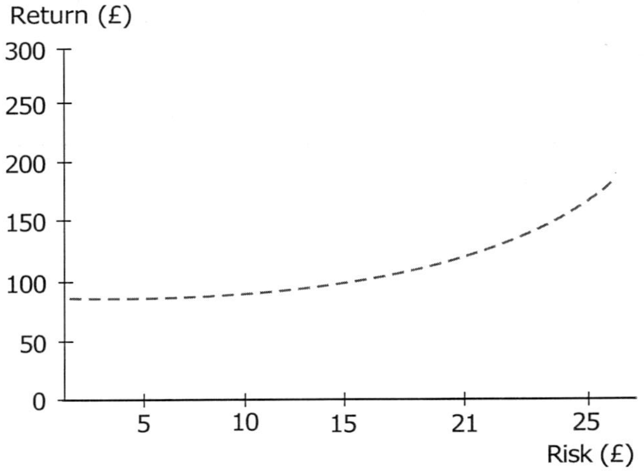


This curve is known as an **indifference curve**, in that our investor would be indifferent between all investments on the curve and a risk-free return of £100.

Clearly, there are plenty of other investment opportunities that do not fall on this line, as so far we have only considered those that would be thought of as equal to a risk-free £100. To get a complete picture of the investor's attitude to risk and return, we would need to establish the curves equivalent to all of the various possible risk-free levels, giving us something like the following.

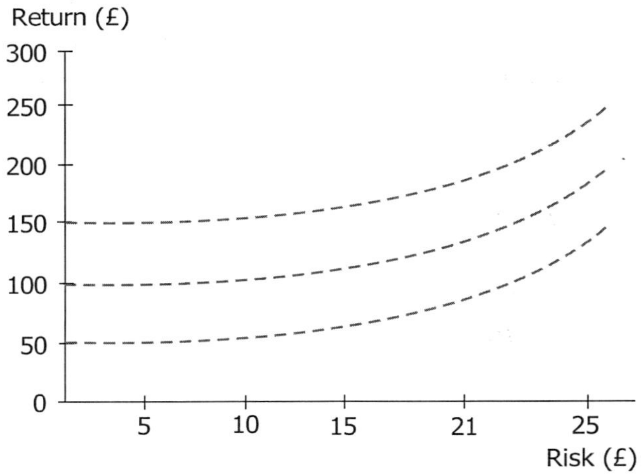


In this way, we could produce a complete series of indifference curves which would show our investor's overall attitude to risk.

**NB:** These indifference curves only represent the attitude of one particular investor and each investor will have a differing attitude and hence a different family of indifference curves. The more risk averse an investor is, the steeper his indifference curves. In other words, for a small increase in risk, a highly risk averse investor will seek a large increase in return.

## Use for investment decisions

Having established the indifference curves for our investor, can they be used to help the investor decide between the two investments, B and D, in the example above?

### SOLUTION

We had shortlisted two alternatives with the following returns and risks.

| Investment | Return £ | Risk £ |
|---|---|---|
| B | 111 | 5 |
| D | 120 | 10 |

Plotting these on a graph to show the indifference curves gives

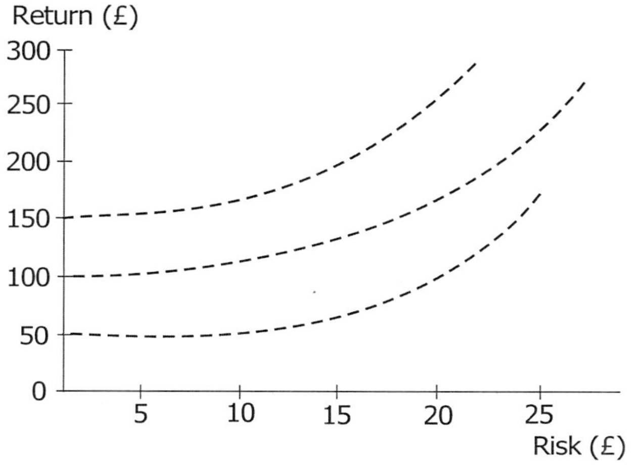


We can see from this that Investment B lies just above the indifference curve equivalent to a £100 return with zero risk, whereas Investment D lies just below it. We may, therefore, conclude that **our investor** would prefer Investment B. For him, the additional return offered by Investment D does not make up for the additional risk.

**NB:** This decision would be reversed by a less risk averse investor with flatter indifference curves. Remember that indifference curves are individual.

In more general terms, what we have seen is that the higher the indifference curve on which a particular investment lies, the more attractive the investment is to our investor.

## Characteristics of indifference curves

The general characteristics of indifference curves are as follows.

- They are upward sloping curves, indicating aversion to risk (a greater risk results in a greater required return).

- The more steeply they curve upwards, the more risk averse the investor (indifference curves are individual).
- All investments on one particular curve are viewed by the particular investor as equivalent to a risk-free investment giving the return shown on the vertical axis where the curve meets it.
- Comparing the risk-free equivalent for investments on each curve shows that the higher the curve, the more attractive it is to the investor.

# 5 Investment Appraisal Problems

What we can say from the above is that, given a single investor or a small group for whom the indifference curves can be established, we can decide between investment opportunities. However, this is not very practical for a large public company. The shareholders of such companies will be constantly changing and it would be impossible to be able to establish accurately an overall indifference curve structure at any point in time.

In the illustration above we saw that the company whose current required return was 10% was considering a project with an expected return of 10.5% and a risk ($\sigma_i$) of 7.399%. This firm had a cost of capital of 10%, which would have been determined to some extent by the risk perceived by the investors to their returns.

If the risk of the company's current operations was 7%, there would be two main problems in deciding whether the project is worthwhile.

- The project has a higher expected return than the current operations, but also a higher risk. A decision can only be reached using indifference curves, but it is important to remember that indifference curves are specific reflections of an individual's risk/return utilities. Therefore, whose indifference curves should be used, given that different curves can give different conclusions?
- We have measured the risk of the project in isolation. However, this may give meaningless information, since the project is not going to exist in isolation. What we should look at is the effect that the project has on the company's overall risk and return.

# 6 Conclusion

- Risk is the level of variability of possible returns offered by a particular investment.
- No investment should be appraised using return alone; it is the combined risk-return profile that is important.
- The risk of an investment may be measured by the standard deviation of its returns about the expected return.
- If one investment offers a higher/equal return for an equal/lower level of risk than another, then the choice between investments is clear. The one investment dominates the other.
- If one investment offers a higher level of return than another, but at a higher level of risk, then indifference curves are needed to decide between them.
- Where such a technique is to be used by a company wishing to appraise a project on behalf of its shareholders, two questions arise.
  - Whose indifference curves should be used?
  - Should the project be appraised in isolation from the company's current operations?

The following section on Portfolio Theory will answer these last two questions by introducing the idea of an 'efficient frontier' and correlation.

## Portfolio theory

We are aware from our study of risk, that consideration of expected returns in isolation is not adequate and that we must consider the overall risk-return profile of an investment opportunity.

We have also noted that we may encounter some problems in determining a suitable cost of capital if the risk of the investment differs significantly from that of the current portfolio of investments or operations of a company.

However, we have not as yet considered the effects of combining investment opportunities into a portfolio as a fund manager does with securities or a company does with projects.

Portfolio theory attempts to enable investments to be appraised by considering this overall risk-return profile and its impact on the current operations of the company or portfolio of the investor.

Portfolio theory enables the investor, given a set of investments from which to choose, to decide which combinations of these securities, or portfolios, give him or her, the best return for the risk involved. He or she can then choose the portfolio that gives the optimal risk-return relationship, depending on his or her individual circumstances.

For example, an individual investor on the stock market may prefer a high-risk, high-return portfolio, whereas a pension fund manager may choose a lower return portfolio because he or she feels unable to accept more than a certain level of risk. Each investor will end up with what is known as an efficient portfolio (which provides the best return for the risk involved), but each investor will probably hold a different efficient portfolio according to his or her individual risk-return preference.

# 7 Combining Investments' Risks and Returns

## Introduction

### Diversification

In essence, portfolio theory is a formalised mathematical expression of the old adage 'don't put all your eggs in one basket'. By holding a portfolio of investments, it is possible to reduce the overall portfolio's risk without significantly reducing its return. It is assumed that a rational investor will always seek to diversify in this fashion.

### Impact of diversification on investment appraisal

When an investor is appraising a new investment, he or she will only be concerned with how the new investment impacts on his or her existing portfolio in terms of the portfolio's overall risk and return. The investment should not be appraised in isolation, since it is not going to be held in isolation.

We can demonstrate this point with a rather simple example.

## TASK

An investor is considering two additional investments, A or B, to add to his existing portfolio. The returns from the investor's existing portfolio of investments and from A and B are dependent on the prevailing economic climate, and are expected to be as follows.

| Economic Condition | Probability | Current Portfolio | A | B |
|---|---|---|---|---|
| | % | % | % | % |
| I | 30 | 0 | 5 | 20 |
| II | 40 | 10 | 10 | 10 |
| III | 30 | 20 | 15 | 0 |

The investor is considering halving the investment in the current projects and investing the cash then freed up in one of the alternatives. Which investment, if any, should the investor accept?

## SOLUTION

From the above data, we can calculate the expected return and risk of the current portfolio, A and B, as follows.

***Current Portfolio***

| Probability (p) | Return ri | Expected Value | $r_i - \overline{r_i}$ | $(r_i - \overline{r_i})^2$ | $p(r_i - \overline{r_i})^2$ |
|---|---|---|---|---|---|
| % | % | % | | | |
| 30 | 0 | 0.0 | (10.0) | 100.0 | 30.0 |
| 40 | 10 | 4.0 | 0.0 | 0.0 | 0.0 |
| 30 | 20 | 6.0 | 10.0 | 100.0 | 30.0 |
| Expected return ($\overline{r_i}$) = | | 10.0 | Variance ($\sigma_i^2$) = | | 60.0 |

Hence

- Expected return $\overline{r_i}$ = 10.0% p.a.
- Risk $\left(\sqrt{\text{Variance}_i}\right) = \sqrt{60} = 7.746\%$

***Investment A***

| Probability (p) | Return $r_a$ | Expected Value | $r_a - \overline{r_a}$ | $\left(r_a - \overline{r_a}\right)^2$ | $p\left(r_a - \overline{r_a}\right)^2$ |
|---|---|---|---|---|---|
| % | % | % | | | |
| 30 | 5 | 1.5 | (5.0) | 25.0 | 7.5 |
| 40 | 10 | 4.0 | 0.0 | 0.0 | 0.0 |
| 30 | 15 | 4.5 | 5.0 | 25.0 | 7.5 |
| Expected return ($\overline{r_a}$) = | | 10.0 | Variance ($\sigma_a^2$) = | | 15.0 |

Hence

- Expected return $\bar{r}_a$ = 10.0% p.a.
- Risk $\left(\sqrt{\text{Variance}_a}\right) = \sqrt{15} = 3.873\%$

***Investment B***

| Probability (p) | Return ri | Expected Value | $r_b - \bar{r}_b$ | $\left(r_b - \bar{r}_b\right)^2$ | $p\left(r_b - \bar{r}_b\right)^2$ |
|---|---|---|---|---|---|
| % | % | % | | | |
| 30 | 20 | 6.0 | 10.0 | 100.0 | 7.5 |
| 40 | 10 | 4.0 | 0.0 | 0.0 | 0.0 |
| 30 | 0 | .0 | (10.0) | 100.0 | 7.5 |
| Expected return ( $\bar{r}_b$ ) = | | 10.0 | Variance ($\sigma_b^2$) = | | 60.0 |

Hence

- Expected return $\bar{r}_b$ = 10.0% p.a.
- Risk $\left(\sqrt{\text{Variance}_b}\right) = \sqrt{60} = 7.746\%$

## Summary

| | Current Portfolio % | A % | B % |
|---|---|---|---|
| **Expected return $\bar{r}$** | 10.0 | 10.0 | 10.0 |
| **Risk $\sigma$** | 7.746 | 3.873 | 7.746 |

At first sight, the answer may appear obvious, since Project A offers the same return as both the current operations and Project B, but at a much lower risk. It would therefore appear that the investor should move into A. However, the important point to the investor is how this fits with his or her other investments. After all, the chosen investment will be combined with the current portfolio, and it is the effects of each investment on the overall portfolio risk-return profile that must be considered.

As you will see, it is not only the individual returns and risks we must consider, but also how they vary in relation to each other. To appreciate this, we must first calculate the expected returns and risks of the various combinations of investments possible, ie the current portfolio by itself, the current portfolio plus A and the current portfolio plus B.

This can be tackled in two ways.

- By calculating each possible combined return and calculating the expected risk and return of these combined returns as before, ie from first principles.
- By using formulae that give the expected risk and return of a combination, given information about the individual investments and how they correlate.

## First principles

This will be illustrated with our example above.

## SOLUTION

***Current Investment + A***

If we calculate the various returns that would result if Investment A was added to the portfolio, we get

| Economic Condition | p | Current Return ($r_i$) | A ($r_a$) | 50:50 Return ($r_i + a$) | Expected Value |
|---|---|---|---|---|---|
| | % | % | % | % | % |
| I | 30 | 0 | 5 | 2.5 | 0.75 |
| II | 40 | 10 | 10 | 10.0 | 4.00 |
| III | 30 | 20 | 15 | 17.5 | 5.25 |
| | | | | | 10.00 |

If we go on to calculate the risk, we find

| Probability (p) | Return $r_i + a$ | Expected Value | $r_i+a-\bar{r}_i+a$ | $(r_i+a-\bar{r}_i+a)^2$ | $p(r_i+a-\bar{r}_i+a)^2$ |
|---|---|---|---|---|---|
| % | % | % | | | |
| 30 | 2.5 | 0.75 | (7.5) | 56.25 | 16.875 |
| 40 | 10.0 | 4.00 | 0.0 | 0.00 | 0.000 |
| 30 | 17.5 | 5.25 | 7.5 | 56.25 | 16.875 |
| Expected return $(\bar{r}_i+a)$ = | | 10.00 | Variance ($\sigma_i^2$) = | | 33.750 |

What we can see from this is that, by combining the current portfolio with an equal amount of Investment A, we can reduce our risk to 5.81% $(\sqrt{33.75})$ whilst still maintaining a 10% return. Hence, accepting Project A would be beneficial.

***Current Investment + B***

If we now calculate the various returns that would result if investment B was added (50:50) to the portfolio, we get

| Economic Condition | p | Current Return ($r_i$) | A ($r_b$) | 50:50 Return ($r_b + a$) | Expected Value |
|---|---|---|---|---|---|
| | % | % | % | % | % |
| I | 30 | 0 | 20 | 10 | 3 |
| II | 40 | 10 | 10 | 10 | 4 |
| III | 30 | 20 | 0 | 10 | 3 |
| | | | | | 10 |

If we go on to calculate the risk, we find the following.

| Probability (p) | Return $r_i + a$ | Expected Value | $r_i+b-\bar{r}_i+b$ | $(r_i+b-\bar{r}_i+b)^2$ | $p(r_i+b-\bar{r}_i+b)^2$ |
|---|---|---|---|---|---|
| % | % | % | | | |
| 30 | 10 | 3 | – | – | – |
| 40 | 10 | 4 | – | – | – |
| 30 | 10 | 3 | – | – | – |
| Expected return $(\bar{r}_i+b)$ = | | 10 | Variance $(\sigma_i^2)$ = | | – |

What we can see from the table above that by combining the current portfolio with an equal amount of Investment B, we can eliminate risk altogether! Our return is 10%, regardless of the state of the economy and will not vary. In other words, it is risk-free as demonstrated by the calculation of the standard deviation.

Our investor now has three options, which we can summarise as follows.

| Portfolio | Return % | Risk % |
|---|---|---|
| Existing portfolio | 10 | 10 |
| Existing + A | 10 | 5.81 |
| Existing + B | 10 | 0 |

It is clear that the best course of action is to invest in B, since in this way the level of risk is dramatically reduced. This is despite the fact that Investment B has more risk than Investment A.

### Conclusion

When considering risk, however, it is not the risk of the investment in isolation that is important, but the effect of the investment on the overall level of risk in the portfolio. This illustrates the portfolio effect, ie that diversifying investments may potentially reduce the level of risk suffered without necessarily reducing the level of return.

## Formulae

### Basic formulae

There are two formulae that permit us to combine returns and risks more quickly. If a portfolio is made up of two investments, as follows,

| | A | B |
|---|---|---|
| **Expected return** | $r_a$ | $r_b$ |
| **Risk** | $\sigma_a$ | $\sigma_b$ |
| **Proportion of funds invested** | $p_a$ | $p_b$ |
| **Correlation coefficient** | $cor_{ab}$ | |

Then, the portfolio will have combined return and risk as set at below.

- Return of combination.

  $$R_a + b = p_a r_a + p_b r_b$$

- Risk of combination.

  $$\sigma_a + b = \sqrt{p_a{}^2 \sigma_a{}^2 + p_b{}^2 \sigma_b{}^2 + 2 p_a p_b \sigma_a \sigma_b cor_{ab}}$$

Before using these formulae, let us examine what they say about combining investments.

- Returns simply combine on a weighted average basis.
- The key to the effect on risk in combination is the correlation coefficient.

## Correlation coefficient

### Introduction

The correlation coefficient measures the extent to which the returns from the two investments move relative to each other. The correlation coefficient always lies between +1 (perfect positive correlation) and –1 (perfect negative correlation).

You can see from the above formula for the risk of the combination that the lower the value of $cor_{ab}$, the lower the combined overall risk, with negative correlation values reducing the total still further. But what do various values of the correlation coefficient actually mean?

### Positive correlation ($cor_{ab} > 0$)

This indicates that if you measured the relative direction of movement in returns from two such investments under changing economic conditions, you would find them generally to be similar. In the extreme case of perfect positive correlation ($cor_{ab} = +1$), they would be identical.

In the case of perfect positive correlation, each investment will simply contribute its risk to the combination in proportion to the amount invested, ie the combined risk would simply be the weighted average of the two individual investment risks.

### Negative correlation ($cor_{ab} < 0$)

In case of negative correlation, the returns will generally be moving in opposite directions. This means that there will be some cancelling out, ie elimination of some of the investments' individual risks when in combination. When one investment is performing well, the other will be performing poorly and vice versa. The resulting combination will have a risk that is lower than a weighted average of the individual risks. This is diversification.

Perfect negative correlation ($cor_{ab} = -1$) is the extreme where the movements are exactly opposite. In this situation, it will be possible to eliminate risk completely.

### Definition and calculation of $cor_{ab}$

Looking at the possible returns from each of our two investments in relation to those of the existing investments, you can see that A tends to move in the same direction (positive correlation), whereas B exhibits negative correlation. Hence, B provides a better fit with the current portfolio. This should be borne out in our calculations.

The correlation coefficient is defined as

$$cor_{ab} = \frac{Covariance(a,b)}{\sigma_a \sigma_b}$$

where the covariance is calculated in a similar way to variance, as follows.

**Current Projects with A**

Based on the figures we calculated above for $(r_i - \overline{r}_i)$ and $(r_a - \overline{r}_a)$, we get

| Probability (p) % | $r_i - \overline{r}_i$ | $r_a - \overline{r}_a$ | $p(r_i - \overline{r}_i)(r_a - \overline{r}_a)$ |
|---|---|---|---|
| 30 | (10.0) | (5.0) | 15.0 |
| 40 | 0.0 | 0.0 | 0.0 |
| 30 | 10.0 | 5.0 | 15.0 |
| | Covariance = | | 30.0 |

Hence

$$cor_{ia} = \frac{30.0}{7.746 \times 3.873} = +1$$

That is, these investment options are perfectly positively correlated.

**Current Projects with B**

Based on the figures we calculated above for $(r_i - \overline{r}_i)$ and $(r_b - \overline{r}_b)$, we get

| Probability (p) % | $r_i - \overline{r}_i$ | $r_b - \overline{r}_b$ | $p(r_i - \overline{r}_i)(r_b - \overline{r}_b)$ |
|---|---|---|---|
| 30 | (10.0) | (10.0) | 30.0 |
| 40 | 0.0 | 0.0 | 0.0 |
| 30 | 10.0 | 10.0 | 30.0 |
| | Covariance = | | 60.0 |

Hence

$$cor_{ib} = \frac{-60.0}{7.746 \times 7.746} = -1$$

That is, these investment opportunities are perfectly negatively correlated.

## SOLUTION

Now using this information in our formulae, we get

***Current Investments + A***

*Return*

$r_i + a = p_i r_i + p_a r_a$

$r_i + a = 0.5 \times 10\% + 0.5 \times 10\% = 10\%$

*Risk*

$$\sigma_i + a = \sqrt{p_i^2\sigma_i^2 + p_a^2\sigma_a^2 + 2p_i p_a \sigma_i \sigma_a cor_{ia}}$$

$$\sigma_i + a = \sqrt{0.5^2 \times 7.746\%^2 + 0.5^2 \times 3.873\%^2 + 2 \times 0.5 \times 0.5 \times 7.746\% \times 3.873\% \times (+1)}$$

$$\sigma_i + a = \sqrt{15 + 3.75 + 15} = \sqrt{33.75} = 5.81\%$$

***Current Investments + B***

*Return*

$$r_{i+b} = p_i r_i + p_b r_b$$

$$r_{i+b} = 0.5 \times 10\% + 0.5 \times 10\% = 10\%$$

*Risk*

$$\sigma_i + b = \sqrt{p_i^2\sigma_i^2 + p_b^2\sigma_b^2 + 2p_i p_b \sigma_i \sigma_b cor_{ib}}$$

$$\sigma_i + b = \sqrt{0.5^2 \times 7.746\%^2 + 0.5^2 \times 7.746\%^2 + 2 \times 0.5 \times 0.5 \times 7.746\% \times 7.746\% \times (1)}$$

$$\sigma_i + b = \sqrt{15 + 15 - 30} = \sqrt{0} = 0.0\%$$

## Application to project appraisal

So far, we have been considering individuals choosing between possible investments. Portfolio theory can also be used to appraise risky projects being considered by companies. The principles are exactly the same, although there are some limitations.

### Limitations

There are limitations to the use of portfolio theory for corporate investment appraisal where we are looking after the interests of a number of shareholders, as follows.

- Unless the decision is unambiguous, the shareholders' indifference curves will be needed. There are two difficulties with this.
  - Obtaining the indifference curves, if the company has more than just a few shareholders.
  - Assessing whether the project will be acceptable (or unacceptable) to all of the shareholders, since they are unlikely to have precisely the same pattern of indifference curves.
- For small private companies, in which the shareholders have most of their wealth invested, the effect of acceptance of a project on the shareholders is going to be fairly accurately measured by looking at the effect on the company's existing pattern of returns, hence portfolio theory would be suitable.
- However, listed companies' shareholders have their wealth invested in a range of different shares. If a listed company were to use portfolio theory to appraise investments, it would not be looking at the impact of the new investment on its shareholders' overall portfolios of investments. Rather, it would only be taking into account that part of the shareholders' wealth invested in the one company. Basing investment decisions on incomplete information in this way may not be in the shareholders' best interests.

We now need to develop portfolio theory such that it has a more general application and can be used by listed companies as well as small private companies. We will do this by first considering how a well-diversified investor will construct his or her required level of risk and return. In the next chapter, we will then see how this knowledge can be used for a listed company to appraise new investments, through the Capital Asset Pricing Model (CAPM).

# 8 PORTFOLIO SELECTION – THE EFFICIENT FRONTIER

## Introduction

We have seen that the correlation coefficient governs the extent of diversification that can be achieved within a portfolio of two investments, but what will be the risk-return profiles of such combinations given different correlation coefficients?

The diagram below illustrates the expected return and risk for possible combinations of two risky investments, A and B (ie different proportions of funds invested in each), assuming three different degrees of correlation.

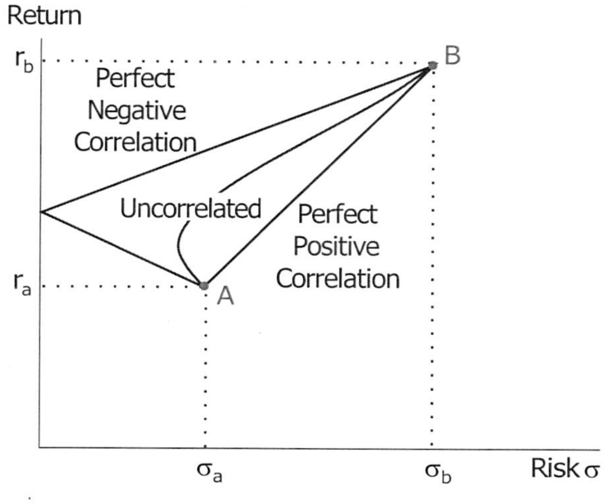


If we have all of our funds invested in B, we will receive all of its returns $r_b$, and face all of its risk $\sigma_b$. As we start to invest in A, we will start to move along the appropriate line towards A. How far along that line we are depends on what proportion of our funds are invested in A. Ultimately, when we are 100% invested in A, we will be at A, ie receive just A's return $r_a$ and face just A's risk $\sigma_a$.

### Perfect positive correlation

With perfect positive correlation the resultant risk and return are calculated from the weighted average of the two investments' risks and returns; there is no benefit from diversification. We saw this to be the case in the above example when we combined Investment A with the current portfolio.

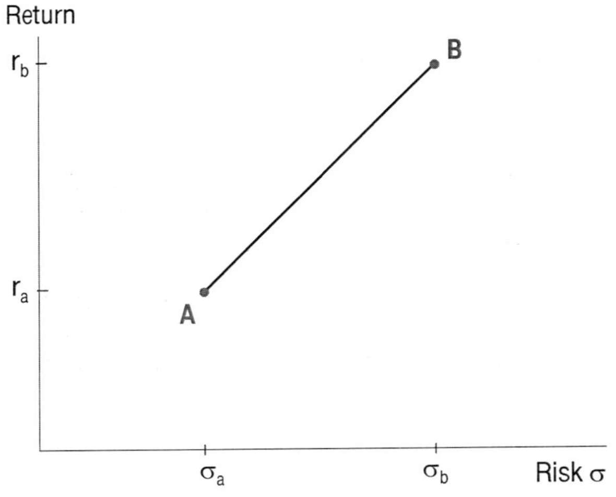


### Perfect negative correlation

When the investments are perfectly negatively correlated, it is possible to find appropriate proportions such that risk is completely diversified away. We saw this to be the case in the above example when we combined Investment B with the current portfolio.

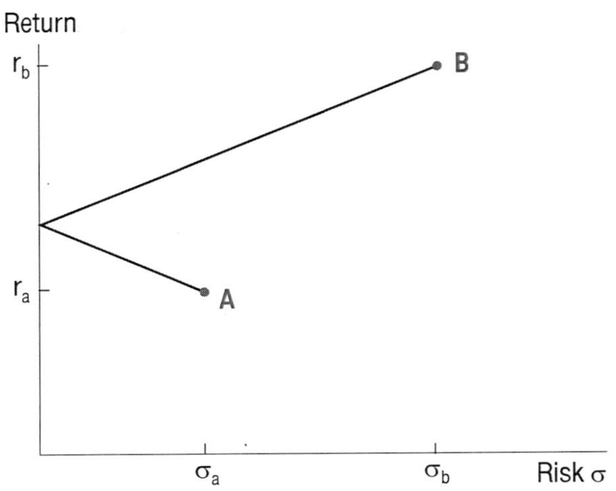


### Imperfect correlation

The middle curved line shows the risk-return profile if A and B are imperfectly correlated ($cor_{ib}$ between –1 and +1), which is the most likely situation.

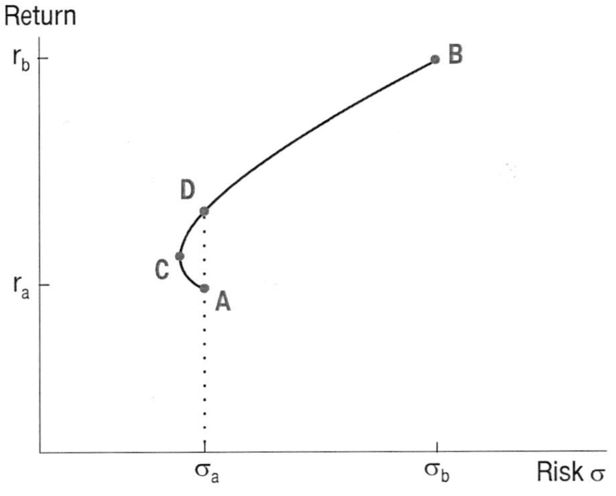

## Portfolio selection

### What portfolio would an investor select?

Assume now that an investor is considering investing in A and B where the two investments exhibit imperfect correlation. The particular choice of portfolio by the investor (ie the split of funds between the two investments) will depend, as always, upon the indifference curves of the investor concerned.

However, some portfolios can be eliminated without knowing about the investor's indifference curves. These are all of those on the curve AC, since they offer lower returns for the same level of risk as those on the curve CD. Any investor would therefore only consider investments on the part of the curve BC, since this part offers the highest possible returns for any given level of risk.

### Indifference curves

If we now consider the possible indifference curves of our investors, we can see from the diagram below that

- The highly risk-averse investor would prefer to hold more of Investment A, which is less risky.
- The less risk-averse investor would prefer to invest more in Investment B.

This is a fairly obvious conclusion, but is now quantifiable. We can calculate specific proportions of investments for each individual investor that will best suit the investor's requirements based on his or her own indifference curves. Remember that a highly risk-averse investor will always exhibit steeper indifference curves than a less risk-averse investor.

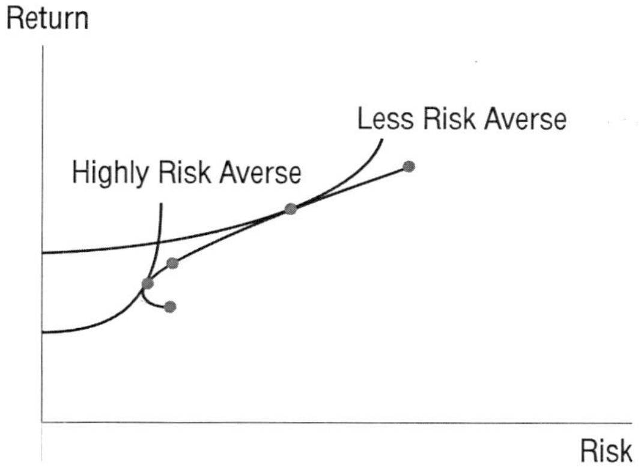


### More than two investments

With more than two investments the number of different portfolios multiplies, introducing various combinations of investments, as well as differing proportions invested in each.

The calculations of combined risks and returns of multiple-investment portfolios becomes more time consuming, but the underlying principle of diversification remains.

Suppose we are considering constructing a portfolio from, say, five risky securities. There will be five possible portfolios of only one security, ten of two, ten of three, five of four and one of all five – 31 possible portfolios in total, each offering an infinite variation of possible proportions invested in each security. The number of possible investment alternatives is enormous, even with just five securities. The diagram below covers the range of risk and return profiles for possible portfolios.

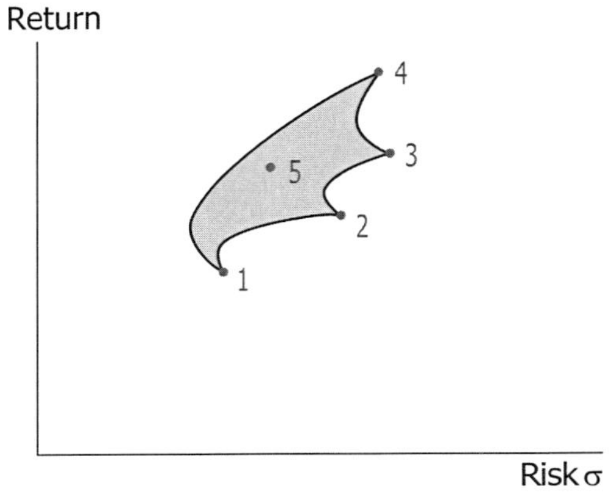


The shaded area, known as the opportunity set, shows the risk-return of the various portfolios that could be constructed from these five securities. Some of the portfolios will involve all five securities, while others will use less.

Of course, an investor may not choose to invest in only five different securities. He or she can choose from all of the securities in the stock market. If a diagram were plotted of risk and return profiles for portfolios constructed from **all** the possible shares that could be bought on the market (rather than just the five above), then the opportunity set that we would obtain would look something like this.

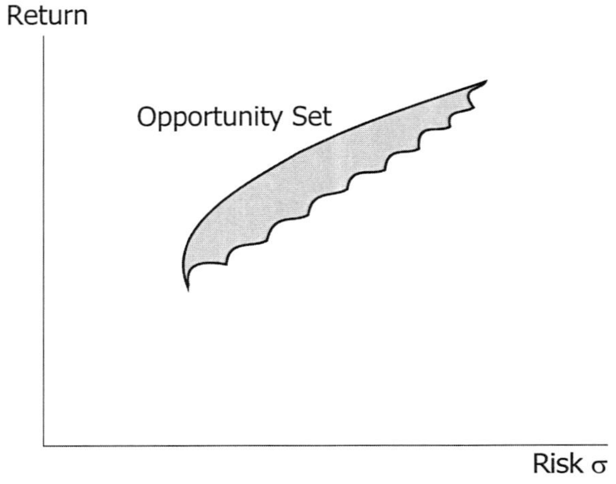


### Implications for the investor

Which of the possible portfolios available would investors actually select?

Even without indifference curves we can rule out all portfolios except those falling on the upper edge of the area between points X and Y below. A portfolio lying on this line gives the highest possible return for a given level of risk. This line is known as the **efficient frontier** because it dominates all other possible portfolios.

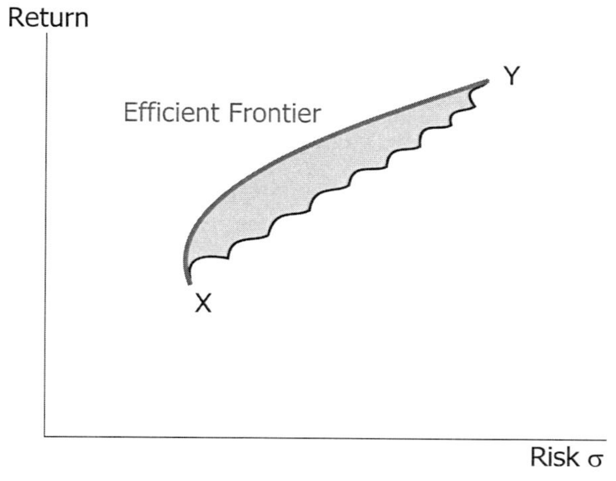


With indifference curves we could go further, but would find (as always) that different investors would prefer different points along the efficient frontier.

We can see from the diagram below that the highly risk-averse investor will choose portfolio a, whereas the less risk-averse individual may select portfolio c, and someone with a mid risk-return preference may choose b – all on the efficient frontier.

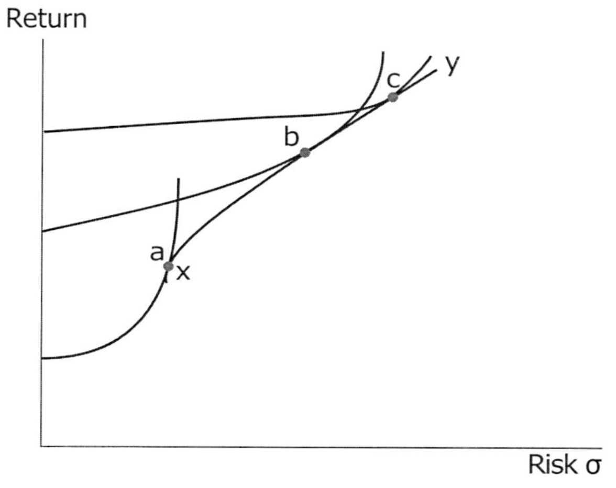


## Size of the optimal portfolio for an investor

The investor, given a set of securities n (number), can now choose the combination of those securities that is optimal for him. It may include only two securities or it may include all n, depending on the correlation of the securities involved. The question that the investor will now no doubt ask is how many securities should he consider in the first place? What would n be?

The benefit of increasing the number of securities in the portfolio is increased diversification and lower risk for a given level of return. The problem is the higher transaction and other costs implicit in holding and monitoring a large number of shares. What an investor will want to do is to hold sufficient shares to grasp most of the benefits of diversification without incurring significant costs in holding the total portfolio.

How quickly does the risk of a portfolio decrease as we increase the number of securities in a portfolio? Experiments have been carried out on different sizes of randomly selected portfolios of UK shares. Portfolios from one to 50 securities were chosen and the **average** risk of each size of portfolio calculated. This average risk was then expressed as a percentage of the average risk of holding only one share.

The results can be shown on a graph.

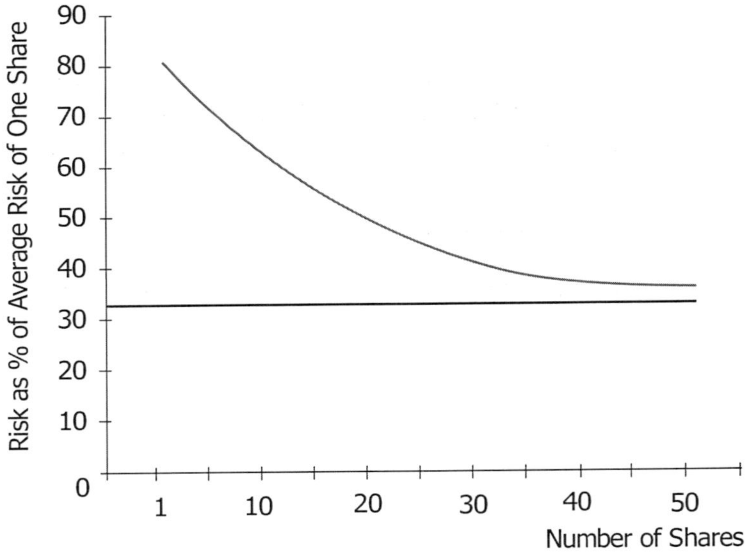


We can see from this that average risk decreases quickly as we increase the number of securities held. Each time another security is added, risk is reduced by a smaller amount. However, no matter how many securities are held, risk cannot be reduced on average to below 34.5% (in this particular study) of the risk of holding only one share. This indicates that there is a certain amount of risk common to all shares quoted on the UK stock market which cannot be diversified away (often referred to as 'market risk' or 'systematic risk'). This is intuitively obvious since if an investor held all quoted UK shares, he or she would not be holding a riskless investment.

These results have two major implications for investors.

- Small investors need only diversify by holding ten to 15 shares to have removed most of the non-market risk from their portfolios. For example, by holding ten randomly selected shares in equal amounts, an investor may, on average, diversify away 90% of the shares' non-market risk.
- Institutional investors do not need to hold vast numbers of securities to achieve satisfactory diversification. The extra reduction in risk gained by holding 150 rather than 50 securities is very small and may well be more than outweighed by the additional transaction and monitoring costs involved in holding the extra 100 shares.

Note that, by limiting the number of individual shares in their portfolios, as suggested above, investors may not actually have a portfolio on the efficient frontier. However, the portfolio achieved will be sufficiently close to the efficient frontier and to move closer to the frontier would entail significant costs.

# 9 Risk-Free Investments – The Capital Market Line

## Introduction

### Risk-free investments

So far, there seems to be no single portfolio preferred by all investors. All we can say is that all investors will construct a portfolio which lies on or around the efficient frontier. However, this is only the case if risky securities alone are included in a portfolio.

Not all securities are risky. In the UK, gilt-edged stocks, for instance, give a certain return if held to maturity (the interest and the capital repayment are known for certain at the time of initial issue and are guaranteed by HM Government).

## Combining risky and risk-free investments

If a portfolio is formed comprising a risk-free investment (say a gilt) and a risky investment (i) then, as we have seen before, the exact risk and return given by the combination will depend on the relative split of funds between the two components. In each case, the average return and standard deviation depend on the relative split of funds.

The relationship between return and standard deviation for different mixes is linear since the risk-free investment, by definition, makes no contribution to the combined risk. This can be proved with the aid of the equations that we established above for combining risk and return, and can be calculated as follows.

### Return

$R_{i+f} = p_i r_i + p_f r_f$

where

$r_i$ = return on the risky portfolio i

$r_f$ = return on the risk-free investment

$p_i$ = proportion of funds invested in the risky portfolio

$p_f$ = proportion of funds invested in the risk-free investment

Now

$p_f = 1 - p_i$

giving

$$\begin{aligned} r_{i+f} &= p_i r_i + (1 - p_i) r_f \\ &= p_i r_i + r_f - p_i r_f \\ &= r_f + p_i (r_i - r_f) \end{aligned}$$

### Risk

$$\sigma_{i+f} = \sqrt{p_i^2 \sigma_i^2 + p_f^2 \sigma_f^2 + 2 p_i p_f \sigma_i \sigma_f cor_{if}}$$

where

$\sigma_i$ = risk of the risky portfolio

$\sigma_f$ = risk of the risk-free investment, ie nil

$cor_{if}$ = the correlation coefficient of $r_i$ and $r_f$

Now

$\sigma_f = 0$, since it is risk free

Hence

$$\begin{aligned} \sigma_{i+f} &= \sqrt{p_i^2 \sigma_i^2 + p_f^2 \times 0^2 + 2 p_i p_f \sigma_i \times 0 \times cor_{if}} = \sqrt{p_i^2 \sigma_i^2} \\ &= p_i \sigma_i \end{aligned}$$

## TASK

Assume the following values.

$r_i$ = 18%

$r_f$ = 10%

i = 4%

An investor has £1,000 to invest. What is the return and risk of the portfolio if the £1,000 is invested

(a) Solely in risk-free investments?

(b) Solely in the risky portfolio?

(c) 50% in risk-free investments and 50% in the risky portfolio?

## SOLUTION

(a) The risk-free investment has a return of 10% and a risk of nil.

(b) The risky portfolio has a return of 18% and a risk of 4%.

(c) The return of this portfolio is given by the equation

$r_{i+f} = r_f + p_i(r_i - r_f)$

$r_{i+f} = 10 + 0.5(18 - 10)$

$r_{i+f} = 14\%$

The risk of the portfolio is given by the equation

$\sigma_{i+f} = p_i\sigma_i$

$\sigma_{i+f} = 0.5 \times 4$

$\sigma_{i+f} = 2\%$

We can see from this illustration that the linear relationship referred to above exists. The investor who invests 50% in risk-free investments and 50% in the risky portfolio achieves a return halfway between the risk-free return and risky portfolio return and a risk that is half the risk of the risky portfolio.

In the illustration above, the investor who invested all his funds in the risky portfolio did so with available funds. It is possible, however, to achieve a portfolio that gives an expected return of greater than this with commensurably higher risk levels. This is done through borrowing money (at the risk-free rate of interest) to invest in the risky portfolio.

Whereas initially with £1,000 we could invest it all in i or in $r_f$, or split it between the two, we could now borrow, say, £500, and put the whole £1,500 available into i which would give the point labelled j below, as could again be demonstrated by the use of the following equations.

$r_{i+f} = 10 + 1.5(18 - 10)$

$= 22\%$

$\sigma_{i+f} = 1.5 \times 4$

$= 6\%$

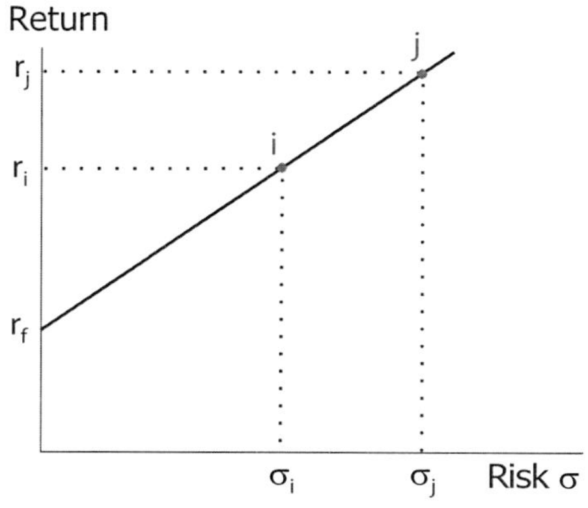


## The capital market line

### What risky portfolio will investors select?

Referring back, we can see how (in the absence of the risk-free stock) each investor selects his portfolio from the wide range of possible choices according to his own preferences. For instance, investors a and c chose points a and c, respectively.

If we now include the possibility of borrowing or lending at the risk-free rate, then each portfolio on the efficient frontier can be combined with risk-free investments, or with borrowing at the risk-free rate to create yet more possible portfolios. As a result, any point falling on a straight line through $r_f$ and any point on the efficient frontier is now also a potential portfolio.

Looking at just two alternatives, using n and m on the efficient frontier, which risky portfolio would an investor choose to combine with risk-free investments? The answer is the one that achieves the better risk-return profile.

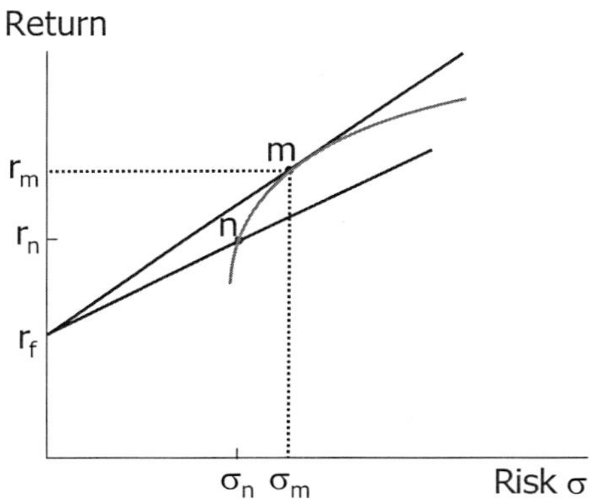


Previously, we have needed to refer to the investors' indifference curves, but this is no longer the case. Regardless of the investor's attitude to risk, portfolios constructed from a combination of $r_f$ and m provide a higher return for the same level of risk as those constructed from a combination of $r_f$ and n and, therefore, must represent the optimal set of opportunities. The line through m gives the greatest possible return at any level of risk. Hence, all diversified investors would choose to invest somewhere along this line, known as the **Capital Market Line** (CML).

The exact proportions in which any one investor would choose to invest could, once again, be determined by reference to his indifference curves, however, all would choose some combination of $r_f$ and m.

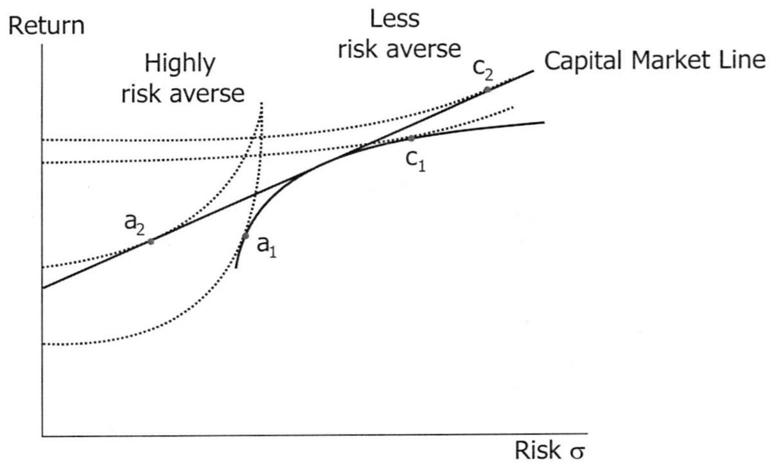


For example, our risk-averse investor who previously invested on the efficient frontier at $a_1$ will now choose to invest on the CML at $a_2$, which puts him on a higher indifference curve. Similarly, the less risk-averse investor who previously invested at $c_1$ on the efficient frontier would now choose to invest at $c_2$.

### The market portfolio

We can conclude from the above that all investors will choose to invest in one combination of portfolio m and risk-free stock, with each investor's utility profile dictating the precise combination chosen.

There remains one question to answer: what is this portfolio m?

Suppose that there was an investment (say x) not contained in portfolio m. Since everyone wants to hold portfolio m in combination with risk-free investments, no one would wish to buy x, so its price would be zero.

But x presumably gives some level of return, so at a price of zero it must be undervalued compared to other securities actually included within m.

If markets are efficient, then investors would sell these other securities and buy the relatively undervalued x until the price of x had risen to the point where it was correctly valued.

This leads us to the conclusion that m must contain a proportion of all investments on the market – it must be a 'scaled-down' version of the market for securities – the 'market portfolio'.

The Capital Asset Pricing Model theory assumes that diversified investors do hold the market portfolio plus risk-free stock. This may seem to be an extremely limiting assumption, since it would clearly be impractical to hold every single security on the market. As we have already noted, however, research has shown that a well-constructed portfolio of even as few as 15 shares is a good approximation to the market portfolio.

### The use of the CML in investment appraisal

The use of the CML is that it gives a benchmark for investment appraisal. An investor can achieve a particular level of return for a given level of risk by investing in the market portfolio plus risk investments/borrowing. This level of return for a particular level of risk is shown on the CML. A new investment's level of risk can be measured and its required return can then be calculated by referring to the return achievable on the CML. This is the subject of the next chapter, the cost of equity and The Capital Asset Pricing Model.

## CHAPTER ROUNDUP

**Module 2, Chapter 9: Understanding Risk and Return**

This chapter introduces some useful concepts to help you understand the application of the Capital Asset Pricing Model, which is examined in the next chapter. You should ensure you are familiar with the principles of portfolio theory and understand how correlation impacts the diversification of an investor's portfolio of investments.

Portfolio theory argues that diversification can lower the risk of investments but maintain returns. This is based on the fact that investments can be correlated with each other. The more the investments are negatively correlated with each other the lower the combined risk.

You should be clear that a well-diversified investor will hold the market portfolio. The Capital Asset Pricing Model assumes that all investors are in this position and are thus well-diversified. An investor thus does not therefore reap any risk reduction benefits, if a company chooses to diversify its activities from its core business. It is often the case that shareholders prefer to diversify themselves rather than invest in conglomerates.

The numerical examples provided in this chapter will not be examined in detail.

# The Capital Asset Pricing Model

chapter 10

Contents


| | | |
|---|---|---|
| 1 | Introduction | 214 |
| 2 | Systematic Risk and Unsystematic Risk | 215 |
| 3 | The Capital Asset Pricing Model | 217 |
| 4 | Betas | 219 |
| 5 | The Impact of Gearing on Project Appraisal | 225 |
| 6 | Modigliani and Miller | 226 |
| 7 | Assumptions and Limitations of the CAPM | 236 |

# 1 Introduction

In our consideration of portfolio theory in the previous chapter, you saw how we can appraise investments from the point of view of companies and individuals by evaluating the impact of the investment on the risk-return profile of the investor's current portfolio.

The primary weakness of the method was that it remained dependent on the individual's risk-return preferences (indifference curves) which, for corporate investment appraisal in particular, is inconvenient as a result of:

- The difficulties involved in ascertaining such risk-return preferences
- The problem caused to a company by an investment which is acceptable to only a section of its shareholders

The introduction of the market portfolio, and the associated idea of well-diversified investors, raised the possibility of avoiding these difficulties.

## The capital market line

We saw in the previous chapter that all diversified investors will choose to hold some combination of the market portfolio and the risk-free investment. Their expected level of return and risk would be given by a point on the Capital Market Line (CML).

If a diversified investor places a proportion of his funds (b) in the market portfolio and the remainder (1 – b) in the risk-free investment, then his expected return and risk can be calculated using the portfolio theory equations as follows.

### Return

$r = br_m + (1 - b)r_f$

giving

$r = br_m + r_f - br_f$

$r = r_f + b(r_m - r_f)$

### Risk

$$\sigma = \sqrt{b^2\sigma_m{}^2 + (1-b)^2\sigma_f{}^2 + 2_b(1-b)\sigma_m\sigma_f cor_{mf}}$$

$$= \sqrt{b^2\sigma_m{}^2 + (1-b)^2 \times 2_b(1-b)\sigma_m \times 0 \times cor_{mf}}$$

$$= \sqrt{b^2\sigma_m{}^2 + 0 + 0}$$

$$= \sqrt{b^2\sigma_m{}^2} = b\sigma_m$$

If an investor puts all of his or her funds into the market portfolio, he or she will receive an expected return in excess of the risk-free return. This excess return ($r_m - r_f$) is the risk premium of the market portfolio and is demanded by investors to compensate them for the level of risk implicit in the market (given by $\sigma_m$) over that of risk-free investments (nil).

## Using the capital market line to appraise new investments

What we can see from the above is that to benefit from a proportion of the **risk premium** $(r_m - r_f)$, we must face the **same** proportion of the market portfolio risk $\sigma_m$.

Alternatively, if we know what proportion of the market portfolio risk we are willing to face, we can establish the level of return that we are likely to achieve. For example, if

$\sigma_s$ = risk we are willing to face

$\sigma_m$ = market portfolio risk

Then, the proportion of funds that we would invest in the market portfolio would be

$$b = \frac{\sigma_s}{\sigma_m}$$

And the return that we could then expect as a diversified investor for this level of risk would be

$$r = r_f + b(r_m - r_f)$$

Clearly, therefore, any alternative investment opportunity with this level of risk must offer a higher return if it is to be attractive to the investor.

Thus, this equation gives the minimum acceptable return for a given level of risk for the diversified investor, ie the required rate of return with which to appraise the investment opportunity.

This, in essence, is the Capital Asset Pricing Model (CAPM), although clearly there is much more to it.

# 2 Systematic Risk and Unsystematic Risk

## Introduction

### The benefits of diversification

We saw in the previous chapter that a share portfolio's total risk could be reduced by increasing the number of investments in the portfolio. You may remember the following graph.

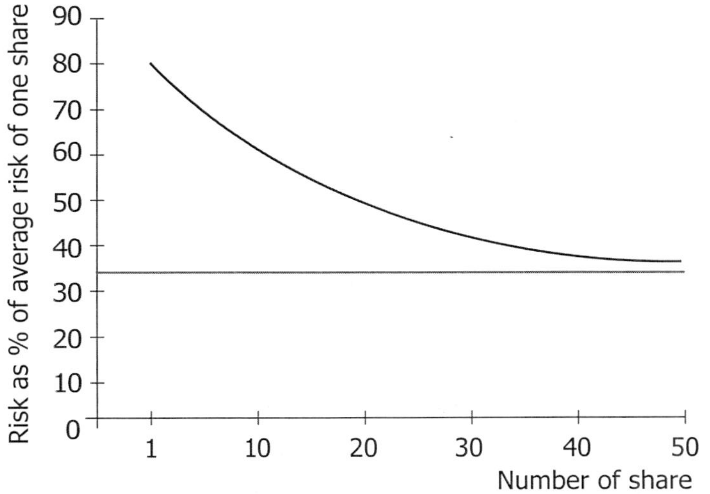


The above graph indicates that, while it is possible to reduce the risk of a portfolio of shares through diversification, the risk cannot be removed altogether. There is always some risk inherent in holding a portfolio of shares. This inherent risk that cannot be diversified away is called systematic risk or market risk. Risk that can be diversified away is called unsystematic or specific risk.

In the same way that a portfolio's overall risk can be analysed into these two components, an individual investment's risk can also be broken down into a systematic and an unsystematic element.

We have seen that an investment's total risk (the variability of its returns about its expected return) can be measured by its standard deviation. This total risk can be split into two components.

## Systematic (or market) risk

This measures the variability in the investment's returns that are caused by general market fluctuations. It cannot be diversified away because it is a 'fact of the market'. Even if an investor held all quoted UK shares, they would still be subject to some risk as history has shown. This risk will be caused by such general economic factors as:

- Inflation rates
- Interest rates
- Tax rates

## Unsystematic (or specific) risk

This is the remainder of the investment's risk that reflects factors specific to one or more of:

- The investment/project
- The company undertaking the project, eg quality of management
- The industry in which the company operates

It is this element of an investment's risk that can be diversified away. Since the unsystematic risk is not common to all projects/companies/segments of the market, it can be eliminated within a well-diversified portfolio.

### Relevance of systematic and unsystematic risk to investment appraisal

The importance of the above to a well-diversified investor is as follows.

#### Unsystematic risk is irrelevant

If an investor is well diversified, unsystematic risk should be of no concern as it will be diversified away within his overall portfolio. In this situation, the only risk the investor is left facing is the systematic risk.

#### The required return for an investment depends on its level of systematic risk

Investors demand a return commensurate with the risk they face. Since our investor faces only the systematic risk of each investment in his or her portfolio, the returns he or she demands will be based on this. This means that the premium for risk will be a function of **systematic** risk only, not the total risk of the investments concerned.

We must measure the level of systematic risk present in any particular investment and use this measure to set a target return that would be sufficient to compensate for that risk. The investment's expected return may then be compared against this required rate to determine whether it should be accepted or rejected.

# 3 The Capital Asset Pricing Model

## Betas and required returns

In our consideration of portfolio theory, we introduced the Capital Market Line (CML). We saw that it shows the best combinations of risk and return that can currently be obtained on the market by diversified investors, through combinations of the market portfolio (m) and risk-free securities. No investor should be content with a portfolio falling beneath the CML.

We can see that if an investment carries a risk of 50% of the standard deviation of $\sigma_m$ ($0.5\sigma_m$) then the return must be equal to $r_f$, plus a risk premium equal to 50% $(r_m - r_f)$ in order to place it on the CML representing an acceptable level of return.

**NB:** The risk referred to here is only systematic risk, as we noted above, since we are assuming unsystematic risk to have been diversified away by the diversified investor.

Now changing the risk axis from an absolute measure (the standard deviation as a percentage) to a relative one where $\sigma_m$ is 1, our investment that has a risk of 50% of $\sigma_m$ will appear with a relative measure of risk of 0.5.

In other words, our horizontal axis is now showing risk represented by a sort of index number, which we call a beta factor ($\beta$) such that for our investment above

$$\beta = \frac{50\% \times \sigma_m}{\sigma_m} = 0.5$$

This change of axis is shown below and you should note that the CML has now become the Security Market Line (SML). The CML shows the expected return for a particular level of risk (measured in absolute terms), which is achieved by investing in a combination of the market portfolio and risk-free investments. The SML shows the required return for a particular investment, given its level of risk relative to market risk, as measured by its $\beta$. The SML is derived from the CML.

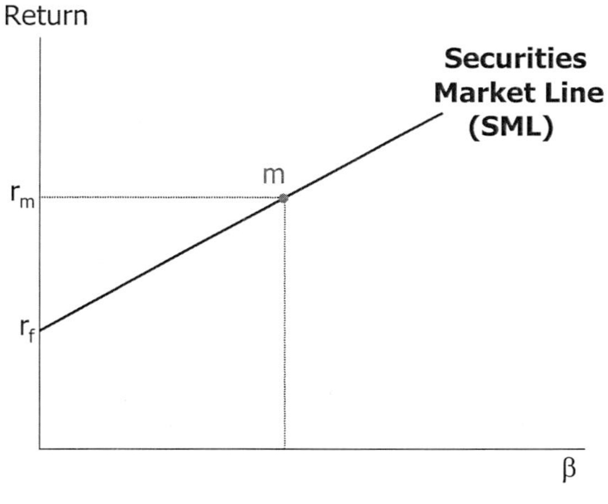


Hence, for an investment whose relative risk is given by $\beta$, the required return is given by the CAPM formula.

$$r = r_f + \beta(r_m - r_f)$$

where

| | | |
|---|---|---|
| $r_m$ | = | the return expected from the market portfolio |
| $r_f$ | = | the return offered by a risk-free security (typically the yield on gilts) |
| $\beta$ | = | the risk of the investment opportunity relative to that of the market portfolio (systematic risk only) |

## TASK

For example, supposing that the risk-free rate of return is 6%, and the market is expected to return 14%, what return would a diversified investor expect from an investment with a $\beta$ of

- 0?
- 0.5?
- 1?
- 1.5?

## SOLUTION

Using

$$r = rf\ \ \beta(rm - rf)$$

gives

$\beta = 0$

$$r = 6\%\ \ 0 \times (14\% - 6\%) = 6\%$$

$\beta = 0.5$

$$r = 6\%\ \ 0.5 \times (14\% - 6\%) = 10\%$$

$\beta = 1$

$$r = 6\%\ \ 1 \times (14\% - 6\%) = 14\%$$

$\beta = 1.5$

$$r = 6\%\ \ 1.5 \times (14\% - 6\%) = 18\%$$

## The security market line (SML)

Investment appraisal under CAPM amounts to plotting investments' expected returns and betas on the SML graph. An investment lying above the SML would be accepted by any investor (or any company) as it is offering a return higher than could usually be expected for that given level of risk, ie it is undervalued. An investment lying beneath the SML would be rejected as its current return is too low, ie it is overvalued. An investment lying on the SML is currently correctly priced in the market. An investor or company should be indifferent to the choice between buying it or not.

## The impact of inflation on the market risk premium

The impact of inflation on the market risk premium is relatively low, as can be seen from the following illustration.

Assume that the nominal yield on gilts is 8%, the nominal yield on the market is 15% and expected inflation is 4%. The market risk premium in nominal terms is therefore 7%.

Given an inflation rate of 4%, the real yield on gilts is 3.8% $\left(\frac{1.08}{1.04}-1\right)$. The real yield on equities is 10.6% $\left(\frac{1.15}{1.04}-1\right)$.

The market risk premium in real terms is, therefore, 6.8%, a minimal difference to the risk premium expressed in nominal terms. The difference will only become significant at higher levels of inflation.

## Cost of equity

From a company's point of view, the return required by its equity investors is the cost of equity for the company. Therefore, r can be replaced by $k_e$ to give the CAPM formula for calculating the cost of equity, as follows.

$$k_e = r_f + \beta(r_m - r_f)$$

# 4 Betas

## Introduction

### What it means

The beta of an investment is a relative measure of the **systematic risk** of an investment.

In general terms:

- The sign of the beta (+/–) indicates whether, on average, the investment's returns move with (+) the market, rising and falling when the market does, or in the opposite direction (–) to the market
- The scale or value of the beta indicates the relative volatility

A beta of +0.5, for instance, would indicate that on average the investment's returns move one half as much as the market's do in the same direction. If the market fell by 6%, we would expect the investment to fall by 3%; if the market rose by 6%, we would expect the investment's returns to rise by 3%, etc.

If the beta were –0.5, then the relative volatility would be the same but the direction of the change in the investment's returns would be the opposite. If the market were to rise by 6%, then the investment's returns would fall by 3%. Note, however, that most investments have positive betas.

### Summary

**$\beta$ > 1**

On average, the investment's returns will move in the same direction as the market's returns, but to a greater extent.

**$\beta$ = 1**

On average, the investment's returns will move in the same direction as the market's returns, and to the same extent.

**$0 < \beta < 1$**

On average, the investment's returns will move in the same direction as the market's returns, but to a lesser extent.

**$\beta = 0$**

The investment's returns are uncorrelated with those of the market. This would be the case if the investment were totally risk free or if all of its risk was unsystematic.

**$\beta < 0$**

On average, the investment's returns will move in the opposite direction to the market, to a lesser extent if $\beta > -1$, to the same extent if $\beta = -1$, and to a greater extent if $\beta < -1$.

## Use of betas

We can use the $\beta$ for an investment to establish from the CAPM formula what the appropriate risk-adjusted required rate of return is in order to appraise the investment.

**TASK**

A new one-year project requires an initial investment of £1m and is expected to give a return of £1.2m at the end of the year.

The current market return is 14%, and risk-free return is 6%.

The project's beta has been estimated at 1.5.

Assuming investors are well diversified, should the project be accepted and what value would the investors place on the investment?

**SOLUTION**

***Required Rate of Return***

The required return given by the CAPM would be

$$k_e = r_f + \beta(r_m - r_f)$$

$$= 6\% + 1.5(14\% - 6\%)$$

$$= 6\% + 12\% = 18\%$$

***Project's Return and Appraisal***

The return on the investment will be 20% (£1.2m return from a £1m investment). Hence, it should be accepted. It is offering a better level of return for its level of (systematic) risk than can currently be obtained elsewhere in the market.

***Net Present Value of the Investment***

To value the project, the investors will use the required rate given by the CAPM as a risk-adjusted discount rate to find the present value of its future returns (the usual market value approach) giving

| Time | Cash Flow £'000 | Discount Factor | Present Value £'000 |
|---|---|---|---|
| 0 | (1,000) | 1 | (1,000) |
| 1 | 1,200 | $\frac{1}{1.18}$ | 1,017 |
| | Net present value | | 17 |

£1.017m is the value of the investment's returns to well-diversified investors (hence, the market value of the investment). It is the maximum price that they should be prepared to pay for such returns.

The investment is accepted because it is worth £17,000 more than it costs. Indeed, it should be accepted by any company whose investors are well diversified.

Although the impact of the investment may differ from quoted company to quoted company (it might correlate positively with some companies' returns, but negatively with those of others), the impact on any company's well-diversified investors is found by looking at the impact on the market portfolio.

If capital markets are efficient, then all quoted shares should be correctly valued (any share that was undervalued would be the subject of buying pressure, which would force its price up to the fair value). CAPM suggests that a share's market value should be that which equates the expected return from the share with the required return for the share's beta.

## Calculation of betas

### Systematic risk

To get a beta, we need to know the systematic risk element of the investment we are considering ($\sigma_S$).

We have said that systematic risk is that part of the total risk that is related to the market portfolio. The correlation coefficient between two investment opportunities is a measure of this relationship, hence

: $\sigma_S = \sigma_i cor_m$

where

$\sigma_S$ = the investment's systematic risk

$\sigma_i$ = the investment's total risk (systematic and unsystematic)

$cor_{im}$ = correlation coefficient between the returns of the investment and those of the market portfolios

For instance, if an investment were perfectly correlated with the market so that all its fluctuations could be fully explained by fluctuations in the market, then all of its risk would be systematic $\sigma_S = \sigma_i$.

If an investment were uncorrelated to the market, then its systematic risk would be zero, and all its risk would be unsystematic.

Between those extremes come varying proportions of systematic and unsystematic risk.

Note that the relationship between these risks (total, systematic and unsystematic) is

$\sigma_i^2 = \sigma_S^2 + \sigma_u^2$

where

$\sigma_i$ = the investment's total risk (standard deviation)

$\sigma_s$ = the investment's systematic risk

$\sigma_u$ = the investment's unsystematic risk

That is, the investment's total variance is the sum of its systematic and unsystematic variances.

### The beta coefficient

Remember that beta is an index number showing the systematic risk of an investment relative to the market portfolio, ie

$$\beta = \frac{\sigma_s}{\sigma_m}$$

and from $\sigma_s = cor_{im}\sigma_i$ above, we can establish

$$\beta = \frac{\sigma_s}{\sigma_m} = \frac{cor_{im}\sigma_i}{\sigma_m} = \frac{cor_{im}\sigma_i\sigma_m}{\sigma_m^2}$$

If the correlation coefficient between the investment and the market can be established, the beta can be calculated. Alternatively, if we establish the systematic risk we can establish the beta.

## Calculation of beta coefficients in practice

### Estimating beta for an existing investment

Beta factors are calculated in practice for shares quoted on the London Stock Exchange and are available from the Risk Measurement Service operated by the London Business School among others.

The method of calculation is largely based on the above ideas regarding the average variability of the returns from investments relative to those of the market, involving the use of linear regression analysis. If the historical return on the FTSE index (representing the market), over and above the risk-free return, is plotted on a scatter diagram against the corresponding returns of a security i, also over and above $r_f$, then the following might be observed.

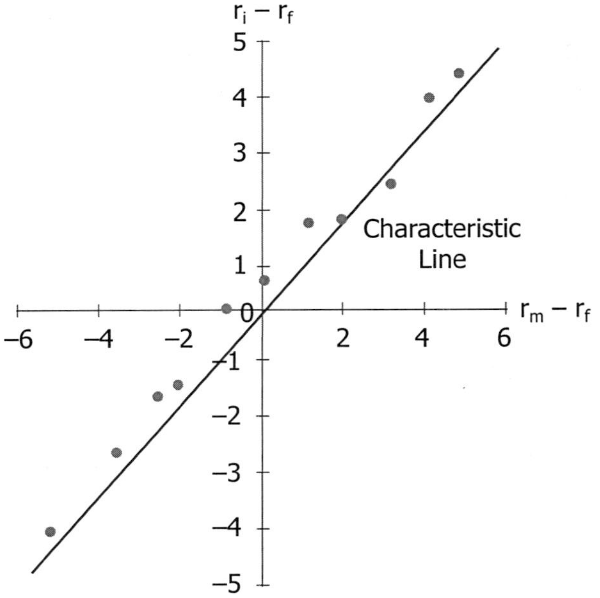


If the linear regression line of best fit is found, it will show the average relationship between the two sets of returns. This line is known as the security's characteristic line.

The results of a regression analysis give the terms for the linear regression equation, (ie y = mx + c).

$(r_i - r_f) = b(r_m - r_f) + a$

where

b = the volatility of i's return relative to the market returns. If the slope is greater than 45%, ie greater than 1, then i's returns tend to be more volatile than those of the market. This is exactly how we have earlier defined an investment's beta factor. Hence, beta is estimated by the slope of the regression line.

a = the intercept on the vertical axis and is known as the alpha factor ($\alpha_i$). It indicates that i has a premium larger than that predicted by the CAPM. (If the expected return from the CAPM equals the actual return, then $\alpha_i = 0$.)

### Estimating beta for a new investment

For a new investment it will not be possible to plot historical returns against the market and calculate the beta coefficient in this way. It may be possible to estimate future returns under likely economic scenarios and to construct an estimate of beta from this, but this would be very involved.

As an alternative, it is probably easier to identify the beta of a similar investment already in existence as an acceptable surrogate.

## Betas for combinations of investments

Although any project or investment must be appraised purely on the basis of its own expected return and beta (without reference, in particular, to the company considering the project), it is possible to work out the impact of accepting the project on the company's own beta.

When two investments are combined, their combination will have a beta equal to the weighted average (by market values) of the individual betas.

**TASK**

An ungeared listed company has a current market value of £20m, and a beta of 0.8. It is considering undertaking a project requiring an investment of £2m to be funded by a rights issue. The project is expected to yield a net cash inflow of £2.5m in one year, the inflows having a beta of 1.5. The expected return from the market is 14% and the risk-free rate is 6%.

Should the investment be accepted, what value will be placed on it and what will be the new market value, β and cost of capital of the enlarged company?

**SOLUTION**

***Required Rate of Return***

From the CAPM formula, we can work out that the appropriate risk-adjusted discount rate to apply to the project is

$k_e = r_f + \beta(r_m - r_f)$

$= 6\% + 1.5(14\% - 6\%)$

$= 6\% + 12\% = 18\%$

***Project's Return and Appraisal***

The return on the investment will be 25% (£2.5m return on a £2m investment), hence it should be accepted. It is offering a better level of return for its level of (systematic) risk than can currently be obtained on the market.

***Net Present Value of the Investment***

To value the project, the investors will use the required rate given by the CAPM as a risk-adjusted discount rate to find the present value of its future returns (the usual market value approach) giving

| Time | Cash Flow £'000 | Discount Factor | Present Value £'000 |
|---|---|---|---|
| 0 | (2,000) | 1 | (2,000) |
| 1 | 2,500 | $\frac{1}{1.18}$ | 2,119 |
| Net present value | | | 119 |

The project would be acceptable to any company with well-diversified investors. We can assume that this is the case for this company, since it is listed (and as such, most of its investors will be large institutional funds).

***New Market Value of the Company***

If the company accepts the project, its market value will rise from £20m (which is the value of the existing expected net cash inflows) to £22.119m, being the value of the original flows plus the flows from the new project. Of this increase of £2.119m, £2m has come from the rights issue, the remaining £119,000 representing the gain from the project.

***New Beta of the Company***

Of the total market value of £22.119m, £20m is the market value of flows with a beta of 0.8, while £2.119m is the market value of flows having a beta of 1.5.

The new overall beta will be the weighted average of 0.8 and 1.5, ie

$$0.8 \times \frac{£20m}{£22.119m} + 1.5 \times \frac{£2.119m}{£22.119m} = 0.867$$

***New Cost of Capital of the Company***

The old cost of equity would have been the required return for a beta of 0.8, ie

$$\begin{aligned} k_e &= r_f + \beta(r_m - r_f) \\ &= 6\% + 0.8(14\% - 6\%) \\ &= 6\% + 6.4\% = 12.4\% \end{aligned}$$

The new cost of equity (once the project is undertaken) will relate to the beta of 0.867, and will therefore be

$$\begin{aligned} k_e &= r_f + \beta(r_m - r_f) \\ &= 6\% + 0.867(14\% - 6\%) \\ &= 6\% + 6.936\% = 12.936\% \end{aligned}$$

**NB:** These two costs of equity are purely of academic interest. The project itself was appraised using $\beta = 1.5$, and any future project would be appraised using its own beta, not that for the company or for the project currently under consideration.

# 5 The Impact of Gearing on Project Appraisal

## Introduction

In our illustrations above, we evaluated investment opportunities undertaken by an all-equity financed company for whom the appropriate cost of capital is the cost of equity. The only risk that we have had to worry about has been that associated with earnings variability or business risk. Would this cost of capital be appropriate if the project was financed differently, ie by a mixture of debt and equity? The answer is clearly no.

In addition, it was stated above that to estimate a new investment's beta, we can often use the beta of a similar investment already in existence. The problem is that the proposed financing for the new investment may be different to that of the existing investment. In such a case, the beta and cost of capital of the existing investment cannot be used directly to appraise the new investment.

We know that gearing impacts on the cost of capital. Somehow we need to take account of this. If we are using the CAPM equation to give the appropriate cost of capital, the $\beta$ must incorporate the effects of the gearing.

## Geared betas

### Introduction

If a company or project is geared, then we could draw up a simple balance sheet with assets on the left and financing on the right as follows.

| | | |
|---|---|---|
| Asset value | Equity value | $MV_e$ |
| | Debt value | $MV_d$ |
| Asset value | Total value | $MV_g$ |

The basic business risk of the operations will cause the asset values and the earnings they generate to vary. Very little, if any, of this variation will be borne by the debt holders, it will all be borne by the shareholders.

With the variation in asset values being spread over much smaller equity values, the percentage variability in this figure for equity will be much larger. As a result, the risk to equity is much higher in a geared company than it would be if the company was ungeared, when the risk to shareholders would simply be the business risk. This additional risk is the effect of financial gearing.

### Definitions

#### Asset/Earnings/Ungeared Beta

The asset/earnings/ungeared beta is a measure of the basic business risk to the asset values/earnings. It, therefore, represents the risk shareholders would face if the company was ungeared.

#### Equity/Dividend/Geared Beta

The equity or dividend beta is a measure of the risk to shareholders in the geared company. The difference between the equity and asset betas will reflect the financial risk.

# 6 Modigliani and Miller

In order to quantify the impact that capital structure has on beta, we need to consider theories on capital structure developed by economists Modigliani and Miller. Modigliani and Miller developed theories on gearing based on a series of highly restrictive assumptions.

(1) **Investors Make Rational Decisions**

Modigliani and Miller assume that investors are rational and hence their actions are logical and can be predicted.

(2) **There are No Dealing Costs When Buying and Selling Securities**

The absence of dealing costs when buying and selling securities enables investors to buy and sell securities on the basis of their value rather than being deterred by transaction costs. It enables arbitrage to take place so that all companies should be valued fairly.

(3) **All Investors Have Costless Access to All Relevant Information**

This again enables companies to be valued fairly by the market place.

(4) **Companies and Individuals Can All Borrow and Lend at One Rate of Interest**

This means that there is no advantage to corporate gearing as opposed to personal gearing so that there is no incentive for an investor to buy shares in a geared company. The lack of a borrowing and depositing spread means that the actions of individuals are not constrained by the transaction cost this implies. Arbitrage can therefore take place to ensure all companies are valued fairly.

(5) **Debt is Risk Free**

This is a simplification that can be relaxed. Its advantage is that it means that a company can never become insolvent, which simplifies any analysis.

(6) **There is No Taxation**

This simplification can also be relaxed, but it is convenient to consider initially the situation where no tax exists before adding in tax refinements.

## Modigliani and Miller's basic theory

### Two equivalent companies

Modigliani and Miller considered two equivalent companies, ie companies that are precisely the same in all respects, except for the fact that one is ungeared (Company U) and one is geared (Company G). The financial results for these two companies are as follows.

| | Company U<br>£ | Company G<br>£ |
|---|---|---|
| Earnings | 1,000 | 1,000 |
| Interest | – | (400) |
| Dividends | 1,000 | 600 |

Both companies pay out all their earnings each year, either as interest to debt investors or dividends to equity investors.

Modigliani and Miller pointed out that the total payouts of both companies are the same at £1,000. Whether these payouts are called dividends or interest is irrelevant. Since both companies generate the same cash flows for their investors, they must have the same total market value. The combined value of Company G's equity and its debt must be equal to the value of Company U's equity.

Any single investor would be indifferent between the choice of owning all of Company U's equity and receiving £1,000, all of which is called a dividend, and owning all of Company G's debt plus equity and receiving £1,000, part of which is called interest and part of which is called dividends. Splitting the ownership between a number of people should still not affect the total market value. The total cake remains the same, however, it is shared out among different investors.

Since the total market values (debt plus equity) of both companies are the same and the total payouts (dividends plus interest) are the same, the WACC for both companies must be the same.

These ideas can be expressed on a graph.

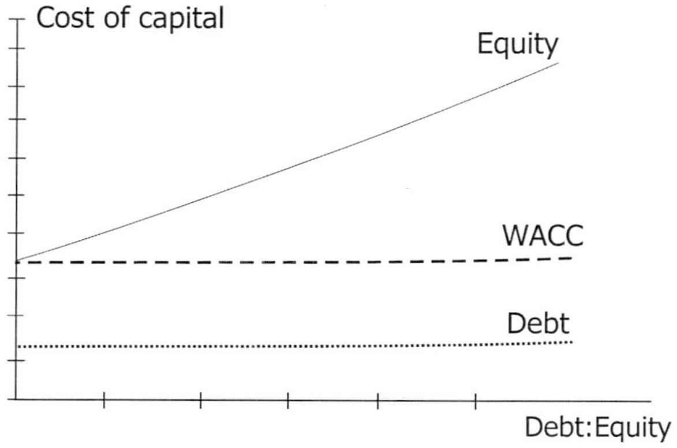


Since debt is risk-free, it has the same cost regardless of the level of gearing. The WACC likewise remains constant whatever the level of gearing, as we have seen above. Given these two lines and the way in which gearing has been defined as $MV_{debt}/MV_{equity}$, it can be shown that the cost of equity will rise in a straight line as indicated.

The benefits of cheap debt finance are counterbalanced exactly by the increased returns required by equity investors, meaning that the company's WACC remains constant.

## Implications for capital structure and investment appraisal

Since a company's market value and its WACC remain constant, regardless of how it has financed itself, the financing decision is irrelevant. All that matters is that any project has a positive net present value when discounted at the company's existing WACC (assuming the project is in the same business risk class as the remainder of the company's investments).

## Formulae

Modigliani and Miller used their rigorous academic approach to develop formulae that will exactly predict the change in the cost of a company's equity and the market value of its equity at different gearing levels. These formulae are as follows.

$$MV_u = MV_{eg} + MV_d$$

where

$MV_u$ = market value of the ungeared company's equity

$MV_{eg}$ = market value of the geared company's equity

$MV_d$ = market value of the geared company's debt

$WACC_u = WACC_g$

where

$WACC_u$ = WACC of the ungeared company (which will also be its cost of equity)

$WACC_g$ = WACC of the geared company

$k_{eg} = k_u + (k_u - r_f) \times MV_d / MV_{eg}$

where

$k_u$ = cost of equity of the ungeared company (which will also be its WACC)

$k_{eg}$ = cost of equity of the geared company

$r_f$ = cost of debt for the geared company, which is the risk-free rate of interest

## TASK

Luigi plc is an ungeared company with a market value of £10m. It pays all of its earnings out as a constant annual dividend of £2m and has a cost of equity of 20%.

It decides to reorganise its capital structure and raises £1m of irredeemable debt at a cost of 5%. It uses the £1m to repay part of its equity.

(a) What is the new market value of the equity?

(b) What is the new cost of equity?

(c) What is the new WACC?

## SOLUTION

(a) Assuming that Modigliani and Miller's theory applies, the market value of the company must remain the same as before, ie at £10m. Since the debt has a market value of £1m, the equity must have a market value of £9m.

(b) The new cost of equity can be calculated as the new dividend divided by the new market value of the equity. The new dividend will be the total earnings of the company of £2m less the interest payment of £50,000 (£1m × 5%), ie £1.95m. The cost of equity is therefore 21.67%.

(c) The new WACC will be given by the calculation

$$WACC = \frac{k_e \times MV_e + k_d \times MV_d}{MV_e + MV_d}$$

$$WACC = \frac{21.67\% \times 9 + 5.00\% \times 1}{9+1} = 20\%$$

***Checking the Equations***

It can be seen that the WACC has remained unchanged at 20%. The formula for the cost of equity can also be checked.

$k_{eg} = k_u + (k_u - r_f) \times MV_d/MV_{eg}$

$21.67 = 20 + (20 - 5) \times 1/9$

This relationship is also true.

The above illustration does not prove that Modigliani and Miller's theories are correct, of course. It merely shows that, given Modigliani and Miller's assumptions and accepting that the total market value of the company cannot change, the equations produced by Modigliani and Miller will hold good.

## Introducing corporation tax

Having established that, in the limited circumstances above, a company's capital structure is irrelevant, Modigliani and Miller considered one of the major limitations in their analysis, the existence of corporation tax. They continued to assume, however, that there was no personal tax.

In the UK, when a company pays interest to debt investors, it is eligible for tax relief, whereas dividend payments to equity investors do not qualify as an allowable expense for the company. The implication of this different tax treatment for the two equivalent companies above can be seen by comparing their earnings streams. Assume corporation tax at 31%.

| | Company U<br>£ | Company G<br>£ |
|---|---|---|
| Earnings | 1,000 | 1,000 |
| Interest | – | (400) |
| Profit before tax | 1,000 | 600 |
| Corporation tax | (310) | (186) |
| Profit after tax = dividends | 690 | 414 |
| Total payouts to investors | | |
| – Interest | – | 400 |
| – Dividends | 690 | 414 |
| | 690 | 814 |

In this case, the geared company can afford to pay out more in total to debt and equity investors than the ungeared company. The difference of £124 is due to the tax relief on the interest of £400 × 31%.

The fact that payouts in total from the geared company exceed payouts in total from the ungeared company means that a rational investor would pay more to acquire the debt and equity together of Company G than the equity of Company U. The total market value of G's debt plus equity exceeds the market value of U's equity.

The effect of this on a company's WACC as it increases its level of gearing can be seen from the following graph.

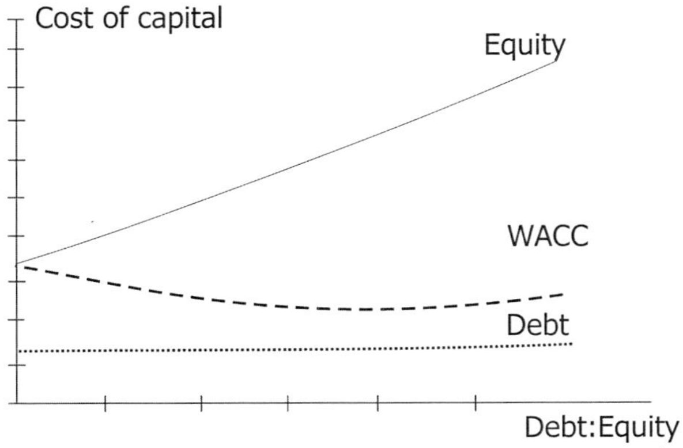


As the company borrows more money and substitutes debt for equity funding, the cost of equity rises to reflect the increased gearing risk. However, due to the tax relief on interest payments, the cost of debt to the company is now cheaper than before. This means that the benefit of cheap debt more than compensates for the increase in the cost of equity. The net effect is that the WACC falls in a curved line, constantly decreasing as the level of debt increases, but never quite falling to the level of the cost of debt.

## Adapting the formulae for corporation tax

The formulae introduced above can be adapted slightly to take account of corporation tax. All the symbols used are as above, with the additional symbol, CT, being used for corporation tax.

$$MV_g = MV_u + MV_d \times CT$$

$MV_g$ = the total value of the geared company, ie $MV_{eg} + MV_d$

This formula confirms what we stated earlier, that the total market value of the geared company exceeds that of the ungeared company. The exact amount by which its market value is higher is given by $MV_d \times CT$.

$$WACC_g = WACC_u(1 - CT \times MV_d MV_g)$$

This formula confirms that the WACC of the geared company is lower than that of the ungeared company. The higher the level of corporation tax, or the higher the level of gearing, the lower the WACC becomes.

$$k_{eg} = k_u + (k_u - r_f)MV_d / MV_{eg} \times (1 - CT)$$

This confirms that the cost of equity in the geared company is higher than that in the ungeared company, due to gearing risk.

Note that in all three equations, if corporation tax is nil, then they become the same as the equations introduced earlier in the absence of corporation tax.

### TASK

Sonny plc is an ungeared company with a market value of £10m. It has constant profits before tax of £4m and suffers corporation tax at a rate of 40%. All post-tax profits are paid out as a dividend. Its dividend is therefore £2.4m and it has a cost of equity of 24% (2.4/10).

Sonny decides to issue £2m of irredeemable debt at the risk-free rate of interest of 5%. It uses the proceeds to repay equity finance.

(a) What is the new market value of Sonny's equity?

(b) What is the new cost of equity?

(c) What is the new WACC?

### SOLUTION

(a) Assuming that Modigliani and Miller applies, the total value of Sonny's equity plus debt will become

$MV_g$ = £10m + £2m × 0.4 = £10.8m

The value of the equity is therefore £8.8m (10.8 – 2).

(b) The new cost of equity will be given by the new dividend divided by the new market value of the equity. The new dividend is the revised profit after tax.

| | £ |
|---|---|
| Earnings | 4,000,000 |
| Interest (£2m × 5%) | (100,000) |
| Profit before tax | 3,900,000 |
| Corporation tax at 40% | (1,560,000) |
| Profit after tax = dividends | 2,340,000 |

The cost of equity is therefore 26.59% (2.34/8.8).

(c) The new WACC is the weighted average of the new cost of equity and the **post-tax** cost of debt of 3% (5% × 0.6).

$$\text{WACC} = \frac{26.59\% \times 8.8 + 3.00\% \times 2.0}{8.8 + 2} = 22.22\%$$

***Checking the Equations***

The new WACC can be predicted as

$$\text{WACC}_g = 24\% \times (1 - 0.4 \times {}^{2}/_{10.8}) = 22.22\%$$

The new cost of equity can be predicted as

$$k_{eg} = 24\% + (24\% - 5\%) \times {}^{2}/_{8.8} \times (1 - 0.4) = 26.59\%$$

As before, we have not proved the validity of Modigliani and Miller's equations. Rather, we have shown that they are mutually consistent.

## Relating asset and equity betas – assuming a tax-free environment

We can use the theories of Modigliani and Miller to assist us in dealing with the impact changes in gearing might have on a company's beta factor.

Suppose we buy all of the firm's debt and equity, then we would own 100% of the assets and their returns. If we assume that there is no difference in value between geared and ungeared companies (based on very restrictive assumptions, set out by Modigliani and Miller, in a world with no tax), then any variability in asset values and earnings in the ungeared company will exactly match the variability of assets and earnings in the geared company, both in absolute and relative terms.

As a result, the asset beta or beta of the ungeared company will equal the beta of the portfolio of debt and equity in the geared company, ie the overall risk of this investment portfolio would be the asset or ungeared beta ($\beta_u$).

We have seen above how betas can be combined. Since we hold all the equity and all the debt, the beta of this combination must be the weighted average of the equity or geared beta ($\beta_g$) and the debt beta ($\beta_d$).

$$\beta_u = \beta_g \times \frac{MV_e}{MV_g} + \beta_d \times \frac{MV_d}{MV_g}$$

where

$\beta_u$ = the asset/earnings/ungeared beta

$\beta_g$ = the equity/dividend/geared beta

$\beta_d$ = debt beta (usually assumed to be nil, ie risk-free debt)

$MV_e$ = market value of the firm's equity

$MV_d$ = market value of the firm's debt

$MV_g$ = the total market value of the firm

We can rearrange this to solve for $\beta_g$ as follows.

$$\beta_u \times MV_g = \beta_g \times MV_e + \beta_d \times MV_d$$

$$\beta_g \times MV_e = \beta_u \times MV_g - \beta_d \times MV_d$$

$$\beta_g = \beta_u \times \frac{MV_g}{MV_e} - \beta_d \times \frac{MV_d}{MV_e}$$

Now, $MV_g = MV_e + MV_d$, hence

$$\beta_g = \beta_u \times \frac{MV_e + MV_d}{MV_e} - \beta_d \times \frac{MV_d}{MV_e}$$

$$\beta_g = \beta_u \times \frac{MV_e}{MV_e} + \beta_u \times \frac{MV_d}{MV_e} - \beta_d \times \frac{MV_d}{MV_e}$$

$$\beta_g = \beta_u + (\beta_u - \beta_d) \times \frac{MV_d}{MV_e}$$

This formula looks familiar in the light of Modigliani and Miller's theory of gearing in the absence of tax that notes that the impact of gearing on the cost of equity is given by

$$k_g = k_u + (k_u - r_f) \times \frac{MV_d}{MV_e}$$

This result is hardly surprising, since the CAPM states that there is a linear relationship between risks and returns. If the returns (the cost of equity) can be linked by this formula, then so can the risks.

What this also highlights, is that the CAPM formula is relevant for establishing a cost of equity regardless of the level of gearing. The result it gives will be the cost of equity for the given level of gearing incorporated in the beta, ie

$$k_u = r_f + \beta_u(r_m - r_f)$$

And

$$k_g = r_f + \beta_g(r_m - r_f)$$

### Introducing corporation tax

You will recall that the above Modigliani and Miller formula relating to the cost of equity was extended to cover the more realistic position of having tax, resulting in

$$k_g = k_u + (k_u - r_f) \times \frac{MV_d}{MV_e} \times (1 - CT)$$

From this, it follows that our beta formula can be extended to

$$\beta_g = \beta_u + (\beta_u - \beta_d) \times \frac{MV_d}{MV_e} \times (1 - CT)$$

which is the general formula for geared betas. If debt is risk-free (an assumption of Modigliani and Miller), then $\beta_d = 0$, and this reduces to

$$\beta_g = \beta_u \left[1 + (1 - CT)\frac{MV_d}{MV_e}\right]$$

## Using geared betas

The above equations allow us to gear up and ungear betas for different levels of gearing in an investment, to take account of the way that gearing amplifies the risk implicit in the earnings. This could be useful for a company entering a new sector of the market and trying to establish an appropriate cost of capital using the CAPM, but it cannot directly enable a calculation of the business risk in that sector.

A way of doing this would be to look up the beta of the shares of a company already in that sector to give a required return from the CAPM for that company. However, the beta reflects that company's level of gearing and therefore may not be appropriate for the new investment.

We need to be able to adjust this beta to reflect the new investment's level of gearing.

**TASK**

A company is considering diversifying into a new sector of the market by forming a new subsidiary at a cost of £4m with a gearing level to be decided on. A company currently in that sector has a dividend risk, described by its beta as $\beta$ = 2.34. This company has a debt to equity ratio of 80% (assume that its debt is risk free). The subsidiary will generate £1m in perpetuity before tax that is at a rate of 30%.

The current return offered by the market is 14% and the risk-free rate is 6%. Should the project be undertaken given its proposed financing?

There are two possible approaches to appraise the project, the **adjusted present value (APV)** approach and the **Weighted Average Cost of Capital (WACC) approach**. Although each approach takes a different route in the appraisal, it will be seen that they both end up with the same solution.

In both cases, we need to decide on the level of debt finance to be raised to fund the project. With the adjusted present value approach, this will be expressed as an absolute level of debt finance to be raised, whereas with the WACC approach we will merely identify the required debt to equity ratio.

### Adjusted present value approach

The adjusted present value approach is to establish the total value of the project and compare that to the value of the finance raised. If the value of the project exceeds the finance raised for the project, it has a positive net present value and should be accepted.

Assume that the project is going to be financed by £2.5m of equity finance and £1.5m of debt finance.

We are looking to establish the market value of the project given its debt finance of £1.5m. The approach is as follows.

(a) Ascertain ku, possibly by ungearing a beta, and applying that ungeared beta to the CAPM formula.

(b) Evaluate the project as if it were ungeared by discounting its cash flows at ku, ie ascertain MVu for the project.

(c) Use Modigliani and Miller's formula

$$MV_g = MV_u + MV_d \times CT$$

to establish the market value of the project ($MV_g$) given its debt financing. This can then be compared to the capital invested.

## SOLUTION

***Establish $k_u$***

Since the debt is risk free, we can use the simplified formula

$$\beta_g = \beta_u \left[1 + (1 - CT)\frac{MV_d}{MV_e}\right]$$

We are given the debt to equity ratio $\left(\frac{MV_d}{MV_e}\right)$ of the comparable company as 80% or 0.8, giving

$$2.34 = \beta_u [1 + (0.8 \times 0.7)]$$

$$= \beta_u \times 1.56$$

$$\beta_u = 1.5$$

From this, we can establish $k_u$ from the CAPM equation

$$k_u = r_f + \beta_u(r_m - r_f)$$

as

$$k_u = 6 + 1.5(14 - 6) = 18\%$$

***Evaluate the Ungeared Project***

Now, discounting the project's perpetuity cash flows, using this rate gives

$$MV_u = \frac{£1m \times 0.7}{0.18} = £3.89m$$

***Gearing-up the Project***

Now, accounting for the project's debt financing using Modigliani and Miller's formula

$$MV_g = MV_u + MV_d \times CT$$

gives

$$MV_g = 3.89 + 1.5 \times 0.3$$

$$MV_g = 3.89 + 0.45 = £4.339m$$

This clearly exceeds the finance raised of £4m (£2.5m + £1.5m), hence the project should be accepted.

### WACC approach

The WACC approach entails discounting the post-tax cash flows of the ungeared investment by the investment's Weighted Average Cost of Capital. This will give the market value of the project in total, which can be compared to the finance raised. The stages to adopt are as follows.

(a) Calculate the geared beta of the investment (and hence its geared cost of equity) based on the investment's target level of gearing.

(b) Calculate the investment's WACC, based on the company's cost of debt, the geared cost of equity and the target level of gearing.

(c) Calculate the market value of the ungeared project's post-tax cash flows, discounted at the WACC.

## SOLUTION

***Target Level of Gearing***

The target level of gearing will usually be based on the investing company's estimate of an acceptable level of debt finance for the new investment. If this target level of gearing gives precisely the same level of debt finance as the above APV approach, then the WACC approach will give the same final net present value. To illustrate this point, we have taken the target level of gearing for the investment as that given by the final gearing level from above, as follows.

| | £ |
|---|---|
| Market value of debt | 1,500 |
| Market value of equity | 2,839 |
| Total market value | 4,339 |

The target debt to equity ratio that we will use is, therefore, 52.84%.

In practice, we would not be able to do this, since we would not have used the adjusted present value approach first of all. We would have to base our target gearing level on what we considered acceptable for that particular investment.

***The Geared Cost of Equity***

$$\beta_g = \beta_u\left[1+(1-CT)\frac{MV_d}{MV_e}\right]$$

$$= 1.5\left[1+(1-0.3)\frac{MV_d}{MV_e}\right]$$

$$= 2.055$$

$$ke_g = 6 + 2.055(14 - 6)$$

$$= 22.44\%$$

***The Weighted Average Cost of Capital***

$$\text{WACC} = \frac{(22.44\times100.00)+(4.2\times52.84)}{100.00+52.84}$$

$$= 16.13\%$$

Note that the calculation takes the 6% risk-free rate of return less the tax relief, ie 6% × 0.7 = 4.2%, to give the cost of debt of 4.2%.

Here, we have calculated the WACC from first principles. We could have used the Modigliani and Miller formula

$$\text{WACC}_g = \text{WACC}_u \times \left(1-CT-\frac{MV_d}{MV_g}\right)$$

$$= 18 \times \left(1-0.3\times\frac{1,500}{4,339}\right)$$

$$= 16.13\%$$

***The Market Value of the Investment***

$$MV_g = \frac{1m \times 0.7}{0.1613} = 4,339$$

This is, of course, the same market value as that arrived at using the APV approach. We can now estimate how much debt we need to borrow to fund the project, since we know the gearing ratio. The required debt level is

$$\frac{52.84}{152.84} \times 4,339,000$$

That is, £1,500,000. This is the same level of debt finance as we used above with the APV approach, as would be expected.

## Comparing the APV and WACC approaches

The benefits of the APV approach are as follows.

- It separates out the benefit received from the project's operating earnings and the method of finance. It therefore helps identify how the company is increasing its market value either through accepting projects – which are good in themselves regardless of how they are financed – or through financing projects with suitable forms of finance.
- This explicit separation of the appraisal of the project's operating earnings and the method of finance used helps to highlight the issue of financial distress. You remember that Modigliani and Miller stated that a firm should gear up to the extent that the marginal benefits of tax relief on debt exceed the marginal costs of financial distress. The above formulae ignore the possibility of financial distress. At low levels of gearing, this is probably not significant. However, the logical conclusion of the above formulae is to finance all projects solely by debt, which is invalid. At higher levels of gearing, the costs of financial distress will affect the decision. One weakness of the WACC approach is that it hides the assumption being used, ie the company gets the benefit of tax relief on debt but does not suffer any costs of financial distress.

The benefit of the WACC approach is that it enables a company to appraise investments based on the company's target level of gearing. No absolute level of debt finance needs to be calculated in advance, and only the ratio of debt to equity finance needs to be known. As a result of this, the WACC approach is normally used in practice. However, it is important to remember that the simplified approach above will not work for higher levels of gearing.

# 7 Assumptions and Limitations of the CAPM

## The CAPM assumptions

The CAPM is based on a number of assumptions. It is important to remember that we assume these apply in any instance where we use the CAPM model to derive the cost of equity and hence undertake equity analysis or corporate valuation.

- Investors are rational and risk averse, as they seek to maximise the expected utility of their wealth.
- Investors are only concerned with a security's expected return and its systematic risk.
- The capital market is perfect and in equilibrium, which means in particular
  - It is not dominated by any individual investors.

- There are no transaction costs, for instance commissions or taxes, or other imperfections.
- All securities are fairly valued, hence rm is a realistic return.
- All investors have the same expectations regarding the probability distributions of returns from each security, thus they have the same opportunity set and efficient frontier.
- There exists a risk-free rate at which all investors may borrow or lend without limit.

The realism and relevance of many of these assumptions may be questioned. The first two are probably not too far-fetched, but the others are clearly invalid. The question is, are the effects of these invalid assumptions significant enough to invalidate the whole theory, or do they just produce minor distortions that can be dealt with separately?

It should be remembered that very similar assumptions underlie Modigliani and Miller's theories of gearing, and whether or not they seriously compromise the CAPM model is a matter for empirical testing of the CAPM's predictions.

It is worth noting that extensions made to that CAPM that seek to relax these basic assumptions give results that are still broadly in line with the basic theory.

Much research has been carried out over the years to try to establish to what extent the CAPM is valid. The results of tests are mixed. However, a large number of tests indicate that beta is not a good explanatory factor for returns.

## The CAPM limitations

Aside from the limitations stemming from the CAPM's assumptions, the following limitations are worth considering.

### Single-period (one-year) model

The required rate of return derived from the model is only valid as long as the inputs ($r_m$, $r_f$, $\beta$) are valid. As a result of annual budgets that tend to effect tax rates and interest rates (through the PSNCR), we can expect that one or more of these factors will change over a year.

Few investment projects last for one year only. However, we can extend the model to more than one time period if we assume that all relevant factors (such as risk-free rate and market rate) remain constant over the period covered.

### Only applicable to large quoted companies

The model assumes that the company's shareholders are representative of shareholders at large and that, as a result, the overall portfolio held by them equates to the market as a whole. If we were dealing with a small private company, then a portfolio theory approach would be more applicable.

### Assumes projects are affected by the same factors as the market

It is likely that projects and companies will be affected by the same factors, since companies are effectively made up of various projects. This will not necessarily be the case for all projects, and in these circumstances it is no longer reasonable to consider the riskiness of a project relative to the market.

In addition, there is evidence that stock returns cannot be explained by a single market factor. Additional factors relating to macroeconomic variables, the industry and specific company features are also relevant.

## Difficult to estimate the β factor for a project

To calculate a β factor for a project, we need to estimate the future returns for the project under different economic conditions. Obviously, this will be extremely difficult to achieve in practice. One solution could be to look at a similar project that had been accepted in the past and calculate its β factor with the benefit of hindsight. This would typically be achieved by looking at the β of a quoted company in a sector which has the same business risk as the project being analysed.

Particular problems with the measurement of beta are as follows.

- The relevance of measuring historical betas for stocks in order to forecast future betas is questionable.
- Even if beta is measured in the past, it is uncertain as to whether it is stable over time.
- If measuring beta historically, the period of time over which observations should be made is uncertain.
- When using historical data, there may be discontinuities. For example, the company may have made an acquisition or a share repurchase part way through the period.
- The beta measure obtained from the process is a sample estimate of the beta of the stock. As such it will be inaccurate. It is, however, possible to make adjustments for known statistical biases.

## Identification of the market risk premium

The model technically requires use of the expected risk premium in the future. This is unobservable, but can be estimated by reference to historical data. This gives rise to the following problems.

- The period of time over which the risk premium should be observed is uncertain. Longer time periods, eg back to 1919, may include irrelevant data while short periods may be unrepresentative.
- The market risk premium may change over time.
- The appropriate statistical method of evaluating the risk premium is uncertain. For example, should the risk premium be estimated using a geometric average or an arithmetic average?

Historically, the risk premium has been between 6% and 8%. However, the current view is that this would be excessive and it is more usual to use a risk premium of around 4%, or even less. This reflects a revised view of the riskiness of markets, due to changing economic conditions, eg lower inflation and an improved understanding of the importance of portfolio theory when assessing risk (previously, the risk of stocks was assessed in isolation).

## Identification of the risk-free rate

There is no pure risk-free rate available in the world. The closest approximation to a risk-free rate would be the T-bill rate. The problem with this is that it represents a very short dated return, for a 90-day period only. As a result, it is more common to use a long government bond yield as the basis for the risk-free rate when doing project appraisal. Although this will include a greater degree of risk (credit, liquidity and inflation risk), it has the benefit of relating to a more appropriate time horizon.

## Chapter Roundup

**Module 2, Chapter 10: The Capital Asset Pricing Model**

- The Capital Asset Pricing Model (CAPM) provides a tool to calculate a company's cost of equity. It uses risk-return benchmarks prevailing in the market to calculate the required rate of return for shareholders.
- All investors are assumed to hold a combination of the market portfolio and risk-free investments. The beta factor makes the calculation 'company-specific' by giving a relative measure of the systematic risk of an investment versus the market.
- You should be able to calculate the cost of equity using CAPM, and be familiar with what source data is required to do this.
- You should be able to list the advantages and disadvantages of using the capital asset pricing model to carry out the calculation of the cost of equity, together with your reservations and assumptions in any given scenario.
- You should be able to quantify and discuss the impact of changing the level of gearing on the cost of equity, via changes to the beta factor. The calculations that enable us to derive adjusted beta factors are based on the theories of Modigliani and Miller and thus rely on the restrictive assumptions that these economists developed.
- You should be able to calculate and apply the Adjusted Present Value (APV) approach to investment appraisal and explain how this differs from the more standard weighted average cost of capital (WACC) approach. You need to identify the relative advantages and disadvantages of both approaches.

# CALCULATING THE COST OF CAPITAL

chapter 11

Contents


| | | |
|---|---|---|
| 1 | Introduction | 242 |
| 2 | The Cost of Equity | 242 |
| 3 | The Dividend Valuation Model | 242 |
| 4 | Arbitrage Pricing Theory (APT) | 247 |
| 5 | Cost of Debt | 248 |
| 6 | Weighted Average Cost of Capital | 251 |

# 1 Introduction

We consider here methods for calculating the cost of capital for a company. We look at firstly approaches to calculate the cost of equity, then cost of debt and finally the weighted average cost of capital (WACC).

# 2 The Cost of Equity

We have seen already that the cost of equity for a company is the return required by its equity investors and that the most common method to calculate this is the Capital Asset Pricing Model (CAPM). We consider now alternative approaches to calculating the cost of equity, namely the Dividend Valuation Model (DVM) and Arbitrage Pricing Theory (APT).

# 3 The Dividend Valuation Model

The Dividend Valuation Method (DVM) is based upon the idea that when shareholders determine the value of a company's equity, they base it on the present value of all their future dividends from the company discounted at their required rate of return. The shareholders' required rate of return is the company's cost of equity.

In order to use this idea to enable us to estimate a company's cost of equity, we first need to identify the market value of the shares and the investors' expectations of future dividends. The cost of equity will then fall out as the missing figure.

## Illustration

The DVM can be illustrated by considering a company that is only going to pay one dividend of £110 in one year's time. The rate of return required by the company's shareholders is 10%. The shareholders will value the company at £100 ($^{110}/_{1.1}$).

### Developing a general formula

If we assume that a company pays an annual dividend to infinity, then a more general expression would be

$$MV_{xd} = \frac{D_1}{(1+k_e)} + \frac{D_2}{(1+k_e)^2} + \frac{D_3}{(1+k_e)^3} \text{ ... etc to infinity}$$

where

$MV_{xd}$ = the market value of the shares (ex-dividend)

$k_e$ = cost of equity

$D_n$ = dividend paid at Time n

If the annual dividend is assumed to be constant, then this equation simplifies to

$$MV_{xd} = \frac{D}{k_e}$$

Note that this will give an ex-dividend market value because the method by which the formula has been derived assumes that the first dividend occurs in one year's time, ie this year's dividend has just been paid. The formula is based on that for calculating the present value of a level perpetuity, ie

$$\frac{\text{Cash flow}}{r}$$

This simple formula is likely to be appropriate for preference shares, where there is a constant annual dividend. However, it is unlikely to be useful for equity shares, where dividend growth is anticipated.

# Introducing dividend growth

## Constant dividend growth

It is relatively easy to accommodate the idea of growth into the dividend valuation model above. The only drawback is that, to keep the model manageable, it is necessary to assume that equity dividends grow at a constant annual rate.

It is clear that in practice equity dividends do not grow at an exactly constant rate each year. However, research has indicated that directors do aim to achieve roughly constant growth and therefore shareholder expectations of constant growth in the short to medium term are not wildly unrealistic.

## A general formula

If dividends are growing at a constant rate (g), then a general expression for a company's equity market value would be as follows.

$$MV_{xd} = \frac{D_1}{(1+k_e)} + \frac{D_1(1+g)}{(1+k_e)^2} + \frac{D_1(1+g)^2}{(1+k_e)^3} \text{ ... etc to infinity}$$

This simplifies down to the following equation, which is known as the **dividend growth model** or the **Gordon growth model**.

$$MV_{xd} = \frac{D_1}{k_e - g}$$

Remember that, in order to use this formula to estimate the shareholders' required rate of return, it is necessary to estimate the prospective dividend to be paid in one year's time ($D_1$), establish the expected annual growth rate and identify the value of the company's equity.

# Estimating dividend growth

There are three main methods of estimating the expected growth rate for a company's dividends that we will consider here.

- Looking at comparable companies and published data.
- Extrapolating from past dividend growth.
- Looking at reinvestment levels.

## Information from comparable companies and published data

One of the simplest approaches is to establish the growth rates of the company itself or other comparable companies with a listing by looking at published forecasts. This information will be available from brokers' circulars and other published information.

## Extrapolation from past dividend growth

An alternative approach is to look at the past dividend growth achieved by the company and assume that this will continue in the future. For example, Michael plc has paid the following dividends over recent years.

| Michael plc – Dividends | |
|---|---|
| **Year** | **£** |
| 2011 | 5,000 |
| 2012 | 5,900 |
| 2013 | 6,950 |
| 2014 | 7,300 |
| 2015 | 8,450 |

Over a four-year period, the dividend has grown from £5,000 to £8,450. Assuming a roughly constant growth rate, the increase in dividends could be shown as follows.

| Michael plc<br>Dividends with Constant Growth | |
|---|---|
| **Year** | **£** |
| 2011 | 5,000 |
| 2012 | 5,000 (1 + g) |
| 2013 | $5,000\ (1 + g)^2$ |
| 2014 | $5,000\ (1 + g)^3$ |
| 2015 | $5,000\ (1 + g)^4$ |

The value of g can be calculated from the equation

$$5,000(1 + g)^4 = 8,450$$

$$(1 + g)^4 = \frac{8,450}{5,000}$$

$$1 + g = \sqrt[4]{\frac{8,450}{5,000}}$$

g = 0.14 or 14%

## Looking at reinvestment levels – the 'rb' model

Instead of looking at past dividend growth as a guide to the future, an alternative approach is to focus on what causes dividends to grow in the first place. Growth in dividends is caused by reinvestment in the business. If we can estimate what future levels of reinvestment are likely to be and what returns those investments are going to achieve, we can predict increases in the company's profitability and its dividend payouts.

## EXAMPLE No reinvestment

Consider a company that does not retain any of its earnings and pays everything out as a dividend. It earns a return of 20% on its existing investments and has existing net assets of £1,000. Earnings will therefore be £200 (1,000 × 20%). Over a number of years, its financial results will look as follows.

***Income plc***

| | Year 1<br>£ | Year 2<br>£ | Year 3<br>£ |
|---|---|---|---|
| Profit after tax | 200 | 200 | 200 |
| Dividends | 200 | 200 | 200 |
| Retained profit | – | – | – |
| Opening net assets | 1,000 | 1,000 | 1,000 |
| Closing net assets | 1,000 | 1,000 | 1,000 |

Since the company is not retaining any of its profits, its asset base remains at £1,000. Since it is generating a return of 20% on net assets, its profits and dividends also remain at £200.

## EXAMPLE Retention of profit

If the company were to retain a constant proportion of its earnings, say 60%, then initially dividends would fall. However, the company's net assets would increase, meaning that future profits and hence future dividends would rise. This can be seen as follows.

***Growth plc***

| | Year 1<br>£ | Year 2<br>£ | Year 3<br>£ |
|---|---|---|---|
| Profit after tax | 200 | 224 | 251 |
| Dividends | 80 | 89 | 100 |
| Retained profit | 120 | 135 | 151 |
| Opening net assets | 1,000 | 1,120 | 1,255 |
| Closing net assets | 1,120 | 1,255 | 1,406 |

In this example, we have assumed that the retained profits earn the same return when reinvested as do the existing net assets. This means that the profit after tax each year can be calculated as opening net assets × 20% (eg £1,120 × 20% = £224). Since the proportion of profits retained is constant and the returns earned on reinvestment are constant, the growth in profits is also constant, in this case 12% a year. The dividends will therefore also grow at a rate of 12% a year.

The growth rate in dividends can be calculated by using the following formula.

$g = rb$

where

$r$ = the rate of return earned on new investment

$b$ = proportion of profits retained each year

In the above example, $g = 0.2 \times 0.6 = 0.12$ or 12%

### The impact of gearing on the rb model

When a company is financed partly by equity and partly by debt, the rb model in its simple form above assumes the ratio of debt to equity finance is kept at a constant figure. This can be illustrated by looking at the example above in more detail.

## EXAMPLE

***Gearing plc – Income Statement***

| | Year 1<br>£ | Year 2<br>£ | Year 3<br>£ |
|---|---|---|---|
| Profit before interest | 350 | 392 | 439 |
| Interest @ 10% | 50 | 56 | 63 |
| Profit before tax | 300 | 336 | 376 |
| Tax @ 33% | 100 | 112 | 125 |
| Profit after tax | 200 | 224 | 251 |
| Dividend | 80 | 89 | 100 |
| Retained profits | 120 | 135 | 151 |

***Gearing plc – Financing***

| | Year 1<br>£ | Year 2<br>£ | Year 3<br>£ |
|---|---|---|---|
| Equity | 1,000 | 1,120 | 1,255 |
| Debt | 500 | 560 | 628 |
| Opening finance | 1,500 | 1,680 | 1,883 |
| Equity | 1,120 | 1,255 | 1,406 |
| Debt | 560 | 628 | 703 |
| Closing finance | 1,680 | 1,883 | 2,109 |

In this case, the ratio of debt to equity is 50%. As the value of the equity increases due to retained profits, the company raises more debt to maintain this ratio. The return on total finance is given by the profit before interest, divided by opening finance for the year in question and is maintained at a constant 23.3%.

It can be seen that the growth in profits and dividends has remained at 12%, as in the previous example for Growth plc.

## Limitations of the DVM

The DVM is obviously fairly simplistic as a means of estimating a company's cost of equity capital. It relies on a number of assumptions and has some limitations. Particular points to note are as follows.

### Market values are only affected by dividend expectations

It assumes that the only factors affecting market values are expected future dividend payments and the shareholders' required rate of return. Although these are both clearly important, other factors are also relevant in practice.

### Shareholder expectations matter

It requires knowledge of shareholder expectations. When we look at a company and try to decide on its cost of equity, we are looking at a market value determined by shareholders, based on their expectations of future dividends. We may feel that we have superior knowledge to the shareholders about dividend growth (particularly if we are the directors of the company wanting to find out the company's cost of equity for investment appraisal purposes). However, our expectations are irrelevant since we are not the ones who are setting the market value.

### Annual dividends

It assumes that dividends are paid annually. This assumption can be relaxed, with dividends being paid semi-annually, for example. The resultant cost of capital would be the cost of capital for semi-annual periods and would need to be adjusted to give an annual figure.

### Taxation

It ignores any impact taxation may have. Since dividends are not allowable as a tax expense for the company, the impact of corporation tax is fairly limited, but different investors may suffer different personal tax treatments for dividends received.

### Dividends are paid to infinity

It assumes that dividends are paid to infinity. Clearly, it is possible that the company will not last forever. However, more distant cash flows have a relatively minor effect on the calculation anyway.

Note that the assumption that the only cash flow an investor receives from the investment in equity shares is dividends when, in reality, investors will sell shares and receive sale proceeds, is not in itself invalid. The sale proceeds are determined by the present value of future dividends at the time of sale. Therefore, the individual shareholder is in effect receiving this stream of dividends as a discounted lump sum at the date of sale rather than waiting to receive the dividends in the future.

## 4 Arbitrage Pricing Theory (APT)

An alternative method to calculate the cost of equity is Arbitrage Pricing Theory (APT).

We have seen already that the Capital Asset Pricing Model only relies on the risk of a company relative to that of the market and its effect on the risk premium to arrive at what is considered to be the required rate of return of shareholders. Proponents of APT argue against this, claiming that shareholders will be concerned (when determining their required rates of return) with a whole range of factors not included in CAPM.

In APT, it is assumed that stock returns are determined by a number of factors such as interest rates, exchange rates, unemployment, and so on. Companies that trade abroad will also face exchange rate influences, while those that serve only the domestic market will not be affected at all. We have to be selective in deciding which factors are influential in determining expected return.

A general equation has been formulated to represent how the return on a company's security, ri, is determined by a host of factors:

$r_i = \alpha + \beta_1F_1 + \beta_2F_2 + ... + \beta_nF_n$, where:

- $\beta_1$, $\beta_2$, etc are coefficients ($\beta_1$ is the sensitivity of $r_i$ to factor $F_1$, for example)
- $F_1$, $F_2$, etc are the other factors determining $r_i$

Thus the main difference between APT and CAPM is that, while the former says that stock returns can be determined by many factors, the latter says that an individual security's return depends only on the return on the market portfolio.

APT shows how it is possible to produce a portfolio of stocks free of the risk arising from the variations in the factors that affect individual stock returns. In this sense, a portfolio constructed in this way would be free of risk and, therefore, earn a risk-free return.

The advantage of APT is that it has wider applicability since CAPM is a special case of the APT. APT also allows for more than one type of risk to be considered. CAPM uses only risk relating to the expected return as a whole. Because APT has many other factors determining the return on a security, it can also specify unique risk associated with each factor. This allows a more complete approach to establishing ri.

APT has no special need to incorporate a 'market portfolio' in the way that CAPM does. In this sense, it deals with more tangible concepts than does CAPM. In addition, APT is applicable to determining rates of return over more than one period, which is not the case with CAPM.

The main disadvantage with APT is the lack of published data necessary to compute the different elements of the equation. As such it is not widely used as a technique to calculate the cost of equity.

# 5 Cost of Debt

## Irredeemable fixed rate debt

A company's cost of debt can be estimated in very much the same way as with equity, using the DVM. The market value of debt is the present value of receipts to investors discounted at their required rate of return. With irredeemable debt that pays a constant amount of interest, we have an analogous situation to a constant dividend.

$$MV_d = \frac{I}{r_d}$$

where

$MV_d$ = market value of debt

$I$ = annual interest payment

$r_d$ = the debt investors' required rate of return

### Example

Fredo plc has in issue some irredeemable debt paying a coupon of 10%. It is quoted at a price of £95 per cent. This means that every £100 nominal value of the stock has a market value of £95 and pays annual interest of £10. The investors' required rate of return is given by the value of $r_d$ in the equation

$$95 = \frac{10}{r_d}$$

$r_d$ = 0.105 or 10.5%

## The impact of taxation

If there were no corporation tax, the cost of debt for Fredo plc would be given by the investors' required rate of return, 10.5%. In order to be able to pay the investors a return of 10.5% on their investment of £95, Fredo plc would need to generate cash of £10.

### Interest is an allowable expense for tax purposes

However, the payment of interest will in fact reduce the company's corporation tax charge, since interest is an allowable expense for tax purposes. This will reduce the net post-tax cost to the company of paying the interest. In the case of Fredo plc, if we assume that corporation tax is charged at a rate of 25%

| | |
|---|---|
| Interest paid to investors | 10 |
| Less: reduction in tax charge | (2.5) |
| Net post-tax cost to Fredo plc | 7.5 |

This means that in order to pay the debt investors their required return of 10.5% ($10/95$), the company only needs to generate post-tax returns of $7.5/95$, ie 7.9%. The cost of debt to the company is therefore lower than the required return of the debt investors.

### Linking the return to debt investors and the cost of debt to the company

A simplistic link between the required return of the debt investors and the cost of that debt to the company is given by

$$k_d = r_d(1 - CT)$$

where

$r_d$ = the investors' required rate of return

$k_d$ = the cost of debt to the company

CT = the corporation tax rate

In the case of Fredo plc, 10.5% × 0.75 = 7.9%

This formula assumes that the debt is irredeemable and the cash flow benefit from the tax relief occurs at the same time as the cash outflow when the interest is paid.

### $K_d$ is the IRR of the cash flows to the company

The above assumptions can be seen to be the case if we consider what we are doing when we calculate the company's cost of debt. In fact, we are calculating the internal rate of return (IRR) of the cash flows to the company. The company's cash flows are as follows.

| Time | Narrative | Flow £ |
|---|---|---|
| 0 | Issue of debt at market value | 95 |
| 1-infinity | Interest payments | (10) |
| 1-infinity | Tax relief | 2.5 |

The IRR is the discount rate where the present value of the future net outflow of £7.5 per year equals the market value of the debt. This is given where

95 = 7.5/IRR

which is exactly the same calculation as for $k_d$.

### Tax relief does not apply to equity and preference shares

Dividends paid by the company, whether on equity or preference shares, are not an allowable expense for tax purposes. Therefore, the required return of the investor and the cost of capital to the company are one and the same.

## Redeemable fixed rate debt

### Another IRR calculation

The approach to finding the cost of redeemable debt is conceptually the same as for irredeemable debt. The market value of the debt is the present value of all future payments to investors (interest and capital), discounted at the debt investors' required rate of return. In order to identify the cost of debt, it is easiest first to calculate the IRR of the flows to the investor and then to use the formula $k_d = r_d(1 - CT)$.

### Illustration

Andolini plc has redeemable debt in issue with a market value of £850,000 and a nominal value of £1,000,000. It is paying a coupon of 10% and is redeemable in three years' time at par. The corporation tax rate is 30%. Tax relief is received in the same year as the interest payments are made.

The required return of the investor is the IRR of the following cash flows.

***Andolini Plc – Cost of Debt***

| Time | Narrative | Flow £000 | Present Value at 16.76% |
|---|---|---|---|
| 0 | Market value | (850) | (850) |
| 1 | Interest | 100 | 86 |
| 2 | Interest | 100 | 73 |
| 3 | Interest and redemption | 1,100 | 691 |
| Net present value | | | – |
| Internal rate of return (ie return of debt investors) | | | 16.76% |

The cost of debt for the company can now be estimated as 16.76% × 0.7 = 11.73%.

If the tax relief occurred in a subsequent year, the cost of debt would need to be calculated as the internal rate of return of the cash flows to the company.

## Floating rate debt

The return to investors for floating rate debt on its reset date will be the new coupon. The cost of debt to the company will be based on the coupon less related tax relief. Assuming instantaneous tax relief, this will be given by the simplistic formula we have seen above.

$$k_d = r_d(1 - CT)$$

A more exact approach would be to calculate the IRR of the cash flows to the next reset date, as follows.

| Time | | Cash Flow £ |
|---|---|---|
| 0 | Par value on reset | 100 |
| 1 | Coupon at say 10% | (10) |
| 1 | Redemption at par | (100) |
| 2 | Tax relief on coupon at say 25% | 2.5 |

Time 1 is the next reset date and Time 2 is when the tax relief is received.

# 6 Weighted Average Cost of Capital

## Calculation of the weighted average cost of capital

The weighted average cost of capital (WACC) is simply an average of all the company's costs of capital for different sources of funds (equity, preference shares, debt, etc), weighted according to the ex-dividend market values of each of the sources.

**Example**

Corleone plc has equity in issue with a market value of £15m and a cost of 20%. It also has irredeemable debt in issue with a market value of £5m. The investors' required rate of return for debt is 12.5% and corporation tax is 20%. The post-tax cost of debt is therefore 10% (12.5% × 80%).

The WACC for Corleone plc is given by the formula

$$\text{WACC} = \frac{k_e \times MV_e + k_d \times MV_d}{MV_e + MV_d}$$

where

$MV_e$ = market value of the company's equity

$MV_d$ = market value of the company's debt

$$\text{WACC} = \frac{20\% \times 15 + 10\% \times 5}{20} = 17.5\%$$

### Alternative method of calculation for irredeemable debt and with constant dividends

Where a company is paying a constant dividend with no growth and debt is irredeemable, an alternative method of calculating its WACC would be to use the following calculation.

$$\text{WACC} = \frac{\text{Total payouts}}{\text{Total market value}}$$

In the above example, the dividend each year would be £3m (20% × £15m) and the post-tax interest on the debt would be £0.5m (10% × £5m). The WACC can be calculated as $3.5/20$ = 17.5%.

## The impact of changes in capital structure on WACC

What will be the effect on the overall value of WACC as the market value of debt increases relative to the market value of equity in this equation?

### Debt is cheaper than equity

Debt is less risky than equity for investors and therefore requires a lower rate of return. The effect of this is that as a company gears up, its WACC will be reduced due to the higher proportion of debt in the company's financial structure.

### Increased gearing increases the risk to equity

Higher debt levels increase the variability of returns to equity. This can be seen from comparing the returns of two companies with different levels of gearing in two different economic scenarios.

| | Company U | | Company G | |
|---|---|---|---|---|
| | Scenario 1 | Scenario 2 | Scenario 1 | Scenario 2 |
| | £ | £ | £ | £ |
| Profits before interest | 1,000 | 500 | 1,000 | 500 |
| Interest | – | – | (400) | (400) |
| Profits after interest | 1,000 | 500 | 600 | 100 |

It can be seen that, whereas returns to equity fall by 50% ($500/_{1,000}$) for the ungeared company, they fall by over 80% ($500/_{600}$) for the geared company.

As a result of the increased risk, equity investors in the geared company will require a higher rate of return. This increase in required returns for equity will tend to increase a company's WACC as it gears up.

### Two conflicting forces

It can be seen that increased gearing affects the WACC in two conflicting ways. It tends to be reduced due to the lower cost of debt finance but pulled up by the increasing cost of equity. The question is, which force is the stronger one?

### An ungeared company

For an ungeared company the WACC will be one and the same as the cost of equity, since such a company only has the one source of finance. At low levels of gearing, the company's cost of equity remains fairly constant. Equity investors are not concerned with low levels of gearing and believe that it does not significantly affect the risk of their investment. Therefore, they do not require any significant extra return to compensate them for the additional gearing risk.

As debt levels increase, however, shareholders will become more concerned about the increased gearing risk attached to their investment. At some stage, this concern will translate into higher required rates of return to compensate equity investors for the additional risk.

When a particular threshold of gearing is exceeded, shareholders demand higher rates of return. This means that, while at low levels of gearing the cost of equity is relatively constant, at higher levels it increases sharply.

### Effect of gearing on the cost of debt

The cost of debt remains constant at low to medium levels of gearing. However, at higher levels it increases to compensate debt investors for increased default risk.

### Overall impact of gearing on WACC

At lower levels of gearing, equity finance is being replaced by cheaper debt finance. However, the cost of the remaining equity does not increase significantly for the reasons noted above. This means that the WACC of the company will fall.

At higher levels of gearing, the introduction of cheap debt still has a downward pull on the company's WACC. However, there is now also a significant upward pull due to increases in the cost of equity. The net effect of these two conflicting forces is that the WACC starts to rise. At very high levels of gearing, increases in the cost of debt means that the WACC increases even more dramatically.

These ideas can be summarised on a graph.

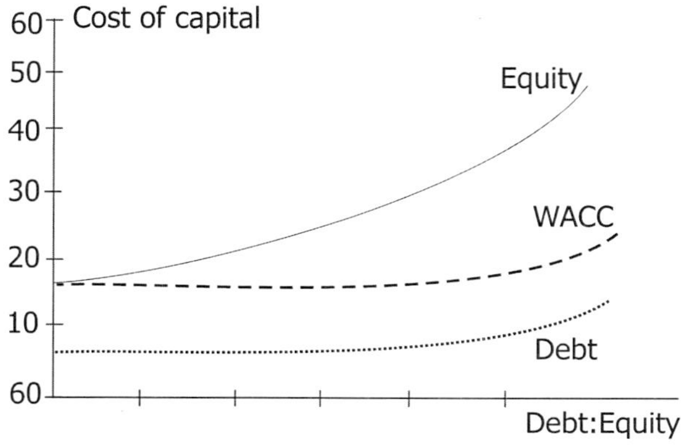


## Implications for capital structure

The implication of the above for a company is that it will have an optimal level of gearing that will minimise its WACC. A low WACC will be beneficial since it will enable the company to accept more projects with positive net present values.

Companies should always raise finance to enable them to move towards their optimal gearing level and their minimum WACC. A company on the far left of the graph should raise debt finance for new projects, while in contrast a company that has gone too far to the right should raise equity finance to reduce gearing levels.

Once the company has hit its optimal capital structure, it should aim to stay there and always raise finance in such a way as to achieve this. Since it would be impractical to constantly raise a mixture of debt and equity for each new project, the company should first issue debt and then issue equity, meaning that it oscillates around its optimal point rather than remaining precisely on it.

## Implications for investment appraisal

### Where a company is already at its optimal level of gearing

In this situation, a company will raise finance so as to maintain its gearing ratio at the existing level. This means that, given the project is in the same business risk class as existing projects, the finance for the new project will be in the same proportion as existing finance, the company's WACC will stay the same and the cost of the new finance will be the existing WACC.

The existing WACC is therefore the relevant discount rate for project appraisal in these circumstances.

### When a company is not already at its optimal level of gearing

When such a company is appraising a project, it needs to consider two factors, namely whether the project itself is worthwhile and whether it should be financed by debt or equity. A worthwhile project is one that has a positive net present value. Worthwhile finance is finance that reduces the company's WACC. If the company has relatively low gearing, the new project should be financed by debt. Where it already has substantial levels of debt, new equity should be issued.

## Task

Antonio plc is at present financed solely by equity with a market value of £10m. It is paying a constant total dividend of £2.5m and has a cost of equity (and hence a WACC) of 25%.

The company is considering a new project in the same business area as its existing investments, which will require investment of £1m and will give annual income of £0.19m to infinity (ignore tax).

The company is considering financing the investment by raising irredeemable debt which will cost 5%. If it does this, then the existing shareholders will perceive additional gearing risk to their investment. As a result, they will require an increased return on their equity of 26%.

Is the project worthwhile and is the financing method appropriate?

## Solution

***The Financing Method***

Considering the finance first of all, it is likely that Antonio plc is correct in wanting to issue debt, since it is at present ungeared. The traditional theory indicates that low levels of gearing cause no problems for the company.

In order to make a more exact evaluation of the financing method, we need to calculate its cost and compare it to the existing cost of capital for the company. If the cost of the new finance is lower than the existing cost of funds, it is a good method of finance and will result in a lowering of the company's overall WACC. If it is higher than the existing WACC, it is bad news and will actually cause the WACC to increase.

***The Marginal Cost of Raising the Finance***

The cost of the new finance comes from two sources. The obvious source is the requirement to pay 5% interest on the borrowings made. If this was the end of the story then the new finance would clearly be much cheaper than the existing 25% cost of equity.

However, an additional cost is the increase in the required return of the equity shareholders that will occur as a result of the increase in borrowings. In order to keep shareholders happy, a higher dividend will need to be paid to compensate them for their additional risk. If the dividend is not increased, then the market value of the shares will fall to £9.6m, being the present value of the existing dividend of £2.5m discounted at a discount rate of 26% (2.5/0.26).

The new total dividend can be calculated as the dividend that would maintain the value of Antonio plc's equity at £10m when discounted at the new required return of 26%. The new dividend will therefore need to be £2.6m (£10m × 26%). Hence, the total cost of the debt finance is

| | £ |
|---|---|
| Interest payments (5% × £1m) | 50,000 |
| Increase in dividends required (£2.6m – £2.5m) | 100,000 |
| Total cost | 150,000 |

Since the company has raised £1m at an annual cost of £150,000, the cost in percentage terms is 15%. This is known as the **marginal cost of the finance**. Since the marginal cost of finance is less than 25% (the existing WACC of the company), the method of finance is good and the WACC of the company will fall after the finance is raised.

***Is the Project Worthwhile?***

The project itself is generating annual returns of £190,000 and therefore gives a return of 19% on the investment required of £1m. If it was being funded by equity, it would clearly not be worthwhile, since equity investors are demanding a return of 25% from an ungeared company in this business area. However, the method of finance being used only needs a return in excess of 15% for the project to have a positive net present value and therefore it can be accepted.

If the project had been giving returns of say £0.3m a year, then it would have been acceptable even with equity finance. However, the company should always aim to maximise its opportunities and, rather than simply remaining ungeared, it should investigate different sources of finance to ensure it raises funds in the most cost effective way possible.

***The New WACC of the Company***

The new WACC of the company can be calculated by using the formula above. The new market value of the company's equity will first need to be calculated, given as the new total dividend is discounted at 26%.

The new total dividend is calculated as follows.

| | £ | £ |
|---|---|---|
| Old dividend | | 2,500,000 |
| Dividends from new project | | |
| Earnings | 190,000 | |
| Less: Interest | (50,000) | |
| | | 140,000 |
| | | 2,640,000 |

The market value of the equity is therefore £10,154,000 (2640/0.26) and the new WACC of the company is

$$\text{WACC} = \frac{26\% \times 10{,}154 + 5\% \times 1{,}000}{10{,}154 + 1{,}000} = 24\%$$

It can be seen that the WACC has fallen.

## Equivalent rates – dealing with inflation

The weighted average cost of capital is calculated based on the cost of debt (bond yields) and the capital asset pricing model. This makes it a nominal (or money) rate ie it includes the rate of return required to compensate for inflation. This WACC can then be used to discount cash flows which are stated on a nominal basis, ie include inflation.

Occasionally you may come across 'real' of return. These rates cannot be used to discount nominal cash flows but must instead be restated to a nominal basis by using effective rates. The nominal discount rate can be calculated as follows.

Effective discount factor $\Rightarrow 1 + m = (1 + r)(1 + i)$

where

| | |
|---|---|
| i | = annual inflation rate |
| m | = money cost of capital (including inflation) |
| r | = real discount rate (excluding inflation) |

## EXAMPLE

Calculate a nominal rate of return, where the real return is 9.5% and inflation is estimated at 1%.

$(1+m) = (1+r)(1+i)$

$m = (1.095)(1.01) - 1$

$m = 1.10595 - 1$

$m = 10.595\%$

## TASK

Hubba plc, an all equity financed food manufacturer, is about to embark on a major diversification into the consumer electronics industry. Its current equity beta is 1.2, while the average equity beta of electronics firms is 1.6. Gearing in the electronics industry averages 30% debt, 70% equity by market values. Debt is considered risk free.

rm = 25% rf = 10% T = 30%

**Required**

Estimate a suitable discount rate for the project if it were financed:

(i) entirely by equity

(ii) by 30% debt, 70% equity (by market values)

(iii) by 40% debt, 60% equity (by market values)

## SOLUTION

(i) **100% equity financing**

The starting point is to find the systematic risk of the electronics industry – measured by the assets beta (ßa)

$$1.6 = ßa\left[1 + \frac{30(1 - 0.30)}{70}\right]$$

ßa = 1.23

ke = 10% + 1.23 (25% – 10%)

ke = 28.45%

ke = WACC, as no debt

(ii) **30% debt, 70% equity**

Project gearing = industry gearing, so use ße = 1.6 to get ke

ke = 10% + 1.6 (25% – 10%)

ke = 34%

kd = 10% (1 – 0.3)

kd = 7%

WACC = (34% × 0.7) + (7% × 0.3)

WACC = 25.9%

(iii) **40% debt, 60% equity**

ßa = 1.23. Adjust to reflect new gearing.

$$\beta e = 1.23\left[1 + \frac{40(1-0.30)}{60}\right]$$

ße = 1.804

ke = 10% + 1.804 (25% – 10%)

ke= 37.06%

kd = 7%

WACC = (37.06% × 0.6) + (7% × 0.4)

WACC = 25.036%

## CHAPTER ROUNDUP

**Module 2, Chapter 11: Calculating the Cost of Capital**

- An alternative approach to calculating the cost of equity, is to use the dividend valuation model (DVM). This uses the relationship between the share price and the expectation of future dividend payments to deduce the required shareholder return. You need to be able to carry out the calculation, including using different approaches to deriving dividend growth, given appropriate market information. You should also be able to provide supporting comments, including the advantages and disadvantages of the approach, together with your reservations and assumptions for the given scenario.
- You should have an awareness of the Arbitrage Pricing Theory and when it might be used and what are its advantages and disadvantages.
- The cost of debt is calculated based on the return required by the investor in the debt instruments. You should be able to calculate this return based on different types of debt and to deal with the impact of taxation on the results. The overall cost of debt depends on the characteristics of the individual debt instruments.
- This chapter also covers deriving the weighted average cost of capital and how changes in gearing will impact the result. This is a very important area and you need to be comfortable with the calculations and the accompanying discussion.

# FREE CASH FLOW

chapter 12

Contents


| | | |
|---|---|---|
| 1 | Introduction | 260 |
| 2 | The Use of Cash-Based Valuations | 260 |
| 3 | What is Free Cash Flow? | 260 |
| 4 | Identifying and Forecasting Free Cash Flow | 265 |
| 5 | Terminal Value | 267 |
| 6 | Discounting the Cash Flows and Terminal Value | 271 |
| 7 | Sensitivity Analysis | 273 |

# 1 Introduction

Discounted cash flow-based valuations are theoretically superior to other valuation methods, since they are based on the fundamental determinant of corporate value, ie cash.

# 2 The Use of Cash-Based Valuations

## An investor acquiring control of the company

The dividend valuation method can be used to value a company on the basis of its cash dividends. As such, it is particularly appropriate to minority investors who only get the dividends determined by the directors. The cash valuation used here focuses on the cash that the business generates before investors have received their returns. It is of use to a controlling shareholder who can decide whether to reinvest this 'free cash flow' of the business or to pay it out as a dividend.

# 3 What is Free Cash Flow?

In order to produce a cash flow-based valuation of a company, it is first necessary to estimate the cash flows the business can generate from its operations. This calculation is often referred to as 'free cash flow' and it can be estimated in the following three ways:

(1) Free cash flow to the enterprise (including capital allowances)

(2) Free cash flow to the enterprise (assuming depreciation is tax deductible)

(3) Free cash flow to equity

We will provide definitions of all three measures, then look at when each might be appropriate to use.

### Definition 1 – Free cash flow to the enterprise, including capital allowances

Free cash flow to the enterprise or free cash flow to the firm (FCFF) is the total amount of cash the company generates after funding purchases of non-current assets and any required increases in working capital, but before any financing flows such as interest, dividends or debt capital repayments. It is termed 'free cash flow to the enterprise' as it gives the flows available to all providers of capital (ie both debt and equity).

A pro-forma calculation for FCFF including capital allowances is as follows:

| FCFF | £ |
|---|---|
| Earnings before interest and tax | x |
| +/– Non-cash items | x |
| **Cash EBIT** | x |
| Less: Cash taxes (Cash EBIT × tax rate) | (x) |
| Add: Tax relief for capital allowances | x |
| Less: Capital expenditure | x |
| Less/add: (Increase)/decrease in working capital | x |
| **Free cash flow to the enterprise** | x |

### Cash EBIT

The starting point for the calculation is the firm's operating profit (EBIT). This is then adjusted for non-cash items, such as depreciation, impairment costs and increases/decreases in provisions. For instance, depreciation and impairment expenses should be added back and the release of an unused provision should be deducted. This gives us a 'Cash EBIT' figure.

### Tax

We can then estimate the cash taxes figure by multiplying the Cash EBIT figure by the prevailing tax rate. The calculated tax figure will differ from the tax charge in the income statement as it is based on a measure of profit pre-financing costs and it excludes accounting adjustments, which are largely disallowable for tax purposes. The calculated tax figure will also differ from the actual tax paid because no credit has been allowed for tax depreciation and this must be adjusted for in the next line in the pro-forma via capital allowances.

### Capital allowances

The company will save tax through capital allowances. Relief is generally available for a company's non-current assets at a rate of 25% on a reducing balance. The impact on the free cash flow calculation will be the tax saving that this represents at the company's marginal cost of taxation.

## TASK

A company purchases a machine for £10,000 which it expects to use for a three-year project at the end of which it will be sold for an estimated £2,000. If the company pays tax at a rate of 30%, what is the impact of the capital allowances on its free cash flow?

| Year | Asset Pool | | Capital Allowances Available | Tax Saving in Free Cash Flow | |
|---|---|---|---|---|---|
| | £ | | £ | £ | |
| 1 | 10,000 | | | | |
| | (2,500) | | 2,500 | 750 | (Time 1) |
| 2 | 7,500 | | | | |
| | (1,875) | | 1,875 | 563 | (Time 2) |
| 3 | 5,625 | | | | |
| | (2,000) | Note 1 | | | |
| | 3,625 | Note 2 | 3,625 | 1,088 | (Time 3) |

Note 1 – the disposal proceeds

Note 2 – the remaining asset value, available for tax relief as a balancing allowance. If the disposal proceeds exceeded the tax written down value of £5,625, the allowances would be clawed back from the company via a balancing charge, giving rise to a cash outflow in the final period.

### Capital expenditure

This is the total amount of cash spent on purchasing new non-current assets less the proceeds from assets disposed of. When analysing past cash flow for a company, total capital expenditure should be included. However, when forecasting, it may be appropriate to limit capital expenditure to a replacement level, on the basis that any additional investment represents an application of free cash flow. This will be the case if a business has reached a state where there is no opportunity for rapid growth in its markets through expansion of the asset base.

### Working capital

Any increase in working capital levels represents increased investment in the asset base of the business and means that a certain amount of profits has not yet been realised in cash. Working capital should only reflect those items that are included in the profit before interest and tax referred to above. This means that it will include inventories, receivables and payables. It will not, however, include short-term investments or cash balances, unless they are an essential part of working capital, eg for a cash retailer. These represent surplus assets in the business and are not linked to operating flows. In addition, it does not include short-term interest bearing liabilities such as bank overdrafts. All of these are dealt with separately in the valuation.

The market value of any deposits or investments is added into the firm's total value. Overdrafts are treated as being part of debt, which is considered in more detail below.

### Non-operating cash flows

Any items excluded from the operating profit figure above need to be taken into account separately for the purpose of the cash flow valuation of the business. Where this is a series of one-off cash flows, they will need to be highlighted and valued as such. Where the cash flows relate to investments and deposits, the market value of the underlying investment is added into the investment, as noted above.

## TASK

Calculate the free cash flow to the enterprise of ABC Ltd, where the following data is given.

| | |
|---|---|
| EBIT | £100m |
| Depreciation | £40m |
| Accounting tax charge | £10m |
| Tax rate | 30% |
| Capital expenditure | £30m |
| Capital allowances available in year | £50m |
| Increase in working capital p.a. | £2m |

## SOLUTION

| | £m |
|---|---|
| EBIT | 100 |
| + Depreciation | 40 |
| Cash EBIT | 140 |
| – Tax (**30% × cash EBIT**) | (42) |
| + Capital allowances relief (30% × 50m) | 15 |
| – Capital expenditure | (30) |
| – Increase in working capital | (2) |
| Free cash flow to the enterprise | 81 |

**Note:** the accounting tax charge is irrelevant since it is not a cash flow.

## Definition 2 – Free cash flow to the enterprise, excluding capital allowances

The second way to calculate free cash flow is commonly used where information on the company's capital allowances is not available.

It is calculated as follows:

| FCFF | £m |
|---|---|
| Earnings before interest and tax | x |
| +/– Non-cash items | x |
| Cash EBIT | x |
| Less: Taxes (**EBIT × tax rate**) | (x) |
| Less: Capital expenditure | x |
| Less/add: (Increase)/decrease in working capital | x |
| **Free cash flow to the enterprise** | x |

The figures used are the same as method (1) above, with the important distinction in the tax calculation. Method (1) based the tax calculation on the **cash EBIT** number and adjusted separately for tax relief on non-current assets ie capital allowances. However, we will not always have access to capital allowance information (for example if carrying out a valuation from publicly available financial information). In this case, method (2) is more appropriate. Here, we base the tax calculation on the **EBIT** number and in doing so assume that depreciation is tax deductible (ie accounting depreciation = tax depreciation). There is thus no need for an additional capital allowances adjustment. We also assume that there are no other tax disallowable items impacting EBIT. In practice, this is not likely to be true – especially for UK companies – but it is generally assumed that the differences are not so significant as to invalidate the overall calculation.

## Definition 3 – Free cash flow to equity

The third calculation is of Free Cash Flow to Equity (FCFE). This calculates the total amount of cash the company generates after funding purchases of non-current assets and any required increases in working capital, and **including** any financing flows such as interest, preference dividends and debt capital repayments. It is termed 'free cash flow to equity' as it gives the flows available to all providers of equity capital (ie after payments to other providers of capital).

It is calculated as follows:

| FCFE | £ |
|---|---|
| Net income | x |
| +/– Non-cash items | x |
| | x |
| Less: Capital expenditure | x |
| Less/add: Changes in working capital | x |
| Less: debt principal repayments | x |
| Add: new debt raised | x |
| **Free cash flow to equity** | x |

The calculation starts from net income, in other words it is already after tax and interest. The non-cash items adjusted for in the next line, will therefore include non-cash operating expenses, finance costs and tax expenses. Capital expenditure and working capital are adjusted for as previously. Finally, as we are calculating free cash flow to equity, changes in debt capital in the year are included, with repayments shown as a cash outflow and any new debt raised as a cash inflow.

## Which method to choose

For valuation purposes, free cash flow to the enterprise is a much more useful calculation. It gives us a valuation independent of the financing structure, which may alter as a result of the proposed acquisition etc. Considering free cash flow to the enterprise enables us to consider the value of the operations as a whole and then consider the financing structure separately.

Importantly, different types of cash flow should be discounted at different discount rates.

- Free cash flow to the enterprise, should be discounted at the weighted average cost of capital to give an enterprise value.
- Free cash flow to equity should be discounted at the cost of equity to give an equity value.

### TASK

You extract the following information from a company's financial statements:

- Earnings before interest and tax (EBIT) $2,000
- Depreciation expense $200
- Interest expense $462
- Tax expense $538
- Capital expenditure $500
- Working capital increased in the year by $100
- Debt repayments totalled $150
- The effective tax rate is 35%

Calculate the company's free cash flow to the enterprise and free cash flow to equity. Can you provide a reconciliation of the two measures of free cash flow?

### SOLUTION

Calculating free cash flow to the firm:

| | $ |
|---|---|
| EBIT | 2,000 |
| + depreciation | 200 |
| Cash EBIT | 2,200 |
| Tax (35% × 2000) | (700) |
| Capital expenditure | (500) |
| Increase in working capital | (100) |
| **Free cash flow to the enterprise** | **900** |

Calculating free cash flow to equity:

| | $ |
|---|---|
| Net income (2000 – 462 – 538) | 1,000 |
| + depreciation | 200 |
| Capital expenditure | (500) |
| Increase in working capital | (100) |
| Debt repayments | (150) |
| **Free cash flow to equity** | **450** |

Reconciling the two measures:

| | $ |
|---|---|
| **Free cash flow to equity** | **450** |
| Interest (net of tax relief) | 300 |
| Debt repaid in the year | 150 |
| **Free cash flow to the enterprise** | **900** |

# 4 Identifying and Forecasting Free Cash Flow

Any cash flow-based valuation necessitates forecasting cash performance for the business. The following key stages need to be followed in a cash flow-based valuation of a business.

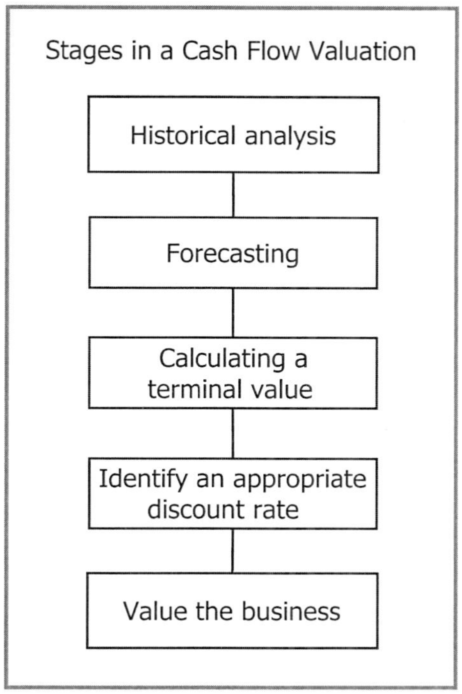


## Historical analysis of cash flows

### Purpose of historical analysis

A company's free cash flow is derived from two main factors:

- Its ability to generate profits from its asset base
- The level of reinvestment in the business

In order to be able to forecast cash flows for the future by analysing these factors, it is important to analyse the past. By understanding how the company has generated cash in the past, we can examine the existing and forecast economic and industrial environment, to establish how it can continue to generate cash in the future.

### Analysis of historical cash flow

Key factors to consider in the analysis will be as follows.

- The company's level of return on its asset base, ie its return on capital employed.

- The amount of profits that have been reinvested in the business each year and the rise in profits this has caused in subsequent years.
- The amount of new external investment each year (debt and equity) and the rise in profits this has caused.

The analysis should go back over a five to ten-year period. The danger with selecting a shorter period for the analysis is that we may fail to identify a trend or cycle that has occurred over a longer period of time. The problem with analysing up to ten years in the past is that the earlier years will give information that may no longer be relevant or applicable.

### Industry and competitor analysis

In conducting any historical analysis, it is important to place the results in context. It is, therefore, necessary to compare the company's performance to other similar companies in the same sector and to identify key factors affecting the sector's performance. Any differences between the company's performance and that of the sector in general should be investigated to identify the reasons for this. It may be that the company is a poor performer and, with good management, the return on capital could be improved substantially in the future. This would need to be taken into account in preparing any forecast.

### Limitations in the historical analysis

It should be remembered that any analysis based on published accounting information is going to be limited. Key limitations to be aware of include the following.

- Accounts are usually prepared on an historic cost basis, with no allowance for inflation. This fact contains many possible risks for an analyst of a set of accounts. For example, the rate of return on assets purchased several years ago will appear artificially high, since current year profits are being compared with the historic cost of purchase. In addition, the depreciation charge in the accounts will be artificially low compared to the revenue that the related assets are generating. Even if inflation is fairly low, say at 5% p.a., the cumulative effect of this could be significant, increasing prices by nearly 30% over a five-year period.
- Various creative accounting techniques may be used to:
  - Increase or smooth profits
  - Understate assets and liabilities ('off balance sheet finance')

Although the above problems are being addressed by the introduction of new Accounting Standards and disclosures, analysis of past accounting data is still going to be of limited use. This highlights the fact that valuation is not a pure science, but involves substantial amounts of judgement. Any conclusions based on the analysis cannot be justified on a purely quantitative basis. The analyst will need to develop an understanding of the company and industry in question and much of the final valuation will be based on judgemental factors.

## Forecasting cash flows

### Free cash flows: the explicit forecasting period

The valuation of the company in question will be based on two main elements, namely the explicit forecasting period and the terminal value. The explicit forecasting period is the period for which detailed cash flow forecasts are completed. The terminal value is a more simplistic forecast for the remainder of the company's life, based on simplifying assumptions for growth and rates of return.

Since the terminal value is based on simplifying assumptions and, hence, may be a less rigorous valuation technique, it is desirable to make it of less significance in the context of the overall valuation. This is achieved by extending the length of the explicit forecasting period, with its more detailed analysis of the company and its cash flows. The problem with extending the explicit period is that any cash flow forecast for years further into the future is inherently less reliable than one for a closer period of time. It may, therefore, be that the additional accuracy obtained from a longer explicit forecast is spurious and a simpler approach is just as good. As always, valuation techniques are not absolute measures and a large element of judgement is required.

A theoretically sound approach is to make the explicit forecasting period the length of time for which the company is able to maintain a level of return on new investment in excess of the required returns to shareholders. The reason for this is considered below in relation to calculating the terminal value. In practice, analysts will usually establish a forecasting period of between five and ten years, depending on whether the company is in a stable or a growing industry.

### Identifying key variables

In developing the forecast, the analyst will need to identify the key factors affecting cash flow over the forecast period. These will include:

- The economic and industry scenario
- The level of investment made by the company
- The return on investment

Having identified the key characteristics of the industry, it is usually the case that demand will be the key limiting factor for the company. Having identified the anticipated level of demand, the level of investment needed to sustain that demand and the level of operating costs can be derived by making assumptions for operating profit margins and asset turnover.

### Synergies

If the valuation is being undertaken for the purpose of an acquisition, any synergies that are expected to arise should be quantified separately in terms of their cash implications. Care needs to be taken relating to the timing of the cash flows. Cash outflows by way of negative synergies, for instance relating to restructuring costs, should not be forgotten. The present value of the synergies should be the maximum level of the bid premium in the transaction.

## 5 Terminal Value

### The purpose of the terminal value calculation

When valuing a company, its total value is usually broken down into two components:

Total value of the company's operations =
Present value of operating cash flows in the explicit forecast period +
Present value of operating cash flows outside the explicit forecast period

The terminal value calculation is designed to estimate the present value of the cash flows outside of the explicit forecast period. It can be incorporated into the cash flow forecast as the value of the business at the end of the explicit forecast period. The present value of the cash flows in the explicit forecast period and the terminal value can then be discounted back using an appropriate cost of capital to give the value of the company today.

**Task**

Brando Limited is expected to generate free cash flow of around £500,000 p.a. for the next five years. The valuer believes that a WACC of 20% is appropriate for Brando Limited's area of business and calculates that an appropriate terminal value is £6m. Calculate the enterprise value of Brando Limited.

## SOLUTION

| Time | Narrative | Cash Flow £'000 | Discount Factor at 20% | Present Value £'000 |
|---|---|---|---|---|
| 1–5 | Cash flow | 500 | 2.99 | 1,495 |
| 5 | Terminal value | 6,000 | $\frac{1}{1.2^5}$ | 2,411 |
| **Enterprise value =** | | | | **3,906** |

The discount factor for times 1 to 5 at 20% has been calculated using the formula

$$\frac{1}{r}\left\{1-\frac{1}{(1+r)^n}\right\}, \text{ ie } \frac{1}{0.2}\left(1-\frac{1}{1.2^5}\right)$$

The terminal value could be viewed conceptually in one of two ways. It could be seen as being the value for which the business could be sold at the end of the explicit forecast period. If an acquirer is planning to hold the business for several years and then dispose of it, then this will be the suitable approach. Alternatively, it could be viewed as being the present value of the future cash flows outside of the explicit forecast period at the end of the explicit period (in the above example, at Time 5). This would be appropriate if an acquirer is aiming to hold the business for the long term.

The enterprise value of Brando Limited is therefore £3,906,000 based on a free cash flow approach.

### Calculation of terminal value

The terminal value can be calculated using a number of different approaches, ranging from the sophisticated to general rules of thumb. It may be appropriate to calculate terminal values using a number of different techniques. The values can then be compared and, if one approach gives a significantly different value, the reason for this can be investigated.

Possible approaches include the following:

- Discounted cash flow-based approach
- Price-to-earnings ratio approach

### Cash flow-based approach – assuming no growth

The cash flow based approach is similar in concept to the dividend valuation approach for valuing shares. The free cash flow is estimated for the year after the end of the explicit forecast period. It may then be assumed that the annual cash flow to infinity remains at this level, ie we have a level perpetuity.

$$\text{Terminal value} = \frac{FCF_{t+1}}{WACC}$$

where

$FCF_{t+1}$ = free cash flow for the year after the end of the explicit forecast period

WACC = Weighted Average Cost of Capital

## Cash flow-based approach – assuming growth

An alternative approach is to assume that the free cash flow will grow at a constant rate to infinity, ie the same as the Gordon growth model for dividends. In this case, the appropriate formula for arriving at the terminal value is as follows.

$$\text{Terminal value} = \frac{ACF_{t+1}}{WACC - g}$$

where

$ACF_{t+1}$ = adjusted cash flow at Time t + 1

g = expected growth rate in cash flows

It is important to note that the adjusted cash flow above is not as high as the free cash flow in the original formula with no growth. The reason for this is that the growth will only be achieved if some reinvestment takes place. It is not possible to create additional cash flows out of thin air. Even if there is inflation giving rise to increases in nominal cash flows, this implies that the money value of the company's asset base will have to increase. This will do so as the cost of replacing fixed assets increases and the level of debtors increases in line with inflation.

## Should growth be incorporated?

It is important to recognise that the two approaches above will only come to a different answer if the expected return on new investment is different from the required return of investors. This can be illustrated by a simple example.

### TASK

Marlon plc, an ungeared company, has free cash flow available of £1,000, at Time 0, ie now. The company is currently paying out all of its annual free cash flow as a dividend to shareholders. The free cash flow is expected to remain constant at £1,000 p.a. to infinity. The shareholders' required rate of return is 10%. Calculate the value of the company today on the basis that Marlon plc decides to

- Maintain its current policy of paying out all of its free cash flow as a dividend.
- Retain 40% of its cash flow each year, starting now, and reinvest this to earn a return of 20%, ie in excess of shareholders' required returns.
- Retain 40% of its cash flow each year but only earn a return on this of 5%, ie below shareholders' required returns.
- Retain 40% of its cash flow each year and earn a return on this of 10%, ie equal to shareholders' required returns.

### SOLUTION

(a) Market value = $\frac{1,000}{0.1} + 1,000 = £11,000$

**Note that the additional £1,000 needs to be added on to reflect the dividend flow at Time 0.**

(b) Growth rate in dividends = rb = 0.2 × 0.4 = 0.08 or 8%

$$\text{Market value} = \frac{600 \times 1.08}{0.1 - 0.08} + 600 = £33{,}000$$

**The value of the dividend at Time 1 is given by the revised dividend of £600 today increased by the growth rate of 8%.**

(c) Growth rate in dividends = rb = 0.05 × 0.4 = 0.02 or 2%

$$\text{Market value} = \frac{600 \times 1.02}{0.1 - 0.02} + 600 = £8{,}250$$

(d) Growth rate in dividends = rb = 0.1 × 0.4 = 0.04 or 4%

$$\text{Market value} = \frac{600 \times 1.04}{0.1 - 0.04} + 600 = £11{,}000$$

The above calculations indicate a conclusion that is not surprising. When a company's new investments earn a rate of return greater than that required by shareholders, the investments have a positive net present value and undertaking the investments increases shareholder wealth. When the new investments earn a sub-standard rate of return, they have a negative net present value (NPV) and reduce shareholder wealth. When the required rate of return equals the expected return, the new investments have a NPV of nil and shareholders are indifferent as to whether or not the investment is made.

### Price-to-earnings ratios

The P/E approach is a fairly rough and ready measure and is more closely linked to the idea that the company is going to be sold at the end of the explicit forecasting period. The analyst will need to identify the expected net operating profits after tax for the last year of the forecast period and apply an appropriate P/E ratio to these profits.

If this approach gives a significantly different valuation to the cash-based approach, the reasons for this will need to be analysed carefully. For example, it may be that the cash-based approach is using a different discount rate than that used by the market to value companies in the sector in general. If this is the case, then the discount rate being used for the cash-based valuation will need to be studied very carefully to ensure that it is appropriate.

### Conclusion on the explicit forecast period

It was stated above that the explicit forecast period should extend over the period during which a company earns supernormal returns on its investments, ie where it is able to achieve a return in excess of that demanded by shareholders. During this period, the level of reinvestment should be relatively high to capitalise on the growth opportunities available. At the end of the period, reinvestment levels will fall, reflecting the lack of profitable new investment opportunities arising.

Given that the explicit forecast period does extend this far, the easiest assumption to make for the terminal value is that cash flows will continue without growth to perpetuity. There is no point in retaining profits for reinvestment and any new investment will have a net present value of nil.

If the explicit forecast period does not extend this far, there are various problems in identifying the terminal value. Some elements of real growth will need to be incorporated, but it will clearly not continue forever – the period when the company has a competitive advantage is finite. In such a case, it may be appropriate to break down the terminal value into two components: the period when supernormal returns are expected; and the period from when expected returns fall to the investors' required returns.

# 6 Discounting the Cash Flows and Terminal Value

## The present value of the free cash flow and the terminal value

Having established the cash flows the company is capable of generating and distributing to investors, these need to be discounted to a present value. The cost of capital used will reflect the risk of the business.

## Identifying the appropriate cost of capital

There are a number of different ways in which to identify the appropriate discount rate to calculate the present values. The usual method, however, is the Weighted Average Cost of Capital (WACC). The key issues to consider are as follows.

- The cost of equity
- The cost of debt
- The level of gearing in the company

## The impact of changing levels of gearing

### Long-term changes in gearing levels

It may be the case that a company is planning to change its gearing ratio in the medium to long-term or that a potential acquirer is planning to alter the level of gearing. What are the implications of this for estimating the company's WACC and calculating a value for the business?

In theory, a separate WACC could be calculated for each period (say, each year), reflecting the spot rate for flows occurring in that year and the expected level of gearing in that year. The present value of each year's flows could then be calculated based on the WACC for that particular year. The problem with this is that it is fairly involved and it is likely that a simpler approach will give a satisfactory answer.

If the company is planning to change its target level of gearing, then it is possible that this proposed change is already known to investors and the current cost of debt and equity will reflect the anticipated changes. This means that the WACC calculation can be based upon the existing cost of debt and equity for the company.

If an acquirer is planning to change the company's level of gearing, then it should first of all calculate the market value of the company using its existing level of gearing as a basis for the WACC, on the basis that investors are not aware that any change in gearing is going to take place. It should then recalculate the value of the company based upon a WACC assuming the revised level of gearing. The difference between the two values indicates the potential increase in value due to the improved gearing level. If this gearing level can only come about as a result of the acquisition, then it represents one of the potential synergies arising from the acquisition.

In this case, care should be taken that the costs of both debt and equity reflect the new level of gearing, rather than being based on historic gearing levels.

### Short-term fluctuations

It may be the case that a company has fluctuating levels of debt through the year, especially if it is involved in a seasonal business. This means that the ratio of debt to equity will vary and the implications of this for estimating WACC should be considered.

As with longer term movements in debt levels, it would theoretically be possible to disaggregate each year into smaller periods and ascribe a WACC for each period based on the relevant spot rates and gearing levels. This would give rise to a very refined calculation but one with a spurious level of accuracy.

An easier approach is to estimate the weighted average level of debt for the year and use this as the basis for the debt to equity ratio in the WACC calculation. This approach has the advantage of reflecting the fact that the interest paid to investors over the year will also reflect the average level of debt outstanding over the year. Hence, the use of the weighted average level of debt will take account of the overall interest cost of servicing debt over the year.

The costs of debt and equity for the company in these circumstances should already reflect any risk implicit in the fluctuating gearing levels.

### Total company value and equity value

The usual approach to discounting future cash flows is to use the Weighted Average Cost of Capital (WACC). The WACC is a discount rate that reflects the overall risk of the company and is applied to the cash flows of company before any interest has been paid out.

This means that the resultant value is the total value of the company's equity and its debt. In order to estimate the value of the company's equity, the value of the debt will need to be deducted from the total value.

## TASK

You wish to establish the fair value of a company to ascertain whether it is an investment opportunity. You have prepared the following free cash flow forecasts for the business and consider it reasonable that the company grows at 1% per annum in the terminal period.

| | £000 |
|---|---|
| Year 1 | 400 |
| Year 2 | 520 |
| Year 3 | 595 |
| Year 4 | 630 |
| Year 5 | 690 |

The company is financed by 30% debt and 70% equity and has a published beta factor of 0.9.

**Additional information**

- Tax is 30%
- The long-dated government bond yield is 4.7% and the yield on the company's own bonds is 6.9%
- The equity risk premium is 4%

**Requirement**

Calculate a fair value for the enterprise.

**SOLUTION**

- **Calculating the discount rate**

  Cost of equity, using CAPM

  Ke = Rf + (beta × Rp)

  = 4.7 + (0.9 × 4) = 8.3%

  Cost of debt, net of tax

  Kd = 6.9 × 0.7 = 4.8%

  Weighted average cost of capital

  WACC = (70% × 8.3%) + (30% × 4.8%) = 7.3%

- **Calculating the primary value**

| Time | Cash Flow | Discount Factor @ 7.3% | Present Value |
|---|---|---|---|
| 1 | 400 | 0.932 | 373 |
| 2 | 520 | 0.869 | 452 |
| 3 | 595 | 0.809 | 481 |
| 4 | 630 | 0.754 | 475 |
| 5 | 690 | 0.703 | 485 |

Total primary value for the business is = 2,266

- **Calculating the terminal value**

$$\text{TV (undiscounted)} = \text{CF} \times \frac{(1+g)}{r-g}$$

$$= 690 \times \frac{(1.01)}{0.063} = 11062$$

TV (discounted) = 11062 × 0.703 = 7777

- **Calculating enterprise value**

  EV = Primary + Terminal value

  = 2,266 + 7,777 = 10,043

# 7 SENSITIVITY ANALYSIS

As with any investment appraisal decision, sensitivity analysis is required to establish the likely impact of a change in a **key variable** on the company's value. Key variables to consider sensitising will include:

- Revenue growth rates
- Operating margins
- The weighted average cost of capital
- The terminal growth rate

Sensitivity analysis should be used to help define the parameters of valuation ranges and to identify where the main risk areas lie in the valuation. Data tables can be used to clearly summarise a range of valuation outcomes given changes in the main valuation inputs. Care must be taken in varying individuals variables, as there is likely to be at least a degree of **interdependence** (for example declines in revenue growth might be expected to also put downward pressure on operating margins).

Another way to carry out sensitivity analysis is by developing different **scenarios** which can incorporate a range of different impacts on the cash flow forecasts and discount rate. This can be used to give a 'base case', 'upside case' and 'worst case' to demonstrate the consequent impact on valuations.

## Chapter Roundup

**Module 2, Chapter 12: Free Cash Flow**

This is a very important chapter. Free cash flow is the cash generated by a company after funding purchases of non-current assets and working capital, but before some or all cash flows relating to the financing of the company. It is a crucial component of any valuation of a business which uses a discounted cash flow approach.

Please ensure you can calculate free cash flow three different ways, depending upon the information that you have been provided with in the exam question. In particular ensure you are able to calculate an appropriate tax figure in each case.

1. Free cash flow to the enterprise, including capital allowances.
2. Free cash flow to the enterprise, assuming depreciation is tax deductible.
3. Free cash flow to equity.

Different measures of free cash flow are discounted at different discount rates:

- Free cash flow to the enterprise, should be discounted at the weighted average cost of capital to give an enterprise value.
- Free cash flow to equity should be discounted at the cost of equity to give an equity value.

To derive a business valuation using free cash flow, forecasts must be prepared for the explicit forecast period and then a terminal value must be included. You should be confident in calculating both the primary and terminal value and combining them to find the overall enterprise and equity value.

You will also need to highlight why sensitivity analysis is important and what approach you might take to sensitising the key variables in any given scenario.

# OTHER VALUATION TECHNIQUES

chapter 13

Contents


| | | |
|---|---|---|
| 1 | Introduction | 278 |
| 2 | Economic Value Added (EVA) | 278 |
| 3 | Real Options and Options-Based Valuation Models | 283 |
| 4 | Methodologies in the Valuation of Mineral Rights | 289 |

# 1 Introduction

This chapter considers other valuation techniques in the syllabus, namely:

- Economic Value Added ('EVA')
- Real options and options-based valuation models
- Valuation of mineral rights

# 2 Economic Value Added (EVA)

## The purpose of shareholder value added techniques

Shareholder Value Added (SVA) is a performance measure of whether a business has added or destroyed value in the period in question. SVA is computed by deriving the company's economic profit using adjusted accounting data. The most widely used SVA technique is Economic Value Added (EVA).

EVA – note that the abbreviation is a registered trademark of Stern Stewart & Co. – is a measure of performance that is designed to identify the economic profit that a company is earning.

It was primarily designed to be a measure of management performance, genuinely assessing the value which management has brought to a company's shareholders through their actions. The benefit of using economic profit for this purpose is that, if carefully calculated, it cannot be affected by accounting choices in the way that accounting profits are. In recent times, it has become fashionable to use EVA as part of an assessment of a company's expected future returns.

The methodology of EVA focuses on the following basic ideas.

- Capital invested
- Cost of capital
- Profitability after allowing for the cost of capital

The idea is that management must generate a positive return to investors after charging an interest charge against profits. The interest charge is based on the cost of capital multiplied by the capital invested in the business.

In other words, management are charged for the capital they are using in the business when their performance is assessed. This should encourage management to use capital efficiently, raising capital where they believe they can earn high returns compared to the cost of capital, and repaying capital if the rate of return on investment is too low.

## Capital invested

### The objective of calculating capital invested

Capital invested is designed to measure the economic book value of all cash invested in the company's business activities. It is based on the accounting balance sheet adjusted for certain items that do not reflect economic reality.

### Definition of capital invested

Capital invested is defined as follows.

| Capital Invested | |
|---|---|
| Current assets | x |
| Less: Non-interest bearing liabilities | (x) |
| Net working capital | x |
| Add: Non-current assets, including goodwill | x |
| Total assets less non-interest bearing liabilities | x |
| **Adjustments to balance sheet figures** | |
| Add: Goodwill previously amortised | x |
| Add: Present value of operating leases | x |
| Add: Cumulative R&D expenditure (to be capitalised and written-off over five years) | x |
| Less: Marketable securities | (x) |
| **Capital invested** | x |

An alternative way of calculating capital invested is to add together all the sources of finance on the balance sheet and make the above adjustments.

In this case, the calculation of capital invested is as follows.

| Capital Invested | |
|---|---|
| Book value of shareholders' funds | x |
| Add: Preference shares | x |
| Add: Minority interest | x |
| Add: Interest bearing liabilities, including finance leases | x |
| Add: Deferred tax provision | x |
| Sources of funds on the balance sheet (= total assets less non-interest bearing liabilities) | x |
| Add: Goodwill previously amortised | x |
| Add: Present value of operating leases | x |
| Add: Cumulative R&D expenditure (to be capitalised and written-off over five years) | x |
| Less: Marketable securities | (x) |
| **Capital invested** | x |

## Cost of capital used in EVA

### Weighted average cost of capital

The cost of capital is the Weighted Average Cost of Capital (WACC) of the firm.

### Obtaining appropriate estimates

The debt to equity ratio is based on the average ratio (in market value terms) over the three preceding years.

The cost of debt is based on the pre-tax cost of debt less the marginal tax rate. The pre-tax cost of debt is based on the yield of long-term bonds issued by companies of similar credit quality to the company in question.

The cost of equity is based on the long-term yield on government bonds plus a risk premium. The risk premium is based on the stock's beta multiplied by the market risk premium.

## Economic value added and economic profit

### Differences between economic and accounting profit

Economic Value Added (EVA) is essentially an economic profit rather than an accounting profit. The major distinctions between economic and accounting profits are as follows.

- Economic profit allows for implicit costs and explicit costs, whereas accounting profit only allows for explicit costs. In particular, economic profit is after charging an implied cost for the use of capital.
- Economic profit recognises revenue and costs on a cash basis, as opposed to an accruals basis.

The terms economic profit and Economic Value Added are synonymous. For convenience, we will consistently use Economic Value Added.

### Definition of economic value added

Economic value added is defined as follows.

| Economic Value Added | |
|---|---|
| Adjusted operating profit before tax (see below) | x |
| Less: Cash taxes on operating profit | (x) |
| **Net operating profit less adjusted taxes (NOPLAT)** | **x** |
| Less: Cost of capital in sterling terms<br>(Capital invested × WACC) | (x) |
| **Economic Value Added** | **x** |

An equivalent definition is as follows.

$$\text{Economic value added} = (\text{Return on capital} - \text{WACC}) \times \text{Capital invested}$$

Return on capital here is defined as NOPLAT ÷ Capital invested.

#### Profit after depreciation

Depreciation **is** deducted when arriving at Economic Value Added because depreciation is viewed as an economic cost, measuring the usage of the asset in the period.

#### Adjusted operating profit

The operating profit figure is based on the reported accounting profits, but is adjusted for the following items.

- Any operating lease rental expense is treated as being partly depreciation and partly interest cost. The implied interest cost is added back to the profit, to avoid making any finance charges against operating profit. The interest cost is estimated by calculating the present value of future operating lease payments using the cost of debt. The interest charge is then the cost of debt multiplied by the present value of the future lease payments.

- Any goodwill amortisation expense is added back to profit. The goodwill is left as an asset on the balance sheet and is not amortised. This is because amortisation of goodwill does not represent a true cost to the business, on the basis that goodwill is not used up like tangible fixed assets.
- Any R & D expenditure charged in the year is added back to profit. In its place an amortisation expense on the R & D asset in the balance sheet is charged. The net of these two adjustments is the amount by which profit is increased (assuming expenditure exceeds amortisation). The net adjustment is referred to as the increase in net capitalised R & D in the period.
- Any investment income is deducted from the profits. Since we are not treating marketable securities as part of the capital invested, we should not include any income relating to these in our profits.

### Cash taxes on operating profit

The tax charge in the accounts will need to be adjusted for two reasons.

- To identify the cash taxes paid in the year, rather than the tax charge in the income statement. Deferred tax effects will therefore need to be stripped out.
- To identify the taxes paid on the operating profit, rather than the income before tax. This means that the tax impact of investment income and interest payable will need to be stripped out.

## Assessing management based on EVA

It was mentioned above that management need to generate positive EVA to justify their existence. Note that this may not be the case every year. Where a company undertakes significant capital investment, it may take time for profits to come on stream.

As a result, management should not be appraised on the EVA of one year, but evaluated based on generation of EVA over their whole time with the firm and possibly beyond.

## EVA return on capital

EVA return on capital is defined as follows.

$$\text{EVA return on capital} = \frac{\text{EVA}}{\text{Capital}}$$

It represents the amount by which the actual return on capital for the year in question exceeds the required return on capital, being the WACC.

The benefits of looking at EVA return on capital instead of purely focusing on EVA as an absolute figure are as follows.

- The EVA return on capital can be tracked through time, identifying how the company is doing now compared to the past.
- The EVA return on capital allows for comparisons across companies with different amounts of capital invested, identifying which company is earning greater excess returns, ie which company has the largest economic profit per pound of capital invested.

An important point to note in relation to the second benefit is that the best company is not necessarily the one that maximises the EVA return on capital. A company may maximise EVA return on capital by only investing in highly restricted projects with very high rates of return. However, it could be ignoring investments that have a rate of return in excess of the cost of capital but by less than the current EVA return on capital of the firm. These investments are good because they have positive net present values, but the firm rejects them because they will reduce the EVA return on capital.

# Market value added

## Definition of market value added

Market Value Added (MVA) is defined as the difference between the market capitalisation of the firm's equity plus debt, less the capital invested.

| Market Value Added | |
|---|---|
| Total market capitalisation of equity plus debt | X |
| Less: Capital invested | (x) |
| **Market Value Added** | X |

MVA measures the amount by which the management have increased the value of the capital invested in the firm. It is achieved by investing in projects with positive net present values, ie where the required return exceeds the WACC.

The MVA is the present value of all the expected future EVA from the firm's operations, as the example in the next section demonstrates.

The performance of the management can be measured by looking at the change in the MVA year on year. If new capital of £1m is added to the firm in the year but the total market value of debt plus equity increases by £1.5m, the management has increased MVA by £0.5m. Hence, they have increased the wealth of stockholders.

# Reconciling EVA with MVA and linking them to NPV analysis

EVA and MVA are simply net present value analysis expressed with a slightly different methodology. This can be seen from a simplified example.

**TASK**

A company has capital invested of £1,000. It is capable of generating net operating profits less adjusted taxes (NOPLAT) of £110 per year to infinity, without changing the level of capital in the business. Its WACC is 10%.

- Value the firm using NPV analysis.
- Identify the MVA of the firm.
- Link the MVA with the expected future EVAs.

**SOLUTION**

**Value of the Firm**

The value of the firm using NPV analysis is the present value of the future free cash flows. Since the company is not changing its level of capital invested, the free cash flow will be equal to the NOPLAT.

$$\text{Value} = \frac{\text{Free cash flow}}{\text{WACC}} = \frac{110}{0.1} = £1,100$$

**Market Value Added**

Market Value Added is the difference between the value of the firm and its capital invested, as follows.

Market Value Added = 1,100 – 1,000 = £100

**Linking MVA to Future EVAs**

The MVA is the present value of all the **future** EVAs, discounted at the WACC.

Each year's EVA is calculated as follows.

| | |
|---|---|
| NOPLAT | 110 |
| Less: Capital charge (10% × 1,000) | (100) |
| EVA | 10 |

The present value of these is as follows.

$$\text{Present value} = \frac{\text{EVA}}{\text{WACC}} = \frac{10}{0.1}$$

Note that, since MVA is determined in part by interest rates, it will change year on year partly as a result of changing interest rates, not just due to changes in the ability of the firm to deliver profits relative to its capital invested.

## Problems in using value added approaches

- There is no standard way of calculating economic profit, with different adjustments to accounting data being possible.
- This ambiguity means that analysts may draw different conclusions about a company due to their different approaches.
- It also means that economic profit may be manipulated, weakening its use as a way of appraising management.
- EVA uses CAPM when identifying WACC. CAPM may not be an adequate approach to use in defining the risk-return relationship.
- Value added approaches involve identification of a market risk premium. The lower the risk premium used, the greater the economic profit.
- Value added approaches also involve other historical estimates, such as the beta.

# 3 Real Options and Options-Based Valuation Models

The value of a firm is generally assumed to come from two different sources, as follows:

- The current assets of the business. Typically, the value of the current assets can be captured in the current cash flows of the firm. We are using the term 'assets' here in a generic, rather than strictly accounting, way.
- The present value of any future growth opportunities. Typically, the value of future growth opportunities is captured by the growth in cash flows in the future.

However, this framework ignores another important source of value – the value attributable to the real options management face in their decision-making about the business. Real options give the right to the management of a company to make future decisions when it is profitable for them to do so. Plans may change because of changes in the underlying business market or in response to the actions of a competitor – both of which are almost impossible to forecast. As a result of these changes, a company may decide to expand faster or slower, defer a project or develop a new strategy. This ability to 'wait and see' is what we term a 'real option'. Real options thus are valuable but are not generating any cash flows and therefore fall outside traditional valuation approaches.

Traditional NPV analysis is carried out upfront, in advance of a decision. Experience shows that companies do invest in projects that offer conventionally-determined negative NPVs. This is likely to be because traditional approaches ignore real options ie opportunities for future value creation.

We can take into account real optionality as follows, with a calculation of modified NPV:

Modified NPV = conventional NPV + option value if greater than zero (>0)

## Possible solutions to the valuation problem

How do we determine option value? There are three possible methods of valuing real options.

- Value the option on the open market. This is only possible if there is a traded market in such options. If there is no active market or if the option is difficult to separate from the other operations of the firm, this approach is not feasible.
- Use a traditional DCF framework and factor in a higher growth rate than would be justified given the existing assets of the firm. The problem with this is that any growth rate used will be subjective. In addition, it expresses contingent cash flows as expected cash flows. It is unlikely that the resulting valuation would be more meaningful than that derived by a conventional method.
- Use an option-based approach to valuation. There are financial models available to value traded financial options and, by accepting their underlying assumptions, the formulae can be applied to value real options.

## Determinants of option values

The value of an option is determined by the following factors:

- The exercise price
- The price of the underlying asset
- The time to expiration
- The volatility of the underlying asset; and
- The interest rate.

The impact that changes in the above factors have upon value, depend upon whether we are considering a call option (right to buy) or a put option (right to sell). Real options can be either call or put options.

The higher the exercise price, the lower the probability that a call option (right to buy) will be exercised. So call prices will decrease as the exercise prices increase. For the put, the effect runs in the opposite direction. A higher exercise price means that there is higher probability that the put will be exercised. So the put price increases as the exercise price increases.

As the **current stock price** goes up, the higher the probability that the call will be in the money. As a result, the call price will increase. The effect will be in the opposite direction for a put. As the stock price goes up, there is a lower probability that the put will be in the money. So the put price will decrease.

Both the call and put will increase in price as the underlying asset becomes more **volatile**. The buyer of the option receives full benefit of favourable outcomes but avoids the unfavourable ones (option price value has zero value).

Both calls and puts will benefit from increased **time to expiration**. The reason is that there is more time for a big move in the stock price. But there are some effects that work in the opposite direction. As the time to expiration increase, the present value of the exercise price decreases. This will increase the value of the call and decrease the value of the put. Also, as the time to expiration increase, there is a greater amount of time for the stock price to be reduced by a cash dividend. This reduces the call value but increases the put value.

The higher the interest rate, the lower the present value of the exercise price. As a result, the value of the call will increase. The opposite is true for puts. The decrease in the present value of the exercise price will adversely affect the price of the put option.

## The Black Scholes pricing model

The most important valuation model for options is the Black Scholes model. It is commonly used in financial markets but the calculation can be applied to valuing real options as well.

### The Black Scholes formula

The Scholes formula for the value of a **European call option** is given by:

$$C = P_a N(d_1) - P_e N(d_2) e^{-rt}$$

where $P_a$ is the current price of the underlying asset

$P_e$ is the exercise price

r is the continuously compounded risk-free rate

t is the time expiration measured as a fraction of one year, for example t=0.5 means that the time to expiration is six months

e is the base of the natural logarithms

$$d_1 = \frac{\ln\left(\frac{P_a}{P_e}\right) + \left(r + 0.5s^2\right)t}{s\sqrt{t}}$$

$$d_2 = d_1 - s\sqrt{t}$$

where s is the standard deviation of S

$\ln\left(\frac{P_a}{P_e}\right)$ is the natural logarithm of the spot price over the exercise price

## Value of European put options

The value of a **European put option** can be calculated in a similar way to a European call option. The result is

$$C_o = P_e N(-d_2)e^{-rt} - P_a N(-d_1)$$

## Value of American call options

Although American options can be exercised any time during their lifetime it is **never optimal** to exercise an option earlier. The value of an American option will therefore be the same as the value of an equivalent European option and the Black-Scholes model can be used to calculate its price.

## Value of American put options

Unfortunately, no exact analytic formula for the value of an American put option on a non-dividend-paying stock has been produced. Numerical procedures and analytic approximations for calculating American put values are used instead.

### TASK Black-Scholes calculation

Consider the situation where the stock price six months from the expiration of an option is $42, the exercise price of the option is $40, the risk-free interest is 10% p.a. and the volatility is 20% p.a. This means $P_2 = 42$, $P_e = 40$, $r = 0.1$, $s = 0.2$, $t = 0.5$.

### SOLUTION

$$d_1 = \frac{\ln(42/40) + \left(0.1 + \frac{0.2^2}{2}\right)0.5}{0.2\sqrt{0.5}} = 0.7693 = 0.77$$

$$d_2 = 0.7693 - 0.2 \times \sqrt{0.5} = 0.6279 = 0.63$$

and

$$P_e^{-rt} = 40e^{-0.1 \times 0.5} = 40e^{-0.05} = 38.049$$

The values of the standard normal cumulative probability distribution can be found from the tables and are:

N (0.77) = 0.7794

N (–0.77) = 1 – N (0.77) = 1 – 0.7794 = 0.2206

N (0.63) = 0.7357

N (–0.63) = 1 – N (0.63) = 1 – 0.7357 = 0.2643

Hence if the option is a European call, its value, is given by:

$c = (42 \times 0.7794) - (38.049 \times 0.7357) = 4.76$

If the option is a European put, its value is given by:

$P = (38.049 \times 0.2643) - (42 \times 0.2206) = 0.81$

The stock price has to rise by $2.76 for the purchaser of the call to break even. Similarly, the stock price has to fall by $2.81 for the purchaser of the put to breakeven.

## Using option pricing models to value real options

When valuing real options, the key inputs for an option pricing will need to be identified, being the underlying asset price, the strike price, the expected volatility of the underlying asset price and the time to expiry. The following approach could be adopted.

- Identify the value of the underlying asset. This will be based on the expected cash flows that the asset can generate. Given the uncertain nature of the cash flows and the distant time periods in which they may arise, it will clearly be difficult to value the underlying asset precisely.

- Identify the standard deviation of the cash flows above. This will again be difficult to identify, due to changes in the potential market for the product, changes in technology etc. It would, however, be possible to use techniques such as scenario analysis. The higher the standard deviation, the more valuable the asset.
- Identify the exercise price of the option. This is the cost of investing in the resources needed to produce the asset. It is typically assumed that this remains constant in present value terms, with any uncertainty being reflected in the cash flows of the asset.
- Identify the expiry date of the option. For example, expiry date of a patent. Any cash flows after this date are expected to have an NPV of zero, since there will be generic competition after patent protection ends.
- Identify the cost of delay. If the project is not implemented immediately, this will reduce the value of the cash flows from the project as competing products will enter the market in future years.

## Benefits and problems of option pricing models

The benefit of using option pricing models is as follows.

- The approach is based on contingent claim valuation, which reflects the situation more precisely than a DCF approach.

The problems of using option pricing models, such as Black Scholes, are as follows.

- They need the underlying asset to be traded. This is because the model is based on the principle of arbitrage, which means that the underlying asset must be easy to buy and sell. This is not a problem when valuing options on quoted shares. However, the underlying asset in the context of product options will not be traded, meaning that arbitrage is not possible.
- They assume that the price of the underlying asset follows a continuous process. While this may be a reasonable approximation most of the time for quoted shares; it is clearly inappropriate in the context of product options. The impact of this is that the model will undervalue deeply out-of-the-money options, since it will underestimate the probability of a sudden large increase in the value of the underlying asset.
- They assume that the standard deviation of price of the underlying asset is known and does not vary over the life of the option. While this may be a reasonable assumption in the context of short-dated equity options, it is not appropriate for long-term product options.
- They assume that exercise occurs at a precise point in time. In the case of product options, exercise may occur over a long period of time. For example, if a firm has the right to mine natural resources, it will take time to extract the resources. This will reduce the present value of the asset.
- Companies have found real options both difficult to use in practice and poorly correlated with observed prices. Usefulness in valuation is broadly confined to two categories of companies: natural resource companies where the price of the underlying product can be tracked continuously (eg oil prices), and companies with very high debt burdens, to the extent that the value of the equity in current terms is zero.

## Example – Using the Black Scholes model to value real options

### TASK

Pandy Inc is considering a project that currently has an NPV of $(3.5m). However as part of this project, Pandy Inc will be developing technology that it will be able to use in five years' time to break into the Asian market. The expected cost of the investment at year 5 is $20m. The Asian project is currently valued with an NPV of 0 but management believes that NPV could be positive in five years' time due to changes in economic conditions.

The standard deviation is 0.25, risk free rate is 5% and Pandy's cost of capital is 12%.

**Required**

Evaluate the value of the option to expand.

### SOLUTION

The value of the project ($P_a$) is $20m at year 5. We therefore have to discount this back to Year 0 to obtain the present value.

$P_a$ = $20m × 0.567 = $11.34m

The other variables are as follows.

$P_e$ = $20m    t = 5    s = 0.25    r = 0.05    $e^{-rt} = 0.779$

$d_1 = [\text{In}(11.34/20) + (0.05 + 0.5 \times 0.25^2) \times 5] / (0.25 \times \sqrt{5})$

$= [-0.5674 + 0.40625] / 0.5590$

$= -0.288$

$d_2 = -0.288 - 0.5590$

$= -0.847$

$N(d_1) = 0.5 - 0.1141 = 0.3859$

$N(d_2) = 0.5 - 0.3023 = 0.1977$

Option to expand = ($20m × 0.3859) – ($11.34 × 0.1977 × 0.779)

= $7.718m – $1.746m

= $5.972m

NPV of the project is now $5.972m – $3.5m = $2.472m

The project now has a positive NPV and should be undertaken.

In this question, a project with a negative NPV becomes feasible due to the value placed on the real option to expand the project into new technology. The company will not receive the value of the real option but the value attached to the option, to use the project to break into the Asian market, is $4.455m.

## Assumptions of the Black-Scholes model

The Black-Scholes model makes a number of assumptions which are discussed below.

(a) Lognormality. The model assumes that the return on the underlying asset follows a normal distribution which means the return itself follows a lognormal distribution.

(b) Perfect markets. This suggests that the direction of the market cannot be consistently predicted and thus the returns on the underlying asset can go up or down at any given moment in time.

(c) Constant interest rates. The risk-free rate is used in the Black-Scholes model and this rate is assumed to be constant and known.

(d) Constant volatility. The model assumes that the volatility of the project is known and remains constant throughout its life.

(e) Tradability of asset. The model assumes that there is a market for the underlying asset and it can therefore be traded.

As we have seen, the two latter assumptions do not necessarily apply to real options. Whilst volatility can be relatively constant in the very short term, it is never constant in the long term. It is not always the case that the underlying asset can be traded therefore this assumption limits the usefulness of the model for valuing real options.

# 4 Methodologies in the Valuation of Mineral Rights

The term 'mineral' applies to elements extracted from the ground, including metals (gold, silver, copper, zinc, lead); energy resources (coal, oil and natural gas); construction materials (sand, gravel, rocks); precious and semi-precious gemstones (diamonds, rubies, emeralds). 'Mineral rights' relate to the rights of a mining company to extract minerals from the ground. The valuation of these mineral rights is complicated by the uncertainties that exist, including the usual lack of upfront knowledge by all parties of the type, quality, location and scale of mineral deposits that are located in the specified area. Timescales are often lengthy, with long research and testing necessary before production commences.

Due to the uncertainties that exist, mining companies often make the commercial decision to lease mineral rights relating to land, rather than enter into an outright purchase of the land. The terms of the mineral rights lease will generally involve the payment of a royalty by the mining company to the owner of the land. This royalty payment is in addition to the specified lease payments. The royalty is payable once production commences and is often calculated based on production volume (eg a fixed amount per ton of minerals produced) or related to production value (eg a percentage of the monetary consideration received).

Mineral rights can be valued using a rule of thumb approach, based on a fixed multiple of the royalties and lease payments received in the prior year. However, as with all standardised approaches, a rule of thumb method is too generalised and can give a materially incorrect conclusion.

Better, is a valuation approach which differentiates between land where there is active development and land where development has yet to commence. Where there is no active development on the property, the value of the mineral right can be estimated to be the present value of the lease payments. Where there is active development, the future potential of development could indicate a value higher than simply the present value of the lease payments. In this case it is usual to forecast expected future free cash flows from development and discount at an appropriate risk-adjusted rate. Such forecasts are highly subjective, given the number of inputs required (eg current and future mineral prices and the distinction between proven and probable reserves). Specialist help will be required to ensure forecasts are reasonable. Sensitivity analysis must be undertaken.

## Chapter Roundup

**Module 2, Chapter 13: Other Valuation Techniques**

The syllabus requires a 'general' level of knowledge for these topics, meaning that the questions you will face in this area will be 'straightforward' as opposed to 'complex'.

You should be clear on the main themes and be able to apply the techniques in a given example.

**Economic Value Added (EVA)**

EVA is a performance measurement tool designed to identify the economic profit that a business is generating. A business' EVA can be computed using a series of prescribed adjustments to the published financial statements of a company. The resulting EVA is a single period result quantifying performance in a particular period.

EVA can be used as a valuation metric by calculating Market Value Added (MVA). MVA measures the amount by which management has increased the value of the capital invested in the firm.

You should be able to compute the EVA and MVA given specific data.

**Options Based Valuation Models**

Real option valuation models apply techniques used to value financial traded options to value the real options faced by a company. Such real options might include the option to expand in a new market, launch a new product, or defer the commencement of a particular product. It would include the option to 'wait and see' what course of action is appropriate, dependent on future market conditions. The approach thus allows value to be attributed to aspects of company operations which cannot be valued in a traditional DCF approach.

You should be able to detail the main inputs required for an options valuation and how these might relate to a real options valuation exercise. You should be able to discuss the benefits and limitations of such an approach.

**Valuing Mineral Rights**

A highly sector-specific approach, but one with increasing market importance. You should be able to discuss how such a valuation might be best undertaken.

MODULE 3

# DEBT AND EQUITY

# Syllabus – Debt and Equity

## Aim

Candidates will be able to explain and evaluate advanced aspects of domestic and international debt instruments and equity issues, to judge when and where to use debt and/or equity, the appropriate mix of debt and equity, and when to use certain types of debt instrument.

Debt and equity questions will make up approximately 20% of the total marks in the examination.

## Syllabus and BPP Study Text coverage

In the assessment, candidates may be required to:

| SYLLABUS | BPP STUDY TEXT |
|---|---|
| **a. Summarise the terms, rights, conditions of use and the factors concerning value of the following instruments:**<br>• **Ordinary shares**<br>• **Preference shares**<br>• **Debt**<br>• **Convertible loans**<br>• **Warrants**<br>• **Options** | Chapter 14 |
| **b. Critically evaluate the following unquoted sources of finance**<br>• **Private equity, including VCTs**<br>• **Private placings**<br>• **Enterprise investment schemes**<br>• **Banks**<br>• **Financial leases**<br>• **Project finance**<br>• **Senior, mezzanine and other debt**<br>• **Sovereign wealth funds**<br>• **Family offices** | Chapter 15 |
| **c. Evaluate the appropriateness of unquoted finance for the following:**<br>• **Start-ups/early stage**<br>• **Development capital**<br>• **Management buy-outs/buy-ins**<br>• **Public companies.** | Chapter 15 |
| **d. Determine financing options, including rights issues, placings and vendor placings, for a company by evaluating a company's financing needs, based on its strategic and operating environment.** | Chapter 16 |

| SYLLABUS | | BPP STUDY TEXT |
|---|---|---|
| **e.** | **Determine financing options for a company by examining the financial implications of pension schemes, with particular reference to: (G)**<br>• **Defined contribution schemes**<br>• **Defined benefit schemes**<br>• **Valuation of assets and liabilities**<br>• **Deficit funding**<br>• **Rights of pension holders**<br>• **Asset based finance**<br>• **Bonds** | Chapter 17 |
| **f.** | **Explain the use of the following derivatives in debt and equity and incorporate these instruments in financing options in straightforward situations: (G)**<br>• **Forwards and futures**<br>• **Options**<br>• **Swaps** | Chapter 18 |

# FINANCIAL INSTRUMENTS

chapter 14

## Contents


| | | |
|---|---|---|
| 1 | Introduction | 296 |
| 2 | Ordinary Shares | 296 |
| 3 | Preference Shares | 297 |
| 4 | Debt | 299 |
| 5 | Bond Pricing and Returns | 303 |
| 6 | Convertible Bonds | 318 |
| 7 | Warrants and Options | 323 |
| 8 | Valuation of Options | 327 |
| 9 | Options – Gearing | 329 |
| 10 | Appendix – Option Strategies | 333 |

# 1 Introduction

The shareholders of a company are the **owners** of the company. Each owner (shareholder) contributes capital and, in return, receives shares (ie share of ownership). The more an individual contributes, the greater the allotment of shares. As the owners, the shareholders take the greatest risks. If the company performs badly, they will lose their money. However, they normally have only a **limited liability**; limited to the amount that they agreed to contribute.

On the other hand, if the company prospers, then the shareholders will reap the rewards. Debt, such as a corporate bond, will only ever receive its interest, or coupon payments and the capital repayment upon maturity, whereas shares do not normally have a fixed return, and participate fully in the remaining profits of the business.

In this chapter, we consider the terms, rights, conditions of use and valuation of ordinary shares, preference shares, debt, convertible instruments, warrants and options.

# 2 Ordinary Shares

**Ordinary shares** are often referred to as **equity shares**. Here, the term equity means that they have an equal right to share in the profits of the company. For example, if a company has 10,000 ordinary shares, each share is entitled to $\frac{1}{10,000}$ of the profits made during any period. These profits may be distributed by way of a dividend, or can be retained within the operation in order to increase the potential for future profit.

## The normal characteristics

The rights of ordinary shares are detailed in the company's constitutional documents and in particular, the **Articles of Association**.

1. It is normal for ordinary shares to carry the **right to vote**. This means that the holder of any ordinary shares may attend, speak and vote at any meetings held by the company. Whilst the day-to-day control and management of the company is dealt with by the directors and managers, the shareholders must retain the right to decide upon the most important issues that affect the business.
2. The shareholders also have an equal right to share in any **dividends** that are distributed by the company. However, a dividend distribution is not guaranteed. If profits for the year are low, the company will be unlikely to pay a dividend. The dividend of a UK company is received net of 10% withholding tax.
3. Additionally, on a **winding-up** of the company, the ordinary shareholders are entitled to participate in any surplus funds available after all the creditors have been paid and preference shareholders have been redeemed.

## Special types of ordinary shares

### Founder shares

A business may find itself requiring additional equity finance but the original, or founding shareholders, may not wish to relinquish control of the company. One solution is to issue a new class of shares to the original shareholders (**founder shares**), with **enhanced voting rights** (say, 100 votes per share) to ensure the original shareholders will retain control of the company whilst still raising additional equity finance. Founder shares are sometimes called '**golden shares**'. Founder shares are usually unpopular with other investors as they do not uphold the principle of 'one share, one vote'. The UK market regulator in particular dislikes them: an important principle to ensure fair operation of markets is that of transparency and to achieve this it is believed that the rights of all ordinary shareholders should be the same.

### 'A' and 'B' class ordinary shares

An alternative to holding shares with enhanced voting rights, in order to maintain control, would be to issue new shares with **no voting rights**. This gives rise to different classes of shares, for example non-voting 'A' class or 'B' class ordinary shares. Again these shares are unpopular with market regulators and are unusual within the UK, although have been common in mainland Europe. They can act as a 'poison pill' deterrent against takeover – for example, any change in control of voting shares, as part of a bid process, causes a change in rights to the non-voting class, making a takeover impossible. 'A' and 'B' shares can also be used by family companies to ensure control remains with family members. Investors generally remain cautious about any organisation which tries to distribute control in a different way from the economic interests of the company. In the UK, directors have a fiduciary duty to act in the best interests of all shareholders and a tiered share capital structure discriminates clearly against non-voting shareholders.

### Deferred shares

The term 'deferred' share applies to a share where the usual rights of the shareholder are deferred in some respect. Commonly, deferred shares have restricted dividend rights and do not rank for dividend until a particular circumstance is satisfied, typically either:

- Until the ordinary dividends have reached a predetermined level; or
- Until a specific period after their issue.

The residual dividend payable is likely to be at a higher rate than the standard dividend and thus additional risks related to deferred shares can be compensated by additional levels of return.

Increasingly senior executives and directors receive deferred shares as part of their remuneration package. The shares are 'deferred' in that they cannot be actively traded until a specified period has passed. If the individual leaves the organization before the end of the vesting period, the shares are forfeited. The shares are therefore issued to help 'lock-in' key employees.

Deferred shares can also be deferred in that they have subordinated rights to the assets of a company undergoing bankruptcy (ie they are paid out after all other ordinary and preferred shareholders are paid).

### Valuing ordinary shares

The methods used to value ordinary shares have been covered in detail in the previous module, 'Valuation'.

## 3 Preference Shares

Ordinary shares carry the full risks and rewards of ownership. **Preference shares** take on debt-like characteristics and offer only limited risks and returns.

## The normal characteristics

A preference share is preferred in two basic ways.

1. The preference share **dividend must be paid out before any ordinary dividend can be paid.** It is conventional for preference shares to be **cumulative** and if the dividend is not paid in any one year, the arrears and the current year's preference dividend must be paid before any ordinary dividend can be paid in the future. The assumption is that preference shares are cumulative unless stated otherwise.

2. The second form of preferencing is on the order of payout on a winding-up. Preference shares **will be redeemed prior to ordinary shares**. On liquidation of the company, the preference shareholders will only ever receive the **nominal value** of the shares. This is not the case for ordinary or equity shares. Equity shares would receive anything that remains after all other investors have been paid (ie in theory it could be more than nominal value).

In order to receive these benefits, preference shareholders must relinquish a number of rights normally attached to shares.

Firstly, the dividend on preference shares is **normally a fixed dividend**, expressed as a percentage of the nominal value. For example, 7% £1 preference shares: these shares would pay a dividend each year of 7p per share. In the UK, the quoted rate on a preference share is net of income tax at 10%.

Secondly, it is conventional for preference shares to carry **no voting rights**. However, most company constitutions contain a clause which states that if the dividend on a cumulative preference share has not been paid for five years, preference shareholders will receive the right to attend and vote at general meetings of the company. It should be remembered that, as with all dividends, the payment is at the discretion of the directors and no shareholder may sue for a dividend.

## Preference shares as investments

As we can see, preference shares offer the rewards one would normally see attached to a debt instrument – a fixed return with no voting rights. However, they carry greater risk since they are nearer the bottom of the liquidation priority table in the event of a winding-up.

There are, however, a number of special features that can be added to preference shares to enhance their attractiveness and make them interesting potential investments for individuals.

## Special types of preference shares

Some preference shares can be specified as **participating shares**. A participating share has a right, when profits reach certain levels, to take a share of those profits as opposed to simply receiving a fixed return. This participation right **may** also apply to the proceeds on a winding-up (liquidation).

Preference shares may also be issued **with conversion rights**. These rights will allow the preference shares to be converted into a specified number of ordinary shares at a specified point in the future. As such, the preference share in this instance is more like a convertible debt instrument than a share.

Finally, preference shares may be given **specified redemption dates**. For the most part, ordinary shares are not redeemable but preference shares frequently carry a redemption date, making them seem once again more like debt than shares.

One key difference between preference shares and debt lies in the **tax treatment of the dividends**. Preference dividends, as well as ordinary dividends, are paid out of the company's after-tax profits and are therefore not allowable deductions for corporation tax. The dividends are subject to income tax, and are paid to the investor net of 10% withholding tax. Interest on debt, by contrast, is paid out of the company's pre-tax profits and is therefore an allowable deduction which reduces the company's profits for corporation tax purposes.

## Valuing preference shares

The choice of valuation method of any financial instrument should reflect the underlying economic substance of that financial instrument. Preference shares have more of the characteristics of debt than equity (ie they do not confer control) and therefore they should be valued as redeemable or irredeemable debt, depending upon whether they have a maturity date. The forecast cash flows, dividend and redemption payment are discounted at the investor's required rate of return.

# 4 Debt

Most companies will, at some point, borrow money from a bank to supplement the equity capital they have raised. Borrowings have the following advantages:

- The shareholders, who may include directors, do not have to give up part of their ownership of the company.
- The interest paid on bank loans is tax-deductible, so that the cost of the bank loan becomes relatively low.

The primary source of borrowings is from a bank. Unquoted debt finance is considered fully in Chapter 2.

## Characteristics of bonds

In the same way that companies may seek to raise equity by selling shares to market investors, they may seek to raise debt by borrowing in the markets. In this case, rather than entering into a negotiated loan agreement with a specific bank or syndicate of banks, they will borrow money through a bank or stock exchange from a wide range of investors. Each investor advances a small proportion of the loan, and in exchange receives a bond.

The main characteristics of bonds are:

- **Term**. Bonds have varying redemption dates: from a year to 99 years or even in perpetuity.
- **Coupon**. The interest on a bond is referred to as a coupon. Most corporate bonds are issued with a fixed coupon rate, paid either annually or semi-annually. The coupon to be received is based upon the nominal value of the corporate bond held, and the fixed coupon rate.
- **Credit rating**. A corporate issuer will usually seek a credit rating for the bond from a ratings agency such as Standard & Poors or Moody's.
- **Certificates**. Bonds are commonly in bearer form, ie the issuer does not maintain a register of owners, and possession of the bond certificate is the only evidence of ownership.
- **Redemption value**. Bonds are normally redeemed at par (nominal value). They may however be redeemed at a **premium to the par value**, particularly when the bond offers a low coupon or none at all (a **zero-coupon bond**). With 'zeros', all of the return to the investor is thus in the redemption value.
- **Security**. Bonds may be secured or unsecured and the security is held by way of a 'fixed' or 'floating' charge.
- **Listing**. Bonds are freely transferable; they may be admitted to listing (ie quoted) on a stock exchange in the same way as equities, or may be traded over-the-counter by agreement with a bank.

## Valuing debt instruments

The value of a debt instrument is calculated as the present value of its expected cash flows, coupon and redemption value, discounted at the investor's required rate of return (the redemption yield). Where the yield reflects market rates, such as a Floating Rate Note (FRN), the market price of the bond will be at or about par.

The market price of a bond will be affected by numerous factors some due to the issuer and some due to the market:

### Issuer factors

- **Yield to the maturity** – for bonds with a fixed rate coupon, changes in the required yield to maturity will change the price of the bond. As the required yield rises, the bond price will fall.
- **Seniority** – the risk associated with a bond depends largely on its seniority in respect to assets in the event of default and as risk and return are closely linked this will drive the price.
- **Structure** – the structure of a bond will give rise to a particular level of risk and hence price. Long dated bonds have more risk than short dated bonds as the cash flows are further out in the future.
- **Credit ratings** – are determined as an indication of the specific issue prospects and likelihood of the company defaulting. Changes in the credit rating will impact the bond's price.
- Bonds from respected issuers and where issues are large tend to be more **liquid** and hence result in lower yields and higher prices.

### Market factors

- Liquid repo markets in a bond will mean that the price of a bond will change rapidly as interest rates vary.
- The market in bonds will generally be strongly linked to market interest rates. As interest rates rise, an investor's required rate of return rises and thus bond prices fall.
- An indication of the market's expectation of future interest rates may be derived from the derivatives market. It is possible to agree today the price of a ten year maturity bond in the derivatives market for up to one year in advance. If there is a significant difference between the prices expected in the futures market versus the cash market, the prices will be brought into line through a process of arbitrage.

## Types of debt

The following types of debt instrument are considered, including their terms, rights, conditions of use and factors impacting valuation:

- Floating rate notes (FRNs)
- Zero-coupon bonds
- Convertible bonds
- Mandatory convertible bonds
- Exchangeable bonds
- MTNs
- Eurobonds

## Floating rate notes (FRNs)

A FRN is a particular types of bond where the coupon is not fixed at the outset, but floats in line with market rates and is re-fixed on a regular basis. Every few months, the market rate of interest is assessed, often using a measure such as LIBOR, and adding to it a margin. LIBOR represents the rate the largest banks are prepared to lend to each other (the interbank deposit rate is called LIBID) and, therefore, provides a benchmark for market interest rates. The margin added reflects the additional risk the investor is taking in lending to a company.

With a fixed rate bond, a change in interest rates will cause the price of the bond to change (so that the yield reflects the market rate of interest). With a FRN, however, the coupon will change in line with market interest rates. This will result in the value of the bond remaining constant at around the par value.

## Zero-coupon bonds

These are bonds that carry no coupon rate but are issued at a discount to their face value. The discount reflects the interest that is liable over the life of the bond. The tax treatment of zero-coupon bonds is that the company receives corporation tax relief on a notional interest charge each year, while the investor suffers income tax (not capital gains tax) on the gain made, but only in the year the bond is redeemed.

The same effect is achieved if the bond is redeemed at a premium to its nominal value. For example, if a bond of £100 nominal value has a redemption premium of 15%, at redemption the issuer will pay back £115.

## Convertible bonds

One way in which a company that is paying a high coupon on its debt may be able to reduce the coupon rate is by attaching conversion rights or warrants to the bond. A conversion right will give the holder of the bond the right, at a date in the future, to convert the bond into shares at a specified rate. In effect, the purchaser of this bond receives two instruments.

Firstly, the holder is the owner of a reasonably low coupon bond and secondly, he has an option into the equity of the company enabling him to convert at a specified price in the future. The attraction of having this option along with the straight bond is that the issuer of convertible stock can obtain a lower yield cost on the bond than would otherwise be the case.

This 'equity kicker' may also come in the form of a warrant. A warrant is a long-term call option, giving the holder the right to buy shares at a specified price up to a certain date in the future. The principal difference between a warrant and a conversion right is that a warrant may be split away from the bond and traded separately. Conversion rights by their very nature must always trade with the underlying bond.

The basic intention of this structure was to make the investor believe that he had a two-way option. If the share prices rose significantly then the conversion right would be a valuable one. However, if the share price were to fall, the investor would always be able to put the bond back to the issuer, at the premium rate. Conversion rights tend to be issued in the belief that they will be exercised. From the point of view of the company issuing the debt, this makes sense because if the conversion right is exercised, there will be no need to refinance the loan when it matures, as at that point, it will be converted into shares.

## Mandatory convertible bonds

However, sometimes the bondholder will be required to convert the nominal value into ordinary shares of the company at a set redemption date. These are known as mandatory convertibles.

For example, equity contract notes will be redeemed for the equivalent of the bond's nominal value in current market value of shares of the company.

The use of mandatory convertibles increased with the weak market for Initial Public Offerings since 2008. The appeal for the investor of 'mandatories' is that the company takes the risk of the share price volatility in the period between issuance and conversion. Mandatories are often issued in conjunction with equity in an IPO to attract investors who would not otherwise be interested in the IPO.

### Exchangeable bonds

Exchangeable bonds are ones that are convertible into the ordinary shares of a subsidiary or associate company of the issuer. This is therefore a **different company to the issuer** of the bond.

The use of exchangeable bonds can be to provide a way for a group to divest an unwanted investment. There is no dilution of control for the shareholders of the issuer.

### Medium term notes/Shelf programmes

Medium Term Notes (MTNs) are not strictly a type of security. Instead, the term describes a facility enabling the issuer to issue a range of stock from one global facility. In the US, the facility can cover short-term, commercial paper out to 30-year debt.

The issuer sets up a **shelf programme**. When the programme is initially set up, relevant documentation is prepared to enable the issuer to issue a wide variety of different instruments in terms of

- Maturity (eg from one week to ten years)
- Currency (sterling, US dollars, euro)
- Coupon (coupon-paying or zero coupon)
- Instrument (commercial paper, long-term bonds)

The implication of this is that the costs of setting up the programme are relatively high compared to the cost of a large Eurobond issue (see below).

However, the benefit is that the programme offers **greater flexibility** and **lower cost** to the issuer **in the long run**. As a result, it is more suitable for issuers who need funding flexibility over a period of time. In contrast, a large issuer might find a one-off large Eurobond issue more suitable.

### Eurobonds

In essence, a Eurobond is a debt instrument issued by a borrower (typically a government or a large company) normally, or predominantly, outside the country in whose currency it is denominated. For example, a US dollar Eurobond could be issued anywhere in the world except for the US. As such, a better name for it might be an 'international bond'. Eurobonds frequently carry no security, other than the name and credit rating of the issuer.

Another important feature of bonds issued in this market is that, for the most part, they are issued in **bearer form**, with no formal register of ownership held by the company. These bearer documents are immobilised at central depositories, such as Euroclear and Clearstream, which provide clearing and stocklending facilities.

It should be noted that for a number of pragmatic reasons, the clearing houses in the Euromarkets do maintain a form of register of ownership. However, this register is not normally open either to government or tax authorities. Combined with the feature of being bearer documents, a vital aspect of the Eurobond is that, unlike most government bonds, it does not attract withholding tax. **Eurobonds pay coupons gross** and usually **annually**.

Most Eurobonds are issued in **bullet form**, redeemed at one specified date in the future. However, a number of issues have alternative redemption patterns. Some bonds are redeemed over a number of years, with a proportion of the issue being redeemed each year. Whilst Eurobonds are not issued in registered form, each will have an identifying number. A **drawing** of numbers is made every year from the pool of bonds in issue. The numbers drawn are published and the bonds are called in and redeemed. This redemption process is known as a drawing on a Eurobond.

# 5 Bond Pricing and Returns

The simplest measure of a bond's return used in the market is the **flat yield**. This is also referred to as the running yield or the interest yield. It looks at the cash return generated by an investment over the cash price. In simple terms, what is the income that you generate on the money that you invest?

$$\text{Flat yield} = \frac{\text{Annual coupon rate}}{\text{Market price}} \times 100$$

For example

5% Loan stock

Redemption date 2010 @ par

Current market price 97.25

The flat yield for the above would be

$$\frac{5}{97.25} \times 100 = 5.14\%$$

## Limitations of the flat yield

This measure is of some use, particularly in the short term, but it has three important drawbacks for the investment markets.

- With all equities and some bonds (FRNs), the return in any one period will vary. If the coupon is not constant, then the measure is only of historic value unless the predicted return is used.
- In addition to the coupon flows, bonds will have return in the form of the redemption monies. Where the bond has been purchased at a price away from par, this will give rise to potential gains and losses.
- Most importantly, the calculation completely ignores the time value of money. If an investor were to be offered the choice between the receipt of £10 now or in two years' time, the logical choice would be to take the £10 now, since the money could then be invested to generate interest.

These limitations combine to make the flat yield of marginal use only.

## Gross redemption yield

The gross redemption yield (GRY) resolves the issue of the redemption values and the time value of money, but is still unable to deal with some of the problems surrounding interim coupon-based cash flows. It is also referred to as the yield to maturity (YTM).

The gross redemption yield considers the flows of money arising from a bond. Each flow is then converted into its present value by discounting the future flow.

$$\text{Current price} = \frac{C_1}{(1+r)} + \frac{C_2}{(1+r)^2} + \frac{C_3}{(1+r)^3} + \ldots + \frac{C_n + R}{(1+r)^n}$$

where

$C_1$ = coupon paid at the end of Period 1

$C_n$ = coupon paid at the end of Period n (maturity)

R = principal repaid at the end of Period n

r = gross redemption yield

For each bond, we have the market price and the coupon flows. The GRY is simply the one rate of interest that, when inserted into the formula, will equate the present values of the coupons with the current market price.

It can be seen that the GRY is simply the internal rate of return of the bond's flows, where the current price is treated as an outflow and the future interest and capital repayment flows are treated as inflows.

For example,

5% Loan stock (annual coupon)

Three years to redemption

Current market price 97.25

The GRY of this bond is 6.03%. This can be demonstrated by calculating the present value of the flows using a discount rate of 6.03%, as follows.

| Time | Cash Flow £ | Discount Factor | Present Value £ |
|---|---|---|---|
| 0 | (97.25) | 1 | (97.25) |
| 1 | 5 | $\frac{1}{1.0603}$ | 4.72 |
| 2 | 5 | $\frac{1}{(1.0603)^2}$ | 4.45 |
| 3 | 105 | $\frac{1}{(1.0603)^3}$ | 88.08 |
| Net Present value | | | – |

## Problems with the gross redemption yield

We have noted that the yield that has been calculated so far is in effect the internal rate of return (IRR) of the flows generated by a bond. As a means of appraising an investment project, the IRR is limited since it ignores the magnitude of the flows.

As a measure of predicted return, the yield is limited, since it assumes that any coupon receipts are reinvested at the same rate as the current yield. If the investor is only able to reinvest the coupon at a lower rate, then the overall return generated by the bond will be lower than the yield.

One further criticism of the yield measure is that it ignores reality – it discounts all flows in the future by the same rate when, as we shall see from the yield curve, the rate of return varies for monies of different maturities.

## The use of spot rates

The spot rate is the rate of interest that the market demands for money of a specific term, eg the rate for six-month or one-year money. It is also referred to as the zero-coupon rate, since it is the rate of interest to be applied to a bond with only one cash flow, that on maturity.

The idea of spot rates argues that it is inappropriate to use one interest rate, the GRY/IRR, to discount all the future cash flows of a bond. Rather, investors will disaggregate the bond into separate flows occurring at different times and use different interest rates to discount each flow.

The interest rate used for flows of a particular maturity is the spot rate for that maturity.

$$\text{Value} = \frac{C}{(1+r_1)} + \frac{C}{(1+r_2)^2} + \frac{C+R}{(1+r_3)^3}$$

where

$r_1$ = spot rate for flows occurring at Time 1

$r_n$ = spot rate for flows occurring at Time n

C = coupon payment

R = redemption proceeds

Effectively, we have three separate zero-coupon bonds here.

### The identification of spot rates

Whilst quotes are available in the money markets, these are only available for relatively short periods. Spot rates for longer maturities are potentially available from the zero-coupon bond or strips market. However, if these markets are not fully developed, then an alternative is to derive the spot rate from the normal bond markets.

## EXAMPLE

Three bonds are selected, with different maturity dates, as follows.

| Bond (Annual Coupon) | Maturity | Price |
|---|---|---|
| 10% | 1 year | 99.50 |
| 11% | 2 year | 98.25 |
| 9% | 3 year | 97.50 |

For the one-year bond, there is a single flow in one year's time of the coupon £10 and the redemption value of £100. The yield on this one-year money is therefore

$$\text{Current price} = \frac{C+R}{(1+r)}$$

This can be rearranged to solve for the yield.

$$(1+r) = \frac{C+R}{\text{Current price}}$$

Inserting the values that we have for the one-year bond, this gives

$$(1+r) = \frac{£110}{£99.5} = 1.1055 \text{ or } 10.55\%$$

This is the yield on one-year money. It is also the spot rate, since the bond is effectively a zero-coupon bond.

For the two-year spot rate, it is necessary to turn to the two-year bond. Here, we have two flows: £11 coupon in one year's time and £111, coupon and redemption, in two years' time.

$$\text{Current price} = \frac{\text{Coupon}}{(1+r_1)} + \frac{\text{Coupon and redemption}}{(1+r_2)^2}$$

We already know from our one-year bond that the spot rate for flows in one year's time is 10.55%. Substituting this into the above equation as $r_1$ and inserting the values for price, coupon and redemption

$$£98.25 = \frac{£11}{(1.1055)} + \frac{£111}{(1+r_2)^2}$$

$$£98.25 = £9.95 + \frac{£111}{(1+r_2)^2}$$

$$£98.25 - £9.95 = \frac{£111}{(1+r_2)^2}$$

$$(1 + r_2)^2 = \frac{£111}{88.30}$$

$$(1 + r_2)^2 = 1.2570$$

$$(1 + r_2) = \sqrt{1.2570} \text{ (or } 1.2570^{1/2})$$

$$(1 + r_2) = 1.1212 \text{ or } 12.12\%$$

The two-year spot rate is therefore 12.12%. In turn, by using the three-year bond, the one and two-year spot rates can be used to derive the three-year spot rate.

$$\text{Current price} = \frac{C}{(1+r_1)} + \frac{C}{(1+r_2)^2} + \frac{C+R}{(1+r_3)^3}$$

In the case of the three-year bond, the coupon in each of the first two years is £9. In the third year, the coupon will be paid with the redemption money making a total payment of £109.

$$£97.50 = \frac{£9}{(1.1055)} + \frac{£9}{1.1212^2} + \frac{£109}{(1+r_3)^3}$$

$$£97.50 = £8.14 + £7.16 + \frac{£109}{(1+r_3)^3}$$

$$£97.50 - £8.14 - £7.16 = \frac{£109}{(1+r_3)^3}$$

$$(1 + r_3)^3 = \frac{£109}{£81.95}$$

$$(1 + r_3) = \sqrt[3]{1.33}$$

$$(1 + r_3) = 1.0997 \text{ or } 9.97\%$$

As mentioned above, it may not be necessary to derive the spot rates using the above formulation. In markets such as the US, where an active strips or zero-coupon market exists, this market will generate the spot rates.

## The relationship between bond prices and interest rates

One of the fundamental correlations in bond markets is that, as the interest rate rises, the price of a bond will fall.

This can be demonstrated either through the flat or the gross redemption yield.

Using the flat yield from above

$$\frac{10}{97.25} \times 100 = 10.283\%$$

If the market interest rate were to rise to 12% then the holders of the bond would be encouraged to sell the bond and invest their money into assets yielding 12%. The result of this would be that the supply of the bond would rise and the demand fall, leading to a fall in the price. As the price falls to £83.33, the yield rises to 12% thereby removing the incentive to switch out of the bond

$$10/83.33 = 12\%$$

The GRY can prove the same result. Using our initial GRY formula

$$\text{Current price} = \frac{C_1}{(1+r)^2} + \frac{C_2}{(1+r)^3} + \frac{C_3}{(1+r)^3} + \frac{C_n + R}{(1+r)^n}$$

If the interest rate increases then the flows received in future periods will have a lower present value and consequently the value of the bond (its price) falls.

## The yield curve

The yield curve is a graphical representation of the structure of interest rates, where the yield offered by bonds is plotted against maturity. It is often calculated by reference to the gross redemption yield.

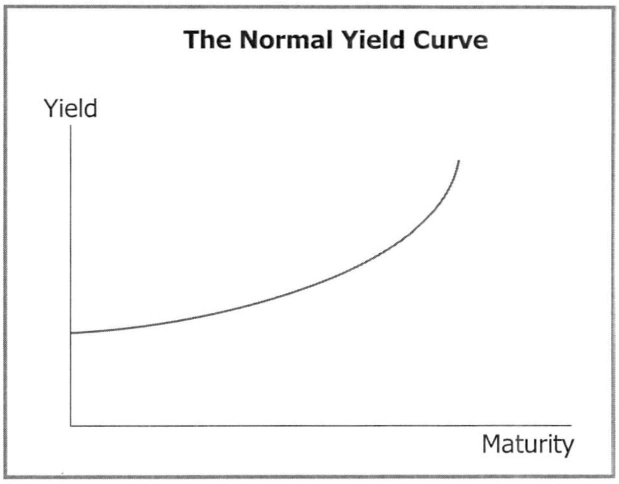


## The shape of the curve

### Liquidity preference

If an investor's money is invested in longer term (and therefore riskier) stocks, then they will require a greater return – **risk premia**. Short-term liquid stocks carry a lower risk and therefore require a lower return. This gives rise to the normal upward sloping yield curve.

### Expectations theory

Expectations theory states that the yield curve is a reflection of the market's expectation of future interest rates. If the market believes that the yield at the long end of the yield curve is high and is likely to fall, then in order to profit from the increase in prices that this will create, it will buy long-dated stocks. As a result, the demand for these stocks will rise and this demand pressure will force the price to rise. As a consequence, the yield will fall, reflecting the expectation of a fall.

On the other hand, if the market believes that rates will have to rise, then the forces will work in the opposite direction and this will lead to a fall in the price and a rise in the yield.

The expectations of the market can clearly be seen in an inverted yield curve.

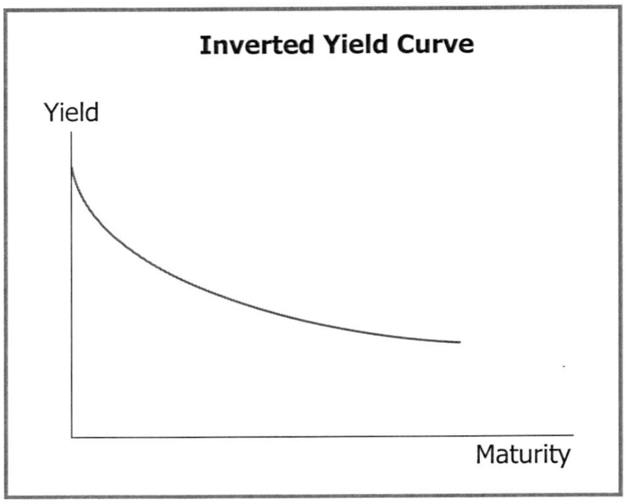


Here, short-term rates are unusually high, but the market anticipates that this cannot last for long. The longer end of the market has anticipated this change by forcing yields down. This can lead to the anomalous situation where the long end of the market remains constant because it has anticipated change and the short end (which is technically the least volatile) exhibits all of the movement.

Another key element of the market's expectations will be the **expectations of inflation**. If the market believes that inflation will rise in the future then the yields on the longer dated stocks will have to rise in order to compensate investors for the fall in the real value of their money. The expectation of inflation is much more of a problem with the long rather than the short end.

### Preferred habitat and market segmentation

Certain maturity ranges are appropriate to particular types of investors. In the UK, the short end of the market is dominated by the financial sector maintaining a proportion of their assets in liquid investments, whereas the long end is dominated by institutional investors such as pension funds. In effect, this gives rise to two markets and may be reflected in a discontinuity, or hump, in the yield curve.

### Supply-side factors

The availability of stocks in certain maturity ranges may lead to either an excess or shortage of stock and consequently an anomalous yield on some stocks.

## Construction of the yield curve

Unfortunately, it is not possible in most markets simply to plot the yields of the available stocks and then fit a curve to the data. This simplistic approach would ignore some of the key factors that affect the yield and mislead the user of the yield curve.

One of the most important distorting factors is the coupon available. In the UK gilts market, for example, there are a large number of issues of the same basic maturity, each with a different coupon. The coupon distorts the yield due to the taxation treatment applied to capital gains in the UK.

### Illustration

There are three stocks with a maturity of approximately four years. The coupons available on these bonds are 3%, 6% and 9%, respectively. If the market is expecting a return of 6% on bonds of this maturity then the 6% bond will be priced at par. However, the 3% bond will be priced at a discount to par. Since it will be redeemed at par in four years' time, realising a gain (which will be tax-free for private investors), this will make it attractive to higher rate taxpayers. The increase in the demand for this stock will force the price up and the yield down.

Therefore, whilst it might be expected that all stocks of a similar maturity and credit risk ought to have the same yield, this will not be the case. **Higher coupon stocks will have higher yields and lower coupon stocks lower yields.** Consequently, the yield information used to plot the yield curve would look like this.

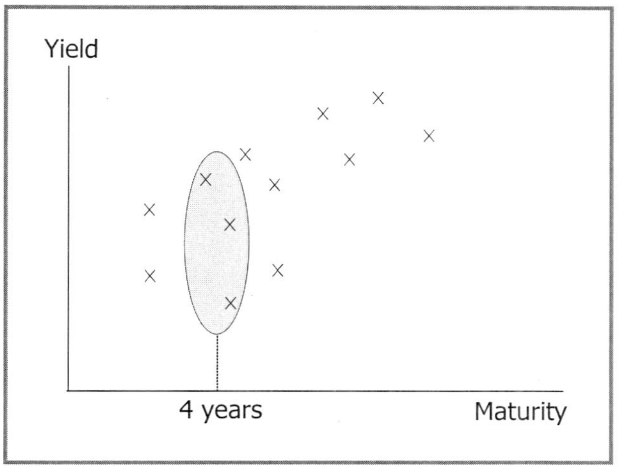


At the four-year range, there are three different yields reflecting the different coupons.

There are various solutions to this problem.

- Restricted coupon yield curves
- The yield surface
- Par yields

### Restricted coupon yield curves

To overcome the problem of coupons and other factors distorting the yield curve, it is possible to construct a restricted coupon yield curve. Here, the yields of a limited number of bonds with coupons in a limited range, say 9% to 11%, are plotted and a curve is then fitted to these data.

The obvious limitation with this approach is that it is not a full picture of the market and may be distorted easily by other variables and maturity gaps in the coupon range.

### The yield surface

A logical extension of restricted coupon yield curves is the yield surface. This is a three-dimensional representation of the yield curve. The normal two-dimensional curve plots yield against the maturity. With a yield surface, the third dimension is the coupon.

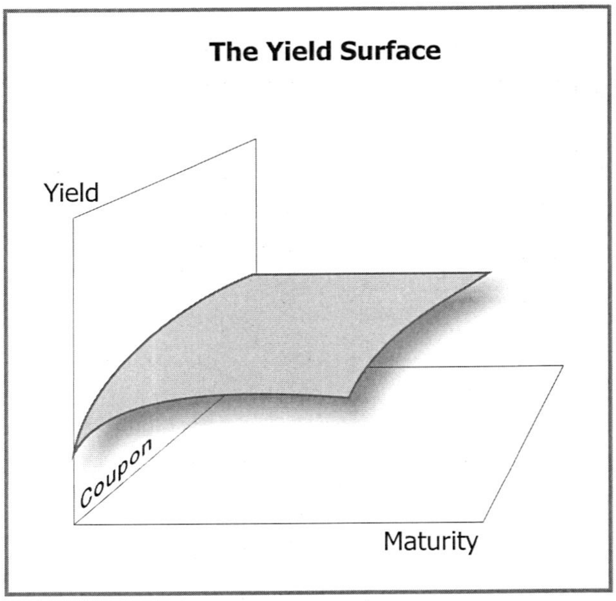


### Par yields

The par yield is the coupon that would have to be offered on a bond in order for it to be priced at par. In this instance, the discount rates used in each period are the appropriate spot rates. If a single discount rate was used, then the par yield would automatically be the same as the discount rate selected.

$$100 = \frac{C}{(1+r_1)} + \frac{C}{(1+r_2)^2} + \ldots + \frac{C}{(1+r_n)^n} + \frac{100}{(1+r_n)^n}$$

where C is the par yield and $r_1$, $r_2$,...$r_n$ are the spot rates for each period.

**EXAMPLE**

Using the spot rates derived earlier in our example, and based on a three-year bond, the par yield is calculated as follows.

$$100 = \frac{C}{(1+0.1055)} + \frac{C}{(1+0.1212)^2} + \frac{C}{(1+0.0997)^3} + \frac{100}{(1+0.0997)^3}$$

$$100 = 0.904C + 0.795C + 0.752C + 75.19$$

$$100 - 75.19 = 2.451C$$

$$\frac{24.81}{2.451} = C$$

10.12%

The par yield curve is particularly useful in the pricing of new issues.

## Understanding the yield curve

The yield on any bond is made up of a number of elements.

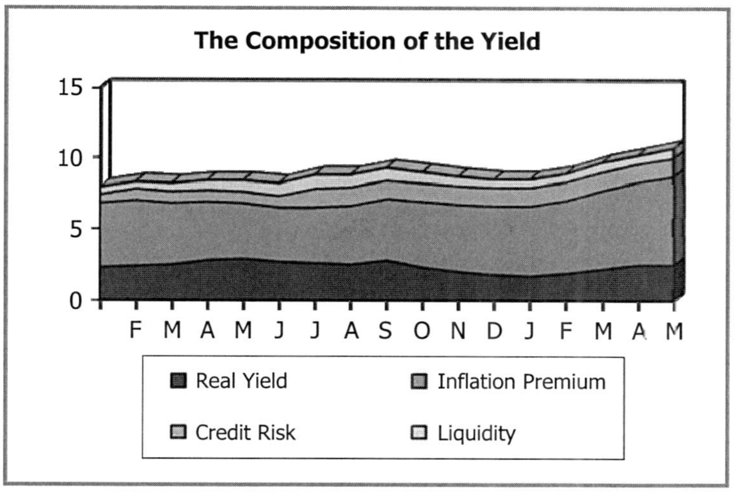


- **The real return** – This is the real rate of return that the investment has to earn. Effectively, it represents the opportunity cost of saving over immediate consumption.
- **Inflation premium** – As inflation rises then the yield on a bond will have to increase in order to compensate the holder. Inflation is basically negative interest, eroding the value of savings, whereas interest adds to them.

Together, the real return and the inflation premium form the yield on government bonds and are therefore said to approximate to the interest rate. In the case of non-government bonds, there are other risks to consider.

- **Credit and default risk** – This is the risk of the issuer defaulting on its obligations to pay coupons and repay the principal. The ratings issued by commercial rating companies can be used to help assess this risk.
- **Liquidity and marketability risk** – This has to do with the ease with which an issue can be sold in the market. Smaller issues are particularly subject to this risk. In certain markets the volume of trading tends to concentrate into the 'benchmark' stocks, thereby rendering most other issues illiquid. Other bonds become subject to 'seasoning' as the initial liquidity dries up and the bonds are purchased by investors who wish to hold them to maturity.
- Even if an issuer has a triple A credit rating and is therefore perceived as being at least as secure as the government, it will still have to offer a yield above that offered by the government due to the smaller size (normally) and the thinner market in the stocks.
- **Issue specific risk** – eg risk of call. If the company has the right to redeem the bond early, then it will only be logical for it to do this if it can refinance at a lower cost. What is good for the issuer will be bad for the investor and, thus, the yield will have to be higher.
- **Fiscal risk** – The risk that withholding taxes will be increased. For foreign bonds, there would also be the risk of the imposition of capital controls locking your money into the market.

## Sensitivity to yield

All of the risks of holding a bond come together in the yield. As we have already seen, there is an inverse relationship between the price of a bond and its yield. It is possible to define this relationship mathematically and predict the way in which a selection of bonds will perform. This is sometimes referred to as the **volatility** of the bond.

The sensitivity of any bond to movements in the yield/interest rate will be determined by a number of factors.

## Sensitivity to maturity

Longer dated bonds will be more sensitive to changes in the interest rate than shorter dated stocks. Consider three bonds with the same coupon but different maturity dates. Given a particular level of coupon and maturity date, the price of each bond can be calculated for each given gross redemption yield, as follows.

| | GRY | | |
|---|---|---|---|
| | **8%** | **10%** | **12%** |
| **Short** | | | |
| 12% 4-year bond price | 113.24 | 106.34 | 100 |
| **Medium** | | | |
| 12% 7-year bond price | 120.83 | 109.74 | 100 |
| **Long** | | | |
| 12% 26-year bond price | 143.23 | 118.32 | 100 |

At a gross redemption yield of 12%, all three bonds have a price of 100. This would be expected, since they all pay a coupon of 12%. As the gross redemption yield falls, the price of all the bonds rises. The greatest rise is for the long dated bond, from 100.00 to 143.23, illustrating that it has the most volatile price.

## Sensitivity to coupon

With regard to the level of coupon, it is the lower coupon stocks that demonstrate the greatest level of sensitivity to the yield. Consider three bonds with the same maturity date but different levels of coupon. As with the above example, the price of each of the bonds can be calculated for different gross redemption yields.

| | GRY | | |
|---|---|---|---|
| | **9%** | **10%** | **11%** |
| 5% 15-year bond price | 67.75 | 61.97 | 56.85 |
| 10% 15-year bond price | 108.0 | 100 | 92.81 |
| 15% 15-year bond price | 148.3 | 138.03 | 128.76 |

In this example, the price of the bond with the lowest coupon exhibits the most volatility.

It should be noted that the relationship between the yield and the price is not symmetrical. This is a relationship that we will return to later and is known as **convexity**.

## The impact of the yield

If yields are particularly high, then the flows in the future are worth relatively little and the sensitivity is diminished. Conversely, if the yield is low then the value of flows in the future is enhanced and the bond is more sensitive to the changing GRY.

### Summary of volatility

| High Volatility | | Low Volatility |
|---|---|---|
| Long Dated | > | Short Dated |
| Low Coupon | > | High Coupon |
| Low Yields | > | High Yields |

Whilst these simple maxims are good indicators of the likely sensitivity to fluctuations in the rate of interest, they do not allow for two bonds to be contrasted. For example, which of the following is likely to be the most sensitive to a rise in interest rates – a high-coupon, long-dated stock, or a low-coupon, short-dated stock? In order to enable two such bonds to be compared, in the 1930s a composite measure of risk was devised – the **duration**.

## Macaulay duration

### What is duration?

This calculation gives each bond an overall risk weighting that allows two bonds to be compared. In simple terms, it is a composite measure of the risk expressed in years.

Duration is the weighted average length of time to the receipt of a bond's benefits (coupon and redemption value), the weights being the present value of the benefits involved. This concept can be shown diagrammatically as follows.

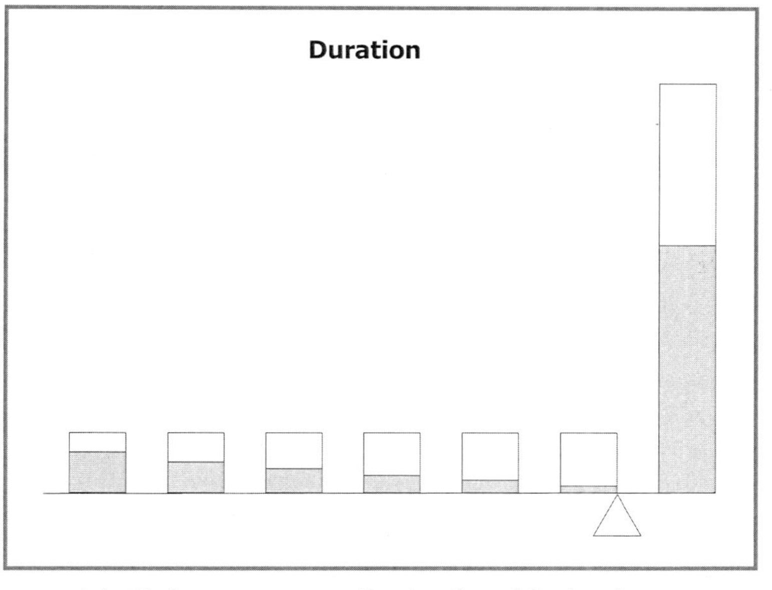


Here, the fulcrum, or point of balance, represents the duration of the bond.

### Calculation of duration

Duration can be expressed mathematically using the following formula.

$$\text{Macaulay duration} = \frac{\sum_{t=1}^{n} t \times PVt}{\sum_{t=1}^{n} PVt}$$

where

PVt = present value of cash flow in Period t (discounted using the redemption yield)

n = numbers of periods

### Illustration

Using an example of 10%, five-year annual coupon bond trading at 97.25 with a GRY of 10.743%, the duration would be as follows.

| | Time Period | | | | |
|---|---|---|---|---|---|
| | 1 | 2 | 3 | 4 | 5 |
| **Flow** | 10 | 10 | 10 | 10 | 110 |
| **Present Value @ GRY** | 9.03 | 8.15 | 7.36 | 6.66 | 66.05 |

Using the above, the duration is

$$\frac{(9.03\times1)+(8.15\times2)+(7.36\times3)+(6.66\times4)+(66.05\times5)}{9.03+8.15+7.36+6.66+66.05}$$

$$\frac{404.3}{97.25} = 4.157 \text{ years}$$

Note that the total present value of the bond's flows of 97.25 is equal to the price, as would be expected.

### Properties of duration

The basic features of sensitivity to interest rate risk will all be mirrored in the duration calculation.

- **Longer dated bonds** will have longer durations.
- **Lower coupon bonds** will have longer durations. The ultimate low-coupon bond is a zero-coupon bond where the duration will be the maturity.
- **Lower yields** will give longer durations. In this case, the present value of flows in the future will rise if the yield falls, extending the point of balance, therefore lengthening the duration.

The duration of a bond will shorten as the life span of the bond decays. However, the rate of decay will not be at the same rate. In our example above, a five-year bond has a duration of 4.157 years. In a year's time the bond will have a remaining life of four years and a duration based on the same GRY of 3.480 years. The life span has decayed by a full year, but the duration by only 0.677 of a year.

## Modified duration

### The use of modified duration

At the same time as the Macaulay duration was being promoted as a means of expressing the sensitivity of a bond to movements in the interest rate, Hicks was developing a formula to explain the impact of yield change on price. Not surprisingly, the two measures are linked.

Hicks' basic proposition was that the change in yield ($\Delta$Y), multiplied by this sensitivity measure, would give the proportionate change in price ($\Delta$P).

$$\frac{\Delta P}{P} = -\text{Modified duration} \times \Delta Y$$

which can also be expressed as

$$\Delta P = -\text{Modified duration} \times \Delta Y \times P$$

### The calculation of modified duration

The modified duration used in this formula is Hick's measure of sensitivity and is simply

$$\frac{\text{Macaulay duration}}{1+\text{GRY}} = \text{Modified duration}$$

Using the example from above

$$\text{Modified duration} = \frac{4.157}{1+0.10743} = 3.753$$

As the modified duration is derived from the Macaulay duration, it shares the same properties.

- **Longer dated bonds** will have higher modified durations.
- **Lower coupon bonds** will have higher modified durations.
- **Lower yields** will give higher modified durations.

The higher the modified duration, then the greater the sensitivity of that bond to a change in the yield.

## Use of duration in asset liability management

### Asset liability management

Asset liability management is where an investor is investing in order to satisfy a liability or stream of liabilities. Examples of this would be pension funds and insurance companies.

The investment objectives of such investors are focused on ensuring that the liability is covered by assets, rather than trying to earn a high return on assets through trading.

Duration analysis can be used to reduce the risk that the assets will be insufficient to cover the liabilities. This technique is referred to as **immunisation**.

Essentially, the approach is based around matching the duration of the liability with the duration of a bond that is designed to cover the liability. Since duration measures changes in value for a change in interest rates, a shift in interest rates will give the same change in value for the asset and the liability, if they have the same duration. Hence, the asset will cover the liability.

**EXAMPLE**

An investor has a liability of £167.35 to meet in four years' time. The maturity of the liability (and also its duration, since it is a single cash flow) is four years.

In order to match the liability, the investor could invest in an annual coupon bond with a price of £114.29. This bond has a coupon of 13.77%, five years to maturity and is currently yielding 10%. Its duration can be calculated as follows.

| Time | Cash Flow £ | DF (10%) | PV £ | TPV £ |
|---|---|---|---|---|
| 1 | 13.77 | 0.909 | 12.52 | 12.52 |
| 2 | 13.77 | 0.826 | 11.38 | 22.76 |
| 3 | 13.77 | 0.751 | 10.35 | 31.04 |
| 4 | 13.77 | 0.683 | 9.40 | 37.62 |
| 5 | 113.77 | 0.620 | 70.64 | 353.22 |
| | | | 114.29 | 457.16 |

Market value = £114. 29

$$\text{Macaulay duration} = \frac{457.16}{114.29} = 4 \text{ years}$$

If this bond is held for four years (its duration) with income reinvested, the value of the fund at the end of that time (its terminal value) for three possible interest rates (9%, 10%, 11%) will be as follows.

| Time | Cash Flow | Comp. Fact. (9%) | Terminal Value (9%) | Comp. Fact. (10%) | Terminal Value (10%) | Comp. Fact. (11%) | Terminal Value (11%) |
|---|---|---|---|---|---|---|---|
| 1 | 13.77 | 1.093 | 17.83 | 1.103 | 18.33 | 1.113 | 18.83 |
| 2 | 13.77 | 1.092 | 16.36 | 1.102 | 16.66 | 1.112 | 16.97 |
| 3 | 13.77 | 1.09 | 15.01 | 1.10 | 15.15 | 1.11 | 15.28 |
| 4 | 13.77 | 1.00 | 13.77 | 1.00 | 13.77 | 1.00 | 13.77 |
| 5 | 113.77 | $\frac{1}{1.09}$ | 104.38 | $\frac{1}{1.10}$ | 103.44 | $\frac{1}{1.11}$ | 102.50 |
| | | | 167.35 | | 167.35 | | 167.35 |

Note that the flows from Times 1 to 3 have been compounded up and the flow at Time 5 has been discounted back to give the value of the flows at Time 4.

It can be seen that, whatever happens to reinvestment rates, the fund value at four years will always be £167.35, and the yield is therefore

$$\text{Yield} = \sqrt[4]{\frac{167.35}{114.29}} - 1 = 10\%$$

This is equal to the original yield on the bond. By holding a bond for its duration, it is possible to lock in the initial yield to maturity, given certain simplifying assumptions (covered later). This investor has managed to achieve a final value of $167.35 in all the circumstances above.

Note that investing in a bond with a duration the same as that of the liability does not guarantee the final return in all circumstances. The above analysis makes simplifying assumptions. For example, it is assumed that the yield curve will only shift in a parallel fashion. If there is a non-parallel shift, the above analysis would change.

Also note that the duration of the bond and the liability will not stay the same over time. Hence, the investor will need to rebalance the portfolio to ensure that the liability remains immunised.

## Convexity

The modified duration predicts a linear relationship between the yield and the price. If the modified duration is –2, then, if yields rise by 20 basis points, the price will fall by

$$-0.40 = -2 \times 0.20$$

If the rise in yields had been 2%, then the fall in price would have been 4%.

**The Price/Yield Relationship Given by the Modified Duration**

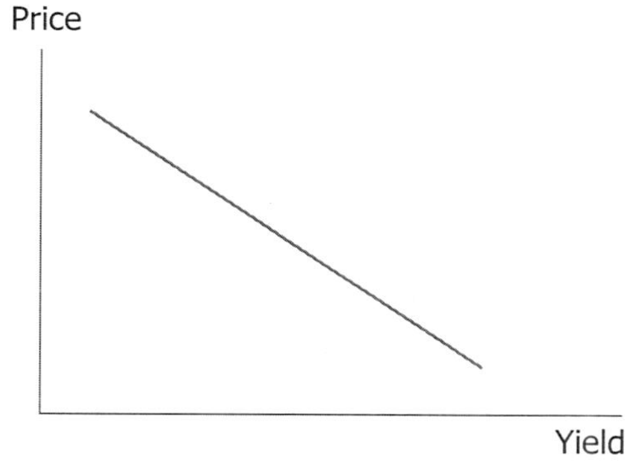


The slope of the line is the modified duration.

In fact, the actual relationship between price and yield is given by the dotted line below.

**Convexity**

The straight line gives the relationship predicted by modified duration. The dotted line gives the actual relationship between price and yield. The difference between the predicted and actual relationships is due to convexity.

The impact of convexity will be that the modified duration will tend to **overstate the fall in a bond's price and understate the rise**. However, for relatively small movements in the yield, the modified duration will be a good estimate. The problem of convexity only becomes an issue with more substantial fluctuations in the yield.

Not all bonds have the same degree of convexity. The general rule is that bonds with a higher duration will exhibit the greatest degree of convexity.

For bonds with the same duration, it will be the higher coupon bonds that will be the most convex. The reason for this is that the lower coupon bonds will have durations that will change little with the alteration in yield. In the most extreme form, the zero-coupon bond will have a duration equal to its maturity and this will not alter as yields move.

Investors may be prepared to pay for convexity. In a volatile market, the convex bonds at any particular maturity interval will outperform the bonds with lesser convexity.

# 6 Convertible Bonds

## The cost of convertibles

As with any source of finance, the cost of convertibles is the internal rate of return of the cash flows to the company. The only additional point to consider on top of standard redeemable debt or equity calculations is that the possibility of conversion needs to be taken into account. The cost of convertibles can be calculated in a simplified fashion that is illustrated in the following example.

### Illustration

A company has equity share capital that has just paid a dividend of 20p per share. Dividends are expected to grow at a rate of 5% per annum. The cost of equity is 20% and the share price is currently 140p.

(This is confirmed by the dividend valuation model, where the share price is calculated as $\frac{21}{0.2-0.05}$)

The company also has convertibles in issue paying a 5% coupon on £100 of nominal value. The debt is convertible into 90 shares per £100 nominal value, or redeemable at par in three years' time. Assume that there is no corporation tax. The current market price of the convertibles is £125 per £100 nominal value.

### Will the investors convert or redeem?

In calculating the cost of the above convertible, some of the cash flows are easy to calculate – both the existing market value and the interest flows are certain. The only other flow to consider is the flow in three years' time. Will the investors redeem and receive cash of £100 or will they convert and receive shares in the company?

In order to decide which is the most likely course of action, we need to estimate the market value of the shares in three years' time. If the market value of 90 shares is greater than £100, then presumably the investors will convert.

We can estimate the value of the shares in three years' time by using our knowledge of the Dividend Valuation Model (DVM). The share price is determined solely by the present value of future dividends and if dividends are growing by 5% per annum then the share price must grow at the same rate. The share price after three years is therefore 162p ($140 \times 1.05^3$).

This can be confirmed by using the DVM. The market value of the shares in three years' time will be the present value at that date of the dividends from the fourth year to infinity.

$$MV_3 = \frac{D_4}{k_e - g}$$

$$MV_3 = 20 \times \frac{1.05^4}{0.15} = 162$$

The value of 90 shares is therefore £145.80, well in excess of £100 and presumably the investors will convert.

### The cost of the convertible

The cash flows relating to the convertible can be summarised as

| Time | Narrative | Flow £ |
|---|---|---|
| 0 | Market value | 125.0 |
| 1–3 | Interest | (5.0) |
| 3 | Conversion | (145.8) |
| Internal rate of return | | 9% |

The cost of the convertibles is therefore 9%.

Note that the issue of shares in three years' time does not in itself constitute a cash flow to the company. The actual cash flows to the company will be all the dividend payments required for new shares in the fourth year and beyond. The value of those payments is given by the share price at the date of issue.

## Pricing of convertibles – the crossover method

When issuing a convertible, a company will need to ensure that it is fairly priced. If the price is too expensive, then investors will not buy the convertible stock and the issue will flop. If the price is very cheap, then the company will be obtaining finance on disadvantageous terms and the value for existing shareholders will fall. Valuation of convertibles is very difficult to do in practice, but various models have been developed. Two common methods are the option pricing method (considered below) and the crossover method (considered here).

The crossover method values convertibles by looking at the cash flows that will accrue to investors and discounting them at the appropriate required rate of return. In the above illustration, the cash flows to the investors are fairly easy to identify since the debt must be either redeemed or converted in three years' time, with no other dates being relevant. In other circumstances, the date of conversion is more difficult to establish, since investors will be given a range of dates on which conversion can occur and so a likely date of conversion needs to be estimated.

The crossover method assumes that conversion takes place when the dividends that would be received from the shares obtained on conversion exceed ('crossover') the interest receipts from the debt. For this reason, it is also known as the income-based approach.

**EXAMPLE**

Antonio plc has an existing share price of 140p. Dividends are currently 20p and are growing at a rate of 5%. The company's cost of equity is 20%. There is some 10% convertible debt in issue that has conversion terms of 40 shares per £100 of nominal value (this can also be called the 'conversion ratio'). What is an appropriate market value for the convertibles? (Ignore tax for this calculation.)

### *The Immediate Conversion Value*

The first stage is to value the convertibles on the basis that they are converted into shares immediately. This would give an 'immediate conversion value' (sometimes called 'parity') of £56.00 (40 shares × 140p). This value represents the present value of all the future dividend payments from one year's time to infinity on the 40 shares.

### *The Income Advantage*

The convertibles will, however, be worth more than the immediate conversion value because for a number of years they will be receiving interest payments of £10 per £100 of nominal value. The dividends on 40 shares are only worth £8 a year at present. The advantage of receiving interest payments rather than dividends can be set out in a table as follows.

| Year | Interest on Debt £ | Dividends (5% Growth) £ | Income advantage £ | Present Value of Advantage Discounted at 5% £ |
|---|---|---|---|---|
| 1 | 10.00 | 8.40 | 1.60 | 1.52 |
| 2 | 10.00 | 8.82 | 1.18 | 1.07 |
| 3 | 10.00 | 9.26 | 0.74 | 0.64 |
| 4 | 10.00 | 9.72 | 0.28 | 0.23 |
| 5 | 10.00 | 10.21 | – | – |
| | | | | 3.46 |

After five years, the dividends exceed the interest receipts and therefore it is assumed that conversion takes place and the investor receives dividends from then on. The value of receiving interest as opposed to dividends for the next four years is £3.18 and hence the total value of the convertible is £59.46 (56.00 + 3.46). Note that the discount rate used to discount the income advantage is arbitrary and is based on market practice, rather than having a theoretical justification.

In practice, when this method is used to price a new convertible issue, the issue price will be set around par and the conversion terms will be adjusted to the appropriate level to ensure that the issue is a success at this price.

**What rate is used to discount the income advantage?**

In the above example, we used a cost of 5% to discount the income advantage. In practice, it is not clear what would be the appropriate discount rate to use. Use of the cost of equity would be overcautious, since the cost of equity assumes that the flows have the same risk as equity dividends. In fact, the flows are more similar to debt-based cash flows, since they are based on the difference between interest and dividends for the four years. When dividends are low, the ability of the convertible investor to receive interest effectively removes the equity risk.

## Pricing of convertibles – option pricing

### Convertibles contain an option to acquire equity

The crossover method of valuation is fairly simplistic and easy to calculate. However, it may not give a sensible answer in valuing a convertible, because it only focuses on the income differential between the debt and equity alternatives. It fails to take into account the true nature of the convertible, which is that it is an option to acquire equity.

As such, a more appropriate method of valuing a convertible would be to use option-pricing theory. This says that the total value of the convertible is its value as straight debt, plus the value of the option to convert into equity. The value as straight debt is sometimes referred to as the convertible's 'investment value' and the value of the option is sometimes referred to as the 'investment premium' or 'bond premium'. The investment premium may be expressed as a percentage of the investment value.

## Factors affecting option values

The value of the option will be determined by a number of factors. These factors are considered further in the section below on options.

- The exercise price of the option
- The actual price of the underlying share
- Expected volatility in the price of the underlying share
- The time to expiry of the option
- Interest rates
- Whether or not a dividend is due to be paid on the share in the option period

## Value of a convertible at its expiry date

A simple example of this technique would be to consider a convertible on its date of expiry. It can either be converted into shares with a value of £120 or redeemed for cash of £100. Clearly, the total value of the convertible is £120.

This is made up of its value as straight debt (£100) plus the value of the option to convert into equity, which must be worth an additional £20. Since the option is at its expiry date, there is no time value and the whole of the £20 is intrinsic value. Remember that intrinsic value is the difference between the market price of the shares (£120) and the exercise price of the option. In the case of a convertible, the exercise price of the option is the lost proceeds from holding the instrument as straight debt – in other words, £100.

## Introducing time value

The above example can be extended to illustrate the idea of time value. Assume that the debt has one year to maturity and will be redeemed for £110 cash. Alternatively, the investor can convert into shares at any time over the next year. The current value of the shares is £120. The cost of straight debt is 10%.

The value of the instrument now as straight debt is the present value of the proceeds as debt of £100 ($^{110}/_{1.1}$). The minimum value of the convertible will therefore be £120, being the value of the straight debt of £100 plus the intrinsic value of the option of £20. It is likely, however, that the total value of the convertible will be higher than this due to time value – the fact that the share price may rise even higher over the next year.

If the value of the shares is significantly less than £100, then the value of the convertible is likely to be its value as debt of £100. The option is significantly out-of-the-money and is almost worthless.

## Evaluation of convertibles

Different techniques have been developed to establish whether or not it is worthwhile to issue a convertible.

## Cheap coupon versus loss on conversion

For a company, the benefit of the convertible is the cheap coupon available for the years prior to conversion. The disadvantage is the obligation to convert into equity. Returning to the previous illustration for the cost of convertibles, we can quantify the impact of each of these.

Following is a summary of the main details.

| | |
|---|---|
| Market value of the convertible | £125.00 per cent |
| Coupon | 5% |
| Period to conversion | Three years |
| Estimated value of equity at conversion | £145.80 |

Assume that if straight debt had been issued at a price of £125.00 per cent to be redeemed in three years' time at par of £100.00, the annual coupon would need to be 12%.

The benefit to the company is the cheap coupon of 5% compared to that for straight debt of 12%. This translates into a cash advantage of £7.00 per year for three years. The present value of this using the cost of debt of 12% is £16.81.

The cost to the company is issuing shares worth £145.80 in three years' time rather than redeeming the debt for £100.00 cash, ie a cost of £45.80. The present value of this at a discount rate of 20% (the cost of equity) is £26.50.

The cost of issuing cheap equity exceeds the benefit of the cheap coupon, meaning that the convertible is not good value for the company and its existing shareholders.

Note that the cost of debt was used to discount the interest flows, on the basis that the 7% saving is guaranteed. The cost of equity is used to discount the loss on conversion since this market value for the shares is a risky value and depends on equity risk factors.

### Dividend growth approach

This method of evaluation calculates the required dividend growth needed for conversion to take place within the investor's desired timescale. For example, assume that a convertible paying annual interest of £5.00 can convert in five years' time into one share. The current dividend on the share is £3.76. In order for conversion to be worthwhile, the dividend will need to grow to at least £5.00 over the five years. The required growth rate is given by the value of g in the following equation.

$$3.76(1 + g)^5 = 5.00$$

$$g = 0.059 \text{ or } 5.9\%$$

Assuming that expected dividend growth is 10%, this would mean that dividends would exceed interest receipts in three years' time. This suggests that conversion is likely to occur.

### Conversion premium

The **conversion premium** is a simple method of evaluating required increases in the share price to make conversion worthwhile.

$$\text{Conversion premium} = \frac{\text{Conversion price} - \text{Current share price}}{\text{Current share price}} \times 100$$

This reflects the current excess of the conversion price over the market price.

## EXAMPLE

A convertible bond that has the right to convert into 25 shares is priced at £110. The current share price in the market is £3.95.

If an investor were to buy the convertible debt and immediately convert into 25 shares, this would give a cost per share of (£110 ÷ 25) £4.40. It would clearly not be worthwhile doing this, since the shares could be bought in the market place for only £3.95. The purchaser of the convertible will not convert immediately, but will hold the debt, hoping that the share price will rise. The conversion premium indicates by how much the share price needs to rise in order to match the price of acquiring the shares through owning the convertible debt.

$$\frac{£4.40 - £3.95}{£3.95} \times 100 = 11.4\%$$

In this situation, the underlying share price is going to have to rise by 11.4% before the conversion right has any intrinsic value.

The investor would need to look at the length of time before which the conversion right expires and decide whether it is likely that the share price will rise sufficiently over the period to make conversion likely and worthwhile.

In addition, the investor could consider the yield advantage, which the convertible is offering over equity, and compare this to the conversion premium. For example, assume that for the above convertible, the dividend yield was 4% and the flat yield on the convertible bond was 6.5%. The current yield advantage is therefore 2.5%. The number of years that it takes for this to repay the conversion premium can be calculated as 11.4 ÷ 2.5 = 4.56 years. This is sometimes referred to as the simple breakeven point for the convertible and it can be compared to the investor's required breakeven point.

# 7 Warrants and Options

## Definition

An **option** is a contract that confers the right, but not the obligation, to buy or sell an asset at a given price on or before a given date.

## Using options

Conventionally, a speculator anticipating a rise in the price of shares would straightforwardly buy 1,000 shares for immediate delivery and then hold them, hoping to sell them for a profit once the price rises. If we imagine that the price of the 1,000 shares is £600, the expenditure would be £600.

Another way of representing the hope of a rise in share prices would be to buy a share option – specifically, an option that would give the right, but not the obligation, to buy 1,000 shares at a price of £600 for a period of, say, three months. The purchase of this option would cost, say, £10.

Remember that an option is a contract for future delivery, so it would not be necessary to pay £600 in the first instance; the only money to be invested at this point is the £10.

One advantage is immediately apparent. Options are cheaper than purchasing the underlying asset.

### Task

If three months later, as expected, the price of the shares has risen from £600 to £700, what will be the position of

- The speculator who bought the actual shares?
- The speculator who bought the share option?

## SOLUTION

### Actual shares

| Table Title | |
|---|---|
| Sale Price | 700 |
| Purchase price | (600) |
| Profit | 10 |

On an investment of £600 the investor has made a profit of £100 in just three months.

### Option

Now let us look at the profit for the options buyer. Three months ago he entered into a contract that gave him the right, but not the obligation, to buy the shares at £600. When purchased, that right cost just £10. With the shares now trading at £700, the right to buy at £600 must be worth at least £100 – the difference between the current price and the stated price in the contract.

This right to buy at £600 was purchased for £10. With the market price at £700 at the end of the option's life, the option will now be worth £100, hence

| Table Title | |
|---|---|
| Sale Price | 10 |
| Purchase price | (10) |
| Profit | 90 |

On an investment of £10, a £90 profit has been achieved. In percentage terms, this profit is spectacularly greater than on the conventional purchase of the shares.

One important thing to note is that options are tradeable instruments. It is not necessary for the underlying share to be bought or sold. What more commonly occurs is that **options** are bought and sold. Thus, an option bought at £10 could be sold to the market at £100, realising a £90 profit without the investor ever having an intention of buying the underlying share.

At this stage, it is necessary to introduce some of the vocabulary used in the options market.

## Terminology

In the definition of an option given earlier, an option was described as being the right, but not the obligation, to **buy** or **sell**. The right to buy and the right to sell are given different names.

- The right to buy is known as a **call option**.
- The right to sell is known as a **put option**.

The rights to buy (call) or sell (put) are held by the person buying the option, who is known as the **holder**.

The person selling an option is known as a **writer**, who is obliged to make or take delivery on or before the date on which an option comes to the end of its life, the **expiry date**.

An option that can only be exercised on its expiry date is referred to as a **European option**. An option that can be exercised on or before its expiry date is referred to as an **American option**.

The price at which the option can be exercised is the **strike price** or the **exercise price**.

**Premium** is the cost of an option. In our example, the premium was £10 and this is paid by the holder and received by the writer.

In return for receiving premium, the writer agrees to fulfil the terms of the contract, which of course are different for calls and puts.

The following diagram shows the relationship between holders and writers.

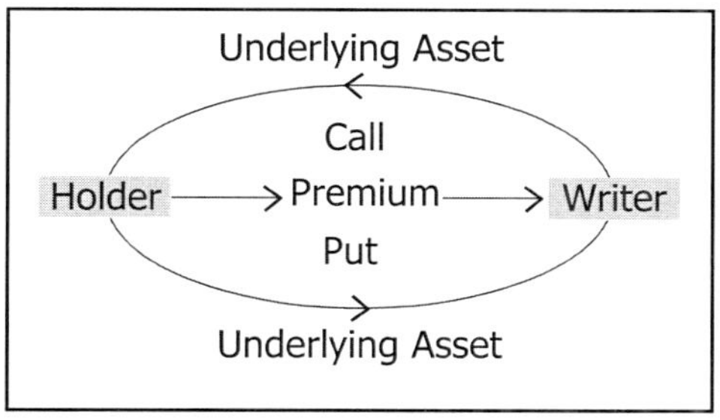


## Call options

Call writers agree to deliver the asset underlying the contract if **called** upon to do so. When options holders wish to take up their rights under the contract, they are said to **exercise** the contract. For a call this means that the writer must deliver the underlying asset for which he will receive the fixed amount of cash stipulated in the original contract.

Thus, for a call option that gives the holder the right to buy 1,000 shares at £600, this would mean that the writer would be required to deliver shares to the holder at £600. The option's holder will only want to buy at £600 when it would be advantageous for him to do so, ie only when the market price of the shares is somewhat higher than £600. If the market price was less than £600, there would be no sense in paying more than the market price.

Call option writers run very considerable risks. In return for receiving the option's premium, they are committed to delivering the underlying asset at a fixed price. As the price of the asset could, in theory, rise infinitely, they could be forced to buy the underlying asset at a high price and deliver it to the option's holder at a much lower value.

## Put options

The dangers for put options writers are also substantial. The writer of a put is obligated to pay the exercise price for assets that are delivered to him. Put options are only exercised when it is advantageous for the holders to do so. This will be when they can use the option to sell their assets at a higher price than would otherwise be available in the market.

If writers price options properly they hope to make money in most instances. Options writing is not for the faint-hearted, nor for those without substantial resources. That said, many conservative users do write options as part of strategies involving the holding of the underlying asset. Such uses are referred to as **covered**.

When investors buy or hold options, the risk is limited to the option's premium. If the market moves against them, they can simply decide not to exercise their options and sacrifice the premium. Remember, options holders have the right, **but not the obligation**, to buy (call) or sell (put). If it does not make sense to buy or sell at the exercise price, the holder can decide to **abandon** the option.

# Traded options

## Introduction

Traded options are available in the shares of major listed companies. As they are traded products, they are very standardised in terms of expiry dates, quantity of shares per option contract, etc.

## Prices of traded options

Prices are quoted in a way illustrated below for call options prices on the shares of a fictitious company, XYZ plc. The options give an entitlement to buy (call) the company's shares. The underlying share price is 76p.

**XYZ calls**

| Exercise Price | Expiry Date | | |
|---|---|---|---|
| | January Premium | April Premium | July Premium |
| 60 | 23 | 28 | 33 |
| 70 | 12 | 18 | 23 |
| 80 | 5 | 8 | 12 |

You will notice that there is a range of exercise prices and expiry dates available. Normally, you would expect there to be exercise prices available both below and above the underlying price.

There is also a range of expiry dates available – this allows investors a choice as to the maturity of their options. As one expiry date passes, a new expiry date is introduced, thus maintaining the choice of dates.

A similar range of exercise prices and expiry dates would be available in XYZ puts. The premiums quoted for calls and puts would, however, be different.

## How much would you pay?

In the table above, the premium quoted for the April 60 call is 28. To find out how much this would be we must know two things. Firstly, how the product is quoted and secondly, the contract size.

Options are traded on a wide variety of assets from currencies, bonds and shares to metals, oils and commodities. Each market has different conventions. For example, crude oil prices are normally quoted in US dollars per barrel, whilst share prices for UK companies are quoted in pence per share.

Governing the operation of options contracts are contract specifications that set out, amongst other things, rules specifying how they are quoted, expiry dates and when exercise prices are introduced. These documents are important because they enable everyone to understand the details of the contract. Exchange traded options are **standardised**, with the method of quotation and contract size being fixed. The only variable is the option's premium.

So, what does a quote of 28 for the April 60 call mean? The premium for shares is quoted in pence, hence '28' means 28 pence per XYZ share.

To determine how much the option costs, we must consult the contract specification again to find out the contract size. This is given as 1,000 shares per contract.

All traded options are traded in standardised lots or contracts. It is only possible to trade in whole numbers of contracts. You could not, for example, buy 1½ April 60 calls.

We know that the quote for XYZ options is in pence per share and that the contract size is 1,000 shares. Therefore, one XYZ April 60 call would cost £280 (£0.28 × 1,000 shares).

### Dividends

The holder of a traded call option is not entitled to receive any dividend on the share unless the option is exercised prior to the share being traded ex-div.

### FTSE index options

Traded options are available not just on individual shares but also on the FTSE 100 Index. These options can be used speculatively. If the investor expects the market to rise, he can buy an option at a particular price for the index. If the market index rises above that price, the option can be exercised profitably. An alternative way of speculating here would be to write put options. If the market rises, then the writer will make a profit through receiving a premium, since the options will not be exercised. However, if the market falls the writer could make substantial losses.

They can also be used to hedge a position. An investor owning a wide spread of shares in the FTSE 100 can buy a put option. If the market falls, the value of the share portfolio will fall, but this will be compensated for by gains on the option.

Writing covered call options (ie where the writer owns the underlying shares) on the index is one way of generating income at the expense of capital growth. If the market rises, the options will be exercised, meaning that the owner of the shares misses out on the increase in share prices. However, they do receive premium income on the options. If the market falls, the capital value of the portfolio falls as the options will not be exercised, but the premium income is still available.

The contract size for the options is £10 × Index value. If the index was at 3,000, then the value of a contract would be £30,000. To hedge a stock market portfolio valued at £300,000 in such a circumstance would involve buying 10 put options on the index. Expiry dates are March, June, September and December plus additional dates so that there are expiry dates for all of the next three months. For example, in February there will be expiry dates available for April and May in addition to the normal expiry dates.

# 8 Valuation of Options

## Factors affecting values

### The underlying share price

The higher the share price, the more attractive it will be to have locked into an option to purchase the shares at a lower price. Hence, the value of call options will increase as the share price rises. The opposite is true for put options, when falls in share price will increase the value of the option to sell at a fixed price.

### The exercise price

The lower the exercise price, the more valuable is a call option. The higher the exercise price, the more valuable is a put option.

### Time to expiry

The longer the time to expiry, the more chance that the option will be exercised to the benefit of the holder. Hence, the longer the time to expiry, the more valuable the option.

### Interest rates

A purchaser of a call option has acquired the right to own a share without paying its full purchase price. Call options are therefore a cheap way of owning shares. If interest rates (and therefore the cost of borrowing) are high, the attraction of buying shares via a call option increases, meaning that call option values increase.

The opposite is true of put options, where high interest rates make it more attractive to sell shares immediately and receive the cash proceeds, rather than taking an option to sell the shares at a later date. This means that increases in interest rates will tend to cause put options to fall in value.

### Expected volatility in the share price

The more volatile the share price, the more likely it is that the option will be exercised. Therefore, high expected volatility will increase option values.

When using option pricing models to value options, volatility is one of the hardest inputs to estimate. A change in the estimate of volatility could change the value of an option significantly. Typically, option pricing models are based on short-dated (three-month) options, making estimating volatility less of a problem. However, it does mean that such models are of less use when pricing longer dated options, since their volatility estimates will be highly suspect for the long term.

### Dividends

The fact that traded options do not receive dividends makes owning shares more attractive than owning the option. If a dividend is due to be paid, the value of call options will be lower than otherwise since it will be more favourable to exercise the option and receive the dividend. The opposite is true for put options.

## Time value and intrinsic value

### Intrinsic value

An option's intrinsic value is the difference between the exercise price of the option and the underlying share price. For example, if a call option entitles the holder to buy shares at a price of £3.00 and the share price is £4.00, then the option has an intrinsic value of £1.00. Intrinsic value is never negative, since the holder of the option is not obliged to exercise it.

### Time value

Time value is the difference between the total value of the option and its intrinsic value. For example, if the price of the above option was actually £1.50 in the market, then the time value would be £0.50. Time value arises because of the prospect that the share price may move even more favourably in the future. The time value of an option is largely determined by the period to expiry of the option and the expected volatility of the share price.

As an option approaches its expiry date, the time value of the option will gradually decrease, a phenomenon referred to as time decay.

### In-the-money options

An in-the-money option is one that has a positive intrinsic value and can therefore be exercised profitably. For a call option, this means that the exercise price is below the share price. For a put option, it means that the exercise price is above the share price.

When an option is in-the-money, it is likely that the option price will track the movement in the share price reasonably closely. This is especially the case when either the option is near to its expiry date or it is very deeply in-the-money. In such circumstances, it has effectively become the same as a share.

### Out-of-the-money options

An out-of-the-money option is one that cannot be exercised profitably. For a call option, this means that the exercise price is above the share price. For a put option, the exercise price would be below the share price.

When an option is out-of-the-money, any value it has will only be its time value. As such, as an option approaches its expiry date or falls significantly out-of-the-money, it becomes almost worthless.

### At-the-money options

An option where the exercise price and the share price are identical is at-the-money.

## 9 Options – Gearing

One of the most attractive, but also dangerous, attributes of options is that they can be used in a geared way.

Gearing describes **the power of such products to control, for a low cost, a much more expensive asset**. This has the effect of magnifying profits and losses.

### Illustration

To demonstrate how gearing works, let us look at an example using options.

**Example**

An investor buys one XYZ January 70 call for 12.

The XYZ share price is 76.

XYZ's share price at expiry is 100 and the call is worth 30. From an investment of 12 a profit of 18 is made. In percentage terms this is

$$\frac{\text{Profit}}{\text{Initial investment}} = \frac{18}{12} \times 100$$

$$= 150\% \text{ profit}$$

If the XYZ share had been bought at 76 and subsequently sold at 100, the figure would be

$$\frac{\text{Profit}}{\text{Initial investment}} = \frac{24}{76} \times 100$$

$$= 31.6\% \text{ profit}$$

As can be seen, the profit from the options trade is very much larger. However, if we imagine a fall in the shares to 70 at expiry, we will see that gearing works both ways.

| | |
|---|---|
| Buy call at | 12 |
| Call at expiry | 0 |
| Loss = | 12 or 100% |

If instead the stock had been bought at 76 and subsequently sold at 70 for a loss of 6, the percentage loss would be

$$\frac{6}{76} \times 100 = 7.9\% \text{ loss}$$

Gearing should therefore be treated with great respect and only investors who understand this attribute should speculate with options. It is very easy to lose your entire investment, or worse.

### Highly geared options

The most highly geared option is one that is deeply out-of-the-money. The reason for this is that it will be very cheap to buy such an option, so it enables the investor to control the whole asset for minimal initial outlay. It is likely that such an option will expire worthless. However, should the share price of the company rise significantly (in the case of a call option), then the holder of such an option has the potential to make huge profits.

### Lowly geared options

The most lowly geared option is one that is deeply in-the-money. The reason for this is that buying the option is tantamount to buying the share. Consider an option to buy a share at a price of 10p when the share price is 1,000p. The value of the option is at least 990p. There is minimal difference between buying the share and buying the option if an investor wishes to acquire control of the share.

## Basic characteristics of warrants

A warrant gives the right to the holder to buy shares from the company that issued the warrant at a specified price on or before a specified date.

It can be seen that a warrant is essentially the same as a call option, giving the right to buy a share. The major difference is that warrants are issued by and exercisable on the company, which will issue new shares on exercise. Traded options are issued by investors and relate to shares already in issue. They are not exercised on the company, which will not issue any new shares.

Warrants have all the characteristics of call options, such as volatility, risk and valuation factors.

## Why issue warrants?

The benefits to a company of issuing warrants include the following.

- Raising immediate cash without the need to finance dividend payments to new shares. The problem is that when the warrants are exercised, the dividend payments in total may increase dramatically.
- Increasing the attraction of a debt issue. Many warrants are attached to a debt issue, giving debt investors the added attraction of an 'equity kicker'. This will translate into lower required yields

on the debt, meaning that the initial financial burden on the company is lower. After the debt is issued, the warrants are usually detached from the debt and traded separately in the market place.

- Capitalising on an overvalued share price. If the company believes that its share price will fall, then any warrants issued are unlikely to be exercised. This means that the company will receive the money on issue of the warrants but anticipates that it will not have to issue any new shares.

## The attractions of warrants for investors

An investor will find warrants attractive for various reasons.

- As a geared investment in a company's shares, it is a cheaper alternative to buying the share itself, much in the same way as for a call option.
- It is also a way of securing an income yield while keeping open the possibility of high equity performance, through buying debt plus warrants from the company. This is similar to the principle of buying a convertible debt issue.

Additional factors to consider include the following.

- The marketability of the warrant.
- The period to expiry, exercise price and current share price, ie basic valuation factors.
- The likelihood that the company's share price will perform adequately.
- The gearing risk implicit in the warrant.
- The risk of a takeover. If a company is taken over, it is often the case that the exercise date of the warrants will be accelerated to the takeover date. This will destroy any time value in the warrant, meaning that an investor could suffer a serious loss. If the warrant is out-of-the-money, having just been issued for example, then it may become worthless.

A warrant holder will not be affected by bonus issues or rights issues because the terms of the warrant will adjust in the same way as the terms of traded options contracts, outlined above.

## Evaluation of warrants

### Gearing ratio

We have already seen that options are highly geared investments. The same is true for warrants. The gearing ratio indicates how highly geared the warrant is. It is calculated as follows.

$$\text{Gearing ratio} = \frac{\text{Market price of the share}}{\text{Market price of the warrant}}$$

Consider two warrants issued by the same company XYZ plc.

| | Warrant 1 | Warrant 2 |
|---|---|---|
| **Company** | XYZ plc | XYZ plc |
| **Share price** | 200p | 200p |
| **Exercise price** | 100p | 300p |
| **Expiry date** | 2000 | 2000 |
| **Price of warrant** | 190p | 30p |

The gearing ratio for each warrant is

**Warrant 1** = $200/_{190} \times 100\% = 105\%$

**Warrant 2** = $200/_{30} \times 100\% = 667\%$

Warrant 1 is deeply in-the-money and warrant 2 is deeply out-of-the-money. The price of warrant 1 is consequently much higher. Warrant 1 is almost certain to be exercised and has in effect become a share. If the share price moves to 201p then the warrant price will probably move to 191p. It is not a highly geared investment and investing in the warrant will give around the same percentage returns as investing in the share itself.

The situation with warrant 2 is very different. A change in the share price from 200p to 201p is unlikely to affect the value of the warrant significantly. If the share price rises significantly, however, then the price of the warrant could also rise significantly, giving a very high percentage return on initial investment.

Warrant 2 is much more highly geared than warrant 1.

### Capital fulcrum point

The capital fulcrum point is the annual percentage increase in share price over the life of the warrant required for the holder of the warrant to obtain the same return in percentage terms as the owner of the share itself.

### Illustration

A warrant has the following characteristics.

| | |
|---|---|
| **Exercise price** | 200p |
| **Share price** | 190p |
| **Warrant price** | 40p |
| **Period to expiry** | 3 years |

If the share price moves to 253p at the end of three years, the shareholder will have earned a gain of 63p or 33%.

With a share price of 253p, the warrant on its expiry date will be worth its intrinsic value of (253p – 200p) 53p. This means that a warrant holder who bought at a price of 40p will have earned a gain of 13p, which is also 33%.

The share price will be required to grow by an average of 10% per year over the next three years to reach 253p. This can be demonstrated by assuming that the share price grows at a constant rate of 10% over the three years.

| Time | Share Price |
|---|---|
| Now | 190p |
| **Year 1** | 209p |
| **Year 2** | 230p |
| **Year 3** | 253p |

If the share price grows by more than 10% per year, then the warrant holder will achieve a higher percentage return than the shareholder. For example, annual growth of 20% per year would give a share price in three years' time of 328p. The shareholder would earn an overall return of 138p or 73%. The warrant price would move to 128p, giving a return of (128p – 40p) 88p or 220%.

If the investor expects the share price to grow by more than the capital fulcrum point, then the warrant should give the higher return, although it will also give higher risk.

# 10 Appendix – Option Strategies

Set out below is an examination of the various different strategies an investor might have regarding options. We also include the different 'pay off' diagrams. Pay off diagrams are charts of the profits and losses for a particular options strategy, prepared in advance of the execution of the strategy. The diagram plots the expected profit or loss against the price of the underlying security.

The appendix contains important information to read in assisting your understanding of options and warrants. You are unlikely to be directly examined on this section.

## The simple uses of options

### Buying a call

This strategy is motivated by a view that the share price will rise.

**Risk** – The investor's risks are limited to the premium he pays for the options. So, if the 80 call could be bought for a premium of 5, this 5 is all he risks. The premium of the call option will only be a fraction of the cost of the underlying share, so the option can be considered less risky than buying the share itself.

Whilst this is true, remember that the whole premium is at risk and it is easy to lose 100% of your investment, albeit a relatively small amount of money.

**Reward** – The rewards from buying a call are unlimited. As the contract gives the holder the right to buy at a fixed price, this right will become increasingly valuable as the share price rises above the exercise price.

Imagine an investor who buys one XYZ call option, which gives him the right, but not the obligation, to buy the XYZ asset at a fixed price of 80 between now and the option's expiry date in January. The cost of this option is 5.

If the share price rises to 120, the right to buy at 80, ie the premium of the 80 call, must be worth at least 40. The net profit for the call would be 35 (40 – 5). Of course, if the price of XYZ falls below 80 at the option's expiry date, the 80 call will be worthless and 100% of the initial 5 invested will be lost. This loss occurs because no sensible person would want the right to buy at 80 if they could buy the share more cheaply elsewhere.

By using graphs, we can show how much an option will be worth at expiry.

On the vertical axis of the graph is profit/loss and on the horizontal axis is the asset price.

**Holder of 1 XYZ January 80 Call – Premium 5**

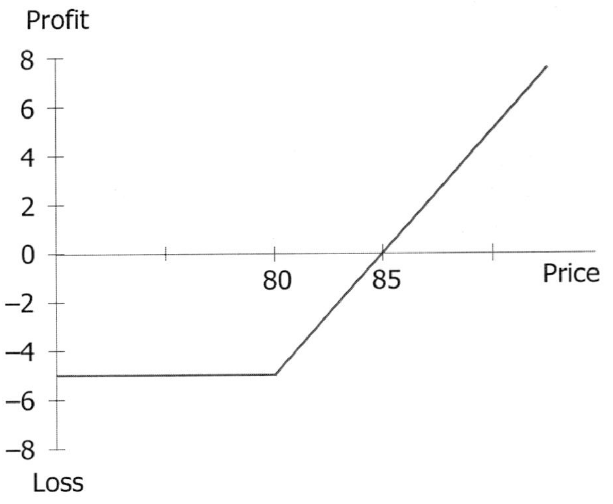


What the graph shows is that losses of 5 are made anywhere below 80, whilst profits emerge above 85. The **breakeven** point is represented by 85. This is the point at which the original investment is recouped and it is calculated by simply adding the premium to the exercise price, eg 80 + 5 = 85. The buying of a call to open a position is known as a 'long call'.

### Selling a call

**Risk** – The selling or writing of a call, without at the same time being in possession of the underlying share, is extremely risky. The risk is unlimited because the writer has a duty to deliver the share at a fixed price, regardless of the prevailing share price. As the share price could, in theory, rise to infinity, the call writer assumes an unlimited risk. This strategy is sometimes called **naked** call writing and as it suggests, can leave you feeling very exposed.

**Reward** – You might ask why someone would assume such an unlimited risk. The answer, of course, is the hope of a profit. The maximum profit the writer can make is the premium he receives. Let us look again at an 80 call with a premium of 5. The seller of this call will receive the 5 premium, and as long as the share price at expiry is less than 80, no-one will rationally want to exercise the right to buy. The graph for selling a call is set out below. You will see that it is the equal and opposite of buying a call.

**Writer of 1 XYZ January 80 Call – Premium 5**

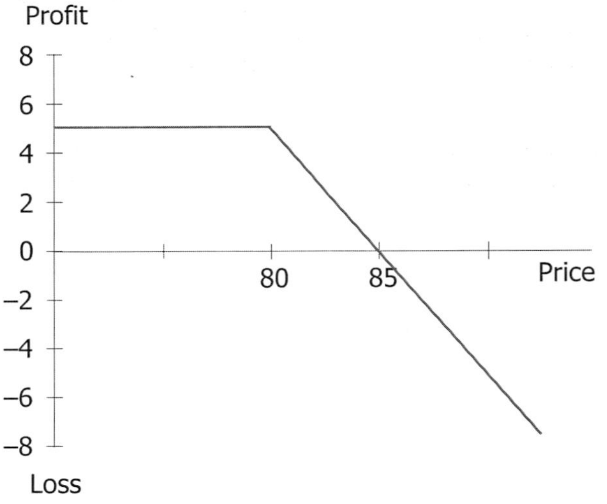

As the graph demonstrates, the call writer believes that the share price is likely either to stay the same or fall. If this happens, the writer simply pockets the premium received and will not have to deliver the share. The selling of a call to open a position is known as a 'short call'.

### Buying a put

**Risk** – As when buying a call, the risk is limited to the premium paid. The motivation behind buying a put will be to profit from a fall in the share price. The holder of a put obtains the right, but not the obligation, to sell at a fixed price. The value of this right will become increasingly valuable as the share price falls.

**Reward** – The greatest profit that will arise from buying a put will be achieved if the share price falls to zero.

**Holder of 1 XYZ July 80 Put – Premium 5**

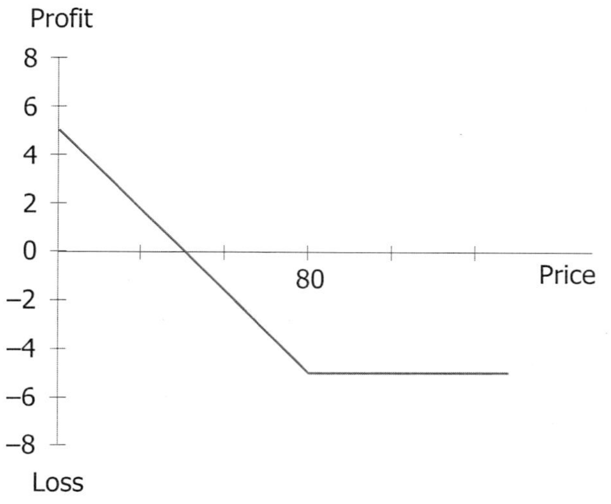


The breakeven point, and maximum profit, is calculated by deducting the premium from the exercise price, eg 80 – 8 = 72. Like the purchase of a call, the premium needs to be recovered before profits are made. The buying of a put to open a position is known as a 'long put'.

### Selling a put

**Risk** – The selling of a put is dangerous as the writer enters into an obligation to purchase a share at a fixed price. If the market price of the share falls, the put writer will end up paying a large amount of money for what could be a valueless share. The worst case will arise when the share price falls to zero. If this happens, the loss will be the exercise price less the premium received.

**Reward** – What the put option writer hopes for is that the put will not be exercised. This will occur if the share has a price above the exercise price at expiry. The maximum reward is the premium received. The selling of a put to open a position is known as a 'short put'.

**Writer of 1 XYZ July 80 Put – Premium 5**

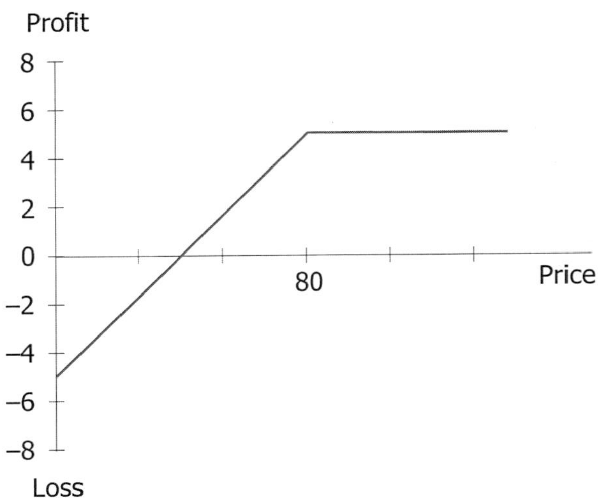


The four basic strategies, outlined above, form the building blocks of all the more complicated option techniques.

## Options combinations

The most common form of option combination strategy is a straddle.

### Long straddle

A long straddle is where a call option and a put option are both purchased, where they both have the same strike price.

Undertake the following cocoa options trade

| | |
|---|---|
| Buy 1 September £19.00 call for | £0.50 |
| Buy 1 September £19.00 put for | £0.45 |
| Total expenditure | £0.95 |

In this trade, the investor is clearly unsure about direction. He buys a call to profit from a rise in cocoa prices and a put to make money from a fall. Whilst unsure about direction, the investor is certain about one thing, namely that volatility will increase.

Before securing a profit, the market must move by at least £0.95, either up or down. This is to recoup the initial cost of both options. The breakeven points are, therefore, £18.05 and £19.95. Beyond these points, there is unlimited profit potential if the price of cocoa rises. If the price of cocoa falls, the investor will profit greatly, to a maximum of £18.05 if cocoa prices fall to zero. This trade is called a **long straddle**.

**Long Straddle Profile**

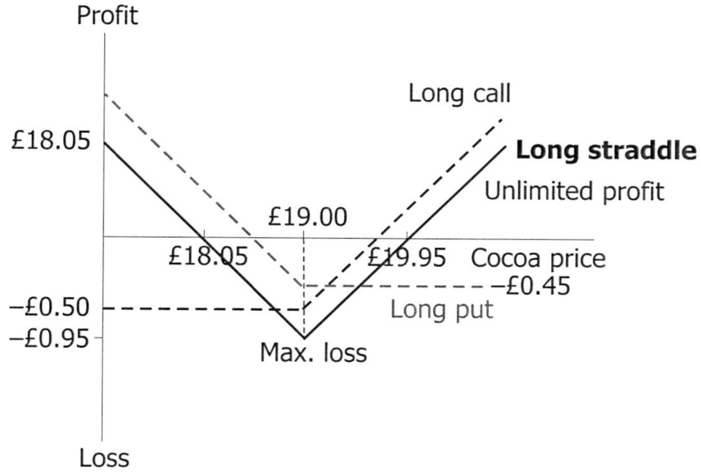


## Short straddle

If the investor's view had been that volatility would decrease, he could sell both a call and a put. In this case, profits would emerge between £18.05 and £19.95. However, if the movement was greater than this, unlimited losses could result. This is a **short straddle**.

**Short Straddle Profile**

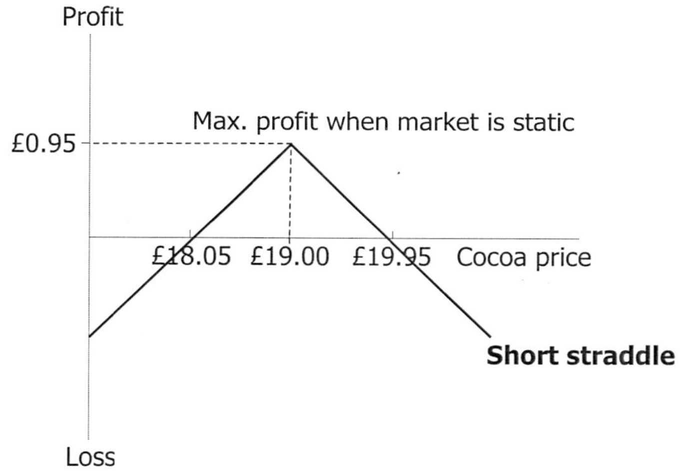

# CHAPTER ROUNDUP

**Module 3, Chapter 14: Financial Instruments**

A thorough revision of this chapter will help ensure you are familiar with the main financial instruments that are used in corporate finance.

You should be able to summarise the terms, rights, conditions of use and factors concerning the value of the following financial instruments:

- Ordinary shares, including special types of ordinary shares:
  - Founder shares
  - 'A' and 'B' shares
  - Deferred shares
- Preference shares
  - Debt
  - Bonds
  - FRNs
  - Zeros
  - Convertibles, including mandatory convertibles
  - Exchangeables
  - MTNs
  - Eurobonds
- Warrants
- Options

You need to be prepared to suggest when each instrument might be a suitable form of financing and what the relative advantages and disadvantages of each source are. The exam is unlikely to ask you to reproduce a list of characteristics, more to ensure you are able to apply the characteristics and see when and why a form of financing might be appropriate for a business.

You will also need to be able to interpret a business' existing financing structure and understand the requirements of the different capital providers, as well as providing suitable valuations.

# UNQUOTED SOURCES OF FINANCE

chapter 15

Contents


| | | |
|---|---|---|
| 1 | Introduction | 340 |
| 2 | Venture Capital | 340 |
| 3 | Approaching Investors – The Business Plan | 346 |
| 4 | The Ideal MBO Candidate | 347 |
| 5 | Sources of Finance and Deal Structuring | 353 |
| 6 | Deal Structuring – Conclusion | 356 |
| 7 | Venture Capital – Exit Routes | 356 |
| 8 | Venture Capital Trusts | 357 |
| 9 | Enterprise Investment Scheme (EIS) | 358 |
| 10 | Seed Enterprise Investment Scheme (SEIS) | 358 |
| 11 | Bank Finance | 359 |
| 12 | Project Finance | 363 |
| 13 | Sovereign Wealth Funds | 364 |
| 14 | Family Offices | 365 |

# 1 Introduction

In this chapter we consider the following sources of unquoted finance:

- Venture capital, including tax relief schemes (Venture Capital Trusts, Enterprise Investment Schemes and Seed Enterprise Investment Schemes)
- Senior, mezzanine and other debt
- Banks: term loans, commercial mortgages, syndicated loans, overdrafts, revolving credits, factoring
- Leasing
- Project finance
- Sovereign wealth funds
- Family offices

# 2 Venture Capital

## What is venture capital?

A venture capitalist is typically someone who invests in the equity of a private company to provide funding for acquisition or expansion purposes. The reward for the venture capitalist is the potential to earn a large capital gain in the medium term. Typically, venture capitalists will aim to realise their investment in three to five years. There are a number of different forms of venture capital, ranging from very risky 'seed capital' (where a business has only just started and aims to develop an idea into a saleable product) to management buyouts (where the business is already well established and generating good cash flows).

## Characteristics of venture capital

### Risk finance

Venture capital investment is very risky. The possibility of business failure is high and even if the business is successful, the investment is illiquid. Shares in a private company are not easily re-sold, and their value will consequently be proportionately less than the market price of shares in a comparable quoted company. In addition, the investments are often not viewed as attractive lending options by traditional bankers for a number of reasons.

- Little asset backing
- Personal guarantees of varying worth, since the directors will already have invested much of their own finance in the business
- Little trading history
- Inexperienced management

As a result, equity finance from investors who are used to dealing with risk and assessing the viability of investments from such a viewpoint is necessary.

### Hands-on management

The venture capitalist will often have financial and organisational skills that will be of value to the company. In addition, the entrepreneur will have given up a sizeable stake of his company to the investor and may expect something more in return than just the initial cash finance. Active management participation and a seat on the board for the venture capitalist will often be attractive to both sides.

### Capital gains

A young company is unlikely to have significant cash surpluses for distribution to investors. Any cash generated is likely to be reinvested in the business to achieve growth or to pay off debt. This means that a venture capital investor will need to achieve most of his return through selling his investment in the future and achieving a high capital gain. Only a small part of the overall return will be in the form of a running yield, through a preference dividend for example.

### Exit routes

Given the investor's need for a capital gain, a feasible exit route is vital from the very start. The exit is likely to be either a flotation, a trade sale to another company or a restructuring whereby the investor's shares are repurchased by the company. The most likely of these is a trade sale since many companies will not be sufficiently large to be floated or may be unsuitable for flotation for some other reason. A share repurchase scheme may not realise a realistic sum unless the company gears up to an unacceptable extent.

### Required rates of return and the principle of leverage

In order to compensate for the high-risk levels, the return on the investment will need to be substantial. The actual return required will vary from investment to investment but an internal rate of return of around 30% to 35% would not be unusual. The venture capitalist will aim to maximise this return by introducing debt funding to help partly fund the purchase price. Since debt finance is repaid at par value on exit, any upside can be for the benefit of the Ordinary shareholders, namely the venture capitalist and the management. This is known as the 'Principle of Leverage'.

## Types of venture capital investment

Venture capital funding can be provided at all stages of a company's development, but typically, is necessary to take the business to a new stage. The existing owners may be unable to fund all the finance the business needs and the banks may be reluctant to lend due to high credit risk.

Venture capital investments can be categorised according to the stage of development the business has reached when risk capital funding is required.

### Seedcorn

Seedcorn funding is invested to help develop a business idea, for example making a prototype or conducting initial market research.

For a venture capitalist investing in seed capital is very high risk. Commencement of trading (and therefore cash generation) is some way off and the feasibility of the business idea is unlikely to be explored fully. Most seedcorn funding will come from the entrepreneurs themselves.

### Start-ups

Financing could be provided to a company in the process of setting up, or at a stage where its product or service has not yet been sold commercially. The product or service exists and, in contrast to a seedcorn business, no research and development (R&D) expenditure is needed before the company becomes operational.

### Other early stage projects

Companies that have completed product development and begun marketing might want more funds to manufacture and sell the product on a commercial scale. These companies will not yet be making a profit, and cannot finance their development out of operational cash flows. They must, therefore, rely on external funding.

### Expansion financing

Finance could be required for the growth and expansion of an established business. A company might wish, for example, to increase its manufacturing capacity, develop its marketing channels or invest more in working capital. Expansion financing is usually low-risk venture capital, compared with early stage investments and turnarounds. Most venture capital investments are for expansion purposes.

### Turnarounds

A company that has been in decline might develop plans for halting the decline and staging a recovery. In the early stage of a recovery programme, the original backers will have to provide the extra finance required. If the recovery appears successful, other venture capitalists could be willing to inject extra funds. Turnaround financing is comparatively rare.

### Refinancing bank debt

An established company burdened by bank debts, possibly reaching maturity, might seek venture capital funding to repay the banks.

### Secondary purchase

In a secondary purchase, existing shares in a company are purchased by one venture capital firm from another, or from another shareholder (or shareholders) in the company. Although venture capital finance is being invested, it replaces existing capital and does not provide any additional capital to the company concerned.

### Acquisitions ('buyouts')

Venture capital funding can be invested to finance a change of control of the company in an acquisition or buyout situation. Two examples of acquisition funding are as follows.

- A management buyout (MBO) is the purchase of an existing company or a business unit by a group of its managers, with the support of external investors.
- A management buy-in (MBI), in contrast, is the purchase of an existing company or a business unit by an external management team, with financing from venture capitalists and banks. The buy-in team must have the necessary experience and/or expertise to run the business they are purchasing.

An alternative is the buy-in management buyout (BIMBO), where the existing management team is supplemented with outside expertise.

### Public to private transactions

A public to private transaction involves the buyout of a quoted company. The following is a list of scenarios when a public to private transaction might be appropriate.

- The company is a small cap share that has been underperforming the market as a result of general underperformance in the small cap sector.
- There is poor liquidity in the shares such that it is difficult for shareholders to realise value other than through some form of offer for the shares.
- There is at least one major shareholder who can influence the outcome of the bid.
- The proportion of shares in public hands falls below a minimum percentage.
- The institutional investors can add something to the company that it does not have in a public context as a separate entity, such as management skills or links to other companies.

### Institutional buyouts (IBOs)

Here, an institution identifies a possible company, arranges the finance and then approaches a potential management team. IBOs tend to be the larger venture capital deals, with management often receiving a very small share of the overall equity.

## Buyouts – regulatory issues

Relevant regulatory issues affecting venture capital-funded acquisitions are as follows.

- There is a conflict of interest arising, since the directors of the company are wishing to buy the company at the lowest price the shareholders will accept. However, they have a duty to the shareholders to act in their best interests.
- The Takeover Code will be relevant for management buyouts of public limited companies.
- There are potential issues to consider in respect of financial assistance under the Companies Act.

### City Code issues

The City Code provisions are only relevant when there is a change of control in a public limited company.

- *Rule 25.2 (note 5)* highlights that the directors of the company subject to the bid face a conflict of interest in their duty to act in the best interest of shareholders, as they are also the offeror.
- *Rule 3* specifies that an independent adviser should be appointed as soon as possible to ensure the shareholders' interests are looked after.
- *Rule 20.3* of the City Code states that, in an MBO, the offeror or potential offeror must, on request, promptly furnish the independent directors of the offeree company or its advisers with all information that has been furnished by the offeror or potential offeror to external providers of finance, whether equity or debt.
- Where there is a competing offer, *Rule 20.2* states that information passed by the offeree company to external providers of finance, whether equity or debt, should be given equally and promptly to the competing offeror, even if that offeror is less welcome. The competing offeror will, however, have to specify exactly what information it requires, rather than asking in general terms for all the information supplied to the external providers of finance for the MBO.
- As with any MBO, the venture capital provider will usually want to incentivise the MBO team by having them take an equity stake in the buy-out vehicle. Rule 16 however prohibits a bidder from making arrangements with shareholders if there are favourable conditions attached which are not available to all shareholders. However, in certain situations, the offeror may wish to retain the services of director shareholders of the offeree and to motivate them by means of an

'earn out' deal where they receive a higher price for their shares if the company's profits hit specified targets.

Such special deals may be permitted as long as relevant details of the arrangements are disclosed and an independent adviser states that, in his opinion, the terms are fair and reasonable. Where the value of the arrangements entered into is significant and/or unusual in the context of industry practice, then the Panel must be consulted and consent to the arrangements be obtained. The Panel may require, as part of this process, that the arrangements be approved at a general meeting of the company's shareholders (Rule 16.2)

- Full details of management shareholdings must be disclosed in the offer document *(Rule 24.2).*

### Financial assistance

The Companies Act 2006 states that it is illegal for a public limited company to give financial assistance for the acquisition of shares in itself or its holding company.

Financial assistance includes gifts, loans, guarantees, indemnities and any other assistance that reduces a company's net assets to a material extent.

Private companies are permitted to give financial assistance for the purchase of their own shares. This exception usually becomes important in the case of management buyouts when the assets of the company are used as security for loans received to buy the company's shares. It is likely that the company subject to the buyout will have to be converted to a private company, prior to the buyout taking place, in order for the financial assistance to be lawful.

In order to convert the company to private status, it will be necessary to have an acceptance condition that the offer is conditional on acceptances being received in respect of 90% of the shares to which the offer relates. This will enable the company to be taken private without any problems from minority shareholders.

## Venture capital organisations

Although venture capital can be provided by individuals and investment institutions, the main providers are specialist venture capital organisations. The major sources of venture capital can be categorised as follows.

There are five broad types.

- Independents
- Captives
- Semi-captives
- Government departments or agencies
- Venture Capital Trusts

They differ in how they raise funds and who controls their investment decisions.

### Independents

Independent venture capital organisations raise their funds from more than one source, mainly institutional investors. No single shareholder or investor has a dominant position in the ownership of the fund. The funds are managed independently, and management is free to choose how the money should be invested. Wholly independent funds can be set up in either of two ways.

- A group of experienced venture capitalists seek backing from several investment institutions. The institutions put money into a fund, which the venture capitalists manage on their behalf.
- A group of financial institutions agree to set up a fund, and recruit a management team to make the investments. The fund managers then decide how to invest the money in business ventures.

Investors in the funds are paid returns out of the proceeds from investing in business ventures, ie dividends on shares, interest on loans and the cash proceeds from the eventual sale or redemption of the investments.

Independent funds have several other features. They are usually 'close-ended', with a specified initial capital base. For example, a £200m fund might be established. After the initial fundraising, no further money will be sought for the fund, and management will invest in business ventures until the money in the fund is used up.

- They are primarily equity oriented, and seek long-term capital gain rather than a regular flow of annual dividend income.
- They are often established with a maximum life, typically ten years. At the end of this time, the fund is liquidated, and the proceeds distributed (in cash or as unsold securities owned by the fund) to the fund investors and managers in a pre-arranged proportion. Management can, if it wishes, set up a new fund to attract fresh venture capital.
- During the life of the fund, management also charges a fee, typically 2%–2½% of the funds invested in a smaller fund, and perhaps 1%–1½% for a larger fund.

Some independents are companies investing their own funds in business ventures. For example, 3i Group plc is a public company with share capital. Funds are obtained by issuing shares, borrowing or reinvesting the proceeds of realised investments in earlier business ventures. Their aim is to make profits on investing in ventures in order to provide a return to their own shareholders.

### Captives

A captive venture capital organisation obtains its funds from a parent organisation, usually a financial institution, and manages them on behalf of the parent. The management is appointed by and accountable to the parent, which expects the fund to provide a suitable return.

Captive funds may be more concerned than independents about an annual 'running yield', ie dividend income, from their investments, although capital gain is an important part of the overall return.

### Semi-captives

A semi-captive venture capital organisation invests funds on behalf of a parent, but also manages independently, funds obtained from other sources. An investment bank or other investment institution could set up a fund and appoint a management team, and then invite a number of other investment institutions to join the fund.

### Government

Some venture capital organisations receive their funds from national or local governments and use the money to invest in businesses in their region.

### Venture capital trusts

Venture Capital Trusts (VCTs) are quoted funds which hold investments in unquoted businesses, and are controlled and managed by venture capital firms. The regulations covering VCTs are considered below.

### Advisory Services

Instead of investing funds under its management, a venture capitalist could also act as adviser to other fund managers or venture capital investors. One example is a 'gatekeeper' that specifically advises investors on funds or provides opportunities to invest in a 'fund of funds'.

# 3 APPROACHING INVESTORS – THE BUSINESS PLAN

When trying to raise funds for his business, the entrepreneur's first point of contact with potential investors will be his business plan. The business plan is a marketing document that aims to make the business seem attractive and a worthy investment opportunity. It will be competing with many other proposals and will need to immediately stand out to the venture capitalist. Key areas to include in the plan are as follows.

- **Executive Summary.** A one-page summary of the document, including the main reasons for the business' likely success, the investment required, the timespan to exit and key financial details, as well as what the unique opportunity is that this investment provides.
- **Company Background.** History and main events in the company's history.
- **The Product or Service.** What it is and why there is demand for it. What advantages it has over rival products/services. Development information.
- **The Market and Demand.** Whether the market is stable, growing or declining. What is the market segment and size? Who constitutes the customer base? What factors affect demand and cause the customers to buy the product? Commercially sensitive information about customers will not be included.
- **Marketing Plan.** How the business is going to be developed and how the customers will be approached and persuaded to do business with the company. The venture capitalist will consider the sales strategy carefully to see how the business could be grown to give a good return on the initial investment.
- **Competition.** Who the competitors are, what size they are, how important the market place is to them, and how likely they are to fight to defend their position against any new entrant. If there is no competition, why this is the case? How can this business meet the competitive threat? What barriers to entry exist?
- **Suppliers.** Who are the principal suppliers for the business, how numerous are they, and are they in a strong position when negotiating prices?
- **Company Structure.** Legal structure and ownership details.
- **Management.** Even if the market is right, it is vital to have a management team capable of developing the business. Many venture capitalists say that the three most important success ingredients for a company are the three M's – management, management and management. Profiles of all key staff and their experience and qualifications for running such a business should be included. A management weakness in one area, such as finance or organisational expertise, can often be filled by the venture capital provider.
- **Operations.** This includes such areas as: production process and capacity; facilities details; and other organisational details that are key to the business, for example, administration facilities.
- **Financial Projections.** The purpose of the financial projections is to estimate
  - How much finance will be needed?
  - Annual revenues, costs and profits of the business.
  - The cash flows, including all capital expenditure and working capital requirements.

  The projections should include a summary profit and loss statement, a cash flow and usually a balance sheet. A forecast period of between three and five years would be typical.
- **Risks and Opportunities.** A summary of the key strengths of the business and the opportunities available to it. Importantly, how they will be capitalised on. Also, the key risks and weaknesses and how they will be mitigated.
- **Investment Required and Exit Routes.** The level of investment required, the time to realisation of investment and how realisation is going to be achieved.

# 4 The Ideal MBO Candidate

The ideal MBO candidate is one where the risks of the investment can be successfully mitigated whilst still allowing the venture capital and debt investors to realise a satisfactory return. Desirable characteristics for a company to have are as follows.

- A stable or growing market place
- Potential for cost saving or synergistic restructuring
- Cash generation
- Large asset backing as security for loans
- The ability to restrict fixed asset expenditure over the years subsequent to the buyout to minimise cash outflows in the critical early years
- The ability to squeeze working capital in the early years to generate additional cash to pay back loan finance
- The existence of surplus assets that can be sold to pay down debt
- A strong, well-balanced management team
- A feasible exit route, ie the company should be of sufficient size to be floated or should be an attractive purchase for other acquisitive companies

## Progressing the deal

### Financiers and advisers

Before making an offer and negotiating with the vendor, the management team should aim to meet with the potential financiers. They can then inspect the business plan and establish whether or not finance is likely to be available.

It may be useful at this stage to use professional advisers, such as accountants or lawyers. The advantage of this is that they will be expert at representing the management's interests. The risk is that heavy fees will be incurred which will have to be met by the management personally if the bid does not succeed.

### Offer to the vendors

After meeting with the potential financiers, an offer can be made to the vendors. This will cover the following points.

- Details of the assets or shares to be purchased.
- Details of trademarks or other brand names to be included in the deal.
- Which employees and attached obligations (such as redundancy payments) are to be included in the deal.
- Pre-conditions for the sale, such as an investigation or tax clearances.
- The purchase price and payment terms.

When setting the price, the management will have to value the company using various valuation techniques. This, however, will only give a base guide and the final price will be determined by a range of factors. The negotiating strength of each party will be paramount.

## Illustration of a venture capital deal

### Initial appraisal

Having established that the venture is a reasonably sound proposition by analysing the business plan, the venture capitalist will identify the total investment requirement in cash terms, how the deal is to be structured (what other sources of finance are likely to be available), and what sort of return he can expect to achieve over the life of the investment. He will then compare the return calculated from the investment to his required return to ascertain whether the deal represents a viable business proposition.

### Profit forecasts

Consider a company that is seeking finance for an MBO and predicts the following income statement figures.

| Income Statement Forecasts | Year 1 £'000 | Year 2 £'000 | Year 3 £'000 | Year 4 £'000 | Year 5 £'000 |
|---|---|---|---|---|---|
| Revenue | 500 | 800 | 1,200 | 1,900 | 2,500 |
| EBIT | 85 | 160 | 300 | 510 | 725 |
| Net income | 30 | 70 | 110 | 150 | 190 |

Net income for the latest year was £26,500.

### Investment required

The capital outlay required is £560,000, which includes the purchase cost of £400,000, paid to the vendors, and expansion capital for the business of £100,000. The remaining £60,000 is estimated to cover fees.

| Funding Requirements | £'000 |
|---|---|
| Purchase consideration | 400 |
| New non current assets (machinery) | 70 |
| Working capital | 30 |
| Costs (professional fees, etc) | 60 |
| Total financing requirements | 560 |

### Sources of finance

As a venture capitalist, you assess that the minimum interest cover ratio (defined as EBIT divided by interest expense) acceptable to the banks, is likely to be 4×. Market rates indicate that loan finance could be raised at a cost of 9.0% per annum. The maximum amount the entrepreneur can afford to invest is £30,000, which he will raise by taking out a second mortgage on his home.

## Financing scheme

A possible financing scheme would be as follows.

| | £'000 |
|---|---|
| Equity (note 1) | |
| Entrepreneur | 30 |
| Venture capitalist – Ordinary shares | 45 |
| Venture capitalist – preference shares | 255 |
| | 330 |
| Debt | |
| Bank debt – term loan (note 2) | 180 |
| Leasing of machinery (note 3) | 50 |
| | 230 |
| Total finance | 560 |

**Note 1 – Equity**

The entrepreneur is only investing £30,000 out of the total financing of £560,000. Although his investment is relatively small compared to the other sources of finance, it is very high in proportion to his overall wealth. His own personal assets are at stake and he will therefore be entitled to a relatively high shareholding in the business to reflect the risk. The entrepreneur will receive Ordinary (voting) shares in return for his investment, based on an ownership split negotiated with the venture capitalist. If we assume management have agreed a 40% stake, then the Ordinary shareholding of the venture capitalist is 60%, ie £45,000 $\left(30 \times \frac{60}{40}\right)$. The balance of venture capitalist funding will be invested as preference shares or loan notes (if gearing covenants permit).

**Note 2 – Debt**

The bank debt is structured as a term loan. This term loan would account for most of the fixed requirements of the business such as leasehold and fixed asset purchases and financing the permanent core of working capital in the business. Repayments would link into the expected cash flows of the business.

The bank would need to justify its lending. Using the assumptions of a minimum interest cover ratio of 4×, and loan finance being available at 9% per annum, we can calculate the maximum debt available to the company.

$$\text{Interest cover} = \frac{\text{Forecast EBIT}}{\text{Maximum interest cost}}$$

$$\text{Maximum interest cost} = \frac{£85{,}000}{4}$$

$$= £21{,}250$$

$$\text{Maximum debt} = \frac{\text{Interest charge}}{\text{Borrowing rate}}$$

$$= \frac{£21{,}250}{0.09}$$

$$= £236{,}111$$

The proposed loan of £180,000 is more than covered by this.

**Note 3 – Leasing**

Leasing is often an excellent way of reducing the initial funding requirements. However, care should be taken that the cost of leasing is not excessive. Leasing companies will often attempt to charge interest rates of 30% or more. Leases will therefore increase the gearing and reduce the interest cover of the business.

## Forecasting free cash flows and debt repayment

We now forecast the cash flow generated by the investment, deducting from this the repayment of interest and debt capital in accordance with the terms of the debt instruments.

Continuing the example above, assume the term loan (£180m at 9% interest) is repayable in equal instalments to include both capital and interest. Assume a tax rate of 30% is applicable.

The annual repayment on the term loan is calculated by dividing the capital sum by the five-year annuity factor at 9%.

Annual repayment $= \frac{£180m}{3.89}$ (see working)

$= £46m$

### Working

Annuity factor $= \frac{1}{r}\left(1 - \frac{1}{(1+r)^n}\right)$

$= \frac{1}{0.09}\left(1 - \frac{1}{1.09^5}\right)$

$= 3.89$

The repayment of capital and interest, together with the associated tax shield on the interest, can be scheduled as follows.

### Scheduling repayment of capital and interest

| Year | Term Loan Balance b/f | Interest (tax relief) | Cash Payment | Term Loan Balance c/f |
|---|---|---|---|---|
| 1 | 180 | 16.2 (4.86) | 46 | 150.2 |
| 2 | 150.2 | 13.5 (4.06) | 46 | 117.7 |
| 3 | 117.7 | 10.6 (3.2) | 46 | 82.3 |
| 4 | 82.3 | 7.4 (2.2) | 46 | 43.7 |
| 5 | 43.7 | 3.9 (1.2) | 46 | – |

We can now forecast the free cash flow from the investment to ascertain if there is sufficient cash flow to repay this debt.

### Forecasting free cash flow

| | Time | | | | |
|---|---|---|---|---|---|
| | 1 | 2 | 3 | 4 | 5 |
| EBIT | 85 | 160 | 300 | 510 | 725 |
| Less tax (30%) | (26) | (48) | (90) | (153) | (218) |
| Free cash flow | 59 | 112 | 210 | 357 | 507 |
| Less: Repayment of capital and interest | (46) | (46) | (46) | (46) | (46) |
| Add: Tax relief on interest | 4.9 | 4.0 | 3.2 | 2.2 | 1.2 |
| Retained cash | 17.9 | 70.0 | 167.2 | 313.2 | 462.2 |

The forecasts make the following assumptions.

- Depreciation is equal to capital expenditure.
- The business has no additional working capital requirements.
- Tax relief is available on the interest as soon as it arises.

The forecasts indicate that the business will have sufficient cash flow to repay the term loan prior to exit at the end of Year 5.

## Calculating the venture capitalist's return

In order to assess whether or not the above deal is acceptable, the venture capitalist needs to assess what his overall rate of return is going to be by calculating the internal rate of return of the cash flows of his investment.

The venture capitalist's internal rate of return (IRR) will largely depend on the value of the business in five years' time, assuming that a sale or flotation occurs at that date.

Assuming the business is exited on a P/E ratio similar to the purchase price.

P/E ratio at entry $= \frac{\text{Purchase consideration}}{\text{PAT (latest year)}}$

$= \frac{400,000}{26,500}$

$= 15.1\times$

P/E ratio at exit $= \frac{\text{Exit value}}{\text{PAT (Year 5)}}$

Exit value $= 15.1 \times £190,000$

$= £2,869,000$

We can now calculate the share of the exit value attributable to the venture capitalist. This calculation assumes all borrowings have been paid off over the life of the investment.

| | £ |
|---|---|
| Total exit value | 2,869,000 |
| Less: Preference shares | (255,000) |
| Balance to equity holders | 2,614,000 |
| Less: Entrepreneur share (40%) | (1,045,600) |
| Venture capitalist (equity) | 1,568,400 |
| | |
| Total venture capitalist cash on exit (Preference and equity shares) | 1,823,400 |

Calculating the IRR of the venture capitalist's cash flows, is as follows.

| Time | | Cash Flow (£) |
|---|---|---|
| 0 | Cash outflow for purchase | (300,000) |
| 5 | Cash inflow on sale | 1,823,400 |

IRR = 43%

As this return is in excess of normal minimum requirements, say, of 30%, the deal is likely to be acceptable to the venture capitalist at this stage.

This calculation assumes that the venture capitalist does not receive a dividend from their shares during the five-year investment period. A dividend would give rise to additional cash flows and therefore increase the overall return of the investment.

## Use of ratchets

The venture capitalist could be prepared to offer incentives to management to motivate them towards making the venture successful. These can take the form of a ratchet.

A ratchet is an arrangement whereby managers get a larger share of the company's equity if the business performs well and achieves certain specified targets in the business plan. The ratchet allows the exact division of the Ordinary share capital between the entrepreneurs and the venture capitalists to be decided after the success (or failure) of the venture is known.

### EXAMPLE

A company is the subject of an MBO. It is currently making annual after-tax profits of £2m, which are forecast to rise to £5m after three years. The venture capital organisation financing the buyout has estimated that to achieve its target return on investment, it would have to own 40% of the company's Ordinary share capital if annual profits are £5m at the end of three years. However, if annual profits are £6m, it will only need to own about 30% of the Ordinary share capital to earn its target return.

#### Analysis

A ratchet arrangement could be agreed whereby for every £100,000 of profits over £5m p.a. after three years, up to a ceiling of £6m, management should be entitled to an extra 0.5% of the equity. If profits reach £6m, management will therefore raise their stake in the Ordinary share capital from 60% to 65%.

Ratchets are often structured using convertible shares.

### Advantages of a ratchet

- A ratchet motivates the entrepreneur, who will probably be optimistic about the business and believe that it will do very well.
- A ratchet also protects the return of the venture capitalist.

### Disadvantages

- A ratchet can encourage short-termism.
- The entrepreneur only concentrates on achieving the ratchet profits to the exclusion of all other considerations.
- The definition of profits can be manipulated.
- If the business does less well, then the entrepreneur may become less motivated since more gains are going to the venture capitalist.

# 5 Sources of Finance and Deal Structuring

The major sources of finance used in venture capital deals are as follows.

- Equity (Ordinary and preference shares)
- Senior debt
- Mezzanine debt
- High yield bonds
- Venture capitalist loan notes
- Vendor loan notes
- Others

## Equity finance

The equity finance will typically be split between the management team and the venture capitalists, although it may be the case that the vendor wishes to retain an interest in the company. The bulk of the finance will be supplied by the venture capitalists. They will largely be concerned to ensure that they earn a satisfactory rate of return on an IRR basis taking into account the risk being incurred. On top of this, they will need to ensure that the management is well motivated to succeed by owning an appropriate proportion of the equity.

Additional elements in the equity package may be as follows.

- **Share Options or Convertible Loan Sock**
  These will enable the financiers to increase their percentage of the company at low cost. The conversion or exercise rights can be altered depending on whether the company achieves agreed performance targets.
- **Redeemable Preference Shares**
  These enable the venture capitalists to obtain repayment of their investment if equity returns are inadequate. They will give a running yield that will increase overall returns. They may include a conversion option.
- **Ratchets**
  These may enable the deal to satisfy both the management team and the venture capitalists.

## Senior debt

Senior debt will be supplied by banks on a secured basis. In order to assess the debt capacity of the company, banks will look at ratios such as the following.

- Interest cover, both on a profits and cash flow basis
- The ratio of free cash flow to total debt repayments (interest + scheduled capital repayments)
- The ratio of total debt to EBITDA

The senior debt lender is likely to specify these ratios for the senior debt facility and also for the total debt of the venture, thereby controlling the total amount of debt raised. For example, the senior debt agreement may stipulate a minimum interest cover of 5× for the senior debt and 2.5× for all debt.

Since the company being acquired is giving a charge over its assets to the banks, there are S151 issues with respect to financial assistance for the purchase of a company's shares. This is considered in more detail in the chapter, Other Takeover Regulations.

## Mezzanine finance

Mezzanine finance is financing that ranks below senior debt for repayment and interest payment, but ahead of equity. It usually takes the form of a loan from a bank or specialist finance house or venture capital firm, at a higher interest rate than the senior debt and with lower or subordinated security. Frequently it will include an 'equity kicker'. This is an entitlement for the lender to take an equity stake in the venture capital investment, usually through the issue of warrants exercisable on the venture capitalist's exit or on repayment of the mezzanine debt.

Mezzanine finance is often part of the funding mix for a buyout. It is popular because debt is inherently cheaper than equity as the interest charge is tax-deductible, and equity providers always seek the maximum leverage compatible with the risk profile of the company, to maximise the returns on equity.

Generally, the team will first establish the maximum amount of senior debt available, based on interest cover and in some cases asset backing. The next step is to establish whether any mezzanine debt can be raised. This will be determined by the attitude of the senior lender, who will have imposed restrictions on the company's overall borrowings in the form of gearing covenants and (most importantly) overall interest cover covenants.

### EXAMPLE

Newco Limited is forecasting EBIT of £1.5m for the current financial year. The senior lender has imposed a senior interest cover of 3× and overall interest cover of 2.0×. Interest rates on secured debt are currently 10%.

The maximum amount of senior debt can be calculated, as interest cannot exceed one third of EBIT of £1.5m. Thus, the maximum interest that can be paid on the senior debt is £500,000. With interest rates at 10%, the maximum senior debt available is £5m.

The maximum mezzanine debt can now be calculated. Total interest cannot exceed half of EBIT of £1.5m, ie £750,000. Of this, £500,000 is being paid to the senior lender, so we have surplus interest capacity of £250,000. Mezzanine debt is typically 3%–4% more expensive than senior debt – say, 14%. The maximum mezzanine debt available is therefore £250,000 @ 14% = £1.785m. To encourage the mezzanine provider to fund the debt more cheaply, an equity kicker might be offered and the terms would be agreed in negotiation.

## High yield bonds in the funding mix

'High yield' bonds are issued by companies with a credit rating below what is called 'investment grade'. High yield bonds are widely used in the funding mix in the US and to a more limited extent in continental Europe, but only used infrequently in the UK. Because bonds are issued to the public through the capital markets, they will only be available to the largest private equity deals, where a company is of potential interest to the public. Typically, however, they will not form a part of the initial purchase consideration, but will be a means of refinancing the buyout shortly after the deal has completed.

This is as a result of the following.

- The time and expense involved in arranging a public offer of securities, which equity investors will not wish to incur until they have actually obtained ownership of the MBO vehicle.
- The timing problem – investors will not wish to lend to a 'Newco' until it has actually acquired the assets.
- The risk of the market for bonds changing adversely prior to the issue, which could wreck the transaction.

Where high yield bonds are available, they are popular as a part of the funding mix because

- Interest is tax deductible and there may be possibilities for structuring the bond tax effectively in other respects.
- Covenants will be limited and therefore less restrictive for the company.
- The overall cost of debt for a large issue is typically lower than mezzanine finance would be (although the initial issue costs are higher).

The maximum amount of high yield bonds that can be issued will be determined in exactly the same way as mezzanine finance, ie by reference to interest cover imposed by the senior lender.

## Venture capitalist loan notes

The venture capitalist may also, if loan covenants on existing debt permit, invest cash as loan notes. This has the following advantages for the company.

- Flexibility. The debt instrument can be structured to the expected cash flow of the business.
- Interest holidays can be used in early years.
- Tax efficiency. Loan interest may be offset against profits to reduce the business' tax liability.

In considering whether the venture capitalist can invest funds as loan notes, it is important to have regard to the loan covenants on debt facilities. The senior lender is likely to specify a minimum interest cover ratio for all borrowing that the venture has outstanding.

## Vendor loan notes

This is where the vendor supplies finance at a reduced rate of interest for several years by accepting deferred consideration. It is more common in a recession, reflecting the inability of vendors to negotiate a better deal with management when no alternative purchasers are available.

## Other sources of finance

Other sources of finance include the following:

- Leasing
- Grants from government and regional bodies
- Sale and leaseback
- Debt factoring

# 6 Deal Structuring – Conclusion

When constructing a financing package for a venture capital transaction, the following principles are usually adhered to.

- Maximise 'cheap' capital for the company.
- Reduce the outlay from the venture capitalist, thereby maximising the venture capitalist's IRR.

Most venture capital deals will usually, therefore, aim to raise the maximum debt compatible with the company's risk profile. Reducing the venture capitalist investment generally gives an increased IRR to the venture capitalist. This is because debt is redeemed at par value and can be paid down over the life of the investment, if cash flows permit. Any upside in the exit valuation is therefore for the benefit of the equity providers alone.

These principles give the following pecking order in raising finance for most venture capital transactions.

1. Maximise cheapest capital first: senior debt.
2. Next cheapest finance: maximum other debt (eg mezzanine) permitted within loan covenants (minimum interest cover ratios and maximum gearing levels will be specified).
3. Management equity stake, based on a negotiated ownership split with venture capitalist.
4. The balance from the venture capitalist as Ordinary shares, preference shares or loan notes.

# 7 Venture Capital – Exit Routes

The two main exit routes whereby investors can realise their capital gain in a successful MBO are the flotation or the trade sale to another company. The attractiveness of each depends to an extent on market conditions.

The factors to take into account when considering which exit route is the more suitable include the following.

| | Flotation | Trade Sale |
|---|---|---|
| **Size of Company** | Large | Any size |
| **Timing of Exit** | Market determined | Flexible |
| **Business weaknesses** | Unacceptable | Can be accommodated |
| **Management Quality** | Essential | Not essential, but will be reflected in the price |
| **Independence** | Arguable | Ends |
| **Realisation** | Partial | Full |
| **Price** | Arguable, but possibly small discount to market | Arguable, but possibly at a premium |

Given the small size of most venture capital transactions, flotation is unlikely to be feasible most of the time. Therefore, most exits are via trade sales. For this reason, venture capitalists are particularly attracted to investments in sectors that are consolidating and therefore offer identifiable potential purchases for the business at exit date.

Alternative exit routes are as follows.

- **Refinancing:** The company is raising new debt to buy out the venture capitalist.
- **Repurchase:** The management buys out the venture capital interest.
- **Secondary purchase:** A second venture capital company buys out the venture capital interest.
- **Insolvency.**

# 8 Venture Capital Trusts

## Introduction

Venture capital trusts (VCT) are a type of UK investment trust company with tax advantages for investors. They invest in new and growing small businesses and allow investors to get indirect exposure to this sector of the market by buying a share in the trust. They thus enable investors to buy publicly traded shares in private company investments.

The tax reliefs are similar to those available for investment in Enterprise Investment Scheme companies.

## The tax relief

On subscription for shares in a VCT, investors receive tax relief against their taxable income at a rate of 30%. This will be clawed back if the shares are not held for five years. The maximum investment that attracts the relief is £200,000 in any fiscal year.

Capital gains on disposal of the shares and dividend income are both exempt from tax, irrespective of the duration of the investment.

Reinvestment relief is also available for investors who wish to defer capital gains tax on other chargeable gains. The shares must be acquired one year before, to one year after, the disposal that generated the gain to be held over.

## Conditions for VCT status

- At least 70% of the trust's instruments will have to be in unquoted trading companies (including AIM).
- A maximum of 15% may be invested in any company or group of companies.
- The trust's Ordinary share capital must be quoted on the London Stock Exchange.
- The income of the trust must be wholly or mainly derived from shares or securities.
- Unlike other investment trusts, a VCT can distribute as dividends any gains arising on the disposal of investments. This enables the VCT to maintain a higher income level than would otherwise be the case, since young companies rarely pay high dividends.

# 9 Enterprise Investment Scheme (EIS)

## Introduction

The Enterprise Investment Scheme (EIS) is a government scheme that is intended to give tax incentives to individuals to invest in new and growing businesses. As with VCTs, the aim is to provide small unlisted companies with a further source of finance which would not otherwise be available.

## The benefits

If an individual invests money in equity shares in certain unquoted companies, then tax relief is available on the investment made at a rate of 30%. Furthermore, any capital gains made on disposal of the shares will not be taxable. Any losses suffered on the investment will be allowable for tax purposes.

The key points to note about the scheme are as follows.

- It must be an investment by an individual in equity shares.
- The company cannot be listed (although AIM companies will qualify).
- The company must be engaged in a 'qualifying trade', which excludes, for example, accountancy, banking and other financial services and property companies.
- The maximum investment in any one year by an individual is £1m.
- Income tax relief will only be given at a rate of 30%.
- The shares must be held for at least three years. If the shares are sold within the three-year period, any tax relief received will be clawed back by the Inland Revenue.
- The investor must not be connected to the company. In essence, this means they must not directly or indirectly control more than 30% of the share capital.

The maximum annual amount that can be invested in an individual company under the EIS scheme is £5m.

# 10 Seed Enterprise Investment Scheme (SEIS)

The aim of the scheme is to provide new sources of finance for smaller newly-formed companies, where traditional sources of finance (eg bank debt) might be less readily available. In return, investors obtain a tax refund of half their investment. Specifically:

- the scheme gives income tax relief at 50% in respect of qualifying SEIS shares up to an annual maximum investment of £100,000; and
- the investment is exempt capital gains tax, as long as SEIS shares are sold more than three years after they are issued.

The investor can be a director of the company but the investor must not be connected to the company (ie they must not directly or indirectly control more than 30% of the share capital).

There are significant restrictions on the company receiving the investment, including:

- The maximum overall amount which can be raised through SEIS is £150,000;
- The gross assets must not exceed £200,000;
- Maximum number of 25 full time employees; and
- Qualifying trade only (not a finance or investment company).

# 11 Bank Finance

We consider below the main forms of bank funding, looking at the main characteristics and uses of each type of finance.

## Term loans

Term loan facilities are suitable for cash flow lending situations in which the loan proceeds are used for long-term needs, such as to finance equipment acquisitions, permanent working investment, stock repurchases, and the refunding of existing maturities of short-term debt as they become due. Some features of term loans are as follows.

- The loan may be **amortised** (ie repaid in instalments over the term of the loan) or **bullet** repayment (ie repaid in one single instalment at the end of the term).
- The interest rate may be **fixed or floating**. The floating rate is expressed as a fixed spread over a variable interest rate such as the London Interbank Offered Rate (LIBOR).
- It may be a **senior** loan or **subordinated.** Senior debt is debt provided by a bank which is designated the senior lender, and which therefore has priority in receiving interest and capital repayments and ranks ahead of other lenders on a winding-up. It is generally secured (see below). Subordinated debt is debt where the rights and returns are subordinated to those of the senior lender. It is therefore typically more expensive for the company than senior debt.

## Commercial mortgage

A commercial mortgage is a flexible method of purchasing or improving a freehold or leasehold property. It may be owner occupied or for investment, commercial or industrial purposes. In essence, it is a long-term loan from the bank, secured on the property concerned. The main features are that it is provided over a long term, the interest base can be either floating or fixed, and the amount granted is based on the open market valuation of the property.

## Syndicated loans

A syndicated loan is a loan provided by two or more banks to one or more borrowers. The loan is syndicated – spread among the banking community – usually because it is for a larger amount that one bank is prepared to lend on its own. The terms and conditions on which the loan is to be made by the banks to the borrower are set out in a loan agreement, to which all lenders and the borrower are a party. Consequently, all lenders are bound by the same terms, which are enforced on their behalf by the lead arranger.

## Overdraft

Some borrowers will borrow on a **demand basis**. This means that the bank itself can demand immediate repayment at any time. The usual mechanism for this is the overdraft – where a company's account is allowed to go into debit up to a certain limit. This is highly flexible for the borrower since it can alter the balance of its borrowings at will. However, it imposes a high degree of risk on the borrower, since the bank can demand repayment immediately (although banks will often quote a non-binding 'review date'), and the borrower would have to seek emergency refinancing from another source. The interest rate for UK overdrafts is normally variable, calculated by reference to a margin above the base rate. Given the flexibility of this source of finance for the borrowing, overdrafts are a relatively more expensive form of funding for a business.

## Revolving credits

A revolving credit is a formal legal agreement in which the bank agrees to lend up to a certain amount for a specific purpose over a specified period of time, usually two to five years. The borrower has complete flexibility in borrowing all or a portion of the total amount as necessary and repaying any amount at any time during the life of the commitment. In other words, revolving credit arrangements do not have set repayment schedules. The interest basis is normally variable, calculated by reference to a margin above LIBOR, payable on the amounts drawn down. Additionally, the borrower must pay a commitment fee on amounts not drawn down.

## Factoring

Factoring means selling trade debts for immediate cash to a 'factor' who charges commission. Most factors offer three basic services, although clients are under no obligation to take them all.

The services provided by a factor are as follows.

- An accounting, credit checking and debt collection service.
- Credit insurance against bad debts, for 'approved' debts.
- The provision of immediate cash against invoices, up to 75–85% of the face value of the invoices and, because of the credit insurance, a guarantee of payment of the remainder within an agreed period of time.

**Invoice discounting** is similar to factoring, except that only the financing service is used; copies of invoices sent to customers are discounted with a financial institution. The trading company still collects the debts as agents for the financial institution and remits the cash on receipt.

In summary, factoring generally refers to purchasing a client's entire turnover (excluding cash sales), whereas invoice discounting refers to purchasing individual debts on a 'one-off' basis.

## Leasing

Leasing is a tax-effective source of finance for the acquisition of a non-current asset. A lease is an agreement in which the owner of an item (eg a business asset) or a piece of real estate allows someone else to use it for a specified time, in return for a rental. The owner of the leased asset is the lessor and the user of the asset is the lessee.

In certain circumstances, it can be seen that leasing is equivalent to raising finance from a bank to purchase an asset. Consider two alternative situations.

### Borrowing money to buy an asset

A plc borrows £100,000 from a bank at a rate of 15%, repayable over three years, with three annual repayments of £44,000. It uses the cash to purchase an asset with a useful life of three years.

### Leasing an asset

B plc takes out a three-year lease on the same asset. The lease payments are £44,000 a year, payable annually in arrears. The lease is not cancellable.

A plc and B plc have the same effective commercial situation. The cash flows for both companies are precisely the same, being three annual outflows of £44,000. The benefits received from the asset are exactly the same for both companies.

Legally, however, the two situations are different. A plc has two separate transactions, borrowing money and buying an asset. B plc has only one transaction, renting an asset.

### Finance leases

The term 'finance lease' has been coined to describe a lease that is virtually equivalent to borrowing money to buy an asset. It is usually a long-term lease, where the lessee is expected to pay over enough cash to have been sufficient to purchase the asset in the first place.

### Operating leases

Operating leases are any leases that are not finance leases, ie they are leases that are not equivalent to borrowing money but are just short-term rental agreements.

## The benefits of leasing

### Tax efficiency

It may be the case that a lease can be structured to benefit the lessor and lessee at the expense of the Inland Revenue. This was the main reason why the leasing industry initially became successful in the United Kingdom.

If a company buys a fixed asset, it is entitled to charge capital allowances (ie depreciation for tax purposes) against its taxable profit, based on the cost of the asset. If the company is not making large profits, it may be unable to take advantage of the whole of its capital allowances entitlement in any one year.

It may be possible for a company making larger profits to buy the asset and receive the capital allowances instead. It can then lease the asset on to the smaller company, which will be allowed to charge the lease rentals paid as a taxable expense instead of the capital allowances.

The lease rentals can be structured to ensure that the smaller company is able to reduce its tax liability efficiently in each year of the lease. The net result is that both the larger and smaller company receive tax relief in a way that is most efficient to them. Both companies can share out the benefits of this arrangement (received at the expense of the Inland Revenue) between them.

It is also possible to construct a 'double dip' lease across national borders. The idea is that both the lessor and the lessee gain tax advantages from the tax treatment of leases in their own tax regime.

### Convenience

Convenience is typically an advantage for a short-term lease. It is much more convenient to rent rather than buy an asset that is only going to be used for the short term.

### Ability to cancel

The ability to cancel a lease on obsolete equipment is valuable to a company. Again, this will typically be the advantage of an operating lease, since finance leases are usually not cancellable until the bulk of the asset has been paid for by the lessee. Otherwise, the lessor would be too much at risk. In the case of the operating lease, the rental payments will be sufficiently large to compensate the lessor for this risk.

### Provision of maintenance

Lessors of specialist equipment are able to include maintenance of the equipment as part of the lease package. They will be able to provide this service relatively cheaply since they are specialists in their own area.

### Low administration and transaction costs

Typically, lenders will have to conduct detailed credit analysis before lending money to a business. The lessor has the advantage that a lease is often based around a saleable object, such as a car. Risk assessment need not focus solely on the lessee but can also focus on the nature of the asset being leased and its likely resale value at various points of time in the lease. If the lessee defaults, the lessor has the automatic right to reclaim the asset, since they are still the legal owner. In addition, the lessor can construct a standard lease agreement to apply to all leases, rather than having separate detailed loan agreements for each borrower.

### Accounting impact

Where a lease is an operating lease, it is not shown on the balance sheet of the lessee and the rental payments are charged as an expense against the profit and loss account. This makes the company's asset base look lower and hence its use of assets to generate turnover and profits (ie return on capital employed) appears superior. In addition, it makes reported gearing levels lower and reduces the interest charge in the profit and loss account compared to when a company borrows money to purchase assets.

When a lease falls into the definition of a finance lease, it is required to be treated as if the company had borrowed money to buy the asset. Consequently, assets and debt levels will increase, meaning that 'off balance sheet finance' is not a possibility.

## Lease evaluation

### Introduction

Leases can be evaluated using discounted cash flow techniques. The basic idea is to identify the impact of the lease on the cash flows of the company and calculate the net present value of the impact. In order to do this, we first need to identify how a lease will affect the cash flows of a company, and secondly what discount rate should be used to appraise the lease. All we then have to do is to calculate its net present value.

### Relevant cash flows

The relevant cash flows to use when appraising a lease are the changes in cash flows that will arise when compared to the alternative, which is borrowing money to buy an asset. The cash flows relating to buying an asset are as follows.

**Cash Flows When Buying an Asset**

| Time | Narrative | Cash Inflow/(Outflow) |
|---|---|---|
| 0 | Purchase asset | (x) |
| 1–n | Tax relief due to capital allowances | x |

**Cash Flows When Leasing an Asset**

The cash flows when an asset is leased are as follows.

| Time | Narrative | Cash Inflow/(Outflow) |
|---|---|---|
| 1–n | Lease rentals | (x) |
| 1–n | Tax relief on lease rentals | x |

**Relevant Cash Flows for Lease Evaluation**

The relevant cash flows to use when evaluating a lease are the **difference** between these two sets of flows, as follows.

| Time | Narrative | Cash Inflow/(Outflow) |
|---|---|---|
| 0 | Saved purchase cost | x |
| 1–n | Lost tax relief on capital allowances | (x) |
| 1–n | Lease rentals paid | (x) |
| 1–n | Tax relief on lease rentals | x |

### Identifying the discount rate

The relevant discount rate to use for investment appraisal is based upon the risk of the cash flows in question. The cash flows of a lease are generally assumed to be in the same risk category as cash flows on debt instruments. This may not be exactly correct, since it assumes that the company in question has sufficient taxable profits to mean that any relevant tax-based flows are effectively guaranteed to occur. However, it is a useful simplification for most companies.

This means that the relevant discount rate to use when evaluating the post-tax flows of the lease as noted above is the company's **post-tax cost of debt**.

## Sale and leaseback

A company may have a significant amount of its net worth represented by non-current assets used in its commercial activities, such as factories or a head office. It may choose to sell one or more of its properties to a property company or bank, and then lease it from the new owners. This will have the effect of raising an immediate cash sum, although the cost of leasing the property back will dilute earnings in future years.

A company might choose to enter into a sale and leaseback agreement when:

- It is seeking to raise cash to repay debt. It will seek to ensure that the leasing costs are lower than the interest on the debt repaid
- It wishes to raise cash for an expansion of the business, or to improve a long-term liquidity position

# 12 Project Finance

Project finance is concerned with the **realization of contracts for infrastructure and other commercial projects**. Internationally, project finance has been used to fund the mining, telecommunications and energy industries. In the UK, project financing principles have been use by the government to build schools, hospitals and prisons under the Private Finance Initiative (PFI). In all cases, the scale and cost of the contract is usually considerable and the time-scale medium to long-term.

A project finance transaction will be led by the '**sponsor**', who will develop a commercial structure and financing package based on the cash flows expected to be generated by the contract. The aim of the financing package will be to attract other investors and lenders on terms so as to mitigate the underlying risks of the project and to give a sufficient return in line with the different investment objectives of the separate financiers.

As with venture capital deals, involvement of banks prepared to commit loan finance to project finance transactions will help maximize returns for equity and other finance investors. Loan finance is generally committed on a non-recourse basis, with capital repayments made from the expected project cash flows.

**Risk identification and allocation** is a key component of project finance. Contracts are often long term which makes forecasting cash flows difficult. In addition, a project may be subject to a number of technical, environmental, economic and political risks, particularly in developing countries and emerging markets. Risk is also introduced by project delay and unexpected cost increases. Risk mitigation can be achieved by having several groups of investors with different capabilities and areas of expertise. Contractors will often possess highly specialist areas of knowledge and it is the role of the sponsor to co-ordinate these skills and to ensure that the risk outstanding is appropriately addressed by the financing structure in place.

Generally, transactions necessitate the establishment of a single purpose project company (**a SPV**), thus limiting recourse to the assets in the SPV and providing a vehicle for raising further equity funds in future. The cash flows generated by the SPV assets will be used to repay debt providers and to generate any further return for other finance providers.

The sponsor will ensure the relevant **documentation** is in place which sets out the work to be undertaken, together with the different responsibilities and rights of different parties in the transaction. The main document is the construction contract which is usually drafted on a 'turnkey' basis – ie requires the contractor to provide the service at a certain pre-determined fixed price, by a certain date, in accordance with certain specifications, and with certain performance warranties.

In addition, there will be an Operation and Maintenance ('O&M') Agreement which deals with the ongoing operation, maintenance and often performance management of the project. The agreement is between the project company and the operator who could be one of the investors/consortium members or a third party operator with relevant expertise.

There will also be shareholder agreements, which cover the relative duties and rights of the investing parties; loan agreements with the bank and other insurance, supply and implementation side agreements.

# 13 Sovereign Wealth Funds

Sovereign wealth funds are **government-controlled investment funds** set up to provide a return on excess liquidity generated from budget or trade surpluses. The source of the funds varies, and includes natural resources, particularly oil; pension investments; foreign exchange assets; and other industrial and financial holdings. The aim of the funds is to maximise long term return as well as to offset potential volatility caused by dependence on a single asset class (eg oil). Each fund has its own unique reason for its creation and all funds have their own objectives. Typical objectives of the funds include: to minimise revenue volatility; to diversify from non-renewable commodity exports; to earn greater returns than on foreign exchange reserves; to assist monetary authorities dissipate unwanted liquidity and to fund social and economic development.

Over the last ten years the number and size of sovereign wealth funds have grown dramatically. The Sovereign Wealth Fund Institute estimates the total market size to be in excess of $4.9 trillion assets. 75% of sovereign wealth funds are located in Asia and the Middle East. Over 50% of funds, initially derived their wealth from natural resources, including oil and gas. Two of the largest funds are the Abu Dhabi Investment Authority (controlling an estimated $627bn assets) and the Norwegian Government Pension Fund (controlling $611bn assets). The origin of both these funds is oil.

Sovereign funds are operating increasingly in the public domain. Following the 2008 financial crisis, the Abu Dhabi Investment Authority became the biggest shareholder in the US banking giant Citigroup. Similarly, Chinese funds bolstered Morgan Stanley and the Qatar Investment Authority acquired a 25 per cent stake in Sainsbury's, though in 2010 a threatened takeover did not transpire.

Some sovereign wealth funds are **non-transparent**, meaning they do not report their holdings or strategies publicly. The concern over lack of transparency was addressed by the International Monetary Fund, which developed the Santiago Principles in 2008. The Principles are a set of 24 voluntary guidelines that assign best practice for the operation of sovereign wealth funds and help to provide a framework for disclosure and governance of the funds.

## 14 Family Offices

A family office is a private company that **centralizes the management of the wealth of a single family**. The purpose of the family office is to effectively transfer established wealth across generations. The family office invests the family's money, manages all of the family's assets, and disburses payments to family members as required. Family Offices will employ staff to manage investments, taxes, philanthropic giving, trusts, and legal matters.

There is **limited regulation** applicable to Family Offices. In 2011, the US Securities and Exchange Commission exempted family offices from being classified as investment advisers, as long as they provide investment advice only to family clients; are wholly owned by family clients and they do not hold themselves out to the public as an investment adviser.

## Chapter Roundup

### Module 3, Chapter 15: Unquoted sources of finance

Venture capital is an important part of the syllabus. You could be asked to structure a venture capital deal, by putting in place suitable sources of capital and estimating overall rates of return for each capital provider. As well as being prepared to prepare a financial model, you also need to understand typical stages in a venture capital deal and the role that a corporate finance adviser might play in progressing the transaction.

Venture capital also incorporates tax relief schemes. You are required to study venture capital trusts, enterprise investment schemes and the new seed enterprise investment scheme.

Other sources of unquoted finance that are available to companies are:

- Bank loans
- Mortgages
- Syndicated loans
- Overdrafts
- Revolving credits
- Factoring
- Leasing
- Project finance
- Sovereign wealth funds
- Family offices

Again, you are expected to be able to apply your knowledge relating to these sources of finance and suggest suitable alternatives for companies when assessing their financing needs.

# PUBLIC EQUITY

chapter 16

Contents


| | | |
|---|---|---|
| 1 | Introduction | 368 |
| 2 | Applying for a Listing | 368 |
| 3 | Key Stages for an Initial Public Offering | 371 |
| 4 | Methods of Bringing Securities to Listing | 372 |
| 5 | Pricing the Flotation | 376 |
| 6 | Secondary Offerings | 378 |
| 7 | Pre-Emption Rights | 381 |
| 8 | Share Repurchases | 383 |
| 9 | Listing Rules Requirements | 386 |

# 1 Introduction

In this chapter on public equity, we initially consider the listing process, together with the rationale for applying for a listing and the advantages and disadvantages of being a listed company. We look at the main stages in an Initial Public Offering (IPO), together with the common methods of issuing shares and methods to price an IPO. We also look at secondary methods of issuing equity, including rights issues, placings, open offers and vendor consideration issues. The chapter concludes with a section on share repurchases.

# 2 Applying for a Listing

## Reasons for wanting a listing

When a new company is formed, particularly with the assistance of venture capitalists, one of the aspirations of the director shareholders may be for the company to seek a stock market listing in the future. In reality, very few companies ever actually come to the market and it is important to consider the reasons why a listing may or may not be appropriate.

### The advantages of a listing

(a) **Exit route**

Flotation of the company could enable investors to realise a large part of their investment and become rich beyond their wildest dreams. Realisation is absolutely vital when the company has some venture capital investors who need to realise their funds in a set time scale. One of the first questions a venture capitalist will ask when assessing a business is the feasibility of various exit routes, including flotation.

(b) **Immediate source of long-term capital for the business**

In addition to existing shareholders realising part of their investment, the company will be able to issue new shares and obtain long-term capital for the business. This will enable the business to expand its markets, make acquisitions and reduce gearing levels.

(c) **Ongoing source of capital**

The ability to issue new shares in the future, subject to investor sentiment, or to issue listed debt will give the company more flexibility in its financing options. This will translate into lower costs and will assist the company in its expansion plans.

(d) **Share-for-share acquisitions**

The ability to issue shares as consideration when making an acquisition will give the company more options when implementing a strategy of growth.

(e) **High profile**

The listing will give the company more credibility with its customers and suppliers and will also be a source of publicity, leading to lower costs and higher revenues.

(f) **Share incentive schemes**

It is easier to introduce share option schemes for employees and directors with a listed company, since there is a readily ascertainable market price and a liquid market in which to dispose of a holding.

(g) **Personal factors**

The directors of the company may feel attracted to the prestige and kudos of being the directors of a listed company.

## The disadvantages of a listing

(a) **Time and cost spent preparing a flotation**

The planning of a flotation is a lengthy procedure and will probably last for at least six months. Throughout this time, a significant amount of management effort will need to be diverted into the flotation process. This will take the management's eye off the underlying business. In addition, advisers will be spending time and charging bills. These may be rolled up and only be payable if the flotation goes ahead, but at some time the cost will come through.

(b) **The cost of the flotation itself**

The flotation process itself is very expensive, involving fees to advisers, the stock market regulator and the underwriters and marketing expenses.

(c) **The ongoing cost of maintaining a listing**

The company must pay annual fees to the stock market regulator. In addition, the directors of the company will need to spend a significant amount of management time communicating with investors and ensuring that the company is being marketed properly.

(d) **Satisfying the needs of external shareholders**

The needs of external shareholders depend on the nature of those investors – whether they want income or capital growth, whether they are pension funds, insurance companies, unit trusts or private investors. The company must identify their needs and tailor the strategy of the company to meet those requirements. This may be at odds with the desires of the directors who previously made decisions by reference to their own personal situations. In particular, the need to achieve short-term results at the expense of the long-term development of the business may be a problem.

(e) **Accountability**

The requirement to have non-executive directors on the board and to justify performance, executive pay and other decisions to outside shareholders may be an interference to directors used to running the company their own way.

(f) **Lack of secrecy**

The disclosure requirements set by the Financial Services Authority and under the Financial Services and Markets Act 2000 (FSMA 2000) and the fact that the company is subject to the scrutiny of analysts and the public, means that the company will not have the benefits of secrecy and discretion accorded to a private company.

(g) **The risk of takeover**

If the directors do not perform satisfactorily, the company may be subject to a hostile bid. Once listed, the directors are answerable to a public shareholder base who may be persuaded by a predator's arguments that a change of control of the company could be in the shareholders' interest.

(h) **Different culture**

The culture of the business is likely to change, since the directors will be answerable to outside shareholders. Previously, the business may have been run as a 'lifestyle' company, with lavish benefits to the directors and their families. Such advantages disappear on listing.

(i) **Tax planning**

The scope for tax planning is much wider in an unquoted company with a small group of shareholders and an uncertain market value. Tax implications are likely to be an important consideration with respect to any possible flotation, and early advice should be sought.

## Alternatives to a listing

Depending on the situation of the company, a number of alternative routes may be available. Each will have advantages and disadvantages.

- **Trade sale to another company**
  The trade sale is the alternative means of realising any investment and is, in fact, the more common occurrence in practice for a successful company. The decision whether to float or sell the company depends on a number of factors. The following table highlights the key differences between the two routes.

| | Flotation | Trade Sale |
|---|---|---|
| **Size of Company** | Large | Any size |
| **Timing of Exit** | Market driven | Flexible |
| **Business Weaknesses** | Unacceptable | Can be accommodated |
| **Management Quality** | Essential | Not essential, but will be reflected in the price |
| **Independence** | Arguable | Ends |
| **Realisation** | Partial | Full |
| **Price** | Depends on market sentiment | Possibly at a control premium |

- **Debt finance**
  Where the purpose of the listing is to raise additional finance, use of debt may be an alternative. The advantages of debt in this context are that it:

  – Is cheap to raise
  – Keeps control of the company with existing shareholders
  – Ensures that all the benefits of success stay with the existing shareholders

  The disadvantages of debt are that it:

  – Is only available in limited quantities up to acceptable gearing levels
  – Exposes the company to the risk of insolvency should operating profits and cash flows fall
  – Is only issued with strict loan agreements defining ratio covenants to which the business must adhere

- **Unquoted equity finance**
  If the company is unwilling or unable to raise sufficient debt, an alternative is to use a provider of equity expansion finance. The key advantage of this approach is that it expands the equity capital base of the company, meaning that additional debt can also be raised and increasing the possibilities for expansion. Furthermore, an equity investor can be selected whose vision for the business matches that of the existing shareholders. For example, a long-term investor may be ideal for a company with expansion plans that involve significant cash outflows but where benefits will only accrue in the distant future. A business with highly volatile earnings, such as in

the airline industry, may find it better to have an investor who understands this and is not going to sell out just because one year's figures are bad.

The disadvantages of such equity finance are that it will dilute the interests of existing shareholders, introduce new investors who will probably want a seat on the board and commit the company to focusing on its new investors' needs. In addition, the level of funds that can be raised in this way is probably less than the level that would be possible by releasing the majority of the company's shares on the market place.

# 3 KEY STAGES FOR AN INITIAL PUBLIC OFFERING

- **Appoint advisers.** Key advisers to appoint are:
  - **Sponsor.** The sponsor will frequently be an investment bank and will co-ordinate the flotation as well as advising on complex issues. The role of the sponsor is discussed in more detail below.
  - **Broker.** The broker will advise on pricing, timing and market conditions, assist in representing the issuer with potential investors, give guidance on the most appropriate method of marketing the issue, advise on FCA, Stock Exchange and any other relevant requirements and ensure that the market for the shares is liquid.
  - **Reporting Accountant.** The reporting accountant will carry out due diligence, as discussed earlier.
  - **Lawyer.** The lawyer carries out the legal due diligence on the company, reviews the issuer's legal status, reviews service contracts, re-registers the issuer as a public company if necessary, completes the document verification process and prepares all other relevant legal agreements. Separate lawyers would normally represent the directors of the company, the issuer and the advisers to the issuer.
  - **Public relations.** Public relations will advise on the selling of the issue to investors, liaise with the press and analysts and ensure that the marketing tone of any documents is appropriate.

  The importance of each of the advisers and the specific role that they adopt will depend on the nature and size of the company to be floated. For example, in a relatively small flotation, the broker can act as the sponsor, lead underwriter and overall co-ordinator of the listing. Alternatively, a firm of accountants or lawyers may take on a more central role.
- **Planning.** This involves preparing a detailed timetable, lists of key documents required, potential problem areas, and clear allocation of responsibilities.
- **Consultation with regulators.** This must be at an early stage, to fix the timing and level of disclosure required, and to confirm suitability for listing.
- **The long form report.** The responsibility of the accountants, this is a very detailed document covering every aspect of the company, its finances and its operations. It will be used by the sponsor to assist in his assessment of the company's suitability for listing and will also be used as a base for much of the information in the prospectus or listing particulars.
- **Draft documents.** The exact scope of the documents required is detailed below. The main documents to be prepared are the long form report, draft prospectus, working capital letter, responsibility letters and derogation letters. The purpose of the derogation letters is to obtain permission from the regulators to omit certain specified information from the prospectus and other documents.
- **Verification.** This is the process of checking on a line-by-line basis that all statements made in the prospectus are fair, accurate and complete, ensuring that the directors have fully discharged their legal responsibilities in respect of the prospectus.
- **Completion meeting.** This is the final meeting when all documents are signed and the final decision to float is taken.

The following table provides an indicative timetable for a listing for a company.

| Application for Listing – Summary Timetable | |
|---|---|
| **Time Before Listing** | **Action** |
| 24 weeks | Appoint advisers<br>Planning<br>Consult regulators (FCA)<br>Commence long form report<br>↓ |
| 8 to 12 weeks | Draft documents prepared<br>Drafts submitted to FCA<br>Public relations campaign starts<br>↓ |
| 1 to 6 weeks | Draft prospectus<br>Verification<br>Formal submission of documents to FCA<br>↓ |
| Final week | Approval of documents by FCA<br>Completion meeting<br>Underwriting agreement signed<br>Investment presentations<br>Allocation lists open and basis of allocation is announced<br>Formal application for listing<br>Listing granted<br>Dealing commences |

# 4 Methods of Bringing Securities to Listing

The methods used to bring securities to listing depend on whether the issuer is a new applicant (ie coming to the market for the first time) or making a secondary offering.

## New applicants for listing

The regulator wishes to ensure that on a new application for listing, the shares will be marketable. The main methods which will ensure this are:

- Offer for subscription or offer for sale
- Placing
- Intermediaries offer
- Introduction
- Reverse takeover

Any other method which is acceptable to the FCA may also be proposed; these methods are not prescriptive and are no longer detailed in the Listing Rules.

### Offer for sale

In an offer for sale the company issues shares to an issuing house (typically an investment bank) which then offers the shares for sale to the retail investing public. These may be shares newly issued by the company, to raise finance for the company, or they may be shares originally held by the existing shareholders, being sold to allow them to realise some of their investment.

The offer for sale can be represented diagrammatically as follows.

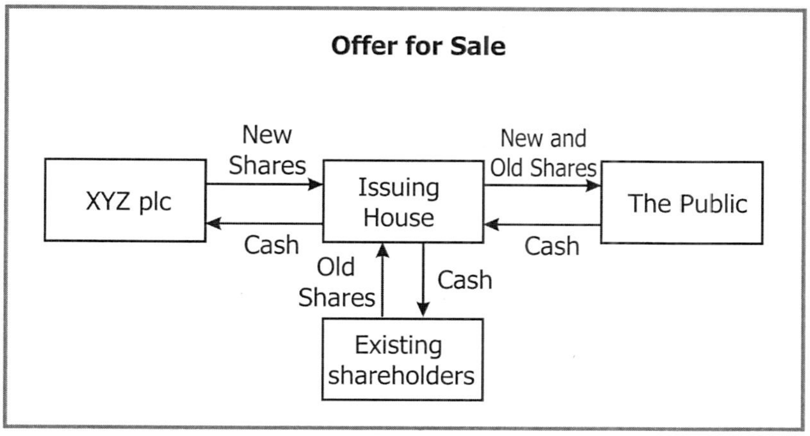


### Offer for subscription

An offer for subscription is similar to an offer for sale, but in this case the company issues new shares to new shareholders directly, in response to the applications for these shares.

This method is most typically used by investment companies. The requirements concerning offers for sale and subscription are the same. It can be represented diagrammatically as follows.

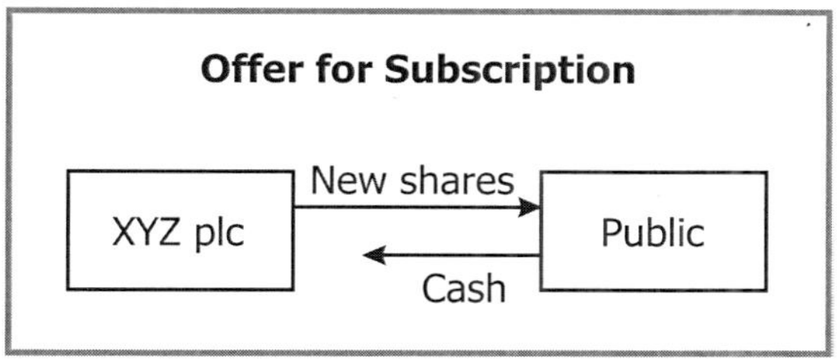


### Placing

It is very common for an offer for sale to be accompanied by a placing. A placing involves the selective identification of interested investors from amongst the issuing house's institutional clients and contacts. Securities are then marketed to this smaller number of larger investors. A placing may be represented as follows.

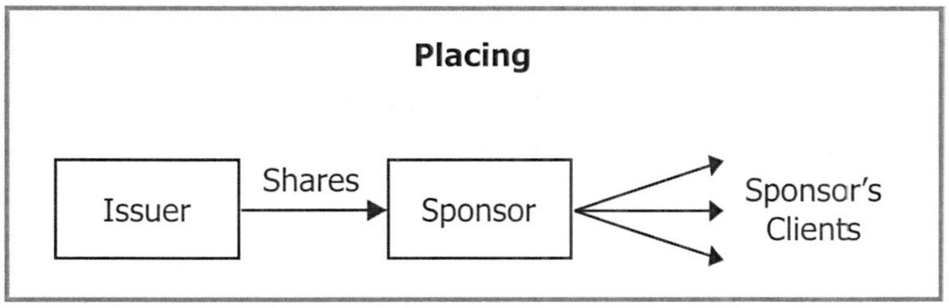

### The advantages of a placing

The main advantages of a placing for the company are

- **Cost.** The placing method is far cheaper than the offer for sale since it involves selling the shares to a limited number of investors rather than having to undertake a widespread general marketing and advertising campaign. In addition, the ongoing costs of maintaining and servicing a share register with a large number of small shareholders will be substantially more.
- **Targeting of investors.** The placing gives the company the opportunity to target an appropriate investor base and to select its shareholders more carefully.
- **Speed.** The placing may be carried out much more quickly than a public offering.

## Intermediaries offer

An intermediaries offer is where the shares are offered only to intermediaries such as stockbrokers, who apply to subscribe for shares on behalf of their own clients for onward sale to them. It is somewhat quicker and cheaper for the issuer than an offer for sale but gives more opportunity for the public to participate than with a placing. It can be represented diagrammatically as follows.

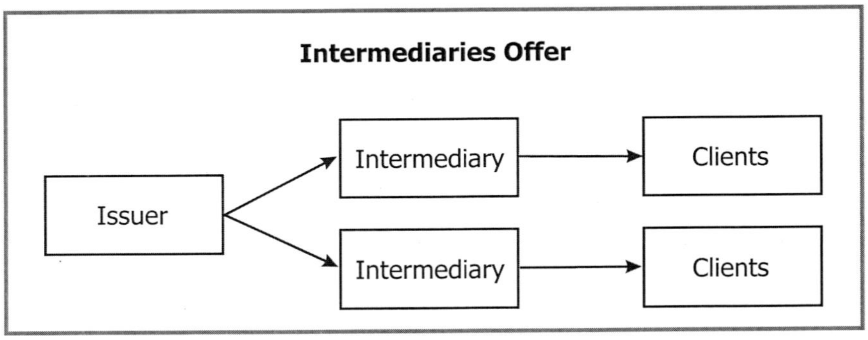


## Introduction

Offers for sale/subscription, placings and intermediaries offers are all marketings of shares in that the company receives cash and issues shares in exchange. Where an issuer is not seeking to raise cash, it may elect to come to the market through an introduction. This does not involve marketing, since no new shares are issued. All that happens is that existing shares continue to be owned by the existing shareholders but are 'introduced' to trading on a Recognised Investment Exchange such as the Stock Exchange.

To ensure sufficient liquidity in the shares, the FCA will therefore only allow an introduction to be used as a means of achieving a listing if the securities are of such an amount and are so widely held that they will be marketable when listed. A shareholder statement confirming this must be submitted to the FCA.

Examples of situations where this may be appropriate include

- A large, perhaps employee-owned, private company that has a substantial shareholder base.
- A demerger, where one listed company distributes shares in a major subsidiary to its own existing shareholders and seeks a listing for that subsidiary.
- An overseas company which already has a listing overseas and wishes to access the UK markets.
- An AIM-traded company seeking to move to the main market.

### Reverse takeovers

A reverse takeover is typically a situation where a listed company makes a share-for-share offer for the shares of an unlisted company. The unlisted company, however, is substantially larger than the listed company making the offer. This means that the unlisted company's management and its shareholders effectively control the new listed company. The major purpose of carrying out the transaction in such a way that the smaller listed company makes the acquisition rather than the other way round is to achieve a listing for the unlisted company.

An example of this was when Star Computer Group plc, a listed company, acquired PizzaExpress Limited, an unlisted company, plus some other smaller companies associated with PizzaExpress, and then renamed itself PizzaExpress plc. In this case, of the 53 million shares in issue in PizzaExpress plc (née Star) after the acquisition, 36 million were issued as a result of the acquisition of PizzaExpress Limited and the other companies. It can be seen that the original shareholders of the listed company had therefore lost control through the acquisition.

**Before**

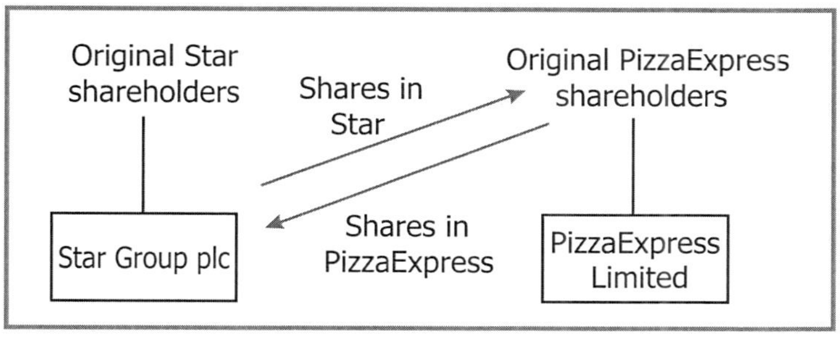


**After**

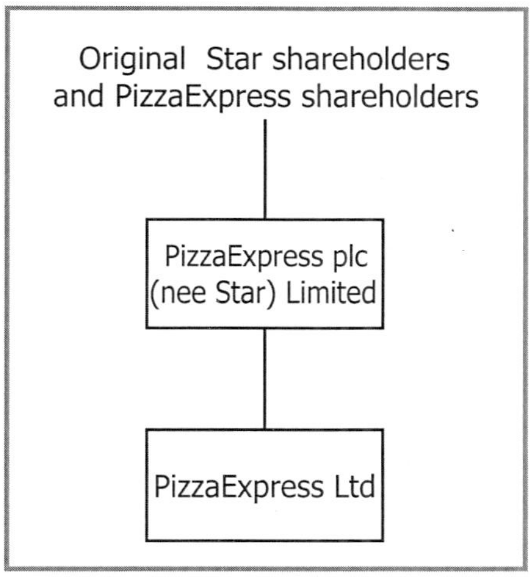


#### Rationale for a reverse takeover

A reverse takeover does not in itself necessarily make obtaining a listing any easier, since the enlarged group must apply for listing for the new shares issued as if it were a new applicant for listing. Unless there are specific benefits related to the reverse takeover, then it may be better for a private company to apply for a listing itself and complete a share issue.

Circumstances that may favour a reverse takeover are as follows.

- An existing listed company has lost its direction and lacks investor confidence with its existing business offering no scope at all.
- The listed company has a large cash balance, which can be released into the private company's business, providing funds for expansion, rather than being paid out to shareholders of the listed company.

- The listed company has a good shareholder base for the private company to access.
- The listed company has tax losses which may become available to the private company to shelter profits.

In these circumstances, the reverse takeover can be useful for both the private company's and the listed company's shareholders. However, there are potential risks, as follows.

- There may be unknown liabilities in the accounts of the listed company.
- There may be a risk that a mandatory offer will arise under Rule 9 of the City Code.
- There may be two sets of advisers' fees to be paid, for both sets of shareholders, leading to increased costs.
- The private company itself must be suitable for listing as an independent entity and, for example, must have three years' results and trading history.

#### Definition of a reverse takeover

A 'reverse' is defined in the Listing Rules *(LR 5.6.4)* as where any of the following ratios give a figure of 100% or more.

- The value of the gross assets acquired by the listed company compared with the gross assets of the acquiring listed company itself.
- Net profit before tax attributable to the assets acquired compared with net profit before tax of the acquiring company.
- The consideration given compared with the market value of the Ordinary share capital of the acquiring company.
- The gross capital (see below) of the acquired assets compared with the gross capital of the acquiring company.

In addition, a reverse takeover will occur where there is a fundamental change in the business or a change in board or voting control for the listed company.

Gross capital for the acquired company is given by the aggregate of the consideration, the value of any shares or debt not being acquired, all other liabilities (excluding current liabilities but including minority interests and deferred tax) and, if applicable, net current liabilities. Gross capital for the acquiring company is calculated in a similar way, being the aggregate of its shares and debt, all other liabilities and, if applicable, net current liabilities.

#### Requirements for reverse takeovers

Once the decision has been taken to complete the reverse takeover, it must be announced publicly. Listing of the acquiring company's shares will then be suspended until, it has prepared and published a class 1 circular, after which it will be restored. The transaction must then be approved by shareholders, at an EGM, following which the new shares will be issued (with listing particulars being prepared).

## 5 Pricing the Flotation

The offer price may be set in either of the following ways.

### Fixed price or tender offer

A fixed price offer is where the price per share is fixed by the company in advance of the offer and the public is invited to subscribe at that price. A tender offer is where the public are invited to tender for shares, offering whatever price they think is appropriate subject to a minimum tender price set by the company. The company will set a strike price for the offer based on tenders received and all successful tenderers will pay the same strike price. Investors who tendered at higher prices will receive preference.

### Illustration of a tender

XYZ plc wishes to issue 1,000 shares by way of tender and sets a minimum tender price of £2.00 per share. The following tenders are received.

| Tendering Investor | No. of Shares Tendered for | Price per Share |
|---|---|---|
| A | 500 | £4.00 |
| B | 700 | £3.00 |
| C | 700 | £3.00 |
| D | 600 | £2.00 |

XYZ plc could theoretically set the strike price at £3.00 per share, issue 500 shares to A and 250 shares each to B and C at this price, with no shares being issued to D. In practice, the price may be set at below £3.00, say at £2.90, in order to stimulate trading in the after market.

### The advantages of each method

The advantages and disadvantages of each method can be compared as follows.

| Fixed Price | Tender |
|---|---|
| Certainty of price | Uncertain price |
| Easier for private investors to understand | Harder for the private investor, but no problem for professionals |
| More difficult to price | Price is set by the market |
| Stagging is possible | Less scope for stagging |

Overall, if the company and its existing investors wish to achieve wide share ownership and to appeal to the public in general, the fixed price offer is likely to be the better alternative. If the company wishes to target its investor base more carefully and to ensure that it issues shares so as to obtain best value for existing shareholders, the tender approach is likely to be superior.

## Bookbuilding

The bookbuilding approach is, to some extent, a merging of the two above methods, the fixed price offer and the tender. It is especially relevant for very large issues of securities that would be difficult to underwrite because of their size. The idea of bookbuilding is that the issuing house gauges demand for the issue prior to setting a fixed price for the offer. Investors are asked to indicate, either on a firm or uncommitted basis, the best price that they will offer and the maximum number of shares that they will buy at particular prices. This information enables the issuing house to build up a demand curve and establish the most appropriate offer price for the issue.

The advantages of using bookbuilding are that it can build up creative tension and increase demand for the shares and the final issue price. It is highly suitable for large issues where underwriting would not be possible due to the size of the risk to which the underwriters would be exposed. It is already well established as a technique in the US and, now that it has been used successfully in a large number of issues, has become accepted in the UK.

The technique does have potential problems. While creative tension may drive the issue price up for a popular share, there is the possibility that investors will all wait to see what others do, particularly with a doubtful issue and uncertain markets. If no-one is prepared to take a lead then the issue may never get off the ground. In addition, it is possible for investors to sell the stock short prior to the issue in an attempt to drive the price down for the new issue. After the issue, the shares can be repurchased at a lower price.

In order to combat these problems, the issuing house must:

- Establish an anchoring market place to get the issue off the ground.
- Have a sophisticated computer system to enable global demand to be accurately tracked on an instantaneous basis.
- Have in place detection techniques to identify sellers of the stock prior to the issue. This will require good relations with market participants so that all sellers can be identified.
- Have the muscle to punish institutions that sell short in the above fashion.
- Have the ability to stabilise the after market, possibly by use of call options on a tranche of shares. This is often referred to as a **greenshoe option**.

### Greenshoe option

A greenshoe option arises where there is an overallocation of shares into the market by the issuing house, typically representing around 15% of the whole issue. The issuing house is short the shares as a result, but is covered through holding a call option on the same number of shares, exercisable on the company. If the share price in the market falls, the issuing house will close its short position by buying shares in the market, hence increasing demand and stabilising the price. If the share price rises, the issuing house will exercise its call option, buying additional shares from the company. In this case, no stabilisation takes place and the company has actually issued more shares into the market.

# 6 Secondary Offerings

If a company already has a listing, the FCA is concerned to protect the interests of existing shareholders. It therefore confirms the pre-emption rights requirement of the Companies Act 2006, which provide that whenever a company issues new shares for cash, these shares are offered in the first instance to the existing shareholders in proportion to their existing shareholders. Thus the main methods for a secondary offering are pre-emptive issues – ie offers to existing shareholders in line with their pre-emption rights. Any non pre-emptive issue must be approved by shareholders.

## Rights issues

A rights issue is an offer to existing shareholders to subscribe for new shares in the company in proportion to their existing shareholdings. Shareholders have the right, but not the obligation, to acquire new shares or to sell their entitlement to the shares. Rules for rights issues are found both in the Companies Act 2006, and in the Listing Rules.

### Procedures for a rights issue

Initially shareholders are sent a circular which provides full details of the rights issue and proposals by the issuer. The contents of the circular are specified by the Listing Rules *(LR 13)* and its issue must be approved by the FCA before posting. The circular is accompanied by a provisional allotment letter (PAL), setting out each shareholder's entitlement to a specified number of new shares, proportionate to their existing holding.

A PAL is a temporary document of title. This means that until definitive share certificates are produced, this letter is proof of the shareholder's entitlement to the new shares. It is renounceable, which means that the shareholder may renounce his entitlement by selling it to someone else. In practice, the holder of the renounceable letter has a number of options.

- Take up the rights to subscribe himself. In this case, he pays the company for the new shares and receives a receipted PAL in exchange. He may then either continue to hold this PAL until definitive share certificates are issued, or sell the receipted PAL to another shareholder, who will then notify the issuer of his right to claim the definitive share certificate instead.
- Without paying for the new shares, simply sell the PAL to a third party. This results in the sale of the rights to subscribe at the set price to that third party; it is then up to the third party to take up the rights issue, pay for the new shares and notify the issuer of his right to receive the definitive share certificates. This is referred to as selling the rights 'nil paid'; the FCA may grant a listing for the securities in nil paid form *(LR 9.5.3 G)*.
- Do nothing. In this case, the company must sell the rights shares attached to the letter in the market place for the best price possible, or place then with underwriters. Any premium achieved over the subscription price is then remitted to the person to whom the rights related and who received the PAL. However, if the surplus is very small (£5.00 or less), the company need not send it to the shareholder but can retain it for the benefit of the company *(LR 9.5.4.R)*.

## Indicative timetable for a rights issue

| Rights Issue – Summary Timetable | |
|---|---|
| **Time** | **Action** |
| **Impact –1** | Board meeting to approve issue<br>Underwriting agreement signed<br>↓ |
| **Impact day** | Announcement<br>Circular posted<br>↓ |
| **+17 days** | EGM for section 551 authority<br>*(if required)*<br>Post provisional allotment letters<br>↓ |
| **+21 days** | Dealings commence nil paid<br>↓ |
| **+38 days** | Last acceptance day<br>Sell rump of issue<br>Place unsold shares with underwriters<br>↓ |
| **+59 days** | Last registration of renunciation<br>↓ |
| **+80 days** | Issue new share certificates |

## Additional rules for rights issues

**Directors' authority to allot shares.** Section 551 of the Companies Act 2006 gives authority for directors to issue and allot shares in the company, provided it is granted by an ordinary resolution of shareholders in general meeting. Such authority may be general or specific. A general authority is granted by shareholders at the company's AGM and is applicable at least for the following year up to a permissible maximum of five years. If general authority has not been granted, an EGM must be called to grant specific authority for the issue of new shares. The notice period for an EGM where only ordinary resolutions are proposed is 14 days.

**Disapplication of pre-emption rights.** Under s571 of the Companies Act, shareholders in listed companies may pass a special resolution disapplying pre-emption rights for a maximum period of **five years**. This maximum period is also confirmed in the Listing Rules.

However, listed companies will normally be allowed to disapply pre-emption rights only for issues of new shares amounting to a maximum of 5% of the issued share capital in any one year, or 7½% on a rolling three-year basis, so long as they obtain shareholder approval. In addition, the Listing Rules do not normally permit non-pre-emptive issues at a discount of more than 10% to the middle market price of the shares. Any discount greater than 10% requires shareholder approval.

The Association of British Insurers, the National Association of Pension Funds and Investment Management Association formed the pre-emption group which has issued a statement of principles relating to disapplying pre-emption rights. The main points are as follows.

A request to issue up to 5% (10% for AIM listed companies) is considered to be routine. Shareholders will have to vote in favour at a special company meeting to disapply routine pre-emption rights. The Pre-emption Group permits a discount of 5% from the market price.

For any secondary offerings outside of these sizes or pricings, the Group requires a strong business case to be presented before approval can be obtained in a general meeting.

**Exemption for overseas companies.** Where an overseas company has a UK listing but does not have pre-emption rights in its own country, the FCA provides an exemption from the requirement for pre-emption rights.

**Disclosure.** The market must be notified without delay of any proposed or completed rights issue, though a Regulatory Information Service (RIS).

**Last acceptance day.** Shareholders must be given a reasonable time to decide on their options, and this is set as at least 21 days after posting of the PAL. No other deadlines are prescribed by law, but must be set by the company and stated in the PAL.

**Last registration of renunciation.** A shareholder who decides to sell his rights to another individual, whether nil paid or paid, must register the renunciation of his rights by a deadline specified by the company in the PAL. Otherwise the new share certificates will be issued in the name of the original holder of the rights.

## Open offers

An open offer is a pre-emptive offer, which is not allotted on renounceable documents. This means that although shareholders are offered shares on a pre-emptive basis, they cannot sell on the right to subscribe for the open offer shares, unlike in a rights issue.

### Requirements for Open Offers

The Listing Rules state that the timetable for an open offer must be approved by the Recognised Investment Exchange (RIE) concerned (*LR 9.5.7 R)*. An open offer will not be permitted where the offer price is at a discount of more than 10% to the middle market price of the shares when the offer is announced *(LR 9.5.10 (1) R)*.

## Placings

Providing shareholders approval the disapplication of their pre-emption rights, a company may issue shares to new investors through an institutional placing. The process here is the same as for a primary placing.

For a company which already has a listing, the FCA will not usually grant permission for a placing which is at a discount of more than 10% unless the issuer obtains specific shareholder approval for that transaction *(LR 9.5.10 R)*. A general authority to disapply the 10% discount rule would not be acceptable. This prevents existing shareholders from losing part of their company at a price significantly lower than its market value.

### Vendor placings

A vendor placing (also called a vendor consideration placing) occurs in the context of an acquisition. The purchaser wishes to pay for the target using its own shares, however, the vendor shareholders wish to receive cash. In order to satisfy both parties to the deal, the acquirer pays for the target in newly issued shares, but arranges through its bankers for the vendor to on-sell those shares to third party investors in a pre-arranged, underwritten deal. Hence they receive the desired cash.

The transaction can be shown diagrammatically.

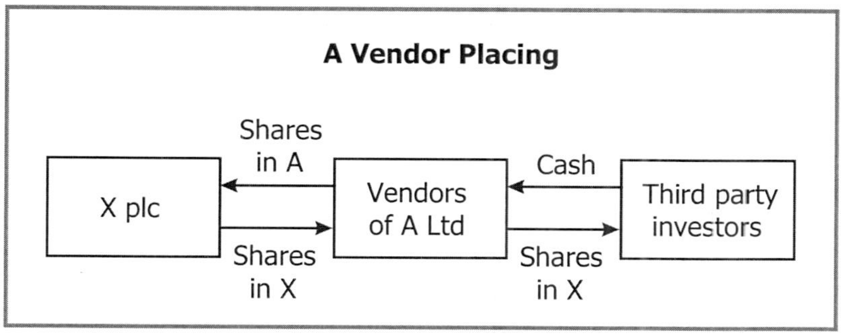


#### Requirements for a vendor placing

The Listing Rules required that all vendor shareholders must have equal opportunity to participate in the placing *(LR 9.5.9 R)*. The placing must not usually be at a discount of more than 10% to the middle market price at the time of the placing, unless permitted by the FCA.

#### Vendor consideration issue

Where the vendors of A Ltd keep the shares in X plc then it is referred to as a vendor consideration issue. Alternative names for this are an acquisition or merger issue, a share-for-share exchange or a paper offer.

#### Clawback

When a company issues convertible loan stock which could increase the equity of the company by more than 10%, then existing shareholders have the right to subscribe for the convertible loan stock in order to protect their investment in the company.

Likewise, when a company completes a vendor placing which increases its share capital by more than 10% or is at a discount to the market price of more than 5%, then the existing shareholders may exercise clawback rights and subscribe for the shares. This will usually be achieved by means of an open offer to shareholders on a pro rata basis to their existing holdings in the company.

## 7 Pre-Emption Rights

### A legal requirement

#### The basic law

Section 561 of the Companies Act 2006 states that where a company issues shares **for cash**, then it is obliged to offer them first to existing shareholders on a pro rata basis to their existing holding in the company. The shareholders must be given at least 21 days to decide whether to purchase the shares. If they do not, then the shares can be sold to outsiders, but the price must not be better than that offered to existing shareholders.

The objective of this law is to protect the interests of existing shareholders and prevent shares in the company being issued by the directors to new shareholders, possibly at cheap prices, thus diluting the existing shareholders' interests.

### Exemption for private companies

A private company is able to exclude the requirement for these pre-emption rights in its Memorandum and Articles if it so desires. However, it is often the case that private company Memorandum and Articles contain even more stringent rules about share issues and transferability of shares than a listed company. This is in order to protect the individual shareholders from being oppressed by a majority of other shareholders.

### Exemption for public companies

The shareholders may pass a special resolution disapplying pre-emption rights for a maximum period of five years, under the Companies Act 2006 and the Listing Rules.

### Exemption for overseas companies

Where an overseas company has a UK listing but does not have to follow pre-emption rights in its own country, the FCA relaxes the requirement to give pre-emption rights to shareholders.

## The advantages and disadvantages of pre-emption rights

### Arguments for pre-emption rights

- Existing shareholders have the right to decide what happens to their ownership of a company, not the directors.
- Issue of shares to new investors will be at a discount to market price, to encourage them to subscribe. This means that shares are being sold on the cheap, resulting in a transfer of value from old to new shareholders.
- Pre-emption rights are a right enshrined in UK statute.

### Arguments against pre-emption rights

- Very few countries actually have pre-emption rights for existing shareholders.
- Pre-emption rights merely perpetuate the stranglehold of UK institutions on UK listed companies.
- Pre-emption rights prevent companies from increasing their shareholder base. An increased shareholder base should result in greater marketability and liquidity for the shares, increasing their price.
- Companies are unable to issue shares into strategically important market places such as the US or Japan, where they have a commercial presence.
- Companies lack the flexibility to issue shares in the most attractive market place where the shares are in most demand.
- High overseas demand for the shares will mean that they do not need to be issued at a significant discount to market value. Any transfer of value is more than offset by increases in share price due to accessing a greater pool of demand and improving the shares

# 8 Share Repurchases

## General rules

Legal requirements covering repurchase of its own shares by a company are contained in the Companies Act 2006. The purpose of the legal rules is to protect creditors of the company by ensuring that the company does not reduce its share capital and non-distributable reserves (known collectively as the **'creditors' buffer'**) as a result of the repurchase.

A repurchase may be completed **off-market** or **on-market**. An off-market purchase is where the shares are either not purchased on a recognised investment exchange (RIE) or purchased on an RIE, but are not subject to a marketing arrangement on that RIE. A marketing arrangement is where the shares are listed on the exchange or the company has been afforded dealing facilities on the exchange.

For an off-market purchase, the terms of the contract of purchase must be approved by special resolution prior to the purchase taking place. For a public company, the authority to make the repurchase must expire within 18 months of the resolution being passed.

For an on-market purchase, an ordinary resolution is required, specifying the maximum number of shares to be purchased, the maximum and minimum prices to be paid and the date on which the authority expires. For a public company, this cannot be greater than 18 months after the resolution is passed.

### Public companies

Public listed companies can repurchase shares and rather than cancel them, hold up to 10% of their issued share capital as treasury shares. The company is then permitted to sell the treasury shares at a later date.

### Private companies

Private companies may repurchase their own shares even if the creditors' buffer is reduced as a result. The extent by which the creditors' buffer is to be reduced is known as the permissible capital payment. However, if a private company wishes to reduce its creditors' buffer, it must comply with certain requirements.

- As much of the repurchase as possible must be financed from distributable reserves, ie the distributable reserves must be zero before the creditors' buffer can be reduced.
- Any capital payment must be approved by special resolution.
- The directors must make a statutory declaration that there are no grounds on which the company could be found unable to pay its debts and can continue as a going concern for the next year. A director who makes such a declaration without having reasonable grounds for doing so is liable to imprisonment and/or a fine.
- An auditors' report must be annexed to the statutory declaration stating that the auditors have inquired into the company's affairs, the capital payment has been properly calculated and they are not aware of anything to indicate that the directors' declaration is unreasonable.

## Accounting requirements

The examples below show the accounting treatment, firstly for a public listed company that repurchases shares and cancels them, and secondly, if the same company repurchases shares, holds them as treasury shares and then subsequently sells them.

## EXAMPLE Share repurchase and cancelling of shares

We will illustrate a share repurchase by considering a company which has 1 million £1 Ordinary shares in issue at a current market price of £3, and which has the following summarised balance sheet.

| Summarised Balance Sheet | £'000 |
|---|---|
| Net Assets | 2,500 |
| Share Capital | 1,000 |
| Share Premium | 500 |
| Profit and Loss | 1,000 |
| | 2,500 |

Our company wishes to repurchase 100,000 shares from a particular shareholder at the current share price of £3. The repurchase will be financed out of cash reserves.

## SOLUTION

*Repurchase Old Shares*

We are repurchasing 100,000 old shares, at a price of £3 per share. Hence, the impact will be

| | £ |
|---|---|
| Cash down | 300,000 |
| Share capital down | 100,000 |
| Profit and loss reserve down | 200,000 |

reducing the creditors' buffer by £100,000.

*Maintain Creditors' Buffer*

The net effect is that our creditors' buffer has been reduced by £100,000 and this now needs to be reinstated by transferring £100,000 from the profit and loss reserve into a capital redemption reserve. The impact of this will be

| | £ |
|---|---|
| Capital redemption reserve up | 100,000 |
| Profit and loss reserve down | 100,000 |

*Summary*

The overall position is illustrated below.

| | Before | Repurchase | Maintain Buffer | After |
|---|---|---|---|---|
| | £'000 | £'000 | £'000 | £'000 |
| Net assets | 2,500 | (300) | – | 2,200 |
| Share capital | 1,000 | (100) | | 900 |
| Share premium | 500 | | | 500 |
| Capital redemption reserve | – | – | 100 | 100 |
| **Creditors' buffer** | **1,500** | **(100)** | 100 | **1,500** |
| Profit and loss | 1,000 | (200) | (100) | 700 |
| | 2,500 | (300) | – | 2,200 |

This illustration shows that the creditors' buffer is being maintained at £1.5m following the repurchase. Also the repurchase itself (costing £300,000) has been financed from the distributable reserves – the profit and loss account (reduced by £300,000) satisfying the general rule above.

## EXAMPLE Share repurchase and holding shares as treasury shares

Using the same company, the following illustrates the accounting if the company were to hold the shares as treasury shares rather than cancel them. We also illustrate what the accounts would look like if the company subsequently sold the treasury shares for £4 each, a higher price than they were acquired for.

*Repurchase Shares*

We are repurchasing 100,000 shares at a price of £3 per share. Hence, the impact will be

| | £ |
|---|---|
| Cash down | 300,000 |
| Profit and loss reserve down | 300,000 |

There is no reduction to the creditors buffer because the shares have not been cancelled and therefore, there has been no impact on the share capital account.

*Subsequent Sale of Shares*

We are selling all 100,000 shares for a higher price of £4. Hence, the impact will be

| | £ |
|---|---|
| Cash ~~down~~ up | 400,000 |
| Share premium up | 100,000 |
| Profit and loss reserve up | 300,000 |

The distributable reserves are replenished up to the amount that they were previously written down on acquiring the shares (£300,000). Any sales proceeds in excess of this amount are included in the share premium account.

*Summary*

The overall position is illustrated below.

| | Before | Repurchase | After Repurchase | Sale | After Sale |
|---|---|---|---|---|---|
| | £'000 | £'000 | £'000 | £'000 | £'000 |
| Net assets | 2,500 | (300) | 2,200 | 400 | 2,600 |
| Share capital | 1,000 | – | 1,000 | – | 1,000 |
| Share premium | 500 | – | 500 | 100 | 600 |
| **Creditors' buffer** | **1,500** | **–** | **1,500** | **100** | **1,600** |
| Profit and loss | 1,000 | (300) | 700 | 300 | 1,000 |
| | 2,500 | (300) | 2,200 | 400 | 2,600 |

This illustration shows that the creditor's buffer is being maintained at £1.5m following the repurchase, just as in the previous example. Also, the repurchase itself has been financed from the distributable reserves. The advantage of holding shares as treasury shares is that when they are subsequently sold, the distributable reserves are replenished up to the amount that they were previously reduced by, as a result of the repurchase (£300,000). However, if in Example 1 the company were to subsequently issue shares, these would have to be brand new shares and the accounts would simply be

| |
|---|
| Cash up |
| Share capital up |
| Share premium up |

Hence, the profit and loss reserve would not be replenished and would still be reduced by £300,000.

# 9 Listing Rules Requirements

## General requirements for buy-backs

The rules relating to share buy-backs apply to companies with equity or preference shares listed.

A decision by a company to seek shareholder permission to purchase its own shares must be disclosed through its RIS without delay, and shareholder approval is required before shares may be repurchased.

Shareholders must be sent a notice of the EGM, together with a circular stating the following (*LR 13.7.1 R)*.

- The directors' intentions, where the authority sought is general (ie where the intention is to buy shares in the market).
- The names of the vendors of the shares and the details of the contract, where the authority is specific (ie where specific vendors are identified).
- Details concerning the maximum and minimum prices to be paid.

In general, no share repurchases may be made in any period prohibited by the Model Code for directors' dealings (*LR 12.2.1 R)*. This is covered in more detail below.

Where less than 15% of the company's share capital is to be repurchased in a year and the purchases are made on market, the price paid must not be more than 5% above the average market price for the five business days prior to the purchases (*LR 12.4.1 R)*. Where 15% or more is to be published, the repurchase must be by means of a tender offer to all shareholders (*LR 12.4.2 R*). Where the repurchase is made by way of tender offer to all shareholders, this pricing limit does not apply.

Where shareholder approval is granted, but prior to any actual purchases, the issuer must disclose the grant of the approval by no later than 07:30 on the day following the approval by shareholders, stating the reason for the purchase, the maximum and minimum price to be paid for shares, the maximum number of shares to be acquired, and the date of expiry of the authority.

Purchases actually made must be disclosed publicly (through an RIS) by no later than 07:30. on the business day following the day of the purchase (*LR 12.4.6 R*). This must state the date of purchase, the number of shares purchased, the average price paid, the number of shares purchased for cancellation and the number to be held as treasury shares.

## Legal requirements for share buy-backs

Public limited companies may generally only fund a repurchase of shares out of distributable profits. A limited company may fund a repurchase out of share capital and undistributable reserves but the directors must make a solvency statement for the company, reported on by the auditors.

Where a company intends to make repurchases on-market, it must seek shareholder approval, through the passing of an ordinary resolution specifying the maximum and minimum price which will be paid and the maximum number of shares to be repurchased.

Where a company intends to make repurchases off-market, the specific purchase contract must be approved by a special resolution of shareholders, requiring a 75% majority voting in favour.

Once shares have been repurchased, the company must give details of the purchases in its next annual report, and must notify the Registrar of Companies of any repurchases made.

## Treasury shares

Companies carrying out a buy-back may hold such shares as treasury shares, as long as the following criteria are met.

- Treasury shares must comprise no more than 10% of the company's issued share capital.
- Shares must be UK listed, AIM shares or EEA listed; private or unlisted companies may not have treasury shares.

If the criteria are not (or cease to be) met, the shares must be cancelled. The company's officers will be liable to a fine if the company is in default.

The company will appear as a member of itself on its share register in respect of the shares; they cannot be held by a nominee on the company's behalf, so may only be held through CREST if the company is a CREST member or sponsored member. Treasury shares do not carry the normal voting, dividend or pre-emption rights associated with their class; however, if the shares are redeemable the company is entitled to redemption proceeds if they are redeemed while in treasury. Any bonus shares allotted in respect of treasury shares are be treated as if they too were treasury shares purchased at the time of allotment.

The treasury shares may not be pledged as security.

The shares will be shown as a deduction to shareholders' equity in the accounts and will reduce the distributable reserves of the business. The company's accounts must show the number and nominal value of any shares held in treasury.

## Selling Treasury shares

Resale of the shares for cash is covered by the Companies Act 2006, whereby existing shareholders' pre-emption rights must be adhered to, unless a disapplication is in place. This excludes shares used to fulfil obligations under an employee share scheme.

ABI guidelines governing the size of non pre-emptive issues (no more than 5% in any one year) also apply to the sale of treasury shares. However, the rolling limit of 7.5% in any three years may be exceeded at the ABI's discretion, to cater for sales or cancellations of treasury shares.

Any sale of treasury shares must be for cash. The corresponding entry in the balance sheet is a restatement of distributable profits. Any excess of the selling price over the buyback price will be credited to the share premium account; otherwise the proceeds are a realised profit.

## General reasons for repurchasing own shares

Reasons for purchasing own shares include the following.

- To pay surplus cash to shareholders as an alternative to dividends.
- To increase the level of financial gearing, borrowing cash to finance the repurchase.
- To signal to investors that the share price is too low and the company is undervalued.
- To increase the share price and earnings per share. (This will be achieved if the interest received on cash surpluses used to finance the repurchase is lower than the returns generated on the main operations of the company.)
- To buy back unwanted share holdings in a private company that cannot be sold on the Stock Exchange.
- To provide an exit route for venture capitalists.
- Part of a capital reorganisation where a company repurchases preference shares and issues new equity shares.
- An employee share scheme where a company buys back the shares from employees when they leave the company.

## Reasons for holding shares as treasury shares rather than cancelling them

Reasons for holding shares as treasury shares are:

- These shares are available for subsequent sale for cash or transfer into an employee share scheme.
- Provides the company with greater flexibility in managing their share capital, leading to a reduction in the cost of funding for the company.
- The accounting treatment is such that a company has the potential to restore the distributable profits used when the shares were bought back. When the shares are sold out of treasury, the sales price replenishes the distributable reserves up to the amount lost on their acquisition.

## Taxation implications

The exact tax implications depend on the precise nature of the transaction. Where the repurchase is considered as off market for tax purposes, investors will receive a tax credit. Where the repurchase is considered as on market, investors will be treated as making a capital gain on disposal of the shares.

## Chapter Roundup

**Module 3, Chapter 16: Public Equity**

This chapter commences with a discussion of the advantages and disadvantages of obtaining a listing. You are unlikely to be asked to reproduce this list verbatim, but more likely to pick out which points apply to a particular company given to you in a scenario. Is there another source of finance that might be more appropriate for a company than a public issue of equity?

As a corporate financier, you will often be the main point of contact in running an IPO for a client. You are expected for the exam, therefore, to be able to discuss the main stages in a flotation and what the specific responsibilities of different groups of advisers are at each stage. You may need to prepare a suitable timetable to listing, adapted to the company circumstances given in the question. We discuss the pricing process and how an IPO price might be set.

This chapter details the mechanics of the different methods of listing, and again you need to be prepared to suggest suitability and any reservations that you have.

We also consider secondary issues and the legal requirements relating to pre-emption rights. You need to understand how a rights issue works and be able to advise a client on the main stages to raise finance.

The chapter finishes off with a consideration of share repurchases. You should be clear on how repurchases are recorded in a company's accounts and what the Listing Rules requirements are relating to buybacks.

# Pension schemes

chapter 17

Contents


| | | |
|---|---|---|
| 1 | Introduction | 392 |
| 2 | Types of Pension Scheme | 392 |
| 3 | Role of the Trustees in Occupational Pension Schemes | 392 |
| 4 | Defined Benefit Schemes | 393 |
| 5 | Using Asset Based Finance to Fund Pension Deficits | 397 |

# 1 Introduction

This chapter examines the financial implications of pension schemes. We look at the financial implications of pension schemes, with particular reference to:

- Defined contribution schemes
- Defined benefit schemes
- Valuation of assets and liabilities
- Deficit funding
- Rights of pension holders
- Asset based finance

# 2 Types of Pension Scheme

There are two main types of company (or 'occupational') pension scheme: defined benefit scheme and defined contribution scheme.

- **Defined contribution schemes**. With defined contribution schemes, the employer (and possibly current employees too) pay regular contributions into the plan of a given or 'defined' amount each year. The contributions are invested, and the size of the post-employment benefits paid to former employees depends on how well or how badly the plan's investments perform. If the investments perform well, the plan will be able to afford higher benefits than if the investments performed less well.
- **Defined benefit schemes**. With defined benefit schemes, the size of the post-employment benefits is determined in advance, ie the benefits are 'defined'. The employer (and possibly current employees too) pay contributions into the plan, and the contributions are invested. The size of the contributions is set at an amount that is expected to earn sufficient investment returns to meet the obligation to pay the post-employment benefits. If, however, it becomes apparent that the assets in the fund are insufficient, the employer will be required to make additional contributions into the plan to make up the expected shortfall. On the other hand, if the fund's assets appear to be larger than they need to be, and in excess of what is required to pay the post-employment benefits, the employer may be allowed to take a 'contribution holiday' (ie stop paying in contributions for a while).

The following table summarises the main differences between Defined Benefit (DB) Schemes and Defined Contribution (DC) Schemes:

| Defined Benefit Schemes | Defined Contribution Schemes |
|---|---|
| Employer takes the risk – guarantees a pension based on final salary levels | Employee takes the risk – pension depends on investment performance and annuity rates available on retirement |
| Risk of losing benefits if change of employment | Easier to transfer |

# 3 Role of the Trustees in Occupational Pension Schemes

Occupational pension schemes are generally established under an **irrevocable trust**, which has the effect of separating the assets of the scheme from those of the employer. The trustees are then the legal owners of the assets and are responsible for the running of the scheme. Given the nature of business, the existence of a trust gives the members of the scheme a considerably greater degree of security than would otherwise be the case, since the assets of the scheme can be seen to be separated from those of the employer. They are therefore protected should the employer get into financial difficulties, or indeed if the employer should become insolvent.

It is the trustees who are responsible for the operation of the scheme, and they will often have **discretionary powers**, at least to some extent, over certain benefits. They are also responsible for the investment of the scheme monies.

However, a pension scheme is different from most other trusts in some ways. Usually the intention is to establish an ongoing arrangement and the provision of benefits under the scheme will be dependent not just upon the money which is already in the scheme, but also on the continued ability and willingness of the employer to input further money. For this reason, certain discretions, for example over the augmentation of benefits under a scheme, are likely to be either the prime responsibility of the employer, or a shared responsibility between the trustees and the employer.

In recent years, both the powers and the responsibilities of trustees have been underlined and reinforced by legislation. The **Pensions Act 2004** introduced for the first time a requirement that all trustees must have knowledge and understanding in relation to various relevant topics.

The trustees are responsible for the proper operation of the scheme, and although they can delegate their duties, they cannot delegate the responsibility for them. The trustees will appoint the professional advisers, including a scheme auditor and, unless the scheme is on a money purchase basis, a scheme actuary is normally appointed. The trustees also have various responsibilities in relation to the communication of information to members, including a statement of investment principle. The trustees are also responsible for ensuring that contributions to the scheme are paid as expected. This involves maintaining a schedule of contributions, which will be audited by the scheme auditor. If expected contributions (employer or employee contributions) are not received on time and the failure is significant (generally if there is a delay of more than thirty days other than as a result of an oversight, or there is a systematic failure), it must be reported to the Pensions Regulator.

The trustees must also ensure that the funding of the scheme is at an acceptable level if the scheme is on a defined benefit basis, and develop a recovery plan if necessary.

## 4 Defined Benefit Schemes

Defined benefit schemes are sometimes termed '**final salary schemes**'. They are often based on a formula such as 1/60th of final pensionable pay for each year of pensionable service. The problem with aiming to provide benefits on this basis is the unpredictability of their cost. The level of future salary increases is uncertain, as are the investment returns which the pension scheme will be able to achieve, and the level of interest rates and life expectancy (which together are the main determinants of the cost of providing a given level of pension income) which will be applicable at the point of retirement. Thus neither the level of benefit nor its cost are certain.

As well as these factors, there is the potential for changes in legislation, which may also impact on cost. For example, the decision in 1997 to withdraw the ability of pension funds to reclaim tax credits on UK dividends inevitably reduced investment returns and therefore increased the cost of providing benefits. Where the employer had decided to provide benefits according to a final salary formula, the cost of doing so increased as a result. Such things are virtually impossible to foresee, yet the employer is faced with meeting the increased cost, possibly sharing the extra cost with members, or alternatively reducing the rate at which future benefits accrue.

Ultimately, it is the employer who stands behind the promise of benefits and is therefore exposed to the risk of cost increases. In recent years, few employers have set up new DB schemes, and those with existing schemes have in many cases either closed them to new entrants, or stopped future accrual entirely. Even in the public sector, schemes are being reconsidered and sometimes benefits are being reduced, or members' contributions increased. In some cases, new defined contribution schemes are being established as an alternative form of provision for new members.

Inevitably, because the assets of a DB scheme and its liabilities are affected by different things, an imbalance can, and frequently, does arise. An employer is required to meet any shortfall (if the employer remains solvent) and this commitment combined with the cost uncertainty of DB schemes is a major factor in the trend away from these schemes.

The cost of a DB scheme can only be estimated. A contribution rate is recommended by the scheme actuary and needs to be agreed between the trustees and the employer. It is expressed as a percentage of the total payroll of members ('pensionable payroll'), sometimes with different contribution rates applying to different membership categories which are subject to different benefit formulae.

The actuary needs to make assumptions about the factors that will affect the scheme in future. The actuarial science behind DB schemes has a long history, and statistical techniques based on experience are used to suggest a contribution rate intended to remain reasonably stable. However, volatile investment and economic conditions have made this increasingly difficult in recent years.

Contributions build up within the fund (which provides for the benefits of all members rather than each member having a personal identifiable fund). They generate investment growth, while at the same time, the employees' benefits build up as a result of their increasing period of employment and any increase in their level of earnings.

## Funding level

When benefits are eventually paid, provision is made for these either through annuity purchase or in some other way, and this is a drain on the fund. Over the life of a pension fund it is therefore necessary to continually scrutinise the relationship between the assets and the current and future liabilities of the pension scheme, with the objective of keeping the two in line. This relationship is often referred to as the funding level of the scheme. A funding level of 100% is ideal because it represents a balance between assets and liabilities.

Various factors can impact on the funding level over time. Some of the most important are as follows:

**Investment returns** – High returns tend to improve funding levels, while poor returns weaken it. Fluctuating investment values can make the funding level difficult to assess in a meaningful way.

**Salary increases** – The rate of increase impacts on the ultimate benefit provided for a member if the scheme is based on a final salary formula. High increases for a particular member can have a significant influence, even if average increases are within expectations, particularly if the member concerned is highly paid, or has substantial benefits because of long service.

**Inflation level** – the level of inflation will affect the rate at which benefits are revalued. It will also affect the inflation proofing requirements in relation to benefits in payment, and preserved benefits for early leavers.

**Interest rates** – The cost of providing income benefits clearly affects liabilities. Some small schemes provide income benefits by annuity purchase while larger schemes usually pay income from the fund. The cost in either case is affected by interest rates and in particular, the return on fixed interest securities.

**Longevity** – The other major influence on the cost of providing income benefits is longevity. Trends are towards increasing longevity, which increases the cost for schemes.

**Staff turnover** – If staff turnover differs from expectations, this can also have an effect, because it will alter the average age and past service of the members, and these factors affect the cost and amount of benefits being provided. Turnover can also affect the balance between men and women, which also affects costs as female life expectancy is greater than male.

**Legal changes** – Changes in the law governing pensions may affect the liabilities of the scheme, or its other conditions and are not always easy to predict.

It is important to recognise that the calculation of the funding level is based to some extent on assumptions, and therefore is not a precise figure. In particular, the present value of liabilities to pay pension benefits in the future can only be estimated based on various assumptions regarding aspects such as future interest rates and trends in longevity.

The relevant factors are also constantly fluctuating, so that the funding level of the scheme is itself in a state of flux. The pension fund may be very large, particularly if it has been in operation for a number of years, and so the emergence of any surplus or deficit within the fund can have serious consequences. If the scheme builds up a deficit, this will have to be dealt with by the employer, either by making a lump sum additional contribution to the scheme, or by increasing the level of regular contributions which are paid.

## Legal requirements

The Pensions Act 2004 brought in pension scheme specific funding requirements, under which a funding strategy is agreed by the trustees with the employer, based on actuarial advice, which can take account of the particular circumstances of the scheme. The statutory funding objective is that the 'technical provisions' of the pension scheme (essentially the cost of providing for liabilities built up to date) should be balanced by the scheme assets. There must be an actuarial valuation of the assets and liabilities at least every three years, with shorter actuarial reports in each of the years between full valuations.

The trustees must prepare and maintain a Statement of Funding Principles setting out their approach. This must be provided to members and must include details of the arrangements with the employer as regards funding and the methods and assumptions used in the calculations. This statement needs to be reviewed every three years (at least) so that it remains relevant to the current state of the scheme.

A schedule of contributions will be agreed by the trustees with the employer, and if contributions are not paid in accordance with this schedule, this will create a debt on the employer which can be enforced by the Regulator. The scheme auditor must disclose whether the employer has adhered to the schedule each year.

## Recovery plan

If the scheme is in deficit, that is, the assets are less than the liabilities, a recovery plan must be prepared, aimed at correcting the position within a defined timescale. The plan should take account of the circumstances of the employer and the scheme. Details must be given to members in the Statement of Funding Principles and a copy sent to the Pensions Regulator.

The regulator can intervene if it is felt that the plan is not appropriate. This can occur if the plan seems unnecessarily 'back-end loaded' in the sense that the expected outcome is that there will be little improvement in the position initially, but then much more speedy progress towards the end of the recovery period. This may be acceptable if justified by the circumstances, but would not be if it was merely an attempt to delay dealing with the issue.

The Regulator will also carefully consider any recovery plan with a recovery period in excess of ten years. There is no maximum period within which a deficit must be cleared, but longer recovery periods can once again indicate an attempt to defer the issue. The objectives of the Regulator include the safeguarding of member rights, and dealing with the issue of recovery plans is an important part of this.

To help make the progress towards meeting the statutory funding objective clear, the recovery plan must specifically show when it is anticipated that half the shortfall will be eliminated.

## Surpluses

It is also possible for a defined benefit scheme to develop a surplus, with assets which exceed liabilities.

There are a number of ways in which the surplus can be used. These are:

- Improvements in benefit
- Contribution holiday for employer (or a reduction in contributions)
- Contribution holiday for employees (or a reduction in contributions)
- Refund to employer (rare and not tax efficient)

These routes are not mutually exclusive, and in practical terms, a combination of two or more may be appropriate. If a surplus is refunded to the employer, an adjustment is made to reflect the fact that tax relief will have been obtained on the contribution, and it will have enjoyed tax-advantaged investment growth for the period of time for which it remained in the fund. The refund will therefore be subject to a special tax charge at the rate of 35%, which is deducted from the refund by the scheme administrator, whose responsibility it is to remit the tax to the tax authorities.

## Winding-up

Although occupational schemes are likely to be established by an employer with the intention of providing benefits over a long period, circumstances can change, and schemes may be discontinued as a result. For example, in some cases, this may be because the employer wishes to save money and is no longer willing to contribute, while in some cases, the ending of the scheme will follow from the liquidation of the employer.

If the employer still exists, the scheme may continue to operate, with no further benefits accruing, but with benefits being provided as members reach retirement. Alternatively, the scheme may be wound-up, which will involve using the fund at that time to provide deferred benefits for members. This may be through a bulk transfer to a new scheme (perhaps where the employer has been taken over by a different company with its own scheme), individual transfers, or the purchase of insured contracts for each member by the trustees.

With a defined benefit scheme, there may be an imbalance between assets and liabilities at the time of winding-up.

- If there is a surplus, this can be used to increase benefits for members. Alternatively, a refund can be made to the employer, but only if this can be done without endangering the security of benefits promised under the scheme. Any such refund to the employer would be subject to tax at 35%, deducted by the trustees of the scheme.
- If there is a deficit, the amount of the deficit is a debt on the employer and the trustees would be expected to pursue legal remedies to recover the debt, to the extent that this was reasonable. This means that if there is no realistic chance of securing repayment because the employer was insolvent, the trustees would not have to waste money on pointless legal action. The potential for the loss of benefits which members regarded as secure is the reason that the government introduced the Pension Protection Fund from April 2005.

### Pension protection fund

The Pension Protection Fund (PPF) is intended to specifically address the issue of security of benefits. Although it has for some time been the case that any under-funding of a pension scheme on winding-up constitutes a debt on the employer, if the employer is insolvent, members of the scheme may in some cases lose a significant part of the benefits that they were expecting.

The PPF was introduced from April 2005 and operates on an insurance basis, with schemes paying a levy which will build up a fund from which compensation claims can be met. Claims can arise under DB schemes where the employer is insolvent and the scheme is unable to meet its liabilities. In addition, claims can arise under DC or DB schemes where there has been a loss as a result of fraud or misappropriation of pension fund assets, and again the employer is insolvent.

The PPF provides compensation of 100% of the pension in payment to existing pensioners who had reached normal pension age under the scheme by the time of the insolvency event. Those who have not yet reached normal pension age will be protected up to a level of 90% of their accrued pension but subject to a limit which is amended each tax year and is dependent on the scheme normal pension age.

# 5 Using Asset Based Finance to Fund Pension Deficits

Increasingly, companies have used asset securitization to fund deficits in their pension schemes. Securitisation allows a company to raise finance by selling assets or income streams into a special purpose vehicle (SPV). The SPV then raises money to pay for these assets by issuing secured bonds. The cash from the bond issue is then transferred to the pension scheme.

Usually assets sold into an SPV have some form of regular income – such as royalties, regular payments from customers or other ongoing revenues. The assets the subject of the transaction can be tangible, such as rental property, or intangible, such as patents or copyright agreements. The assets remain fully in use and controlled by the business, although they are now owned by the SPV. Securitisation reduces the cost of financing for a company as, generally, the interest rates payable on the securitised bonds sold by the SPV are lower than those on corporate bonds. The credit risk of the SPV reflects the quality of the assets transferred. The assets in the SPV are protected, even if the business gets into financial problems, including insolvency, which reduces the credit risk for investors.

The Pensions Regulator has for a while accepted tangible assets for pension fund investment and has more recently accepted less traditional assets including many different forms of intellectual property. Given that much of the value of a company is 'intangible', this opens up a whole new source of financing for companies.

The following is a list of asset-based financing examples:

**Interserve** transferred PFI contacts into a SPV, with resulting cash inflows for its pension fund.

Engineering firm **GKN** transferred a mix of assets, including its trademark, into an SPV. Pension trustees to receive payments of £30m per annum for 20 years, which can be used to satisfy future service contributions if the pension plan moves into surplus in the future.

**Diageo** used barrels of whisky to fund its pension deficit. Diageo transferred maturing whisky reported to be worth around £500m into an SPV. Diageo pension trustees to receive an annual income of £25m for 15 years, followed by a bullet payment to remove the deficit up to a maximum of £430m.

The following is an extract from the **Kingfisher** plc Annual Report relating to the sale by Kingfisher of property assets to its pension fund.

**Kingfisher plc: UK pension scheme interest in property partnership**

On 28 January 2011 the Group entered into an arrangement with the pension scheme Trustee to address an element of the current pension scheme deficit. The Group established a partnership, Kingfisher Scottish Limited Partnership ('Kingfisher SLP'). The partnership interests are held by the Group and by the pension scheme ('scheme'), the latter resulting from a £78m investment made by the scheme Trustee. This investment followed a Group contribution of the same amount into the scheme. Under IAS 19, 'Employee benefits', the investment held by the scheme in Kingfisher SLP does not represent a plan asset for the purposes of the Group's consolidated financial statements. Accordingly the pension deficit position does not reflect the £78m investment. The Group has control over the partnership and therefore it is consolidated in these Group financial statements. Accordingly, advantage has been taken of the exemptions provided by Regulation 7 of the Partnerships (Accounts) Regulations 2008 from the requirements for preparation, delivery and publication of the partnership's accounts.

UK property assets with a market value of £83m were transferred into the partnership and leased back to B&Q plc. The Group retains control over these properties, including the flexibility to substitute alternative properties. The Trustee has a first charge over the properties in the event that Kingfisher plc becomes insolvent. The scheme's partnership interest entitles it to the majority of the income of the partnership over the next 20 years. These future payments to the scheme by Kingfisher SLP will be reflected as Group pension contributions on a cash basis. At the end of this term, Kingfisher plc has the option to acquire the Trustee's partnership interest in Kingfisher SLP.

As this last example illustrates, the assets transferred will not always be shown as assets under the pension scheme and thus reduce the reported deficit in the balance sheet. For the asset to be classified as a pension scheme asset, the assets in the SPV must be transferable to a third party.

## Chapter Roundup

**Module 3, Chapter 17: Pension Schemes**

The syllabus requires a 'general' level of knowledge for these topics, meaning that the questions you will face in this area will be 'straightforward' as opposed to 'complex'.

The main required areas of knowledge are:

- Defined contribution schemes
- Defined benefit schemes
- Valuation of assets and liabilities
- Deficit funding
- Rights of pension holders
- Asset based finance
- Bonds

# Derivatives

chapter 18

Contents


| | | |
|---|---|---|
| 1 | Introduction | 402 |
| 2 | Interest Rate Risk | 402 |
| 3 | Foreign Currency Risk | 403 |
| 4 | The Foreign Currency Market | 405 |
| 5 | The Impact of Inflation and Interest Rates on Exchange Rates | 407 |
| 6 | Use of Derivatives to Hedge Interest Rate and Foreign Currency Risk | 408 |
| 7 | Foreign Currency Forward Contracts | 413 |
| 8 | Foreign Currency Futures | 415 |
| 9 | Interest Rate Futures | 416 |
| 10 | Currency Options | 416 |
| 11 | Interest Rate Options | 417 |
| 12 | Equity Derivatives | 418 |

# 1 Introduction

We consider in this chapter the use by companies of derivatives as risk management tools. The main risks that companies use derivatives to hedge against are **interest rate risk**, the variability in cash flows that comes from changes in underlying interest rates and **foreign currency risk**, the variability in cash flows that results from changes in underlying exchange rates. In addition, a company may choose to hold equity derivatives to hedge against the systematic risk of the market which cannot be eliminated by holding a diversified portfolio of shares. Businesses may choose to develop a hedging strategy to reduce or remove this variability by using derivative instruments such as forwards, futures, options or swaps.

# 2 Interest Rate Risk

A company faces interest rate risk on both its floating rate and fixed rate borrowings. Floating rate debt exposes a company to the risk of underlying variability in the interest charges it faces on its borrowings. As market interest rates increase or decrease, the floating rate on the company's borrowings will also rise or fall, tracking the movement in the underlying rate. Choosing fixed rate debt removes this variability risk; however, a company can end up paying a higher fixed rate than prevailing market rates. Fixed rate debt thus leaves a company open to changes in the fair value of its debt capital, as market rates change in relation to the fixed interest rate attached to the borrowings. A company thus faces interest rate risk on both fixed and floating rate debt.

**Example** Interest rate risk

**Extract from Kingfisher plc 2014/2015 Annual Report**

*Interest rate risk*

Borrowings arranged at floating rates of interest expose the Group to cash flow interest rate risk, whereas those arranged at fixed rates of interest expose the Group to fair value interest rate risk. The Group manages its interest rate risk by entering into certain interest rate derivative contracts which modify the interest rate payable on the Group's underlying debt instruments, principally the Medium Term Notes and other fixed term debt.

## Borrowing at fixed versus floating rate

There are various factors which businesses will consider when deciding whether to borrow at fixed or floating rate:

1. **Expectations of interest rate movements** will determine whether a company chooses to borrow at a fixed or floating rate. The term structure of interest rates – the rates available on loans of different length – should help businesses determine the market's view on how interest rates are likely to move in the future.

2. **The finance term**. The longer the term the more difficult interest rates are to predict and therefore the more likely the business will be to choose a fixed rate. If finance is required to meet long term funding needs the business will be less concerned about the 'fair value' risk highlighted above. The main concern will be to manage the volatility risk on the coupon.

3. The borrower's **fixed to floating spread**. The difference between the fixed and floating rates available to the company will be considered, plus arrangement costs for new finance. Fixed rate

debt generally attracts a higher effective cost, given that it provides predictability of finance costs. The company will consider whether the additional cost compensates for the removal of the likely variability of interest volatility.

4 The **risk tolerance of the directors**.

5 The **existing debt mix**. Most firms will have an optimal ratio of fixed versus variable borrowings and new borrowings will be raise in this proportion.

6 **Current pressures on liquidity**. If the business has liquidity constraints, it may prefer to take the lower rate available on floating rate debt. In doing so, it is accepting the risk that rates may rise and borrowing eventually become more expensive. However the directors are calculating that if this happens, the company will have accumulated sufficient cash to be able to bear the higher rates.

## Managing interest rate risk

Once the fixed/floating proportion is deciding on, the company can seek to hedge the interest rate risk by using derivatives. The main hedging instruments that can be used are forward rate agreements, futures, swaps and options. Alternatively where the magnitude of the risk is immaterial in comparison with the company's overall cash flows or appetite for risks, the company may decide to do nothing.

The company may also decide to do nothing if risk management costs are excessive, both in terms of the costs of using derivatives and the staff resources required to manage risk effectively. Appropriate products may not be available and of course the company may consider hedging unnecessary as it believes that the chances of an adverse movement are remote.

The company's tax situation may also be a significant determinant of its decision whether or not to hedge risk. If hedging is likely to reduce variability of earnings, this may have tax advantages if the company faces a higher rate of tax for higher earnings levels. The directors may also be unwilling to undertake hedging because of the need to monitor the arrangements, and the requirements to fulfill the detailed disclosure requirements of IASs 32 and 39 and IFRSs 7 and 9.

The different characteristics of the interest rate derivatives are detailed in the sections below, together with a consideration as to which instrument is likely to be most appropriate in a given scenario.

# 3 Foreign Currency Risk

Changes in underlying exchange rates gives rise to foreign currency risks. Generally, exposure to foreign currency risk can be categorised as transaction exposure, translation exposure and economic exposure.

## Transaction exposure

### What is transaction risk?

Transaction risk is the risk of adverse exchange rate movements occurring in the course of normal international trading transactions. Transaction exposure occurs when a company has a future transaction that will be settled in a foreign currency. Such exposure could arise for example as the result of a US company operating a foreign subsidiary. Operations in foreign countries encounter a variety of transactions for example, purchases or sales or financial transactions that are denominated in a foreign currency. Even when foreign subsidiaries operate independently of the parent company, without relying on the parent company as a source of cash, they will ultimately remit dividends to the parent in the home currency. Once again, this will require a conversion from foreign to home currency.

### Hedging against transaction risk

Transactional risk gives rise to variability in cash flows which can be managed via foreign currency derivatives. Appropriate derivatives are forwards, futures, options and swaps. The use of these instruments is considered in the sections below.

## Translation exposure

### What is translation risk?

Translation exposure occurs in multinational corporations that have foreign subsidiaries with assets and liabilities denominated in foreign currency. Translation exposure occurs because the value of these accounts must eventually be stated in domestic currency for reporting purposes in the company's financial statements. In general, as exchange rates change, the home currency value of the foreign subsidiaries' assets and liabilities will change. Such changes can result in translation losses or gains, which will be recognised in financial statements.

### Hedging against translation risk

Translation gains/losses will not have an impact on the firm's cash flow unless the assets are sold. Translation risk is predominantly a presentational issue and as such the risks are best managed by 'natural hedges' such as matching assets and liabilities in the same currency.

## Economic exposure

### What is economic risk?

Economic risk is the risk that exchange rate movements might reduce the international competitiveness of a company. It is the risk that the present value of a company's future cash flows might be reduced by adverse exchange rate movements. Economic exposure differs from transaction exposure in that exchange rate changes may affect the value of the firm even though the firm is not involved in foreign currency transactions. For example, if a company trades only in the UK but sterling strengthens significantly against other world currencies, it may find that it loses UK sales to an overseas competitor who can now afford to charge cheaper sterling prices.

### Hedging against economic risk

Various actions can reduce economic exposure, including the following.

(a) **Matching assets and liabilities**

A foreign subsidiary can be financed, as far as possible, with a loan in the currency of the country in which the subsidiary operates.

(b) **Diversifying the supplier and customer base**

For example, if the currency of one of the supplier countries strengthens, purchasing can be switched to a cheaper source.

(c) **Diversifying operations worldwide**

On the principle that companies which confine themselves to one country suffer from economic exposure, international diversification is a method of reducing such exposure.

(d) **Changing prices**

The amount of scope a company has to change its prices in response to exchange movements will depend on its competitive position. If there are numerous domestic and overseas competitors, an increase in prices may lead to a significant fall in demand.

**EXAMPLE Foreign currency risk**

**Extract from Kingfisher plc 2014/2015 Annual Report**

*Currency risk*

The Group's principal currency exposures are to the Euro, US Dollar, Polish Zloty and Russian Rouble. The Euro, Polish Zloty and Russian Rouble exposures are operational and arise through the ownership of retail businesses in France, Spain, Portugal, Germany, Ireland, Poland and Russia. In particular, the Group generates a substantial part of its profit from the Eurozone, and as such is exposed to the economic uncertainty of its member states. The Group continues to monitor potential exposures and risks, and consider effective risk management solutions.

It is the Group's policy not to hedge the translation of overseas earnings into Sterling. In addition, the Group has significant transactional exposure arising on the purchase of inventories denominated in US Dollars, which it hedges using forward foreign exchange contracts. Under Group policies, the Group companies are required to hedge committed inventory purchases and a proportion of forecast inventory purchases arising in the next 12 months, and this is monitored on an ongoing basis.

# 4 THE FOREIGN CURRENCY MARKET

Before we look at foreign currency derivatives, we need to understand more about how the market in foreign currency operates.

## Spot transactions

The spot market is the forex market for immediate currency trades. These trades will settle in two business days. This will exclude public holidays in the countries of the two parties to the trade and also in the country of the currency. For example, a German bank dealing in the sterling market with an American bank would have to take into account public holidays in Germany, the US and the UK.

The market has no formal market place and trading takes place via telephones with prices being quoted on screen services. The spot market quotes bid offer prices in the form of a spread, normally based against the dollar. The main exception to this is £/$ (known as **cable**) where the dollar is quoted against the pound.

| £\$ Spot Rate | |
|---|---|
| 1.4275 – | 1.4385 |
| The buyer's rate | The seller's rate |
| £1 will get $1.4275 | $1.4385 will get £1 |

It may be useful to remember that the bank will always give the customer the worse of the two rates. When selling you dollars, they will only give you $1.4275, instead of $1.4385. When buying dollars from you, they will give you £1 for each $1.4385 you give them, rather than $1.4275.

## Forward transactions

The forward market is a market in currencies at an agreed date in the future. It enables you to agree a rate today (the forward rate) at which the currencies will be exchanged on the agreed future date. The benefit of this is certainty – although you do not need the foreign currency until three months' time, you can fix an exchange rate today.

Forward rates are quoted as premiums (pm) or discounts (dis) to the spot rate. It is possible for rates to be quoted at par where the spot and forward are the same.

### TASK

| | |
|---|---|
| Spot | 1.4275–1.4385 |
| One month forward | 0.37–0.35c pm |
| Three month forward | 1.00–0.97c pm |

What is the one-month forward rate?

### SOLUTION

It is important to remember that these rates are quoted in cents, whereas the spot rate is quoted in dollars.

To obtain the forward rate, the **premium is subtracted** from the spot rate or the **discount is added**.

Based on the above figures, the one-month forward rate is

| | |
|---|---|
| Spot rate | 1.4275–1.4385 |
| **Less** premium | 0.0037–0 0035 |
| | 1.4238–1.4350 |

One important factor to remember about this market is that it in no way reflects an expectation of what the rate will be in three, six or nine months' time. It is simply a **mathematical result of the difference in interest rates** in the two countries. The currency that has the lower interest rates will be at a premium in the forward market.

### TASK

Sterling interest rates are 8% and US dollar interest rates are 5%. The spot rate is 2:1. What will be the one-year forward rate?

### SOLUTION

Assume that we have £100, which is equivalent today to $200, given a spot rate of 2:1.

| | £ | £ |
|---|---|---|
| Current values | 100 | 200 |
| Interest for one year at 8% ÷ 5% | 8 | 10 |
| Values in one year's time | 108 | 210 |

The one-year forward rate today will be 1.9444 (210 ÷ 108). If this were not the case, it would be possible to generate an arbitrage profit in the markets.

### Interest rate parity formula

As an alternative to the involved calculation above, it is possible to use the interest rate parity formula, as follows.

$$\text{Forward rate} = \frac{1 + r\$}{1 + r£} \times \text{Spot rate}$$

In this case

$$\text{Forward rate} = \frac{1.05}{1.08} \times 2$$

$$\text{Forward rate} = 1.9444$$

# 5 The Impact of Inflation and Interest Rates on Exchange Rates

## Interest rates

The impact of interest rates on forward rates has been seen above. If the forward rate is assumed to be a good, unbiased indicator of the change in spot rates over time, then it can be stated that low interest rates will indicate that a currency is strengthening against currencies with higher interest rates. This can be justified by arguing that weakening currencies will need to offer high interest rates to remain competitive. This is observable in practice, as soft currencies usually offer high returns. The high interest rates are compensating for foreign exchange losses on the capital value for the investor.

## Purchasing power parity (PPP)

Purchasing power parity argues that currencies suffering high inflation will tend to devalue to maintain relative purchasing power across currencies. For example, if the sterling/dollar exchange rate is 1.5:1, then £100 or $150 can theoretically purchase the same basket of goods. If the UK suffers inflation at 10%, then in one year's time, the same basket of goods will cost £110. If the US has no inflation, the basket will still cost $150. Purchasing power parity argues that the exchange rate will become 1.36 (150 ÷ 110).

# 6 USE OF DERIVATIVES TO HEDGE INTEREST RATE AND FOREIGN CURRENCY RISK

We consider below:

- Swaps – interest rate and currency
- Forwards – FRAS and foreign currency forwards
- Futures – currency and interest rate
- Options – currency and interest rate

## Interest rate swaps

In their simplest form, interest rate swaps enable a company to raise funds on a fixed basis and subsequently convert the interest basis to a floating rate. Alternatively, a payment stream that is originally on a floating rate basis may be converted to a fixed rate stream.

The benefits of interest rate swaps include the following.

- The ability to exploit pricing inefficiencies between different market places to end up with a lower overall cost of funds. For example, a company borrowing on a fixed rate basis may usually have to pay 10%. By borrowing floating rate and swapping into fixed rate, it may achieve a cost of less than 10%. The reason for this is that the fixed rate market place is overpricing the company's debt compared to the floating rate market place and a swap enables the company to exploit this inefficiency.
- The ability to restructure the company's payment profile from fixed to floating or vice versa. A company may wish to do this as a result of its view on the future direction of interest rates, for example.

**EXAMPLE**

Company A may have borrowed £5m on a floating rate basis in the past, paying LIBOR + 2% on an annual basis. The maturity of the debt is five years. It now wishes to convert this to a fixed rate basis. It achieves this by taking out a five-year interest rate swap based on a notional principal of £5m. The swap is based on the company paying a fixed rate amount of 8% × £5m to the swap dealer and receiving LIBOR × £5m from the dealer. Under the swap, the company either pays or receives the difference between these two payment streams.

The cash flows can be represented diagrammatically as follows.

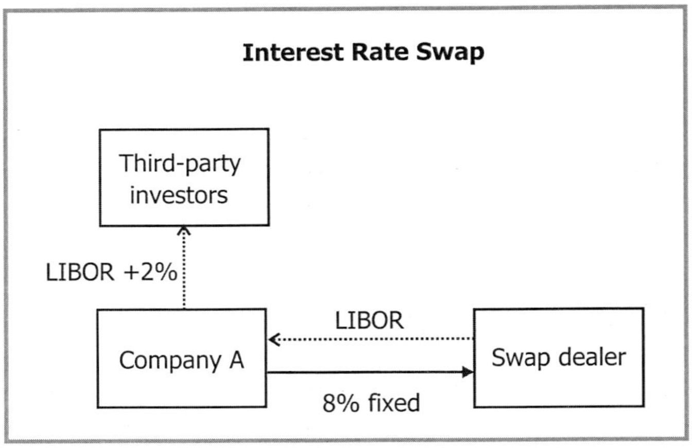


In net terms, company A is now paying 10% fixed, since the LIBOR element has cancelled out. For example, assuming that LIBOR is 9%, the company will pay its third party investors 11% and receive from the swap dealer the difference between LIBOR and 8%, ie 1%. The net cost is therefore 10%.

### Advantages of interest rate swaps

(a) **Flexibility and costs**
Swaps are flexible, since they can be arranged in any size, and they can be reversed if necessary. Transaction costs are low, particularly if no intermediary is used, and are potentially much lower than the costs of terminating one loan and taking out another.

(b) **Credit ratings**
Companies with different credit ratings can borrow in the market that offers each the best deal and then swap this benefit to reduce the mutual borrowing costs.

(c) **Capital structure**
Swaps allow capital restructuring by changing the nature of interest commitments without renegotiating with lenders.

(d) **Risk management**
Swaps can be used to manage interest rate risk by swapping floating for fixed rate debt if rates are expected to rise. Swaps can also be used to swap a variable rate for a fixed rate investment if interest rates are expected to fall.

(e) **Convenience**
Swaps are relatively easy to arrange.

(f) **Predictability of cash flows**
If a company's future cash flows are uncertain, it can use a swap to ensure it has predictable fixed rate commitments.

### Disadvantages of interest rate swaps

(a) **Additional risk**
The swap is subject to counterparty risk; the risk that the other party will default leaving the first company to bear its obligations. This risk can be avoided by using an intermediary.

(b) **Movements in interest rates**
If a company takes on a floating rate commitment, it may be vulnerable to adverse movements in interest rates. If it takes on a fixed rate commitment, it won't be able to take advantage of favourable movements in rates.

(c) **Lack of liquidity**
The lack of a secondary market in swaps makes it very difficult to liquidate a swap contract.

## Currency swaps

In their simplest form, currency swaps enable a company to raise funds in one currency and to convert these funds into another currency. The rationale for such swaps is similar in principle to interest rate swaps, ie exploiting market inefficiencies and enabling the company to restructure the currency profile of its debt.

**EXAMPLE**

Company B raises $10m with a maturity of four years from third party investors, paying a fixed cost of 7%. It swaps this into sterling for four years, receiving £6.5m in exchange for the $10m (based on an exchange rate of 1.538). Over the four years, Company B receives 7% × $10m and pays 8% × £6.5m in interest. In four years' time, the swap is reversed. Company B pays the swap dealer £6.5m and receives $10m. It then uses this $10m to repay the third party investors.

Effectively, Company B has raised sterling funds for four years, paying a fixed rate of interest of 8%. The transaction can be viewed diagrammatically as follows.

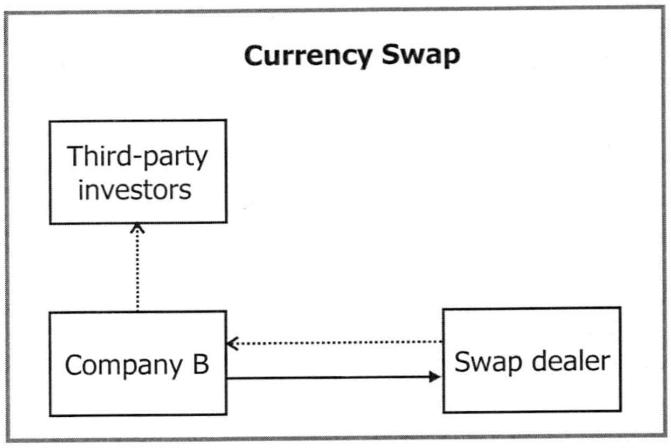


In this case, all interest payments were fixed rate flows. It is also possible to have cross-currency interest rate swaps, where one of the payments is fixed and the other is floating.

## Advantages of currency swaps

(a) **Flexibility**

Swaps are easy to arrange and are flexible since they can be arranged in any size and are reversible.

(b) **Cost**

Transaction costs are low, only amounting to legal fees, since there is no commission or premium to be paid.

(c) **Market avoidance**

The parties can obtain the currency they require without subjecting themselves to the uncertainties of the foreign exchange markets.

(d) **Access to finance**

The company can gain access to debt finance in another country and currency where it is little known, and consequently has a poorer credit rating, than in its home country. It can therefore take advantage of lower interest rates than it could obtain if it arranged the currency loan itself.

(e) **Financial restructuring**

Currency swaps may be used to restructure the currency base of the company's liabilities. This may be important where the company is trading overseas and receiving revenues in foreign currencies, but its borrowings are denominated in the currency of its home country. Currency swaps therefore provide a means of reducing exchange rate exposure.

(f) **Conversion of debt type**

At the same time as exchanging currency, the company may also be able to convert fixed rate debt to floating rate or vice versa. Thus it may obtain some of the benefits of an interest rate swap in addition to achieving the other purposes of a currency swap.

(g) **Liquidity improvement**

A currency swap could be used to absorb excess liquidity in one currency which is not needed immediately, to create funds in another where there is a need.

### Disadvantages of currency swaps

(a) **Risk of default by the other party to the swap (counterparty risk)**

If one party became unable to meet its swap payment obligations, this could mean that the other party risked having to make them itself.

(b) **Position or market risk**

A company whose main business lies outside the field of finance should not increase financial risk in order to make speculative gains.

(c) **Sovereign risk**

There may be a risk of political disturbances or exchange controls in the country whose currency is being used for a swap.

(d) **Arrangement fees**

Swaps have arrangement fees payable to third parties. Although these may appear to be cheap, this is because the intermediary accepts no liability for the swap. (The third party does however suffer some spread risk, as they warehouse one side of the swap until it is matched with the other, and then undertake a temporary hedge on the futures market.)

## Forward rate agreements (FRA)

Interest rate swaps are usually appropriate for longer term interest rate exposures and are often used for maturities of between two and five years, possibly going out even further. Forward rate agreements (FRAs) are usually appropriate for shorter term hedging strategies. They enable a company to fix its interest cost for a particular payment period.

A forward rate agreement (FRA) does not involve the actual transfer of capital from one party to another. A FRA is an agreement to borrow/lend a notional amount for up to 12 months at an agreed rate of interest (the FRA rate). The 'notional' sum is the amount on which the interest payment is calculated. Only the interest on the notional amount between the rate dealt (that is the rate when the FRA is traded) and the rate prevailing at the time of settlement (the reference rate) actually changes hands.

If there is a rise in interest rates between the time that the FRA is traded and the date that the FRA comes into effect, the borrower is protected from paying the higher interest rate. If interest rates fall during that time, the borrower must pay the difference between the traded rate and the actual rate on the notional sum.

If a borrower wishes to hedge against an increase in interest rates to cover a three month loan starting in three months' time, this is known as a 3 × 6 FRA. A three month loan starting in one month's time would be a 1 × 4 FRA etc.

### EXAMPLE

A company has borrowings of £5m, with interest payable quarterly, at a rate of LIBOR + 2%. It is concerned that in three months' time interest rates will rise, increasing its interest cost for the period from three months' time to six months' time. Accordingly, it buys a 3 v 6 FRA with a notional principal of £5m at an interest rate of 8%. This effectively locks it into a LIBOR rate of 8%, giving an overall cost of 10% (LIBOR + 2%).

In three months' time, LIBOR is 10%. On its borrowings, the company now has an interest cost of £5m × 3% (12% × $\frac{3}{12}$). Under the FRA, it receives a payment from the FRA dealer equivalent to

£5m × 0.5% ({10% – 8%} × $\frac{3}{12}$). Its net cost is therefore 2.5% for the three months, or 10% on an annual basis.

Note that the actual receipt under the FRA will usually take place at the beginning of the period to which it relates, whereas interest is usually paid in arrears. As a result, the payment under the FRA is actually the discounted value of the sum above, the discount rate being the appropriate market rate of interest. This can be seen as follows.

Difference under the FRA = £5m × 0.5% = £25,000

Relevant discount rate = 10% × $\frac{3}{12}$ = 2.5%

Actual payment made = 25,000 × $\frac{1}{1.025}$ = £24,390

### Advantages of FRAs

(a) **Protection provided**. An FRA would protect the borrower from adverse interest rate movements above the rate negotiated.

(b) **Flexibility**. FRAs are flexible; they can in theory be arranged for any amounts and any duration, although they are normally for amounts of over $1 million.

(c) **Cost**. The cost of forward rate agreements is negligible.

### Disadvantages of FRAs

(a) **Rate available**. The rate the bank will set for the forward rate agreement will reflect expectations of future interest rate movements. If interest rates are expected to rise, the bank may set a higher rate than the rate currently available.

(b) **Falling interest rate**. The borrower will not be able to take advantage if interest rates fall unexpectedly.

(c) **Term of FRA.** The FRA will terminate on a fixed date.

(d) **Binding agreement**. FRAs are binding agreements and are not easy to sell to other parties.

## TASK

Rumple Inc will shortly be making a short-term investment and wants to borrow $4m for three months, starting in three months' time. However interest rates are currently volatile and it is worried about adverse movements in these rates before it takes out the loan.

LIBOR (the base rate) is currently 3.5% and Rumple has been offered a 3–6 FRA for 3.75%. Rumple can currently borrow at approximately 1% above the base rate.

**Required**

Advise Rumple of the likely outcome of the FRA if the base rate in three months' time is

(a) 4%

(b) 3%

**SOLUTION**

(a) The actual base rate is above the FRA rate therefore the bank will pay the difference as compensation to Rumple – that is, 0.25%.

Rumple will borrow at the best available rate, which is base rate + 1% – that is 5% (4 + 1).

Net cost to Rumple = 5% - 0.25% = 4.75%

(b) As the actual base rate is below the FRA rate, Rumple will pay compensation of 0.75% to the bank.

Rumple will borrow at the best available rate – that is 4% (3 + 1).

Net cost to Rumple = 4% + 0.75% = 4.75%

This amounts to 0.0475 × 3/12 × $4m = $47,500

# 7 FOREIGN CURRENCY FORWARD CONTRACTS

A forward contract enables a company to agree an exchange rate today (the forward rate) for delivery of the currency at an agreed date in the future. This can be used by exporters and importers to fix the sterling value of overseas receipts and payments. It can also be used to fix the sterling value of dividend payments from overseas investments.

### Problems with forward contracts

The advantage of a forward contract is that it locks into a fixed rate of exchange in the future. There are, however, a number of problems.

- Since the exchange rate is now fixed, the investor is protected against adverse rate movements, but cannot profit from favourable movements.
- The forward contract is for a fixed amount. If the amount of foreign currency received or paid is different to the amount specified in the forward contract, the difference will represent an outstanding exposure.
- It is necessary to estimate the expected future payment or receipt, which may not be easy.
- A series of flows, say dividends from overseas investments, would each need a separate forward contract, increasing costs and administration.
- If the underlying cash flow does not emerge, then the contract becomes an exposure in itself.

**TASK** **Hedging foreign currency risk using forwards**

Weft is an importer/exporter of textiles and textile machinery. It is based in the UK but trades extensively with countries throughout Europe, particularly in the eurozone. It has a small subsidiary based in Germany. The company is about to invoice a customer in Germany for 750,000 euros, payable in three months' time. Weft's treasurer is considering two methods of hedging the exchange risk. These are:

**Method 1**

Borrow €750,000 for three months, convert the loan into sterling and repay the loan out of eventual receipts. The interest payable on the loan will be purchased in the forward exchange market.

**Method 2**

Enter into a 3-month forward exchange contract with the company's bank to sell €750,000. The spot rate of exchange is £1 = €1.6006

The 3-month forward rate of exchange is £1 = €1.5935

Annual interest rates for three months' borrowing and lending are: euro 3%, sterling 5%.

**Required:**

(a) Which of the two methods is the most financially advantageous for Weft?

(b) What are the other factors to consider before deciding whether to hedge the risk using the foreign currency markets?

## SOLUTION

**Method 1**

Weft borrows euros 750,000

| | EXPORTER | |
|---|---|---|
| | **UK £** | **€** |
| **Now** | **4** pay € loan into UK bank account €744,417/1.6006 = £465,066 | **3** take out € loan €750,000/1.0075 = €744.417 |
| | 5% × 3/12 = 1.25% (ie 1.0125) | 3% × 3/12 = 0.75% (ie 1.0075) |
| **Three months** | **5** to compare to a forward £465,066 × 1.0125 = £470,900 | **1** receive € from export €750,000<br>**2** pay off € loan with export revenue (€750,000) |

Using the money market hedge, Weft will receive £470,900.

**Method 2**

The exchange rate is fixed in advance at €1.5935 by the forward contract. Cash received in three months is converted to produce €750,000/1.5935 = £470,662.

**Conclusion**

On the basis of the above calculations, Method 1 gives a slightly higher receipt. However, the difference is quite small, and banker's commission has been excluded from the calculation.

(b) Factors to consider before deciding whether to hedge foreign exchange risk using the foreign currency markets

**Defensive strategy**

The company should have a clear strategy concerning how much foreign exchange risk it is prepared to bear. A highly risk-averse or 'defensive' strategy of hedging all transactions can be expensive in terms of commission costs, but recognises that exchange rates are unpredictable, can be volatile and so can cause severe losses unless the risk is hedged.

**Predictive strategy**

An alternative 'predictive' strategy recognises that if all transaction exposures are hedged, the chance of making gains from favourable exchange rate movements is lost. It might be possible to predict the future movement in an exchange rate with some confidence. The company could therefore attempt to forecast foreign exchange movements and only hedge those transactions where losses from currency exposures are predicted. For example, if inflation is high in a particular country, its currency will probably depreciate, so that there is little to be gained by hedging future payments in that currency. However, future receipts in a weak currency would be hedged, to provide protection against the anticipated currency loss.

A predictive strategy can be a risky strategy. If exchange rate movements were certain, speculators would almost certainly force an immediate fall in the exchange rate. However, some corporate treasurers argue that, if predictions are made sensibly, a predictive strategy for hedging should lead to higher profits within acceptable risk limits than a risk-averse strategy of hedging everything. Fewer hedging transactions will also mean lower commission costs payable to the bank. The risk remains, though, that a single large uncovered transaction could cause severe problems if the currency moves in the opposite direction to that predicted.

**Maximum limit**

A sensible strategy for a company could be to set a maximum limit, in money terms, for a foreign currency exposure. Exposures above this amount should be hedged, but below this limit a predictive approach should be taken or, possibly, all amounts could be left unhedged.

Before using any technique to hedge foreign currency transactions, receipts and payments in the same currency at the same date should be offset. For example, if the company is expecting to receive €750,000 on 31 March and to pay €600,000 at about the same time, only the net receipt of €150,000 needs to be considered as a currency exposure.

Matching can be applied to receipts and payments which do not take place on exactly the same day by simply hedging the period and amount of the difference between the receipt and payment, or even by using a currency bank account. A company that has many receipts and payments in a single currency such as the euro should consider matching assets with liabilities in the same currency.

# 8 Foreign Currency Futures

Futures are standardised contracts that are traded on an organised exchange such as the Chicago Mercantile Exchange or London International Financial Futures and Options Exchange (LIFFE). They fix the exchange rate for a set amount of currency for a specified time period.

When entering into a foreign exchange futures contract, no one is actually buying or selling anything – the participants are agreeing to buy or sell currencies on pre-agreed terms at a specified future date if the contract is allowed to reach maturity, which it rarely does. Futures are a derivative (their value derives from movements in the spot rate).

Futures are generally more liquid and have less credit risk than forward contracts as organised exchanges have clearing houses that guarantee that all traders in the futures market will honour their obligations.

Futures contracts are assumed to mature at the end of either March, June, September or December. One of their limitations is that currencies can only be bought or sold on exchanges for US dollars.

A futures market hedge attempts to achieve the same result as a forward contract, that is to fix the exchange rate in advance for a future foreign currency payment or receipt. Forward contracts are agreed 'over the counter' between a bank and its customer. Futures contracts are standardised and traded on futures exchanges. This results in the following advantages and disadvantages.

## Advantages of currency futures

(a) Transaction costs should be lower than for forward contracts.

(b) The exact date of receipt or payment of the currency does not have to be known, because the futures contract does not have to be closed out until the actual cash receipt or payment is made. In other words, the futures hedge gives the equivalent of an 'option forward' contract, limited only by the expiry date of the contract.

(c) Because future contracts are traded on exchange regulated markets, counterparty risk should be reduced and buying and selling contracts should be easy.

### Disadvantages of currency futures

(a) The contracts cannot be tailored to the user's exact requirements.

(b) Hedge inefficiencies are caused by having to deal in a whole number of contracts and by basis risk.

(c) Only a limited number of currencies are the subject of futures contracts (although the number of currencies is growing, especially with the rapid development of Asian economies).

(d) The procedure for converting between two currencies neither of which is the US dollar is twice as complex for futures as for a forward contract.

(e) Using the market will involve various costs, including brokers' fees.

In general, the disadvantages of futures mean that the market is much smaller than the currency forward market.

## 9 Interest Rate Futures

Interest rate futures are a similar method of hedging to FRAs, except that the terms, amounts and periods are standardised. For example, a company can contract to buy (or sell) $100,000 of a notional 30-year bond bearing an 8% coupon in, say, six months' time at an agreed price. The basic principles behind such a decision are:

(a) The futures price is likely to vary with changes in interest rates. This acts as a hedge against adverse interest rate movements.

(b) The outlay to buy futures is much less than for buying the financial instrument itself.

## 10 Currency Options

A forward exchange contract is an agreement to buy or sell a given quantity of foreign exchange, which must be carried out because it is a binding contract. However, some exporters might be uncertain about the amount of currency they will earn in several months' time.

An alternative method of obtaining foreign exchange cover, which overcomes much of this problem, is the currency option. A currency option does not have to be exercised. Instead, when the date for exercising the option arrives, the importer or exporter can either exercise the option or let the option lapse.

The exercise price for the option may be the same as the current spot rate, or it may be more favourable or less favourable to the option holder than the current spot rate.

As with other types of option, buying a currency option involves paying a premium, which is the most the buyer of the option can lose. The level of option premiums depends on the following factors:

- The exercise price
- The maturity of the option
- The volatility of exchange and interest rates
- Interest rate differentials, affecting how much banks charge

**EXAMPLE**

It is now 1st March. Robin Inc anticipates that it may receive €6m from the sale of a European investment in June. It wishes to hedge this potential receipt using options. The current spot rate is $1 = €0.7106. June options with a value of €6m and an exercise price of €0.7200 can be purchased for a premium of $150,000.

**Required**

What will the outcome of the hedge be in each of the following scenarios?

- The spot exchange rate in June is €0.6500
- The spot exchange rate in June is €0.7500
- The sale of the investment does not take place

**SOLUTION**

(a) The spot rate is better than the option rate therefore the spot rate is used. This will give a value of $9,230769 or $9,080,769 after the premium (which is paid up front).

(b) The option rate is better than the spot rate therefore the option will be exercised. This will give a value of $8,333,333 (or $8,183,333 after the premium).

(c) If the sale of the investment is abandoned then the option is no longer necessary. It will be abandoned (as in (a) above). There is no point in exercising the option as it would cost $8,443,568 to purchase the Euros but Robin Inc would only receive $8,333,333 at the option price (before taking the premium into account). The cost to the company of abandoning the option will be the premium of $150,000.

## Options in practice

In corporate finance, we are concerned with hedgers who purchase options in order to reduce risk. So, given that we are normally going to purchase options, should we purchase puts or calls? Consider each of the following scenarios:

(a) **A US company receiving £ in the future.** The US company will wish to sell £ in the future, and can therefore hedge by purchasing £ put options (ie options to sell £).

(b) **A US company paying £ in the future.** The US company wishes to buy £ in the future and can therefore hedge by purchasing £ call options (ie options to buy £).

(c) **A UK company receiving $ in the future.** The UK company wishes to sell $ in the future and cannot hedge by purchasing $ put options as they don't exist. The company therefore has to purchase £ call options.

(d) **A UK company paying $ in the future.** The UK company wishes to buy $ in the future and cannot hedge by purchasing $ call options as they don't exist. The company therefore has to purchase £ put options.

# 11 INTEREST RATE OPTIONS

An interest rate option grants the buyer of the option the right, but not the obligation, to deal at an agreed interest rate (strike rate) at a future maturity date. On the date of expiry of the option, the buyer must decide whether or not to exercise the right.

Clearly the buyer of an option to borrow will not wish to exercise it if the market interest rate is now below that specified in the option agreement. Conversely an option to lend will not be worth exercising if market rates have risen above the rate specified in the option by the time the option has expired.

Tailor-made 'over the counter' interest rate options can be purchased from major banks, with specific values, periods of maturity, denominated currencies and rates of agreed interest. The cost of the option is the 'premium'. Interest rate options offer more flexibility – and are more expensive – than FRAs.

Exchange traded options are also available. These have standardised amounts and standard periods.

### Advantages of interest rate options

(a) Upside risk – the company has the choice not to exercise the option and will therefore be able to take advantage of falling interest rates.

(b) Over the counter options – these are tailored to the specific needs of the company and are therefore more flexible than exchange traded options for a more exact hedge.

(c) Exchange traded options are useful for uncertain transactions – for example you may be unsure if a loan will actually be needed. If it becomes evident that the option is not required it can be sold.

### Disadvantages of interest rate options

(a) Premium – the premium cost may be relatively expensive compared with the costs of other hedging instruments. It will be payable whatever the movement in interest rates and whether or not the option is exercised.

(b) Collar – if the company has a collar, this will limit its ability to take advantage of lower interest rates to the lower limit set by the cap.

(c) Maturity – the maturity of exchange traded options may be limited to one year.

(d) Traded options – if the company purchased exchange traded options then the large fixed amounts of the available contracts may not match the amount to be hedged. The large amounts of the contracts will also prohibit organisations with smaller amounts to be hedged from using them.

## 12 Equity Derivatives

We have already discussed risk in the context of shares in earlier chapters. Remember that risk is the variability in future returns as measured by the standard deviation ($\sigma$). What causes returns to vary? What risk is there in holding a share? As a reminder, we need to break risk into two components. The total risk of a security ($\sigma i$) is made up of unsystematic risk ($\sigma u$) and systematic risk ($\sigma s$).

Unsystematic risk, or **specific risk** as it is also called, relates to risk factors specific to a particular company. These would be factors such as management, products, location, etc. These factors will influence a company's returns to some extent. These specific risk factors can be eliminated by holding a diversified portfolio. This is a concept known as diversification that we do not need to discuss in any more detail here.

Having eliminated unsystematic (specific) risk of investments through holding a diversified portfolio, for example a portfolio of the FTSE 100 Index stocks, we are still left with the systematic risk of the shares in the portfolio. It is clear that if an investor holds the market portfolio, ie FTSE 100 stocks, there is still variability in returns, as evidenced by the movement in the FTSE 100 Index from one day to the next. This variability, or risk, is a function of the market (rather than being a function of things specific to a particular company). It cannot be eliminated by diversification. It is this risk that is eliminated by equities hedging with a suitable derivative, such as the FTSE 100 Index future. What we are saying is that the risk or variability associated with the market (FTSE 100 Index) is eliminated by using a future based on the price movement, or variability, of that index.

In the UK, to achieve an equities hedge with index futures the fund manager will look to sell FTSE Futures. If the equity market were to fall, the short futures position should generate profits to offset the loss on the equity position.

If we wish to hedge a portfolio that does not match the market we need to consider the beta of the portfolio. The beta of a stock or portfolio is defined as the ratio of the expected change in the price of the stock/portfolio to changes in the market itself. It is obtained by regressing stock prices against the overall market over time. A beta of 1.2, for example suggests, at least historically, that the stock has moved at 1.2 times the rate of the market. If the market were to move by 10%, the stock would be expected to move by 10% × 1.2 or 12%.

## Chapter Roundup

**Module 3, Chapter 18: Derivatives**

The syllabus requires a 'general' level of knowledge for these topics, meaning that the questions you will face in this area will be 'straightforward' as opposed to 'complex'.

Derivatives are used in corporate finance to manage risk.

Tools to manage **interest rate risk**:

- Interest rate swaps
- FRAs
- Interest rate futures
- Interest rate options

Tools to manage **foreign currency risk**:

- Currency swaps
- Foreign currency forwards
- Foreign currency futures
- Foreign currency options

You may face numerical examples testing your understanding of how these instruments work or a discursive question asking you to recommend which risk management tools are appropriate.

MODULE 4

# Mergers, acquisitions and disposals

# SYLLABUS – MERGERS, ACQUISITIONS AND DISPOSALS

## Aim

Candidates will be able to assess how, and whether, value is created by domestic and international mergers, acquisitions and disposals, including the effect on a group's financial statements (including IBO's, management buy-outs and other variants).

Mergers, Acquisitions and Disposals questions will make up approximately 20% of the total marks in the examination.

## Syllabus and BPP Study Text coverage

In the assessment, candidates may be required to

| SYLLABUS | BPP STUDY TEXT |
|---|---|
| **a. Evaluate or construct commercial and financial rationale for acquisitions and disposals in a given scenario** | Chapters 19 & 21 |
| **b. Explain in detail how the following disposal processes are carried out and apply this knowledge to a given scenario**<br>• **The sale process (initiation only)**<br>– **Traditional and alternative disposal methods**<br>– **Identifying and short-listing purchasers**<br>– **Approaching potential purchasers**<br>• **The auction process**<br>– **No-names teasers**<br>– **Confidentiality undertakings**<br>– **The information memorandum**<br>– **Inviting and evaluating offers** | Chapter 21 |
| **c. Explain in detail how the following stages in an acquisition are carried out and apply this knowledge to a given scenario:**<br>• **Identifying potential acquisition targets**<br>• **Initial evaluation of targets**<br>• **Approaching the target: considerations and best practice** | Chapter 19 |

| SYLLABUS | BPP STUDY TEXT |
|---|---|
| **d. Explain in detail the following aspects of mergers, acquisitions and disposals and apply this knowledge to a given scenario:** | Chapter 22 |
| • **Public deals**<br>– **Transaction process overview**<br>– **Outline of regulatory issues**<br>– **Defence and bid strategies** | |
| • **Due diligence**<br>– **Scope of due diligence**<br>– **Vendor due diligence and data rooms**<br>– **Purchaser due diligence** | Chapter 19 |
| • **Legal documentation**<br>– **Heads of agreement**<br>– **Break clauses and exclusivity agreements**<br>– **Sale and purchase agreement**<br>– **Warranties, indemnities, representations and disclosures**<br>– **Conditions precedent and subsequent**<br>– **Exchange and completion**<br>– **The completion meeting and problem areas**<br>– **'Locked box' mechanisms versus completion accounts**<br>– **Other post completion mechanisms** | Chapter 19 |
| • **Deal structuring**<br>– **Buying and selling assets versus shares**<br>– **Cash, loan stock, shares and alternatives as consideration**<br>– **Earn-outs, options and deferred consideration**<br>– **Tax considerations for the vendor and purchaser**<br>– **Hedging foreign exchange rate risk**<br>– **Hedging interest rate risk** | Chapter 20 |

# MAKING ACQUISITIONS

chapter 19

Contents


| | | |
|---|---|---|
| 1 | Introduction | 426 |
| 2 | Synergies | 426 |
| 3 | Quantifying Synergies | 427 |
| 4 | Motivations for Making Acquisitions | 428 |
| 5 | Why do Acquisitions Fail? | 430 |
| 6 | Attaining Growth by Alternative Methods | 431 |
| 7 | The Acquisition Process | 432 |

# 1 Introduction

This chapter evaluates commercial and financial justifications for acquisitions, starting with a consideration of synergies. We highlight the main motivations for making acquisitions, including motivations not directly connected to enhancing shareholder value. We look at the main reasons acquisitions fail and how growth might be achieved other than by acquisition. We conclude by considering the acquisition process, focussing in this chapter on the acquisition of unlisted companies.

# 2 Synergies

In considering whether an acquisition is appropriate or not, a company should always address the underlying rationale. The key reason given in empirical studies why most acquisitions fail is that they are not planned properly and insufficient thought is given to the financial benefits likely to arise from the transaction. In all cases, an acquirer should be able to isolate and quantify the anticipated synergies. Value creation only arises from purchasing fairly priced assets, if the assets are more valuable under new management and/or in combination with existing assets. Otherwise the change in control equates to constructing a portfolio, and investors are able to do this themselves.

Synergies are the financial benefits arising as a result of a transaction. They are derived from four sources.

- Cost savings
- Revenue enhancement
- One-off cash inflows
- Real optionality

## Cost savings

Synergistic cost savings can arise in the combined operations from operational reasons, such as eliminating duplication in the merged entity, as well as improvements in the financing structure of the business.

Examples of both types of cost savings are as follows.

- Reducing head-count in administrative functions.
- Economies of scale leading to improved production efficiencies.
- Gaining critical mass and market dominance, giving ability to set prices and negotiate bulk ordering discounts.
- Eliminating excess production capacity.
- Reducing the group's effective tax rate. The value of this synergy is the present value of the tax savings that accrue because of this merger. Tax synergies could be achieved by:
  - Acquiring foreign operations that are taxed at a lower rate than the group's domestic tax rate;
  - Utilising tax losses across the group, although often such losses will be 'ring-fenced' to prevent acquisitions where the sole motivation is to gain tax losses; or
  - A write-up in the valuation of the assets of the firm being taken over, leading to higher tax savings from depreciation in future years.
- Improving free cash flow. The acquisition may have the effect of reducing business seasonality, and thus making cash flow less volatile. This can lead to an improvement in the entity's credit

rating and an overall cheaper cost of debt. It can also increase the overall debt capacity of the enlarged group.

## Revenue enhancement

The merged entity can benefit from the following.

- Cross-selling products to two separate customer bases
- Common distribution channels
- Common advertising, sales promotion and warehousing

Revenue synergies are more difficult to quantify than cost synergies. When companies merge, cost synergies can be relatively easy to assess pre-deal and to implement post-deal. But revenue synergies are more difficult. It is hard to be sure how customers will react to the new entity, whether customers will actually buy the new expanded 'total systems capabilities,' and how much of the company's declared cost savings they will demand in price concessions. Nevertheless, revenue synergies must be identified and delivered. The stock markets will be content with cost synergies for the first year after the deal, but it is really only revenue synergies that can deliver growth.

## One-off cash flows

Non-recurring cash savings arise from the following.

- Disposal of surplus assets
- One-off tax credits
- Disposal of non-core elements of the business

One-off cash flows can also be cash outflows, from business restructuring, redundancies etc. In most transactions, there will be one-off negative cash outflows in the early years.

## Real optionality

Real optionality synergies come from the added flexibility created by the acquisition. Creating the combined entity might establish new opportunities, for example the flexibility to expand into new markets or develop new products. These options would not exist if the businesses were not under common ownership.

# 3 Quantifying Synergies

Once the source of the synergies has been highlighted, it is necessary to estimate the financial effect and also the timing of the cash flows. A discounted cash flow forecast can then be prepared which computes a present value of the synergies. The valuer should also consider the negative impact of the transaction, for example, cash outflows arising due to reorganisation and redundancies or delays in anticipated revenue streams being realised. Quantifying synergies that arise from real optionality requires the use of option valuation models which will include accepting the list of underlying assumptions. The valuation of real options has been covered in the Valuation section.

The present value of the synergies amounts to the financial gains expected from the acquisition and will be an important reference point in structuring the deal – in particular in deciding upon the size of the bid premium and the nature of the consideration available to the target company shareholders. This is considered further in the next chapter.

# 4 Motivations for Making Acquisitions

Possible motivations for acquisitions that could lead to the realisation of synergies, include the following.

## Horizontal integration

Acquire a company in a similar line of business. This may give access to different geographical markets or new market segments. It could also protect market position by helping eliminate the competition.

## Vertical integration

Acquire a supplier or customer. Such integration may enable a company to secure an important source of supply for its business. It may enable a company to obtain supplies more cheaply than its competition. Alternatively, it may enable a company to control its outlets to the final buying public, as with, say, breweries and public houses.

## Purchase an undervalued company

It may be that the target is currently undervalued by the market and that there is an opportunity to buy it cheaply. If the acquirer thinks that this is the case, then he should have very good justification for his view as opposed to the general view of the market.

## Acquire to gain expertise

Acquire technical or other expertise. This could enable a company to seize market share from competitors or retain competitive edge in a sector facing rapid technological change.

## Market penetration

Market penetration means developing new and larger markets for a company's existing products. A market penetration policy will often be used within markets that are becoming more international or globalised. Cross-border mergers and acquisitions can be a means of becoming a major player in such markets.

## Acquire for growth

The quickest way of achieving growth is usually by acquisition. In the short term, it is probably the most expensive of all the options. It does, however, enable a company to acquire new expertise, avoid the need to build a market presence gradually and may result in synergies that give extra benefit to the company as a whole.

## Financial rationale for acquisitions

The acquisition could be made in order to generate potential financial benefits for the purchaser, for example:

- Improved earnings quality (consistency of annual profits) through acquiring a more consistently or counter-seasonally profitable business.
- Greater and cheaper access to financing through acquiring a more cash generative subsidiary.
- Possible use of tax losses of the target company. However, as most tax authorities dislike acquisitions which are entered into simply in order to reduce tax, these tax losses may not be usable post acquisition.
- Enhanced asset backing for the bidder's shares (where the bidder has a lower ratio of net assets to share price than the target company). This would increase the assets available to secure loans, thereby probably improving the terms and amounts of any borrowing.

## Some dubious motivations for acquisitions

### Diversification

Diversification is achieved by acquiring a business that faces different risks from an entity's existing operations. Diversification may bring benefits to a group, for example by reducing the overall beta of the group and thus its equity cost of capital.

However, diversification is not, in itself, necessarily a sufficient reason for an acquisition. If investors are already fully diversified, then the acquiring company is not bringing any benefits to its shareholders by diversifying its business portfolio. The shareholders have already done this for themselves. With the globalisation of capital markets, it is increasingly easy for investors to diversify for themselves rather than relying on companies to do it for them.

In certain circumstances, diversification can be detrimental for a business, where the acquiring company has little or no expertise in the area into which it is diversifying. An inexperienced management may be unable to devote sufficient time or have the inside business knowledge to develop the acquired operations to their best potential.

Inclusion in a larger group that does not understand its business will merely demotivate a new subsidiary's management and probably result in higher administration and other overheads.

### Accounting considerations

It has been possible for acquisitive conglomerates to achieve growth in earnings per share solely by acquiring new companies every year. Since accounting earnings are less important than the fundamentals of the business and its cash flows, acquisitions made on this business cannot be guaranteed to succeed in the long term.

### To avoid takeover

The larger the company, the less likely it is to be the subject of a bid itself. However, recent experience has indicated that size is not necessarily a deterrent to a determined bidder, who may see benefits in acquiring the group and breaking it into smaller segments.

### Empire building

Existing management may feel that the existing group is too small for their talents or the nature of the businesses is not interesting enough for them. In such a situation, rather than returning any surplus cash to shareholders by way of dividend, they may reinvest the cash in new businesses to enable them to demonstrate their management skills fully.

# 5 Why do Acquisitions Fail?

Success of mergers can be judged by reference to the returns generated post-acquisition versus those received by the acquirer's shareholders pre-acquisition. What reasons can be identified where acquisitions fail to generate value?

## Diversification into an area outside company expertise

The acquirer's management do not understand the business they now control and are not able to expand it in order to maximise possible returns.

## Premium priced transaction

The acquirer overpaid for the target. Insufficient synergies are generated by the combined entity post-acquisition to justify the bid premium paid. Experience fails to deliver the financial benefits that were quantified prior to the deal completing.

## Inappropriate financing structure

The capital structure put in place to fund the transaction is inappropriate. In particular, the combined entity post-acquisition generates insufficient cash flow to service the borrowings necessary to fund the transaction. Borrowings as a source of funding are cheaper for the company than equity, however, borrowings require a fixed cash payment relating to the interest charge for servicing the debt and a repayment of the capital amount outstanding. The greater the volatility of the underlying operational cash flows the more problematic it will be to service the debt finance. Riskier acquisitions should always be funded by a higher proportion of equity, which is a more permanent source of finance.

## Ineffective rationalisation

In order to integrate two or more organisations effectively there must be effective integration management and a recognition that successful integration takes time. Where management is poor or there is an attempt to do too much too soon, potentially successful mergers can actually fail. Inflexibility in the application of integration plans drawn up prior to the event can be damaging. Once the merger has taken place, management must be prepared to adapt plans in the light of changed circumstances or inaccurate prior information.

Poor man-management can be detrimental to successful integration. Keeping staff informed is important. Lack of communication of goals and future prospects of employees, and failure to recognise and deal with uncertainties and anxieties can lead to employees being unclear of what is expected of them. Hostilities may develop between the two groups of staff, with an unwillingness to adapt to new procedures and practices.

# 6 Attaining Growth by Alternative Methods

The quickest way of achieving growth is usually by acquisition. Acquisition also entails many risks. For example, the acquirer may pay too high a price, may buy a very poor company with hidden liabilities or may buy into an area that it does not really understand and which becomes a drain on its resources.

Growth can be achieved in different ways. Three alternatives are considered below, namely organic expansion, licensing, and joint ventures.

## Organic expansion

The company may aim to expand its existing operations through increasing production and marketing. If it is aiming to develop a new business area, it may start up from scratch.

The advantage of this approach is that it may be relatively cheap and involve limited investment. However, growth will be achieved more slowly. There is also a risk that a start-up in a new business area may not succeed against established competition.

This method of growing the business is most likely to be appropriate in areas where the company already has substantial expertise and a good reputation. In such circumstances, the risk of failure and the costs of the venture are minimised.

## Licensing

Licensing involves establishing an agreement with another business in return for a royalty stream, for example selling the license to manufacture a product under an owned brand name.

The advantage of this approach is that it reduces cash outlay, for example it avoids the need to fund capital expenditure necessary to establish manufacturing facilities. In return, the licenser receives a steady income stream at a small proportion of the start-up costs. The main disadvantage is that there may be control issues over the quality and speed of production and it will be necessary to estimate and monitor the level of royalties payable.

## Joint ventures

Joint ventures can be particularly appropriate for large projects or where the company has limited expertise in a specific area. Their benefit is that they spread the costs and the risks of the new venture with other parties. In addition, the other investors can bring their own skills and expertise to the deal, reducing overall risk significantly. The other investor may be a local company in an overseas market or a company that is already involved in a particular industry where the expanding company has little expertise at present.

The disadvantage of joint ventures is that gains are limited due to the existence of a partner and a 'partner' may simply be stealing expertise, intending eventually to set up in competition by himself.

Joint ventures can be established using different legal structures.

- The joint venture can be an **incorporated company**, with each party holding 50% of the shares. Such a structure gives limited liability for the shareholders, but the entity will be subject to corporate tax on profits generated.
- An equal **partnership** could be set up between two companies. A partnership is not a separate legal entity like a company and so the structure gives flexibility and confidentiality as to the financial affairs and constitution of the operations. However, the partners face unlimited liability and joint and several liability for the debts of the operations.

- A **limited partnership** has the flexibility benefits of a partnership, but provides protection for the partners in the form of limited liability. However, the limited partners cannot be involved in the day-to-day management of the partnership and at least one partner must be a general partner with unlimited liability.
- A **Limited liability partnership** (LLP) is a more recent possible structure (governed by the Limited Liability Partnership Act 2000). It offers the flexibility of a partnership with limited liability and it is treated as a body corporate with a separate legal identity from its members. With this structure, the two partners are bound like directors running a company and are required to file accounts but the partnership agreement is a private document.

# 7 The Acquisition Process

## Identifying potential acquisition targets

Having decided that the acquisition route is the most effective, a search to highlight suitable companies can commence. It is likely that the directors of the acquisitive company will be able to identify some candidates just by considering their own competitors and through general industry knowledge.

In addition, information about companies can come from a variety of sources, including the following.

- Financial information services and online databases
- Industry surveys that have been published
- Asking individuals with a specialised knowledge of a sector, for example the financial adviser.
- For smaller acquisitions, reference can be made to 'Business for Sale' websites and columns in newspapers

The aim of the initial search is to construct a list of suitable candidates and ensure all relevant possibilities have been considered. The list will then need to be examined to provide a shortlist of companies.

## Analysis of targets

The initial analysis of the companies will be fairly brief and only focus on key details. The objective will be to exclude candidates which for some reason or another (for example poor profitability) are unlikely to be satisfactory targets. As such, only summarised information need be obtained from a financial database about each of the companies being considered.

Once the initial screening process is over, it is likely that two or three companies will stand out as being attractive. These companies can then be analysed in more depth, drawing on more detailed information from a wider range of sources. Areas to cover in the analysis will include the following.

- **Financial Analysis.** A detailed analysis of trading, profitability, financial position and cash flows for the last three to four years. This period should be sufficient to give a trend without getting too historic so as to be irrelevant. The information will be available from the annual reports.
- **Shareholder Information.** Relevant information will include the total number of shareholders, an analysis by proportion of shares held and identification of any key stakes, including directors' holdings. Unusual voting or dividend rights and the existence of 'A' shares or preference shares should be noted.
- **Information on Directors and Advisers.** The backgrounds of directors and advisers should be noted in case this may afford an easy means of contacting the company through a mutual acquaintance.

- **General Information.** Other company information, such as brochures, will help to give an understanding of the company and its business. Premises can be visited discretely and information obtained from casual conversations. A press cuttings search may also yield results.
- **Initial Valuation.** At this stage, an initial valuation of the company can be prepared using a range of different methods covered in the Valuations section. The most important method will usually be cash flow based. Consideration should also be given as to how the acquisition will make commercial sense for both the acquirer and the vendor.

After this process has been completed, the company should have a good idea as to which company it wishes to approach, how much it is prepared to pay and why the acquisition makes sense. It can then consider how it is going to approach the target and, hopefully, negotiate a successful acquisition.

Where the target company is a public listed company, the 'due diligence' carried out on the acquisition will be largely performed at this stage. For an unlisted company, there will be much less information in the public domain, and a further due diligence process must take place following the initial approach.

## The approach

### Regulation

Where the target is a public limited company (plc), the manner and timing of the approach will be governed by the City Code on Takeovers and Mergers. If the acquisition is to fall under the remit of the Code, then the rules and principles set out therein should be adhered to.

Even if the City Code does not specifically apply to the transaction, any advisers should conduct themselves in such a way as to follow best market practice and, hence, should remember the main provisions of the City Code. Failure to do so may cast doubt on their integrity and their authorisation by the FCA.

The details below relate largely to a private company negotiation. Offers for public limited companies are considered in later sections.

## Approaching the company

### Obtain the approval of the target's board

The approach to any company should typically be to the board of directors. In the case of a small limited company, it is likely that the directors are significant shareholders and have great influence over the remaining shareholders. It is, therefore, important to convince them of the merits of the offer. Because of the lack of separation in a limited company between the board and the shareholders, a hostile bid is unlikely to be successful.

### Use of contacts

The initial approach may be made by one of the directors of the acquirer or by a financial adviser, who will probably have to identify the principal in the transaction quickly. It may be the case that a mutual contact between the acquirer and the target can be identified, such as a partner in a firm of solicitors. This will often help to smooth the initial approach.

# Confidentiality

## The confidentiality agreement

If the target company board is not averse to the initial approach, then negotiations may be taken further. At this stage it is likely that a confidentiality agreement will be signed by both parties. The objective of this is to ensure that any information released as part of the negotiations is not misused by the recipient, although other clauses may also be inserted. For example, the acquirer may attempt to obtain sole negotiating rights with the target for a period of time.

## Contents of the confidentiality agreement

Typical points that would be covered in the confidentiality agreement include the following.

- The nature of information that will be disclosed by each party.
- To whom the information will be made available in each company and who will not be permitted to see it.
- A prohibition on photocopies or scans being made of information passed over and an agreement to return all originals should negotiations fail.
- A prohibition on any information made available being used by the recipient for the benefit of their own business, unless they had already received the information from another source.
- Agreement not to disclose the existence of negotiations to other parties and stressing the secrecy of the proceedings.

## Enforceability of the confidentiality agreement

It is clear that it is difficult to enforce many of these points in practice. However, it does provide some form of safeguard and helps to prevent blatant abuse of any information obtained.

# Due diligence

The acquirer's accountants, typically their auditors, will usually conduct a detailed investigation of the company to be acquired. This investigation forms what is known as 'due diligence' and the final conclusions are often prepared by the accountants in the form of a 'Long Form Report'. The report will normally cover the following areas.

- An appraisal of the **corporate structure** of the company, including a review of incorporation documents, minute books, partnership agreements and documents of legal title.
- A detailed examination of the company's **products and industry** and of how the market place has developed and is expected to develop in future. This will include an understanding of the industry size, growth rates and barriers to entry, as well as technological developments that are expected.
- Details of competing firms and an assessment of the acquiree company's **competitive position** in its market place.
- A list of **non-current assets** and any intangible assets such as patents or copyright agreements. Details of premises occupied, leases, etc.
- Details of the company's **operations** in general, including an investigation of the production process, including any capacity constraints and management information systems.

- A detailed examination of **supplier and customer contracts**, including contract terms and provisions such as warranty claims.
- An analysis of the **management team**, how effective they are and whether they are essential to the company's success.
- Details of **other employees**, including identification of any key employees and an organisation chart to understand different roles and responsibilities within the company.
- An **historical financial summary** of income statements, balance sheets and cash flows. The accounting policies, along with any proposed or recent changes to these.
- An examination of the **internal controls** of the company, along with the internal management reporting system.
- An examination of any profit or other **forecasts** made by the company, considering how reasonable they appear to be. Comparison of forecast and actual position and an assessment of budgetary variances.
- An understanding of the **liquidity position** of the business, including working capital management and access to liquidity through committed but undrawn facilities.
- Details of the current **financing structure**, together with the terms and cost of any borrowings.
- An examination of the **tax position**, including review of tax returns and an assessment of future tax liabilities.
- **Other key contracts** of the business, including employment, insurance documentation and relevant government permits. Any franchise or licence agreements must be carefully reviewed.
- Details of any **legal claims** outstanding against the company.
- A consideration of **environmental matters** and the outcome of any environmental audits that have taken place.
- Details of any other **contingent claims** or **capital commitments**.

This information and analysis will be obtained by examining company documents but also via meetings with key parties, especially the acquiree company current auditors. The need to gather information via face-to-face meetings must be counterbalanced with the importance to keep proceedings secretive at this stage.

The conclusions of the due diligence exercise will be presented in a 'long form report'.

Any issues identified in the report will be examined. The conclusions of the due diligence exercise may lead the purchasing company to abandon the acquisition or to a reassessment of initial valuation estimates to reflect the new information.

## Heads of Agreement

If the initial due diligence exercise is satisfactory then further negotiations will take place between the acquirer company and the directors of the company to be acquired. If negotiations are successful, a preliminary agreement containing the terms of the acquisition will be reached. These will be summarised in the form of heads of agreement (also referred to as 'heads of terms' or a 'letter of intent'). This is not usually a legally binding contract but merely formulates the key terms of the agreement. It is a memorandum of understanding between the two parties. It will usually be subject to the final contract being agreed, after a detailed investigation of the acquisition target has been completed.

### Contents of heads of terms

The heads of terms will usually cover the following points.

- The names of the acquirer and the vendor.
- Brief details of what is being sold, specified assets or equity.
- The price to be paid.
- The structure of the consideration, eg deferred consideration.
- Any key warranties made by the vendor. A warranty provides a form of protection for the purchaser of the business. It is a statement by the vendor that a particular statement of affairs is correct. For example, the vendor may warrant that it has good legal title to the assets of the business (and therefore is permitted to sell the assets on to a third party).
- Possible exclusivity provisions (see below)
- Conditions, such as:
  - Completion of satisfactory due diligence
  - Buyer's financing being put in place
  - Tax clearances being obtained
  - No material contracts terminated or adversely changed in the vendor's business.
  - No material adverse change in the vendor's business.

## Break clauses and exclusivity agreements

The heads of terms may include an exclusivity clause or be accompanied by a separate exclusivity agreement. This will seek to prevent the seller from negotiating with, or soliciting offers from, other parties for a fixed period of time. An exclusivity agreement thereby provides the prospective buyer with a time-frame in which to complete its due diligence, negotiate and hopefully complete the proposed transaction, without competition from other parties.

Exclusivity agreements are sometimes accompanied by a clause relating to break fees, whereby financial compensation is payable to the potential purchaser by the vendor if the period of exclusivity is not upheld by the vendor ie if discussions are entered into with another potential purchaser or the transaction is terminated for some reason. In the UK, the use of break clauses is effectively prohibited by The Takeover Code for the purchase of public limited companies as they are viewed as not being in the interest of offeree company shareholders.

The target company gets little in return for its grant of exclusivity, other than the (legally unbinding) comfort of the Heads of Agreement document.

## The sale and purchase agreement

### Contents

The final contract of sale is termed the 'sale and purchase agreement'. It will typically be prepared by the acquirer's solicitors and will be a substantial document, aiming to cover all eventualities. The exact terms may be varied by a process of negotiation between the acquirer and the vendor and their respective legal representatives. The final contract will reflect the negotiating strength of each of the parties and will usually contain the following details.

- What is being sold
- The identities of the vendor and acquirer
- The price to be paid, how it is to be satisfied and the exact structure of the deal

- Any warranties, representations and indemnities made by the vendor
- A disclosures letter
- Any conditions of the contract: both conditions precedent and subsequent
- Termination provisions and any break-up fee if the contract does not complete
- The completion date of the contract

## Warranties and representations

The purpose of the warranties and representations made in the contract is to protect the acquirer. They are statements given by the vendor of the business to the acquirer, which give greater comfort about the business being bought.

Specifically, the **representations** are statements about the business given by the vendor, and the **warranties** are assurances from the vendor that those statements are true and accurate. Representations are wide-ranging and cover the areas focussed on by due diligence. A seller will generally not make representations regarding its future financial performance or its prospects.

Warranties are more specific assurances, for example as to:

- Completeness of liabilities in the accounts
- Good title to assets, particularly properties
- Warranties regarding the tax position of the company

Where a warranty is found to be incorrect, the acquirer may sue the person giving the warranty for compensation if the acquirer has suffered losses as a result of the incorrect statement.

There is no such contractual provision to rely on in the case of breach of representations. Most sale and purchase agreements will expressly exclude liability of the seller for innocent or negligent misrepresentation, provided the exclusions are reasonable in the circumstances. The exception to this is for fraudulent misrepresentation in any contract. A misrepresentation will be classed as fraudulent where it is made knowingly by a seller; it is made without belief in its accuracy; it is made recklessly; and it is made with the intention that the purchaser shall act upon it. Care needs to be taken therefore with what representations are included in the contract.

## Indemnities

**Indemnities** provide for compensating the acquirer for any losses suffered due to specific liabilities mentioned in the sale agreement. This may include, for example, certain contingent liabilities. They will probably include indemnities in respect of tax liabilities.

Indemnities provide a stronger form of protection for an acquirer than warranties. An acquirer need only prove that the state of affairs envisaged by the indemnity has arisen, without the need to quantify that a loss has been suffered as a result.

Usually a minimum and maximum indemnity claim is specified, although there may be specific exclusions to this. There can also be a time limit as to when indemnity claims are valid.

As part of the terms of the contract, the acquirer may require the seller to deposit an agreed amount (can be up to the amount of the maximum indemnity claim) into an escrow account to back up any indemnification claims.

## Disclosures

The **disclosure letter** is needed to highlight specific exceptions to the warranties. Disclosures are made by the vendor regarding the business to be sold. Where a warranty is found to be incorrect, the acquirer may sue the person giving the warranty if the acquirer has suffered losses as a result of the incorrect statement. It is not possible for the acquirer to seek legal redress concerning items included in the disclosure letter.

## Conditions precedent and subsequent

**Conditions Precedent** must be met prior to completion of the transaction. Failure by one party to complete a condition, allows the other party to walk away from the transaction. Usually, the condition will relate to a specific matter like the signature of financing documentation, the receipt of regulatory clearances or completion accounts. Once a condition is satisfied, then in order to confirm the transaction and make sure that there is a binding agreement between the parties, the matter needs to be documented within the relevant time period.

**Conditions Subsequent** do not need to be fulfilled for the transaction to become binding. They do however allow the acquirer to terminate the agreement if the conditions are not fulfilled within a specified time limit.

## Locked box mechanism versus completion accounts

A locked box is a mechanism whereby the acquisition price of a business is agreed between the acquirer and vendor upfront, before completion, and 'locked' at a point in time. Usually an acquirer makes an offer on 'a debt free, cash free' basis and leaves the final determination of purchase price until completion accounts are available, and the cash, borrowings and working capital position of the business at the completion date is finalised. With a locked box mechanism, the final price is based on a historic balance sheet, where the amounts of cash, borrowings and working capital are known with certainty. There is thus an agreed up-front enterprise value for the business being sold. The relevant date used is often the date of the most recently available management accounts.

A locked box price works in favour of the vendor of the business. The acquirer has the risks and rewards from the locked date. The requirement is removed for the seller to prepare and negotiate completion accounts. It also gives a certain transaction value upfront, thereby saving time and cost associated with final price negotiations once completion accounts come through.

A locked box structure will be less suitable for a business with very volatile funding requirements, especially if working capital requirements cannot be estimated with certainty.

The locked box mechanism was developed when M&A markets were very active and there were plentiful buyers and not enough good businesses to buy. Potential acquirers were prepared to accept locked box structures, and the additional risk this entailed, in order to get the deal done. It has been a popular structure with private equity vendors who wish to maintain control over the pricing process.

As part of the locked box structure, the acquirer will negotiate protections in the sale and purchase agreement to prevent vendors extracting value from the business between the locked box date and the completion date when they relinquish control of the business. Such extractions of value could include the payment of dividends, returns of capital paid to the seller, capital expenditure commitments and excessive expenses incurred by the vendor relating to the transaction and any other payments other than necessary for the normal course of business. Indemnities may be put in place to protect the acquirer, covering any non-permitted extractions of value by the vendor.

## CHAPTER ROUNDUP

**Module 4, Chapter 19: Making Acquisitions**

Synergies are the financial benefits arising as a result of a transaction. They are derived from four sources.

- Cost savings
- Revenue enhancement
- One-off cash inflows
- Real optionality

You should be able to list examples of each and be able to discuss appropriate valuation methods.

This chapter has considered motives for making acquisitions and how these might tie into a value-enhancing strategy. We have also looked at alternative methods to achieve growth.

As a corporate financier, you will be expected to 'run' the acquisition process. This chapter has considered the main stages in private company acquisitions:

- Identifying potential acquisition targets
- Initial evaluation of targets
- Approaching the target: considerations and best practice
- Due diligence
- Legal documentation
  - Heads of agreement
  - Break clauses and exclusivity agreements
  - Sale and purchase agreement
  - Warranties, indemnities, representations and disclosures
  - Conditions precedent and subsequent
  - Exchange and completion
  - The completion meeting and problem areas
  - 'Locked box' mechanisms versus completion accounts

# DEAL STRUCTURING

chapter 20

Contents


| | | |
|---|---|---|
| 1 | Introduction | 442 |
| 2 | Structuring the Deal | 442 |
| 3 | Offer Consideration | 443 |
| 4 | Earn Outs and Deferred Consideration | 444 |
| 5 | Analysing Deal Effects | 445 |
| 6 | Sharing of Merger Gains | 449 |
| 7 | Calculating Control Premia | 450 |

# 1 Introduction

This section considers the relative merits of a share purchase versus structuring a deal as the purchase of assets. We also examine different forms of transaction consideration and why each might be appropriate to use. We finish off looking at deal effects and how the rationale for a transaction can be substantiated by financial analysis.

# 2 Structuring the Deal

## Shares versus assets purchases

When buying a business in a private deal, it is possible to acquire either the shares of the company that is conducting the business or to buy the business and the related assets from the company. The factors to consider in deciding which route to follow include the following.

### Share deal

- The transaction will put the cash directly in the hands of the vendor, whereas selling assets would keep the cash in the company selling the assets. Taking the cash out of the company will involve additional tax charges. Receiving cash directly will only incur capital gains tax liabilities. If the consideration being paid is not cash, but shares or loan stock, then any capital gains tax liability may be deferred.
- The share deal will preserve tax losses in the business being sold, if applicable. Selling the business would mean that the acquirer would probably be unable to use these losses.
- Transferring shares may make it easier to keep the business of the target company intact, eg preserving long-term contracts with key customers.
- Given the business is transferring intact, the sale and purchase agreement will include detailed warranties and indemnities regarding the nature of the business to be sold.
- Transferring shares will avoid potential problems with loss and clawback of capital allowances that may occur with an asset sale.

### Assets purchase

- The acquirer can pick and choose which business assets he wishes to buy. The exception to this is the target company's staff, who will transfer automatically in the UK under 'TUPE' employment regulation – Transfer of Undertakings (Protection of Employment) Regulations 2006.
- The target company's liabilities are not transferred without explicit agreement.
- The business can be put into a 'clean' company and, hence, there is no risk of unpleasant surprises or liabilities in the future. This avoids the need for many of the detailed warranties and indemnities in the sale agreement.
- If the acquirer has previously disposed of certain business assets, such as land and buildings or plant and machinery, then it may be able to claim roll-over relief when it replaces these by purchasing the assets of the target company.
- Purchase of assets will result in different capital allowances being received when compared to the purchase of shares in the company, which may be disadvantageous.
- Purchase of assets will create goodwill in the acquirer's accounts, whereas this may be avoided in the case of a shares purchase.

- The target company will remain in existence, unless liquidated.
- The vendor effectively is subject to two tax charges: there will be an immediate gain on the asset sale arising in the target company, amounting to the difference between the sales price and the book value of the assets. A subsequent gain will arise if the proceeds are distributed to shareholders in the form of a dividend or a liquidation distribution.

# 3 Offer Consideration

We are concerned here with how the offer is to be financed. This will usually be a choice between cash or equity.

## Cash bid

- The vendor's connection with the company is severed. He will, therefore, feel no concern as to whether or not the company does well in the future. Cash consideration provides the vendor with an exit route from the business and a way to realise his investment.
- The vendor will have to pay capital gains tax immediately on any gain.
- The acquirer's gearing will increase, if borrowings have been raised to finance the purchase. For a group with little debt, this may have the desirable effect of lowering the overall WACC of the company. For a highly geared company, the increase in financial risk of the entity may have a negative impact on credit rating and therefore overall cost of capital. In the latter scenario, it may be appropriate to raise the cash via a rights issue, termed a 'cash underpinning'.
- The earnings of the acquiring group will be boosted by the profits of the target but reduced by the additional interest expense on increased borrowings or the lower interest income due to reduced cash balances. The net effect is likely to be an increase in earnings per share, but the quality of the earnings will have fallen as a result of the increased gearing.
- All the gains of the acquisition after allowing for the cost of the deal will go to existing shareholders of the acquirer. Their interest in the group has not been diluted through the introduction of additional shareholders.

## Shares bid

- The fortunes of the vendor are tied in with the acquirer. It is, therefore, in his interests to ensure that the company does well in the future. It provides a way for the acquirer to incentivise the existing owners to maximise value in the post-acquisition period. Typically, the vendor of a private company will not be allowed to sell the shares for several years via a 'lock-in' arrangement.
- The vendor will be able to roll over any capital gains tax liability until the shares are disposed of. This will assist in tax planning.
- The gearing of the acquirer will reduce as a result of issuing shares, although this does depend on the level of gearing in the acquired company.
- The earnings of the acquirer will be boosted by the profits of the acquired company, but these will be spread over more shares, with the effect on earnings per share being uncertain. Generally, if a company acquires another company on a P/E ratio lower than its own, then the earnings per share subsequent to the acquisition should improve.
- It may be possible to use merger accounting in the group accounts as an alternative to acquisition accounting. This will give the acquirer more flexibility in how it prepares its accounts. Merger accounting is only available for share-for-share deals.

- The gains arising from the acquisition will have to be shared with the new shareholders. The interests of the existing shareholders will have been diluted by the issue of new shares to outsiders.
- The total dividend will need to be increased in order to maintain dividend per share after the acquisition.

### Loan stock

Instead of borrowing from outside providers of finance to fund a cash bid, the acquirer may issue loan stock to the vendor. Loan stock is an 'IOU' from the acquirer to the target company shareholders. Loan stock enables the vendor to defer any capital gains tax liability until the loan stock is disposed of. It may also reduce the effective price of the acquisition if the coupon on the loan stock is below a market rate of interest.

## 4 Earn Outs and Deferred Consideration

### Advantages of earn outs

It is possible for a transaction to be structures so that the final consideration for a deal is paid several years after completion and is linked to the profit performance of the acquired company. This is termed as 'contingent' consideration or using an 'earn out'. The obvious advantage for the acquirer is that it ensures that a full price will only be paid if certain financial targets are met in the post-acquisition period. It will also often mean that the vendor will stay on to manage the acquired company for several years. This will ensure continuity of management, enable a smooth transition to be made in terms of management over the period of the earn out and keep in the company an individual who may well be instrumental in the company's past success.

Deals can also be structured using deferred consideration where there is certainty at the outset as to the total consideration to be paid; however this is paid in instalments, thus helping the cash flow of the bidding company.

### Problems of earn outs

- Calculation of profits for the purpose of working out the deferred consideration will need to be exactly defined. The temptation is for both sides to adjust the profits to suit themselves. The vendor, who is still the key director of the acquired company, may argue for reduced provisions for doubtful debtors, etc, whereas the acquirer may seek to impose excessive management charges against the company.
- The level of integration of the subsidiary with the group will need to be established. The group will want to integrate it as fully as possible in order to realise the anticipated benefits of the acquisition. However, it will need to be kept separate for the purposes of profit calculations. If central services are provided by the group, then this will reduce the costs in the subsidiary but a management charge will be made. Such charges can be difficult to negotiate and be seen as fair.
- The acquiring company's directors will seek to control the direction in which the subsidiary is heading, for the benefit of the overall group. This may conflict with the desire of the vendor to maximise profits over the period of the earn-out. It will be difficult to ensure goal congruence between the vendor and the acquirer.
- The vendor will find it difficult to operate within the constraints of a large organisation and with budgets imposed from outside. His or her ability to run a successful business may have stemmed

from the ability to make decisions quickly without reference to any outsiders. Furthermore, the vendor's status in the company will have changed and this may be hard for him or her to take.

- Earn outs can work against the long-term good of the business. The managers may be incentivised to focus too much on short-term profit targets and avoid making difficult decisions that have a detrimental impact on profit today but benefit the business as a whole in the long term. For example, if targets are based on a measure of free cash flow, capital expenditure could be put off until after the earn-out period is completed.

# 5 Analysing Deal Effects

When commentators are appraising public company acquisitions, they will look to financial analysis to substantiate the commercial justification for the transaction. Pro-forma numbers are helpful here. Pro-forma numbers calculate key ratios to provide a comparison between a company on a stand-alone basis and as part of a pro-forma merged entity. This makes a direct comparison possible – is there a direct financial justification for the deal? We often use the latest historical financial results for the calculation, to develop some 'what if?' scenarios for consideration. The most common deal effects that are computed are:

- Pro-forma earnings per share
- Pro-forma gearing
- Pro-forma statement of net assets

Other factors that commentators consider are the size of any bid premium, the P/E ratio post-acquisition and dividend policy.

## Calculating pro-forma earnings per share

Commentators will want to know if a transaction is earnings 'enhancing' or 'accretive' (EPS is improved) or if it is earnings 'dilutive' (EPS worsens). For an acquisition, we can make this conclusion by comparing the earnings per share of the acquirer on a standalone basis, versus the pro-forma earnings per share of the enlarged entity.

- Where the earnings per share of the acquirer < the earnings per share of the acquirer and target on a pro-forma basis, the transaction is said to be **earnings enhancing**
- Where the earnings per share of the acquirer > the earnings per share of the acquirer and target on a pro-forma basis, the transaction is said to be **earnings dilutive**

When calculating the pro-forma earnings per share of the combined entity, bear in mind the following considerations:

- The post-tax impact of any **synergies** should be included. For the EPS calculation, we are looking at the impact on earnings and thus synergies need to be incorporated on an accruals basis. Remember that synergies can be negative, as well as positive.
- The post-tax impact of the **financing structure on earnings** needs consideration. For example, the interest on new borrowings should be factored in, as well as the interest receivable lost on cash consideration paid out as part of the transaction terms.
- The pro-forma number of **ordinary shares** must take account of the financing structure ie any new shares to be issued as offer consideration must be included.

In the current low interest rate climate, potential acquirers have found that many acquisitions are earnings enhancing, given the poor return that businesses earn on their retained cash.

For a transaction where the consideration is new acquirer shares, if the target company has a higher P/E ratio than the acquirer, then the transaction will be earnings dilutive. This is because the acquirer has to pay more for each pound of target company earnings than the market currently rates its own earnings. In terms of the calculation, the pro-forma number of shares (denominator) will go up by more than the pro-forma earnings (numerator), causing EPS to decline.

## Example

Giant Inc takes over Tiddler Co by offering two shares in Giant for one share in Tiddler. Details about each company are as follows.

| | **Giant Inc** | **Tiddler Co** |
|---|---|---|
| Number of shares | 2,800,000 | 100,000 |
| Market value per share | $4 | – |
| Annual earnings | $560,000 | $50,000 |
| EPS | 20p | 50p |
| P/E ratio | 20 | |

By offering two shares in Giant worth $4 each for one share in Tiddler, the valuation placed on each Tiddler share is $8, and with Tiddler's EPS of 50c, this implies that Tiddler would be acquired on a P/E ratio of 16. This is lower than the P/E ratio of Giant, which is 20.

If the acquisition produces no synergy, and there is no growth in the earnings of either Giant or its new subsidiary Tiddler, then the EPS of Giant would still be higher than before, because Tiddler was bought on a lower P/E ratio. The combined group's results would be as follows.

| | **Giant group** |
|---|---|
| Number of shares (2,800,000 + 200,000) | 3,000,000 |
| Annual earnings (560,000 + 50,000) | 610,000 |
| EPS | 20.33c |

If the P/E ratio is still 20, the market value per share would be $4.07 (20.33 × 20), which is 7c more than the pre-takeover price.

The process of buying a company with a higher P/E ratio in order to boost your own EPS is known as bootstrapping. Whether the stock market is fooled by this process is debatable. The P/E ratio is likely to fall after the takeover in the absence of synergistic or other gains.

You might think that dilution of earnings must be avoided at all costs. However, there are three cases where a dilution of earnings might be accepted on an acquisition if there were other advantages to be gained.

(a) Earnings growth may hide the dilution in EPS.

(b) A company might be willing to accept earnings dilution if the quality of the acquired company's earnings is superior to that of the acquiring company.

(c) A trading company with high earnings, but with few assets, may want to increase its assets base by acquiring a company which is strong in assets but weak in earnings so that assets and earnings get more into line with each other. In this case, dilution in earnings is compensated for by an increase in net asset backing.

## Calculating pro-forma gearing

Pro-forma gearing ratios assess the change in financial risk as a result of the transaction. A comparison is made between the acquirer's existing gearing ratio, calculated as interest-bearing borrowings divided by shareholders' funds and the pro-forma gearing ratio, which considers the borrowings and shareholders' funds of the enlarged group. If the gearing ratio has increased, the acquirer's shareholders will need to be convinced that forecast cash flows for the combined entity are sufficient to service the levels of borrowings. They will be mindful of the existing operating leverage of the business (how volatile are earnings?) and the current asset-backing. Combining different earnings streams can reduce volatility and therefore the risk appetite of shareholders for debt may increase.

The following considerations impact the calculation:

- The pro-forma debt number should be based on the borrowings of the enlarged entity, namely the acquirer borrowings and any borrowings necessary to fund the transaction.
- The pro-forma equity number should include any new equity to be issued. In addition, shareholders' funds should be adjusted to include accrued profits in retained earnings, between the balance sheet date and the date of the transaction.
- Gearing ratios can be distorted by accounting policy choices and therefore the ratios should be computed eliminating accounting policy differences between the two companies.

## Calculating pro-forma net assets per share

Pro-forma net assets per share gives an idea of the relative size of the enlarged entity, versus the acquirer. It also provides the basis for other calculations, for example, pro-forma gearing and pro-forma return on equity.

The following considerations are relevant:

- The net assets of the two companies need to be added together, taking account of fair value adjustments and aligning accounting policies.
- The net assets need to be adjusted for profit accruals between the last balance sheet date and the proposed transaction date.
- Any goodwill arising on the acquisition should be capitalised as an intangible asset, calculated as the difference between the fair value of the acquisition consideration and the fair value to the acquirer of the net assets of the business that is to be acquired.

### TASK Analysing deal effects

Blackbird plc is about to buy Tornado Limited, but is concerned about the effect on its earnings per share of the deal it has negotiated. The facts are as follows:

| **Blackbird** | **Tornado** |
|---|---|
| 3,000,000 shares in issue | 100,000 shares in issue |
| Share price £2/share | Purchase price £1.8m in Blackbird shares |
| Latest reported net income £600,000 | Latest reported net income £120,000 |

Calculate if the deal will be earnings enhancing for Blackbird. Would your conclusion be different if the transaction was financed by cash instead of shares. Make any assumptions you feel are necessary to do the calculation and state any reservations you have with the calculation.

## SOLUTION

**Equity deal**

| | |
|---|---|
| Blackbird's existing earnings per share | = 600,000/3,000,000 = 20 pence |
| Pro-forma earnings per share | = (600,000 + 120,000)/(3,000,000 + 900,000) |
| | = 18.5 pence |

Based on the numbers provided, the transaction will **dilute earnings by 7.5%** for Blackbird. However, the calculations exclude the impact of any synergies which are expected to arise and which should be quantified separately. In addition, the calculation is based on historic earnings. Investors may be less concerned about earnings dilution, if the deal is expected to be earnings enhancing based on forecast earnings.

**Cash deal**

We assume that the deal is financed from retained cash on the balance sheet of Blackbird.

Assumed rate of return on the cash = 3%. Assumed tax rate = 25%

| | |
|---|---|
| Pro-forma earnings per share | = {600,000 + 120,000 – (£1.8m × 0.03 × 0.75)}/ 3m |
| | = (720,000 – 40,500)/3m |
| | = 679,500/3m |
| | = 22.7 pence |

Based on the numbers provided, the transaction will **enhance earnings by 13.5%** for Blackbird. Again, the calculations exclude the impact of any synergies which are expected to arise and which should be quantified separately.

## Other factors

Other factors that commentators consider are the size of any bid premium, the P/E ratio post-acquisition and dividend policy.

### Bid premium

Where the target company is listed, the acquirer will consider the size of the bid premium. The bid premium is calculated as the increase in bid price over the pre-announcement share price of the target company. The share price chosen is the last closing share price prior to a market announcement relating to the transaction. Sometimes, the bid premium is calculated by comparing the bid price to the average of the target's share price over a period time, often six months', in the pre-announcement period. This is to ensure the impact of any market rumours is excluded. Once computed, the bid premium can be compared to comparable market transactions to see if it is reasonable.

### P/E ratio post acquisition

A combine P/E ratio for the combined entity can be calculated by weighting the existing P/E ratios of both companies by their market values. This gives a basic means to assess the market rating of the new entity.

**EXAMPLE**

| | |
|---|---|
| Acquirer market value | = \$2.1bn, with a P/E ratio of 9× |
| Target market value | = \$250m, with a P/E ratio of 6× |
| Combined P/E | = {(2,100 × 9) + (250 × 6)}/ (2,100 + 250) |
| | = 8.7× |

### Dividend policy

Commentators will assess the relative dividend policy by looking at the payout ratios of the two businesses. The payout ratio is calculated as the dividend per share divided by the earnings per share. A view can then be taken on what the likely payout ratio of the combined group will be.

## 6 Sharing of Merger Gains

The financial gains expected to arise from the acquisition will not necessarily all accrue to the acquirer company shareholders. The nature of the acquisition consideration will determine the basis of sharing of merger gains between acquirer and target company shareholders.

This concept is best illustrated by an example.

**EXAMPLE**

Africa plc pays €1.2m cash consideration to purchase Botswana plc. The existing market value of Africa is €10m and existing market value of Botswana is €875,000. Africa has 1 million shares in issue and anticipate that €500,000 merger gains will arise from the transaction.

(i) What is the bid premium?
(ii) What proportion of total acquisition gains go to Africa shareholders?
(iii) What would be the bid premium if the transaction was instead funded by 120,000 new Africa shares?

**SOLUTION**

| | | |
|---|---|---|
| (i) | Bid premium | = acquisition consideration – market value of target (pre-bid) |
| | | = 1,200,000 – 875,000 |
| | | = €325,000 |
| (ii) | Gains to Africa | = 500,000 – 325,000 |
| | | = €175,000 |

(iii) With equity consideration, Botswana shareholders will now participate in the future gains and losses of the combined entity.

| | |
|---|---|
| New bid premium | = original bid premium + B's share of A's merger gains |
| | = 325,000 + {(120/1,120) × 175,000} |
| | = €343,750 |

# 7 Calculating Control Premia

The per share value for a controlling stake is greater than the per share value for a minority stake. A controlling stake gives the power to decide business strategy; acquisitions and disposals; the level of dividends; who to appoint as a director; how much to pay directors; which business options to pursue. A minority stake gives only the right to receive dividends and capital gains.

When an acquirer agrees the deal consideration, the acquisition price should include a control premium. A control premium is often quantified by looking at comparable transactions. However establishing true comparability is very difficult due to differences in individual circumstances caused by different synergies; strategies etc. In addition, unless the comparable transaction is very recent, comparability is likely to have been eroded by changing market conditions.

The control premium must be justified to acquirer shareholders by a quantification of deal synergies. The bid premium should never exceed the present value of the estimated synergistic benefits that are expected to arise.

In practice, the need to apply a control premium to the valuation that is computed, will depend on the valuation method chosen. The following table provides guidance for you on this matter:

| Valuation Method | Control premium? |
|---|---|
| Discounted cash flow | A DCF calculation values a business on a controlling basis already. There is therefore no need to add on a separate control premium |
| Comparable company multiples | Comparable company multiples assume a minority holding. A separate control premium must be added on to the valuation |
| Comparable transaction multiples | Already includes a control premium |
| Discounted cash flow | A DCF calculation values a business on a controlling basis already. There is therefore no need to add on a separate control premium |

## Marketability discounts

For valuations of unlisted companies, a marketability discount is sometimes applied to the final valuation to reflect the fact that there is not an active market in which to trade the company's shares. It is therefore harder to value the company and the investment is illiquid.

In practice, the marketability of all investments has improved, as markets become more homogenous and liquid. The appropriate size of a marketability discount is thus getting smaller. The size of discount in any scenario (if any) is therefore up for individual negotiation. If appropriate, marketability discounts should be applied to valuations computed by both discounted cash flow and multiples methods.

# CHAPTER ROUNDUP

**Module 4, Chapter 20: Deal Structuring**

Deal structuring is concerned with how a transaction is brought about – by buying the assets or the shares.

Deal structuring also entails deciding on the consideration package, be it cash, loan stock, shares or alternatives. Consideration can be paid using earn-outs, options or deferred arrangements.

You need to discuss suitability of each in a given scenario, including thinking about tax considerations for the vendor and purchaser and hedging foreign exchange and interest rate risk.

The examiner may ask you to consider the 'deal effects' resulting from a transaction. What you are doing here is summarising how a particular transaction might be viewed by shareholders and the market generally. Various headline figures are often used to substantiate the merits of a transaction. You should be prepared to calculate:

- Pro-forma earnings per share
- Pro-forma P/E ratio
- Pro-forma gearing
- Pro-forma dividend; and
- Pro-forma net assets.

All measures provide an indication of financial performance of the enhanced group and can be useful figures to emphasis your conclusions on a deal. Analysis is more meaningful when substantiated by appropriate ratios.

# Disposals and Demergers

chapter 21

Contents


| | | |
|---|---|---|
| 1 | Introduction | 454 |
| 2 | Motives for Disposal | 454 |
| 3 | Preparing the Business for Sale | 455 |
| 4 | The Auction Process | 457 |
| 5 | Demergers | 458 |
| 6 | Methods of Achieving a Demerger | 461 |

# 1 Introduction

The chapter examines the process entailed in conducting disposals and demergers. We examine motives for the transaction and the actual mechanics of undertaking a disposal.

# 2 Motives for Disposal

Having considered the motives for acquisitions, we consider now the motives for disposals. It is important to identify the reasons why a business is for sale. Once these are known, it will be possible to establish whether the business is actually saleable, how much it can be sold for and to whom it can be sold.

## Corporate disposal of a subsidiary or division

Corporate disposals should be determined by strategic considerations. The same strategic ideas that determine whether a company should make acquisitions and in what area to expand, will be relevant for disposals. The only difference is that the company should be disposing of businesses which do not fit into its strategic plans and which are non-core to the group.

Where a company, usually a large group, wishes to dispose of just one part of its business, this can be achieved by a trade sale, spin-off or equity carve-out.

In a **trade sale** or **divestiture**, the disposal will be of the division or subsidiary as a whole to one acquirer. This will be of the assets and liabilities of the division as a going concern.

In a **spin-off**, the shares of the subsidiary company, currently 100% owned by the parent company in the group and therefore not publicly traded, are distributed to the parent company shareholders in the form of the dividend. No money is exchanged; whereas before one firm existed, two exist after the distribution, and they are run as separate businesses with separate management teams. There is now greater transparency to the two different operations and thus the assessment of their value should be easier.

A spin-off can be compared to an **equity carve-out**. Again the business to be sold is organised in a separate legal entity but here shares in this entity are sold to the public, thus generating cash for the parent. With a spin-off, shareholders are initially the same, but with a carve-out new shareholders purchase the equity. The sale doesn't necessarily need to involve 100% of equity; the parent may retain a shareholding in the company.

## Personal disposal of a family business

A disposal of a business by an individual is unlikely to be motivated by strategic considerations of core businesses and growth areas. It is more likely that the entrepreneur has developed the business over a number of years and now wishes to realise his or her capital gain.

The motives of such a vendor may include the desire to:

- Realise a cash sum after building up a business
- Achieve a level of security
- Let the business grow through combining with a larger concern
- Obtain status through becoming a director of a listed company
- Exit the business due to personal reasons, eg retirement
- Get out while the going is good, anticipating the demise of the business

The motives of the vendor will determine what is a satisfactory form and level of consideration. A vendor who wishes to realise a cash sum and believes that the company is not going to prosper is going to want a cash deal and will possibly be prepared to sell for a smaller sum than would otherwise be the case. A vendor who believes that the company will continue to be successful, wants continued involvement in the business and wants to ensure the continued well-being of his staff, will probably only accept a higher price and may be happy to have an earn out deal and shares consideration.

## Private company disposals

Private company disposals are not governed by stock market considerations. Individual sales processes will thus differ significantly and depend upon the individual objectives of the vendors of the businesses and also the specific circumstances of the businesses to be sold.

In all cases, the objective of the vendor should be to keep the sales process as controlled as possible. This will be achieved by a 'rifle shot' approach to targeting a few selected acquirers rather than contacting and meeting with a large number of possibly interested companies. The more companies that are contacted, the greater the time spent in meeting people unnecessarily and the more information that is released to time-wasters who are only interested in seeing the details of the company for sale rather than making a purchase. There are two main methods of negotiation: a controlled auction and a managed bid.

### Controlled auction

A controlled auction, as the name suggests, gives the greatest control to the vendor over the disposal process. This method will usually be applicable where the business for sale is extremely attractive and there are a few, serious potential acquirers.

The potential acquirers are given details of the company for a sale and a deadline by which to reply with an offer, subject to final investigation and the final contract being agreed.

The advantage of this approach is that it keeps the seller in control and forces interested companies to make a serious offer upfront. In order to make it work, the sales document will need to be detailed enough to enable the acquirer to make an offer.

### Managed bid

The managed bid is where the vendor arranges to meet potential acquirers prior to their making an offer for the company. No timescale is fixed and the vendor can deal with several potential acquirers at the same time.

This method of conducting the sale takes control out of the hands of the vendor and puts it into the hands of the acquirer to an extent. It allows acquirers to move further down the line before pulling out of the action. It should only really be used when the company for sale is not sufficiently attractive for a controlled auction to be possible.

# 3 Preparing the Business for Sale

There are a number of important issues to be considered to prepare a subsidiary or group business for sale.

## Interdependence of group companies

One factor to consider is how interdependent individual subsidiaries are in the group. For example, the division to be sold may depend on another group company for provision of a central service. Alternatively, the division may have another subsidiary of the group as a vital customer. Yet again, it may itself be a vital customer of another group customer.

Such situations will need to be recognised before the business is sold. If the business will lack any vital services, then it will have to plug this gap itself prior to the sale or find a buyer to whom such a deficiency is not important. If the business to be sold has an important trading relationship, then a contract may need to be negotiated to protect the relationship for several years.

## Legal structure

A business for sale that is already an autonomous legal entity will not present a problem. However, it is possible that the division to be sold is merged with other divisions within the same subsidiary. In this case a disposal will necessitate a group reorganisation to align the elements of the business that will be divested.

A reorganisation may take many different forms, such as a 'hive down'.

### Before

Y Holdings plc is the holding company of a subsidiary company, Z Ltd. Z Ltd has two separate businesses, one of which is for sale.

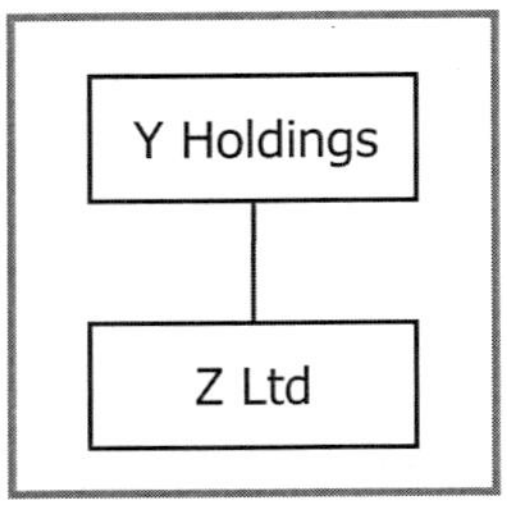


### The reconstruction

Y Holdings plc creates a new subsidiary (Newco) and transfers the business for sale into Newco.

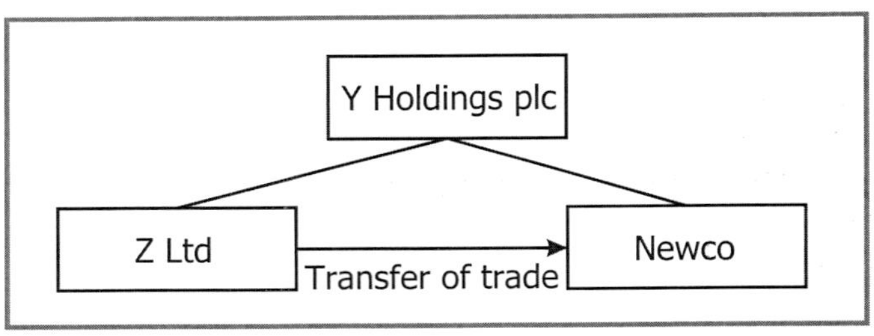


The business can now be sold as a separate legal entity, Newco.

## Regulatory requirements

It should be ensured that the sale of the company to a particular acquirer will not cause problems with regulatory authorities, such as the competition regulators. It may be possible to restructure the business to avoid this problem by the acquirer agreeing to sell one part of the business, for example, or by the acquirer disposing of different parts separately. Advice will need to be sought on the tax position.

# 4 The Auction Process

## No-names teaser

Having established the exact structure of the company for sale and to whom it is likely to be attractive, a selling document can be prepared which is accurately targeted to the desired acquirers.

The detailed selling document is proceeded by a 'teaser' document. This is prepared by the vendor to provide a potential buyer with outline information on the business to be sold, whilst at the same time withholding important information, including the company name and details of business operations and customers so as to protect the confidentiality of the sale. The teaser is used to gauge a potential buyer's interest prior to providing them with more details, in the form of an information memorandum. The document is outline in nature and brief.

The vendor, or more likely the vendor's advisers, draw up a list of potential purchasers and will send out the no-names teaser document to try and provoke a response.

Acquirers can be identified in the same ways as potential vendors can be sought by companies seeking to make an acquisition. The initial approach should be to either the finance director, business development director or managing director of the company. Certain potential buyers may be excluded from the list for competitive reasons and the wish not to disclose information that will give a competitor a strategic advantage.

## Information memorandum

If a potential purchaser responds to the no-names teaser with a request for more information, the sales process can be developed further. The potential acquirer can apply to receive the full selling document, which is termed the Information Memorandum (IM). Before the IM is despatched, potential purchasers must sign a Confidentiality Agreement, which is a legal document that provides undertakings regarding the use of the information that will be provided.

An Information Memorandum is like a detailed business plan. The information memorandum should give a potential acquirer sufficient information to make a decision about whether to buy the business and how much to offer, subject to an accountant's investigation. As an information memorandum, it should portray the business in a compelling light. However, it should be remembered that S397 of FSMA 2000 makes it a criminal offence to make a false statement dishonestly or recklessly in order to induce someone to enter into an investment agreement. It is also an offence to withhold information dishonestly or recklessly for the same purpose. The document should, therefore, be prepared with due care and attention.

The IM will be a detailed document, enabling comprehensive financial analysis and valuations to be undertaken. However, the vendor should be careful not to reveal all confidential details until he is assured as to the seriousness of the acquirer's intent. For this reason, certain details will be omitted, for instance terms of key customer contracts. The key contents will be as follows.

- An overview/executive summary
- Sales marketing and product information
- Suppliers
- Directors, senior management and employee details
- Administration systems and related details
- Locations of key premises
- Existing shareholders and their percentage holdings
- General company information, such as the registered office, company registration number, etc

- Financial details, being recent profit and loss accounts, balance sheets and cash flow forecasts. Budgets and forecasts for coming years may also be appropriate
- Suggestions as to how the acquirer can develop and add value to the business

Potential buyers are given a period of time, usually a few weeks, to assess the memorandum before submitting an indication of interest.

## Letters of Intent

Expressions of interest from potential purchasers usually take the form of a letter of intent. This is a non-binding letter from potential buyers that discuss how much they are willing to pay for the company, how the purchase will be financed and a description of their experience with making acquisitions. The letters of intent are considered and the most credible purchasers are identified. If the process is a competitive one, an adviser can apply pressure on buyers to offer their highest price and maximize value for the company.

## Due diligence

The remaining buyers, perhaps one or two depending on the case, are invited to conduct more detailed due diligence on the acquisition company. Due diligence should to be conducted at a company's data room: a location where very detailed information on the company is available for potential buyers to view and analyze. Now, data rooms have been replaced by documents held online on a secure website for potential buyers to view. The vendor can use these websites to monitor the usage by potential purchasers of this information, for example what information has been viewed and for how long. Based on this due diligence, potential purchasers will submit their final bids.

## Heads of Terms

At this point, final negotiations commence between the vendor and potential purchasers. The outcome of the negotiation is usually a 'heads of terms' document, which sets out the position of both parties as agreed by discussion. The heads of terms will include the purchase price, the purchase consideration, details of what is being sold (ie assets or shares), conditions of the sale, including warranties, indemnities and representations. The heads of terms document provides a basis for the completion document, the Sale and Purchase Agreement.

# 5 DEMERGERS

A demerger is when one large listed company is split into two smaller listed companies, with shareholders receiving shares in both companies in proportion to their holdings in the original group.

## The benefits of demerging

There are a number of possible benefits in demerging a company, which include the following.

### Focus on central strategy

In the past, there have been trends for companies to diversify their interests. The logic of this was that it reduced the variability of the company's earnings stream and the increased size of the company made it more resilient to takeover. In recent years, this trend has been reversed, with companies returning to their core businesses. The logic of this has been twofold.

Firstly, it is often the case that large conglomerates are not necessarily desirable. Shareholders can diversify their investments themselves to reduce variability of returns if they so desire. Companies that diversify their interests do not therefore perform a service to their shareholders. Indeed, since they may be less effective at managing the acquired businesses than the original owners, they may actually be committing a disservice. Thus, companies should stick with what they know best and concentrate on core interests and central strategy.

Secondly, it has been seen that size is not necessarily a defence against takeover, when many companies have large war chests and even small companies can raise substantial amounts of debt to make acquisitions. Since one of the first actions of predators will be to sell off non-core divisions to reduce the cost of the acquisition, disposal of these will make the company less attractive to them.

### Elimination of cross-subsidies

It may be the case that one profitable part of a group is subsidising the poor performance of another part. Forcing the less profitable division to stand on its own two feet will mean that both divisions can make decisions that fit their own situations – with the profitable division concentrating on growing its market while the unprofitable division concentrates on eliminating unnecessary costs and returning to profitability.

### Reduction of foreign currency exposure

If investors seek foreign currency exposure, they can invest in overseas companies directly. Notwithstanding this, it may be that companies can take on foreign exposure more cheaply than investors, meaning that it may be worthwhile for companies to have exposure to the US dollar, for example.

### Separating out very different businesses

It is unlikely that there are significant synergies in combining two very different businesses. It is more likely that central management is more expert in one area than the other, meaning that one division's performance suffers as a result. In addition, shareholders may find it difficult to separate the performance of the two very different parts. As a result, the performance of the more successful of the two divisions may find its stock market rating tarnished by its association with the less profitable division.

Separating out the businesses will enable each to make decisions solely by reference to its own needs and its own strategy. For example, Cadbury demerged into its confectionery and its beverages businesses. Cable and Wireless demerger into its business and consumer telecommunications businesses.

### Capital market factors

The company may find it has greater access to capital markets post-divestiture. Investors may decide that the strategy of the company is now more clearly defined and thus fits within it investment objectives.

### Defence against takeover

As noted above, a raider may acquire a company with the intention of 'unbundling' its different divisions, ie selling off some of the divisions to reduce the acquisition cost and being left with the core business at a very attractive price. One defence against this is for the target company to unbundle itself.

### Motivation of management

The management of a subsidiary may find it difficult to perform well when dominated by a board largely interested in the other part of the group. Releasing the subsidiary to make its own way in the world may enable management to make better decisions for the benefit of the shareholders.

### Cultural differences

Two very different businesses may require very different cultures in order to succeed. Inclusion in the same group where one corporate culture prevails may hold back one of the divisions.

### Increases in market value

The ultimate reason for a demerger is that the aggregate value of the two separate divisions may be worth more than their combined value. All the reasons above should give rise to increases in value.

## The problems of demerging

### Internal reorganisations

The company will need to reorganise the whole group to enable the demerger to go ahead. For example, the existing legal structure of the group may be geographically based. When the demerger takes place, the different group companies will need to be owned by the relevant holding company. This reorganisation has potential tax and legal problems and will need to be managed carefully.

### Tax

There are potential capital gains tax (CGT) charges arising from the transfer of assets within the group into the subsidiary to be demerged. It is unlikely, pre-demerger, that all assets the parent company wishes to demerge are in a single legal entity. Thus, there may well be considerable intergroup transfers that could crystallise capital gains tax liabilities.

In addition, it is necessary to mitigate in advance CGT for the parent on transfer of the assets to the shareholders, and income tax and CGT for the shareholders themselves.

The tax consequences are effected by the method of demerger which is chosen (see below).

### Size of the independent companies

The smaller companies may find that their shares lack marketability and that they are subject to takeover pressures that did not previously exist.

### Credit ratings

The credit ratings of the separate companies may fall substantially, resulting in higher borrowing costs. There is also a risk that existing loan covenants will be breached when the demerger takes place. For example, covenants forbidding disposals of significant business assets or material adverse change clauses may be invoked.

### Use of central services

Before the demerger, both divisions will probably have used the same central services for treasury, tax, etc. It will be important to establish the length of time both companies will continue to use these services together and how the cost of such services will be allocated. Additionally, at some time in the future, the divisions will ultimately need to stand alone.

### Employees

The interests of employees will need to be protected. Pension rights, for example, will need to be established.

### Costs

The cost of preparing the demerger, both in terms of management time and professional advice, will be substantial.

# 6 Methods of Achieving a Demerger

There are three methods of achieving a demerger.

- The dividend approach
- By scheme of arrangement
- By liquidation

## Demergers – dividend approach

Here, a demerger is achieved by paying shareholders a dividend comprising the shares of the entity being demerged. This is known as a dividend 'in specie'. This means that all shareholders will automatically receive their pro rata share of the division to be demerged.

The parent company instigating the demerger must have sufficient distributable reserves to cover the book value, though not the market value, of the demerged shares.

The dividend must be declared indirectly to ensure it is classified as a 'scheme of reconstruction', thereby avoiding the capital gains tax charge that the company effecting the demerger would otherwise be liable to. An indirect dividend involves the issue of the shares to the shareholders by the demerged entity itself, as opposed to a transfer by the parent company making the divestment.

The investor receiving the shares will be subject to income tax on the dividend, unless the distribution is classified as an 'exempt' transfer under the 2010 Corporation Taxes Act. Classification as such requires proof that the transaction is for 'bona fide' commercial purposes (ie not tax evasion) and, pre-transaction, the parent owns over 75% of the shares of the subsidiary to be demerged.

FCA approval must be gained for the listing of the new shares of the demerged entity. The shares will be listed via an Introduction.

## Demergers – scheme of arrangement

The scheme of arrangement method is allowed under company law and involves the holding company, the subsidiary and the shareholders coming to an 'arrangement' and redistributing shares based on this. A scheme of arrangement avoids the need for sufficient distributable reserves in the parent company effecting the demerger.

Arrangements will be conducted under part 26 of the Companies Act 2006. The key requirements are as follows.

- Court approval must be obtained.
- Shareholders must approve a special resolution, requiring a 75% majority in value of the shareholders voting.
- Creditors must approve.

If all of the above are satisfied, then the arrangement becomes binding on all creditors and shareholders.

As with the above approach, the transfer of the demerged shares must be done indirectly to avoid potential CGT charges for the parent.

## Demergers – liquidation method

This method arises under the Insolvency Act 1986. The procedure is that the parent is put into voluntary liquidation and its assets are distributed to two new companies (Newco 1 and 2). Newco 1 and 2 pay for the assets by distributing shares that are given to the shareholders of the liquidated parent.

The problems with this method are that it entails paying off all creditors before assets are sold or reassigning their debts to the new company. The position of employees needs to be resolved, since their old contracts will be at an end. All legal or contractual obligations of the company being liquidated need to be terminated or reassigned.

Due to these problems, this method is probably only easy to achieve in the case of a fairly small company.

No income tax charge should arise for investors because of a specific exemption for distributions made on a winding up.

## Chapter Roundup

**Module 4, Chapter 21: Disposals and Demergers**

We consider motivations for disposals. In the exam you may need to comment on these and discuss a disposal as part of a value-enhancing strategy.

You need to be able to explain the different ways of achieving a private company disposal and which method might be appropriate in a particular scenario. Consider how a vendor might prepare a business for sale, including a re-organisation of the legal structure.

We have looked at

- The sale process
  - Traditional and alternative disposal methods
  - Identifying and short-listing purchasers
  - Approaching potential purchasers
- The auction process
  - No-names teasers
  - Confidentiality undertakings
  - The information memorandum
  - Inviting and evaluating offers

The chapter concludes by looking at the practical ways to achieve a demerger:

- The dividend approach
- A scheme of arrangement
- The liquidation method

# PUBLIC DEALS

chapter 22

## Contents


| | | |
|---|---|---|
| 1 | Takeovers of Public Limited Companies | 466 |
| 2 | Takeover Offer | 466 |
| 3 | Schemes of Arrangement | 467 |
| 4 | Agreed or Hostile Bid | 467 |
| 5 | Hostile Bid Tactics | 468 |
| 6 | Defence Strategy and Tactics | 470 |
| 7 | Bid Defence | 471 |

# 1 Takeovers of Public Limited Companies

There are two main methods to takeover public limited companies in the UK: **a takeover offer** to the shareholders of the target company or a **scheme of arrangement**. A takeover offer is structured as an invitation to the offeree shareholders by the offeror and a scheme of arrangement is a proposal by the target company to its own shareholders and/or creditors.

For a takeover offer to be successful, offeree company shareholders amounting to the specified acceptances level must vote to accept the offer. For a scheme to be successful, offeree shareholders must vote in a general meeting to accept the scheme and the scheme needs court approval.

If successful, both methods will result in the takeover of the offeree by the offeror and both methods are subject to the provisions of the City Code on Takeovers and Mergers.

The following section of the material, Regulation, Governance and Ethics, considers the provisions of the City Code in detail. In this chapter, we concentrate on the overall process of a public company takeover and consider how this differs from the private company acquisition process covered earlier.

# 2 Takeover Offer

We have looked already at the acquisition process for private companies. By necessity, this process is collaborative, and the terms of the transaction are worked out in negotiation between the offeror company and the offeree directors. With public companies, it is likely that there is a separation between the offeree company directors and offeree shareholders (who have ownership). Offers for public companies thus follow a different process, with the offeror appealing directly to the offeree shareholders who will determine the bid outcome. Offeror shareholder approval is also necessary if the transaction is particularly material for the offeror (required by the Listing Rules).

All takeover offers for UK public limited companies (both listed and unlisted) are covered by the City Code on Takeovers and Mergers. The City Code contains detailed provisions relating to the way an offer is conducted to ensure fair treatment of offeree shareholders and to avoid the creation of a false market in offeree company shares during the course of the bid. Offeree directors are required to communicate their views on the offer to the shareholders, but are prevented from undertaking action designed to frustrate the bid. Shareholders must be allowed to decide for themselves on the merits of the bid. In addition, the offeror must treat all offeree shareholders of the same class, as far as possible, equally – so no special deals with significant shareholders are allowed.

The takeover offer is an invitation by an offeror company to the shareholders of the offeree public limited company. The offer will include the price and terms of the offer, including the nature of the consideration to be paid. The offer will also incorporate an acceptances condition. The acceptances condition will specify the percentage of share capital which the offeror requires for the offer to be declared 'unconditional as to acceptances'. This acceptances level can be chosen by the offeror; it must be a minimum of 50%, but is usually set at 90%. A 90% level of acceptances, allows an offeror to evoke the compulsory purchase provisions available under the Companies Act 2006, thus gaining 100% of the offeree company.

The main due diligence exercise carried out by the offeror is undertaken from publicly available information prior to the launch of the offer. Due diligence is limited once the offer process commences. In particular, offeree companies will be mindful of the provisions of the City Code, which state that information given to one offeror or potential offeror must also be given on request to another offeror or bona fide potential offeror, regardless of whether or not their offer is welcome *(City Code, Rule 20.2)*. The offeror must request the information specifically and cannot frame a request in general terms.

Public company takeovers do not have a sale and purchase agreement, as is used in private company acquisitions. The legal document is the 'offer document' which contains the offer conditions, such as regulatory clearances and information that is to be furnished to the offeror. In a voluntary offer, the offeror can include whatever conditions they wish to, provided that the conditions do not depend solely on subjective judgements by the directors of the offeror or if the fulfilment of the condition lies in their hands *(City Code, Rule 13)*. If this proviso were not in existence, it would be easy for offerors to withdraw their offers at will and at any time by setting subjective conditions. If the conditions are met, the transaction completes and a change in ownership is affected.

# 3 Schemes of Arrangement

A Scheme of Arrangement is a statutory procedure, under Part 26 (Sections 895-901) of the Companies Act 2006, which allows a company to make an arrangement or compromise with its shareholders or creditors. Once the Scheme is approved by the requisite majority of shareholders or creditors and sanctioned by the court, the Scheme is binding on all, whether or not they have voted in favour of it. The requisite majority is 75% in value of members or creditors present and voting at the relevant court meeting, either in person or by proxy. Schemes can be used to effect a number of processes, including a takeover, an alteration of the rights of creditors, share buybacks , a debt restructuring and a compulsory purchase of minority shareholdings.

In a takeover context, the offeree company's shares are cancelled and then reissued to the bidder, in return for which the bidder pays the consideration to the target's shareholders. A scheme of arrangement can really only be used for an agreed bid, because the application to the court must be made by the company whose shares are being re-organised (ie the offeree). A Scheme does, however, have some advantages for the offeror: for example, there is a greater finality of outcome – either the scheme will be agreed or not. The offeror does not risk being left with a large stake but not 100% ownership. Once a scheme is sanctioned, the offeror is guaranteed 100% control of the target. Minority shareholders are bought out under the terms of the Scheme, whether they like it or not.

The need to seek court approval adds extra complication to a takeover via a Scheme, as opposed to a takeover offer. Scheme documentation is lengthy and complex, containing the same information as a takeover offer document, and also the relevant notices for shareholder meetings and the court hearing. As such, a Scheme is most expensive to effect in terms of advisers' fees and regulatory costs. However, on almost all Schemes stamp duty (at 0.5 per cent of the target's value at the offer price) can be saved. A takeover offer would generally be expected to provide the offeror with control of the offeree company quicker than a scheme. However acquiring, dissenting, outstanding minority shareholdings could substantially extend the timetable of the takeover offer beyond that of the scheme.

Schemes are less suitable to use where changes in terms of the offer are expected mid-way through the process. Changing offer terms, for example because a rival bidder has emerged, requires changing the terms of a scheme mid-way through the process and is likely to require the parties to go back to court.

Takeovers of UK public limited companies via Schemes of Arrangement are still subject to the provisions of the Takeover Code. Specific rules for Scheme of Arrangement takeovers are in Appendix 7 of the Code.

Recent years have seen a significant increase in the number of takeover deals effected by Schemes of Arrangements.

# 4 Agreed or Hostile Bid

## Private companies

In the case of a bid for an unlisted company, it is highly likely that the bid will need to be approved by the board of the company. This is because the board will probably own a significant number of shares and other shareholders will tend to follow the board's lead. If the board does not approve the bid, then the chances of success are usually so low that it will be best to find a different target.

### Listed companies

A bid for a listed company does not need to be approved, since the directors will probably not own a significant number of shares and the shareholder base is unlikely to have emotional or other attachments to the company. Instead, it is the fiduciary duty of directors to advise whether the bid is in the best interests of shareholders. If the bid is recommended by directors, it is termed an 'agreed' offer. If directors do not support the bid, then it is 'unrecommended' and, if to proceed, will do so on a 'hostile' basis.

### Advantages of an agreed offer

Notwithstanding this, there can be advantages in obtaining board approval for a bid, as follows

- There is a greater chance that shareholders will accept the bid.
- It may act as a disincentive for a hostile bidder to join the fray or persuade them to pull out.
- It will avoid the risk of the bidding company coming out worse in a public relations battle and damaging its reputation.
- More information will be forthcoming on the target company and make for an easier due diligence process.
- Integration of the target into the acquiring company's group may be easier.

### Problems with trying to achieve an agreed offer

Against this, certain disadvantages must be considered.

- If talks fall through, then the bidder will have probably released information about itself to the target.
- It will give the target advance warning of the impending bid and, should the approach fail, enable the board to prepare their defence.

Surprisingly perhaps, obtaining board approval for a bid does not make it any cheaper for the bidder to acquire the company. It is true that, in a hostile situation, the bidder will be obliged to make the price sufficiently attractive to overcome opposition to the bid. However, in an agreed bid, the price will need to be set sufficiently high to deter other bidders from coming in. It will also need to ensure that the bid can be sold successfully to the target's shareholders without accusations of their board negotiating a bad deal.

## 5 Hostile Bid Tactics

A number of tactics can be adopted to enhance the chances of a bid's success as follows

### Stakebuilding

This can either be undertaken gradually or rapidly, via a dawn raid. In the case of the gradual build-up of interests, the danger is that the demand for the shares will be picked up by the company which will use its powers under S793 of the Companies Act 2006 to identify the acquirer. In any case, if 3% or more of the company is acquired, then the acquirer will be legally obliged to notify the company of its interests. This regulation sacrifices any element of market surprise.

In the case of a dawn raid, the company will quickly be identified and may be unable to acquire a significant number of shares if the market becomes aware of what is happening. It can be very time-consuming to accumulate shares from daily trading of the free float in the market.

## Tender offer

A bidder can consider making a tender offer directly to target shareholders. This is an invitation to shareholders to sell their shares to the bidder at a certain price within a specified time frame. In the UK, the Takeover Panel's consent is required for any tender offer. This consent is unlikely to be forthcoming for a tender offer for over 30% of the share capital of the target company. Tender offers have been used extensively in other jurisdictions, for example the United States, as a way to circumvent management and gain control even when managers oppose the takeover.

## Advertising

The City Code prohibits advertising of a controversial nature about the bid *(Rule 19.4)*, but the company's image can be improved by selected and tasteful advertising of a more general nature.

## Lobbying

In order to persuade politicians that the bid will be in the target's and the country's interests and prevent a referral to the Competition Commission or a subsequent blocking of the bid.

## Public relations campaign

This may obtain press support and favourable press comment.

### Investor relations

This may persuade the bidding company's own shareholders of the validity of the bid and assure the target's investors of the bid's advantages.

### Offer document

In the case of superior performance of the bidder and its management, which will be relevant if the offer is shares and not just cash. It will also criticise the past performance of the target and illustrate the benefits of the bid for the target's shareholders.

### Offer price

It is important to ensure that the price is sufficiently competitive to:

- Make it unattractive for competing bidders to enter the fray or to stay in the frame, if already bidding
- Encourage target shareholders to accept

However, the price should not be so expensive as to result in the company overpaying.

### White Knight

A bidder can portray itself as the saviour of the company subsequent to another hostile bidder announcing an offer.

# 6 Defence Strategy and Tactics

## General housekeeping before a bid

The most effective method of defence is to ensure that the company is not perceived as being a bid target in the first place. The way to achieve this is to ensure that the company is fully and fairly valued by investors. If this is the case, then it is unlikely that any company will be motivated to bid, since there will be no prospect of satisfactory gains to be made from the acquisition. There are various ways of achieving this.

## Investor relations

Effective communication with the company's investor base will ensure that they understand its business and strategy, appreciate the reasons for short-term falls in profitability and will not sell out on the cheap just before results start to improve.

## Investor management

This will ensure that the shareholder base is appropriate for the company, so that they will be happy to stay committed for the longer term and not sell out at the first opportunity. It may be appropriate to develop friendly shareholdings with other companies. The danger of this is that a cross-holding ties up capital and a large shareholder who was originally perceived as friendly may either sell out on a bid or use its stake to launch a bid itself.

## Group strategy

Developing a clear and consistent group strategy will add value to the company and increase the share price. This strategy will, of course, need to be explained and communicated to investors.

## Public relations

The company should ensure that announcements, interim statements and final published accounts are produced in an attractive way that fully emphasises the strengths of the company. In addition, it should ensure that announcements are followed up appropriately with interviews and analysts' meetings.

## Dividend policy

The company should ensure that its dividend policy is suitable for its earnings stream and reflects investors' needs and expectations.

### Specific bid preparation

In addition to the above points, techniques which can be used specifically to assist in defending against a bid include:

- Checking the share register for undesirable investors and identifying trends in share transactions. Powers to investigate shareholdings under S793 of the Companies Act 2006 can be used to identify undesirable shareholders.
- Keeping a draft defence document ready to be tailored to meet a specific bid situation.
- Keeping files of information on possible bidders ready for use.
- Having a contingency plan ready for a bid, to be put into action at a moment's notice. This will include allocation of responsibilities for defence, setting up a defence committee and allocating everyday tasks in managing the business to others who will be less concerned with the bid defence. The details are often maintained in what is commonly referred to as a company's Defence Manual or 'Black Book'.

## 7 Bid Defence

After the bid has been launched, the company will only have a limited amount of time (around 60 days) to conduct its defence against the specific bidder. By contrast, the bidder may have spent a substantial amount of time identifying the target and putting together an attractive and feasible bid. This underlies the importance of good housekeeping before a bid to ensure that the company is as prepared as possible. Once the bidder has been identified, possible tactics include the following. There are rules relating to the contents and other matters related to Defence Document and Profit Forecasts released by a company in a potential transaction to which the Takeover Code applies.

### Defence document

It is, of course, vital to have a well-argued and cohesive defence document subsequent to receiving the offer document from the bidder.

### Profit forecast

The company may decide to issue a profit forecast. The danger with this is that it will need to be sufficiently optimistic in order to prevent the bidder's offer from seeming attractive, but must not be too ambitious. Otherwise it will either lose credibility in the short-term or act as a hostage to fortune in the longer term, when the company has to achieve those results.

### Attack as a form of defence

In a share bid, attacking the bidder's management, strategy and accounting policies (used to show improving profits) can be particularly effective.

### Public relations

Lobbying, effective public relations and advertising may assist in turning the tide of investor opinion or may cause the bid to be referred to the Competition Commission.

## Restructuring

The company may announce an intention to restructure itself, by selling off a major division or demerging the company into separate divisions, each with a listing.

## White knight

The company could encourage a counter bid from a friendly bidder or white knight, although this will mean that the company will lose its independence. An alternative would be the purchase of a large block of target shares by a 'white squire', who does not take control but agrees to vote in alignment with target management. The white squire can disrupt the hostile takeover process and help the company retain its independence.

## Dividend increases

Increases in dividends may pacify investors. However, this may be seen as too little, too late. Also, if the increase is too large, it may beg questions as to why it has only been done now and raise doubts as to whether the larger dividend is sustainable in the future.

## Frustrating action

The City Code prohibits the board of the target company from taking actions which would frustrate a bona fide offer or prevent its shareholders from deciding on the bid's own merits. Therefore, actions such as disposals of significant business assets in the course of a bid will need shareholder approval. In addition, preferential treatment of certain shareholders will go against the basic principle of equal treatment for all offeree shareholders. This means that many frustrating action techniques used in other jurisdictions (eg the US), would not be possible in the UK.

Examples of frustrating action:

- Changes to a company's constitutional documents that limit the ability of a predator to gain control. For example, changes in the voting rights of shares in the event of a hostile bid to effectively block a predator gaining control or the use of dual class voting shares.
- Golden parachutes, granting management generous severance payments if they lose their jobs in the event of a hostile bid.
- Crown jewels defence; where key assets are sold from the business prior to a hostile bidder gaining control.
- Leveraged recapitalisation; the target company draws down a significant amount of debt and uses it to pay a special dividend to shareholders. This means the bidder acquires a much larger debt burden than expected. Leveraged recapitalisations can be structured to include 'poison puts' whereby the debt becomes immediately repayable on a change of control of the company.
- Greenmail. Here the target company buys back shares from the bidder at an inflated premium not available to other shareholders. Greenmail will temporarily repel an intruder but will not stop other potential purchasers. Again, under the Takeover Code this is not permitted, as it is against the interests of the other shareholders of the offeree.

## CHAPTER ROUNDUP

**Module 4, Chapter 22: Public Deals**

Takeovers of public companies in the UK are governed by the City Code on Takeovers and Mergers, which is covered in detail at the start of the next module. This chapter should be read in conjunction with the regulatory chapters. The regulation will determine the way the bid is conducted and the roles of the offeror and offeree company at the different stages of the timetable.

There are two methods to achieve a takeover of a public limited company in the UK.

A takeover offer is an invitation by an offeror company to the shareholders of the offeree public limited company. Offeree shareholders vote on the proposals, and, dependent on the outcome, the offer will become 'unconditional as to acceptances'.

A scheme of arrangement is a statutory procedure, driven by the offeree company, where a rearrangement of share capital is sanctioned by the court.

The outcome of the two methods can be the same – with the offeror company gaining control of the offeree.

This chapter also considers the difference between agreed and hostile bids and examines the defence tactics that can be used by the offeree company to try and thwart a hostile bidder.

MODULE 5

# REGULATION, GOVERNANCE AND ETHICS

# SYLLABUS – REGULATION, GOVERNANCE AND ETHICS

## Aim

Candidates will be able to describe UK regulation and the regulatory regimes in different jurisdictions, recognise the applicability of regulation in given scenarios and apply that knowledge to given scenarios.

Regulation, Governance and Ethics questions will make up approximately 20% of the total marks in the examination.

## Syllabus and BPP Study Text coverage

In the assessment, candidates may be required to

| SYLLABUS | BPP STUDY TEXT |
|---|---|
| a. **Specific rules and practice statement will be tested. All candidates should be able to describe the following aspects of the Takeover Code and assess their relevance to a given scenario**<br>• **The structure of the Code**<br>• **The spirit of the Code**<br>• **The structure of the Panel and its powers**<br>• **Statutory status**<br>• **Companies to which the code applies**<br>• **Independent advice**<br>• **Irrevocable undertakings**<br>• **Financing arrangements**<br>• **Offers for different classes of shares**<br>• **Concert parties**<br>• **Special deals and management incentives**<br>• **Accuracy and content of documents**<br>• **The creation of false markets**<br>• **Restrictions and frustrating actions**<br>• **Consideration**<br>• **Mandatory offers**<br>• **The timetable of an offer**<br>• **EU implications**<br>• **Consulting the Panel**<br>• **Schemes of arrangement** | Chapters 23 |

| SYLLABUS | BPP STUDY TEXT |
|---|---|
| **b. Listing:** | Chapter 24 |
| **(i) Describe the following aspects of the Listing Rules and assess their relevance to a given scenario** | |
| • **The structure of the UK Listing Authority rules** | |
| • **Standard and premium listing options** | |
| • **The minimum requirements for listing** | |
| • **Prospectuses** | |
| • **Timetable for listing** | |
| • **Sponsor's obligations** | |
| • **Announcements and circulars to shareholders** | |
| • **Continuing obligations** | |
| • **Class tests** | Module 3: chapter 16 |
| • **Share buybacks** | Module 3: chapter 16 |
| • **Secondary offerings** | |
| • **Prospectus rules** | |
| **(ii) AIM and PLUS rules** | Chapter 24 |
| **c. Describe the following areas relevant to corporate finance activity and assess their relevance to a given straightforward scenario (G)** | |
| • **Corporate governance** | Chapter 25 |
| – **The UK Corporate Governance Code (including the implications for smaller companies)** | |
| – **The overlap with the FCA Disclosure Guidance and Transparency Rules** | |
| – **EU implications** | |
| • **Competition regulation** | Chapter 25 |
| – **The general purpose of competition regulation** | |
| – **EU implications** | |
| • **Ethics** | Chapter 26 |
| – **Fiduciary duties to the client** | |
| – **Bribery Act** | |
| – **CISI Code of Conduct or ICAEW Code of Ethics** | |
| • **Market abuse** | Chapter 26 |
| – **Insider trading** | |
| – **Price sensitive information** | |
| – **Misleading statements** | |
| – **Financial promotions** | |
| • **Companies Act** | |
| **Candidates should be able to demonstrate an awareness of US and other extraterritorial regulations which might impact upon a UK transaction** | |

# THE TAKEOVER CODE

chapter 23

Contents


| | | |
|---|---|---|
| 1 | The Panel on Takeovers and Mergers | 480 |
| 2 | When Does the Code Apply? | 480 |
| 3 | The Spirit of the Code | 481 |
| 4 | The Offer Process | 482 |
| 5 | The Offer and Defence Documents | 484 |
| 6 | The Offer Document | 484 |
| 7 | The Defence Document | 486 |
| 8 | Profit Forecasts and Earnings Enhancement Statements | 486 |
| 9 | Restrictions on Share Dealings | 488 |
| 10 | The Mandatory Offer | 492 |
| 11 | The Voluntary Offer | 496 |
| 12 | Conduct During the Offer | 499 |
| 13 | Timetable of an Offer | 503 |
| 14 | Restrictions Following Offers | 506 |
| 15 | Conflicts of Interest and Management Buyouts | 507 |
| 16 | Partial Offers | 508 |

# 1 The Panel on Takeovers and Mergers

The Panel on Takeovers and Mergers ('the Panel') is responsible for regulating takeovers in the UK. Backing the Panel is the Bank of England, which appoints the Chairman and Deputy Chairmen. In addition, its membership draws from representatives of key City institutions. The purpose of the Panel is to monitor adherence to the general principles and detailed rules laid down in the City Code on Takeovers and Mergers ('the City Code' or 'the Code'). The Code is designed to provide an orderly framework within which takeovers are conducted. In addition, it is designed to promote, in conjunction with other regulatory regimes, the integrity of the financial markets.

The Panel has statutory authority from the Companies Act 2006. In addition, it has the support of regulatory authorities such as the Financial Conduct Authority (FCA), meaning that adherence to the City Code is indicative of best market practice. The FCA requires that all investment businesses follow best market practice and it may be that anyone who breaches the Code could have the facilities of the market withdrawn from them ('cold shouldering').

The Panel operates via a system of consultation and the City Code requires advisers and parties to a bid to discuss in advance any course of action related to a bid if there is uncertainty as to how the Code might apply. There are a number of advantages of the system of Takeover Regulation administered by the Panel, as follows.

- **Flexibility** – the Code can quickly be adapted to take account of changing circumstances. The law can only be changed very slowly.
- **Consultation in advance** – the Panel can be consulted in advance to ensure that the rules in the City Code are not going to be broken, albeit unintentionally.
- **Quick decisions** – due to the system of consultation, the Panel can come up with speedy judgements.
- **Focus on principles** – the Panel applies general principles of fairness in making its decisions. Companies must comply with the General Principles which represent the 'spirit' of the code. An action can be deemed inappropriate if it does not uphold these principles.
- **Practitioner involvement** – this makes the City Code and its application more realistic, acceptable and effective.
- **Links with other regulatory bodies** – the FCA requires compliance with the City Code and may cold-shoulder people who are severely censured by the Panel.

# 2 When Does the Code Apply?

All UK, Channel Island and Isle of Man incorporated public companies which have securities admitted to trading on a multilateral trading facility (which includes AIM and the ISDX Growth Market) in the UK are subject to the Takeover Code, **irrespective of the company's place of central management and control**. The Code applies to all public and private companies if:

- They are registered in the UK, the Channel Islands or the Isle of Man; and
- Their securities are admitted to trading on a UK multilateral trading facility

regardless of the location of that company's central management or control.

The Code also applies to offers for any private limited company (Ltd) resident in these areas if

- The company's equity share capital has been listed on the London Stock Exchange at any time during the ten years prior to the offer being announced.
- Dealings and/or prices in the company's shares have been published on a regular basis for a continuous period of at least six months in the last ten years.
- The company's shares have been afforded dealing facilities on a recognised investment exchange in the last ten years.
- The company has filed a prospectus to issue equity shares in the last ten years.

The objective of these rules is to cover any company where the public may have had an opportunity to purchase shares in the recent past.

It should be noted that if the Code applies to a transaction, then it will apply to **all parties** involved with that transaction (including the directors of the offeror and offeree and all of the professional advisers) regardless of where the offeror is incorporated or based.

The Code applies to all takeover and merger transactions, including partial offers for less than 100% of a company's shares and situations where **control** of a company is to be obtained or consolidated. However, it does not usually relate to offers for non-voting or non-equity shares.

Control is defined in the definitions as where **at least 30%** of the company's voting rights are held. Although, strictly speaking, control only becomes legally possible when more than 50% of the voting rights are held, the Panel believes that effective control can be achieved at this much lower percentage.

### Waiver of the Code

The Panel has indicated that it is prepared to consider a waiver of the Code for a public company in the following circumstances.

- There are ten or less shareholders in the company; and
- All shareholders have confirmed in writing that they are happy to waive their rights under the Code.

Waivers are only available for specific transactions and not as a 'general' waiver. Panel permission to seek a waiver from shareholders must be sought in advance.

## 3 The Spirit of the Code

The main overriding principle of the Code is that all shareholders of the target company ('offeree shareholders') are treated fairly during the offer process and are not denied an opportunity to decide on the merits of a takeover.

There are six General principles of the Code. The existence of the Principles recognises that it is impossible to devise rules that cover every situation. The General Principles assist companies and the Panel in interpreting and applying the spirit of the Code. Three key propositions of the Code sum up the spirit of the Code:

- Equal treatment for all offeree company shareholders
- Adequate and timely advice and information
- No false markets

### Equal treatment for all shareholders

General Principle 1 states that all holders of securities of an offeree company of the same class must be afforded equivalent treatment; moreover, if a person acquires control of a company, the other holders of securities must be protected.

### Adequate and timely advice and information

General Principle 2 states that shareholders must have sufficient time and information to enable them to reach a properly informed decision. General Principle 3 states that the board of an offeree company must act in the interests of the company (as opposed to, for instance, the directors' personal interests). They must allow shareholders the opportunity to consider the merits of the bid. Unapproved frustrating action is not permitted.

General Principle 6 states that the offeree company must not be hindered in the conduct of its affairs for longer than is reasonable by a bid for its securities. Takeover offers must be conducted in reference to the bid timetable set out in the Code.

### No false markets

General Principle 4 provides that false markets must not be created in the securities of the offeree company, of the offeror company or of any companies concerned by the offer, in such a way that the rise or fall of the prices of the securities becomes artificial and the normal functioning of the markets is distorted. As a further point, General Principle 5 states that an offer should be announced by an offeror only once it can fulfil in full any cash consideration, if offered, and after taking all reasonable measures to secure the implementation of any other type of consideration.

## 4 The Offer Process

The method in which a company should make an offer is included in section D of the City Code. This covers how approaches should be made, what announcements are required and what advice should be sought by the offeree board.

### The approach (Rule 1)

Any approach must first be made to the board of the offeree company or to its advisers. The identity of the offeror must be disclosed.

### Announcements (Rule 2)

In order to prevent leakage of price-sensitive information, it is vital that absolute secrecy is maintained prior to an offer being announced *(Rule 2.1)*. The advisers to the offeror or offeree should always warn their clients of the importance of this. They are required to draw their clients' attention to the Code and to highlight the rules restricting share dealings (these rules are dealt with below). This is to ensure a false market does not develop in offeree company shares.

### When an announcement is required

An announcement is required in the following circumstances *(Rule 2.2)*. Consultation with the Panel to clarify whether an announcement is required is encouraged.

(a) A firm intention to make an offer has been notified to the offeree board from a serious source. The offeree board is obliged to make an announcement that it has received the offer regardless of its attitude to the offer.

(b) The offeror should make an announcement where an obligation to make an offer has arisen as a result of *Rule 9*, manadatory offers. The announcement should be made immediately after the obligation has been incurred.

(c) Where there is rumour and speculation or the offeree's share price moves untowardly (for example, by more than 5% in any one day or by more than 10% above the lowest price since an approach was made to the potential offeree), an announcement may be required in the following circumstances.

 – If there has been an approach to the offeree company, in which case the offeree board should make an announcement.

- If no approach has yet been made but the potential offeror has reason to believe that its actions are causing the rumours or price changes, in which case the offeror should make an announcement. Where there is any doubt in this respect, the Panel should be consulted.

(d) Where negotiations or discussions are being extended to include more than a very restricted number of people outside of those in the company who need to know and their immediate advisers, then the offeree should make an announcement.

(e) Where a purchaser is being sought for a holding or aggregate of holdings which have 30% or more of the voting rights in the company or where a company is seeking potential offerors, then the offeree company will be required to make an announcement in any of the following circumstances.

- The company is subject to rumour and speculation or there is untoward movement in its share price.
- The number of offerors being approached is increasing beyond a very restricted number.

## Contents of the announcement of a firm offer

Where there is a firm intention to make an offer, a detailed 'firm intention' announcement is required. The announcement should contain details of the terms and conditions of the offer, the identity of the offeror and any existing holdings in the offeree which the offeror (or people acting in concert with him) owns, controls or has options to buy *(Rule 2.7)*.

## Contents of an announcement of a possible offer

All 'possible offer' announcements made under *Rule 2.4* of the Code, which commence an offer period, will be required to identify a potential bidder. The possible offer announcement, whether released by the prospective offeror or offeree, will trigger an automatic 28 day 'put up or shut up' deadline by which time the named bidder must either commit to a 'firm intention to make an offer' announcement, or publicly withdraw from the offer process (*Rule 2.6*).

## Offeror's obligations

An offeror should only announce an offer if he knows that he has the ability to see the offer through, for example financing arrangements are in place. After an announcement has been made, an offeror must proceed with the offer unless permitted to withdraw by the Panel *(Rule 2.7)*. Once an offeror has stated that he does not intend to make an offer, he will normally be bound by that statement for at least six months or until there is a material change in circumstances *(Rule 2.8)*.

The purpose of this rule is to avoid uncertainty and the possibility of vexatious offers, which may create a false market in the offeree's shares.

## Independent advice (Rule 3)

After an offer has been received, the offeree board must obtain **competent and independent advice** on the offer *(Rule 3.1)*. The substance of this advice must be made known to their shareholders. This is particularly important in the case of a management buyout (MBO), where the MBO directors will have a conflict of interest and will be unable to give advice to their shareholders.

If an adviser receives a fee dependent on the failure of a hostile bid, this will give an impression of a conflict of interest. Such an adviser will normally be disqualified from acting as a *Rule 3* adviser. In addition, the Panel will require such arrangements to be disclosed in a defence document.

### Reverse takeovers

A reverse takeover is typically a situation where a listed company makes a share offer for an unlisted counterpart. As a result of the offer, the original shareholders of the unlisted company end up owning more than 50% of the shares of the listed company. Effectively, the unlisted company becomes the acquirer and obtains a listing through being taken over in this way.

Where the offer is effectively a reverse takeover or the offeror directors have a conflict of interest, then the **offeror** must also obtain competent independent advice *(Rule 3.2)*. The basis of this is that the offeror is effectively the offeree.

## 5 The Offer and Defence Documents

### General obligation as to information

Documents from the offeror and offeree boards are covered in section J of the Code. *Rule 23* states that shareholders must be given sufficient information and advice to enable them to reach a properly informed decision as to the merits of an offer. This information must be made available early enough for them to make a decision in good time.

The offer and defence documents are both essentially sales documents. As such, much of the required information below, which is not necessarily exciting to shareholders, will be relegated to the small print at the back of the document.

### The responsibility of the directors

Any document or advertisement issued in connection with an offer must state that the directors of the offeror or offeree company, as appropriate, accept responsibility for the information contained in the document. It must also state that, to the best of the directors' knowledge, the information is in accordance with the facts and does not omit anything likely to affect the importance of the information *(Rule 19.2)*.

If the information relates to another company and has been taken from published sources, then this responsibility is limited to ensuring that the information is correctly and fairly reproduced *(Note 3 to Rule 19.2)*.

## 6 The Offer Document

The offer document must be sent to offeree shareholders within 28 days of the announcement of a firm's intention to make an offer (*Rule 24.1*). On the day of publication, the offeror must publish the offer document on a website (usually its own) in accordance with *Rule 30.4*; and announce via a RIS that the offer document has been so published.

The principal contents are as follows.

(a) **The intentions of the offeror for the offeree company and its employees (*Rule 24.2*).**

This will include any major changes to be introduced and plans for continued employment of employees. The document should give the long-term commercial justification for the bid.

Typically, offer documents will make rather bland statements concerning the offeror's plans for existing employees. For example, they may just state that the existing rights of employees will be safeguarded. The commercial justification for the offer will be more fully developed, particularly in a share for share offer.

(b) **Financial and other information on the offeror and offeree company *(Rule 24.3)*.**

- Names of directors
- Nature of the business and the financial and trading prospects
- The website address where the audited consolidated accounts for the last two years have been published
- The website address where an interim statement and/or preliminary announcement made since the date of the last published audited accounts have been published
- For a securities exchange offer, a description of any known significant change in the financial or trading position that has occurred since the end of the last financial period
- A pro-forma statement of earnings and net assets for the offeror
- Details of material contracts for the offeror for the two year period prior to the offer
- Rating agencies' outlooks and any changes made during the offer period

(c) **Offer conditions** *(Rule 24.3d)*

(d) **The terms of the offer** *(Rule 24.3d)*, including the consideration offered and how this is to be paid.

(e) **Share price comparisons.** The offeree historic share price for the first business day in the each of the six months immediately before the date of the offer document and for the last business day before the commencement of the offer period and for the last date before the publication of the offer document *(Rule 24.3d).*

It is often the case that the value of the offer is compared to the share price of the offeree. If this is done, there must be a comparison with the offeree share price on the last business day before the offer was announced along with any other comparison that may be made. This is meant to prevent solely unfair comparisons being made. *(Rule 24.3g)* The problem is that the share price of the offeree will often have moved before the announcement in anticipation of the offer. As a result, this share price will already contain an element of bid premium, reducing the validity of the comparison.

(f) **How the offer is to be financed *(Rule 24.3f)*.**

There must be details of how the offer is to be financed and the source of any finance. This includes details of any debt instruments entered into in order to finance the offer.

Where the offer is for cash or includes an element of cash then the offeror's bankers or another appropriate adviser should confirm that resources are available to satisfy full acceptance of the offer *(Rule 24.8)*.

(g) **Details of any relevant shareholdings and dealings *(Rule 24.4)*.**

These include shareholdings in the offeree by the offeror company and shareholdings in the offeror or the offeree company by the offeror's directors or people acting in concert with the offeror. It also includes dealings in derivatives referenced to the shares.

(h) Whether and in what manner the **emoluments of the offeror directors** will be affected by the acquisition of the offeree company or other associated transaction *(Rule 24.5)*.

(i) **Responsibility statement *(Rule 19.2)*.**

A statement that the directors of the offeror accept responsibility for the information contained within the document must be included in each document the offeror sends to shareholders.

(j) Fees and expenses (*Rule 24.16*). The offer document should contain an estimate of the fees and expenses expected to be incurred by the offeror, analysed by different fee categories.

# 7 The Defence Document

The defence document should be sent to shareholders within 14 days of the publication of the offer document *(Rule 25.1)*. On the day of publication, the offeree company must publish the document on a website (usually its own) in accordance with Rule 30.4; and announce via a RIS that the defence document has been so published.

The main contents of the defence document are as follows.

- **The views of the offeree board** on the offer and their reason for this view. An opinion on the effects of the implementation of the offer on the company's interests, including employment and an opinion on the offeror's strategic plans for the offeree company *(Rule 25.2a)*.
- Substance of the advice received by the board from the Rule 3 **independent adviser** *(Rule 25.2b)*.
- a description of any known **significant change in the financial or trading position** of the offeree company which has occurred since the end of the last financial period for which either audited financial information or interim financial information has been published, or the directors need to give an appropriate negative statement *(Rule 25.3)*.
- **Relevant shareholdings and dealings** should be disclosed *(Rule 25.4)*. These include shareholdings in the offeror held by the offeree or its subsidiaries and any shareholdings in the offeror or offeree company held by the offeree's directors or people acting in concert with the offeree. It also includes derivatives referenced to the shares.
- **Directors' service contracts**, including the name of the relevant director and the remuneration payable under the contract *(Rule 25.5)*.
- **Responsibility statement** *(Rule 19.2)* is also required.

# 8 Profit Forecasts and Earnings Enhancement Statements

There are specific regulations in the City Code regarding the inclusion of financial forecast information in published documents. The subjectivity associated with making forecasts necessitates clear reporting requirements regarding the forecast and how it has been prepared to ensure shareholders understand the information that has been provided.

The Code distinguishes between 'profit forecasts' and 'earnings enhancement statements'.

## Definition of a profit forecast

The definition of a profit forecast is fairly wide-ranging and is covered in *Rule 28.6*. A statement that includes no figures, but indicates how the profits have performed may constitute a forecast. Key factors to consider include whether the statement:

- Puts a ceiling or floor on the possible profit
- Gives information enabling an approximate profit figure to be calculated

For example, a statement that profits will be higher than last year is likely to be considered a forecast.

Even if the period for which the estimate of profit is being made has already expired, the estimate will still be a forecast. However, preliminary or interim announcements made by companies that comply with the Listing Rules' requirements for such announcements will not be treated as forecasts. Likewise, dividend forecasts will not normally be included unless they are accompanied by an estimate of dividend cover.

## Requirements relating to profit forecasts

A profit forecast must be compiled with due care and consideration by the directors *(Rule 28.3)*. It must be fairly presented to the highest standards of accuracy. The responsibility for this lies with the directors making the forecast, but the advisers must satisfy themselves that it is the case.

The assumptions upon which the forecast has been based must be stated in the document giving the forecast *(Rule 28.4)*.

Where an offer is solely for cash, then any forecast made by the offeror need not be reported on *(Rule 28.1)*. In all other cases, the accounting policies and calculations for the forecast must usually be examined and reported on by the auditors for the company. If another financial adviser has been mentioned in the document, then that person must also report on the forecast.

A report by a financial adviser will not confirm that the profit forecast is correct. It will typically state that the adviser has discussed the bases and assumptions relating to the forecast with the directors of the company and that he considers the forecast to have been prepared after due and careful enquiry.

The accountant's report is likewise fairly limited in its scope. It merely states that the accountant has confirmed that the figures in the forecast have been properly compiled on the basis of the assumptions made by the directors and that the report has been prepared on a basis consistent with the usual accounting policies of the company.

The reports must be published in the document giving the forecast *(Rule 28.1)*. The reports must be accompanied by a statement that those making them have given and not withdrawn their consent to publication. If a company's forecast is published first in an announcement, it must be repeated in full, together with the reports, in the next document published in connection with the offer by that company.

### Exception

The Takeover Code has been changed so that third party advisers' confirmation reports are not required on profit forecasts made outside an offer period.

Instead, a directors' confirmation regime applies *(Rule 28.1c)*. Directors must confirm that:

- The forecast has been properly compiled on the basis of the assumptions; and
- The basis of accounting used is consistent.

The rationale behind the change is to encourage listed companies to provide greater guidance to the market about their future expectations, thus improving market transparency and valuations, without the company worrying about the Takeover Code implications on profit forecasts if an unforeseen offer materialises in the future.

If an offer does subsequently arise, any document or announcement published during the offer period which refers to the profit forecast must:

- Repeat the forecast and include certain confirmations from the directors; or
- Include a statement by the directors that the forecast is no longer valid and an explanation as to why that is the case; or
- Include a new forecast for the relevant period, which will then need to be accompanied by the relevant third party advisers' reports.

However, where a company **regularly publishes 'earnings guidance' statements** as part of their normal shareholder communications the need for third party reports may not arise. The new rules allow that if all parties agree (or the Takeover Panel considers reporting would be disproportionate), the profit forecast need not be reported on and only the directors' confirmations set out above for pre-approach forecasts are required.

The Panel will normally grant a waiver from *Rule 28* reporting regimes for a forecast relating to a future financial period, which ends more than 15 months from the date of publication. Instead directors' confirmations must be provided. However, if a subsequent offer document or announcement repeats the forecast, the document must include a profit forecast for the current year and any intervening year and these forecasts are potentially subject to the *Rule 28* reporting regime.

*Rule 28* reporting requirements will always apply in an MBO scenario: in other words third party reports are required and directors' confirmation statements alone are insufficient.

## Quantified Financial Benefits Statements

### Quantified financial benefits statements

Where a party makes a statement concerning the expected financial benefits of a takeover or merger (for example by quantifying the synergies expecting to arise), the following disclosures are required *(Rule28.6)*.

- The bases of the belief supporting the statement (including sources of information)
- Reports by financial advisers and accountants
- An analysis and explanation to enable shareholders to understand the statement
- A base figure for any comparison drawn

These requirements also apply to target companies quantifying financial benefits from cost savings and all quantification of financial implications should a bid fail. Those wishing to make quantified financial benefits statements should consult the Panel in advance.

# 9 Restrictions on Share Dealings

## Restrictions on the offeror and concert parties during the offer period (Rule 4.2)

During the offer period, the offeror or persons **acting in concert** (see below) may not sell securities in the offeree without prior permission from the Panel, and only then after 24 hours' public notice has been given that the sales may take place. If the bid is a mandatory bid under *Rule 9* (see below), then no sales will be allowed at all.

If there is an announcement that sales may be made, then no further purchases of securities will be permitted and it is highly unlikely that the Panel will permit the offer to be revised. This means that the only way the offeror can acquire shares in the offeree after the announcement will be if shareholders accept the existing offer.

The rationale behind these rules is to prevent an offeror from driving up the price of a target's shares via announcing an offer and then selling subsequently at a profit.

## Acting in concert

The definition of acting in concert for the purpose of the City Code (section C) includes persons who, pursuant to an agreement or understanding, cooperate to acquire shares in a company to obtain or consolidate control. Note that this is not the same as the legal concept of acting in concert, which merely refers to an agreement between two or more people to acquire interests in shares (Companies Act).

### Specific examples

In certain cases, people will be deemed to be acting in concert unless it is shown to be otherwise. Specific examples include the following.

(a) A company, together with its parent, subsidiaries and fellow subsidiaries plus any company that is an associated company of any of the above, or a company which itself owns 20% of any of the above. An associated company is defined as a company in which the investing company owns at least 20% of the voting rights.

The relationships described above can be demonstrated on a diagram.

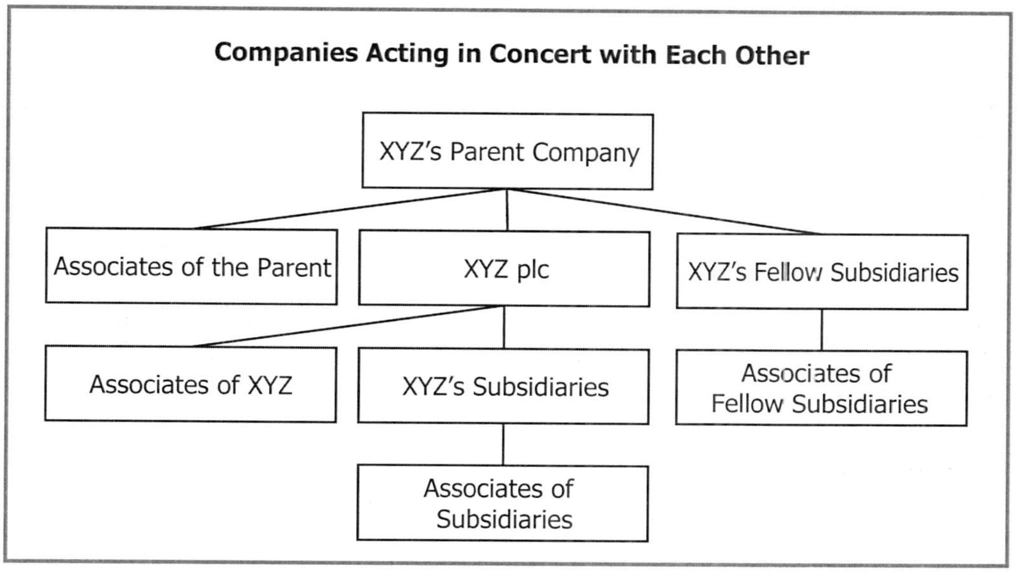


Each of the above companies will be presumed to be acting in concert with any other member of the total grouping.

(b) A company will be presumed to be acting in concert with its directors and their close relatives.

(c) The directors of a company subject to, or likely to be subject to, an offer, are presumed to be acting in concert.

(d) A company with any of its pension funds, or any pension funds of the companies mentioned in (a) above.

(e) A 'connected' adviser with its client. This normally relates to a financial adviser and corporate broker advising an offeror or offeree or concert party on a specific transaction. It excludes exempt fund managers and exempt principal traders acting in such capacity.

(f) A fund manager (including an exempt fund manager) is presumed to be acting in concert with any person whose investments it manages on a discretionary basis.

## Standstill agreements

A standstill agreement is an agreement between a company and a shareholder which maintains the status quo, ie restricts a shareholder's ability to acquire further shares in the company or to sell any shares in the company.

If a standstill agreement is in place, the Panel will not normally consider a concert party to exist between the parties to the agreement, provided that the agreement does not restrict any of those parties from either accepting an offer for the company's shares at any stage or agreeing to accept any offer for the company's shares either before or after announcement (Practice Statement 16). The Panel should be consulted.

## Dealings by connected exempt principal traders and connected exempt fund managers

A principal trader is a person who:

1 Is registered as a market-maker with a recognised investment exchange, or is accepted by the Panel as a market-maker; or

2 Is a member firm of a recognised investment exchange dealing as principal in order book securities. An exempt principal trader is recognised by the Panel as exempt for the purposes of the Code.

An exempt fund manager is a fund manager who deals on a discretionary basis for clients and is recognised as such by the Panel.

Fund managers, who manage investment accounts on a discretionary basis, and principal traders must apply to the Panel to obtain 'exempt' status. Exempt status is only relevant if the sole connection between a fund manager or principal trader is that they are in the same group as a financial adviser or corporate broker to an offeror, offeree or concert party thereof.

The main effect of having exempt status is that the definition of acting in concert will not apply.

Connected, exempt principal traders must comply with *Rule 38* of the Code. A principal trader, who is connected with the offeror or offeree, must not carry out dealings with the purpose of assisting the offeror or offeree company *(Rule 38.1)*. An offeror and persons acting in concert must not deal as principal with a connected exempt principal trader *(Rule 38.2)*.

If a principal trader or fund manager is connected but not exempt, *Rule 7.2* of the Code applies. On commencement of the offer period both connected principal traders and connected fund managers will be presumed to be concert parties and Code restrictions on dealings will be relevant *(Rules 5, 6, 9, 11, 36)*.

## Dealings in offeree securities by financial advisers of the offeree (Rule 4.4)

Financial advisers to the offeree, apart from exempt principal traders and exempt fund managers, may not do the following during the offer period.

- Purchase any securities of the offeree or deal in derivatives and options referenced to the securities during the offer period on their own account.
- Lend money to others to enable them to deal in the shares other than on normal commercial terms.
- Enter into any agreement to induce someone else to deal or refrain from dealing in the shares.

This rule prevents advisers from purchasing shares or adopting other related methods designed to prevent the offeror from obtaining sufficient acceptances to declare the bid unconditional.

## Prohibited dealings by people other than the offeror (Rule 4.1)

### Dealing in the shares of the offeree

Any person who possesses confidential price-sensitive information concerning an offer or possible offer is prohibited from dealing in any way in the securities of the offeree, including dealing in options. In addition, they are also prohibited from making recommendations to other people to deal.

### Dealing in the shares of the offeror

Dealings in the securities of the offeror company will be permitted so long as the offer is not price sensitive to the relevant securities, for example, in a wholly cash bid.

### Insider dealing

This rule reinforces the Criminal Justice Act 1993, which broadly states that nobody in possession of inside information may deal in the relevant company's securities.

## Summary: dealings in offeror and offeree securities

The table below summarises the main provisions relating to dealings in offeror and offeree securities in the offer period.

| Dealings by | Offeror Securities | Offeree Securities |
|---|---|---|
| Offeror | N/A | • Sales – prohibited<br>• Purchases – allowed subject to *Rules 5, 9, 6* and *11* |
| Financial Advisers to Offeree | N/A | Dealings – prohibited |
| Any holder of Price-Sensitive Information | Dealings – prohibited* | Dealings – prohibited |

* Unless the offer is not price-sensitive to the offeror

## Restrictions on acquisitions

### Restrictions on obtaining control

The Code contains restrictions on companies amassing substantial shareholdings in target companies without making an offer for all of the shares. Two Code rules work together here – Rules 5 and 9.

The objective of *Rule 5* is to prevent a person obtaining control or consolidating control over a company except in a number of acceptable circumstances. The basic rule states that when a person (including people acting in concert with him) holds shares or rights over shares that carry less than 30% of the voting rights in a company, he may not acquire any shares or rights over shares, which would mean that he would hold 30% or more of the voting rights in the company.

It should be noted that the definition of 'effective control' as being control of 30% of the voting rights is essentially arbitrary. The Panel has considered changing this percentage in the past but has concluded that the 30% test has 'stood the test of time'.

If a person already holds shares or rights over shares with between 30% and 50% inclusive of the voting rights then he may not increase his percentage holding in the company.

### Exceptions to the restrictions

There are a number of exceptions where the above basic rule does not apply, allowing a stake of over 30% to be acquired. These are as follows *(Rules 5.1 and 5.2)*.

(a) Where a person already holds shares with more than 50% of the voting rights, since they already have legal control *(Note 1 to Rule 5.1)*.

(b) Where there is a vote of independent shareholders, ie excluding the acquirer, which approves the acquisition *(Note 4 to Rule 5.1)* – a 'whitewash' – see dispensations from *Rule 9* later in this chapter.

(c) Where the purchase of shares or rights over shares is from a single shareholder and it is the only purchase in a seven-day period *(Rule 5.2a)*. Where such a purchase is made, then no subsequent purchases will be permitted unless the situations given below apply *(Rule 5.3)*.

(d) Where the purchase is immediately before or at any time after a firm announcement to make an offer or during an offer and either the offer itself or a competing offer will be/has been recommended by the offeree board *(Rule 5.2b/c)*. Where the purchase is immediately before the announcement, it must be conditional on the offer being made.

(e) Where an offer has been announced, and the first closing date of the offer or a competing offer has passed *(Rule 5.2c)*.

(f) During an offer that is unconditional in all respects *(Rule 5.2c)*.

(g) Where the acquisition is by way of a shareholder accepting an offer, as opposed to selling in the market *(Rule 5.2d)*.

(h) Where the acquisition replenishes a previously held shareholding, as long as it is a very small purchase (less than 1% of issued voting share capital) *(Rule 9.1, note 11)*.

### Rights over shares

It should be noted that *Rule 5* refers to shares or rights over shares. This will include options over existing shares but will not include warrants to subscribe for new shares in the company or convertible debt (since the shares are not yet in existence in these cases). Exercise of such warrants or conversion rights would, however, be relevant for the purpose of *Rule 5*, when they would be treated as an acquisition from a single shareholder. The exercise of options over existing shares would not be relevant, since the options themselves have already been included as rights over shares.

**EXAMPLE**

| Table Title | Before % | Exercise Options % | Exercise Warrants % |
|---|---|---|---|
| Shares owned | 25 | 29 | 32 |
| Options over existing shares | 4 | – | – |
| Total for *Rule 5* purposes | 29 | 29 | 32 |
| Warrants over shares | 3 | 3 | – |

Since the options are already included in the *Rule 5* total, the exercise of the options has no effect on the holder's position. By contrast, exercise of the warrants increases the shares and rights over shares held and brings the total to 30% or over. This in itself would be permitted by *Rule 5*, since the exercise of the warrants is treated as a purchase from a single shareholder. However, the restrictions on future purchases outlined above would subsequently apply.

## 10 The Mandatory Offer

The mandatory offer is required by *Rule 9* of the Code. Where a person obtains control of a company, then he must make an offer for the shares of all other shareholders. This means that other shareholders will not

- Be forced to keep a shareholding in a company where somebody else effectively controls the company's operations and financial policy; or
- Have to sell shares subsequently at a lower price that reflects the fact that there is a dominant investor who does not intend to make an offer for the other shares.

## When the mandatory offer is required

### Acquiring or consolidating control

*Rule 9* covers two situations.

- When a person originally acquires effective control of a company (defined as holding 30% or more of the voting rights).
- When a person consolidates control (defined as increasing a holding of between 30% and 50% inclusive of the voting rights by any percentage).

The rule specifically states that

- Where a person acquires shares which, when taken in aggregate with his existing holdings and those of people acting in concert, carry 30% or more of the voting rights of a company; or
- Where a person or people acting in concert already hold shares with between 30% and 50% (inclusive) of the voting rights and the person or people acting in concert acquire shares which result in an increase in their percentage holding,

then that person must make an offer to all the holders of any class of equity share, or voting non-equity share in which he or people acting in concert have a holding.

### Contrast to Rule 5

This rule links in strongly with *Rule 5*. There are, however, some important distinctions between the two. *Rule 5* basically prohibits purchases that take a holding to 30% or over except in certain circumstances. If a person takes advantage of one of the exceptions, they can purchase the shares. However, they will still be subject to *Rule 9* and will be required to make a mandatory offer for the company in question.

A second difference is that *Rule 5* refers to shares or rights over shares (such as options) but *Rule 9* refers to shares. Thus, a purchase of options taking a person over 30% would be relevant for *Rule 5* purposes, but would not usually be covered by *Rule 9*, unless the buyer of the option had effectively acquired control of the shares *(Note 10* to *Rule 9.1)*. If the options were exercised, however, then the resultant acquisition of shares could trigger a *Rule 9* bid.

**EXAMPLE**

| Table Title | Before % | Exercise Options % | Exercise Warrants % |
|---|---|---|---|
| Shares owned | 25 | 25 | 31 |
| Options over existing shares | – | 6 | – |
| Total for *Rule 5* purposes | 25 | 31 | 31 |
| Warrants over shares | 3 | 3 | – |

The purchase of the options has no effect on the total for *Rule 9* purposes and hence no mandatory offer is required. It will, nevertheless, be relevant for *Rule 5* purposes. If the options are purchased from more than one shareholder, then the purchase would probably not be permitted. If the purchase was from only one person, then it would be permitted but subsequent acquisitions would not usually be possible, in accordance with *Rule 5*.

The later exercise of the options is irrelevant for *Rule 5* purposes, but increases the total of shares to 30% or over. Hence, a mandatory offer will probably be required under *Rule 9*.

### Moving from a voluntary offer to a mandatory offer

Note that a person may make an offer on a voluntary basis and then purchase shares in the market bringing his holding in the company to 30% or more. This will trigger *Rule 9* and mean that the offer will become mandatory. Mandatory offers can only have a limited number of conditions attached and must have a cash alternative (see below).

Should an offeror plan to incur such an obligation, it should consult the Panel in advance *(Note 9 to Rule 9.1)*.

### Acquisitions of shares by people acting in concert

The prime responsibility for making a mandatory offer rests with the person who made the purchase that took the total concert party holding to 30% or over and triggered the offer *(Rule 9.2)*. The obligation may, however, be extended to include any other member of the concert party, especially where the person with prime responsibility is a relatively minor member of the group.

### Reduction or dilution of a controlling shareholding

It may happen that a controlling stake of between 30% and 50% is diluted as a result of a new issue of shares by the company or by a sale of part of the shareholding. In these circumstances, the controlling shareholder (or concert party) is permitted to make limited purchases without incurring a *Rule 9* obligation *(Note 11 to Rule 9.1)*.

Such shareholders may purchase up to 1% of the shares in any one year, subject to the proviso that the total percentage owned does exceed the highest percentage owned in the previous 12 months. As a result, such controlling shareholders will not be able to increase their percentage holdings from one year to the next. They can only reinstate the holding to its previous percentage level. For example, if a holding was reduced from 37% to 36.5%, it could be reinstated to a maximum level of 37% within the next year.

### Advisers with recognised intermediary status

Shares held by a recognised intermediary acting in a client-serving capacity will not be treated as interests in shares for the purpose of deciding if a *Rule 9* bid is required *(Note 1 to Rule 7.2)*. Note that the shares must be held by the intermediary in a client-serving capacity and as such this exclusion would not apply to shares held by an intermediary for proprietary trading purposes. If any part of the trading operations of a bank or securities house wishes to be accepted by the Panel as a recognised intermediary, it must apply to the Panel to be granted such status and it will have to comply with any requirements imposed by the Panel as a condition of its granting such status.

## Dispensations from making a mandatory offer

The dispensations from *Rule 9* give a number of situations when acquiring 30% or more of the voting rights in a company, or increasing a holding with 30% or more of voting rights by any percentage, will not necessarily trigger a mandatory offer. In all cases, the dispensation is not an automatic right but is granted by the Panel.

### Whitewash

Where there is an issue of new securities by the company as consideration for an acquisition and a shareholder is set to acquire 30% or more of a company. No mandatory offer will be required if there is a vote of independent shareholders, ie not including the person making the acquisition or people acting in concert with him, which approves the shareholding. This type of proposal is known as a 'whitewash'. A 'whitewash will also be given provided there has been a vote of independent shareholders, in cases involving the underwriting of an issue of shares.

### Foreclosure on security for a loan

Where a lender forecloses on security for a loan and takes control of 30% or more of the company. This exception will not apply if the lender had reason to believe that foreclosure was likely when the loan was made.

### Rescue operations

Where a person acquires 30% or more of a company as a result of a rescue operation when the company is in financial difficulty.

### Inadvertent mistake

Where the person made a genuine mistake in incurring an obligation to make an offer. However, the shares must be sold in a limited period of time to people unconnected to the original purchaser.

### Where 50% of shareholders will not accept

Where holders of shares carrying 50% or more of the voting rights in the company have confirmed in writing that they will not accept any offer. This would mean that a mandatory offer would be bound to fail, since it must be a condition of the offer that the offeror and people acting in concert end up with more than 50% of the voting rights (see below).

### Enfranchisement of non-voting shares

Where shares that were previously non-voting are enfranchised, giving a person 30% or more of the voting rights. However, the person should not have acquired the shares with reason to believe that they would be enfranchised.

### Repurchase of shares

Where a company repurchases its own shares and a person not acting in concert with the directors ends up owning 30% or more of the company as a result. Such a person will not be required to make an offer for the company, unless he acquired the shares with the expectation of the share repurchase taking place (*Notes 1 and 2 to Rule 37.1*). Note that a director obtaining 30% or more of the company may be required to make a mandatory offer in such a situation, unless there is a whitewash vote.

## Required conditions for a mandatory offer

There are only two conditions permitted with a mandatory offer:

### Referral to Competition and Markets Authority or the European Commission

The mandatory offer must be made subject to a referral to the CMA or the European Commission, before the later of the first closing date of the offer and the date that it becomes unconditional. If the bid is referred before this date, it will lapse *(Rule 9.4)*.

### Acceptances condition

It must also be conditional on the offeror and people acting in concert holding shares with more than 50% of the voting rights after the offer *(Rule 9.3)*.

## Required consideration to be offered

The offer must be for cash or with a cash alternative *(Rule 9.5)*. The cash offer must be at a price not less than the highest price paid for shares in the offeree in the last 12 months by the offeror or persons acting in concert with him.

# 11 THE VOLUNTARY OFFER

A voluntary offer is any offer not subject to *Rule 9*, Mandatory Offers. There are required conditions for a voluntary offer, and then the offeror may choose to add in additional conditions.

### Referral to the CMA

Where an offer comes within the statutory provisions for a referral to the CMA or to the European Commission, then it must be a term of the offer that it will lapse should such a referral take place before the later of the first closing date of the offer and the date that the offer becomes or is declared unconditional *(Rule 12)*.

### Acceptance condition

The offer must contain an 'acceptances condition'. A usual condition of the offer is that it will not become unconditional as to acceptances unless the offeror has acquired or agreed to acquire shares such that he will hold more than 50% of the voting rights in the company *(Rule 10)*.

Although the acceptance condition must specify that the offeror holds more than 50% of the company, it may specify a higher percentage. A typical acceptance condition would state the following.

> The offer is conditional upon the offeror acquiring 90% or more of the shares to which the offer relates (or such lesser percentage as the offeror sees fit), so long as the offeror holds more than 50% of the voting rights in the offeree.

### Contrast between voluntary offer and mandatory offer acceptance provision

In a mandatory offer, there is no option to have an acceptance level in excess of 50%.

Note that the offeror in a voluntary offer will be required to control more than 50% of the shares himself, excluding any people acting in concert. This is a contrast to *Rule 9* where the requirement is that the offeror together with persons acting in concert control more than 50% of the shares. If there are reasons why a person acting in concert cannot or will not transfer the shares to the offeror, this will make it easier for the mandatory offer to succeed than the voluntary offer.

### Illustration

An illustration of this would be a situation where B plc, an associated company of A plc, owns 29.4% of X plc. A plc wishes to bid for X plc, but to leave at least 25% of the shares in public hands, in order to maintain X plc's listing. The problem is that, if A plc makes a voluntary offer, it will have to acquire more than 50% of X plc's shares. This means that a maximum of <20.6% of the shares will remain in public hands, after taking into account A plc's holding of >50% and B plc's holding of 29.4%.

A solution may be for A plc to purchase an additional 0.6% of X plc's shares in the market. Together with the associate's holding of 29.4%, this comes to a total of 30% and incurs a mandatory offer requirement. In this case, it would be possible to acquire only an additional 21% of the shares, since B plc's holding can be taken into account for the purpose of the acceptance condition, leaving well over 25% of the shares in public hands. The deal would of course need to be structured to make it attractive for existing shareholders not to fully accept the offer and leave A plc owning all of the shares in X plc.

In the actual case from which this illustration was drawn, the offeror gave investors two choices as part of the mandatory offer. They could either sell all their shares or they could sell $3/5^{ths}$ of their holding and retain the other $2/5^{ths}$. The second alternative, which was the preferred option for the offeror, would mean that only $3/5^{ths}$ of the remaining shares would need to be purchased, ie ($3/5 \times 70\%$) 42%, leaving a total of 28% of the shares in public hands.

Note that such an offer may be considered to be a partial offer by the Panel and, hence, be covered by the rules on partial offers, covered below.

### Other possible conditions

In addition to the above, the offeror can set any conditions he wants, provided that the condition does not depend solely on subjective judgements by the directors of the offeror or if the fulfilment of the condition lies in their hands *(Rule 13)*. If this proviso were not in existence, it would be easy for offerors to withdraw their offers at will and at any time by setting subjective conditions.

## Minimum price to be offered

Where an offeror or people acting in concert have purchased shares in the offeree within the three months prior to the announcement, then the offer price should be on terms no less favourable than for those purchases *(Rule 6)*. Note that, even if the purchases are for cash, there is no requirement in these circumstances for a cash alternative.

The Panel may extend the three-month period if it feels that this is necessary to ensure similar treatment to all shareholders, as required in the first general principle *(Note 1 to Rule 6)*. An example of this may be where purchases were made from directors of the offeree company in the fourth month prior to the offer.

### Purchase of shares in the offer period

If the offeror or people acting in concert purchase shares after the announcement of the offer at higher than the offer price, then the offer must be revised to at least the highest price paid for the purchases *(Rule 6.2)*. The revised offer will apply to all offeree shareholders, including those who have already accepted the offer *(Rule 32.3)*. This prevents the offeror arranging a better deal with a particular shareholder by waiting until other shareholders have accepted an inferior offer and then purchasing his shares in the market place.

## Requirement for a cash alternative

This requirement usually arises where the offeror or people acting in concert have either purchased any shares for cash during the offer period or have purchased for cash shares with 10% or more of the voting rights in the company in the 12 months prior to the announcement of the offer *(Rule 11)*.

Where shares have been purchased for cash during the offer period but the 10% threshold has not been breached, the offer must be for cash or there must be a cash alternative to the offer at a price not less than the highest price paid by the offeror or persons acting in concert during the offer period. Where the 10% threshold is breached, the offer must be for cash or have a cash alternative set at not less than the highest price paid by the offeror or persons acting in concert in the last 12 months.

The Panel may, in addition, require a cash offer or cash alternative in any circumstances where it feels this is necessary to ensure similar treatment for all shareholders. This will be in similar circumstances to those noted above for the minimum price to be offered, eg where directors have sold their shares for cash.

## Requirement for a securities alternative

When an offeror has acquired 10% of shares in the last three months in exchange for securities, securities must be offered to all other shareholders.

## Similar treatment for all shareholders

General principle 1 of the Code requires that all holders of the securities of an offeree company of the same class must be afforded equivalent treatment. This principle must be adhered to for all offers, mandatory and voluntary.

### Different classes of share capital and convertibles

All classes of share capital must be given comparable (but not necessarily identical) treatment *(Rule 14.1)*. In addition, the interests of convertible debt and warrants investors should be safeguarded *(Rule 15)*.

### Special deals with favourable conditions

Favourable conditions should not generally be extended to any particular group of shareholders *(Rule 16)*. However, in certain situations, the offeror may wish to retain the services of director shareholders of the offeree and to motivate them by means of an 'earn out' deal where they receive a higher price for their shares if the company's profits hit specified targets.

Such special deals may be permitted as long as relevant details of the arrangements are disclosed and an independent adviser states that, in his opinion, the terms are fair and reasonable. Where the value of the arrangements entered into is significant and/or unusual in the context of industry practice, then the Panel must be consulted and consent to the arrangements be obtained. The Panel may require, as part of this process, that the arrangements be approved at a general meeting of the company's shareholders *(Rule 16.2)*.

## Summary of differences between mandatory and voluntary offers

| | Mandatory Offer | Voluntary Offer |
|---|---|---|
| **Nature of Consideration** | Cash or cash alternative required | No cash offer required except under *Rule 11* |
| **Price to be Offered** | Highest price paid by the offeror in the last 12 months | Highest price paid by the offeror in the last three months, unless *Rule 11* applies |
| **CMA Referral Condition** | Yes | Yes |
| **Acceptances Condition** | Offeror and concert parties own more than 50% of the voting rights in the offeree | Offeror sets acceptance condition, subject to it being at least owning more than 50% of the voting rights in the offeree |
| **Other Conditions** | No | Yes, so long as not subjective and fulfilment does not lie in hands of offeror's directors |

# 12 Conduct During the Offer

## Disclosure of shareholdings

### Opening position disclosure

An offeror *(Rule 8.1a)*, an offeree *(Rule 8.2a)* and a 1% security-holder in any party to the offer *(Rule 8.3a)* must make an Opening Position Disclosure relating to its interests in or rights to subscribe for any relevant securities of any party to the offer. Shares or other securities of a cash offeror will not be treated as 'relevant securities' for the purposes of *Rule 8 (Rule 8, note 1)*. The Opening Position Disclosure must be made by no later than 12 noon on the day falling 10 business days after the commencement of the offer period or the announcement that first identifies the offeror *(Rule 8, note 2)*.

## Dealings during the offer period

As well as the Opening Position Disclosure, announcements are required relating to relevant dealings during the offer period. Public dealing disclosures must be made by certain parties, including:

- The offeror *(Rule 8.1b)*
- The offeree *(Rule 8.2b)*
- Any person who holds an interest in 1% or more of any class of relevant securities of any party to the offer *(Rule 8.3b)*
- Any person acting in concert with a party to the offer dealing for his own account or for the account of discretionary investment clients *(Rule 8.4)*

Shares or other securities of a cash offeror will not be treated as 'relevant securities' for the purposes of *Rule 8 (Rule 8, note 1)*.

The disclosure is required to be made no later than 12 noon on the business day following the day of dealing.

Both the offeror and offeree are obliged to assist the Panel in identifying those persons interested in 1% or more of any class of relevant securities of the offeror or offeree *(Rule 22)*. The offeror and offeree have a responsibility to send those persons an explanation of their disclosure responsibilities under *Rule 8*.

## Irrevocable commitments

Irrevocable commitments and letters of intent are commitments to accept or not to an offer, and often include a commitment to vote in a certain way relating to the shares. An irrevocable undertaking may be either hard (binding in all circumstances), soft (ceases to be binding if a higher offer emerges) or semi-hard (ceases to be binding if a higher offer emerges which exceeds the existing offer by an agreed amount).

An irrevocable commitment which relates only to acceptance of an offer will not, in itself, normally result in a shareholder being considered to be acting in concert with an offeror under the definition of 'acting in concert' in the Code.

However, the Panel considers that a shareholder who enters into an irrevocable commitment to accept an offer, which includes a voting undertaking, to be acting in concert with the offeror, if the voting undertaking is restricted to the period of the offer or it is limited to matters which relate to ensuring that the offer succeeds.

During an offer period, if any party to the offer or any person acting in concert with it procures an irrevocable commitment or a letter of intent, the relevant party to the offer must publicly disclose the details in accordance with the Notes on *Rule 2.11*. The announcement must be made no later than 12 noon on the business day following the date of the transaction.

Any irrevocable commitments or letters of intent received before the commencement of the offer period, must be disclosed in the Opening Position Disclosure *(Rule 2.11* and *Rule 8, note 5a (viii))*.

## Standards of care and responsibility

### Highest standards of accuracy and fair presentation

Whenever any document or advertisement is issued or any statement is made during the course of an offer, the highest standards of accuracy must be satisfied and any information must be presented adequately and fairly *(Rule 19.1)*. Parties to an offer or potential offer must take care not to issue statements which, although not inaccurate, may mislead shareholders and the market or create uncertainty *(Rule 19.3)*.

It may be the case that a document is true and correct but nevertheless misleading. Consider the following graph of a company's earnings per share performance.

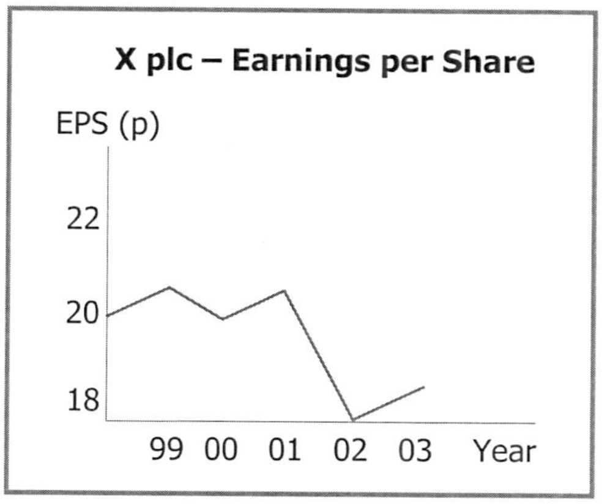


While the graph may truthfully portray the earnings per share performance of the company, the decision to make 18p the base line of the y-axis means that the presentation may be misleading, giving the impression that the earnings have almost fallen to nil.

Similarly, the selection of the base year when calculating dividend growth rates, for example, must be made with care to ensure that misleading growth rates are not quoted.

### The responsibility of the directors

Any document or advertisement issued in connection with an offer must state that the directors of the offeror or offeree company as appropriate accept responsibility for the information contained in the document and that to the best of their knowledge the information is in accordance with the facts and does not omit anything likely to affect the import of the information *(Rule 19.2)*.

If the information relates to another company and has been taken from published sources, then this responsibility is limited to ensuring that the information is reproduced correctly and fairly *(Note 3 to Rule 19.2)*.

## Advertisements

In the past, a number of controversial advertisements have threatened to reduce the credibility of the City in the eyes of the public and to trivialise takeover bids. As a result, advertisements connected with the offer may not be published unless they fall within a number of specific categories *(Rule 19.4)*. These include the following.

- Product advertisements not bearing on the offer. The advert will need to be cleared with the Panel in advance of publication if in doubt.
- Corporate image advertisements not bearing on the offer.
- Advertisements confined to non-controversial information about an offer, eg a reminder of closing dates.
- Advertisements comprising preliminary or interim results and their accompanying statements, so long as the statement does not contain argument or invective about the offer.
- Advertisements giving information that is required or specifically permitted to be published by the FCA.

## Telephone campaigns

There is an obvious danger that telephone calls by overzealous salesman may result in misleading information being released to offeree shareholders or additional information being made available to some shareholders, but not to others. The purpose of the City Code is to ensure that all callers are properly briefed about their responsibilities under the Code.

Telephone campaigns should only be conducted by staff of the financial adviser who are fully conversant with the requirements of and their responsibilities under the Code *(Rule 19.5)*. The Panel may consent to other callers being used, but only if they have a prepared script and information from which they are not allowed to depart.

Only previously published information that is still accurate may be used during the telephone call. Shareholders must not be put under pressure and must be encouraged to consult their own advisers.

## Interviews and debates

The unscrupulous nature of some editors in pursuing the art of sensational television leads to risks that fairly ordinary interviews may be rearranged so that they are no longer a fair representation and will appear controversial as a result.

When interviewed, parties involved in the offer should seek to ensure that the sequence of the interview is not broken by the insertion of comments by others not made during the interview *(Rule 19.6)*. Joint interviews and confrontations between the offeror and offeree or competing offerors should be avoided.

## Equality of information to all shareholders and to competing offerors

Information about companies involved in the offer must be made available, as far as possible, to all shareholders at the same time and in the same manner *(Rule 20.1)*. Notwithstanding this, an offeree company can make available information on a confidential basis to a potential offeror or vice versa.

### Interviews and meetings

There is a clear danger that, when meeting with important shareholders, new information may be released that is not yet available to all shareholders. *Rule 20* aims to ensure that new information is not released or, if it has been, that it is then immediately made available to all shareholders.

*Rule 20* states that great care must be taken during interviews and meetings to ensure that no significant new information is released *(Note 3 to Rule 20)*. If significant new information does emerge, then a circular must be sent to shareholders as soon as possible.

A representative of the company's financial adviser should **always** attend meetings and confirm in writing to the Panel by 12 noon of the next business day whether in their opinion significant new information was forthcoming at the meeting.

### Information to different offerors

Information given to one offeror or potential offeror must also be given on request to another offeror or bona fide potential offeror, regardless of whether or not their offer is welcome *(Rule 20.2)*. The offeror must request the information specifically and cannot frame a request in general terms.

For example, it would not be possible for one offeror to request 'all the information given to company Y'. Rather than such a general request, the offeror would have to list a specific series of questions. It is of course possible for the offeror to compile an exceedingly long list of questions!

The objective of making sure that information is disseminated equally is to ensure that all offerors are in a position to make a fair offer. This will ensure that the offeree shareholders are not disadvantaged and forced to accept a lower offer than might otherwise have surfaced.

### Frustrating action

If an offer is in process, or the board of the offeree company has reason to believe that an offer is imminent, then the board must not attempt to frustrate the bid without the permission of the shareholders by any of the following actions *(Rule 21.1)*.

- Issue any authorised but unissued shares or grant options on these shares.
- Issue securities with the right to convert into shares.
- Sell, dispose of or acquire/agree to sell, dispose of or acquire assets of a material amount. The Panel will normally consider relative values of 10% or more as being of a material amount.
- Enter into contracts other than in the ordinary course of business.

### Inducements

An inducement fee is where the offeree company agrees to pay an offeror a sum of money should certain events cause the offeror's bid to fail. For example, a fee might be payable if the offeree company's directors recommend a competing bid that is higher.

Under *Rule 21.2*, any commitment by a prospective target to pay the bidder a break fee, or inducement, should a transaction abort is prohibited under the Code. There are some very limited exceptions: payments to a 'white knight' coming in to rescue a target from a hostile bidder, or where a potential target puts itself up for auction, and in both cases subject to a 1% de minimis limit.

## 13 Timetable of an Offer

### Summary bid timetable

The following summary highlights the main dates in an offer. These and other important dates are dealt with in more detail below.

**Summary Bid Timetable**

| | |
|---|---|
| **28 days** | Announcement of offer |
| | ↓ |
| **'D' day** | Publication of offer document |
| | ↓ |
| **D + 14** | Posting of defence document |
| | ↓ |
| **D + 21** | First closing date |
| | ↓ |
| **D + 39** | Last date for announcements by offeree |
| | ↓ |
| **D + 46** | Last date for revision of the offer |
| | ↓ |
| **D + 60** | Last day an offer can be declared unconditional as to acceptances |

## Posting the offer document ('D' Day)

The offer document should normally be sent to shareholders within 28 days of the announcement of a firm intention to make an offer *(Rule 24.1)*.

## Offeree board circular (D + 14)

The defence document should be sent to shareholders within 14 days of the publication of the offer document *(Rule 25.1)*.

## First closing date (D + 21)

The offer must initially be open for at least 21 days following the date on which the offer document is posted *(Rule 31.1)*. If there is any announcement of an extension to the offer, then the next closing date must be stated *(Rule 31.2)*. If the offer has been declared unconditional as to acceptances, then a statement may be made that the offer will remain open until further notice. In this case, at least 14 days' notice must be given in writing to shareholders who have not yet accepted before the offer is closed.

## Purchase of shares in the market

After the first closing date has passed and provided that the bid has not been referred to the CMA, the restrictions on purchasing shares carrying more than 30% of the votes in *Rule 5* is lifted *(Rule 5.2)*. However, such purchases could trigger a mandatory offer.

## Unconditional acceptance period

After an offer has become or is declared unconditional as to acceptances, the offer must remain open for acceptance for at least 14 days after the date it would otherwise have expired, unless it has been unconditional from the outset *(Rule 31.4)*.

## Fulfilment of conditions

Except with the consent of the Panel, all conditions must be fulfilled or the offer must lapse within 21 days of the later of the first closing date and the date the offer becomes or is declared unconditional as to acceptances *(Rule 31.7)*.

## Withdrawal of acceptances

If an offer has not become unconditional by 21 days after the first closing date, then an acceptor must be entitled to withdraw his acceptance from this date *(Rule 34)*.

## Offeree board announcements (D + 39)

The offeree board should not, without the Panel's consent, announce any material new information (including trading results, profit or dividend forecasts and any material acquisition or disposal) after the 39th day following the posting of the initial offer document *(Rule 31.9)*. Where such an announcement is made, the Panel will normally be prepared to grant an extension to 'Day 46' and/or 'Day 60'.

## Revision of offers and final revision date (D + 46)

There is no requirement for an offer to be revised or extended *(Rule 31.3)*. However, if an offer is revised, then it must remain open for at least 14 days following the date the revised offer document is posted *(Rule 32.1)*. This means that the latest possible date that an offer can be revised is 46 days after the initial offer, since the time limit for the bid is 60 days after that date (see below).

On revision of an offer, all shareholders who accepted the original offer must be entitled to the revised consideration *(Rule 32.3)*.

Where it has been stated that an offer will not be extended or increased, then only in exceptional circumstances will the Panel permit the offer to be extended or increased *(Rules 31.5 and 32.2)*. It is usual for a 'no extension' or 'no revision' statement to be accompanied by a rider stating that the offeror specifically reserves the right to extend or revise the offer, should a competing offer emerge. The Panel will normally accept this *(Notes 2 and 4 to Rule 31.5)*.

When an offer includes shares, the offeror will have to ensure that it does not release information after D + 46, which will affect the value of the share consideration. For example, the issue of interim results that are better than expected might increase the share price and effectively revise the offer. Release of such sensitive information will only be possible if it: fits in with the offeror's normal results timetable; every effort was made to ensure that the release date was not after Day 46; and it is not likely to affect, materially, the outcome of the offer.

### Final time limit (D + 60)

An offer may not become or be declared unconditional as to acceptances after midnight on the 60th day after the day the initial offer document was posted: without the Panel's consent *(Rule 31.6)*. The Panel will normally consent to an extension beyond this if:

- There is a competing offer, in which case both offerors will normally have to follow the timetable of the competing offer
- The board of the offeree company consents to the extension
- The board of the offeree company has made an announcement of material new information more than 39 days after the initial offer document was posted

In establishing whether acceptance conditions have been satisfied, the offeror can only take into account acceptances or share purchases where the relevant documents are received by its receiving agent by 13:00 on the 60th day.

### Settlement of consideration

The consideration must be posted within 14 days of the later of:

- The first closing date
- The date the offer becomes or is declared unconditional
- The date an acceptance is received *(Rule 31.8)*

### Impact of CMA investigation on timings

It is often the case that there is a significant delay before a decision is made subsequent to an investigation by the competition authorities. In such a case, the Panel will typically rule that, should the offer be cleared, Day 39 will be two days after the clearance and subsequent dates will be adjusted accordingly to maintain the usual relationship thereafter *(Note 5 to Rule 31.6)*.

## 14 Restrictions Following Offers

### Delay of 12 months before making new offer

Where an offer is unsuccessful or an announcement is made that raises the possibility of an offer but no offer is forthcoming within a reasonable period, then the offeror or any person acting in concert with it should not within 12 months *(Rule 35.1)*.

- Make an offer for the company.
- Acquire shares in the company if this would result in an obligation to make an offer under *Rule 9.*

### Partial offers

The above restrictions also apply where a partial offer has been made that could have resulted in a holding of between 30% and 50% inclusive of the voting rights of the offeree, regardless of whether the offer has been successful or not *(Rule 35.2)*.

### Dispensations

The 12-month waiting period may be dispensed with if the Panel consents. Circumstances when consent is likely to be forthcoming include where *(Notes a* and *b* to *Rules 35.1* and *35.2)*:

- A new offer is to be recommended
- A competing offer has been announced
- A 'whitewash' proposal, whereby another shareholder will acquire 30% or more of the company without the requirement to make a mandatory offer, is announced
- There has been a material change in circumstances

### Delay of six months before buying shares above the offer value

If a person or people acting in concert hold shares carrying more than 50% of the voting rights of a company, then they may not acquire shares in the company or make an offer for it on better terms than those available under a previous offer within six months of the closure of the previous offer which became unconditional *(Rule 35.3)*. Should they do so, then the Panel may require that the better terms are offered to the shareholders who accepted the previous offer.

As with the rules concerning purchases above the offer price during the offer period, the purpose of this is to ensure equality of treatment for all offeree shareholders.

## 15 Conflicts of Interest and Management Buyouts

### Independent advice and conflicts of interest

*Rule 3.1* states that the board of the offeree company must obtain competent independent advice on any offer. The Panel will not regard as being independent either of the following *(Rule 3.3)*:

- Someone from the same group as the financial adviser to the offeror company.
- Someone who has a significant interest or financial connection with either an offeror or the offeree company so as to create a conflict of interest.

This means that any directors who will continue as part of the management team are unlikely to be able to offer advice to their existing shareholders. In addition, any adviser working for a management buyout team will be unable to give independent advice to the shareholders.

Where the transaction is a reverse takeover or the directors of the offeror company have a potential conflict of interest, then the board of the offeror must also seek independent advice *(Rule 3.2)*.

### Management buyouts

Clearly, a management buyout (MBO) presents special problems in ensuring that shareholders are given a fair deal. The MBO directors will possess a level of knowledge about the company and its value to which shareholders can only aspire. In addition, the directors are unlikely to be keen to pay the full market value of the company.

*Rule 20.3* states that, in an MBO, the offeror or potential offeror must, on request, promptly furnish the independent directors of the offeree company or its advisers with all information that has been furnished by the offeror or potential offeror to external providers of finance, whether equity or debt.

Where there is a competing offer, *Rule 20.2* states that information passed by the offeree company to external providers of finance, whether equity or debt, should be given equally and promptly to the competing offeror, even if that offeror is less welcome. The competing offeror will, however, have to specify what information it requires, rather than asking in general terms for all the information supplied to the external providers of finance for the MBO.

# 16 Partial Offers

## Panel's consent

### Offers for less than 30% of a company

The Panel's consent is required for any partial offer *(Rule 36.1)*. This will normally be granted if the offer will not result in the offeror holding shares with 30% or more of the voting rights in the offeree.

### Offers for 30% or more

Consent will not normally be granted for offers for 30% or more when the offeror or persons acting in concert have acquired significant numbers of shares in the offeree in the 12 months preceding the application for consent *(Rule 36.2)*.

## Share dealings around the offer period

The offeror and persons acting in concert may not purchase shares in the offeree company during the offer period *(Rule 36.3)*. They are also not permitted without Panel consent to make purchases in the 12-month period after the offer if the offer is successful. Panel consent will normally be granted where the original offer resulted in a holding of less than 30%.

The objective of this is to ensure fair treatment for all shareholders, preventing the offeror from buying all the shares from one shareholder and only making a partial offer to other shareholders.

## Offers for between 30% and 50%

### Acceptance condition

Where the offer could result in a holding of between 30% and 50% inclusive, then the precise number of shares offered for must be stated and the offer can only be declared unconditional when acceptances are received for at least the stated number of shares *(Rule 36.4)*.

### Shareholder approval

An offer for 30% or more of the company should be made conditional on shareholders carrying at least 50% of the voting rights not held by the offeror or persons acting in concert indicating that they approve of the offer *(Rule 36.5)*.

# Tender offers (Appendix 5)

## Fixed and maximum price tenders

A fixed price tender is where the offeror agrees to buy shares for cash at a fixed price of, say, £2.50 per share. People can submit tenders if they believe this price to be attractive. A maximum price tender is where the offeror invites people to submit the price at which they are prepared to sell their shares, subject to a defined maximum price that the offeror is prepared to pay. The final strike price of the tender will depend on the prices submitted by the existing shareholders.

## Oversubscription for a tender

If the tenders received exceed the number offered for, then with a fixed price offer all the tenders must be scaled down pro rata. If a maximum price tender is oversubscribed, then the striking price will be the lowest price at which the number of shares offered for is met. All who tender at or below that price will receive that price. Tenders made at the striking price will be scaled down pro rata if necessary.

Consider the following example where the offeror wants to purchase 1,000 shares in XYZ plc and has specified a maximum tender price of £5.00 per share. The following tenders to sell shares to the offeror are received.

| Tendering Shareholder | Number of Shares Tendered | Price at which Tendered |
|---|---|---|
| A | 400 | £2.00 |
| B | 500 | £4.00 |
| C | 500 | £4.00 |
| D | 200 | £5.00 |

The minimum price at which 1,000 shares can be purchased is £4.00 per share. This becomes the common strike price for all successful tenders. The offeror, therefore, buys 400 shares from A at a price of £4.00, and 300 shares each from B and C at a price of £4.00. D's offer to sell 200 shares at a price of £5.00 each is not taken up.

## Undersubscription for a tender

If the tender is undersubscribed, then all tenders will receive the maximum or fixed price, subject to the minimum acceptance condition in (d) above.

## Code regulation on tender offers

The Panel's consent is required for any tender offer. The Panel's consent will normally be granted where:

(a) The tender offer could not result in the offeror and concert parties being interested in shares carrying 30% or more of the voting rights of the company on the closing date of the tender; or

(b) The tender offer is by a person holding shares carrying more than 50% of the voting rights of a company, is for less than all the shares carrying voting rights held by the minority and the Panel believes the circumstances justify the use of a tender offer.

### Advertising requirements

Any tender offer must be published by a paid advertisement in two national newspapers and the advertisement must include the following details.

- The name of the offeror and its broker
- The name of the offeree
- The maximum number of shares being offered
- A statement that if tenders totalling less than 1% (or higher if the offeror wishes, but not usually over 5%) of the offeree's voting rights are received, then the tender will be void (no other conditions will be allowed)
- The fixed or maximum price offered
- Details of the offeror's existing holding in the offeree
- The closing day and time for the tender

### Minimum duration of a tender offer

The minimum period for which a tender offer can remain open is eight calendar days, from the date it is advertised to the date it closes (inclusive).

## Schemes of arrangement (Appendix 7)

A scheme of arrangement is a transaction effected by means of statutory provisions in the Companies Act 2006. The provisions of the Code apply to offers effected by schemes of arrangement in the same way as they apply to contractual offers, except as set out in Appendix 7.

The offer document should normally be sent to shareholders within 28 days of the announcement of a firm intention to make an offer *(Rule 24.1)*. This rule also applies to the scheme document. A scheme must include a term that it will lapse if there is a competition reference before the shareholder meetings.

There is no maximum time limit for the holding of shareholder meetings and/or the fulfilment of other scheme conditions in the absence of a competitive situation. So there is no equivalent to the 60 day limit *(Rule 31.6)* as there is for contractual offers.

Section 5 of Appendix 7 requires the offeree to make announcements following three key events in a scheme, namely (a) the shareholder meetings (b) the court sanction hearing and (c) the date of effectiveness of the scheme. In relation to the announcement following the shareholder meeting, the announcement should specify whether the resolutions had been passed by the requisite majorities, the voting results and, in relation to the court-convened meeting and the number of shareholders who voted for and against the resolution.

Section 10 of Appendix 7 requires consideration to be posted to offeree shareholders within 14 days of the effective date of the scheme. It also requires the terms of the scheme to reflect this, so it may be enforced by offeree shareholders.

An obligation to make a mandatory offer under *Rule 9* may not be satisfied by a scheme of arrangement unless the Panel consents. The factors that the Panel would take into account when considering giving their consent would include the likely timetable and the views of the offeree board and its Rule 3 adviser.

There is a specific obligation on an offeror to consult the Panel when it is considering announcing an offer (or possible offer) to be implemented by a scheme, but without first obtaining the support of the offeree board. This requirement is set out in section 13 of Appendix 7.

### Practice Statements

Practice Statements are issued by the Panel Executive to provide informal guidance to companies involved in takeovers and practitioners as to how the Executive normally interprets and applies relevant provisions of the Takeover Code in certain circumstances.

Practice Statements do not form part of the Code. Accordingly, they are not binding on the Executive or the Panel and are not a substitute for consulting the Executive to establish how the Code applies in a particular case.

Tutors' note

You are expected to be familiar with the content of the Practice Statements for your exam. It is recommended that you read the Practice Statements in full. The current up to date version of the statements can be found on the Panel's website at www.thetakeoverpanel.org.uk.

# CHAPTER ROUNDUP

**Module 5, Chapter 23: The Takeover Code**

This examination requires a detailed and thorough understanding of the UK Takeover Code. UK public deals are governed by the City Code and the examiner will expect you to be able to apply the regulation and advise your 'client' on the regulatory ramifications of particular courses of action.

The syllabus specifies that you understand the following areas of the Code:

- The structure of the Code
- The spirit of the Code
- The structure of the Panel and its powers
- Statutory status
- Companies to which the code applies
- Independent advice
- Irrevocable undertakings
- Financing arrangements
- Offers for different classes of shares
- Concert parties
- Special deals and management incentives
- Accuracy and content of documents
- The creation of false markets
- Restrictions and frustrating actions
- Consideration
- Mandatory offers
- The timetable of an offer
- EU implications
- Consulting the Panel
- Schemes of arrangement
- Practice Statements

You should expect the examiner to devise scenario-based questions here; a more advanced skill than a fact-based requirement to describe the rule.

# THE LISTING RULES

chapter 24

Contents


| | | |
|---|---|---|
| 1 | The Structure of the Listing Rules | 514 |
| 2 | Standard and Premium Listings | 514 |
| 3 | Minimum Requirements for Listing | 516 |
| 4 | Prospectuses | 517 |
| 5 | Pathfinder Prospectus | 520 |
| 6 | Publication of the Prospectus | 521 |
| 7 | Timetable to a Listing | 521 |
| 8 | The Sponsor | 522 |
| 9 | Continuing Obligations | 524 |
| 10 | Announcements to Shareholders | 524 |
| 11 | Significant Transactions | 527 |
| 12 | Related Party Transactions | 530 |
| 13 | Class Tests Summary | 531 |
| 14 | Directors' Obligations | 531 |
| 15 | AIM and ISDX | 534 |

# 1 The Structure of the Listing Rules

The Financial Conduct Authority is the UK Listing Authority (UKLA) and, as such, has overall responsibility for regulating the UK stock market. The London Stock Exchange operates two markets: the Main Market and the Alternative Investment Market (AIM). FCA regulation relating to Main Market listings is set out in the Listing Rules, contained within the FCA Handbook.

To be able to list on the Main Market, a company must satisfy the admission for listing requirements from the Listing Rules. In addition, the company will also need to apply to the London Stock Exchange for admission to trading of its shares. The Stock Exchange has its own trading rules, which act in conjunction with the FCA's Listing Rules.

The Listing Rules are organised into three sections:

- **Listing Rules**. This includes twenty chapters of provisions for listing and continuing obligations, with rules and guidance shown in a single text.
- **Disclosure Rules**. This provides rules and guidance for the dissemination of price-sensitive and other information, compliant with the EU Market Abuse Directive.
- **Prospectus Rules**. This contains the rules on the format, content and approval of prospectuses, in line with the EU Prospectus Directive.

# 2 Standard and Premium Listings

Companies listing on the main market can choose between two types of listing: a 'premium' or a 'standard' listing. **Premium listings** are only available for listing equity shares and require adherence to a set of 'super-equivalent' rules which provide a higher regulatory hurdle than the EU minimum requirement for listing.

**Standard listings** cover the issuance of shares, Global Depositary Receipts (GDRs), debt and securitised derivatives that are required to comply with EU minimum requirements. A Standard listing allows issuers to access the Main Market by meeting EU harmonised standards only rather than the higher hurdle for premium listings.

Both Premium and Standard listings are available to UK and overseas domiciled companies. Both Premium and Standard listings require that a prospectus is prepared in line with the Prospectus Rules.

The Listing Rules apply to Premium and Standard listings but not all of the provisions apply to Standard listings. The following table summarises the main regulatory between the two types of listing.

| Rule | Premium Listing | Standard Listing |
|---|---|---|
| Country of domicile | Any | Any |
| Inclusion in UK indices | Yes | No |
| Minimum market capitalisation | £700,000 | £700,000 |
| Free transferability of shares required | Yes | Yes |
| Historical audited financial information | Required for the last three years | Not required |
| Three year revenue earning record | Required for 75% of business | Not required |
| Three year control over majority of assets | Required | Not required |
| Working capital statement | Required | Not required |
| Proportion of shares in public hands | 25% | 25% |
| Sponsor required? | Yes | No |

| Rule | Premium Listing | Standard Listing |
|---|---|---|
| Publish a prospectus for admission | Yes – Prospectus Rules apply | Yes – Prospectus Rules apply |
| Publish preliminary and interim financial results | Yes | Yes |
| Announce price sensitive information | Yes | Yes |
| Corporate governance | Compliance with Combined Code required | A corporate governance statement should be made |
| Rules on directors' share dealings | The Model Code applies | No |
| Significant transaction rules apply | The Class Tests apply | No |
| Stock Exchange trading rules apply | Yes | Yes |

A premium listing thus encompasses much more comprehensive regulatory requirements and compliance with the Listing Rules provisions therefore is more expensive and time-consuming. The additional cost of a premium listing may be offset by a reduction in the cost of capital due to greater investor confidence from compliance with the 'gold standard' rules.

## Listing principles

The purpose of the Listing Principles (*LR 7.2)* is to set out the overall responsibilities of listed companies in maintaining market confidence and ensuring fair and orderly markets. The Listing Principles apply to companies with a premium listing for equity shares *(LR 7.1.1 R).*

The Listing Principles state that:

1 A *listed company* must take reasonable steps to establish and maintain adequate procedures, systems and controls to enable it to comply with its obligations.

2 A *listed company* must deal with the *FCA* in an open and co-operative manner.

There are additional listing principles for Premium Listed Companies as follows:

1 A *listed company* must take reasonable steps to enable its *directors* to understand their responsibilities and obligations as *directors*.

2 A *listed company* must act with integrity towards the holders and potential holders of its premium listed shares premium listed shares.

3 All *equity shares* in a class that has been admitted to *premium listing* must carry an equal number of votes on any shareholder vote.

4 Where a *listed company* has more than one class of *equity shares admitted* to *premium listing*, the aggregate voting rights of the shares in each class should be broadly proportionate to the relative interests of those classes in the equity of the *listed company*.

5 A *listed company* must ensure that it treats all holders of the same class of its listed equity shares that are in the same position equally in respect of the rights attaching to those listed equity shares.

6 A *listed company* must communicate information to holders and potential holders of its listed equity shares in such a way as to avoid the creation of a false market in those listed equity shares.

The Listing Principles are designed to ensure adherence to the spirit – as well as the letter – of the rules in the interests of promoting a transparent and fair market.

# 3 Minimum Requirements for Listing

The basic conditions for a listing are given in Chapters 2 and 6 of the Listing Rules. They are divided into generic requirements for all issuers of securities (Chapter 2) and additional requirements for commercial companies seeking a premium listing (Chapter 6). Key requirements are as follows.

## The issuer

The applicant must be incorporated *(LR 2.2.1 R)* as a public limited company (for UK issuers only). Private limited companies (those designated Limited or Ltd) are not permitted to issue shares to the public. Therefore, a private company must re-register as a public limited company (plc) before it can apply for a listing.

There are some additional requirements for premium listings:

- **The business must have a trading history.** Apart from in exceptional circumstances, the applicant must have published audited accounts which cover at least three years (LR 6.1.3 R) and the latest accounts must be in respect of a period ended not more than six months before the date of the listing particulars. This requirement exists to ensure that there is evidence of a company's stability and likely future success.
- **The business must be independent.** Apart from in exceptional circumstances, the applicant must be an independent revenue generating business supported by a historic revenue earning record covering at least 75% of its business and with control over the majority of its assets throughout at least the last three years *(LR 6.1.4 R)*.
- **The business must be liquid.** The applicant must supply a working capital statement that indicates that the company will have sufficient working capital for at least the next 12 months *(LR 6.1.16)*.

Companies that cannot meet the additional Premium listing criteria will still be eligible to apply for a standard listing.

## The shares/securities

These regulations apply to both premium and standard listings:

- Securities must **conform to the law** in the company's place of incorporation *(LR 2.2.2 R)*.
- The whole class of securities **must be admitted to trading** on the London Stock Exchange *(LR 2.2.3 R)*.
- The securities must be **freely transferable** *(LR 2.2.4 R)*. Many private companies' Articles stipulate that shares may only be transferred with the approval of the board of directors, or that shares to be sold must first be offered to existing shareholders prior to being made available to outsiders. Both of these conditions prevent free transferability and are not permitted for listed companies.
- The securities must have a **market capitalisation of at least £700,000 in the case of shares and £200,000 in the case of debt** securities *(LR 2.2.7 R)*. These limits may be disapplied if the FCA is satisfied that securities of a lower market value would be adequately marketable, although this would be unusual.
- **All of** the **securities** of any **class** must be **listed** *(LR 2.2.9 R)*.
- **Convertible securities** are only to be admitted to listing if the securities into which they are convertible (or the securities to which they relate) are already or will be listed. *(LR 2.2.12 R)*.

There are additional regulations for premium listings only:

- A **sufficient number of the shares must be in the hands of the public**, to ensure that the secondary market for the shares is sufficiently liquid and the shares are marketable (*LR 6.1.19 (3) R*). This requirement is known as the 'free float' requirement and will be satisfied where at least 25% of the shares are in public hands. A lower percentage than 25% may be permitted if the shares will nevertheless be sufficiently marketable.
- **Warrants or options to subscribe for shares must not exceed 20% of the issued equity**. Rights under employee share schemes are not included in this *(LR 6.1.22)*.
- In the case of UK applicants, shares must be **eligible for electronic settlement** *(LR 6.1.23)*.

# 4 PROSPECTUSES

## When is a prospectus required?

The Prospectus Rules section of the Listing Rules details when a prospectus is required, the contents and format of a prospectus, the processes for approval, publication and advertising, and other relevant provisions.

A prospectus is a detailed document required by the Prospectus Directive, in the following circumstances:

- **When an offer of securities is made <u>to the public</u> in any EU member state**. An 'offer' includes any 'communication to persons in any form and by any means, presenting sufficient information on the terms of the offer and the securities to be offered, so as to enable an investor to decide to purchase or subscribe to these securities'. 'Securities' means transferable securities – eg equities and debt securities, or tradable warrants or options – not stock options.
- **When securities are admitted to trading <u>on a regulated market</u> in the EU**. This includes admission to trading on domestic 'second markets' and trading facilities, provided that they are a 'regulated market' as defined in the Investment Services Directive. This does therefore include Premium and Standard listings on the Main Market of the London Stock Exchange; but not the Alternative Investment Market, which is an 'Exchange-Regulated Market'.

There are a number of exceptions to this requirement. In particular, issues of securities with a maturity of less than 12 months such as short-dated debt instruments are excluded; so are corporate issuers offering debt and equities where the total size of the offer is less than €2.5m over a 12-month period.

Additionally, the Prospectus Directive provides a number of exemptions which apply as long as the securities are **not** admitted to trading on an EU regulated market. In particular, these include

- Offers to 'qualified investors' only. Qualified investors are defined as legal entities which are authorised or regulated to operate in the financial markets, as well as other entities whose corporate purposes are solely to invest in securities, national and regional governments and central banks.
- Offers to fewer than 100 people per EU member state, excluding qualified investors.
- Offers where the minimum subscription per investor, or minimum denomination per unit of stock, is at least €50,000 ('wholesale' issues).
- Offers where the total consideration is under €100,000 over a 12-month period.

Further exemptions from the requirement for a prospectus apply where the securities **are to be** admitted to trading on an EU regulated market. These apply to secondary issues in certain circumstances, such as:

- Conversion of existing securities
- Merger and takeover issues

- Employee share issues
- Admission to trading of shares involving less than 10% of a class already issued, over a 12-month period

Generally speaking, then, primary issues of equity, most significant secondary issues of equity, and substantial issues of debt, **will** require the production and approval of a prospectus whose format and content is in line with the Prospectus Directive.

## Format of the prospectus

The prospectus can be a single document or comprise three separate documents *(PR 2.2.1 R)*. The prospectus must contain: a **summary** of approximately 2,500 words using non-technical language which gives information on the directors, advisors, financial performance, reasons for the offer, risks and prospects; a **registration document** containing the detailed information on the issuer and valid for up to twelve months; and a **securities note** containing a description of the securities for which listing is sought *(PR 2.2.2 R)*.

Where a three-part prospectus is used, the issuer may file a registration document in advance, with or without approval by FCA. At the time of issue of securities, the issuer must then seek approval for its securities note and summary (and registration document, if not already approved). Each must be approved separately, but jointly they comprise a valid prospectus.

All necessary information must be provided in the documents to enable investors to make an informed assessment of various factors *(PR 2.1.1 R)*. It is also acceptable to incorporate information by reference, meaning that the prospectus could refer potential investors to recently published documents, for example financial statements *(PR 2.4.1 R)*.

## Contents of the prospectus

The Prospectus Rules set out the minimum information to be included in a prospectus, but this varies according to the type of issuer, the nature of the securities and the size of the issue.

Appendix 3 to the Prospectus Rules provides a building block approach, whereby issuers consult a number of different Annexes, according to the type of securities to be issued and the circumstances involved, to extract the information requirements for the relevant section of their particular prospectus.

### (1) Persons responsible

There will be a declaration by those accepting responsibility for the document, stating that it is in accordance with fact and that there are no material omissions. Primary responsibility for the document rests with the directors of the issuer. This will be accompanied by details of the auditors and any other advisers (for example the sponsor, bankers or legal advisers) whose statement or report forms part of the prospectus.

### (2) Information relating to the issuer

The detailed requirements include:

- Incorporation details
- Domicile and legal form
- Summary of important events in history
- Investments
- Business overview (including principal activities and markets)

- Organisational structure
- Operating and financial review
- Significant assets
- Capital resources
- Details of directors, including experience and remuneration policies
- Board structure and practices
- Corporate governance information, including internal controls and statement of compliance with regulation
- Major shareholders
- Related party transactions

### (3) Trend information

Details of significant historical trends and information about the issuer's prospects in the current financial period. Forecast information does not have to be included but, if it is, assumptions must be detailed and the forecast must be accompanied by an accountants' report.

### (4) Risk factors

There must be prominent disclosure of risk factors that are specific to the issuer or its industry.

### (5) Financial information

- The latest audited three year historic accounts, accompanied by the audit reports
- Most recent interim results if applicable
- Pro-forma financial information, to show how the transaction is expected to impact the balance sheet and income statement of the issuer
- Details of dividend policy
- Details of any significant change to the trading or financial position from the latest reporting period end

### (6) The issuer's share capital

- Details of issued share capital, and authorised but unissued share capital
- Changes to share capital in the last three years
- Details of outstanding convertibles, warrants etc

### (7) Material contracts and display documents

There needs to be included a summary of all material contracts entered into in the last two years and details of all documents available to be inspected (including the memorandum and articles of association, directors' service contracts and previous years' audited accounts).

## Omission of information

The FCA permits information to be omitted from a prospectus, where the inclusion of it would be against the public interest, or it is of minor importance, or would be seriously detrimental to the interests of the issuer. Additionally, the Prospectus Directive allows omissions of information which is inappropriate to the issuer's legal form, its activity, or the securities concerned *(PR 2.5.1–2 R/D)*. FCA permission to omit must be sought in advance of publication of the prospectus.

## Approval of a prospectus: 10/20 day documents

Where a prospectus is required for an offering of shares, it must be approved by FCA in advance. In this respect, a wide range of documents needs to be submitted to the FCA in draft form. In a primary (initial) offering, or where there are complex issues involved, the deadline is 20 business days prior to the intended publication of the prospectus *(PR 3.1.3 R)*. Where a company is not a new applicant, but is seeking admission to listing of additional new securities, the drafts need to be submitted 10 business days in advance. The documents required must be submitted in draft but substantially in final form, and in duplicate in hard copy or electronic format. They are as follows *(PR 3.1.1 R)*.

- A completed 'Form A' seeking approval
- The prospectus
- A cross-reference sheet, linking items in the prospectus to those in the schedules and building blocks in the PD Regulation
- Any letter seeking the authorisation of omission of information from the prospectus
- A non-applicable letter confirming that items excluded from the prospectus are not applicable to the issuer
- Contact details for individuals within the issuer's firm who are knowledgeable and available to answer queries (between the hours of 7am and 6pm)
- Any other information required by FCA
- The fee required for approval of the prospectus

This information must also then be submitted to the FCA in final form before midday on the day when approval is required to be granted.

## Passporting

Under the Prospectus Directive, prospectuses approved in one EU member state may be 'passported' into another 'host' member state. If an issuer wishes to take advantage of this, he may request a 'certificate of approval', either on filing the application for approval of the prospectus, or after the approval. In the former case, the certificate will be granted within one day of the approval of the prospectus; in the latter case, it will be issued within three days of the request. In either case, the certificate is provided to the competent authority in the host member state.

Where it is in the best interests of investors to do so, the FCA has the power to transfer the responsibility for approving a prospectus to a competent authority in another EU member state, at the request of the issuer or the competent authority.

# 5 Pathfinder Prospectus

The FCA may formally approve the issue of pathfinder prospectuses in certain circumstances. A pathfinder is a 'preliminary offering circular' or draft prospectus which is, broadly speaking, the entire text of the prospectus omitting only the final pricing details. Pathfinder documents must be approved by the FCA if they are to distributed beyond a 'tightly limited' number of investors. These must therefore include information as required in the Prospectus Rules.

The Prospectus Directive permits the approval of prospectuses where the final offer price and amount of securities to be offered remain to be determined; but these must contain information set out in the prospectus rules.

## 6 Publication of the Prospectus

Once the prospectus is approved, it must be filed with the FCA and made available to the public as soon as practicable, and before the offer of securities to the public or the admission to trading of the securities (*PR 3.2.2–3 R).*

## 7 Timetable to a Listing

The typical stages in a listing are summarised below.

| Application for Listing – Summary Timetable | |
|---|---|
| **Time Before Listing** | **Action** |
| 24 weeks | Appoint advisers<br>Planning<br>Consult FCA<br>Commence long form report<br>↓ |
| 8 to 12 weeks | Draft documents prepared<br>Drafts submitted to FCA<br>Public relations campaign starts<br>↓ |
| 1 to 6 weeks | Draft prospectus<br>Verification<br>Formal submission of documents to FCA<br>↓ |
| Final week | Approval of documents by FCA<br>Completion meeting<br>Underwriting agreement signed<br>Investment presentations<br>Allocation lists open and basis of allocation is announced<br>Formal application for listing<br>Listing granted<br>Dealing commences |

An issuer will initially appoint a team of advisers. The primary adviser in a listing is the '**sponsor**'. The sponsor will co-ordinate the other advisers, as well as advising the issuer on regulatory issues and ensuring the directors are aware of their responsibilities. The sponsor will take the lead in all communications with the FCA.

All primary listings and some other transactions require an issuer to appoint an independent sponsor on the FCA list of 'approved' advisers – investment banks and similar organisations, with a track record in listings and possessing appropriate expertise. The role of the sponsor is considered further below.

Typically the advisory team will also contain the following advisers:

- **Broker.** The broker will advise on pricing, timing and market conditions, assist in representing the issuer with potential investors, give guidance on the most appropriate method of marketing the issue, advise on FCA, Stock Exchange and any other relevant requirements and ensure that the market for the shares is liquid.
- **Reporting accountant.** The reporting accountant will carry out due diligence and prepare the long form report, and will assist with information required for the prospectus.
- **Lawyer.** The lawyer carries out the legal due diligence on the company, reviews the issuer's legal status, reviews service contracts, re-registers the issuer as a public company if necessary, completes the document verification process and prepares all other relevant legal agreements. Separate lawyers would normally represent the directors of the company, the issuer and the advisers to the issuer.
- **Public relations.** Public relations will advise on the selling of the issue to investors, liaise with the press and analysts and ensure that the marketing tone of any documents is appropriate.

The importance of each of the advisers and the specific role that they adopt will depend on the nature and size of the company to be floated. For example, in a relatively small flotation, the broker can act as the sponsor, lead underwriter and overall co-ordinator of the listing. Alternatively, a firm of accountants or lawyers may take on a more central role.

The **initial planning** stage involves preparing a detailed timetable, lists of key documents required, highlighting potential problem areas, and ensuring there is a clear allocation of responsibilities. The **FCA must be consulted** with at an early stage, to fix the timing and level of disclosure required, and to confirm suitability for listing.

Prior to the listing, a **detailed due diligence** exercise will be undertaken, to ensure that all the regulatory requirements are complied with and that the appropriate information is disclosed in the prospectus. The accountants will prepare a long form report, which is a very detailed document covering its past financial performance, the current net asset position and an assessment of the reliability of its forecasts. The long form report will be used by the sponsor to assist in his assessment of the company's suitability for listing and will also be used as a base for much of the information in the prospectus.

Selected contents from the long form report will be input into the draft prospectus and **other documentation** must be prepared, including the working capital letter, responsibility letters and derogation letters. The purpose of the derogation letters is to obtain permission from the FCA to omit certain specified information from the prospectus and other documents.

All documents must be **verified** before they are finalised. Verification is the process of checking on a line-by-line basis that all statements made in the prospectus are fair, accurate and complete, ensuring that the directors have fully discharged their legal responsibilities in respect of the prospectus.

A **completion meeting** is held to finalise all documents and ratify the final decision to seek a listing for the shares.

# 8 The Sponsor

## Obligations of a sponsor

The sponsor is the primary adviser to an issuer of equity securities in the UK. A sponsor has responsibility for guiding the issuer as to the regulatory requirements in the Listing Rules, Prospectus Rules and Disclosure Rules. The sponsor is required to report to the FCA that the issuer has met its responsibilities under the Listing Rules *(LR 8.3.1 R)*. The FCA expects the Sponsor to be its main point of contact in relation to the proposed listing *(LR 8.3.2 G)*.

A sponsor is required for an issuer seeking a premium listing of shares where *(LR 8.2.1 R)*:

- An issuer makes an application for listing of equity securities that requires production of a prospectus, or equivalent document
- An issuer produces a circular in connection with a Class One transaction, a reconstruction or a major share buyback, or is proposing to undertake a substantial or related party transaction
- A transfer of listing from a Standard listing to a Premium listing
- The issuer has breached listing rules and the FCA decides that a sponsor is needed to advise the company

A sponsor is needed to report to the FCA in relation to a particular transaction. For example, if a prospectus contains a profit forecast, then a sponsor must confirm to the FCA that the forecast has been prepared after due and careful enquiry.

Issuers are encouraged to retain, on an ongoing basis, a sponsor fully experienced in market practice but this is not mandatory. For transactions other than those listed above, a sponsor is not required.

## Qualifications of a sponsor

A sponsor must be authorised by the FCA, or a member of a designated professional body. To qualify, a firm must satisfy the FCA that it is competent to act as such and has appropriate systems and controls to carry out its duties *(LR 8.6.5 R)*.

The FCA will consider a sponsor to be competent if it has a broad range of relevant expertise in providing advice to listed companies and on the listing rules *(LR 8.6.7 R)*.

## Principles for sponsors

The Listing Rules set out principles for sponsors, as follows *(LR 8.3.3–6 R)*.

- The sponsor is required to provide all of its services, including guidance or advice to an issuer in relation to the rules, with **due skill and care**.
- Where the sponsor gives advice or guidance to an issuer on the application of the rules, it must take all reasonable steps to satisfy itself that the directors **understand** the nature and extent of their responsibilities in this regard; and it should provide **updates** to the issuer where there are major changes to the listing or disclosure rules, or when a new director is appointed to the board.
- It should deal with the FCA in an **open and co-operative way**; deal with all enquiries raised by the FCA promptly; and disclose promptly to the FCA any material information of which it has knowledge which addresses non-compliance with the Listing Rules or Disclosure Rules.
- It should identify and manage **conflicts of interest** that could adversely affect its ability to perform its role, by putting in place adequate organisational and administrative arrangements eg Chinese walls. Disclose of the existence of a conflict is not enough.

### Specific responsibilities of the sponsor

On an application for listing, the sponsor should ensure that:

- The company has satisfied all conditions and requirements for listing *(LR 8.4.2 R)*
- The directors of the company have established procedures which enable them to comply with the Listing Rules and Disclosure Rules on an ongoing basis *(LR 8.4.2 R)*

- In the case of a new applicant, the directors have established procedures to enable them to make proper judgements on an ongoing basis as to the financial position and prospects of the company *(LR 8.4.2 R)*
- The directors have concluded that the company has adequate working capital for its present requirements and the confirmation has been made after due and careful enquiry by the directors *(LR 8.4.2 R)*
- All matters relevant to the application for listing have been disclosed with sufficient prominence in the prospectus *(LR 8.4.3 (3) R)*

# 9 Continuing Obligations

We examine here the obligations of a company once it is listed. We will look at the following areas:

- **Announcements to shareholders** – inside information and when other announcements are required
- **Significant transactions** – the existence and application of the class tests
- **Related party transactions** – definition and additional regulatory requirement
- **Directors' obligations –** directors' statutory obligations and the operation of the Model Code, including prohibited dealings

# 10 Announcements to Shareholders

The Disclosure Rules provide rules and guidance for the dissemination of price-sensitive and other information, compliant with the EU Market Abuse Regulation. The rules apply to a premium and a standard listing on the Main Market, but not to AIM.

The overall purpose of the Disclosure Rules is stated as being to 'promote prompt and fair disclosure of relevant information to the market; and set out specific circumstances when issuers can delay public disclosure of inside information and requirements to ensure that such information is kept confidential in order to protect investors and prevent insider dealing' (*DR 2.1.3 G).*

This reinforces S397 of the Financial Services and Markets Act (FSMA), which makes it a criminal offence to conceal information dishonestly in order to create a false market, or to take a course of action which has the effect of distorting the market. In addition, Section 118 of FSMA states that action or inaction which abuses the markets is a civil offence.

## Announcements of inside information

The primary rule within the Disclosure Rules is that an issuer must notify a Regulatory Information Service (RIS) as soon as possible of any inside information which directly concerns the issuer *(DR 2.2.1 R).*

Information is deemed to be 'inside' if it meets each of the tests set out in the S118 of FSMA. Specifically, these are as follows. Information which is:

- **Of a precise nature and not generally available.** The Code of Market Conduct states that generally information is available if it has been disclosed to the market, in public records, available via the internet or by payment of a fee or observable without infringing any rights of privacy. And either
- **For investments other than commodity derivatives** – relates directly or indirectly to one or more issuers of the investment or to one or more qualifying investment and would if generally

available be likely to have a significant effect on the price of the investments (or related investments); or

- **For investments which are commodity derivatives** – relates directly or indirectly to such derivatives and users of the relevant markets would expect to receive that information in accordance with accepted market practices on **those** markets.

The definition of accepted market practice would require consideration of the level of transparency in the relevant market, the need to ensure a proper operation of supply and demand and what the regulators in that country have indicated accepted market practice is.

In addition the rules make clear that inside information could include information which that client has conveyed in connection with an order, eg to a broker. This would be the case where the information indicates circumstances that may exist and is specific enough to enable a conclusion to be drawn as to the possible effect of those circumstances on the price of qualifying or related investments.

The rules provide guidance on how issuers should interpret this definition, in deciding whether disclosure is required in each circumstances. Disclosure will generally be required, however, **where the information would be likely to be used by a reasonable investor**, and would therefore be likely to have a significant impact on the price of the qualifying investments (known as the 'reasonable investor test') *(DR 2.2.4 G)*. To apply the reasonable investor test, issuers must exercise their own judgement, but should take into account the size, status and position of the company concerned in deciding what information would be significant to an investor, whilst assuming the investor is acting to maximise his own economic interests. Further, the issuer's directors and advisers should continuously monitor changes in the issuer's position, to check whether and when announcements should be made.

Specific factors to take into account include

- The assets and liabilities of the issuer
- Expectations of future performance
- The issuer's financial position
- The course of business of the issuer
- Any major new developments in its business
- Information already disclosed to the market

## Dissemination of inside information

The prescribed method of dissemination of inside information is that all disclosures should be made as soon as possible, through a Regulatory Information Service (RIS) (*DR 2.2.1 R)*. An issuer's disclosure obligation is fulfilled as soon as the relevant announcement has been forwarded by them to the RIS.

In addition, issuers must publish all inside information disclosed through an RIS, on its own internet site no later than the close of the business day following the RIS announcement, and this information should be available on the issuer's website for at least one year following the posting. This is not an alternative to the RIS disclosure, nor should it be posted here in advance of the RIS disclosure (*DR 2.3 R)*.

Where possible, all inside information disclosed should be announced at the same time in all jurisdictions where its investments are traded or listed.

## Exceptions

There may be cases where public disclosure of inside information would be **detrimental to the legitimate interests of the issuer**. This might include impending developments or negotiations in progress, in particular in relation to refinancing. In these circumstances, the issuer may delay the disclosure, provided that the delay would not be likely to mislead the public, and that the issuer is able to ensure the confidentiality of the information. Moreover, if any person (such as an adviser) receives this information, it is regarded as having a duty of confidentiality towards the issuer. However, any decision to delay disclosure of information remains the responsibility of the issuer.

Delay will not be permissible when there is rumour or speculation in the market about the inside information, where the price of investments is already reacting, or where the issuer cannot ensure the confidentiality of the information (*DR 2.6.2R)*. It is also not permissible to delay public disclosure of worsening financial condition, or financial difficulty.

Where disclosure is reasonably delayed, the issuer may selectively disclose this inside information to persons owing it a duty of confidentiality, provided that this is in the normal course of his duties; this would include advisers to that transaction, interested regulators, etc.

## Control of inside information

Issuers have an obligation to have in place effective systems and controls, to ensure *(DR 2.6 R)*:

- Preservation of the confidentiality of the information, by preventing unauthorised third parties gaining access to it
- Disclosure via a RIS of all inside information revealed to any third party, subject to the exemptions available above
- Immediate disclosure via a RIS, where it becomes impossible to maintain the confidentiality of the inside information
- All persons with access to inside information understand and acknowledge the duties, and the sanctions available

## Insider lists

Under the Market Abuse Directive the issuer is required to maintain an insider list. This is a list of those persons working for the issuer, whether employees, advisers or otherwise, who have access to inside information relating directly or indirectly to the issuer, whether regularly or occasionally (*DR 2.8.1 R).* The list should show the identities of the insiders, the reason for their being on the list, and the date the list was last updated. It must be provided to the FCA on request.

Where the company includes an adviser on its insider list, it must record the name of the principal contact at that firm on its own list, and make contractual arrangements for the adviser to also maintain a list of those of its staff and associates who are also insiders in relation to that issuer, to be provided to the issuer on request. Persons on the list must be both acting for the issuer and have access to inside information. Moreover, all employees on the insider list must be trained as to the rules in relation to insider dealing.

The list should be updated whenever there is a change to the list and it should be kept for at least five years from when it was last updated.

## Other announcements

The Listing Rules and Disclosure Rules detail a number of specific announcements that must be made by issuers, which include the following.

- **Changes in share capital and capital structure**, such as new issues or redemptions of equity or debt securities *(LR 9.6.4 R).*
- **Corporate actions**, including details of dividends to be paid *(LR 9.7A.2 R).*
- **Changes** to the company's name, board of directors, details of directors, reporting dates, key advisers or directors' responsibilities *(LR 9.6.11 – 19 R).*
- **Financial results**, including a requirement for interim results to be announced no later than two months from the period end (DTR 4.2.2). The company must publish its annual report and

accounts as soon as possible after they have been approved, and in any event no later than four months from the financial year end *(DTR 4.1.3 R)*. The consolidated accounts must be prepared in accordance with IFRS *(DTR 4.1.6 R)*.

# 11 Significant Transactions

Shareholders in listed companies delegate responsibility for the company's day-to-day decisions to directors. However, when the directors wish to enter into a material acquisition or disposal, outside the normal day-to-day activities of the company, it may require separate shareholder approval. The FCA is concerned to capture all transactions by **premium listed** companies outside the normal course of business that change a shareholders' economic interest in the assets and liabilities of the company.

Whether the transaction requires shareholder approval is dependent on its materiality, which is established by comparing the size of the business/assets being bought/sold to the size of the listed company, using a number of different means of measuring size. These measures are known as the **Class Tests**, as they allow us to divide transactions into a number of classes, each with different requirements.

Transactions covered by the Class Tests include acquisitions and disposals outside the ordinary course of business, of assets or businesses by the issuer or by its subsidiaries. It also includes entering into joint ventures, where the entire joint venture is compared to the size of the issuer.

## The tests

The tests used to determine the materiality of a transaction are

(a) **Gross assets**

The gross assets which are the subject of the transaction, divided by the gross assets of the listed company. This refers to the total fixed assets plus the total current assets of each of the listed company and of the subject of the transaction, irrespective of the percentage interest being bought or sold.

(b) **Profits**

The profit before taxation and extraordinary items attributable to the assets acquired or disposed of, divided by those of the listed company. Note that if the transaction involves an interest in a subsidiary company which would be or is consolidated, the whole of the profit of the business acquired or disposed of should be included in the test, regardless of the actual interest bought or sold.

(c) **Consideration to market capitalisation**

The consideration (including the maximum amount of any deferred consideration) divided by the aggregate market value of all the ordinary shares (excluding treasury shares) for the listed company at the close of business on the day before the announcement of the transaction. If no maximum consideration is shown, then the transaction is treated automatically as a Class 1 transaction.

(d) **Gross capital**

The gross capital of the company or business being acquired compared with the gross capital of the listed company. Note that this test only applies to **acquisitions** of a company or business. Gross capital for the acquired company is given by the aggregate of the consideration, the value of any shares or debt not being acquired, all other liabilities (excluding current liabilities but including minority interests and deferred tax) and, if applicable, net current liabilities. Gross capital for the listed company is calculated in a similar way, being the aggregate of its shares and debt, all other liabilities and, if applicable, net current liabilities.

## Results – classifying transactions

### Class 1

If any test amounts to 25% or more, the transaction is usually a Class 1 transaction.

### Class 2

If any test amounts to at least 5% but all are less than 25%, it ranks as a Class 2 transaction.

### Class 3

Any transaction where none of the tests comes to 5% ranks as a Class 3 transaction.

### Related party transactions

Chapter 11 of the Listing Rules provides additional requirements for related party transactions. Any transaction with a director or other closely connected person is a related party transaction, and requires shareholder approval if any one of the tests shown above comes to 5% or more. These are discussed further below.

### Reverse takeovers

In the case of acquisitions of unlisted companies, where any of the tests come to 100% or more, the transaction is classed as a reverse takeover.

## Other points

Where an **anomalous result** would arise due to the application of these tests (eg where the test would involve comparing profits with losses), the FCA has the discretion to substitute other relevant indicators of size.

When considering the class of transaction, the FCA will **aggregate all transactions** with the same person or with connected persons, or involving a particular business or new business line, entered into **in any 12 month period**. If the aggregated transactions require shareholder approval, this is required only for the latest transaction.

## Class 3 transactions

Class 3 transactions do not require any announcement unless the transaction involves an acquisition, where the consideration to be paid includes securities for which admission to listing will be sought or a press release is to be made to the public. If an announcement is made, it must include details of any securities being issued and brief details of the transaction.

## Class 2 transactions

### Announcement

A Class 2 transaction requires disclosure without delay once terms have been agreed. The announcement should give details of the following.

- The business being acquired and its trade.
- The consideration being paid and how it is to be satisfied.
- The net profits and net assets attributable to the business.
- The expected benefits from the transaction.
- For a disposal, the application of the sale proceeds.
- If the consideration for a disposal includes shares or securities, a statement as to whether these will be sold or retained.

Shareholder approval, of the premium listed company undertaking the transaction, is not required.

## Class 1 transactions and reverse takeovers

### Announcement, Circular to Shareholders and Shareholders' Approval

Reverse takeovers and Class 1 transactions are sufficiently material to require all of the following.

- An announcement in the same form as for a Class 2 transaction.
- A circular to be sent to shareholders, after approval by the FCA.
- The **transaction to be made conditional on approval by shareholders in general meeting** (ordinary resolution).
- On the completion of a reverse takeover where the target is an unlisted company, UKLA will generally cancel the listing of the securities and require the company to re-apply for listing as if it were a new applicant.

## Contents of the circular to shareholders

The circular to shareholders must be approved by the FCA before it may be sent to shareholders (*LR 13.2.1 R)*. It comprises a letter from the chairman of the listed company explaining the transaction to its shareholders, and seeking approval by shareholders in a general meeting. It is further backed up by detailed additional information on the issuer and the target of the transaction.

The main contents of the circular are as follows.

- The information contained in the announcement.
- A summary of the acquired company's income statement record for the last three years, in the case of an acquisition of a new subsidiary.
- A summary of the acquired company's most recent balance sheet, in the case of an acquisition of a subsidiary.
- For disposals and other smaller acquisitions, a summary of any relevant financial information and confirmation that the value of the relevant business justifies the consideration received or paid.

- A working capital letter covering the adequacy of working capital for the new group, after taking into account the acquisition or disposal.
- Statement of indebtedness.
- The combined group's prospects.
- A statement of the effect of the acquisition or disposal on the earnings and assets and liabilities of the group (typically a pro forma statement).
- A statement by the directors acknowledging responsibility for the information contained in the circular.
- Where any profit forecast has previously been published, this profit forecast must be either included or disclaimed.
- Where any synergy statement or profit forecast is included in the circular, this must be reported on by the company's advisers, and the figures included in the next published annual accounts; if the results for the period differ by 10% from the forecast, issuers should also include an explanation of the difference.

If the company to be acquired is unlisted and there has been a significant change in its business or its accounts have been qualified or unaudited in the last three years, an accountant's report must be prepared, and included in the circular.

## 12 Related Party Transactions

A related party transaction refers to a transaction, or an arrangement, between the company and a related party, other than one of a revenue nature in the ordinary course of business.

A related party is a director (of any company in the group); 50:50 joint venture partner and its subsidiaries; a substantial shareholder (10% or more); or an associate of each of these.

An associate is a spouse, a child, a trustee of a trust in which the related party is interested or a company where he or she (plus spouse and children) owns 30% or more of the voting rights or has control of the Board.

Where the related party is a joint venture partner, transactions requiring approval include any amendments to the joint venture agreement, exercise of any put or call options in relation to the agreement, and further investment in the joint venture.

### Announcement, circular to shareholders and shareholders' approval

When a company with equity shares listed agrees to enter into a related party transaction, the FCA will normally require that an announcement is made, a circular is sent to shareholders and shareholder approval is obtained for the transaction. The circular should explain the nature of the transaction and contain a statement that the directors have been advised by an independent adviser that the transaction is fair and reasonable. An ordinary resolution must be passed at an extraordinary general meeting of the company.

The related party, and its associates, should abstain from any vote in relation to the transaction.

### Exceptions to the rule

The rules relating to related party transactions do not apply to a company if:

(a) It does not have equity shares listed.

(b) It is a standard listed company.

(c) The transaction relates to the issue of securities for cash that is available to other holders of securities of the same class on the same terms or relates to the conversion of or subscription rights attached to a class of security.

(d) The transaction involves the receipt of shares by the director or is the grant of an option to the director under an employee share scheme that does not confer benefits only or mainly on directors.

(e) The transaction is giving of credit on commercial terms or on terms no more favourable than to other employees of the company.

(f) The transaction is the granting of indemnity for the director to protect him when conducting business for the company.

(g) The transaction is a normal commercial underwriting transaction.

(h) The transaction is small, where the tests for class purposes above all come to 5%. However, if any of the tests reaches 0.25% the transaction must be notified to UKLA, together with written confirmation from an independent adviser acceptable to the FCA that the terms of the transaction are fair and reasonable so far as the shareholders are concerned. In this case details of the transaction must also be included in the next published financial accounts.

## 13 Class Tests Summary

| Transaction | Approval of Shareholders | Circular to Shareholders | RIS Announcement |
|---|---|---|---|
| Related party transaction | Yes | Yes | Yes |
| Reverse takeover | Yes | Yes | Yes |
| Class 1 | Yes | Yes | Yes |
| Class 2 | No | No | Yes |
| Class 3 | No | No | If new equity issued or if announced to the press |

## 14 Directors' Obligations

The implied duty of a director is as an agent of the company and therefore one of skill and care. In exercising their powers, directors must demonstrate fiduciary duties. If directors fail to use their powers appropriately, they can end up finding themselves personally liable for their actions. This liability may fall due to the members of the company (the shareholders, for the negligent use of the company's assets) or indeed maybe to third parties where the third party, in dealing with the company, has incurred a loss.

With regard to the liability to third parties, the extent of a director's authority is set out in several key documents.

- Articles of Association
- Service Contracts
- Special Resolutions of a Company

All of these are publicly available documents.

## Directors' duties

The duties of directors arise from both the common law and statute. Additional obligations apply to directors of listed companies, and these are found within the Listing Rules.

### Common law

Under a common law there is a general duty of skill and care attached to any agent. The level of skill and care required from a director is difficult to define and does depend very much on the director and the firm involved.

### The fiduciary duties of directors

Directors have a duty of utmost good faith to the Company (not to the shareholders). There are three broad areas where this applies.

- Directors are to exercise their powers for the benefit of the company as a whole.
- Directors are not to make secret profits; and
- Directors are to avoid conflicts of interest.

This final point is covered by statute in the form of the Companies Act, which requires directors to state their interests in any contract into which the company enters. The Companies Act has wide powers to excuse Directors for negligence, default, breach of duty or breach of trust, provided that the Director acted reasonably and honestly.

## General obligations imposed by the listing rules

Additional obligations for directors of listed companies are dealt with in Chapter 9 – *Continuing Obligations* of the Listing Rules. Key areas are as follows.

### Board changes

Changes in the composition of the Board or the significant roles or responsibilities of its members must be notified without delay through the company's RIS *(LR 9.6.11 R)* and by no later than the end of the following business day following the decision or receipt of notice by the company.

In respect of any new director appointed, or existing director, the company must announce details of *(LR 9.6.13 R)*

- Any directorships held by him in any other quoted company during the last five years, including his current status;
- Any unspent convictions in relation to indictable offences;
- Details of any receiverships, administrations, compulsory liquidations etc in relation to companies where the director was an executive director at the time or in the previous 12 months, or for partnerships where he was a partner in the same timescale; and
- Details of any public statutory or regulatory criticisms of the director, including designated professional bodies and whether he has ever been disqualified as a director.

The disclosure must be made within five business days of the decision to appoint the new director, or as soon as possible in the case of an existing director.

### Disclosure of directors' interests

Under the Disclosure Rules, all transactions in the shares of the company by the issuer's senior executives and their close associates, must be disclosed by them to the issuer within four business days of the day of the transaction. The disclosure must show the name of the person and issuer concerned and full details of the transaction in the shares.

Senior executives includes directors and also those who are not directors but who have regular access to the company's inside information, and the authority to make managerial decisions.

Close associates include any relative who has shared the same household as a director or senior executive in the preceding 12 months, and any company connected with a director or a senior executive.

Once an issuer receives such a notification, it is required to disclose it as soon as possible via a RIS, and not later than the end of the business day following the receipt of the disclosure.

## Directors dealing in their own company's securities – the Model Code

It is desirable that directors should own shares in their company, to align their interests with those of the company that they run. However, due to the privileged level of knowledge possessed by directors, restrictions must be placed on their dealings in shares. It is not sufficient for directors to have integrity in their share dealings; they must also be seen to have integrity.

Listed companies are therefore required to have internal rules which restrict the ability of directors to trade freely in the shares of that company. The Listing Rules provide that a listed company must *'require every person discharging managerial responsibilities, including directors, to comply with the Model Code and to take all proper and reasonable steps to secure their compliance.' (LR 9.2.8 R)*

A listed company may impose more rigorous obligations than those required by the Model Code. *(LR 9.2.9 G)*

## Prohibitions on dealing

The Model Code requires that directors of the listed company should not deal in its shares on considerations of a short-term nature (eg an investment with a maturity of one year or less).

Additionally, employees of the listed company or its subsidiaries who, by virtue of their position in the company, are likely to receive price sensitive information will be treated in the same way as directors for the purpose of the Model Code, and are referred to as relevant employees. Jointly, they are referred to as restricted persons.

Specifically, a restricted person will not be allowed to deal in the shares of his own company

- In the 60 days immediately preceding the preliminary announcement of the company's annual results or half year results or, if shorter, the period between the financial period end and the results announcement. This is known as the **close period**.
- For companies reporting on a quarterly basis, in the 30 day period prior to the announcement of results or, if shorter, the period from the financial period end to the announcement (except for the last quarter of the year, which is covered by the point above). Where relevant this would also be included in the close period.
- Prior to the announcement of matters of an exceptional nature involving unpublished price sensitive information.

- At any time when in possession of price sensitive information about the shares and hence prohibited from dealing by insider dealing legislation (this, together with the close period, is known as the **prohibited period**).
- Without notifying the Board of his intention to deal and receiving clearance.

### Procedures to be followed on dealing

If a restricted person wishes to deal in the company's shares, then he must first notify the chairman of the company or a designated director of his intention to do so and receive clearance in advance of the trade. Clearance or refusal to trade must be given within five business days of the request. Once clearance is given, the restricted person must deal within two business days of it being received.

For persons below Board level, the company secretary may grant or withhold approval to deal.

Clearance should not be given in any situation where the above prohibitions apply, even if the restricted person is not aware of the reason for the prohibition.

The company must keep written records to show that notification was received and clearance was given to the restricted person concerned, and a copy given to the restricted person concerned.

### Exceptions to the rules

The following dealings may be permitted.

- Exercise of share options or convertible securities where the expiry date falls within a prohibited period.
- Dealings in an approved employee share scheme.
- Taking up entitlements to rights.
- Acceptance of a takeover offer.
- Selling (but not buying) shares to meet a director's pressing financial commitment that can only be satisfied through the sale of the securities, provided that disclosure of the dealing and the circumstances is made through an RIS. The disclosure of this dealing is only required in the close period, but not in the prohibited period when the disclosure would create speculation in the market. The FCA should be consulted at an early stage in this case.

## 15 AIM AND ISDX

### Alternative Investment Market

The Alternative Investment Market is regulated by the London Stock Exchange and provides an alternative market place for companies to trade their shares publicly. AIM offers similar benefits to a full listing but without imposing the full regulatory burden of listing on the main market. **AIM Rules are more flexible and less complex** than the Listing Rules which apply to premium and standard listings on the main market.

An admission to trading on AIM used to be regarded as a stepping stone towards obtaining a full listing. Companies now choose to remain on AIM rather than progress to the Main Market; indeed recent years have seen an increase in traffic of companies transferring the other way - from the main market to AIM, attracted by the lighter touch regulation and also the **tax advantages offered to investors**. Shareholders in an AIM-listed company only need to pay Capital Gains Tax on gains of 10 per cent, rather than the usual 40 per cent. Certain AIM holdings are also free from inheritance tax.

## Market data

Since its launch in 1995, AIM has played host to more than 3,500 companies with more than £88 billion having been raised. Of those currently on the market, about a quarter are from overseas. Many of these companies do not fit the traditional 'niche' profile of AIM companies. As at November 2015, 22 AIM companies had a market capitalisation exceeding £500m. The largest of these was Asos plc with a market capitalisation of £2.8bn. Most AIM companies have a market capitalisation in the range £5–50m.

## Regulation

All AIM companies must appoint a **nominated adviser** (termed a 'nomad') to advise on the company's admission to AIM and then the on-going responsibilities of meeting the AIM requirements. The nomad must advise the London Stock Exchange on the company's initial suitability for listing to gain admission to AIM. Otherwise, there are limited initial listing requirements, for example there is no free float threshold, nor minimum market capitalisation required.

A comparative summary of listing regulation is shown below, to help you understand how the AIM requirements to compare to those of the main market.

| Rule | Main market: Premium listing | Main market: Standard listing | AIM |
|---|---|---|---|
| Minimum market capitalisation | £700,000 | £700,000 | None |
| Track record required? | Yes | No | No |
| Free transferability of shares required | Yes | Yes | No |
| Requirement for 25% of shares in public hands | Yes | Yes | No |
| Working capital statement required | Yes | Yes | Yes |
| Sponsor/ nomad required | Yes | No | Yes (at all times) |
| Corporate governance requirements | Yes | Yes | Yes |
| Class tests apply | Yes | No | Yes (light – 10% threshold) |
| Related party rules apply | Yes | No | Yes (light – 5% threshold) |
| Disclosure rules apply | Yes | Yes | No |
| Requirement to announce price sensitive information without delay? | Yes | Yes | Yes |
| Prospectus rules apply | Yes | Yes | Only for public listings, otherwise an admission document is required |
| Half yearly financial reporting required? | Yes | Yes | Yes |

# ISDX

**ISDX (ICAP Securities and Derivatives Exchange)** was created in late 2012 after the inter-dealer broker ICAP acquired and re-branded PLUS Stock Exchange (PLUS-SX), which has been described as London's third stock market after the LSE main market and AIM. The market is lightly regulated and was established (as PLUS-SX) to help smaller companies raise capital. However, PLUS-SX struggled to attract listings thanks, in part, to the success of AIM. ISDX has said it is targeting entrepreneurial companies typically seeking access to equity capital of between £150,000 and £5 million. This would place its target market at the lower end of the companies on AIM.

ISDX describes itself as a London-based stock exchange providing UK and international companies with access to European capital through a range of fully listed and growth markets.

## ISDX Growth Market

The **ISDX Growth Market** aims to provide growing **small- and medium-sized enterprises (SMEs)** from all industry sectors with a source of equity finance for companies coming to a public market for the first time, as well as being a venue for existing issuers to raise further funds.

ISDX admits companies to its ISDX Growth Market in accordance with the ISDX Growth Market Rules for Issuers, which include its application requirements and continuing obligations requirements. A fast-track admission procedure is available to applicants from the Alternative Investment Market of the London Stock Exchange (AIM), and the Access Market of the Munich Stock Exchange (Bayerische Boerse).

ICAP now have three market makers (including Peel Hunt and Shore Capital) making continuous two-way prices to maintain liquidity provision on the venue and to ensure that it operates as a primary and secondary market.

ISDX faces the prospect of competition as a **listing venue for SMEs** from NYSE Euronext's Entrepreneurial Exchange (launched in May 2013), and from the LSE, which is believed to be considering possibilities of improving opportunities for SMEs to raise equity.

Benefits of ISDX (for issuers and investors)

- Reduced regulatory requirements – there is no requirement for companies to issue a full prospectus to join ISDX.
- Lower cost – ISDX is, for some companies, a cost effective flotation venue which compares favourably with other Stock Markets including AIM.
- No minimum market capitalisation – The ISDX rules currently do not stipulate the minimum size of company that may be admitted to the market.
- No minimum trading record – There is no minimum trading history required for companies prior to joining the market.
- Tax incentives – Investors in ISDX companies benefit from a range of tax advantages as ISDX is an unquoted market for tax purposes.
- A potential exit route for existing Shareholders – ISDX provides existing shareholders in the company with a potential exit or part exit route if required, either at the time of the flotation or at a later time of their choosing.

The main negative associated with listing on ISDX is the lack of liquidity in the market, with more delistings than listings since the market was launched at the end of 2012.

**Entry requirements**

Companies are required to publish an 'ISDX Growth Market Admission Document'. This is the key admission document that will contain information about the company, its operations and its strategy. Although the ISDX admission document is comprehensive, it is considerably less onerous than undertaking the preparation of a full prospectus.

In addition, the following rules apply:

- Companies are required to publish audited financial reports no more than nine months prior to the date of their admission to ISDX.
- Companies must demonstrate appropriate levels of corporate governance including having at least one independent Non-Executive Director on their board, (currently AIM companies require two Non-Executive Directors).
- Companies are required to demonstrate that they have at least 12 months adequate working capital.
- No restrictions are permitted on the transferability of shares.
- Company shares must be traded via electronic settlement.

## ISDX main board

The **ISDX main board** is an **EU regulated market** aims to provide companies and other issuers with lower-cost admission to trading through the UKLA's Official List, or other European Competent Authority.

Issuers will be subject to the Listing Rules and the regulator's Disclosure and Transparency Rules. To join the ISDX Main Board, issuers will be required to produce a prospectus approved by the UK Listing Authority (UKLA), or other EU body that is a competent authority under the Prospectus Directive.

The application for admission to the ISDX Main Board will be made in conjunction with the issuer's application to the UKLA (or other EU competent authority for listing) for admission to the Official List under a Premium or Standard Listing.

## Chapter Roundup

**Module 5, Chapter 24: The Listing Rules**

This examination requires a detailed and thorough understanding of relevant sections of the UK Listing Rules, Disclosure Rules and Transparency Rules. The examiner will expect you to be able to apply the regulation and advise your 'client' on the regulatory ramifications of particular courses of action.

The syllabus specifies that you understand the following areas of the rules:

- The structure of the UK Listing Authority rules
- Standard and premium listing options
- The minimum requirements for listing
- Prospectuses
- Timetable for listing
- Sponsor's obligations
- Announcements and circulars to shareholders
- Continuing obligations
- Class tests

You should expect more 'scenario-based' questions rather than a straight-forward re-statement of the facts. The examiner is looking to ascertain your ability to apply the knowledge and add value for your 'client' in the comments that you make.

# OTHER CORPORATE FINANCE REGULATION

chapter 25

## Contents


| | | |
|---|---|---|
| 1 | Introduction | 540 |
| 2 | The UK Regulatory Regime | 540 |
| 3 | The 2014 UK Corporate Governance Code | 544 |
| 4 | The Main Principles | 544 |
| 5 | The Supporting Principles and Provisions | 544 |
| 6 | Contents of the Corporate Governance Code | 544 |
| 7 | Overlap with the FCA Disclosure Rules and Transparency Rules | 548 |
| 8 | UK Competition Regulation | 549 |

# 1 INTRODUCTION

This chapter considers other corporate finance regulation, namely corporate governance rules and the framework that exists for competition investigations. It also considers the financial services regulatory structure in the UK.

# 2 THE UK REGULATORY REGIME

## The Financial Conduct Authority (FCA)

The late 2000s was a period of turmoil for the international financial services sector, stemming in large part from excessive lending by banks, particularly to sub-prime borrowers, and from the 'securitisation' or packaging of mortgages by lenders for selling on to investors who were insufficiently aware of the risks attached to the securities.

In mid-2010 it was announced by the Conservative-Liberal Democrat coalition that there was to be a complete overhaul of the regulation of the UK financial services industry and that the Financial Services Authority (FSA) in its existing form would be abolished. The changes came into force with the enactment of the 2012 Financial Services Act, which came into effect in 2013.

The main provisions of the Act were as follows:

- **Bank of England**. Significant new powers were granted to the Bank of England. The Bank is now responsible for identifying potential crises and developing and implementing contingency plans. The Bank has been made **responsible for ensuring the stability of the financial system**, and is empowered to lead the response in a financial crisis. Responsibility for regulating settlement systems and recognised clearing houses has been transferred to the Bank of England.
- The **Financial Policy Committee (FPC)** was established within the Bank of England, with responsibility for macro-prudential oversight of the regulatory system. The FPC has more flexibility regarding appointments of committee members to allow for swift changes in membership. The Government renews the FPC's remit annually. In an effort to make its workings transparent and accountable, records of FPC meetings are published. The FPC publishes two **Financial Stability Reports (FSRs)** a year, including a summary of its activities and an assessment of the effectiveness of its actions in the period since the last report. (The FPC can exclude confidential or market-sensitive information from what it publishes.) The Role of the FPC is considered further below.
- The **Prudential Regulation Authority (PRA)** was set up as a **subsidiary of the Bank of England** to conduct prudential regulation of firms which manage significant balance sheet risk as a core part of their business. This includes banks, insurers and the more complex investment firms. The PRA has the power to designate firms that should fall within its scope, subject to certain procedural safeguards. The role of the PRA is considered further below.
- The Financial Services Authority (FSA) legal entity became the **Financial Conduct Authority (FCA)**, which is now responsible for consumer protection in financial services, the regulation of conduct of business (including in firms regulated by the new PRA) and market conduct. The **FCA** specialises in protecting customers and promoting confidence in financial services and markets, and promoting competition. The listing function (hitherto performed by the FSA in its UKLA role) is conferred on the FCA. The role of the FCA is considered further below.
- The reforms emphasised the need for **coordination between the regulatory bodies**, as well as extensive **coordination with other bodies**, such as the Financial Ombudsman Service (FOS) and the Bank of England.

- The **Financial Ombudsman Service (FOS)** is one of a **range of organisations** that has the power to raise with the FCA **matters causing significant detriment** and the FCA is required to consider appropriate action, which may include consumer redress.
- **Financial promotions power**. The FCA has the power to take regulatory action to prevent consumers from being misled and to publicise the action taken. Safeguards have been introduced to reflect concerns raised by respondents over potential reputation damage to them in the use of this power.
- **Competition scrutiny**. The Government made the competition scrutiny regime, which will applies to the PRA and FCA, more up-to-date and effective. The regime allows the competition authorities to monitor the impact of regulatory practices and provisions upon competition in financial services. While the promotion of competition is a key duty of the FCA, the Authority's primary objective remains as the protection and enhancement of the UK financial system.

## The Financial Policy Committee (FPC)

The creation of the **Financial Policy Committee** was motivated by the perception that the absence of any effective macro-prudential agency was a major failing in the UK, EU and US before the 2008 financial crisis. This lack was highlighted with the inability of the authorities to deal with asset price bubbles, especially in the property market, and the accumulation of debt and leverage across the financial system.

The FPC includes the FCA Chief Executive and representatives from HM Treasury. The FPC also has some external representation and meets four times annually and at times of crisis.

S9C Bank of England (BoE) Act 1998 (as amended by FSA 2012) provides that the FPC is to exercise its functions with a view to:

- Contributing to the achievement by the Bank of England of the **Financial Stability Objective**; and
- Subject to that, supporting the economic policy of the Government, including its objectives for growth and employment.

The BoE's **Financial Stability Objective** is stated in s2A Bank of England Act 1998 (as amended by FSA 2012), which states that an objective of the Bank shall be: **To protect and enhance the stability of the financial system of the UK**.

The responsibility of the Committee in relation to the achievement by the Bank of the Financial Stability Objective relates primarily to the identification of, monitoring of, and taking of action to remove or reduce, **systemic risks** with a view to protecting and enhancing the resilience of the UK financial system (s9C(2) BoE Act 1998).

Those systemic risks include, in particular:

- Systemic risks attributable to structural features of financial markets, such as connections between financial institutions
- Systemic risks attributable to the distribution of risk within the financial sector; and
- Unsustainable levels of leverage, debt or credit growth (s9C(3) BoE Act 1998).

**Systemic risk** here means a risk to the stability of the UK financial system as a whole or of a significant part of that system, whether the risk arises in the UK or elsewhere.

The **FPC** has the following **tools** at its disposal:

- Setting system-wide cyclical capital requirements, reducing capital buffers required in a crisis while toughening them in more favourable economic times
- Altering risk weights, enabling the Bank to force banks to hold more capital against specific classes of assets in apparently frothy markets

- Setting limits on leverage as a backstop against excessive lending where changing risk weights might not be effective
- Requiring forward-looking loss provisioning to prepare for future losses when lending growth is strong
- Setting limits on borrowing, eg with maximum loan-to-value ratios for mortgages
- Setting limits on lending through regulation

The **Chancellor of the Exchequer** retains the right to **overrule the Bank of England Governor** in a crisis.

## Prudential Regulation Authority (PRA)

The PRA – established in 2013 as a subsidiary of the Bank of England – is responsible for the prudential regulation of banks, insurance companies and large investment firms.

The PRA has a statutory **general objective** that is fundamentally different from that of earlier regulatory regimes:

**Promoting the safety and soundness of PRA-authorised firms**

The PRA meets this objective primarily by seeking to minimise any adverse effects of firm failure on the UK financial system and by ensuring that firms carry on their business in a way that avoids adverse effects on the system.

The PRA focuses on the stability of the system overall, albeit through the mechanism of the supervision of individual firms. This requires close coordination with the **Financial Policy Committee** whose role is to manage the risks in the system as a whole. The PRA is a key contributor to the information and analysis on which the Financial Policy Committee bases its judgements.

The PRA's supervisory efforts relating to financial stability focuses particularly on **large international banks**. In the case of UK subsidiaries of overseas banks, links of the UK entity with the group as a whole as well as the group's viability are an integral part of the PRA's supervisory assessment.

In order to deliver its objective of stability of the financial system, the PRA uses a new framework to assess risks to financial stability.

**Key elements of PRA risk assessment framework**

- Potential impact on the financial system of a firm coming under stress or failing
- Impact on the viability of a firm's business model of the macroeconomic and business risk context
- A firm's overall safety and soundness, which may act to mitigate the potential risk a firm poses to financial stability

**Key mitigants assessed by the PRA**

- Degree of resolvability of a firm (working closely with the Bank's Special Resolution Unit)
- The firm's financial strength (including its ability to generate capital through earnings, its capital held against future risks, the quality of its liquid assets and its liquidity management)
- The quality of a firm's risk management and governance (including the competence of its senior management)

Risks to a firm are identified using:

- Baseline monitoring
- Investigation and assurance
- The macroeconomic and business context

The PRA takes a forward-looking and **judgment-based approach to supervision**. Baseline monitoring isundertaken for all firms, including those that can be resolved with minimal disruption to the financial system (eg credit unions and small deposit-takers). This monitoring includes a review of a firm's resolvability (at least) once a year, analysis of a firm's financial position, discussions with senior management and ensuring compliance with minimum prudential standards for capital, liquidity and large exposures, as well as early interventions where necessary.

## Financial Conduct Authority (FCA)

The **Financial Conduct Authority (FCA)** is the **conduct regulator** for the UK financial services industry. The FCA also has responsibility for the **prudential regulation** of investment exchanges, many investment firms and other financial services providers.

Although set up by statute, the FCA is not regarded as acting on behalf of the Crown. Its members, officers and staff are, therefore, not Crown or civil servants. Like its predecessor – the FSA – the FCA is structured as a **company limited by guarantee**, and is given its powers by FSMA 2000.

The FCA is **accountable to the Treasury** and, through the Treasury, to **Parliament**.

The FCA is governed by a **Board** that is appointed by the Treasury. The majority of the Board members are non-executive. One of the non-executive members is a senior non-executive.

The FCA's Board sets the policy of the Authority. Day-to-day decisions and staff management are the responsibility of the FCA's **Executive Committee**.

The Authority is operationally independent of Government and is funded entirely by the firms it regulates.

The FSA 2012 gives the **Financial Conduct Authority (FCA)** a single **strategic objective**:

**'Ensuring that the relevant markets function well'** (s1B(2) FSMA 2000, as amended by FSA 2012)

'Relevant markets' include the financial markets and the markets for regulated financial services.

The strategic objective of the FCA is supported by three **operational objectives** (s1C-E FSMA 2000):

- **The consumer protection objective**: securing an appropriate degree of protection for consumers
- **The integrity objective:** protecting and enhancing the integrity of the UK financial system
- **The competition objective**: promoting effective competition in the interests of consumers in the market for regulated financial services and for services provided by a recognised investment exchange

The Authority also has duties to **promote competition** (which may involve analysing pricing) and to **address financial crime**.

A spokesperson for the regulator explained that the FCA was set up to work with firms with the aim of ensuring that they put consumers at the heart of their business.

Underlining this are three outcomes:

- Consumers get financial services and products that meet their needs from firms they can trust.
- Firms compete effectively with the interests of their customers and the integrity of the market at the heart of how they run their business.
- Markets and financial systems are sound, stable and resilient with transparent pricing information.

# 3 The 2014 UK Corporate Governance Code

Corporate governance is the system by which companies are directed and controlled. In the UK, the Listing Rules requires Premium listed companies to comply with the 2014 UK Corporate Governance Code, which applies regardless of where the companies are incorporated. Boards of directors are responsible for the governance of their companies. The shareholders' role in governance is to appoint the directors and the auditors and to satisfy themselves that an appropriate governance structure is in place.

# 4 The Main Principles

The Corporate Governance Code is not part of the Listing Rules. It is published by the Financial Reporting Council, and consists of '**Principles**' (both Main and Supporting) and '**Provisions**'. The Principles are the core of the Code and adherence with these ensures that companies adopt the 'spirit' of the regulations.

The **Listing Rules require companies to apply the Main Principles** and to report to shareholders on how they have done so. *(LR 9.8.6 (5)R).*

# 5 The Supporting Principles and Provisions

Each Main Principle is accompanied by Supporting Principles and Provisions which help demonstrate how the Main Principles should be applied. The Supporting Principles provide guidance for companies, together with detailed provisions on the design of performance-related remuneration, the duties of non-executive directors, and disclosure of corporate governance arrangements. In addition, there are guidance and good practice suggestions. The Listing Rules do not require companies to comply with the Supporting Principles or Provisions, but it is recognized that in most cases best corporate governance practice will be to adhere to the letter of these provisions.

The **Listing Rules requires disclosure of compliance** throughout the accounting period **with all relevant provisions set out in the Code**. If all provisions have not been complied with, then the company needs to set out:

(i) Those provisions, if any, it has not complied with;

(ii) In the case of provisions whose requirements are of a continuing nature, the period within which, if any, it did not comply with some or all of those provisions; and

(iii) The company's **reasons for non-compliance** *(LR 9.8.6 (6) R).*

The corporate governance system therefore is set up around a 'comply or explain' approach.

# 6 Contents of the Corporate Governance Code

The Code is set out in five sections. The Main principles are set out below, followed by a summary of relevant guidance provisions.

## Section A: Leadership

### Main principles

- Every company should be headed by an effective board which is collectively responsible for the long-term success of the company.
- There should be a clear division of responsibilities at the head of the company between the running of the board and the executive responsibility for the running of the company's business. No one individual should have unfettered powers of decision.
- The chairman is responsible for leadership of the board and ensuring its effectiveness on all aspects of its role.
- As part of their role as members of a unitary board, non-executive directors should constructively challenge and help develop proposals on strategy.

### Guidance on Section A

The board should meet regularly and disclose the number of its meetings and attendance at meetings. Whereas all directors have a duty to monitor the company's performance, non-executive directors have the duty to monitor also the performance of the Board as a whole and to inform shareholders if they are not satisfied. Non-executive directors are responsible for monitoring financial controls and for setting executive directors' remuneration. The roles of chairman and chief executive should not be exercised by the same individual.

## Section B: Effectiveness

### Main principles

- The board and its committees should have the appropriate balance of skills, experience, independence and knowledge of the company to enable them to discharge their respective duties and responsibilities effectively.
- There should be a formal, rigorous and transparent procedure for the appointment of new directors to the board.
- All directors should be able to allocate sufficient time to the company to discharge their responsibilities effectively.
- All directors should receive induction on joining the board and should regularly update and refresh their skills and knowledge.
- The board should be supplied in a timely manner with information in a form and of a quality appropriate to enable it to discharge its duties.
- The board should undertake a formal and rigorous annual evaluation of its own performance and that of its committees and individual directors.
- All directors should be submitted for re-election at regular intervals, subject to continued satisfactory performance.

### Guidance on Section B

Except for smaller companies, at least half of the board should comprise independent non-executive directors. Independent non-executive directors must be identified in the Annual Report. The following factors are provided as circumstances which might suggest that a director is **not** independent. The individual:

- Has been an employee of the company or group within the last five years;
- Has, or has had within the last three years, a material business relationship with the company;
- Has received or receives additional remuneration from the company apart from a director's fee, participates in the company's share option or a performance-related pay scheme, or is a member of the company's pension scheme;
- Has close family ties with any of the company's advisers, directors or senior employees;
- Holds cross-directorships or has significant links with other directors through involvement in other companies or bodies;
- Represents a significant shareholder; or
- Has served on the board for more than nine years from the date of their first election.

Directors falling into the above categories may still serve as independent non-executive directors, but the company should disclose the basis on which it determines that a director is independent notwithstanding the existence of conflicting relationships or circumstances.

Non-executive directors should be appointed for fixed terms with a maximum term usually set at six years. Any non-executive serving a term beyond six years should be subject to rigorous review, with annual re-election required for non-executives serving more than nine years.

A full time executive director should have a maximum of one non-executive directorship of a FTSE 100 company. No individual should be chairman of more than one FTSE 100 company.

Directors of FTSE 350 companies should be subject to annual election by shareholders. All other directors should be subject to election by shareholders at the first annual general meeting after their appointment, and to re-election thereafter every three years. There should be a formal and transparent procedure for appointment of new directors.

A nomination committee should be established, comprising mainly independent non-executive directors.

## Section C: Accountability

### Main principles

- The board should present a balanced and understandable assessment of the company's position and prospects.

The board is responsible for determining the nature and extent of the principal risks it is willing to take in achieving its strategic objectives. The board should maintain sound risk management and internal control systems. The board should establish formal and transparent arrangements for considering how they should apply the corporate reporting and risk management and internal control principles and for maintaining an appropriate relationship with the company's auditor.

### Guidance on Section C

The directors should give a responsibility statement in the annual report. The effectiveness of internal controls should be reviewed at least annually and this must be reported to shareholders. The directors should confirm in the annual report that they have carried out a robust assessment of the principal risks facing the company, including those that would threaten its business model, future performance, solvency or liquidity. The directors should describe those risks and explain how they are being managed or mitigated.

The company should appoint an audit committee, comprising at least three independent non-executive directors (two for smaller companies). The role of the committee is to monitor the integrity of the financial statements and any statements made by the company relating to financial performance, as well as responsibility for internal financial controls and the relationship with the external auditor.

## Section D: Remuneration

### Main principles

- Levels of remuneration should be sufficient to attract, retain and motivate directors of the quality required to run the company successfully, but a company should avoid paying more than is necessary for this purpose. A significant proportion of executive directors' remuneration should be structured so as to link rewards to corporate and individual performance.
- There should be a formal and transparent procedure for developing policy on executive remuneration and for fixing the remuneration packages of individual directors. No director should be involved in deciding his or her own remuneration.

### Guidance on Section D

Remuneration should be established by the remuneration committee, comprising at least three independent non-executive directors (two for smaller companies). Directors should have objective service contracts with notice periods of a maximum of one year.

The performance-related elements of executive directors' remuneration should be stretching and designed to promote the long-term success of the company. Guidance is provided by the Code into designing performance-related remuneration for executive directors. The guidance gives minimum vesting periods for executive share options schemes (three years) and the requirement to get shareholder approval for any new long-term incentive schemes.

Non-executives should not usually be remunerated via share options or have remuneration packages which contain any other performance-related elements.

The annual report should contain a statement of remuneration policy and details of the remuneration of each director.

## Section E: Relations with Shareholders

### Main principles

- There should be a dialogue with shareholders based on the mutual understanding of objectives. The board as a whole has responsibility for ensuring that a satisfactory dialogue with shareholders takes place.
- The board should use the AGM to communicate with investors and to encourage their participation.

### Guidance on Section E

The chairman should discuss governance and strategy with major shareholders. The senior independent non-executive director should meet with shareholders to ensure there is awareness and understanding of shareholder issues. Independent non-executive directors should make themselves available for meeting with shareholders if requested to do so.

## 7 Overlap with the FCA Disclosure Rules and Transparency Rules

The following table shows the overlap between the Corporate Governance Code and requirements in the FCA's Disclosure and Transparency Rules relating to corporate governance matters. References to the source rules are provided for information.

| | UK CORPORATE GOVERNANCE CODE | FCA DISCLOSURE AND TRANSPARENCY RULES |
|---|---|---|
| **Composition of the audit committee** | The board should establish an audit committee of at least three, or in the case of smaller companies, two independent non-executive directors. The board should satisfy itself that at least one member of the audit committee has recent and relevant financial experience *(Provision C.3.1)* | At least one member of the audit committee or equivalent body must be independent and at least one member must have competence in accounting and/or auditing. *(D.T.R 7.1.1 R )* |
| **Responsibility of the audit committee** | The recommended minimum terms of reference for the audit committee are:<br>• To monitor the integrity of the financial statements of the company and any financial announcements;<br>• to review the company's internal financial controls and risk management systems;<br>• to monitor and review the effectiveness of the company's internal audit function;<br>• to make recommendations to the board, in relation to the appointment, re-appointment and removal of the external auditor and to approve the remuneration and terms of engagement of the external auditor;<br>• to review and monitor the external auditor's independence and objectivity and the effectiveness of the audit process; and<br>• to develop and implement policy on the engagement of the external auditor to supply non-audit services.<br>*(Provision C.3.2)* | The audit committee or equivalent body should:<br>• monitor the financial reporting process;<br>• monitor the effectiveness of the issuer's internal control, internal audit where applicable, and risk management systems;<br>• monitor the statutory audit of the annual and consolidated accounts;<br>• review and monitor the independence of the statutory auditor, and in particular the provision of additional services to the issuer.<br>*(D.T.R 7.1.3 R)* |

| | UK CORPORATE GOVERNANCE CODE | FCA DISCLOSURE AND TRANSPARENCY RULES |
|---|---|---|
| **Disclosures related to the audit committee** | The annual report should identify members of the board committees. *(Provision A.1.2)*<br><br>The annual report should describe the work of the audit committee. *(Provision C.3.3)* | The composition and function of the audit committee or equivalent body must be disclosed in the annual report. *(D.T.R 7.1.5 R)*<br><br>DTR 7.1.7 R states that compliance with Code provisions A.1.2, C.3.1, C.3.2 and C.3.3 will result in compliance with DTR 7.1.1 R to DTR 7.1.5 R. |
| **Statement relating to internal controls** | The Board must report that a review of the effectiveness of the risk management and internal control systems has been carried out. *(Provision C.2.1)* | The corporate governance statement must include a description of the main features of the company's internal control and risk management systems in relation to the financial reporting process. *(D.T.R 7.2.5 R).* |
| **Statement relating to board committees** | • The annual report should include a statement of how the board operates. *(Provision A.1.1)*<br>• The annual report should identify members of the board and board committees. *(Provision A.1.2)*<br>• The annual report should describe the work of the nomination committee. *(Provision B.2.4)*<br>• The annual report should describe the work of the audit committee. *(Provision C.3.3)*<br>• A description of the work of the remuneration committee should be made available.<br>*(Provision D.2.1)* | The corporate governance statement must include a description of the composition and operation of the administrative, management and supervisory bodies and their committees. *(DTR 7.2.7 R)*<br><br>DTR 7.2.8 R states that compliance with Code provisions A.1.1, A.1.2, A.4.6, B.2.1 and C.3.3 will result in compliance with DTR 7.2.7 R. |

# 8 UK Competition Regulation

The UK competition authority is the Competition and Markets Authority (CMA). The CMA's primary duty is to seek to promote competition, both within and outside the UK, for the benefit of consumers.

Under the Act, the CMA has a function to obtain and review information relating to merger situations, and a duty to refer for an in-depth 'Phase 2' investigation any relevant merger situation where it believes that it is or may be the case that the merger has resulted or may be expected to result in a substantial lessening of competition in a UK market.

A relevant merger situation occurs where the following three criteria are met first, either, two or more enterprises must cease to be distinct, or there must be arrangements in progress or in contemplation which, if carried into effect, will lead to enterprises ceasing to be distinct, and second, either:

- The UK turnover associated with the enterprise which is being acquired exceeds £70 million
- The enterprises which cease to be distinct supply or acquire goods or services of any description and, after the merger, together supply or acquire at least 25% of all those particular goods or

services of that kind supplied in the UK or in a substantial part of it. The merger must also result in an increment to the share of supply or acquisition

and third, either

- The merger must not yet have taken place; or
- It must have taken place not more than four months before the day the reference is made.

After starting an investigation, the CMA is in most cases required to decide whether the test for reference is met within a timetable of 40 working days.

The CMA must bring to the attention of the Secretary of State any merger it is investigating at Phase 1, which it believes raises a material public interest consideration. The public interest considerations that the Secretary of State may take into account are those relating to:

- National and public security
- Newspaper and other media mergers; and
- The stability of the UK financial system.

The Secretary of State has the power to add further public interest considerations.

Under the EU Merger Regulation, the European Commission has jurisdiction over those mergers that have an 'EU dimension'

Mergers that are deemed to be concentrations under the EU Merger Regulation fall under the jurisdiction of the Commission where they have an EU dimension, that is where they satisfy one of two alternative sets of jurisdictional thresholds:

Either

- The combined aggregate worldwide turnover of all the undertakings concerned is more than €5 billion, and
- The aggregate EU wide turnover of each of at least two of those undertakings is more than €250 million

or

- The combined aggregate worldwide turnover of all the undertakings concerned is more than €2.5 billion, and
- In each of at least three Member States, the combined aggregate turnover of all those undertakings is more than €100 million, and
- In each of at least three of the Member States included for the purposes above, the aggregate turnover of each of at least two of the undertakings concerned is more than €25 million, and
- The aggregate EU wide turnover of at least two of the undertakings concerned is more than €100 million

unless

- In relation to either situation above, each of the undertakings concerned achieves more than two-thirds of its aggregate EU wide turnover within one and the same Member State.

## Chapter Roundup

**Module 5, Chapter 25: Other Corporate Finance Regulation**

The syllabus requires a 'general' level of knowledge for these topics, meaning that the questions you will face in this area will be 'straightforward' as opposed to 'complex'.

The chapter looks at the financial services regulatory regime which is in operation in the UK, in particular the establishment of the Financial Conduct Authority and enhanced regulatory powers for the Bank of England.

The Corporate Governance Code in the UK is also considered, giving an overall summary of the main regulations.

We have also considered competition regulation, including transactions with an EU dimension.

You are required to describe these areas as they are relevant to corporate finance activity and to assess the relevance of the regulation in a given straightforward scenario.

# ETHICS AND MARKET ABUSE

chapter 26

## Contents


| | | |
|---|---|---|
| 1 | Introduction | 554 |
| 2 | Ethics | 554 |
| 3 | Ethical Behaviour in Corporate Finance | 556 |
| 4 | The Bribery Act 2010 | 557 |
| 5 | Insider Dealing | 558 |
| 6 | Misleading Statements and Practices | 559 |
| 7 | Financial Promotions | 560 |
| 8 | Market Abuse | 562 |
| 9 | The Companies Act 2006 | 566 |

# 1 Introduction

We consider the importance of an ethical code of conduct in relation to the work of corporate financiers. We also look at the Bribery Act and rules on insider trading, misleading statements and market abuse provisions. In each case we consider how each of the regulations applies in practice, together with the relevant defences and remedies that are available.

# 2 Ethics

Ethics are the moral principles that govern a person's conduct. Ethical behavior in the financial services industry has come under scrutiny in recent years, particularly in light of a series of financial scandals and business collapses which has turned the spotlight on the way the financial services industry operates.

Poor ethical standards clearly have detrimental effects. They pose risks to market confidence and consumer protection. They can increase the scope for financial crime and have a negative impact on public awareness and confidence.

Behaving ethically in a business scenario can run counter to personal interest. A finance professional is in a position of trust with the client, employer and general public. Consequently, the highest standards of professional behavior are expected. Written codes have been formulated in an attempt to systematize standards of ethical behavior and provide practical examples of the ethical dilemmas that could arise.

## Ethics – CISI Ethics

Members of the Chartered Institute for Securities & Investment (CISI) are required to meet the standards set out within the CISI's 'Lord George' Principles.

| The Principles | | Stakeholder |
|---|---|---|
| 1 | To act **honestly** and **fairly** at all times when dealing with clients, customers and counterparties and to be a good steward of their interests, taking into account the nature of the business relationship with each of them, the nature of the service to be provided to them and the individual mandates given by them. | **Client** |
| 2 | To act with **integrity** in fulfilling the responsibilities of your appointment and to seek to avoid any acts, omissions or business practices which damage the reputation of your organisation or the financial services industry. | **Firm –** Industry |
| 3 | To **observe applicable law, regulations and professional conduct standards** when carrying out financial service activities, and to interpret and apply them to the best of your ability according to principles rooted in trust, honesty and integrity. | **Firm –** Industry, Regulator |
| 4 | To observe the standards of **market integrity**, good practice and conduct required or expected of participants in markets when engaging in any form of market dealings. | **Market –** Participant |
| 5 | To be alert to and **manage fairly** and effectively and to the best of your ability **any relevant conflict of interest**. | **Client** |
| 6 | To attain and actively manage a level of **professional competence** appropriate to your responsibilities, to commit to continuing learning to ensure the currency of your knowledge, skills and expertise and to promote the development of others. | **Client –** Colleagues, Self |

| The Principles | | Stakeholder |
|---|---|---|
| 7 | **To decline to act in any matter about which you are not competent** unless you have access to such advice and assistance as will enable you to carry out the work in a professional manner. | **Client** – Firm, Industry |
| 8 | To strive to uphold the **highest personal and professional standards**. | **Self** |

The CISI state that material breach of the Code of Conduct would be incompatible with continuing membership of the CISI and may result in disciplinary action.

Members who find themselves in a position which might require them to act in a manner contrary to the Principles are encouraged by the CISI to:

1. Discuss their concerns with their line manager
2. Seek advice from their internal compliance department
3. Approach their firm's non-executive directors or audit committee
4. If unable to resolve their concerns and, having exhausted all internal avenues, contact the Chartered Institute for Securities & Investment for advice at principles@cisi.org

## Ethics – ICAEW Ethical Code

The Institute of Chartered Accountants in England and Wales has developed a Code of Ethics, effective from 2011. The Code is based around five fundamental principles as follows. A professional accountant shall comply with the following fundamental principles:

- **Integrity** – to be straightforward and honest in all professional and business relationships.
- **Objectivity** – to not allow bias, conflict of interest or undue influence of others to override professional or business judgments.
- **Professional competence and due care** – to maintain professional knowledge and skill at the level required to ensure that a client or employer receives competent professional services based on current developments in practice, legislation and techniques and act diligently and in accordance with applicable technical and professional standards.
- **Confidentiality** – to respect the confidentiality of information acquired as a result of professional and business relationships and, therefore, not disclose any such information to third parties without proper and specific authority, unless there is a legal or professional right or duty to disclose, nor use the information for the personal advantage of the professional accountant or third parties.
- **Professional behaviour** – to comply with relevant laws and regulations and avoid any action that discredits the profession.

## Ethics – FCA's ethical framework

The Financial Services and Markets Act 2000 and the FCA's principles and commitments embody a framework of core values. In summary they can be seen as:

- Being open, honest, responsive and accountable;
- Being committed to acting competently, responsibly and reliably; and
- Relating to colleagues and customers fairly and with respect.

The following questions are set out in the FCA paper 'An Ethical Framework for Financial Services', published in 2002. The questions are designed to help practitioners recognise, apply and balance values in everyday decisions and actions:

**Open, honest, responsive and accountable**

- Who is left out or kept in the dark? Why?
- How happy are we to be associated with our decisions/actions?
- Are we listening or just hearing?
- What can we learn? How do we help others to understand us?
- How do we recognise and deal with conflicts of interest?

**Relating to colleagues and customers fairly and with respect**

- Do we treat everyone as we would like to be treated?
- Do we deal with people with respect and without prejudice?
- How do we keep rights and obligations in balance and proportionate?
- When do we hold to our commitments and resist 'fudging'?
- Who benefits and who loses out? Should they?

**Committed to acting competently, responsibly and reliably**

- Do we do what we say we will do?
- Under pressure do we swap co-operation for coercion?
- Do we dither or delay? How is error treated?
- Do people trust us? If not, why not?
- Can we meet our commitments and plans?

# 3 Ethical Behaviour in Corporate Finance

Some key themes can be developed out of the above codes of conduct that impact particularly on corporate finance work.

## Conflicts of interest

Conflicts of interest prevent an adviser **acting objectively**, or, as importantly, **being perceived to be acting objectively**. Conflicts of interest can arise between the adviser and the client or between two different clients of an adviser.

### Conflicts between the adviser and the client

A conflict can exist due to some arrangement which an adviser has entered into which might prevent them giving a client unbiased and objective advice. An example might be an arrangement whereby the adviser receives commission from introducing the client to a third party, or from performing some other service. Any such arrangements must always be disclosed to the client.

### Conflicts between two different clients of an adviser

If the interests of two clients are in dispute with each other (for example different sides of a takeover bid) the objectivity of the adviser may be perceived to be impaired. Conflicts can sometimes be managed via internal arrangements, for example by using separate advisory teams and proper record keeping, but if a material conflict exists an appointment should be declined. The Takeover Code requires that offeree shareholders be represented by an independent (Rule 3) adviser and a material conflict of interest would prevent the adviser being perceived as independent.

A disclosure to the client that a conflict of interest exists is not always sufficient to ensure that the perception of objectivity is upheld.

### Confidentiality

A corporate financier is privy to much confidential information about a client. This information should not be disclosed without express consent from the client, unless there is a legal duty to disclose the information, for example if breaches of the law come to light. Confidential information acquired in the course of professional work should neither be used nor appear to use that information for personal advantage or for the advantage of a third party. In some situations disclosing confidential information can be a crime; legislation exists in respect of insider dealing and market abuse.

Corporate financiers are often dealing with price sensitive information. The takeover code sets out the importance of secrecy relating to all matters concerning a bid prior to initial announcement to prevent false markets in the company's shares.

### Fee arrangements

Fee arrangements with clients must not be designed in a way that might be perceived to detract from the impartiality and objectivity of the advice that is given. Fee estimates should be set out in advance of work being undertaken and should specify the scope of work that is expected. It is acceptable to charge differential fees with different rates for different services that are to be undertaken. It is acceptable to charge fees on a percentage or contingent basis. However, contingent fees may give rise to a self-interest threat to objectivity. The significance of this threat should be evaluated and safeguards considered. Success fees payable to advisers are likely to prevent an adviser being seen as 'independent' under Rule 3.2 of the takeover code.

## 4 The Bribery Act 2010

The Bribery Act was enacted in 2010 to modernize the regulations on bribery and became effective in July 2011.

Bribery is defined as **giving someone a financial or other advantage to encourage that person to perform their functions or activities improperly or to reward that person for having already done so**. A bribe therefore does not have to be monetary in nature but could include an offer of employment, other contractual entitlement or gift. **Function or activity** includes any function of a public nature and any activity connected with a business. **Improper** performance of functions occurs where the expectation of good faith or impartiality has been breached, or when the function has been performed in a way not expected of a person in a position of trust.

The Act is very wide in jurisdiction and will apply if any part of an organisation's business takes place in the UK, regardless of where the organisation is incorporated and regardless of where the bribe took place. The offence applies to both making and receiving bribes.

The penalties for committing bribery are a maximum of ten years' imprisonment, along with an unlimited fine, and the potential for the confiscation of property under the Proceeds of Crime Act 2002, as well as the disqualification of directors under the Company Directors Disqualification Act 1986.

The Act also introduces a **corporate offence** of failure to prevent bribery. A company may be guilty even if no one within the company knew of the bribery. There is a defence, if the company can show that it has in place 'adequate procedures designed to prevent persons associated with (the organization) from undertaking such conduct.' The government has provided guidance as to what constitutes 'adequate procedures' and each organisation needs to have a code of conduct in place that appropriately reflects this guidance and to ensure its personnel are fully conversant with the risks and adequately trained. Failure by an organization to prevent bribery is punishable by an unlimited fine.

# 5 Insider Dealing

Insider dealing is the offence of acting with information that is not freely and openly available to all other participants in the market place. This is an offence under the Criminal Justice Act 1993. The Act makes it a criminal offence for connected persons who receive inside information to act on that information. The penalties are imprisonment for a maximum of seven years and/or an unlimited fine.

The legislation covers the following instruments.

- Shares
- Debt securities issued by the private or public sector
- Warrants
- Depository receipts
- Options, futures or contracts for a difference on any of the above

An insider is defined as an **individual** (not a company) who has **information** in his possession that he **knows** is **inside information** and **knows** is from an **inside source.** Inside information in this context refers to unpublished price-sensitive information that is specific or precise and relates to a security or its issuer.

For the purposes of determining what is **published** information the following information is deemed to be published.

- Information published via a regulated market, eg an RIE
- Information contained in public records
- Information that can otherwise be readily acquired by market users, eg in the financial press
- Information derived from public information
- Information that can only be acquired by expertise or by the payment of a fee
- Information that is published only to a section of the public, rather than the public in general, or published outside the UK
- Information that can be acquired by observation, eg a factory burning down

An **inside source** is an individual and would include a director, employee or shareholder of an issuer of securities or a person who has access to the information by virtue of their employment, office or profession. A person will also be an inside source if he receives the information directly or indirectly from one of the above and in addition satisfies the general definition above.

If a person satisfies the definition of an insider it is an offence to:

- **Deal** in the affected securities either on a regulated market or through a professional intermediary
- **Encourage another** person to deal with reasonable cause to believe that dealing would take place on a regulated market or through a professional intermediary
- **Disclose the information** to another person other than in the proper performance of their duties

An individual is not guilty of insider **dealing** if he can show:

- That he did not, at the time, expect the dealing to result in a profit attributable to the fact that the information was price sensitive
- That, at the time, he believed on reasonable grounds that the information had been disclosed widely enough to ensure that none of those taking part in the dealing would be prejudiced by not having the information
- That he would have done what he did even if he had not had the information

A similar series of defences are available to the charge of **encouraging** another to deal in price-affected securities.

An individual is not guilty of insider dealing by virtue of a **disclosure** of information if he shows:

- That he did not, at the time, expect any person, because of the disclosure, to deal in securities either through a regulated market or via a professional intermediary
- That although he had such an expectation at the time, he did not expect the dealing to result in a profit attributable to the fact that the information was price sensitive in relation to the securities

An individual is not guilty of insider dealing if he can show:

- He acted in good faith as a market maker
- The information, gained as an insider, was market information and it was reasonable to act in that way despite having information as an insider
- That he acted in connection with an acquisition or disposal and the information was market information arising directly from the involvement with the acquisition or disposal
- He acted in conformity with the price stabilisation rules

# 6 MISLEADING STATEMENTS AND IMPRESSIONS

### Misleading statements

s89 of 2012 Financial Services Act covers misleading statements. Under s89, it is an offence to

(a) Make a statement which the person making the statement 'P' knows to be false or misleading in a material respect

(b) Make a statement which is false or misleading in a material respect, being reckless as to whether it is; or

(c) Dishonestly conceal any material facts whether in connection with a statement made by P or otherwise.

P commits an offence if P makes the statement or conceals the facts with the intention of inducing, or is reckless as to whether making it or concealing them may induce, another person:

(a) To enter into or offer to enter into, or to refrain from entering or offering to enter into, a relevant agreement; or

(b) To exercise, or refrain from exercising, any rights conferred by a relevant investment.

### Misleading impressions

s90 of 2012 Financial Services Act covers misleading impressions.

A person ('P') who does any act or engages in any course of conduct which creates a false or misleading impression as to the market in or the price or value of any relevant investments commits an offence if P intends to create the impression.

### Manipulation of Benchmark Rates

Finally, in response to the LIBOR scandal section 91 creates a new offence which deals with the manipulation of benchmark rates. In summary, offences are committed if misrepresentations are made in the course of setting the benchmark, or if false impressions as to the value of an investment may in due course have an impact upon the benchmark rate.

### Penalties

This is a criminal offence and the maximum penalty is **seven years'** imprisonment and/or an unlimited fine. The fine is often referred to as the 'statutory fine'.

## 7 Financial Promotions

A **financial promotion** is an **invitation** or **inducement** to engage in investment activity. The term therefore describes most forms and methods of marketing financial services. It covers traditional advertising, most website content, telephone sales campaigns and face-to-face meetings.

The purpose of regulation in this area is to create a regime where the quality of financial promotions is scrutinised by an authorised firm who must then comply with lengthy rules to ensure that their promotions are **clear**, **fair and not misleading** (Principle 7) and that customers are treated **fairly** (Principle 6).

### Application of the financial promotions rules

The financial promotions rules apply to a firm:

- Communicating with a **client** in relation to **designated investment business** other than a third party prospectus
- **Communicating** or **approving** a **financial promotion** (with some exceptions in respect of: credit promotions, home purchase plans, home reversion schemes, non-investment insurance contracts and unregulated collective investment schemes)

The financial promotion rules **do apply** to corporate finance contacts and venture capital contacts.

### Fair, clear and not misleading

A firm must ensure that a communication or financial promotion is **fair, clear and not misleading**, and is **appropriate** and **proportionate** considering the means of communication and the information to be conveyed.

Some specific interpretations of this are as follows.

- If a product or service places a client's capital at risk, this should be made clear
- Any yield figure quoted should give a balanced impression of both short term and long term prospects for the investment
- Sufficient information must be provided to explain any complex charging arrangements, taking into account recipients' needs
- The regulator (FCA) should be named, and any non-regulated aspects made clear
- A fair, clear and not misleading impression should be given of the producer for any packaged or stakeholder products not produced by the firm

A firm must ensure that a **financial promotion** addressed to a **client** is clearly **identifiable as such**.

## Excluded communications

A firm may rely on one or more instances which make a communication into an **excluded communication** for the purposes of the rules. The exclusions include

- A financial promotion that is subject to, or exempted from, the Takeover Code or to the requirements relating to takeovers or related operations in another EEA State.
- A **'one-off' financial promotion** that is not a cold call. The following conditions indicate that the promotion is a 'one-off', but they need not necessarily be present for a promotion to be considered as 'one-off'.
  (i) The financial promotion is communicated only to one recipient or only to one group of recipients in the expectation that they would engage in any investment activity jointly.
  (ii) The identity of the product or service to which the financial promotion relates has been determined having regard to the particular circumstances of the recipient.
  (iii) The financial promotion is not part of an organised marketing campaign.

## Financial Promotions Order

**S21** Financial Services and Markets Act 2000 makes it criminal for someone to undertake a financial promotion, ie invite or induce another to engage in investment activity, unless they are either:

- An **authorised firm** (ie **issuing the financial promotion**); or
- The content of the communication is **approved** by an authorised firm.

Contravention of section 21 is punishable by up to **two** years in jail and an **unlimited** fine.

There are a number of exemptions from s21 set out in the **Financial Promotions Order**. The effect of being an **exemption** is that the promotion would **not** need to be issued or approved by an authorised firm. It would therefore not have to comply with the detailed financial promotion rules.

The main examples are as follows. (Other exemptions cover certain one-off and purely factual promotions.)

| Exemption | Comments |
|---|---|
| Investment professional | A communication to an authorised or exempt person. |
| Deposits and insurance | Very limited application of COBS. |
| Certified high net worth individuals | Anyone may promote **unlisted securities** to persons who hold certificates of high net worth (normally signed by their accountant or employer, however, these can be self-certified by an individual) and who have agreed to be classified as such. Requirements for a certificate are that a person must have a net income of £100,000 or more, or net assets (excluding principal property) of £250,000 or more. |
| Associations of high net worth individuals | Anyone can promote non-derivative products to associations of high net worth investors. |
| Sophisticated investors | Anyone can promote products to a person who holds a certificate indicating that they are knowledgeable in a particular stock (signed by a firm or self-certified) and who have signed a statement agreeing to be such. |
| Takeover Code | Promotions subject to the Takeover Code. |

# 8 Market Abuse

Certain types of behaviour, such as insider dealing and market manipulation, can amount to market abuse. Types of conduct constituting market abuse are set out in section 118 of the Financial Services and Markets Act 2000 and in the Market Abuse Directive.

In June 2014 new European legislation seeking to strengthen the fight against market abuse was agreed. The Market Abuse Regulation (MAR) came into effect in the UK and across the EU on 3 July 2016.

Market abuse is a civil offence under s118 of FSMA which provides an alternative civil regime for enforcing the criminal prohibitions on insider dealing and market manipulation. The UK market abuse rules implement the EU Market Abuse Directive.

The **territorial scope** of market abuse is very wide. It covers everyone, not just authorised firms and approved persons. Furthermore, firms or persons outside the UK are also covered by the offence.

As market abuse is a **civil offence**, the FCA must prove, on the balance of probabilities, that a person:

- Engaged in market abuse; or
- By taking or refraining from action required or encouraged another person to engage in market abuse.

## The definition of market abuse

Market abuse is behaviour, whether by one person alone or by two or more persons jointly or in concert, which occurs in relation to

- Qualifying investments admitted to trading on a prescribed market; or
- Qualifying investments in respect of which a request for admission to trading on a prescribed market has been made; or
- Related investments of a qualifying investment (strictly, this is only relevant to the offences of 'Insider Dealing' and 'Improper Disclosure', see below).

And falls within one or more of the offences below.

## The seven 'offences' of market abuse

The seven types of behaviour which can constitute market abuse are

1 **'Insider Dealing'**. This is where an insider deals, or attempts to deal, in a qualifying investment or related investment on the basis of inside information.

2 **'Improper Disclosure'**. This is where an insider discloses inside information to another person otherwise than in the proper course of the exercise of his employment, profession or duties.

3 **'Misuse of Information'**. This fills gaps in '1' or '2' above and is where the behaviour

(a) Is based on information which is not generally available to those using the market but which, if available to a regular user of the market, would be regarded by him as relevant when deciding the terms on which transactions in qualifying investments should be effected; and

(b) Is likely to be regarded by a regular user of the market as a failure on the part of the person concerned to observe the standard of behaviour reasonably expected of a person in his position.

4 **'Manipulating Transactions'**. This consists of effecting transactions or orders to trade (otherwise than for legitimate reasons and in conformity with accepted market practices) which

(a) Give, or are likely to give a false or misleading impression as to the supply, demand or price of one or more qualifying investment; or

(b) Secure the price of one or more such investment at an abnormal or artificial level.

5 **'Manipulating Devices'**. This consists of effecting transactions or orders to trade which employ fictitious devices or any other form of deception.

6 **'Dissemination'**. This consists of the dissemination of information by any means which gives, or is likely to give, a false or misleading impression as to a qualifying investment by a person who knew or could reasonably be expected to have known that the information was false or misleading.

7 **'Misleading Behaviour'** and **'Distortion'**. This fills any gaps in '4', '5' and '6' above is where the behaviour

(a) Is likely to give, a regular user of the market a false or misleading impression as to the supply of, demand for or price or value of, qualifying investments; or

(b) Would be regarded by a regular user of the market as behaviour that would distort the market in such an investment and is likely to be regarded by a regular user of the market as a failure on the part of the person concerned to observe the standard of behaviour reasonably expected of a person in his position.

## Qualifying investments and prescribed markets

Behaviour will only constitute market abuse if it occurs in the UK or in relation to qualifying investments traded on a prescribed market. The term 'behaviour' is specifically mentioned as the offence of market abuse can cover both action and inaction.

Qualifying investment means any investment traded on a UK RIE or a regulated market. Regulated markets cover the main European exchanges.

The definition of prescribed market and qualifying investment are amended slightly with reference to the offences of 'Misuse of Information' and 'Misleading Behaviour' and 'Distortion'. Here, a prescribed market means any UK RIE. Thus these offences are only relevant to the UK markets.

As behaviour must be in relation to qualifying investments, the regime is not limited to on-market dealings. For instance, abusive trades on foreign exchanges could constitute market abuse if the underlying instrument also trades on a prescribed market. This makes the regime much wider than the criminal law offences.

## Defences

Under S123 of FSMA, the FCA may not impose a financial penalty in relation to market abuse where it is satisfied that the person believed, on reasonable grounds, that his behaviour did not amount to market abuse or he took all reasonable precautions and exercised all due diligence to avoid engaging in market abuse.

The FCA also has a Code of Market Conduct which sets out:

- Descriptions of behaviour that, in the opinion of the FCA, do or do not amount to market abuse. Descriptions of behaviour which do not amount to market abuse are called 'safe harbours'
- Descriptions of behaviour that are or are not accepted market practices in relation to one or more identified markets
- Factors that, in the opinion of the FCA, are to be taken into account in determining whether or not behaviour amounts to market abuse

The Code does not exhaustively describe all types of behaviour that may or may not amount to market abuse.

## Enforcement and penalties

The FCA may impose one or more of the following penalties on those found to have committed market abuse:

- An unlimited fine
- Issue a public statement
- Apply to the court to seek an injunction or restitution order
- Where an authorised/approved person is guilty of market abuse, they will also be guilty of a breach of the FCA's Principles and they could, in addition to the above penalties, have disciplinary proceedings brought against them, which may result in withdrawal of authorisation/approval

Note that as market abuse is a civil offence, offenders cannot be sent to prison unlike the criminal laws of insider dealing and the rules on misleading statements and impressions. Civil offences are also easier to prosecute.

In addition to being able to impose penalties for market abuse, the FCA is given criminal prosecution powers to enforce insider dealing. The FCA has indicated that it will not pursue both the civil and criminal regime. In terms of the enforcement process for market abuse, this is the same as the FCA's disciplinary process.

## Reporting suspicious transactions (market abuse)

A firm which has reasonable grounds to suspect that a transaction might constitute market abuse must notify the FCA without delay. The notification must include a description of the transaction and reasons for the suspicion. The firm must not inform any other persons of this notification, in particular the person on behalf of whom the transaction has been carried out.

## Statutory exceptions

If a person is within one of the statutory exceptions set out in the Code of Market Conduct (also known as safe harbours) they are not committing market abuse. Generally, there are no rules in the Takeover Code which permit or require a person to behave in a way which amounts to market abuse.

However, the following rules provide safe harbour meaning that behaviour conforming with that rule does not amount to market abuse.

### FCA rules

Behaviour caused by the proper operation of a Chinese wall or behaviour which relates to the timing, dissemination or content to a disclosure under the Listing Rules will not amount to market abuse.

### Takeover Code

Behaviour conforming with any of the rules of the Takeover Code about the timing, dissemination or content of a disclosure does not, of itself, amount to market abuse. This is subject to the behaviour being expressly required or permitted by a rule and provided it conforms to the General Principles of the Takeover Code.

## Price stabilisation

Behaviour which conforms with the Buyback and Stabilisation Regulation (in the Market Conduct Sourcebook of the FCA's Handbook) will not amount to market abuse.

However, buyback programmes which do not follow the Buyback and Stabilisation Regulation are not automatically seen as market abuse, but do not have an automatic safe harbour.

The Market Conduct section of the FCA Handbook sets out how and when a lead manager in an initial public offering may purchase securities to stabilise a price without abusing the market.

- Where the offer is for cash
- Where the offer is public on a qualifying exchange
- When it is for a limited period
- When adequate prior disclosure is given to the market in the prospectus
- When information on stabilising activity is given to the issuer, although this would not include identifying individual clients

Price stabilisation is often achieved through a process of over-allotment, backed up by a greenshoe option over further shares for the stabilising manager.

By allotting to new investors more than 100% of the shares actually created by the issuing company, the stabilising manager has left itself 'short' of these extra shares it has sold but does not yet have. This means the manager will go into the market and buy these extra securities from any new shareholders willing to sell their allocation. This creates an artificial demand to support the price.

Of course, this leaves the stabilisation manager exposed to having to buy the extra shares needed at above the issue price, incurring a loss. To protect against this risk, the manager will hold 'greenshoe' options to buy more shares from the issuing company at the issue price.

Greenshoe options may be used for other purposes besides stabilisation, but the reason must be disclosed to the issuer.

**Market Abuse Regulation (MAR)**

MAR seeks to increase market integrity and investor protection, while ensuring a single rulebook and level playing field across the EU. MAR contains the following main provisions.

**Inside information and disclosure:** the definition of inside information is broadly unchanged, but has been widened to capture inside information for spot commodity contracts. Issuers must notify the regulator after delaying disclosure of inside information, and financial institutions must seek consent from the regulator prior to delaying disclosure due to financial stability concerns.

**Insider dealing and unlawful disclosure**: it is clarified that the use of inside information to amend or cancel an order shall be considered to be insider dealing. It is also clarified that recommending or inducing another person to transact on the basis of inside information amounts to unlawful disclosure of inside information.

**Market manipulation:** the manipulation offence has been extended to capture attempted manipulation. Benchmarks, and in some situations spot commodities, are now in scope of the manipulation offence. Examples of behaviours and activities that shall be considered as market manipulation are set out eg acting in collaboration to secure a dominant position over the supply or demand of a financial instrument, and certain algorithmic trading strategies which disrupt the functioning of a trading venue.

**Market soundings:** introduces a framework for persons to make legitimate disclosures of inside information in the course of market soundings.

**Buy-back programmes and stabilisation measures:** makes revisions to the existing framework for conducting buy-back programmes and stabilisation measures.

**Accepted market practices (AMPs):** continues to permit regulators to establish an accepted market practice which is subject to certain criteria and conditions.

**Insider lists:** places an obligation on issuers to draw-up and maintain a list of all those persons working for them that have access to inside information. Issuers on SME growth markets will only be required to draw up a list when it is requested by the regulator.

**Suspicious transaction and order reports (STORs):** extends the existing obligation to report suspicious transaction reports, to include suspicious orders too. Trading venues are also caught by the obligation to submit STORs.

**Managers' transactions:** persons discharging managerial responsibilities within issuers (PDMRs), and persons closely associated with them, must notify the issuer and the regulator of relevant personal transactions they undertake in the issuer's financial instruments. The issuer in turn must make that information public within three business days.

**Investment recommendations:** continues to require persons producing or disseminating investment recommendations to ensure information is objectively presented, and to disclose any conflicts of interest.

**Whistleblowing:** places requirements on regulators and firms to be able to receive whistleblowing notifications.

MAR will apply from July 2016.

# 9 The Companies Act 2006

The Companies Act includes the following key provisions, which can impact corporate finance transactions:

- Requiring information about interest in own shares
- Company meetings
- Alterations to capital structure
- Financial assistance
- Company investigations
- Minority shareholder protections
- Duties of directors in relation to conflicts of interest

## Requiring information about interest in own shares CA06 S793

In the UK, all shares are issued in registered form. However, the use of nominee names and delays in the settlement process may result in companies being unaware of the ultimate owner of particular shares. Section 793 gives a **public company** the power to require shareholders to give information regarding their shareholding. The investigation notice can be sent to existing shareholders asking them to reveal the ultimate owner of any shares held in their names. It may also be sent to a particular individual asking whether he has, in the **last three years**, been an owner of shares in the company, **either directly or through concert parties**. If the shareholder has sold their shares in the last three years, they should identify the person they sold them to.

In the absence of a response, companies may remove the voting/dividend rights of defaulting shareholders during the course of an investigation. If false information is provided the person is liable to a minimum penalty of two years in jail and/or an unlimited fine.

## Company meetings

Whilst directors are responsible for making decisions regarding the day-to-day running of the business, decisions which affect the structure of a company or the rights of members are decided upon in a meeting of the shareholders.

### Types of meetings

The Companies Act provides general provisions as to the conduct and structure of company meetings which will apply in the absence of any provisions to the contrary in the company's Memorandum and Articles.

The two varieties of meeting are Annual General Meetings (AGMs) and Extraordinary General Meetings (EGMs). AGMs must be held by public companies once a year with a maximum time between AGMs of 15 months. An EGM may be held at any other time as required.

The Companies Act 2006 removed the requirement for private companies to hold AGMs. All private company meetings are now on 14 days' notice (unless the Articles say otherwise) and it requires 90% of voters to agree to hold meetings at shorter notice.

### Public companies

All members and directors of a public company must be informed in writing (which includes posting on a website) in advance of the meeting and of the nature of the business to be transacted. This notice differs according to the type of meeting. An AGM requires **21 calendar days'** notice, whereas an EGM requires **14 calendar days**. The notice may be reduced, and an AGM held on short notice, if 100% of members entitled to attend a meeting vote in favour. This figure becomes 95% of members in the case of reduced notice for an EGM.

Members may require the company to circulate a statement regarding business at the meeting of up to 1,000 words provided that it is requested by either:

- Members representing at least 5% of voting rights; or
- At least 100 shareholders holding at least £100 paid up shares each.

### Resolutions

Decisions are made at company meetings via resolutions. **Ordinary resolutions** require only a **simple majority** (>50%) of votes cast at the meeting to be carried. **Special resolutions** cover more unusual matters, such as changes to a company's constitution or structure. Any meeting voting on special resolutions requires a **75%** majority of votes cast to be passed. Unless specified to the contrary in the company's constitution, each member will be entitled to one vote in respect of each share held.

Resolutions may be proposed by the members provided they are legal and not defamatory, frivolous or vexatious. The request must be from:

- Members representing at least 5% of voting rights; or
- At least 100 shareholders holding at least £100 paid up shares each.

The costs of circulating the notice of this resolution must be paid by the requesting members unless notice is given before the end of the previous financial year.

### Meeting conduct

Directors normally call the meeting and send out the required notice. However, members holding **at least 10%** of a company's voting shares may requisition that the directors call an EGM. Directors must send out notice within 21 days of such a request, thereby convening a meeting. In exceptional circumstances, the courts may order that a meeting be held.

A meeting can only validly pass resolutions if it is quorate, a **quorum** is two members. Any member so elected may act as Chairman at any meeting.

### Proxies

Any member entitled to attend and vote at a company's meeting is entitled to appoint another person (who may not be a member) as his proxy to attend and vote in his place. In a public company, a proxy may attend and vote, but may not exercise the member's right to speak.

## Alterations to capital structure

The funds which a company raises from the issue of shares are generally maintained within the company as a permanent source of finance rather than being returned to shareholders. This concept of capital maintenance is of great importance within the Companies Act. However, there are various exceptions contained within the Companies Act, whereby capital may be reduced.

A company may carry out a **reduction of share capital**, provided the Articles of Association permit and a special resolution is passed in favour of the reduction. Private limited companies complete a solvency statement and plcs need confirmation by the court. It can be done for any reason, but the Act specifically mentions three instances.

(a) Extinguish or reduce the liability of shareholders or shares which are not fully paid up.

(b) Cancellation of share capital which has been permanently lost, and is thus no longer represented by assets.

(c) Return of capital to shareholders, which is in excess of the company's needs.

## Financial assistance

**S678** of the Companies Act 2006 provides that it is illegal for a company directly or indirectly to give financial assistance for the purchase of its own shares (or those of its holding company). The reason for this is the principle of capital maintenance. If a company provides financial assistance to allow a third party to buy its shares, it reduces its own assets without receiving compensation in exchange, and potentially reduces its ability to meet its debts as they fall due.

Financial assistance would include:

- A gift
- Provision of a guarantee, security, indemnity, release or waiver
- Any other form of assistance, whereby the company's net assets are reduced to a material extent

Thus, many transactions are caught under these definitions, not just direct cash payments.

### Consequences of contravention

Any financial assistance in contradiction of these rules is void. In other words, all contracts in connection with it have no legal effect.

The company and its officers may be liable to a fine and/or two years' imprisonment.

Directors who are in breach of their duties are liable to the company for any losses.

### Exceptions

There are various exceptions when transactions that would satisfy the definition of financial assistance are permitted.

- If the principal purpose of the transaction is not the provision of financial assistance
- If the financial assistance is an incidental part of a larger purpose
- When the assistance is lending in the ordinary course of business
- Where a loan is made to employees as part of an Employee Share Scheme
- The restriction **does not apply to private companies**, but only to public companies

## Company investigations by inspectors

The Companies Act s1035-1039 gives members the right to apply to the UK Department for Business, Innovation and Skills (BIS) for an inspector to investigate the company's affairs.

An inspector may be appointed by the BIS on application of:

- At least 200 members or holders of at least 10% of issued shares
- The company itself, if it has passed an ordinary resolution approving such an action

Any applicant must provide £5,000 security for costs and must furnish the BIS with evidence to support their claim.

The Companies Act also gives the BIS the power to exercise their investigative powers at their discretion in the following three circumstances.

- The company has been conducting its affairs with intent to defraud auditors or in a manner prejudicial to members, or for unlawful or fraudulent purposes.
- The promoters or managers have been guilty of fraud or any other act of misconduct.
- The company has failed to provide proper information to the members.

The BIS has no obligation to warn the company or reveal the circumstances which led to the investigation.

The inspectors have very wide powers to obtain and require disclosure of information. They may also question any person on oath, obtain a warrant to search premises and finally inform the Secretary of State for Business, Innovation and Skills of any matters coming to their attention during the investigation.

The Secretary of State has the power to:

- Give directions to an inspector as to the subject matter to be investigated (eg area of operation, specific transactions or a period of time)
- Terminate an investigation where criminal offence matters have been passed to a prosecuting authority
- Set requirements for the contents and time limit of the inspector's report

## Minority shareholder protections

Sections 974–985 of the Companies Act 2006 make provisions for the protection of members against unfair prejudice. If members believe that their company or large shareholders are taking action against their interests they may seek redress through the courts. This may result in the courts ordering the majority shareholder to buy out the minority shareholders at a fair price.

Under Companies Act 2006, s985 protects a minority in giving them the right to insist that a successful bidder buys them out within three months of the end of their bid – **known** as a '**sell out**'.

In contrast, if a bidder is successful enough to secure a total of **90%** or more of the voting rights of a company, then under s979 they can compulsorily purchase ('**squeeze out**') the remaining minority shares.

## Duties of directors in relation to conflicts of interest

A company's directors have a duty under section 175 of the Companies Act to avoid situations which bring about a conflict of interest between the directors and the company, either directly or indirectly. Where the situation would not be regarded as likely to give rise to a conflict of interest or the dealings have been authorised by the directors then this duty will not be considered to have been breached.

Examples of where such a conflict may arise include:

- A director having an interest such as a shareholding in a competitor whose interests conflict with the company with whom they hold the directorship.
- A director in company A, also holding the position of director in company B, whose services are used by company A. This would present possible conflicts of interest.
- Where the director offers services to the market in a personal capacity in direct competition to the company for whom they act as a director.

## Chapter Roundup

**Module 5, Chapter 26: Ethics and Market Abuse**

The syllabus requires a 'general' level of knowledge for these topics, meaning that the questions you will face in this area will be 'straightforward' as opposed to 'complex'.

We look at three ethical codes which set out standards of behaviour as relevant to the corporate financier:

- The CISI Ethical Principles
- The ICAEW Ethical Code
- The FCA's Ethical Framework

The Codes have similar themes and should be drawn upon to substantiate your answer concerning ethical standards of behaviour in the corporate finance arena.

Other areas of regulation which are in the syllabus: the Bribery Act; Insider Dealing regulation; the Market Abuse Directive and FCA rules on misleading statements.

You are unlikely to get detailed questions in this area but you need to understand the relevance of the rules and be prepared to discuss in a straight-forward scenario.

# INDEX

## A

Acceptance condition, 497
Accounting for associates, 64
Accounting for disposals, 70
Accounting for investments, 44
Accounting for tax, 76
Accounting policies, 128
Accounting rate of return, 166
Accrued income, 9
Acting in concert, 488
Adjusted resent value, 233
Alternative investment market (AIM), 534
American option, 325
Announcement of a firm offer, 483
Announcement of a possible offer, 483
Announcements, 482, 524, 526
Arbitrage pricing theory, 247
Articles of association, 296
Assets, 23
Asset beta, 225
Asset cover, 108
Asset purchase, 442
Asset turnover, 93
Asset turnover ratio, 93
Asset-based valuations, 170
Assets 'held for sale', 70
Associate, 64

## B

Bank of England, 540
Bed and breakfast transactions, 129
Betas, 217, 219
Betas for combinations of investments, 223
Black Scholes, 285
Bond prices, 307
Bonds, 299
Bonus issue, 113
Bookbuilding, 377
Break clauses, 436
Bribery Act 2010, 557
Business plan, 346
Buying a call, 333
Buying a put, 335

## C

Call option, 324, 325
Capital asset pricing model, 217
Capital employed, 90
Capital expenditure, 102
Capital fulcrum point, 332
Capital invested, 278
Capital Market Line (CML), 206, 214
Capital structure, 104, 568
CAPM assumptions, 236
CAPM limitations, 237
Cash, 15
Cash alternatives, 498
Cash equivalents, 15
Cash flow analysis, 100
Cash flow from operations, 100
Cash flow statement, 14, 133
Cash flows, 15
Circular transactions, 128
CISI's 'Lord George' Principles, 554
City Code, 480
Class tests, 527
Clawback, 381
Commercial mortgages, 359
Common size statements, 132
Companies Act, 566
Company investigations, 569
Company meetings, 567
Competition and Markets Authority (CMA), 549
Competition objective (FCA), 543
Competition regulation, 549
Component of an entity, 71
Concert parties, 488
Conditions precedent, 438
Conditions subsequent, 438
Confidentiality, 557
Confidentiality agreement, 434
Conflicts of interest, 507, 556, 570
Consignment inventory, 24
Consolidated accounts, 46
Consolidated balance sheet, 66
Consolidated income statement, 60, 66
Consolidating control, 493
Control premia, 450
Controlled auction, 455
Convertible bonds, 301
Convexity, 317
Corporate Governance Code, 544
Corporation tax, 76
Correlation coefficient, 197
Cost of convertibles, 318
Cost of debt, 248
Costs to sell, 70
Criminal Justice Act 1993, 558
Currency options, 416
Currency swaps, 409
Current ratio, 96

## D

Deal effects, 445
Dealings by connected exempt principal traders, 490
Dealings during the offer period, 500
Deductible temporary differences, 80
Defence document, 486
Deferred consideration, 444
Deferred income, 9

Deferred shares, 297
Deferred tax, 79
Deferred tax assets, 80, 85
Deferred tax liabilities, 80, 84
Defined benefit schemes, 392, 393
Defined contribution schemes, 392
Demergers, 458
  dividend approach, 461
  liquidation method, 462
  scheme of arrangement, 461
Diluted earnings per share, 117
  convertibles, 117
  options and warrants, 119
Directors' obligations, 531
Disclosure letter, 438
Disclosure of shareholdings, 499
Disclosure rules, 514, 524, 548
Discontinued operation, 71
Dispensations from making a mandatory offer, 495
Disposal, 454
Diversification, 215
Dividend cover, 126
Dividend growth model, 243
Dividend valuation model, 242
Dividend yield, 125
Double tax relief, 79
Due diligence, 434, 458

**E**

Earn outs, 444
Earnings before interest and tax multiple, 176
Earnings before interest, tax, depreciation and amortisation multiple, 176
Earnings per share, 111, 165
  bonus issues and share splits, 113
  full price issue, 112
  post-balance sheet events, 116
  rights issue, 114
Earnings yield, 125
Economic profit, 280
Economic risk, 404
Economic value added (EVA), 278
Enterprise investment scheme (EIS), 358
Enterprise value, 172
Enterprise value multiples, 123
Equity accounting for associates, 69
Equity beta, 225
Equity method, 64
Equity shares, 296
Equity value, 173
Equivalent rates, 255
Ethics, 554
  CISI ethics, 554
  FCA's Ethical Framework, 555
  ICAEW Ethical Code, 555
Eurobonds, 302
European option, 325
EVA return on capital, 281
Exchangeable bonds, 302
Excluded communications, 561
Exclusivity agreements, 436
Exempt fund manager, 490
Expectations theory, 308
Expected return, 186
Expenses, 24
Explicit forecasting period, 266

**F**

Factoring, 360
Factoring of receivables, 28
Fair value, 4, 57, 70
Family offices, 365
Fee arrangements, 557
Fiduciary duties, 532
Final salary schemes, 393
Finance leases, 32, 38
Financial advisers, 490
Financial assistance, 344, 568
Financial Conduct Authority (FCA), 540, 543
Financial Ombudsman Service (FOS), 541
Financial Policy Committee (FPC), 541
Financial promotion, 560
Financial promotion rules, 560
Financial promotions order, 561
Financial Services Authority (FSA), 540
Financial stability objective, 541
Financial stability reports (FSRs), 540
Financing activities, 15
Flat yield, 303
Floating rate debt, 250
Floating rate notes (FRNs), 301
Forecasting free cash flow, 265
Foreign currency forward contracts, 413
Foreign currency futures, 415
Foreign currency market, 405
Foreign currency risk, 403
Forward rate agreements (FRA), 411
Forward transactions, 406
Founder shares, 296
Free cash flow, 260
Free cash flow to equity, 263
Free cash flow to the enterprise, excluding capital allowances, 263
Free cash flow to the enterprise, including capital allowances, 260
Frustrating action, 472, 503

## G

Geared betas, 225, 233
Gearing, 104, 105
General principles of the Code, 481
Golden shares, 297
Goodwill, 50, 54
Gordon growth model, 243
Greenshoe options, 378, 565
Gross redemption yield (GRY), 303

## H

Heads of agreement, 435
Heads of terms, 435, 458
Hire purchase agreement, 32
Holding period return, 182
Hostile bid tactics, 468

## I

IAS 11 Construction Contracts, 7
IAS 12 Income Taxes, 76
IAS 17 Leases, 31
IAS 28 Investments in Associates, 64
IASB Framework, 23
Immunisation, 315
Income, 24
Indemnities, 437
Independent advice, 483
Indifference curves, 188
Inducements, 503
Information memorandum, 457
Initial Public Offering (IPO), 368
Inside information, 524
Insider dealing, 558, 562
Insider lists, 526
Institutional buyouts (IBOs), 343
Integrity objective (FCA), 543
Interest cover, 107
Interest in own shares, 566
Interest rate futures, 416
Interest rate options, 417, 419
Interest rate parity formula, 407
Interest rate risk, 402
Interest rate swaps, 408
Intermediaries offer, 374
Internal rate of return, 160
Intrinsic value, 328
Introduction, 374
Inventory turnover, 97
Investing activities, 15
Investors' ratios, 111
Irredeemable fixed rate debt, 248
ISDX, 536
ISDX growth market, 536
ISDX main board, 537

## J

Joint control, 64
Joint ventures, 69, 431

## L

Leases, 32
Leasing, 360
Lenders' debt to equity ratio, 106
Letters of intent, 435, 458
Liability, 23
Licensing, 431
Limited liability partnership, 432
Liquidity, 128
Liquidity ratios, 95
Listing principles, 515
Listing rules, 514
Loan transfers, 31
Locked box mechanism, 438
Long form report, 435
Long straddle, 336
Long term contracts, 6

## M

Macaulay duration, 313
Maintainable earnings, 116
Managed bid, 455
Mandatory convertible bonds, 301
Mandatory offer, 492
Market abuse, 562
Market risk premium, 218
Market segmentation, 308
Market value added, 282
Marketability discounts, 450
Medium term notes, 302
Merger gains, 449
Methods of listing, 372
Mezzanine finance, 354
Minority interests, 49
Minority shareholder protections, 569
Model Code, 533
Modified duration, 314
Modified internal rate of return, 164
Modigliani and Miller, 226
Motivations for making acquisitions, 428
Multivariate ratio, 133

## N

Negative correlation, 198
Negative goodwill, 53
Net asset value, 126
Net assets per share, 126
Net debt to equity ratio, 106
No-names teaser, 457
Normalized EPS, 166

**O**

Off-balance sheet financing, 22
Offer consideration, 443
Offer document, 484
Offer for sale, 373
Offer for subscription, 373
Offeror's obligations, 483
One-off financial promotion, 561
Open offers, 380
Operating activities, 15
Operating lease, 32, 38
Operational gearing, 94
Operational gearing ratio, 94
Option strategies, 333
Options, 323
Options-based valuation models, 283
Ordinary shares, 296
Other points, 528
Overdraft, 359
Overseas tax, 78

**P**

Panel on Takeovers and Mergers, 480
Par yields, 310
Partial offers, 508
Passporting, 520
Pathfinder prospectus, 520
Pay off diagrams, 333
Payables' payment period, 99
Pension deficits, 397
Pension protection fund, 396
Pension scheme, 392
Placings, 373, 380
Portfolio selection, 201
Portfolio theory, 193
Positive correlation, 198
Pre-emption rights, 381
Preference shares, 297
Premium listings, 514
Prescribed markets, 563
Price to book ratio, 168
Price to earnings ratio (P/E), 122, 171
Price to sales ratio, 170
Pricing of convertibles – option pricing, 320
Pricing of convertibles – the crossover method, 319
Profit forecast, 486
Profit margin, 92
Profitability, 128
Profitability ratios, 89
Pro-forma earnings per share, 445
Pro-forma gearing, 447
Pro-forma net assets per share, 447
Prohibited dealings, 490
Project finance, 363
Prospectus rules, 514
Prospectuses, 517
Prudential Regulation Authority (PRA), 542
Public to private transactions, 343
Purchasing power parity (PPP), 407
Put options, 324, 325

**Q**

Qualifying investments, 563
Quantified financial benefits statements, 488
Quick ratio, 97

**R**

'rb' model, 244
Ratchets, 352
Ratios, 37, 88, 89
Real options, 283
Receivables' collection period, 98
Recognition, 24
Recoverable amount, 70
Redeemable fixed rate debt, 250
Reduction of share capital, 568
Related party transactions, 530
Representations, 437
Resolvability (of a firm), 542
Responsibility statement, 485
Restricted coupon yield curves, 309
Restrictions following offers, 506
Restrictions on obtaining control, 491
Return on capital employed, 89, 166
Return on equity, 121
Return on equity ratio, 121
Return on investment, 166
Revenue, 4
Revenue recognition, 4
Reverse takeovers, 375
Revolving credits, 360
Rights issues, 114, 378
Risk, 184

**S**

Safe harbours, 563, 564
Sale and leaseback, 363
Sale and purchase agreement, 436
Sale and repurchase agreements, 26
Scheme of arrangement, 466, 510
Secondary offerings, 378
Securities alternative, 498
Securitisation, 30
Security Market Line (SML), 217, 218
Seed Enterprise Investment Scheme (SEIS), 358
Selling a call, 334
Selling a put, 335
Share repurchases, 383
Shareholder value added, 278
Shares purchases, 442

Shelf programme, 302
Short straddle, 337
Significant influence, 64
Sovereign wealth funds, 364
Special Resolution Unit, 542
Sponsor, 522
Spot rates, 304
Spot transactions, 405
Squeeze out, 570
Standard deviation, 187
Standard listings, 514
Standstill agreements, 489
Syndicated loans, 359
Synergies, 178, 426
Systematic risk, 215, 216, 221
Systemic risk, 541

**T**

Takeover Code, 564
Takeover offer, 466
Tax base, 80
Taxation
  permanent differences, 77
  temporary differences, 80
  timing differences, 77
Tender offers, 376, 509
Term loans, 359
Terminal value, 267
Time value, 328
Timetable for a rights issue, 379
Timetable of an offer, 503
Timetable to a listing, 372, 521
Transaction risk, 403
Transaction value, 172, 175
Translation risk, 404
Transparency rules, 548
Treasury shares, 387
Trend statements, 130

**U**

Unsystematic risk, 215, 216

**V**

Valuation of mineral rights, 289
Valuation of options, 327
Value in use, 70
Variance, 187
Vendor consideration issue, 381
Vendor placings, 381
Venture capital, 340
Venture capital trusts, 357
Voluntary offer, 496

**W**

Waiver of the Code, 481
Warrant, 330
Warranties, 437
Weighted average cost of capital, 251
White knight, 470, 472
White squire, 472
Window dressing, 128
Working capital, 101
Working capital cycle, 100

**Y**

Yield curve, 307, 308, 310
Yield surface, 309
Yield to maturity, 303

**Z**

Zero-coupon bonds, 301
Z-scores, 133